Understanding Financial Risk Man

Financial risk management is a topic of primary importance in financial markets and, more generally, in life. Risk can be seen as an opportunity if related to the concept of compensative return. It is therefore important to learn how to measure and control risk, in order to get exposure to as much risk as is necessary to achieve some level of compensation, without further useless exposure.

This book analyses the various types of financial risk a financial institution faces in everyday operations. Each type of risk is dealt with using a rigorous mix of analytical and theoretical approaches, describing all the major models available in the literature, with an innovative look at the topic.

This book covers the following aspects of risk and provides introductory overviews of the most relevant statistical and mathematical tools:

- market risk
- interest rate risk
- credit risk
- liquidity risk
- operational risk
- currency risk
- volatility risk.

Understanding Financial Risk Management offers an innovative approach to financial risk management. With a broad view of theory and the industry, it aims at being a friendly, but serious, starting point for those who encounter risk management for the first time, as well as for more advanced users.

Angelo Corelli is Assistant Professor of Finance, Bursa Orhangazi University, Turkey.

Routledge Advanced Texts in Economics and Finance

Understanding Financial Risk Management

Angelo Corelli

LONDON AND NEW YORK

First published 2015
by Routledge
2 Park Square, Milton Park, Abingdon, Oxon, OX14 4RN

and by Routledge
711 Third Avenue, New York, NY 10017

Routledge is an imprint of the Taylor & Francis Group, an informa business

© 2015 Angelo Corelli

British Library Cataloguing in Publication Data
A catalogue record for this book is available from the British Library

Library of Congress Cataloguing in Publication data
Corelli, Angelo.
  Understanding financial risk management / Angelo Corelli.
    pages   cm. – (Routledge advanced texts in economics and finance)
  Includes bibliographical references and index.
  1. Financial risk management. 2. Risk management. I. Title.
  HD61.C668   2014
  658.15′5–dc23
  2014008863

ISBN: 978-0-415-74617-5 (hbk)
ISBN: 978-1-315-79753-3 (ebk)
ISBN: 978-0-415-74618-2 (pbk)

Typeset in Times New Roman
by Out of House Publishing

Printed and bound by CPI Group (UK) Ltd, Croydon, CR0 4YY

**Alla mia famiglia
Giuseppe,
Rina,
e Mauro**

Contents

Figures

xiv   *List of figures*

Tables

Preface

A modern approach

Understanding Financial Risk Management offers an innovative approach to financial risk management. With a broad view of theory and the industry, it aims at being a friendly, but serious, starting point for those who encounter risk management for the first time, as well as for more advanced users.

The focus is no longer on the mere measurement, but on the whole package. Risk is also opportunity, and when managing it, one should reach the right balance between opportunity and loss. That is why we propose a new approach that starts from the basic knowledge of classic theory and methodologies and moves to the latest findings in measurement and hedging.

Many books are more exhaustive in covering some of the topics that are treated in this book, but most of them do not offer the wholesome coverage on the horizon of financial risk management as the present book does.

There is no doubt that a deeper analysis of many concepts is possible, but no book in the actual market is able to collect all risks and the managing of them in one single essay. This book is definitely an all-included piece or work that guides the reader from the beginning to the end without ever losing focus on what is more important for good risk management knowledge.

An innovative pedagogy

The foundations of the book rely on three main blocks: theory, analytics and computational. They all merge in a way that makes it easy for students to understand the exact meaning of the concepts and their representation and applicability in real-world contexts. Examples are given throughout the chapters in order to clarify the most intricate aspects; where needed, there are appendices at the end of chapters that give more mathematical insights about specific topics.

Learning comes from the correct combination of the three pillar elements, none of which should be excluded. The trinity stands as the foundation of the whole project.

Preferably, students have a solid background in financial mathematics, statistics and basic econometrics. Indeed, students facing financial topics for the first time may benefit from using the book as a medium-level introduction to some aspects of financial theory and practice.

In this sense, practitioners represent a possible share of the users of the book. In recent years, due to the global financial crisis, the demand for links between academics and private industry has increased substantially. For this reason, practitioners nowadays like to explore the work done in academic research, and this book provides useful information for managers who want to increase their knowledge about risk management and understand what may have been lacking in their own systems.

A selected audience

The book is meant for third or fourth year undergraduate students of business finance, quantitative finance and financial mathematics. Most of the universities that the book would target offer the kind of training in mathematics and statistics that would be prerequisites for the successful completion of a course using *Understanding Financial Risk Management*. Potential users include students of universities, technical schools and business schools offering courses in financial risk management.

This book offers a unique approach and represents a clear improvement on existing textbooks in the field of finance. Most textbooks on financial risk management focus on measurement or on some specific kind of risk. There is no challenge or criticism in them, and there is no drive for understanding risk management in the critical sense. That is exactly what this book will offer.

Quantitative approaches now incorporate a more critical view and contribute to a vision that does not blindly rely on numbers, but takes into account the variety of (sometimes unpredictable) situations that characterize financial markets.

Certainly, it is not an easy book, but it is a book that never abandons the reader. Even in the most complicated parts, the student is guided through the processes and given the tools he needs; nothing is cryptic.

A reliable partner for instructors

Understanding Financial Risk Management is tailored mostly for in-class lectures, and it has the best effect if combined with good quality lecture slides from the instructor. Second, given its overall flexibility (a result of its simple structure), it can also be used for online learning. However, the medium-high level of difficulty of the book suggests the need for a closer relation with the instructor and the possibility of in-person explanations.

The structure of *Understanding Financial Risk Management* lends itself to a typical Swedish course of approximately six ECTS. The ten chapters, of at most 60 pages each, can fit a course design of about 14–16 lectures of 1.5 hours' effective teaching. That would also fit an overall international standard of a course with two lectures per week spanned over a two-month teaching term. The overall contents in the book can fill approximately 40–60 hours of teaching.

Richness in content

This book is the ultimate tool for understanding the many aspects of financial risk management, and it comes with a solid theoretical set.

This first edition has been edited to help educators around the world, suiting users dealing with financial risk for the first time, as well as more advanced users looking for an innovative approach.

As a textbook, the richness in content, exercises and applications makes the book the perfect partner for the students of all areas in the world, all shaped in a book featuring:

a.   14 chapters.
b.   70 major and 126 detailed learning outcomes.
c.   Numerous tasks (questions and exercises).
d.   Snapshots and appendices where relevant.
e.   Numerous selected references.

Every chapter follows the same structure, where the full text is complemented by snapshots relating to cutting edge research and up-to-date news. At the end of each chapter, there is an exercise section with targeted tasks.

After that, there is a list of the references that serve as a convenient bibliography and appendices, where relevant.

1 Risk: an overview

Financial markets are typically characterized by transparent pricing and specific trading regulations. The costs, fees and market forces determine the price of traded securities, and the risk embedded in any single trade.

Risk can be defined as the possibility of negative outcome as a consequence of specific choices. In all fields of life, including business and financial activities, actions that lead to a loss can be defined as risk. Various types of risk daily affect a business, but when it comes to money they can be mainly classified into two types: business risk and financial risk.

Financial risk in particular involves the financial structure of the corporation. It generally arises by variability of prices and returns on financial markets. Movements can involve any kind of security as stocks, currencies, derivatives and interest rates.

Financial risk managers have the duty to perform identification, measurement and hedging of risk, if necessary. Financial instruments can be used for the purpose but it is not always necessary to do that, since often risk entails the opportunity of a good expected return in exchange.

It is not possible to prevent all possible risks, given some of them are unpredictable and not identifiable sufficiently in advance. However, for many types of risk, the analytical, computational and numerical tools available in the literature can offer a way of reducing uncertainty.

After studying this chapter you will be able to answer the following questions, among others:

1. What is financial risk and how does it differ from other types of risk?
2. What are the various types of financial risk and how do they link to each other?
3. What are the differences among risk in banks, corporations and insurances?
4. How can we define the process of risk management, and what steps does it involve?
5. What are the most common types of strategies and instruments involved in risk management?

The first section of the chapter is an introduction to the definition of risk, and how it arises in different types of business. The second section is about the various types of financial risk and their interconnection. The final part aims at introducing the process of risk management, as identification, measurement and mitigation and/or transfer.

1.1 Introduction

Learning outcomes

1. Distinguish between uncertainty and risk.
2. Learn about generic concepts in utility theory.
3. Acquire generic knowledge about different types of risk.

1.1.1 Randomness and uncertainty

Financial risk management has its roots in the history of commercial and financial trades, but it is still a modern quantitative discipline. Its development began during the 1970s, on the premises of the first Basel Accord, between the G10 countries, which covered the regulation of banking risk.

Modern financial markets are constantly subject to speculative attacks and external shocks, given the uncertainty of the actual worldwide economic environment. Financial risk management is therefore in a state of confusion, and gained focus, in recent years, on the minimization of capital charges and corporate risk.

Managing risk is about making decisions under uncertainty, with decisions involving a large share of investors, and determining the outcome of investing strategies for even bigger investors, like banks.

It is now clear that old-fashioned financial risk management has contributed in generating the most severe financial crisis the world ever experienced, due to common use of static risk measurement methodologies and unrestrictive regulatory provisions. As a consequence of the lacks in regulation and modelling efficiency, the policies of banks and financial institutions have fed the bubble until it burst, with the effects of the explosion spreading all over the world.

The subprime mortgage affair in the US turned quite fast into a global crisis, involving all sectors of the financial and real economy. At some point it was clear that something was wrong in how risk assessment of new assets had been managed until then.

One of the first definitions of the difference between uncertainty and risk was given by Knight, in 1921. He argued that uncertainty differs from risk for the important reason that risk can be measured precisely.

This difference also plays a crucial role in financial markets, given that, if risk were the only relevant feature of randomness, it could have been possible for financial institutions properly equipped, to price and market insurance contracts based on risky phenomena only. The role of uncertainty is to create frictions that cannot be easily accommodated.

Uncertainty then refers to the situation where an event has an unknown probability, and individuals tend to choose gambles with precise expected outcomes, compared to gambles with unknown odds.

Both uncertainty and risk define a random environment and affect individuals and their choices. The behaviour of individual agents is often counterintuitive, if confronted with the classic expected utility model, and research has focused on that aspect.

Based on the fact that, if uncertainty is so influential on individual behaviour, an equilibrium outcome should exist, Knight claims that, as opposed to risk, uncertainty cannot be insured.

The presence of uncertainty causes a departure from standard utility theory and sets an environment where insurance markets may break down, while the randomness of probabilities does not allow for precise pricing of risky claims.

Randomness drives risk and uncertainty, and the two concepts are strictly linked to each other but with some differences. Risk entails the existence of a measurable probability associated with the event.

Probabilities are calculated directly or by induction, depending on the availability of observable variables. Calculation by induction is made via analytical models or by analysis of the past information.

In a few words, risk is a quantifiable variable, while uncertainty is not. This is the main distinction between risk and uncertainty. The purpose of financial analysis is to assess risk based on available information.

When a choice must be made, both uncertainty and risk apply. In financial literature most of the work has been done on risk, given its calculability. It is anyway not appropriate to fully ignore uncertainty.

Example 1.1: Consider two portfolios traded on a market. The first portfolio, *A*, is a risk-free investment on government bonds, while the second portfolio, *B*, includes risky complex securities written on a market index. If the expected return on portfolio *A* is 2.5%, and the expected return on portfolio *B* is 9.5%, that means investors are demanding an extra 7% to move their money from a risk-free investment to a risky investment.

The concept of risk spans different disciplines from insurance and engineering to classical economic theories like portfolio theory. Each discipline defines risk in a different way. Some of these definitions are in terms of:

a. Probability and consequences: This definition of risk focuses on the likelihood of an event to happen and the consequences of the event. Both aspects are involved in ranking the risk level of an event. Consider for example a tsunami: it has a very small probability of happening, but when happening, it will carry severe consequences. Therefore it would be ranked as a high-risk event.

b. Risk or threat: There is a difference between a threat and a risk. Threat is considered to be a very low probability event with extremely large negative outcomes and no possibility for analysts to assess the probability of that event to happen. Risk on the other hand is similar, but it involves events happening at a higher probability, where it is possible to assess both probability and outcome.

c. Positive and negative outcome: Definitions of risk may involve both positive and negative variability around the mean, or just focus on the downside scenarios. A fair definition of risk in this sense is the product of probability of an event occurring and the assessed value of the outcome. In the following chapters, it will be clear how this is the main definition of risk underlying the financial analysis.

To be more specific, in finance risk is defined as the (positive or negative) variability of financial returns on some type of investment, around some expected (mean) return. It is then fundamental to understand how to define risk broadly, in order to include both the positive and negative side of the variability.

The general rule of thumb is that there is a direct link between risk and reward. High levels of positive outcome can be obtained only by getting exposed to considerably large risk. The principle is that there is no free lunch in life, and especially in finance. In fact, the link between risk and return is a foundation of classical and modern finance theory.

In the following chapters this concept will become very clear. Just for now, it is primarily important to consider, as an example, the difference between investing on financial markets. Stocks are much riskier than bonds, and give a higher expected return.

The concept can be extended to all aspects of life. Therefore, for any business the key to success is the reliability of the decision on which type of risk it is worthwhile taking, and how much of it.

Protecting the business against all risk, in some sense results in limiting the profit opportunities. On the other hand, being exposed to the wrong type of risk can lead to even worse scenarios.

That's why a crucial part of good business management is about making the right choices on how to face different types of risk. Good risk management is a crucial part of good corporate management.

A typical example of risk and uncertainty in finance is the classical portfolio problem. Consider an agent endowed with a wealth of amount w, to invest. The market is very simple, being composed of a risk-free asset paying a fixed rate r and a risky asset with random return x. The random return is distributed according to a cumulative density function $F(x)$. The utility function of the investor u is assumed to be concave (this is very important for the existence of a risk measure, as will become clearer in the next sections).

The total wealth is invested by the individual, by dividing it between an amount m of the risky asset, and an amount $w - m$ in the risk-free asset. Therefore, the resulting portfolio value is given by the combination of the stochastic return on the risky asset, and the deterministic return on the risk-free asset, and can be written as

$$p = mx + (w - m)r$$

The problem of asset allocation, among the assets in the market, entails an optimization program, which maximizes the expected utility from the investment strategy as described.

The investor maximizes the portfolio value given the utility function, and the program is defined as

$$\max \int u\left[mx + (w - m)r\right]dF(x)$$

The first order condition for the program is

$$\int u'\left[m(x - r) + wr\right](x - r)dF(x) = 0$$

If the investor is risk neutral, there is no need of compensation for the risk taken, and the resulting utility function is linear and directly proportional to the value of the risky asset, in the form

$$u(x) = \lambda x$$

where

λ is some constant.

This means the marginal return on the investment is given by the sum of returns on both the risk-free and the risky part of the investment.

$$r_M = \lambda r (w - m) + \lambda m E(x)$$

where

$E(x)$ is the expected return on the risky asset,

which is equivalent to

$$r_M = \lambda w r + \lambda m \left[E(x) - r \right] \tag{1.1}$$

Equation (1.1) shows that returns are always positive if $E(x) > r$ and always negative otherwise. The logical consequence is that a risk-neutral investor will always invest all the wealth in the asset with highest expected return.

Given this result, the concavity of the utility function also implies that the marginal return given by investing a bit more in the risky asset is always positive. This is a very important result, implying that a risk-averse investor will choose to not put all the wealth on just the risk-free asset.

All types of investors will always choose to put at least a small bit of their wealth in the risky assets. In terms of insurance, this means that a risk-adverse agent will never choose to buy full insurance, unless insurance prices are equal or below the fair actuarial level, where the fair actuarial price is the price corresponding to a zero net present value.

1.1.2 Rationality and risk aversion

The theory of rational expectations is a foundation of modern economics and finance. It includes assumptions on how the investors (agents) process the available information to form their expectations.

There are some firm points in the theory of rationality and information, which is scarce on the markets, so that it is important to keep track of the relevant knowledge. Investors form their expectations in a way that depends on the structure of the economic system, and the information history embedded in market prices.

In finance, the outcome of many situations depends on the expectations of investors. Often prices depend on the trading decision of the investors, which in turn depend on how the investors behave on the market.

People tend to rush in selling and buying assets, following the predictions they have on the market price. Financial markets tend to adjust very quickly to new information and investors must be quick in implementing their strategies.

There is a two-way flow of influences between expectations and outcomes, so that people try to make forecasts of what will occur, and base their expectations on that.

Better forecasts mean better profits.

Investors adjust their expectation and the way they interpret the information is highly dependent on the past outcome of the process. They adapt the forecasting rules to previous errors, to eliminate them.

Rational expectations theory states that outcomes do not differ from people's predictions, when these are based on rational processing of the universally available information. Singularly taken, the investors can make mistakes, but the various sides of the market will adjust rapidly and those mistakes will not be persistent.

The theory is based on the assumption that people behave in order to maximize their utility and this belief is the core of a theory that tries to predict future outcomes of an economic system, based on past decisions of the agents.

Rational expectations are at the basis of many theories, like the random walk theory of financial assets, the efficient market hypothesis, economic theories of consumption, public economic policies, and more.

The efficient market hypothesis applies rational expectations to efficient markets and asset pricing. It concludes that, after adjusting for discounting and dividends, the changes in a stock price follow a random walk process.

The main bug in classical consumer choice theory is that all the results are drawn in a framework of certainty. However, as mentioned above, the real world is characterized by uncertainty, so that bad things may happen, and agents must adapt to it.

Investors make choices in a context of uncertainty and the outcomes are often unpredictable. But there is a need to look forward, and make predictions somehow. In order to get a realistic model of choice, it is necessary to model uncertainty.

A standard gamble has the following expected payoff:

$$E(x) = p_+ x_+ + (1 - p_+) x_-$$

where

p_+ is the probability of a positive outcome
x_+ is the positive outcome
x_- is the negative outcome.

If asked about entering a fair gamble with positive payoff, most people behave in such a way that they would reject a gamble even if it has an expected positive payoff, when the uncertain prospects are worth less in utility terms than certain ones, even when expected tangible payoffs are the same.

Example 1.2: Assume you are offered a fair gamble. A coin is tossed with a positive payoff (win) of €1,000 if it is heads and a negative payoff (loss) of €850 if it is tails. The expected value is

$$E(x) = 0.5 \times 1,000 - 0.5 \times 850 = €75$$

A positive value suggests the gamble is worth being accepted. However, the downside potential loss is so consistent, compared to the winning amount, that most people would reject the gamble.

In order to characterize mathematically the utility maximization framework, leading to the definition of risk and risk measurement, define a world with $1,2,...,n$ possible states associated with probabilities $p_i = p_1, p_2,..., p_n$. The expected value is defined as

$$E(x) = \sum_{i=1}^{n} p_i x_i$$

Dispersion (variance) is measured as

$$Var(x) = \sum_{i=1}^{n} p_i \left(x_i - E(x) \right)^2$$

Example 1.3: A stock has a 25% probability, in one year, of being worth €400 and a 75% probability of being worth €200. The expected value is

$$E(x) = 0.25 \times 400 + 0.75 \times 200 = €250$$

and the variance is

$$Var(x) = 0.25 \times (400 - 250)^2 + 0.75 \times (200 - 250)^2 = 7500$$

By standard theory of utility, a utility function on the real domain $U \mid_{\mathbb{R}}$ has an expected utility form if it is possible to assign values $u_1, u_2,..., u_n$ to the outcomes of a simple lottery. The expected value of the lottery is then given by

$$E(x) = \sum_{i=1}^{n} p_i u_i$$

where

p_i is the probability of outcome i in the simple lottery.

Consider also the compound lottery defined as $(l_1, l_2,..., l_J; \pi_1, \pi_2,..., \pi_J)$ being the set yielding the lottery l_j with probability π_j. A utility function has the expected utility form if and only if

$$u\left(\sum_{j=1}^{J} \pi_j l_j \right) = \sum_{j=1}^{J} \pi_j u(l_j)$$

The shape of the utility function determines the different relationships between expected outcomes and the utility they give. In particular, for a lottery with n outcomes, the main distinction is between the expected value of the utility, defined as

$$E\big[u(x)\big] = \sum_{i=1}^{n} p_i u(x_i)$$

and the utility of the expected outcome, which is given by

$$u\big[E(x)\big] = u\left(\sum_{i=1}^{n} p_i x_i\right)$$

The risk premium involved in the choice is defined as the difference between the wealth after entering the gamble, and the certain amount.

Example 1.4: Suppose an investor has an initial wealth $w = €100$ and utility function $U(w) = \sqrt{w}$. The risk premium associated with a gamble with 50% probability to get to a wealth of €120 and 50% of lowering the wealth to €80, is given by calculating the expected utility first, as

$$E\big[u(w)\big] = 0.5\sqrt{120} + 0.5\sqrt{80} = 9.95$$

Since $u(w) = \sqrt{w} \Rightarrow w = \big[u(w)\big]^2$, the wealth associated with it is given by

$$w = 9.95^2 = €98.99$$

And the risk premium is given by

$$RP = 100 - 98.99 = €1.01$$

The relationship between the expected utility and the utility of the expectation determines the risk attitude of the investors. It turns out that if

$$E\big[u(x)\big] = u\big[E(x)\big]$$

where

$u(.)$ is a concave utility function, the investor is risk neutral. If, instead,

$$E\big[u(x)\big] > u\big[E(x)\big]$$

the investor is a risk-taker. Finally, if

$$E\big[u(x)\big] < u\big[E(x)\big]$$

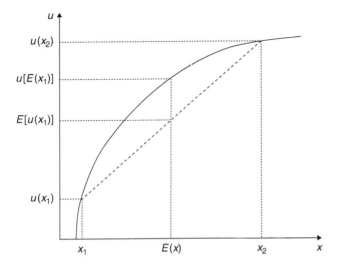

Figure 1.1 A concave utility function implies the investor is risk averse. Notice by comparing points D and E that the concavity of the elementary utility function implies that the utility of expected income, u[E(x)] is greater than expected utility E(u).

the investor is risk-averse.

To see the point mathematically, following Levin (2006), define a lottery by some cumulative distribution function, where the minimum amount x to be paid out is received with probability $F(x)$. Given that preferences are represented by the expected utility u, it holds that

$$u(F) = \int u(x)dF(x), \quad \forall F(x)$$

Defining $E(F)$ as a degenerate lottery giving a sure reward, an investor is said to be risk averse if, given the certain amount

$$E(F) = \int xdF(x)$$

the investor has a strict preference for the certain amount instead of the random lottery F. The risk-aversion relationship can be mathematically defined by means of Jensen's inequality

$$\int u(x)dF(x) \leq u\left[\int xdF(x)\right], \quad \forall F$$

so that the investor is risk averse if and only if the utility u is concave (Figure 1.1).

From the definition of certainty equivalent of a lottery F, given by

$$CE_u = \int u(x)dF(x)$$

it follows that when u is concave, the following holds:

$$u_C \leq E(F)$$

The certainty equivalent provides a measure of the degree of risk aversion among different investors. Given two investors, with Bernoulli utility functions u and v, it can be said that u is more risk averse than v if

$$CE_u \leq CE_v$$

The risk aversion is proportional to the concavity of the utility functions, which are anyway not uniquely defined. A measure that stays constant up to affine transformations of the utility function is therefore needed, to measure risk aversion.

Following all the above considerations, it is possible to define the Arrow-Pratt coefficient of absolute risk aversion, which stays constant up to affine transformations of the utility function, and is given by

$$AR_x = \frac{-u''(x)}{u'(x)}$$

which relates the risk aversion of the investor to the shape of the utility function.

Another coefficient of risk aversion is given by multiplying AR_x by the value of x, to give

$$RR_x = \frac{-xu''(x)}{u'(x)}$$

which is a still valid measure of risk aversion, also accounting for changes in the concavity of the utility function from risk aversion to risk taking, as x varies.

1.1.3 Types of risk

Risk can arise from multiple sources. As said above, there are many different types of risk a corporation faces during daily activity. Some of them involve non-economic aspects of the business operations. The ones of interest to this section are the types of economic risk associated with the company.

The purpose of this section, in fact, is to give a list and insight on the major types of financial risks, that will be dealt with more completely in the following chapters. Each source is very peculiar and entails a different approach to the risk process.

First of all, financial risk can be divided into two sub-categories, which are not related to the source of the risk itself, but to the possibility of eliminating it or not.

Systematic risk influences the whole market where an asset is traded. Big external shocks (i.e. political events, natural disaster) that are not company related, may have an impact on systematic risk, affecting the prices of most stocks in the market. Getting protection against this type of risk is virtually impossible.

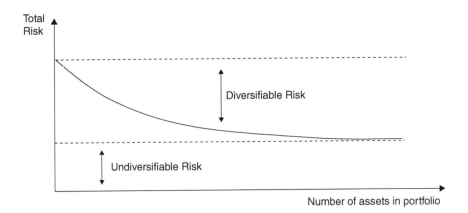

Figure 1.2 The effects of diversification on the riskiness of a portfolio of assets. By adding assets in the portfolio the diversifiable risk decreases while the systemic (undiversifiable) risk cannot be reduced.

Specific (unsystematic) risk is company (asset) specific, and can be reduced through diversification, due to the covariance effect of assets moving in opposite directions, leading to a reduction of volatility compared to the sum of the volatilities of the single assets.

Factors that have an impact on it range from employees' behaviour, to production issues, profit warnings, and more. From a portfolio management point of view, specific risk is diversifiable. Adding more assets to the portfolio reduces the risk, and virtually eliminates it beyond some level of diversification (Figure 1.2).

Financial risk is mainly caused by adverse movement of many factors, and can be classified into various types. Major risk sources include, but are not limited to, Market Risk, Interest Rate Risk, Credit Risk, Liquidity Risk, Operational Risk, Currency Risk and Volatility Risk.

Financial risk comes from many different sources. Most chapters of the book are dedicated to detailed analysis of the single sources of risk. Here is a list with introductions to all of them.

Market risk is the core of Chapter 5. It is the risk of loss on portfolio value due to movements in market prices. Market prices entail stock prices, interest rates, exchange rates and commodity prices.

Any change of the reference variable results in a gain or loss in the value of the portfolio. Other forms of risk like liquidity and credit risk can amplify market risk, since all risks are interconnected.

Every bank, investor and other institution should assess in advance how much market risk they are willing to assume. This is an issue that relates to the levels of risk capital for risk coverage. Often the amount of capital to set aside is determined by regulators.

As an example, consider a bank willing to manage optimally its market risk. First of all some factors must be taken into consideration.

•   Conditions of market and the economy where the bank is operating.
•   Ability to perform profitable business in the reference market.
•   The composition of the portfolio of assets.

All these factors can determine how much market risk an investor or financial institution is willing to bear, and how the right balance of several positions on the markets can be reached.

Measurement of market risk typically involves the use of Value at Risk (VaR) methodology. VaR is a well-established risk management technique based on the normal distribution. It contains a number of limiting assumptions that constrain its accuracy. In the following chapters, VaR and its limitations are explored.

Interest rate risk (Chapter 6) is the risk of a decrease in value of an investment due to an adverse change in interest rates. This risk mainly affects debt securities like bonds, and only marginally equity securities like stocks.

Bond prices and yields are inversely related. When the interest rate rises, bond prices go down, and vice versa. This is the core of the interest rate risk disclosure. The bond yield to maturity of a bond shows the return on investing in that bond.

Holding a bond until maturity involves scarce concern about interest rate fluctuations during bond life, since at maturity the par (face) value will be paid, which is a contractual fixed amount, carrying no risk.

Interest rates are therefore connected to bond trading before maturity, and their direction and level are affected by various factors. In a growing economy interest rates go up, while they fall in time of recession. Also inflation has an impact on the level of interest rates, with a direct relationship. When inflation rises, interest rates rise.

Ignoring interest rate risk may not be a problem, but sometimes can be a very bad decision. In fact, a large amount of money invested in fixed income may result in huge losses even for small movements of interest rates.

Credit risk can take many forms, given the many different types of counterparties and the many different types of obligations available. There are important factors in common for all types of credit risk:

•   Default Probability (DP) is the likelihood that a company or investor will default on its payments at some time point before maturity. Risky companies have a higher default probability than safe ones. Therefore high default probabilities entail higher risk and higher expected return.
•   Expected Exposure (EE) is the amount at risk in case the default occurs, at a specified point of time.
•   Recovery Rate (RR) is the part of the loss that can be recovered in case default occurs, as a fraction of the total loss, going bankrupt or through other forms of settlement.

The risk depends on the quality of the obligation, which depends itself on the creditworthiness of the counterparty. The quality is represented by the uncertainty connected to the obligation. When repayment is very uncertain, risk perception increases, and the risk associated, accordingly.

Credit risk is the focus of Chapter 7. It is the risk that a counterparty will not be able to face its debt obligations, failing to pay back the due interest and capital. Credit risk is common for bond holders, since bonds represent the debt of a counterparty (company or government), therefore they carry credit risk.

In Western markets, mainly populated by countries with a strong economy, government bonds are usually considered to be less risky, being safer than corporate bonds.

Therefore they have a lower return, while corporate bonds usually have higher risk and higher return. Bonds are considered to be investment grade when they have a low chance of default, while being considered junk bonds when they have a high chance of default.

The simplest forms of credit risk measurement are credit scoring, soft data, information gathered prior to the transactions. The information is processed using a formula that produces a number, called a credit score. Given the calculated value of the credit score, the lending institution can decide whether or not to grant a credit extension. Other forms are complicated and require less standardized approaches. This is typically the case of large counterparties and/or amounts of transactions.

Foreign exchange risk (Chapter 9) refers to the possibility of market movements of exchange rates, when investing in a foreign currency. Foreign exchange risk affects any financial instruments that are denominated in a currency other than domestic.

An investment in foreign currency exposes the investor to currency risk. If the exposure is not hedged, changes in the exchange rate may have substantial effects on the expected return from the investment.

In theory, currency risk, like any other risk, can be good or bad according to the amount of risk borne by the investor. However, there is some empirical evidence in the literature that exposure to currency risk does not reward investors with higher returns.

Transactions in international trade usually involve a delayed transfer of funds, that happen at a different point in time. Therefore the currency risk is also attached to a time delay that creates uncertainty about what the exchange rate will be at payment day.

Foreign currencies are traded in organized markets. The spot market hosts trades in the actual currencies, while future and forward markets are the place for the transactions in currency that will happen at some point in the future. A common practice is in fact for companies to enter contracts to transfer to a counterparty the right to receive currency payments at a future time.

Chapter 8 deals with liquidity risk, which is due to an inability to execute transactions. It can be divided into two sub-categories:

- Funding risk relates to the ability of the corporation to have enough cash to pay the daily liabilities. There are good indicators of the liquidity situation of the firm, like the current ratio or quick ratio.
- Market liquidity risk is the risk arising when an asset is illiquid. In this case, it is very difficult to close a long position selling back the asset for cash. The realized value on the asset is significantly lower, due to lack of buyers. Assets like stocks, bonds and derivatives usually carry a low liquidity risk. The opposite holds for alternative assets.

Market liquidity risk can be a function of several factors like the market microstructure (some markets are more liquid than others), the type of asset traded (alternative assets are illiquid due to their complexity), asset substitution (the possibility to replace an asset with some other increases liquidity), time horizon (urgency of selling generates a rush and consequently carries liquidity risk).

Operational risk (Chapter 9) arises out of operational failures or technical failures. A common classification of operational risk includes Fraud Risk, which arises due to lack of controls and Model Risk, due to incorrect model application.

The Basel Committee defines operational risk as 'the risk of direct or indirect loss resulting from inadequate or failed internal processes, people and systems or from external events'. The definition does not include strategic and reputational risk.

Measurement of operational risk focuses on the right calculation of capital for operational risk, in the form of internal calculations and regulatory compliance. Some companies are not subject to regulatory requirements and include the operational risk capital in the bunch of the whole strategic capital allocation.

Processing failures are just a subset of operational risk. These risks are usually not uncertain, therefore they carry relatively low losses and can be easily managed. Failures which are not typical drive the real operational risk. Among others, these failures comprise illegal practices and general violation of moral standards.

The key to modern operational risk management is about developing a consistent process incorporating risk control, and reward, to align it with standard risk expectations of investors and stakeholders.

It is not easy to develop a structured process for risk management. There are consequences for any different risk category. A multidimensional approach is crucial in order to assess the potential losses associated with the various categories.

Snapshot 1.1
Common forms of utility functions

It is possible to define some specific forms of utility function, and derive the absolute and relative risk-aversion coefficients for them.
The simplest case is the Linear utility, which is given by

$$u_L(x) = \beta x, \quad \beta > 0$$

The first and second derivative of the linear utility are given by

$$u'_L(x) = \beta, \quad u''_L(x) = 0$$

The second derivative is equal to zero, so that both ARA and CRA are equal to zero.
   The Constant Absolute Risk Aversion (CARA) is defined as

$$u_A(x) = 1 - e^{-\beta x}, \quad \beta > 0$$

The first and second derivative of the CARA utility are given by

$$u'_A(x) = \beta e^{-\beta x} > 0, \quad u''_A(x) = -\beta^2 e^{-\beta x} < 0$$

So that the ARA and RRA are defined as

$$ARA_A = -\frac{-\beta^2 e^{-\beta x}}{\beta e^{-\beta x}} = \beta, \quad RRA_A = -\frac{-x\beta^2 e^{-\beta x}}{\beta e^{-\beta x}} = x\beta$$

The Constant Relative Risk Aversion (CRRA) is defined as

$$u_R(x) = \frac{x^{1-\beta} - 1}{1 - \beta}, \quad \beta > 0$$

The first and second derivative of the CRRA utility are given by

$$u_R'(x) = x^{-\beta} > 0, \quad u_R''(x) = -\beta x^{-\beta-1} < 0$$

So that the ARA and RRA are defined as

$$ARA_C = -\frac{-\beta x^{-\beta-1}}{x^{-\beta}} = \frac{\beta}{x}, \quad RRA_C = -\frac{-x\beta x^{-\beta-1}}{x^{-\beta}} = \beta$$

1.2 The process of risk management

Learning outcomes

1. Describe financial risk in different types of business.
2. Learn about the risk management process.
3. Implement various risk response strategies.

1.2.1 Risk in corporations and financial institutions

There are two main categories of risk that a business has to face in its daily activities. Business risk and financial risk, as opposed to how they are commonly known, are not the same. That is why it is important to know the differences between these risks, in order to manage them appropriately and keep the company profitable.

The difference is important also from an investor relationship perspective. When it comes to speaking with financial investors, institutions and actors having an interest in the company, the distinction becomes crucial.

Business risk involves all the forms of risk related to business decisions besides financial decisions. Examples of business risks are the risk of entering a new market, entering into a partnership with another business.

The assessment of risk is done internally by calculating efficiency and assessing the convenience of entering a new project by calculating how the value of the company will be affected by it.

Among the factors affecting the business risk in a company there are fluctuations in demand for certain products or services, competition from other companies introducing similar products on the same market, cutting down the sales of the first company.

Other examples relate to external factors, like authorities' new interventions, changes in consumers' preferences and utility. Internal factors like the change of profitability ratios (gross margin, net margin, profit margin) are also potential sources of business risk.

Financial risk relates to how the capital of the company is structured. The focus is usually on corporate debt, and companies having huge amounts of debt financing are considered to be very risky, even if the assessment must also take into account the profitability generated by the investments financed by that debt.

Financial risk can be affected by many factors, including the features and structure of the financial market hosting the activities of the corporation. In case of a poor economy, the macroeconomic factors like undeveloped financial markets, high level of interest rates and underrated currency may result in high risk, independently of the company structure and operations.

In more developed countries, usually risk is associated with the level of debt in the company capital structure. The leverage of a company (ratio of debt over equity) can be used to assess the riskiness of the business. Companies with high leverage usually entail higher levels of financial risks.

Among the various risks a company is exposed to, here the focus is on the economic risks that can arise during the daily life of the firm. The risk management process is composed of

1. Identification
2. Measurement
3. Mitigation and/or transfer

The aim of this part is to analyse the general methods of risk management in a financial institution. Corporate stockholders are ready to accept that success for the business relies on taking appropriate risks.

Given that risk is well rewarded, why then should companies try to manage it? There are many reasons behind the choice of hedging corporate risk. One of the main issues for a company is the riskiness of its debt.

If the company can no longer face its obligations, it may incur default, with consequent direct and indirect costs that a firm should try to avoid.

Direct costs are directly related with the default of the company, and they mostly involve the expenses of reorganizing the business through a bankruptcy process. Indirect costs are related to negative effects of default, like the difficulties in attracting new customers, or in general entering contracts with economic agents.

One must consider that there are opportunity costs arising even if default never occurs. The riskiness itself generates costs, and that's why it is optimal to hedge risk most of the time.

Managers could decide to behave unethically when default approaches. Usually on behalf of shareholders, managers tend to make suboptimal decisions when the situation starts to deteriorate.

Decisions include underinvesting in profitable projects, when those are only beneficial to bondholders, as well as investing in negative net present value projects, that carry risks only for bondholders.

Classic theory shows how it is possible to reduce likelihood to default by reducing the variability of cash flows, as well as through reduction of the leverage. On the other hand, the tax shield attached to debt holding makes it convenient to leverage the capital structure until some fair amount.

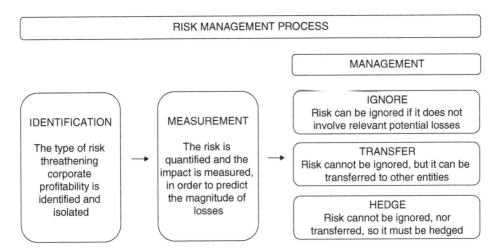

Figure 1.3 An example of risk management process for a typical corporation.

The earnings must exceed interest payments in order for the tax shield benefits to be effective, and generally it is possible to transfer the benefits to subsequent years. Anyway in general the process involves loss of value, making it optimal to hedge risk in order to reduce the likelihood of losses.

Managers are usually compensated according to the performance of the business they care about. Therefore managers are usually risk averse, since their revenue is tied to the profitability of the firm.

There is a common interest of hedging risk for both managers and the company. The company will also pay less aggregate compensation to managers, due to the fact that risk-averse employees are willing to accept lower compensation if the whole employment package is less risky.

Sometimes risk has an impact on the price of shares, especially when publicly traded. Uncertainty about the ability of the firm to meet its earnings and cash-flow targets drives investors to react on financial markets. That generates high variability on the stock price that cannot be explained by market fluctuations.

Hedging against negative performance ensures stock prices are stable and/or just positively affected by new information. This is of primary importance especially considering the asymmetry in investors' reaction that usually follows these kinds of signals.

Securing good revenues and cash flows also creates a source of capital at a very cheap cost. When a company needs capital for new projects the external sources are usually quite expensive.

Both equity and debt financing involve a cost, whereas having cash in place due to stable positive revenues allows fresh capital to be accessed at no cost.

Financial institutions have to process their risk exposure adequately in order to keep profitability and safety of investors at a high level. Moreover there are social implications in the riskiness of financial institutions, especially banks.

In the following parts of the chapters, the various types of risk are introduced and commented on. Limiting the analysis to banks, the risks that are typically faced and need monitoring are:

1. Credit risk
2. Market risk
3. Operational risk

Further risks are secondary to a bank, while becoming very important for financial investors, and will be discussed later on. Banks must assess the three types of risk continuously in order to succeed.

As seen above, credit risk relates to possible losses from a credit portfolio. Losses can be divided into expected and unexpected losses.

Market risk and operational risk are easier to calculate since there are more data available.

After all risk categories have been addressed, the last step is aggregation. In order to perform an accurate risk measurement, correlation effects must be taken into account. The correlation among counterparties and among risks plays a crucial role in assessing the right amount of aggregate risk for each bank.

Aggregation happens among different risks, and among different departments for the same risk. The management has then the chance to grasp the overall risk of a complex system and use the information to plan future activities and business.

Risk management is the process to be used by corporations to address the uncertainty surrounding their core activities. Diversification and balance ensure the portfolio of activities is profitable and fairly safe.

Good risk management relies on identification and management of all risks, in order to add value to the corporation. It entails good understanding of the variability associated with the factors affecting the outcome of business. Successful business goes through good risk management, which should run as a continuous process, developing parallel to the development of business activities.

1.2.2 Identification, measurement and mitigation

Risk process is an important task for managers, as important as good business plans. The first step in the risk process is identification. Companies should identify the different types of risk, analyse the risk factors and possibly evaluate the consequences.

To analyse financial risk in the corporation there are several methodologies. The most widely used is fundamental financial analysis. The tool is based on information about the firm, where the information mainly comes from the financial statement of the company.

The analysis of balance sheet, income statement and cash-flow statement is an important step in order to assess the risk exposure of the corporation.

Using the data in the financial statement, it is possible to identify the causes of exposure to any specific factor. Consequently the relation between each factor and the company risk exposure drives future decisions.

This type of analysis can be done either for limited internal use or even for external purposes, in the form of communications and reports to the stakeholders and the public. Potential investors in a firm are always concerned about the riskiness of the business. It is not surprising that big companies dedicate a lot of resources to it.

The first element of the financial statement is the balance sheet presenting the company's assets and the liability and equity claims against those assets.

The capital structure of the company is crucial to the degree of risk it is exposed to. Therefore the balance sheet analysis is based on ratios calculated on the assets and liabilities lines. The most important are:

- Debt on Equity ratio shows the financial leverage of the firm. The higher the ratio, the higher the risk.
- Debt on Asset ratio shows what part of the firm's capital is financed through debt.
- Return on Asset (ROA) describes how much capital is financed by the profits, therefore independently of debt sources and recapitalizations.
- Long-term debt on total debt describes the structure of company liabilities.

Other ratios refer to the liquidity of the company and include current ratio, cash ratio (cash divided by current liabilities) and quick ratio. All ratios are static, being based on the balance sheet. Other ratios can be calculated on the income statement.

Another important element is the net working capital (difference between current assets and current liabilities).

Both long-term and short-term financial entries give important information to be translated into ratios and risk awareness. The rule is that the company should at least manage to finance fixed assets by fixed capital. This should keep the risk very low.

Some companies operate internal risk management departments, but nowadays it is quite common for some companies to outsource the risk management tasks and engage outside consultants.

The professionals can give a competent view in terms of risk assessment. In particular they offer many advantages. For example risk can be handled without distracting important resources from the core business.

External consultants are able to identify risk forms that are not visible to insiders, and require an external eye and a broader view on the company. Moreover, usually inside risk management tends to underestimate some types of risk.

In general, the process of risk management requires lots of time and resources. In some specific periods of the company life, carrying out a risk analysis can be a very cumbersome task. External consultants help to assess risk with a consistent efficiency throughout the whole life of the firm.

Risk assessment involves analysing the likelihood and consequences of possible risk events, in order to prioritize which of them should receive proper treatment. The criteria to evaluate the risk likelihood can be summarized in Table 1.1.

After the likelihood of the risk event occurring has been established, it is also important to establish the severity of the consequences of the event on the corporation. This is represented in Table 1.2.

Merging the information from the previous tables, the result is an aggregate table, showing complete information about the riskiness of each event, in terms of the potential impact on the profitability of the firm. This is usually represented in the risk priority table (Table 1.3).

Table 1.1 An example of how the likelihood of a risk event can be classified. Several levels of likelihood correspond to different probabilities for an event to happen.

Level	Likelihood of event
5	**Almost certain**: The event will occur with a probability very close to 100%
4	**Very likely**: High probability that the event will occur in the short-medium term
3	**Possible**: Reasonable likelihood that the event will occur in the medium-long term
2	**Unlikely**: Low probability of an event, even in the medium-long term
1	**Rare**: The event will occur with a probability very close to 0%

Table 1.2 An example of the impact a shock may have, given that the event has occurred. Several levels of impact severity correspond to higher damages to the business.

Level	Impact
5	**Disaster**: The desired outcome will not be achieved at all
4	**Severe**: The outcome is heavily affected by the shock, with big losses
3	**Moderate**: The business is partially affected, with moderate losses
2	**Minor:** The impact of the shock does not play a major role on the outcome
1	**Negligible**: The impact is so small that it can be ignored

Table 1.3 The likelihood and impact scales can be combined to get a table of the different combinations of risk.

	Catastrophe	Major	Moderate	Severe	Disaster
Almost certain	Extreme	Extreme	Major	Major	Medium
Very likely	Extreme	Extreme	Major	Medium	Minor
Possible	Extreme	Major	Major	Medium	Minor
Unlikely	Major	Major	Medium	Minor	Minor
Rare	Medium	Medium	Minor	Minor	Minor

After identification, risk must be dealt with appropriately. A good risk mitigation program can address the responsibility for the monitoring of the various risks. This includes mitigation of any material weaknesses in processes that serve to uncover or control risks.

The company board should implement recommendation from the identification stage in order to reduce the risk exposure. This happens through monitoring the change within an organization and recognizing that unplanned change can serve as a warning for a variety of risks.

Vigilance against signals of inappropriate governance should be effective. Moreover board members should formalize controls and make them effective. Transparent Financial Reporting is another important issue, translating into a clear and accessible report of the firm's financial situation and exposure.

1.2.3 Risk response strategies

In risk management, risk response is the strategy to be implemented to deal with risk after it has been identified and measured. Risks are first quantified and ranked in terms of impact and severity.

Response to risk is based on risk tolerance. When the level of risk is below tolerance, two possible reactions are avoidance and acceptance. In case tolerance is overtaken and an active strategy is needed, the two possible strategies are mitigation and transfer.

Many factors must be considered in order to choose the right strategy to adopt. For example, if a task is connected to other dependent tasks, the riskiness of the first can involve also the others. In this case, if severity is measured only on the first task, it could be underrated compared to the cumulative risk.

Acceptance implies risk severity is so low that it is not worth doing anything until the risk event occurs. That also means risk is lower than tolerance level and when the risk event occurs, it is worth fixing the problem. Low severity and acceptance of risk in fact do not mean nothing will be done against the event. It only means that no preventing actions will be taken until the event occurs. Many insignificant risks fall into this category and they are not the focus of our discussion.

Acceptance can be active or passive. Active acceptance implies the risk can be accepted but anyway a plan should be made about what to do if the risk occurs. The point is to have a plan well in advance to not rush at the last moment.

Passive acceptance happens when there is no planning at all to face the event. The risk is too small to generate a real concern, therefore actions are taken in real time when needed, and not planned before.

Another form of response is transfer. It involves externalizing the responsibility for the risk. One way to transfer risk is to refuse parts of a project, simply because they carry too much risk. The risky parts can be transferred onto other projects.

Another way to transfer risk is through demand of goods or services at a fixed price. Negotiating a fixed price means the contractor working on the project bears the risk of extra costs on the project realization.

Vendor reaction is usually to increase the fixed price compared to what a fair price could be, in order to include a risk quote in the fixed price itself, taking into account what could be normal compensation for possible risk.

This way to deal with risk introduces the concept of risk premium, that is useful to understand how risk compensation works in financial markets, as well as in ordinary business transactions.

The most common way to transfer risk is through insurance. Insurance involves paying a relatively small amount of money in order to transfer the risk to the insurance company. This amount is significantly small compared to the cost of the risk itself and the insurance pays if the risk event happens.

Another form of response is risk avoidance, which consists of eliminating completely the possibility of risk. Risk can be eliminated from any project at the beginning, or dealt with after.

It should be clear that eliminating risks at the beginning is also a way to reduce the possible profits from a project or investment. Therefore it is not a straightforward strategy to implement, but requires a proper assessment. In project design, risk can be sometimes avoided just by designing the project around it.

Risk mitigation is another form of response. It involves dealing with unacceptable risk in a way to reduce it below the tolerance level. The mitigation is obtained usually by reducing the probability of the risk event to happen. This reduces the expected loss associated with the risk and therefore requires less capital to be put in it.

The trick is to spend some small amount of money to rework the project or investment in order to reduce the risk and avoid future large expenses due to losses.

In general all responses cost some money. Avoidance requires money to redesign the investment, and no money must be then allocated for the risk. Acceptance on the other side does not involve initial cost, beside planning, and requires money to be allocated for contingencies.

Risk mitigation involves setting up a budget in order to face a risk event, but also requires some initial amount of money in order to finance the mitigation activities. Risk transfer requires a small amount of money to be given to the insurance or to the sub-contractor.

1.3 Theory of markets

Learning outcomes

1. Acquire basic knowledge about information and rationality on financial markets.
2. Learn and master the concept of arbitrage.
3. Understand the Brownian Motion.

1.3.1 Arbitrage

A central concept in financial theory is the absence of arbitrage. Arbitrage is the practice of buying and selling the same good in different markets in order to take advantage of price differences, and profit on it without taking any risk.

In order for an arbitrage to exist on the market, one of the following conditions must be satisfied:

- An asset is traded at different prices on different markets.
- Two assets with same cash flows are traded at different prices.
- The actual market price of an asset is different from the discounted future price.

If a market is free of arbitrage, prices cannot imply risk-free profits without taking any risk. Arbitrage theory is a central component of market normality, and explains most of the price movements in financial markets.

There are two types of financial arbitrage:

- Arbitrage of the first kind is the opportunity to make investments with null expenditure today, yielding a positive profit in the future. Short sell one asset and use the proceeds to buy another one to make the portfolio riskless.
- Arbitrage of the second kind instead is the opportunity to make investments with a negative investment today (a positive cash inflow), and a future non-negative cash flow.

The principle of no-arbitrage requires a sufficient number of individuals in the market to be rational enough and money oriented in order to take advantage of possible arbitrage opportunities and have enough resources to eliminate them quickly from the market. Any mispricing in fact can be eliminated by putting sufficient pressure on the price, in order to invert its trend towards equilibrium.

It is not so easy to establish in a continuous time setting whether prices of a given portfolio are arbitrage free. It all depends on the information available for developing trading strategies on the assets, which determine how arbitrage can be defined.

Example 1.5: Suppose the EUR/GBP exchange rate is simultaneously 0.84 in New York City and 0.85 in London. An investor can purchase €1,000,000 in New York for £840,000 and simultaneously sell €1,000,000 in London for £850,000. The investor faces no risk and yet earns a profit of £10,000 for simultaneously buying and selling Euro. This is an arbitrage, meaning the foreign exchange market is not in equilibrium. If a large number of investors try to buy Euro in New York and sell them in London, the exchange rate will rapidly rise in New York and fall in London until both exchange rates are identical. The market will then be in equilibrium and the no-arbitrage condition will be satisfied.

If the prices on the market do not allow for any arbitrage profit, the market is said to be normal, or arbitrage-free. Absence of arbitrage is a foundation of market equilibrium. In finance the no-arbitrage condition is widely used to calculate the risk-neutral prices of assets (derivatives in particular).

Example 1.6: Consider a stock trading at €52 on the London Stock Exchange and at €50.50 on the Frankfurt Stock Exchange. Profit could be guaranteed by purchasing the stock in Frankfurt and simultaneously selling the same amount of stock in London, assuming the price difference is sufficient to cover the commissions too. In order to exploit arbitrage, various security could be used, including stock and options, or convertibles and stock.

Conditions for an arbitrage to be effective are to buy or sell a product on one market and sell it on another market at a different price. The actions must take place simultaneously, without time delay. In practice, this is only possible when trading electronically, and even in that case, a small delay of even seconds would result in price changes due to market risk.

A common way to spot an arbitrage strategy is to observe a market with highly correlated assets. If one of the assets rapidly changes in price, while the other stays stable, it is very likely that soon also the second asset will follow in the price change. It is then possible to perform some trading strategy on the asset which is going to adjust, in order to profit from the price change.

There are many types of arbitrage, according to the markets and securities involved. Risk arbitrage comes typically in the following forms.

Fixed Income Arbitrage happens when an investor borrows at a low short-term interest rate and invests the proceedings at a high long-term rate, so to practise arbitrage on maturities.

Derivatives arbitrage refers to another type of arbitrage involving the use of financial derivatives related to some underlying asset. Derivatives prices should be always syncronized with the price of the underlying asset. Sometimes, the disequilibrium of supply and demand on the markets makes the sync not perfect, leaving space for arbitrage opportunities on the mispricing.

There are arbitrage arguments also for funds. Funds invest in portfolios of assets, with high diversification. When two funds are managing exactly the same portfolio, they should also have the same value. But sometimes this is not the case, and the funds may have different values. In this case, an arbitrage is possible.

Financial markets are full of arbitrage opportunities and most of them come from the fact that there are many ways to trade essentially the same asset, and many different assets are influenced by the same factors.

A common stock market arbitrage involves spotting indices or stocks that usually are highly correlated, and trading on them when they are out of sync. If one of the stocks moves in an opposite direction to the other, it is almost certain that sooner or later they will fall back in sync with each other again.

The strategy is then to sell the overvalued stock, and buy the one that is lagging. The resulting profit on the winning side will offset the loss on the other side. Many classes of investors apply this strategy very often, and the opportunities last for a very short time.

The major difference between true and risk arbitrage is that a different security is traded in the latter case. The risk arises because the two securities considered are different, even if they might be related, where the relationship can change at any time.

Another difference is that true arbitrage takes place in real time, with an instantaneous settlement, while risk arbitrage is on a much longer time horizon, and may take weeks or months to be fully exploited.

The no-arbitrage condition is fundamental for financial markets to function properly and be in equilibrium, and it is a foundation of modern financial theory. Any investor that bears zero risk and invests zero wealth must earn zero profits.

1.3.2 The efficient market hypothesis

Information flows continuously on the market. Investors react to that information and trade on assets accordingly, meaning the price adjusts almost immediately to hits of information on the market.

That means stock prices react only to new information, therefore they are independent of past information. New information is unpredictable, otherwise it would be incorporated in previous information through a prediction.

The logical consequence is that asset prices move unpredictably, and this is the core of the theory of random walk. Prices follow a random walk, reflecting the competition of investors to discover and process the relevant information on the market.

The trick to win on the financial market is to become aware of new information before any other investor does. Beating the market is the key to success and random walk assumption ensures that prices react only to new information.

The notion that all the past information is already incorporated in today's prices is called the Efficient Market Hypothesis (EMH), developed by Roberts (1967) and Fama (1970) among others, which comes in three different forms.

The weak-form version of the hypothesis states that stock prices already reflect all information derivable by past prices and volumes. Therefore technical analysis on past trends is useless.

Information signals lose value as they are received by the investors and processed into buy or sell signals. Prices adjust immediately.

According to the weak-form theory, prices are composed of three elements: past stock price, expected return on the stock and a random error component. The error component represents new information hitting the markets in the period observed.

$$S_t = S_{t-1} + E(r) + \varepsilon_{t-1}$$

where

S_t is the stock price at time t
$E(r)$ is the expected return on the asset
ε_{t-1} is a normally distributed, zero-mean error uncorrelated to R, $\forall t$.

Weak-form efficiency is a prerequisite for many asset pricing models like the Capital Asset Pricing Model and for option valuation models following the Black-Scholes-Merton framework.

The semi-strong-form version of EMH states that all the information that is publicly available must be reflected in the stock prices. Compared to the weak form, it adds information as firm statements, product quality, earnings forecast and more to the information available from past prices.

Again, if investors have access to public information, then prices will adjust immediately to it, due to investor reaction on the market.

The strong-form version of the theory states that prices reflect all possible information available about the company, including the most private information available only to company insiders.

It is an extreme version which is controversial since one can claim private information rarely becomes public. When this happens, it is a slow process so it does not make much sense to assume prices will reflect that kind of information.

Authorities are focused on preventing insider trading, making the point quite relevant in practice. Defining insider trading is not always easy, however. After all, stock analysts are in the business of uncovering information not already widely known to market participants.

Example 1.7: Assume a company stock is selling on the market at €20 per share. The company experiences an expected increase of profit due to a successful new product. The price is then expected to rise to a new target price of €40. In such a case the price will move to €40 right away, not slowly over time. Because any purchase of the stock at a price below €40 will yield an immediate profit, we can expect market participants to bid the price up to €40 without delay.

The main implications of the strong-form version are:

- When a change in some important factor is announced, markets react immediately, and investors react by changing their expectations on the future values of the variable, even anticipating the actual change.
- Expectation can fail in being strong-form rational if the investors do not use all available information, or they manage to use it but fail to process it optimally.

The speed and accuracy of information does not always allow fast adaptation of investors. Different investors give different estimates of the information they get, resulting in different target prices.

Correct prices are not an obvious consequence of EMH, as well as not all market participants are necessarily rational. Empirical evidence shows most agents trade with limited rationality, and their way to process information is biased.

Prices would not be correct even in the extreme case of full rationality of utility-maximizing agents. If all prices would be correctly determined as present value of future cash flows, there would be uncertainty on their realization.

Future profits, sales, earnings are subjects to estimate error and this leads to bias in pricing of actual assets. On top of that, risk premiums are not stable, varying over time. In some cases it is easy to determine if an asset is under-priced or over-priced. In some other cases it is more complicated, and the judgement is subject to error.

Mispricing happens in presence of complex investment structures. When many types of different assets are included in the target portfolio, and there are huge amounts of securities involved, pricing errors are more likely to affect the predictability of portfolio value.

As an example of mispricing, consider the real estate bubble at the basis of the actual financial crisis. Incentives were issued to mortgage issuers and bankers to foster the housing market, at the expense of the correct pricing of assets. Financial institutions ended up holding a huge amount of toxic assets. The topic is the focus of Chapter 13, on financial crisis and securitization.

All forms of EMH can be considered as a sequence of information subsets (Figure 1.4). EMH has been widely criticized and in recent years empirical studies have shown evidence against it. For example there is evidence in the literature of abnormal returns, too high when considering for all the risks involved.

Theories in support of the small firm effect rely on the low liquidity of small firms stocks, frequent rebalancing of portfolios by investors, and more. Anyway, this is to date an evident violation of the EMH.

Another phenomenon associated with small firms is the so-called 'January effect'. Prices on financial markets tend to rise consistently between December and January. This is due to the fiscal convenience of closing positions before the end of the year. When the markets open in January, it is then appropriate to buy back the shares.

Market overreaction to news is another source of anomaly. Sometimes, when a firm announces profit warnings or change in earnings, markets may react with a magnitude much higher than expected.

This violates the efficient market hypothesis, because an investor could earn abnormally high returns, on average, by buying a stock immediately after a poor earnings announcement and then selling it after a couple of weeks when it has risen back to normal levels.

EMH has been criticized, especially in the last decades, even if in 1978 Jensen wrote: 'There is no other proposition in economics which has more solid empirical evidence supporting it than the EMH.'

Most of the criticisms about EMH point to the rationality aspects, claiming that evidence does not support the statement that investors are rational, with decisions driven by the calculation of present values of discounted cash flows.

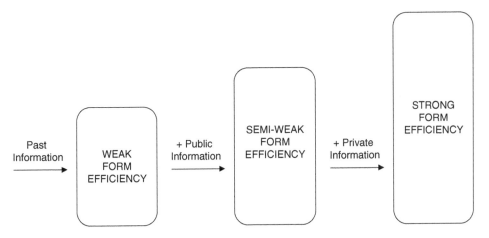

Figure 1.4 EMH versions and level of information involved.

Moreover, it has been alleged that historical data on stock prices show controversial patterns. The most famous effects are the small firm effect, the January effect and the mean reversion effect.

The small firm effect was described by Banz in 1981, who observed that the stocks of small capitalization firms delivered higher returns than those of big companies. Even if the reasons for that effect are unclear, there was a clear persisting trend in the data.

The January effect refers to the tendency of the small-cap high returns effect to happen in successive Januarys, which also appeared as a clear trend in the data, not just a temporary effect.

The mean reversion effect refers to the tendency of some asset prices in the market to follow some periods of time underperforming or overperforming, and revert afterwards, going back to some long-term average.

Anyway, despite all the work done in the area, there is no universally accepted risk measure in the context of investment holdings. This is why supporters of EMH, when interrogated about fallacies of the theory, state that pricing anomalies observed in the markets are more apparent than real, as they may be based on inaccurate measures of risk.

1.3.3 The Brownian motion

A stochastic process is a Markov process when the only value that is relevant for predicting the future of the process is the current value. The past history of the process is not relevant to the future realizations of the process. The condition can be mathematically formulated as

$$\Pr\left(X_n = x_n \mid X_{n-1} = x_{n-1}, X_{n-2} = x_{n-2}, \dots, X_0 = x_0\right) = \Pr\left(X_n = x_n \mid X_{n-1} = x_{n-1}\right)$$

Example 1.8: Consider a bowl containing two red balls and one blue ball. Assume that, without replacement, one ball was drawn in the past, one ball is drawn today and a third ball will be drawn in the future.

There is no information about the colour of the past ball, and today's ball is red, so that the chance that tomorrow's ball will be red is ½, since the blue ball and a red ball are left in the bowl. If there is information that both past and present extraction be a red ball, then it would be 100% sure to get the blue ball in the future. It is clear that the probability distribution for the tomorrow-ball's colour is affected by the information about the past. This stochastic process of observed colours does not have the Markov property.

The British botanist R. Brown in 1827 observed the movement of pollen grains suspended in the water, using a microscope, and observed it was following a zig-zag path. Even the pollen grains that had been stored for a century moved in the same way.

The first theory of Brownian motion (Wiener process) was developed by L. Bachelier in 1900, in his PhD thesis, and soon thereafter A. Einstein, using a probabilistic model, could sufficiently explain Brownian motion.

Einstein could observe that under kinetic energy of fluids, the water molecules moved at random, receiving a random number of impacts from random directions, from other molecules, in any short period of time.

A convenient way to understand Brownian motion is as a limit of random walks with ever smaller steps taking place more and more often.

A classical random walk is a sum process in which each process step is a Bernoulli variable, a random variable which can only take the values +1 or −1, with equal probability

$$S_T = X_1 + X_2 + ... + X_T$$

where

$$X_t = \begin{cases} +1 & \text{with probability } 1/2 \\ -1 & \text{with probability } 1/2 \end{cases}$$

with expected value and variance given by

$$E(S_T) = 0$$
$$Var(S_T) = T$$

The central limit theorem shows that in the limit, for $T \to \infty$, it holds that

$$\frac{X_T}{\sqrt{T}} \to N(0,1)$$

Define them a piecewise constant random function z_{tT}, on an interval T with $n = \dfrac{T}{t}$ subintervals, such that

$$y_{tT} = \frac{X_{\lfloor tT \rfloor}}{\sqrt{T}}, \quad t \in [0, \infty)$$

where

$\lfloor tT \rfloor$ is the largest interest which is lower than the product tT.

It is possible to show that, in the limit for $n \to \infty$, the process y_{tT} converges to a stochastic process W_t, such that

$$\Delta W = \varepsilon \sqrt{\Delta t}, \quad \varepsilon \sim N(0,1)$$

where

$$E(\Delta W) = 0$$
$$Var(\Delta W) = \sqrt{\Delta t}$$

Osborne (1959) showed that the logarithms of common-stock prices have a close analogy with the ensemble of coordinates of a large number of molecules. Using a probability distribution function and the prices of the same random stock choice at random times, he was able to derive a steady state distribution function, which is precisely the probability distribution for a particle in Brownian motion.

The basic properties of the Brownian motion are

1. $W_0 = C$
2. $W_t \sim N(0,t)$
3. The paths of the process are continuous function of time $t \in [0, \infty)$.
4. For any set of time points s, t, such that $0 \le s \le t$, it holds that

$$E(W_t^2) = Var(W_t) + \left[E(W_t)\right]^2 = t + 0 = t$$
$$E(W_t - W_s) = E(W_t) - E(W_s) = 0 - 0 = 0$$
$$E\left[(W_t - W_s)^2\right] = E(W_t^2) + E(W_s^2) - 2Cov(W_t, W_s)$$
$$= t + s - 2\min(W_t, W_s) = |t - s|$$

5. The covariance between the process at two different points in time is $Cov(W_t, W_s) = \min(s,t)$
6. Process increments on non-overlapping intervals are independent, meaning that
   a. The distribution of $W_t - W_s$ depends on $t - s$ only.
   b. If $0 \le u \le s \le t$, the random variables $W_t - W_s$ and W_u are independent.

The process path over a long interval T is such that $W_T - W_0$ is the sum of n small changes in Δt of the process, and it is equal to

$$W_T - W_0 = \sum_{i=1}^{n} \varepsilon_i \sqrt{\Delta t}$$

so that

$$E(W_T - W_0) = 0$$
$$Var(W_T - W_0) = n\Delta t = T$$

It is possible to derive several important properties that allow for simplifications when solving the mathematics of Brownian motions. First of all, consider the model expressed in continuous time, dW, and recall that, for $\Delta t \to 0$, the time interval becomes very small and equal to dt. Recall that

$$E(dW) = 0$$
$$E(dWdt) = E(dW)dt = 0$$
$$E(dW^2) = dt$$

Further analysis shows that

$$Var(dW^2) = E(dW^4) - \left[E(dW^2)\right]^2 = 3(dt)^2 - (dt)^2 = 0$$
$$E\left[(dWdt)^2\right] = E\left[(dW)^2\right](dt)^2 = 0$$
$$Var(dWdt) = E\left[(dWdt)^2\right] - \left[E(dWdt)\right]^2 = 0$$

Since for all elements, the variance and second order moment are zero, their actual value is the same as the expected value, and since the square of dt is supposed to converge to zero even faster than dt, it is possible to conclude that

$$dW^2 = dt$$
$$dWdt = 0$$
$$dt^2 = 0$$

Introducing a drift term in Δt, a new Δx process is defined as

$$\Delta x = a\Delta t + b\varepsilon\sqrt{\Delta t}$$

where a and b are constants, and

$$E(\Delta x) = a\Delta t$$
$$Var(\Delta x) = b^2 \Delta t$$

The model expressed in continuous time is

$$dx = adt + bdW_t$$

which is called generalized Brownian motion.

An Itô process is defined as a generalized Wiener process in which *a* and *b* are not constant, but dependent on *x* and *t* respectively

$$dx = u(x,t)dt + b(x,t)dW_t$$

The generalized Wiener process is the leading process in defining stock price movements in the markets. It would be simple to assume stock prices follow a generalized Wiener process, with constant drift and volatility.

But this is not true since an important feature of stocks is that the expected return demanded by investors is independent of the stock price.

So the assumption of constant expected drift rate must be replaced by the assumption that the expected return, which is the ratio between expected drift and stock price, must be constant.

If *S* is the stock price at time *t* the expected drift is assumed to be μS for some constant parameter μ. In a short time interval Δt the expected increase in *S* is $\mu S \Delta t$. The parameter μ is then the expected rate of return on the stock.

The process for the stock is therefore given by the geometric Brownian motion, which is given by

$$\frac{dS}{S} = \mu dt + \sigma dW_t$$

which expresses the return provided by the stock, on the left hand side, as the sum of the mean of return (drift) and the standard deviation multiplied by the Brownian motion.

Snapshot 1.2
Sampling of Brownian motion paths in Excel

Random paths of generalized Brownian motion can be samples through Monte Carlo simulation. The process contains constant parameters, and the only stochastic element is the $\varepsilon \sim N(0,1)$ associated with the variance term.

The Excel routine to simulate the paths of the process involve the following commands:

- RAND( ) is the function that returns a sample between 0 and 1.
- NORMSINV is the function of the inverse cumulative normal distribution.

Therefore

- NORMSINV(RAND( )) is the function producing a random sample from a standard normal distribution.

It is possible to extend the analysis to multiple variables driven by correlated stochastic processes, in the form

$$dx_1 = a_1 dt + b_1 dz_1$$
$$dx_2 = a_2 dt + b_2 dz_2$$

also definable in their discrete time versions as

$$\Delta x_1 = a_1 \Delta t + b_1 \varepsilon_1 \sqrt{\Delta t}$$
$$\Delta x_2 = a_2 \Delta t + b_2 \varepsilon_2 \sqrt{\Delta t}$$

When simulating the processes, the stochastic elements ε_1 and ε_2 should be sampled individually, using the above functions, given the assumption of no correlation between the two processes, which is the most convenient one.

In case of a correlation ρ, the ε_1 and ε_2 must be sampled from a bivariate normal distribution, assuming the marginals are both standard univariate standard normal distributions.

In this case it is possible to set

$$\varepsilon_1 = u$$
$$\varepsilon_2 = \rho u + \sqrt{1 - \rho^2} v$$

where
u and v are uncorrelated samples from a standard normal distribution.

Summary

Uncertainty, randomness and risk are related concepts but with some differences. Measurable probabilities associated with events determine risk.

There is a direct link between risk and reward. Positive outcomes are obtained just by getting exposed to adequate levels of risk. There is no free lunch in life and finance, and the risk-return connection is at the basis of financial theory.

Information is an important element in the markets and it is scarce, and the investors form their expectations based on the structure of the economic system and the actual amount of information available.

Expectations of investors drive the outcome of many situations, and prices depend on the trading decision of the investors, based themselves on investors' behaviour on the market.

Several sources of risk are possible, and a corporation faces risks of many different kinds during daily activity. Some of these risks have a non-economic nature, while others are explicit economic risk associated with the firm.

Factors affecting financial risk include the features and structure of the financial market domestic to the activities of the corporation. Times of recession are characterized by the downturns in financial markets, high level of interest rates and underrated currency, which may result in high risk, independently of the company structure and operations.

Risk process is a crucial task and it is divided into several steps, including identification, measurement and treatment. Rules apply to the management of corporate risk and both external and internal standards apply to the single firm.

Absence of arbitrage is a key feature of well-functioning markets. Any mispricing involves pressure on the market, which is often sufficient to invert the trend towards equilibrium.

The main step in assessing arbitrage and risk is to establish an analytical form for the process of the asset prices. Brownian motion is the mathematical tool that helps describing the dynamics of prices and interest rates on the markets.

Bibliography

Austrian Financial Market Authority. 2004. Credit Approval Process and Credit Risk Management. *Guidelines on Credit Risk Management.*

Bebzuc, R.N. 2003. *Asymmetric Information in Financial Markets: Introduction and Applications.* Cambridge University Press.

Bessis, J. 2010. *Risk Management in Banking.* Wiley. 3rd Edition.

Bjork, T. 2009. *Arbitrage Theory in Continuous Time.* Oxford University Press.

Blavatskyy, P.R. 2008. Risk Aversion. *Institute for Empirical Research in Economics*, Working Paper Series.

Butler, K.C. 2012. *Multinational Finance: Evaluating Opportunities, Costs, and Risks of Operations.* Wiley. 5th Edition.

Damodaran, A. 2007. *Strategic Risk Taking: A Framework for Risk Management.* Pearson Prentice Hall.

Eberlein, E., Frey, R., Kalkbrener, M. and Overbeck, L. 2007. Mathematics in Financial Risk Management. *Jahresbericht der Deutschen Mathematiker Vereinigung*, 109: 165–193.

Eeckhoudt, L., Gollier, C. and Schlesinger, H. 2005. *Economic and Financial Decisions under Risk.* Princeton University Press.

Fama, E.F. 1970. Efficient Capital Markets: A Review of Theory and Empirical Work. *The Journal of Finance*, 25(2): 383–417.

Field, P. 2003. *Modern Risk Management: A History.* Risk Books.

Global Association of Risk Professionals (GARP). 2009. *Foundations of Banking Risk: An Overview of Banking, Banking Risks, and Risk-Based Banking Regulation.* Wiley Finance.

Hasbrouck, J. 2007. *Empirical Market Microstructure: The Institutions, Economics, and Econometrics of Securities Trading.* Oxford University Press.

Jensen, M. 1978. Some Anomalous Evidence Regarding Market Efficiency. *Journal of Financial Economics*, 6: 95–101.

Knight, F.H. 1921. *Uncertainty and Profit.* Houghton Mifflin.

Kwon, W.J. 2009. *Risk Management and Insurance: Perspectives in a Global Economy.* Wiley-Blackwell.

Levin, J. 2006. *Choice Under Uncertainty.* Stanford University.

Muth, J. 1961. Rational Expectations and the Theory of Price Movements. *Econometrica*, 29(3): 315–335.

Nelson, S.C. and Katzenstein, P.J. 2014. Uncertainty, Risk, and the Financial Crisis of 2008. *International Organization*, 68(2): 361–392.

Osborne, M.F.M. 1959. Brownian Motion in the Stock Market. *Operations Research*, 7: 145–173.

RBC Royal Bank. 2009. *Managing Risk for Business.*

Rejda, G.E. 2010. *Principles of Risk Management and Insurance.* Prentice Hall. 11th Edition.

Roberts, H. 1967. Statistical versus Clinical Prediction of the Stock Market. Unpublished manuscript.

Schachermayer, W. 2008. The Notion of Arbitrage and Free Lunch in Mathematical Finance. *Aspects of Mathematical Finance*, 15–22.

Schmidt, A.B. 2011. *Financial Markets and Trading: An Introduction to Market Microstructure and Trading Strategies*. Wiley Finance.

Exercises

Questions

1. What are the characteristics of an efficient market?
2. In a world with absolutely no risk, would there be positive interest rates on bonds? Why would a financial deal involve a positive interest rate in such a world?
3. Explain the meaning of an agent being risk averse. Why are some agents risk averse, and others are risk takers?
4. What does it mean for an agent to maximize expected utility? Is there any possible case of an agent not willing to maximize expected utility?
5. What is the primary assumption behind the experience approach to forecasting?
6. Describe the three forms of market efficiency. Give an example of each one in the context of the equity market.
7. Consider two agents with same age and same level of wealth. One has a high-salary job and the other has a low-salary job. What agent should hold a higher fraction of total wealth in stock? Explain.
8. What is risk aversion? If common investors are risk averse, how can the fact that they often invest in very risky assets be explained?
9. Explain why agents prefer to get full insurance against uncertain situations even when the premium paid exceeds the expected value of the loss being insured against.
10. When is it worth paying to obtain more information to reduce uncertainty?
11. Is it true, false or uncertain to say that 'Human fear is the source of stock market crashes, so these crashes indicate that expectations in the stock market cannot be optimal'? Explain.
12. If every investor in the world becomes convinced that the efficient market hypothesis holds, would it stay true? Explain.
13. Someone stated that in a world without information and transaction costs, financial intermediation would not exist. Is it true or false?

Problems

1. Calculate the expected value and variance of a fair roll of a standard dice with six faces.
2. A lottery sells 500,000 tickets, with one main prize of €750,000, 100 intermediate prizes of €7,500 and 10,000 minor prizes of €1.
    a. Calculate the expected value of winnings from a single ticket.
    b. Calculate the variance of the winnings from a single ticket.
3. An investor has a company whose earnings in good times are of €10,000. In bad times, the earnings are of €2,500. The probability of a good year is 60%.

a. Calculate the expected value and variance of the income.
b. Assume the investor has a wealth $w = 0$ and a utility function $U(w) = \sqrt{w}$, and an offer comes to lease the business for a certain €6,500 per year. Should the offer be accepted?
4. A coin-toss lottery gives a payoff of 2^n where n is the number of tosses until getting a tail. Show that such a lottery has an infinite expected value.
5. An investor has an initial wealth $w = $€150, and a utility function $U(w) = \ln w$. A gamble offers the possibility to raise the wealth up to €200 with probability 50% or decrease it to €100 with the same probability. Calculate the risk premium associated with the gamble.
6. An investor is risk averse and must choose between a certain €50 or a gamble with likely outcomes €50 − x and €50 + x. Show on a graph that the investor's risk premium is increasing in x.
7. Consider the utility function given as $U(x) = -(x+1)^{-2}$
a. Compute the absolute risk aversion.
b. Compute the relative risk aversion.
c. Are the coefficients increasing or decreasing in x?
8. Suppose F is uniformly distributed over $[1,a]$ for $a > 1$, with p.d.f. equal to $1/(a-1)$. Calculate the risk premium for the following utility functions.
a. $U(x) = \ln x$
b. $U(x) = \sqrt{x}X$
9. Given a Brownian motion z_t, with

$$\Delta z = \varepsilon\sqrt{\Delta t}, \ \varepsilon \sim N(0,1)$$

a. Prove that $\operatorname{cov}(z_t, z_s) = \min(s,t), \ s \le 0 \le t$

10. Given a Brownian motion z_t check if the following are Brownian motions as well:
a. $\dfrac{tz_1}{t}$
b. $\sqrt{t}z_t$

Appendix: Types of market failure

Market efficiency is a foundation element of modern economic theories. Also financial matters are strongly relying on market efficiency. But there are cases when markets are not efficient.

Market inefficiencies are usually addressed through regulation, since their peculiar nature does not allow for the existence of a point of efficiency. Correction of market imperfections is crucial for the markets to work efficiently and benefit the social surplus.

The first type of market failure to be addressed is the natural monopoly. This happens when a company is able to produce and offer goods or services at a lower cost than all of its market competitors. Economies of scale play a crucial role in the natural monopoly.

In such a situation usually the monopolist tends to raise prices in order to maximize the profit, since there is no incentive to efficiency.

A natural monopoly does not necessarily imply market inefficiency. Under some conditions, the markets are such that the monopolist has no incentive in behaving inefficiently and resulting prices are close to optimality. Sometimes it is the direct choice of the monopolist to use customer-friendly policies in order to benefit both the client and maximize profits anyway. Sometimes monopoly is gained through competitive bidding, and that enhances efficiency, as well.

Externalities are another form of inefficiency. They happen to be when producers of a good or service face more costs or less benefit than originally planned, due to external factors. A positive externality happens when the producer cannot benefit from all the output of production, thus having an incentive in underinvesting. Negative externalities involve excess production, for example in case of pollution. Since external costs do not enter the calculation made by the producer, the production exceeds the level that is socially beneficial. Such externalities can be eliminated through regulation.

Public goods are such that consumption by one person does not reduce the availability to other people. Most public goods, like infrastructures, roads and more are provided by governments. In some cases the private sector can supply public goods. This is mostly the case of leisure goods like radio or television.

The main problem with public goods is the revelation of preferences. If customers are asked to pay for the good based on their valuations, they will tend to waive payments and leave it to others. That is why public goods are often funded by taxation or compulsory tariffs.

Market failures can also arise from transaction costs. When economic actors face a cost in order to gather information and complete market transaction, markets are no longer efficient. Again, regulation is the tool to reduce costs and enhance efficiency.

Another common source of inefficiency is asymmetry of information. When agents have different information when entering a negotiation, markets may not perform efficiently. For a given good, an uninformed buyer may want to pay the average price on the market for that good, independently of its quality. That gives an incentive to sellers to only sell bad quality goods, which are overpaid, while good quality goods would be underpaid, at average prices. Therefore sellers with bad quality goods will fill the market while sellers of good quality goods will disappear. That is clearly inefficient.

Also insurance is a field of common application of that principle. If an insurance company is not able to assess the riskiness of a customer, different levels of risk are pooled together and offered the same price. Therefore, only risky individuals have an incentive to buy insurance, while the safer customers do not buy it. This leaves the insurance with only highly risky customers, generating inefficiency. This phenomenon is also known as adverse selection and can be addressed requiring prior examination of possible customers in order to acquire the missing information about their riskiness.

How does adverse selection impact financial markets and economic issues? Besides the case of the insurance policies there are several implications of market inefficiency in financial matters.

In financial markets failures translate into frictions. In credit markets, borrowers often know much more about their creditworthiness, compared to the lenders. That generates an information asymmetry. If the bank cannot distinguish between bad and good borrowers, it will end up offering the same interest rates on loans to everybody. That will penalize good borrowers and will incentivize bad borrowers to take a lot of money. The final result is a global increase in interest rates due to riskiness, that generates inefficiency.

Financial instability is a severe issue in credit markets and high interest rates will likely cut off the market to the good borrowers, aggravating the problem. The problem can be solved through better investigation on creditworthiness and asking for collateral as a guarantee on the loans. More extreme measures include credit rationing.

Moral hazard is another phenomenon related to inefficiency. It refers to the situation where an individual has an incentive to behave in a way that generates cost she/he does not have to bear. The individual usually acts without any consideration of the consequences of the actions, and in particular without taking any preventive measure to avoid the cost. Health insurance giving full coverage to an individual gives the incentive to not take any preventive action against illness, having full access to unlimited care. As for adverse selection, a response to the moral hazard problem is again through regulation. The key is to structure the system in order to impose behaviour that generates efficiency despite the lack of incentives. This, combined with monitoring of behaviour, ensures optimality.

2   Financial markets and volatility

A financial market is an aggregate of possible investors, willing to buy or sell financial securities, commodities and other fungible items, as well as the transactions, that generate volatility on the markets.

Investors tend to go for anticipated future returns that cannot be predicted precisely. Any feasible investment is always associated with some degree of risk, and realized returns on the investments will always deviate from the expected return anticipated at the beginning of the investment period.

Risk can be broadly defined as the chance that an investment will yield a profit sensibly different than expected. Standard measures of profit and variability are the expected return and volatility of the associated distribution.

Generally a low risk is associated with low potential outcome. Risk is not only bad. It is an opportunity. Being willing to bear some risk is an important prerequisite to the chance of having high returns from any possible investment.

An important principle in financial markets is that securities with higher risk must offer a higher expected return in order to attract investors, while securities with lower risk are demanded by less risk-taking investors, and offer a lower return.

The risk-return trade-off is at the foundation of modern finance, and finding the right balance between return demand and risk exposure is at the basis of good management of a business.

After studying this chapter you will be able to answer the following questions, among others:

1. What are the foundations of financial economics theory?
2. What are the main analytical models for risk and how can they be used to describe the risk-return trade-off?
3. What information can be gathered by graphical representation of market efficiency?
4. What is volatility, how can it be measured and what is its role in assessing risk?
5. What is correlation, how can it be measured and what is its role in assessing risk?

The first section of the chapter is an introduction to the relationship between risk and return, and how it translates into distributional matter. The second section is about the Capital Asset Pricing Model, as the main analytical model to describe the risk-return trade-off. The final part introduces the concepts of volatility and correlation, with insights on data autocorrelation and the use of matrices for multivariate framework.

2.1 Modern portfolio theory

Learning outcomes

1. Understand the trade-off between risk and return on financial markets.
2. Learn about market efficiency.
3. Understand the main concepts of Modern Portfolio Theory.

2.1.1 The risk-return trade-off

The most influential theory in financial economics was developed in the 1950s by Harry Markowitz. Modern Portfolio Theory (MPT) claims it is not enough to look at just the risk and returns of the single assets included in a portfolio.

Diversification reduces the risk of the portfolio, and MPT quantifies the benefits modelling the mathematical relationship between risk and return of the assets in a normal market.

The major risk in investing is that the investor will get a lower return than expected. Therefore the standard deviation is the key measure of risk in the MPT framework, since it quantifies the deviations from the mean (expected) return.

MPT relies on assumptions on distribution of prices and returns. In particular, they are assumed to follow a normal distribution. So in order to understand the relationship between risk and return, it is important to recall the basic properties of the normal distribution.

a.   The distribution is symmetric, bell shaped.
b.   It is continuous for all values of X between $-\infty$ and ∞ so that every interval of real numbers has a non-null probability.
c.   The distribution is totally defined by two parameters, μ and σ, that determine the shape of the distribution.
d.   The probability density function is

$$f(x) = \frac{1}{\sqrt{2\pi\sigma^2}} e^{-\frac{(x-\mu)^2}{2\sigma^2}}$$

where
μ is the mean of the distribution.
σ is the standard deviation of the distribution.
e.   About two-thirds of all cases fall within one standard deviation from the mean, that is

$$\Pr(\mu - \sigma \leq x \leq \mu + \sigma) \approx 0.68$$

f.   About 95% of cases lie within 2 standard deviations from the mean, that is

$$\Pr(\mu - 2\sigma \leq x \leq \mu + 2\sigma) \approx 0.95$$

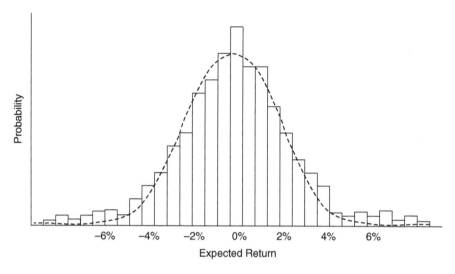

Figure 2.1 Financial returns of most securities are normally distributed. In this case the graph shows an average return of almost 2% for that particular security.

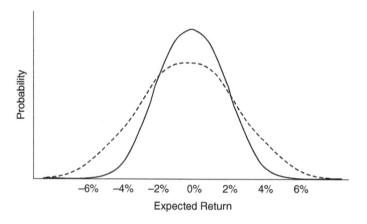

Figure 2.2 Distribution of possible returns of two different investments. They both have the same expected return but one of them (dashed line) offers a wider spread of possible outcomes, making other investments safer and more attractive for most of the investors.

A Gaussian (normal) distribution is completely defined by its two parameters, the mean and standard deviation. Assuming financial returns are normally distributed, the mean of the distribution corresponds to the expected return and the standard deviation to the volatility of returns.

The result is that the most straightforward idea of the relationship between risk and expected return of some financial investments is given by the relationship between the mean and standard deviation of the distribution of the returns. If we assume prices and/or returns are normally distributed, we can infer the properties of the normal distribution.

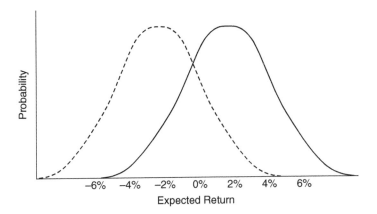

Figure 2.3 Distribution of possible returns of two different investments. They both have the same standard deviation but one of them (dashed line) offers lower expected return, making the other investment safer and more attractive for most investors.

Example 2.1: If we have a time series of normally distributed financial returns, with mean 0.04 and standard deviation 0.22, we can say that the asset associated with that particular series of data has an expected return of 4% (over the time horizon considered) and a volatility (risk) of 22%.

The distributional properties as seen above clearly indicate that risk and return are directly proportional. As explained later, in complete (normal) markets the higher the risk (volatility) of an investment, the higher the expected return (mean).

Investment returns reflect the degree of risk carried by the investment, and investors should be able to determine what level of return is appropriate for a given level of risk.

Define the portfolio value as

$$V_t = \sum_{i=1}^{n} \frac{\alpha_i}{S_{i,0}} S_{i,t}$$

where

α_i is the amount invested in asset i
$S_{i,0}$ is the value of asset i at time 0
$S_{i,t}$ is the value of asset i at time t.

The return of a portfolio composed by many assets can be calculated as the weighted average of the returns of the single assets, where the weights are based on the proportion of each asset's value on the total value of the portfolio, and is given by

$$r_p = \frac{V_t - V_{t-1}}{V_{t-1}}$$

$$= \dots$$

$$= \sum_{i=1}^{n} w_i r_i$$

(2.1)

where:

r_i is the expected return on stock i
n is the number of stocks in the portfolio
w_i is the weight (proportion) of asset i in the portfolio.

Example 2.2: Suppose stocks A and B have expected returns $E(r_A) = 12.5\%$ and $E(r_B) = 20\%$. The expected return of the portfolio composed by 75% of stock A and 25% of stock B is given by

$$E(r_p) = 0.75 \times 12.5\% + 0.25 \times 20\% = 14.38\%$$

Differently from the expected return, the standard deviation of the portfolio does not reflect only the volatility of the single assets in the portfolio. In order to assess the cumulative volatility, the co-movements of asset returns must also be taken into account. To measure how the returns of two pairs of securities vary together, the covariance and the correlation coefficient can be used.

The variance of the portfolio is given by

$$
\begin{aligned}
\sigma_p^2 &= E\left[\left(r_p - E(r_p)\right)\right]^2 \\
&= \dots \\
&= \sum_{i=1}^{n}\sum_{j\neq i=1}^{n} w_i w_j \sigma_{ij}
\end{aligned}
\tag{2.2}
$$

where:

σ_i^2 is the variance of the i-th asset
w_i is the weight of an asset i in the portfolio
w_j is the weight of an asset j in the portfolio
σ_{ij} is the covariance between asset i and j.

Equation (2.2) can be written in matrix notation as

$$\sigma_p^2 = \mathbf{w}^T \Sigma \mathbf{w}$$

where
$\mathbf{w} = (w_1, w_2, \dots, w_n)$ is the vector of weights of assets in the portfolio.

$$
\Sigma = \begin{pmatrix}
\sigma_1^2 & \cdots & \sigma_{1,n} \\
\vdots & \ddots & \vdots \\
\sigma_{n,1} & \cdots & \sigma_n^2
\end{pmatrix}
\text{ is the covariance matrix of the portfolio.}
$$

The covariance between any couple i,j of asset returns is given by

$$
\begin{aligned}
\sigma_{ij} &= E\left\{\left[r_i - E(r_i)\right]\left[r_j - E(r_j)\right]\right\} \\
&= \dots \\
&= E(r_i r_j) - E(r_i) E(r_j)
\end{aligned}
$$

The calculation of the correlation coefficient between the returns on two stocks is given by

$$\rho_{ij} = \frac{\sigma_{ij}}{\sigma_i \sigma_j}$$

where

σ_i is the standard deviation of asset i
σ_j is the standard deviation of asset i.

Example 2.3: Suppose stocks A and B have expected returns $E(r_A) = 12.5\%$, $E(r_B) = 20\%$ and standard deviations $\sigma_A = 5.12\%$, $\sigma_B = 20.49\%$, correlation coefficient is $\rho_{AB} = -1$. First we compute the covariance to be

$$\sigma_{AB} = \frac{-1}{0.0512 \times 0.2049} = -0.0105$$

The variance of a portfolio of 75% stock A and 25% stock B is

$$\sigma_p^2 = (0.75)^2 (0.0512)^2 + (0.25)^2 (0.2049)^2 + 2 \times 0.75 \times 0.25 \times -0.0105 = 0.00016$$

2.1.2 Optimal portfolios of risky assets

Financial investors aim at maximizing the expected return, given some acceptable level of risk. The Modern Portfolio Theory defines the analytics of the relationship between risk and return in a complete market.

The Modern Portfolio Theory was developed by Harry Markowitz in 1952, and suggests the hypothesis that investors minimize the risk (volatility) of the portfolio, for a given level of return.

The point is achieved by choosing the right amount of each security to include in the portfolio, so that the total portfolio variance is minimized, taking into consideration how the price of an asset changes in comparison to that of every other security in the portfolio, rather than choosing securities individually.

The theory uses a mathematical approach to construct the ideal portfolio for an investor minimizing risk given some fixed return, taking into consideration the relationship between risk and return.

The theory states that each security has its own risks and that a portfolio of many securities should be less risky than a single security portfolio, due to the diversification effect, emphasizing the importance of diversifying to reduce risk.

The Markowitz model comprises a set of procedures to select the optimal portfolio in a context of wealth-maximizing, risk-adverse investors. The model is graphed on a risk vs return space.

All investors minimize the risk given some fixed expected return. The model allows for different investors having different risk tolerance and return requirements. Taking into consideration the utility function of the investors, the model identifies a set of feasible risk-return combinations.

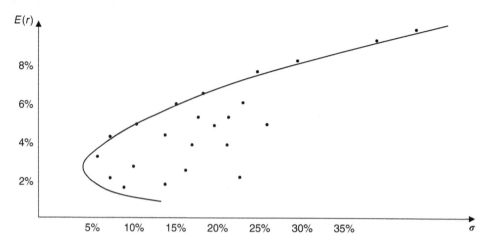

Figure 2.4 Efficient frontier for portfolio or risky assets. Various combinations of available assets generate different portfolios, with different combinations of risk and return (dots). The portfolios lying on the upper side of the curve are efficient.

Securities can be combined in portfolios (and portfolios of portfolios) in a way to minimize the risk for some level of return. The set of portfolios with minimum variance for a given return is called efficient frontier.

Large portfolios are not easy to handle with linear algebra. It is much easier to use matrix algebra, to simplify the calculations. Matrix algebra formulas are faster to process and much easier to implement on the computer.

The efficient frontier can be derived analytically from an optimization problem that minimizes the portfolio variance given some fixed expected return. The derivation shown here is in vector algebra, but can be easily adapted to linear algebra.

The minimum variance portfolio with expected return μ is the solution of the following minimization program

$$\min\left(\frac{1}{2}\mathbf{w}^T \Sigma\, \mathbf{w}\right)$$

subject to

$$\mathbf{w}^T \mathbf{1} = 1$$
$$\mathbf{w}^T \mathbf{r} = \mu_P$$

where:

    $\mathbf{w}$ is the vector of weights assigned to each asset
    Σ is the variance-covariance matrix of the asset returns
    $\mathbf{r}$ is the vector of the expected returns of the assets
    $\mathbf{1}$ is a vector of ones
    μ_P is the expected return of the portfolio.

In order to reduce the amount of constraints in the problem, short selling is allowed so that weights can also take a negative value, but the model could be further complicated by not allowing for short selling, meaning setting a constraint of all weights being positive.

The Lagrangian function of the problem is

$$L \equiv \frac{\mathbf{w}^T \Sigma \mathbf{w}}{2} + \lambda_1 \left(\mu_P - \mathbf{w}^T \mathbf{r} \right) + \lambda_2 \left(1 - \mathbf{w}^T \mathbf{1} \right)$$

where

λ_1 and λ_2 are the Lagrange multipliers

with first order conditions given by the partial derivatives of the Lagrangian function with respect to the weights vector, and the Lagrangian multipliers, which can be written as

$$\frac{\partial L}{\partial \mathbf{w}} = \Sigma \mathbf{w} - \lambda_1 \mathbf{r} - \lambda_2 \mathbf{1} = 0$$

$$\frac{\partial L}{\partial \lambda_1} = \mu_P - \mathbf{w}^T \mathbf{r} = 0$$

$$\frac{\partial L}{\partial \lambda_2} = 1 - \mathbf{w}^T \mathbf{1} = 0$$

It can be shown that the solution set, represented by the vector of optimal weights, which minimize the variance of the portfolio, is then given by

$$\mathbf{w}^* = \lambda_1 \left(\Sigma^{-1} \mathbf{r} \right) + \lambda_2 \left(\Sigma^{-1} \mathbf{1} \right) \tag{2.3}$$

Following the usual notation in the literature, it is now possible to simplify the notation by indicating the following

$$\begin{aligned}
A &= \mathbf{1}^T \Sigma^{-1} \mathbf{r} > 0 \\
B &= \mathbf{r}^T \Sigma^{-1} \mathbf{r} > 0 \\
C &= \mathbf{1}^T \Sigma^{-1} \mathbf{1} > 0 \\
\Delta &= BC - A^2 > 0
\end{aligned} \tag{2.4}$$

Notice that $\Delta > 0$ by the Cauchy-Schwarz inequality, given that the covariance matrix is non-singular and all assets do not have the same mean, so that

$$\mathbf{r} \neq k\mathbf{1}.$$

where

k is some constant.

From the constraints of the problem, and using the notation and results in (2.4), the Lagrange multipliers can be written as

$$\lambda_1 = \frac{C\mu_p - A}{\Delta}$$

$$\lambda_2 = \frac{B - A\mu_p}{\Delta}$$

Following Merton (1972), as an additional result to the equation of the minimum variance portfolio, the variance as resulting from the optimization is then given by

$$\sigma^2 = \frac{C}{\Delta}\left(\mu_p - \frac{A}{C}\right)^2 + \frac{1}{C}$$

This is the equation of a parabola, representing the efficient frontier in the return-volatility space. The most interesting application of the program is its implementation with some software and real data, in order to draw the efficient frontier of the market analysed and conclude about efficiency of single portfolios.

Substituting for the explicit values of the Lagrange multipliers into (2.3), the vector of portfolio weights, solution of the optimization program, can be written as

$$\mathbf{w}^* = \left(\frac{C\mu_p - A}{\Delta}\right)(\Sigma^{-1}\mathbf{r}) + \left(\frac{B - A\mu_p}{\Delta}\right)(\Sigma^{-1}\mathbf{1})$$

$$= \frac{1}{\Delta}\left[\mu_p\left(C\Sigma^{-1}\mathbf{r} - A\Sigma^{-1}\mathbf{1}\right) + \left(B\Sigma^{-1}\mathbf{1} - A\Sigma^{-1}\mathbf{r}\right)\right]$$

The vector represents a portfolio which minimizes the variance for some specific value of the portfolio expected return. It is possible to show that the minimum variance portfolio is obtained for a value μ_p corresponding to

$$\mu_p = \frac{A}{C}$$

so that the optimal portfolio is given by

$$\mathbf{w}^*_{OPT} = \frac{1}{\Delta}\left[\frac{A}{C}\left(C\Sigma^{-1}\mathbf{r} - A\Sigma^{-1}\mathbf{1}\right) + \left(B\Sigma^{-1}\mathbf{1} - A\Sigma^{-1}\mathbf{r}\right)\right]$$

2.1.3 *Optimal portfolios with risk-free asset*

Once the efficient frontier is derived, the analysis can be extended to a market with a risk-free asset. Since the risk-free asset is like a constant in the model, the following holds.

$$\sigma^2_f = \sigma_{if} = 0$$

where

σ_f^2 is the variance of the risk-free asset.

σ_{if} is the covariance between the risk-free and the risky asset.

Consider two portfolios, Π_1 and Π_2, lying on the efficient frontier, and a convex combination of the two, such that

$$\alpha\Pi_1 + (1-\alpha)\Pi_2, \quad \forall \alpha, \quad -\infty < \alpha < \infty$$

Consider the minimum variance portfolio (MVP), as derived in the space of only risky assets, having expected return r_p and variance σ_p^2.

Investing α in the MVP and $(1-\alpha)$ in the risk-free rate, the new portfolio Π has new expected return and variance. The expected return of the portfolio is defined as

$$E(r_\Pi) = \alpha E(r_i) + (1-\alpha)r_f$$

where

$E(r_i)$ is the expected return on the risky asset

and the variance can be written as

$$\sigma_\Pi^2 = \alpha^2 \sigma_A^2 + (1-\alpha)^2 \sigma_f^2 + 2\alpha(1-\alpha)\sigma_{A,f}$$
$$= \alpha^2 \sigma_A^2$$

A new frontier is obtained for different values of α, with tangent portfolio r_m, covering all the portfolios with expected return in the range between zero and $E(r_m)$, for $0 < \alpha < 1$.

When $\alpha > 1$, the frontier includes portfolio with an expected return higher than $E(r_m)$. These are leveraged portfolios which are created by borrowing money at r_f and investing it into the tangent portfolio.

Consider a portfolio composed of a proportion w_f of the risk-free asset and a proportion $w_i = (1 - w_f)$ of the risky asset.

According to the properties of the variance of a portfolio of uncorrelated asset, it follows that

$$\sigma_p^2 = (1 - w_f)^2 \sigma_i^2$$

where σ_P^2 is the portfolio variance. Straightforward mathematics shows that the portfolio weights can be expressed as

$$w_f = 1 - \frac{\sigma_p}{\sigma_i}$$

$$w_i = \frac{\sigma_p}{\sigma_i}$$

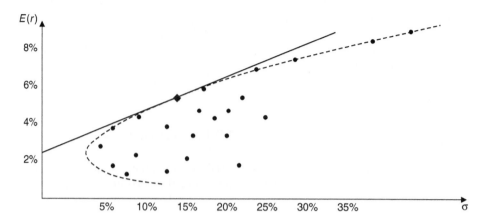

Figure 2.5 Introducing a risk-free asset in the market allows choosing efficient portfolios on the straight line. Combinations of risk-free assets and risky assets lead to different points on the line.

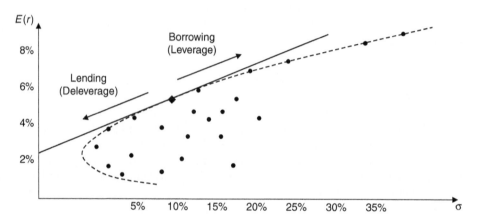

Figure 2.6 Lending and borrowing money it is possible to leverage or deleverage the position over the optimal portfolio.

Therefore we can calculate the portfolio return as

$$E(r_p) = \left(1 - \frac{\sigma_p}{\sigma_i}\right) r_f + \left(\frac{\sigma_p}{\sigma_i}\right) E(r_i)$$

The Capital Market Line takes the form

$$E(r_p) = r_f + \left(\frac{\sigma_p}{\sigma_i}\right)\left[E(r_i) - r_f\right]$$

Including risk-free asset r_f in the previous optimization (which included only the risky one) adds a zero-risk element in the market. Including r_f in the portfolio, the efficient frontier expands, increasing the range of investment opportunities.

The model changes from the efficient frontier (a curve) to the CML (a line). The CML represents the capital allocation between the risk-free security and the risky asset. The optimal portfolio is the tangency point of the curve and line. The tangency portfolio is known as the market portfolio.

The CML is the line drawn from the vertical intercept (risk-free rate) to the tangency point, as said above. The new line is considered dominant to the efficient frontier because the inclusion of a risk-free asset in the economy allows for better portfolios to be formed.

How can an investor move on the line? Introducing the risk-free rate allows for borrowing and lending funds in order to leverage or deleverage the investment portfolio. That means the investor can borrow funds to invest in the risky asset or sell back some of the risky asset and lend the money. The tangency point represents a portfolio of only risky assets.

There are some important implications to the theory. First of all risk-averse investors end up wanting to hold portfolios consisting of a combination of the risk-free asset and the same (tangency) risky portfolio.

Since all investors hold the same risky portfolio this must be the market portfolio, containing all the risky assets in the market. The only choice left to risk-averse investors is the proportion to put in the risk-free asset.

Snapshot 2.1
Portfolio optimization in Excel

In order to apply portfolio optimization in Excel, first of all it is necessary to create a matrix of the *n* observed returns for the chosen *m* assets in the market, and the covariance matrix, as in the following example:

E(R)	0.178	0.216	...	0.049	**Var(R)**	0.178	0.216	...	0.049

Using the formulas from Markowitz Portfolio Theory, the following step is to calculate, from the expected return and variances of the *m* single assets, the portfolio expected return and portfolio variance

R(P)	0.178	**Var(P)**	0.178

In order to set for the optimization, a line of weights of the assets in the portfolio must be filled.

	1	*2*	...	*m*
Weights	0.111	0.223	...	0.015

It is then possible to start the program, using the Solver Tool in Excel, and implementing the following steps:

1. Set your desired portfolio return
2. Start the Excel Solver and
3. Minimize the Portfolio Variance
4. Change 'By changing variable cells' to the range of cells containing the Portfolio Allocation
5. Set the constraints (the total portfolio allocation must add up to one, and the portfolio return should be your desired value)
6. Click Solve

Once the set of optimal weights is obtained, they can be used to build efficient portfolios for different combinations of expected return and variance. In order to get the efficient frontier, it is sufficient to plot the line crossing these portfolios, using the graph function in Excel.

2.2 The Capital Asset Pricing Model

Learning outcomes

1. Understand the Capital Asset Pricing Model.
2. Draw and describe the Capital Market Line and Security Market Line.
3. Acquire introductory knowledge of advanced factor models for asset pricing.

2.2.1 Main assumptions

The next step after developing the CML is to find a way to measure systematic risk, given that diversification can eliminate only part of it. MPT does not answer the question about how systematic risk can be measured and what is the right compensation for it.

Systematic risk is the only one to be compensated, therefore it is crucial to get a measure of it. The Capital Asset Pricing Model (CAPM) solves the issue through mathematical modelling of systematic risk.

CAPM starts from the risk-free rate as benchmark, and a risk premium added in order to get the right expected return for the asset. The premium is a compensation for the risk borne by the investor. The risk premium is then multiplied by a coefficient (beta) relating the asset risk to the market risk. This is the link between the expected return on the asset and the risk premium in the market.

The main question of this part is to determine what is the expected return on a portfolio of assets.

The main points of MPT can be recalled as:

*   Diversify to eliminate non-systematic risk.
*   Investors hold only combinations of the risk-free asset and the tangency portfolio.
*   Systematic risk is measured as the proportion of the market risk related to the asset.
*   An asset's risk premium is proportional to its systematic risk.

The CML describes a linear relationship between excess return of the asset and excess return of the market.

$$r_i - r_f = \beta\left(r_m - r_f\right)$$

where

r_m is the return of the market
β is the dependence factor between market and asset.

The key of CAPM is to identify the tangency portfolio as the market portfolio, and consequently price any asset as a function of the market. The market portfolio is the portfolio composed of all the assets traded in the market.

Consider a model where there are n assets in the market. Each asset $i = 1,...,n$ has a market capitalization

$$Mcp_i = V_i n_i$$

where

V_i is the price per share of asset i
n_i is the number of shares outstanding of asset i.

It follows that the total capitalization of the assets in the market is

$$Mcp_m = \sum_{i=1}^{n} Mcp_i$$

As said above, the market portfolio is composed of all the risky assets in the market. Each asset has a proportion of

$$w_i = \frac{Mcp_i}{\sum_{i=1}^{n} Mcp_i} = \frac{Mcp_i}{Mcp_m}$$

The CAPM relies on some assumptions. In order to derive the model, some conditions must be fulfilled.

1. The markets are complete and competitive. There are perfectly competitive securities, and the investors are price takers.
2. There are no frictions in the market, meaning no taxation or transaction costs.
3. All investors have the same holding period.
4. Lending and borrowing are unlimited and happen at the risk-free rate. Assets other than financial are not in the set of possible investments.

5. Investors are fully rational and mean-variance optimizers, following the Markowitz portfolio selection method.
6. Information is the same for all investors, and all investors process the information in the same way.
7. Estimation of the expected return and variance-covariance matrix is homogeneous among all investors.

The idea behind CAPM is that every investor splits funds between risk-free assets and the tangency portfolio. All investors hold the risky assets in the same proportions (tangent portfolio). Therefore the tangent portfolio is the market portfolio.

The CAPM states that if an investor holds some amount of the market portfolio, the risk compensation for single assets should be a consequence of how the single asset behaves compared to the market.

If a single asset has a variability exactly equal to the market, then the expected return should be the same for both, and so on. To model it in formulas, suppose σ_M^2 is the variance of the market (and is a proxy for market risk), then the risk premium per unit of risk λ will be given as

$$\lambda_P = \frac{\left[E(r_m)-r_f\right]}{\sigma_m^2}$$

The risk premium is directly proportional to the excess return on the market, and inversely proportional to the risk (variance) of the market. In order to calculate the right compensation for each asset, one needs to analyse how the asset covaries with the market.

The expected premium on asset i should be equal to the risk premium per each unit of risk multiplied by the relationship of the asset with the market, expressed in the form of covariance.

$$E(r_i)-r_f = \sigma_{im}\frac{\left[E(r_m)-r_f\right]}{\sigma_m^2}$$

When the asset has zero covariance with the market, it carries no risk, therefore it earns the risk-free rate. When the covariance is equal to one, the asset moves exactly like the market, and it earns the market return.

The formula of the CAPM simplifies in

$$E(r_i)= r_f +\sigma_{im}\frac{\left[E(r_m)-r_f\right]}{\sigma_m^2}$$

And rearranging terms it follows

$$E(r_i)= r_f +\frac{\sigma_{im}}{\sigma_m^2}\left[E(r_m)-r_f\right]$$

The expected return on the asset is equal to the risk-free rate plus a risk premium proportional to the market risk premium. The proportionality is shown by a multiplying factor $\dfrac{\sigma_{im}}{\sigma_m^2}$ called the beta β (beta) of the asset. The resulting model is the CAPM and is typically written as:

$$E(r_i) = r_f + \beta_i \left[E(r_m) - r_f \right]$$

Example 2.4: Suppose the covariance of some stock A with the market is 15% and the variance of A is 12%. The market expected return is 11% and the risk-free rate is 5%. We can calculate then the expected return of A applying the CAPM

$$E(r_A) = 0.05 + \frac{0.15}{0.12} [0.11 - 0.05] = 0.125$$

The expected return for the stock is 12.5%.

An issue in reality is how to practically implement CAPM. In fact in real life it is almost impossible to consider a portfolio of all assets in a regulated market. A good proxy of the market portfolio in this case is given by index funds.

Such a fund is a sort of smaller portfolio representative of the market. The assets included are the most dominant assets, capturing the essence of it. One of the most famous stock indices in the world is the Standard & Poor's (S&P) 500.

The index is made up of 500 assets as a proxy of the market. In this specific case CAPM implementation goes through an elaborated model that applies to reality. For example consider an asset $i = 1, 2, ..., m$ for which we wish to estimate the beta. Consider a discrete time horizon of n time points. For every $k = 1, 2, ..., n$. The average (expected) return for the asset i in this case is

$$\hat{\bar{r}}_i = \frac{1}{n} \sum_{k=1}^{m} r_{i,k}$$

where

$\hat{\bar{r}}_i$ is the average return of asset i
r_{ik} is the k-th sampled value of asset return
$r_{SP,k}$ is the k-th sampled value of the S&P 500 index return.

For the index is

$$\hat{\bar{r}}_{SP} = \frac{1}{n} \sum_{k=1}^{m} r_{SP,k}$$

The estimation of the index variance σ_{SP}^2 is

$$\hat{\sigma}_{SP}^2 = \frac{1}{n-1} \sum_{k=1}^{m} \left(r_{SP,k} - \hat{\bar{r}}_{SP} \right)^2$$

And the covariance σ_{SPi} between asset i and the index is estimated by

$$\hat{\sigma}_{SPi} = \frac{1}{n-1}\sum_{k=1}^{m}\left(r_{SP,k} - \hat{\bar{r}}_{SP}\right)\left(r_{ik} - \hat{\bar{r}}_i\right)$$

The beta value estimation is finally given by

$$\hat{\beta} = \frac{\hat{\sigma}_{SP}^2}{\hat{\sigma}_{SP}}$$

2.2.2 The Security Market Line

The result of the CAPM is the appropriate rate to discount future cash flows of the asset in order to get the correct price. Beta is the risk measure associated with each stock and when it is higher than one, the asset riskiness is quite high.

The higher the riskiness of the asset, the higher the beta associated with it. Stocks with a high beta will have a high discount rate for the cash flows, therefore yielding a lower present value for the asset. Stocks that are less sensitive are characterized by a lower beta, and discounted at a lower interest rate.

Summarizing, the main findings of CAPM are:

1. The market portfolio is the tangent portfolio.
2. The risk of a single asset is determined by its covariance with the market portfolio.
3. Systematic risk cannot be diversified away and must be compensated, according to the relationship between excess return of the asset and excess return of the market.

The CAPM was developed in the early 1960s by William Sharpe, Jack Treynor, John Lintner and Jan Mossin. Before their work there was no asset pricing model built on preferences and fully capable of predicting risk and return of any given asset on the market. The following is the derivation of Sharpe.

The proof is based on portfolio composition. Assume investing an amount w_i in a risky asset I, and an amount $w_m = (1-w_i)$ in the market portfolio m. The portfolio p formed has an expected return

$$E\left(r_p\right) = w_m E\left(r_m\right) + w_i E\left(r_i\right)$$

where

$E\left(r_m\right)$ is the expected return of the market
w_m is the weight of the market in the portfolio.
And the standard deviation is

$$\sigma_p = \sqrt{w_m^2 \sigma_m^2 + w_i^2 \sigma_i^2 + 2w_i w_m \sigma_{im}}$$

where

σ_m^2 is the variance of the market
σ_{im} is the covariance between the market and the asset.

The proof then continues taking into account the topology of the efficient frontier and CML. In particular, the point is to analyse the slope of the curve and the line at tangency point. At the point of tangency between the CML and the market portfolio, the slope of the CML is given by

$$\text{Slope}_{CML} = \frac{\left[E(r_m) - r_f\right]}{\sigma_m}$$

The following step is to derive an expression for the slope of the efficient frontier, the curve. The slope is calculated again at tangency point. Note that asset (portfolio) i does not have to be necessarily efficient.

The slope of the curve can be expressed differentiating the expected portfolio return $E(r_p)$ with respect to portfolio variance σ_p. The variable σ_p is not included in the expression for r_p, therefore it is necessary to use a chain rule

$$\text{Slope}_{EFR} = \frac{\partial E(r_p)}{\partial \sigma_p} = \frac{\dfrac{\partial E(r_p)}{\partial w_i}}{\dfrac{\partial \sigma_p}{\partial w_i}}$$

The above chain can be solved piece by piece. The first part is the derivative of the expected return with respect to the weight of asset i

$$\frac{\partial E(r_p)}{\partial w_i} = E(r_i) - E(r_m)$$

The second part is the derivative of the standard deviation, again with respect to the weight of asset i

$$\frac{\partial \sigma_p}{\partial w_i} = \frac{1}{2}\left[w_m^2 \sigma_m^2 + w_i^2 \sigma_i^2 + 2w_i w_m \sigma_{im}\right]^{-\frac{1}{2}} \times \left[-2w_m \sigma_m^2 + 2w_i \sigma_i^2 + 2(1 - 2w_i)\sigma_{im}\right]$$
$$= \frac{\left[-w_m \sigma_m^2 + w_i \sigma_i^2 + (1 - 2w_i)\sigma_{im}\right]}{\sigma_p}$$

The maths now is quite cumbersome. The ratio of the two derivatives is complicated to solve. So the properties of the model must be used to simplify the calculation. Recall at tangency point all investors choose the market portfolio.

Therefore the proportion of asset i is zero and the variance of the portfolio turns into the variance of the market, the only variable left. Therefore the derivative of the variance with respect to the weight w_i becomes

$$\left. \frac{\partial \sigma_p}{\partial w_i} \right|_{\substack{w_i=0 \\ \sigma_p=\sigma_m}} = \frac{\sigma_{im} - \sigma_m^2}{\sigma_m}$$

It is now possible to implement the chain rule efficiently and obtain an expression for the slope of the efficient frontier:

$$\text{Slope}_{EFR} = \frac{\dfrac{\partial E(r_p)}{\partial w_i}}{\dfrac{\partial \sigma_p}{\partial w_i}}$$

$$= \frac{E(r_i) - E(r_m)}{\dfrac{\sigma_{im} - \sigma_m^2}{\sigma_m}}$$

$$= \frac{\left[E(r_i) - E(r_m) \right] \sigma_m}{\sigma_{im} - \sigma_m^2}$$

The key of the equilibrium at tangency point is that both slopes must be equal. In fact, recall the definition of the market portfolio as the most efficient portfolio, dominating all other portfolios.

$$\frac{\left[E(r_i) - E(r_m) \right] \sigma_m}{\sigma_{im} - \sigma_m^2} = \frac{\left[E(r_m) - r_f \right]}{\sigma_m}$$

so that

$$E(r_i) = r_f + \beta_i \left[E(r_m) - r_f \right]$$

where

$$\beta_i = \frac{\sigma_{im}}{\sigma_m^2}$$

as described in 2.2.1.

The equation defines the relation between the expected risk premium of any asset in the market and the respective beta. The line graphing the relation is called the Security Market Line (SML). The SML is the line where all efficient portfolios lie.

In the standard context of a concave utility function of the investors, the CAPM is consistent with the intuition of the direct relationship between the risk borne by the investor and the expected return to compensate for the risk.

The beta can be estimated using a regression model relating stock returns to market returns. The regression formula includes an intercept α and a zero-mean, normally distributed error term

$$r_{i,t} = \alpha_{i,t} + \beta_{i,t} r_m + \varepsilon_{i,t}$$
$$\varepsilon_i \sim N(0,\sigma^2)$$

where

$\beta_{i,t}$ is the beta of asset i at time t.

Reworking the CAPM formula, the expected return can be written as

$$E(r_i) = r_f(1-\beta_i) + \beta_i\left[E(r_m)\right]$$

The estimated α can be compared to $(1-\beta_i)$ in order to compare the performance of the actual stock with the CAPM prediction. This is why alpha is said to measure the abnormal rate of return on an asset in excess of its equilibrium prediction given by CAPM.

The coefficient gives a reliable indication on how an investment has performed after accounting for the risk it involved. The golden rule therefore is:

- When $\alpha < 0$ the asset return has been too low for the risk taken, therefore it is a not a good investment. Usually it is recommendable to sell such an asset.
- When $\alpha = 0$ the asset return has been adequate for the risk taken, no action is recommended.
- When $\alpha > 0$ the asset return has been higher than expected for the risk taken, therefore it is a good investment. Usually it is recommendable to buy such an asset.

It is interesting to analyse the variance of the return, as from the regression.

$$\sigma_i = \beta_i^2 \sigma_m + \sigma_\varepsilon \tag{2.5}$$

where

σ_ε is the volatility of the error term.

The formula separates the variance of the market return from the variance of the error term. This is called variance decomposition of returns, and allows us to distinguish between the systematic risk, related to the market, and the diversifiable risk, related to the error term.

When the error term is close to zero, the portfolio is well diversified, and no more action is needed in order to eliminate risk. Only systematic risk is left and it is rewarded by the market, according to the beta of the asset.

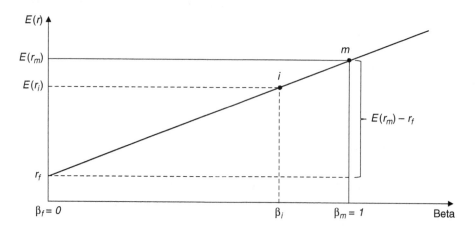

Figure 2.7 The CAPM relation identifies the Security Market Line (SML) on which all the efficient combinations of expected return and asset betas lie. The slope of the curve identifies the relation between asset and market excess return.

For an equally weighted portfolio p of N assets, equation (2.5) turns into

$$\sigma_p = \beta_p^2 \sigma_m + \frac{1}{n}\sigma_p^2$$

where

β_p is the beta of the portfolio.

The last term proves that portfolio variance can be reduced by adding more assets in the portfolio, through the diversification effect. Some mathematics also shows that, given 2.5, the covariance between any couple of assets i and j can be expressed as

$$\sigma_{i,j} = \text{cov}\left[\alpha_i + \beta_i r_m + \varepsilon_i, \alpha_j + \beta_j r_m + \varepsilon_j\right]$$
$$= \dots$$
$$= \beta_i \beta_j \sigma_m^2$$

2.2.3 Beyond CAPM

The Consumption-based Capital Asset Pricing Model (CCAPM) is a derivation of the Capital Asset Pricing Model (CAPM), expanding the analysis to consumption as a factor for calculating the expected return on an investment.

The main implication of CCAPM is that the expected risk premium on a risky asset (excess return on the risk-free return) is proportional to the covariance between the asset return and the level of consumption in the period of the return.

Consider a multi-period model with an infinitely lived representative household, and an expected lifetime utility function defined as

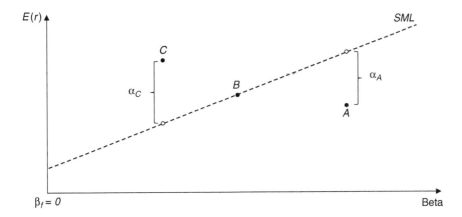

Figure 2.8 The Security Market Line plots the expected return of an asset against its beta. Points that are not on the SML indicate inefficiency of the CAPM condition for that market, and positive and negative alphas are generated, indicating investment opportunities.

$$E(u_t) = u(c_t) + E\left[\sum_{i=1}^{\infty} d^i u(c_{t+i})\right], \quad 0 < d < 1$$

where

$u(c_t)$ is the utility associated with consuming at time t
d is a discount function
$u(c_{t+i})$ is the utility associated with consuming at time $t+i$.

The household chooses at each time t the corresponding level of current consumption c_t, subject to a budget constraint. Assume the level of prices for a financial security is p_t, and the household can buy the security and redeem later at $t+1$, to finance consumption at that time.

The optimal quantity of financial security desired by the investor can be derived from the first order condition

$$dE\left[c_{t+1}u'(c_{t+1})\right] - u'(c_t)p_t = 0 \tag{2.6}$$

where

c_t is the consumption at time t.

The FOC is the utility gained from the consumption at $t+1$ financed by redemption of marginal unit of the security, minus the marginal utility lost from not consuming, due to the purchase of the security.

The one-period return on the security is given by

$$r_{t+1} = \frac{c_{t+1}}{p_t} - 1$$

Equation (2.6) becomes then

$$dE\left[c_{t+1}u'(c_{t+1})\right]-u'(c_t)p_t = 0$$
$$\Rightarrow dE\left[\frac{c_{t+1}}{p_t}u'(c_{t+1})\right]-u'(c_t) = 0$$
$$\Rightarrow dE\left[(1+r_{t+1})u'(c_{t+1})\right]-u'(c_t) = 0 \tag{2.7}$$
$$\Rightarrow dE\left[(1+r_{t+1})\frac{u'(c_{t+1})}{u'(c_t)}\right] = 1$$

which is the standard equation of CCAPM. In equilibrium, the expected value of the asset return plus one, multiplied by the marginal rate of substitution of the utilities from consumption over time, is equal to one.

The equation is valid for all assets, and in particular for the risk-free asset as well. In this specific case, the formula of CCAPM takes the form

$$d(1+r_f)E\left[\frac{u'(c_{t+1})}{u'(c_t)}\right] = 1 \tag{2.8}$$

In order to express the model in terms of the excess return of the asset, equation (2.8) must be subtracted from (2.7), in order to obtain

$$dE\left[(1+r_{t+1})\frac{u'(c_{t+1})}{u'(c_t)}\right]-d(1+r_f)E\left[\frac{u'(c_{t+1})}{u'(c_t)}\right] = 0$$
$$\Rightarrow \dots$$
$$\Rightarrow E\left[(r_{t+1}-r_f)\frac{u'(c_{t+1})}{u'(c_t)}\right] = 0$$

meaning that the expected value of the excess return multiplied by the marginal rate of substitution of consumption is equal to zero.

The CAPM is a single factor model, when one parameter (beta) must be used to implement the model, or estimated from the data, running the model in the form of linear regression.

A step further is possible, adding more factors to the analysis. The best known approach like this is the three-factor model developed by Eugene Fama and Kenneth French. After empirical analysis of financial returns, they found out that two classes of stock have the tendency of performing better than average.

Both small capitalization stocks and high book-to-value ratio stocks showed excess returns compared to the average of all classes of stocks. Therefore they remodelled the CAPM in order to match this fact.

In order to gather exposure to the above factors they calculated returns of small minus big (SMB) capitalization stocks, and high minus low (HML) book-to-value stocks. The resulting model is a three-factor formula in the form

$$E(r_i) = r_f + \beta_i\left[E(r_m)-r_f\right]+\beta_{i,SMB}SMB+\beta_{i,HML}HM$$

where

> SMB is the expected excess return on SMB factor
> HML is the expected excess return on HML factor
> $\beta_{i,SMB}$ is the beta of small capitalization stock factor, for asset i
> $\beta_{i,HML}$ is the beta of high-minus-low book-to-value factor, for asset i.

The relationship between risk and return in principle stays the same as CAPM. The Fama-French model still considers high returns as being a reward for taking a high level of risk.

Looking at the formula, the model enriches the analysis with new information. It is interesting to study the dynamics of the regression. When returns increase with book-to-value, stocks with a high ratio must be more risky than average.

There is actually uncertainty on how book-to-value can measure risk. Few interpretations are possible, like conditions of distress that cause selling at low price. In any case, empirical evidence supports the findings of the model, revealing it to be more accurate than single-factor CAPM.

The strength of the multi-factor model is mostly in the great diversity of the factors included, which make the analysis based on heterogeneous variables. A strong point is that indices weigh stocks according to capitalization, meaning that factor actually defines the market portfolio of reference.

The Arbitrage Pricing Theory is a multifactor model developed by Stephen Ross in 1976. It is based on the idea that asset returns can be predicted by relating them to many common risk factors.

Compared to CAPM, the APT does not require that all investors have the same behaviour, nor does it claim that the tangency portfolio is the only risky asset that will be held by the investors.

APT starts from the consideration that expected returns on a security should be related to the security's covariance with the common factors. Investors can construct portfolios to diversify idiosyncratic risk.

Suppose that returns are driven by a set of factors $F_1, F_2, ..., F_m$. The model in case of m factors can be expressed in the form

$$E(r_i) = r_f + \beta_{i,F_1}\left[E(r_{F_1}) - r_f\right] + \beta_{i,F_2}\left[E(r_{F_2}) - r_f\right] + ... + \beta_{i,F_m}\left[E(r_{F_m}) - r_f\right]$$

where

> $E(r_{F_j})$ is the expected return on factor j
> $\beta_i^{F_i}$ is the beta of factor j, for asset i.

The parameters estimation can be performed through a regression function similar to CAPM

$$r_i = \alpha_i + \beta_{i,F_1}r_{F_1} + \beta_{i,F_1}r_{F_2} + ... + \beta_{i,F_1}r_{F_m} + \varepsilon_i$$

APT estimation is based on multivariate regression analysis.

2.3 Volatility and correlation

Learning outcomes

1. Describe and comment on the various types of volatility measurement.
2. Learn the differences and similarities between correlation and covariance.
3. Understand the principle and use of Maximum Likelihood Methods.

2.3.1 Types of volatility

Financial volatility is a fundamental input for many uses in finance, and in particular for risk management. It is therefore crucial to learn about how volatility can be measured, and what are the economic drivers of volatility in financial markets.

The aim of any financial manager is to understand the determinants of volatility on financial markets, and that also allow him to uncover the connections between market price movements and risk factors causing them.

There are several methods to measure volatility, according to the approach used. The main approaches are the historical volatility measurement, and the implied volatility calculation.

Historical volatility can be defined as the standard deviation of the logarithmic price changes, measured at regular time intervals. In order to estimate volatility from historical data, usually one must start from the observation of the market prices at fixed time intervals. Prices can be observed daily, weekly, monthly and so on, according to the purpose of the analysis.

Assume n prices are observed at some point in time. Each price is observed in correspondence at the end of any interval i in the time range. In order to compute the variance, the returns for each interval are needed. Each of the returns r_i is calculated on prices, so that for a total of $n+1$ prices, it is possible to compute n returns. Define

$$r_i = \ln(S_i) - \ln(S_{i-1})$$
$$= \ln\left(\frac{S_i}{S_{i-1}}\right), \quad i = 1, 2, ..., n$$

Where

S_i is the stock price at the end of i-th interval (time i)
S_{i-1} is the stock price at the end of $(i-1)$-th interval (time $i-1$).

The measurement of volatility follows the basic statistical properties of variance and standard deviation. In particular, it is convenient to define the sum of square deviation from the mean d^2 as

$$d^2 = \sum_{i=1}^{n} (r_i - \bar{r})^2$$

where $\bar{r}$ is the mean of the returns over time, calculated as

$$\bar{r} = \frac{1}{n}\sum_{i=1}^{n} r_i$$

Once d^2 is defined, the standard deviation estimator can be derived as the square root of the unbiased sample variance.

$$s_\sigma = \sqrt{\frac{\sum_{i=1}^{n}(r_i - \bar{r})^2}{n-1}}$$

Recall from basic statistics that s is a biased estimator of the standard deviation of the population σ. In fact, while s^2 is an unbiased estimator for the population variance σ^2, its square root is not. Since the square root is a concave function, it follows from Jensen's inequality that the square root of the sample variance is an underestimate.

It is not straightforward to choose the right value for n. The advantage of choosing a high number of observation is to increase the accuracy of calculation. However, including data that go too far back in time can bias the analysis since the distant past may be irrelevant.

As above mentioned, the periodicity of observation can be of any kind. It is also possible to scale the volatility so as to get to an annualized volatility from any periodicity of observations. The yearly estimate of standard deviation therefore is

$$\hat{\sigma} = s_\sigma \sqrt{m}$$

where m is the number of reference periods in a year, so that $m = 252$ for daily observations, $m = 52$ for weekly observations, $m = 12$ for monthly observations, and so on. The standard error of the estimation is approximately equal to $\hat{\sigma}/\sqrt{2n}$.

A high measured implied volatility means the stock price has been fluctuating a lot. A low volatility shows the price has been quiet over time. Comparison with volatility of other stocks or indices gives a measure of the relative volatility.

Volatility is changing over time, but it is possible to identify long-term values that tend to be almost fixed or contained in between narrow boundaries. In order to do that a technique is to measure volatility over different time windows and average it.

This analysis is also useful to determine the trend of the volatility over time. For example a high short-period low volatility combined with a long-period high volatility means the stock has recently calmed down in price fluctuations. Studying changes in the volatility of an asset can help identify a normal volatility range, deviations from it and, subsequently, trading opportunities.

Another type of volatility widely used in finance is the Implied volatility. As the name suggests, it is a volatility measure implied by an analytical model. More specifically, it is the volatility implied by the Black-Scholes-Merton (BSM) model.

The analysis of the BSM model is dealt with in Chapter 4. The purpose of this part is to introduce the concept of implied volatility and analyse the use of it in financial analysis.

According to the BSM model, the price of a European call option written on a stock is given by

$$c = SN(d_1) - Ke^{-rT}N(d_2)$$

with

$$d_1 = \frac{\ln\left(\dfrac{S}{K}\right) + \left(r + \dfrac{\sigma^2}{2}\right)\Delta t}{\sigma\sqrt{\Delta t}}$$

$$d_2 = d_1 - \sigma\sqrt{\Delta t}$$

where

S is the price of the stock, as observed in the market at the time of calculation
K is the strike price, as specified in the option contract
σ is the volatility of the underlying stock
r is the risk-free rate
Δt is the time left until maturity of the option
$N(.)$ is the cumulative normal distribution.

The volatility parameter σ enters the model as a constant. The rationale behind implied volatility analysis is to invert the BSM model in order to get the volatility implied by the actual market price of the option.

In order to achieve the measurement, numerical procedures are needed, since the BSM formula cannot be inverted analytically. However, advanced financial mathematics develops approximation formulas for the calculation of implied volatility.

Among the various approximation methods, a straightforward one has been developed by M. Brenner and G. Subrahmanyam. They proposed the formula

$$\sigma = \sqrt{\frac{2\pi c}{S\Delta t}}$$

The approximated volatility obtained is valid for at-the-money options, for what the condition $(S = Ke^{-rT})$ holds.

Another approximation method is the Direct Implied Volatility Estimate (DIVE) developed by C.E. Curtis and G.L. Carriker in 1988. In this case the formulas in (2.6) become

$$d_1 = \frac{\sigma\sqrt{\Delta t}}{2}$$

$$d_2 = -\frac{\sigma\sqrt{\Delta t}}{2}$$

The BSM formula then becomes

$$c = S\left[N\left(\frac{\sigma\sqrt{\Delta t}}{2}\right) - N\left(-\frac{\sigma\sqrt{\Delta t}}{2}\right)\right]$$

$$= S\left[N\left(\frac{\sigma\sqrt{\Delta t}}{2}\right) - \left(1 - N\left(\frac{\sigma\sqrt{\Delta t}}{2}\right)\right)\right]$$

$$= S\left[2N\left(\frac{\sigma\sqrt{\Delta t}}{2}\right) - 1\right]$$

This formula can be inverted in order to get the implied volatility as

$$\sigma = \frac{2}{\sqrt{\Delta t}} N^{-1}\left(\frac{c+S}{2S}\right)$$

where

$N^{-1}(.)$ is the inverse of the cumulative normal distribution.

Investors use implied volatilities to keep track of the market's opinion about the volatility of a particular stock. Some investors calculate implied volatility on actively traded options, then manipulate it in order to price less actively traded options on the same underlying stock.

The third type of volatility is the one defined by econometric models. Chapter 3.3.1 is dedicated to the definition, estimation and analysis of ARCH and GARCH variance. Econometric models offer the chance to model variance in a framework of autoregressive (dependency on past values) returns and heteroscedastic (non-constant) conditional variance.

2.3.2 Correlation vs covariance

Covariance and correlation describe the relation between two variables, if it is positive or inverse, and the degree to which the variables tend to move together, in the same or opposite direction.

Recall the variance of a random variable x with mean μ is given by

$$\sigma^2 = E\left\{\left[x - E(x)\right]^2\right\}$$
$$= E\left[(x-\mu)^2\right]$$
$$= \int(x-\mu)^2 f(x)dx$$
$$= \int x^2 f(x)dx - \left[\int xf(x)dx\right]^2$$
$$= E(x^2) - E^2(x)$$

Using the integration method it is then possible to describe the covariance between two variables X and Y, which is given by

$$\begin{aligned}
\sigma_{x,y} &= E\big[(x-\mu_x)(y-\mu_y)\big]\\
&= E(xy) - E(x)E(y)\\
&= \int\int xyf(x,y)dxdy - \Big[\int\int xf(x,y)dxdy\int\int yf(x,y)dxdy\Big]\\
&= \int\int xyf(x,y)dxdy - \Big[\int xf_x(x,y)dx\int yf_y(x,y)dy\Big]
\end{aligned}$$

where

$f(x,y)$ is the joint density
$f_x(x,y)$ and $f_y(x,y)$ are the marginal densities.

Correlation is another measure of relation between two variables, adding the information about the degree to which the variables are related, an information that is not possible to get from covariance.

The correlation coefficient ranges from −1 to +1, making it a standardized measure of the interdependence between two variables. When the coefficient is 1, the two variables are positively perfectly correlated. The variables are not related at all for a value equal to zero, and they are perfectly negatively correlated for a value of −1.

The correlation coefficient, denoted by $\rho_{x,y}$, of random variables x and y is defined to be

$$\rho_{x,y} = \frac{\sigma_{xy}}{\sigma_x \sigma_y}$$

where

σ_{xy} is the covariance between x and y
σ_x is the standard deviation of x
σ_y is the standard deviation of y.

The coefficient is independent of the measurement unit, and has the same sign of covariance.

Example 2.5: Assume the joint density of two random variables x and y is

$$f(x,y) = \begin{cases} y^{-2x} & x \geq 0,\ 0 \leq y \leq 1\\ 0 & \text{otherwise} \end{cases}$$

Integration leads to

$$E(x) = \int_0^{\infty} x f_x(x, y) dx = \ldots = \frac{1}{2}$$

$$E(y) = \int_0^1 y f_y(x, y) dy = \ldots = \frac{1}{3}$$

$$E(xy) = \int_0^{\infty} \int_0^1 xy f(x, y) dx dy = \ldots = \frac{1}{12}$$

The covariance is given by

$$\begin{aligned}
\sigma_{x,y} &= E(xy) - E(x)E(y) \\
&= \frac{1}{6} - \frac{1}{12} \\
&= \frac{1}{12}
\end{aligned}$$

The correlation between x and y is simply the expected product of the corresponding standard scores as can be shown by

$$\begin{aligned}
\rho_{x,y} &= \frac{\sigma_{x,y}}{\sigma_x \sigma_y} \\
&= \frac{E\{[x - E(x)][y - E(y)]\}}{\sigma_x \sigma_y} \\
&= E\left\{\left[\frac{x - E(x)}{\sigma_x}\right]\left[\frac{y - E(y)}{\sigma_y}\right]\right\}
\end{aligned}$$

The correlation coefficient between two financial assets plays a major role in determining the effectiveness of diversifying a portfolio.

The correlation coefficient can be expanded to give a measure of the correlation between two assets, starting from the historical realized returns based on n observations, as described by

$$\hat{\rho}_{x,y} = \frac{n \sum_{i=1}^{n} x_i y_i - \sum_{i=1}^{n} x_i \sum_{i=1}^{n} y_i}{\sqrt{\left[n \sum_{i=1}^{n} x_i^2 - \left(\sum_{i=1}^{n} x_i\right)^2\right]\left[n \sum_{i=1}^{n} y_i^2 - \left(\sum_{i=1}^{n} y_i\right)^2\right]}}$$

which provides the sample correlation coefficient of the two assets rather than the population coefficient.

Example 2.6: Consider the following table with five observation of the returns of two assets x and y.

Stock	n=1	2	3	4	5
x	13.2%	-2.35%	4.53%	10.42%	-3.44%
y	10.3%	3.45%	-1.23%	8.33%	1.21%

Calculation yields

	x_i	y_i	$x_i y_i$	x_i^2	y_i^2
1	13.2%	10.3%	1.36%	1.74%	1.06%
2	-2.35%	3.45%	-0.08%	0.06%	0.12%
3	4.53%	-1.23%	-0.06%	0.21%	0.02%
4	10.42%	8.33%	0.87%	1.09%	0.69%
5	-3.44%	1.21%	-0.04%	0.12%	0.01%

So that

$$\sum_{i=1}^{n} x_i = 22.36\%, \ \sum_{i=1}^{n} y_i = 22.06\%, \ \sum_{i=1}^{n} x_i y_i = 2.05\%,$$

$$\sum_{i=1}^{n} x_i^2 = 3.21\%, \ \left(\sum_{i=1}^{n} x_i\right)^2 = 5.00\%, \ \sum_{i=1}^{n} y_i^2 = 1.90\%, \ \left(\sum_{i=1}^{n} y_i\right)^2 = 4.87\%$$

and the sample correlation is given by

$$\hat{\rho}_{x,y} = \frac{(5 \times 2.05\%) - (22.36\% \times 22.06\%)}{\sqrt{[(5 \times 3.21\%) - 5.00\%][(5 \times 1.90\%) - 4.87\%]}} = 0.7416$$

2.3.3 Maximum likelihood methods

Maximum Likelihood Estimation (MLE) is a general method for estimating the parameters of an econometric model. The method involves a random variable with some probability density whose form is known, but not the parameter vector.

Consider a random variable $x_i = x_1, x_2, ..., x_n$ with probability density function $f(x_1, x_2, ..., x_n; \theta)$. Maximum likelihood involves choosing the values of the parameters giving the highest probability to match the observed data. The likelihood function must be valuable for all admissible values of the parameter set θ.

The time series can be viewed as drawn from probability distributions. Assume there are n random variables conditional on n parameters. The joint probability density function is given by

$$f(x_1, x_2, ..., x_n; \theta_1, \theta_2, ..., \theta_n)$$

The key point is that the above function is usually seen as f being a function of the variable x, for given parameters θ. In the case of MLE the interpretation is reversed and the aim is to look at f as a function of the parameter given the value of the variable.

MLE and likelihood functions become unbiased minimum variance estimators as the sample becomes bigger. Moreover, it is common to use maximum likelihood as a general framework for hypothesis testing.

Both time series models and replicated experiments benefit from MLE which is a versatile tool in statistics. Assume a variable x with observations $x_1, x_2 ..., x_n$ and a joint probability density $(x_1,..., x_n) \mapsto p_{n,\theta}(x_1,..., x_n)$ that depends on a parameter θ, the likelihood function is the stochastic process

$$\theta \mapsto p_{n,\theta}(x_1,...,x_n)$$

The ML estimator for θ is the value of the parameter that maximizes the likelihood function. Repeated conditioning allows us to represent the likelihood appropriately. The likelihood corresponding to the observations $x_1,..., x_n$ as $\theta \mapsto p_\theta(x_1,..., x_n)$ can be decomposed as

$$\theta \mapsto p_\theta(x_1,...,x_n) = p_\theta(x_1) \times p_\theta(x_2 | x_1) \times ... \times p_\theta(x_n | x_{n-1},...,x_1)$$

This is the factorization of the likelihood of an i.i.d. sample, but its components can be distributed in any form, not necessarily i.i.d.

Consider a continuous random variable x with probability density function $f(x; \theta_1, \theta_2,..., \theta_k)$ depending on k unknown parameters $\theta_1, \theta_2,..., \theta_k$. From an experiment draw n independent observations $x_1, x_2,..., x_n$.

The likelihood function associated with the experiment is

$$L(x_1, x_2,..., x_n | \theta_1, \theta_2,..., \theta_k) = \prod_{i=1}^{n} f(x_i; \theta_1, \theta_2,..., \theta_k)$$

The term on the right-hand side is cumbersome to calculate, being a product of density functions. Therefore it is convenient to work with the log of the likelihood. As is well known, the log function preserves the concavity of the target function, so that the maximization problem is not compromised.

The log-likelihood function is given by:

$$\ell(x | \theta) = \ln L(x_1, x_2,..., x_n | \theta_1, \theta_2,..., \theta_k)$$
$$= \sum_{i=1}^{n} \ln f(x_i; \theta_1, \theta_2,..., \theta_k)$$

So, maximizing the log-likelihood is much easier than the likelihood L, and the MLEs of $\theta_1, \theta_2,..., \theta_i$ are given by the simultaneous solutions of k equations such that

$$\frac{\partial \ell(x | \theta)}{\partial \theta_j} = 0, \quad j = 1, 2,..., k$$

For finite samples, MLE is not the best tool, since other estimators have greater fit to the true parameter value. Maximum likelihood is very attractive as the samples increase to infinity. In this case, ML estimators show some interesting properties:

- Consistency is the convergence in probability of the MLE to the value being estimated.
- Asymptotic normality is the tendency to the normal distribution of the MLE as the sample increases.
- Efficiency means the MLE has lower asymptotic mean squared error than other estimators when approaching the Cramer-Rao lower bound, a lower bound on the variance of estimators of a deterministic parameter. An unbiased estimator achieving the lower bound is said to be fully efficient with lowest possible mean squared error, therefore being the minimum variance unbiased estimator.

MLE is commonly used to estimate parameters of known distributions. An example is the use with the Normal distribution. To obtain the MLE estimate for the mean μ and the standard deviation σ for the normal distribution, the first step is to recall its probability density function

$$f(x) = \frac{1}{\sigma\sqrt{2\pi}} e^{-\frac{1}{2}\left(\frac{x-\mu}{\sigma}\right)^2}$$

Assume the observations $x_1, x_2, ..., x$, are realizations of a normally distributed variable x. The likelihood function is given by

$$L(x_1, x_2, ..., x_n | \mu, \sigma) = \prod_{i=1}^{n} \left[\frac{1}{\sigma\sqrt{2\pi}} e^{-\frac{1}{2}\left(\frac{X_i-\mu}{\sigma}\right)^2} \right]$$

$$= \frac{1}{\left(\sigma\sqrt{2\pi}\right)^N} e^{-\frac{1}{2}\sum_{i=1}^{N}\left(\frac{X_i-\mu}{\sigma}\right)^2}$$

The log–likelihood is

$$\ell(x | \theta) = -\frac{n}{2}\ln(2\pi) - n\ln\sigma - \frac{1}{2}\sum_{i=1}^{n}\left(\frac{x_i-\mu}{\sigma}\right)^2$$

The first order conditions are defined by setting the partial derivatives with respect to mean and standard deviation equal to zero.

$$\frac{\partial(\ell)}{\partial\mu} = \frac{1}{\sigma^2}\sum_{i=1}^{n}(x_i-\mu) = 0$$

$$\frac{\partial(\ell)}{\partial\sigma} = -\frac{n}{\sigma} + \frac{1}{\sigma^3}\sum_{i=1}^{n}(x_i-\mu)^2 = 0$$

Solving the two equations simultaneously gives the solution

$$\hat{\mu} = \frac{1}{n}\sum_{i=1}^{n}x_i$$

$$\hat{\sigma} = \sqrt{\frac{1}{n}\sum_{i=1}^{n}(x_i - \mu)^2}$$

The estimators are correct in the limit, meaning their accuracy increases with the size of the sample. When the sample equals the whole population, the estimators are true values. As for the general MLE the above estimators have in-the-limit properties, being unbiased, sufficient, consistent and efficient.

Snapshot 2.2
The covariance matrix of financial returns

The covariance matrix of stock returns is an input to the mean-variance optimization process. For the minimum-variance strategy, the resulting portfolio is highly sensitive to the covariance matrix estimate. A misspecification of covariance matrix could lead to an undesirable portfolio.

The covariance matrix of a vector of random returns $\mathbf{r} = (r_1, r_2, \ldots, r_n)$, with the mean returns vector $\mu = (\mu_1, \mu_2, \ldots, \mu_n)$, is defined as

$$\Sigma = E\left[(\mathbf{r} - \mu)(\mathbf{r} - \mu)^{\mathrm{T}}\right]$$

with each (i, j) element of the matrix defined as

$$\sigma_{ij} = E\left[(r_i - \mu_i)(r_j - \mu_j)\right]$$

and the matrix can be written as

$$\Sigma = \begin{pmatrix} \sigma_1^2 & \sigma_{12} & \cdots & \sigma_{1n} \\ \sigma_{21} & \sigma_2^2 & \cdots & \sigma_{2n} \\ \vdots & \vdots & \ddots & \vdots \\ \sigma_{n1} & \sigma_{n2} & \cdots & \sigma_n^2 \end{pmatrix}$$

The diagonal entries of a covariance matrix are the variances of the assets, therefore all positive, so that the trace of the matrix is positive too. Moreover, it is symmetric, given the symmetry property of the covariance, so that

$$\sigma_{ij} = \sigma_{ji}$$

The covariance matrix is positive semidefinite, meaning that

$$\Sigma = E\left\{\left[(\mathbf{r}-\mu)^{\mathrm{T}}\mathbf{a}\right]^2\right\} = E\left\{\left[(\mathbf{r}-\mu)^{\mathrm{T}}\mathbf{a}\right]^{\mathrm{T}}\left[(\mathbf{r}-\mu)^{\mathrm{T}}\mathbf{a}\right]\right\} \geq 0$$

$$E\left[\mathbf{a}^{\mathrm{T}}(\mathbf{r}-\mu)(\mathbf{r}-\mu)^{\mathrm{T}}\mathbf{a}\right] \geq 0$$

$$\mathbf{a}^{\mathrm{T}}\Sigma\mathbf{a} \geq 0, \quad \mathbf{a} \in \mathbb{R}^n$$

Summary

Portfolio theory was developed in the 1950s as the founding element of modern finance, introducing the concept of diversification and aggregate consideration of the risk-return combination of assets.

Diversification results in risk reduction and its benefits can be mathematically modelled in order to clearly identify the risk-return relationship of all assets in the market, and their contribution to the overall portfolio risk.

Investors want to maximize returns, for some acceptable level of risk. Large portfolio must be handed with matrix algebra to simplify the calculation, and sometimes, computational power is required.

The efficient frontier is the result of an optimization algorithm minimizing the portfolio variance for a fixed expected return. The Capital Market Line is drawn from the risk-free intercept on the vertical axis, to the curve of the efficient frontier, which is then expanded upwards.

The Capital Asset Pricing Model expresses the expected return of a stock as a multiple of the excess return on the market. The premium is a compensation for the risk taken by an investor, and it is multiplied by a specific beta factor.

The CAPM is based on the idea that investors split their funds between risk-free and risky assets, and all investors hold a proportion of the market portfolio. The line graphing the CAPM relationship is called the Security Market Line. In a CAPM-efficient market, all portfolios lie on the SML.

Financial volatility is the main input for defining risk applications in finance. It is very important to learn how volatility can be defined, measured and describe the factors that drive volatility on actual markets.

Volatility can be calculated from historical data, or as implied by analytical models. Maximum Likelihood Estimation gives estimation of parameters of econometric models, involving random variables with known probability density.

Bibliography

Best, M.J. 2010. *Portfolio Optimization (Chapman & Hall/CRC Finance Series)*. Chapman & Hall/CRC.

Brealey, R. and Myers, S. 2003. *Principles of Corporate Finance*. 7th Edition. McGraw-Hill.

Brenner, M. and Subrahmanyam, M. 1988. A Simple Solution to Compute the Implied Standard Deviation. *Financial Analysts Journal*: 80–83.

Cochrane, J.H. 2005. *Asset Pricing*. Revised Edition. Princeton University Press.

Connor, G., Goldberg, L.R. and Korajczyk, R.A. 2010. *Portfolio Risk Analysis*. Princeton University Press.

Esch, L., Kieffer, R., Lopez, T., Berbe, C., Damel, P., Debay, M. and Hannosset, J.F. 2005. *Asset and Risk Management: Risk Oriented Finance*. John Wiley & Sons Inc.

Glasserman, P. 2003. *Monte Carlo Methods in Financial Engineering*. Springer.

Green, W. 2011. *Econometric Analysis*. 7th Edition. Prentice Hall.

Grinblatt, M. and Titman, S. 2002. *Financial Markets & Corporate Strategy*. McGraw-Hill.

Jackel, P. 2002. *Monte Carlo Methods in Finance*. Wilcy Finance.

Lettau, M. and Van, N.S. 2008. Reconciling the Return Predictability Evidence. *Review of Financial Studies*, 21: 1607–1652.

McLeish, D.L. 2005. *Monte Carlo Simulation and Finance*. Wiley Finance.

Merton, R. 1972. An Analytic Derivation of the Efficient Portfolio Frontier. *Journal of Financial and Quantitative Analysis*, 7: 1851–1872.

Milne, F. 1995. *Finance Theory and Asset Pricing*. Clarendon Press.

Renneboog, L. 2006. *Advances in Corporate Finance and Asset Pricing*. Elsevier.

Roll, R. and Ross, S. 1984. The Arbitrage Pricing Theory Approach to Strategic Portfolio Planning. *Financial Analysts Journal*, 40(3): 14–19.

Satchell, S. 2007. *Forecasting Expected Returns in the Financial Markets*. Elsevier Academic Press.

Schneeweis, T., Crowder, G.B. and Kazemi, H. 2010. *The New Science of Asset Allocation*. John Wiley & Sons, Inc.

Schuyler, J.R. 2001. *Risk and Decision Analysis in Projects (Cases in Project and Program Management Series)*. Project Management Institute.

Shreve, S.E. 2004. *Stochastic Calculus for Finance II: Continuous-Time Models*. Springer Finance.

Wenzelburger, J. 2010. The Two-Fund Separation Theorem Revisited. *Annals of Finance*, 6(2): 221–239.

Exercises

Questions

1. Briefly explain the risk-return relationship.
2. Why do some investors put a large portion of their portfolios into risky assets, while others invest largely in the risk-free asset?
3. Explain why the following assumptions in particular are required for the Capital Asset Pricing Model to hold:
   a. A single investor cannot impact the share price.
   b. Time horizon is the same for all investors.
   c. All assets are marketable and infinitely divisible.
4. Is it entirely correct, as an analyst recently commented, that market crashes are never advertised in advance?
5. Recall that criticisms of EMH claim that the rate of return on small-cap stocks tend to be higher than for large-cap.
   a. Is this compatible with CAPM?
   b. How could such a claim be tested?
6. Assume beta coefficients are estimated for a large number of assets, finding that average rates of return of assets and their beta coefficients are not significantly correlated.
   a. What does the result imply in terms of validity of the CAPM?
   b. Would it make sense to completely reject the CAPM on the basis of this evidence?
7. What happens to the riskiness of a portfolio if assets with very low or negative correlations are combined?

8.   Comparing diversifiable and non-diversifiable risk, which one do you think is more important to financial managers in corporations?
9.   Discuss financial risk from the perspective of the CAPM.
10. What features define the points on the efficient frontier? Do portfolios exist above the frontier?
11. Explain the concept of beta, its calculation and meaning.
12. What does the SML indicate? What are the main differences with the CML?

Problems

1.   Derive the intermediate passages to solve equation (2.1) in the chapter.
2.   Consider the following investments

Investment	Expected return	Standard deviation
A	5%	10%
B	7%	11%
C	6%	12%
D	6%	10%

Which investment would you prefer between the following pairs?
   a.   A and D
   b.   B and C
   c.   C and D
3.   Derive the intermediate passages to solve equation (2.2) in the chapter.
4.   Assume two assets A and B for which the following estimates have been derived:

$$E(r_D) = 8\%, \ \sigma_D = 12\%$$

$$E(r_E) = 13\%, \ \sigma_E = 20\%$$

Consider the portfolios that can be formed investing 50% of total wealth in A and 50% in B. What is the portfolio's standard deviation if the assets are perfectly positively correlated?

5.   A portfolio consists of the following assets.

Stock	Investment	Beta
A	€200,000	1.25
B	€300,000	−0.75
C	€500,000	1.25
D	€1,000,000	0.87

The market return is 15% and the risk-free rate is 4%.
- a. Calculate the beta of the portfolio.
- b. Calculate the required rate of return of this portfolio.

6. Assume the market portfolio has an expected return of 5% and a volatility of 21%. There is a risky asset i on which limited information is available. It is known that the expected return of the asset is 4%, the volatility is bounded between 20% and 40%, and the covariance between the asset and the market is bounded between 0.0168 and 0.03.
- c. Find the interval of possible values of $\rho_{i,M} = Corr(r_i, r_M)$ and of β_i.
- d. What range of values for the risk-free rate do you find realistic? Give an interval in which the risk-free rate should be. Then, find the interval of risk-free rates implied by the CAPM in the above system.
- e. How would you price an asset with the same risk characteristics as asset i?

7. Denote by X a stock and by M the market. The correlation coefficient $\rho_{P,M}$ between the stock and the market is 0.80. The volatility of stock X is 25% and the volatility of the market is 12%.
- f. Calculate the systematic variance, the unsystematic variance, and β_P.
- g. Show that the beta of a portfolio equals the weighted average of the assets' betas.

8. When estimating CAPM from data, a regression error must be taken into account and the formula modified accordingly. The error is normally distributed. Suppose there are three risky assets with the following betas and values of $\sigma_{\varepsilon_j}^2$ in the CAPM.

j	β_j	$\sigma_{\varepsilon_j}^2$
A	1.3	0.008
F	1.1	0.012
E	0.6	0.010

Suppose also that the market excess returns have a variance of 0.016.
- a. What is the beta of an equally weighted portfolio of these three assets?
- b. What is the variance of the excess return on the equally weighted portfolio?
- c. What proportion of the total risk of asset A is due to market risk?

9. Consider the following data for a one-factor economy. All portfolios are well diversified.

Portfolio	$E(R_i)$	Beta
A	10%	1.0
B	4%	0
C	9%	2/3

a.   Is there any arbitrage opportunity in the market?
    b.   If so, what would the arbitrage strategy be?
10. The weight measurement of individuals picked in two different areas of the world
    X and Y are given in the following table

i	X_i	Y_i
1	71	69
2	68	64
3	66	65
4	67	63
5	70	65
6	71	62
7	70	65
8	73	64
9	72	66
10	65	59
11	66	62

a.   Calculate the sample correlation of the weight in the two areas of the world.

Appendix: The table of the standard normal distribution

Z	0.00	0.01	0.02	0.03	0.04	0.05	0.06	0.07	0.08	0.09
0.0	0.5000	0.5040	0.5080	0.5120	0.5160	0.5199	0.5239	0.5279	0.5319	0.5359
0.1	0.5398	0.5438	0.5478	0.5517	0.5557	0.5596	0.5636	0.5675	0.5714	0.5753
0.2	0.5793	0.5832	0.5871	0.5910	0.5948	0.5987	0.6026	0.6064	0.6103	0.6141
0.3	0.6179	0.6217	0.6255	0.6293	0.6331	0.6368	0.6406	0.6443	0.6480	0.6517
0.4	0.6554	0.6591	0.6628	0.6664	0.6700	0.6736	0.6772	0.6808	0.6844	0.6879
0.5	0.6915	0.6950	0.6985	0.7019	0.7054	0.7088	0.7123	0.7157	0.7190	0.7224
0.6	0.7257	0.7291	0.7324	0.7357	0.7389	0.7422	0.7454	0.7486	0.7517	0.7549
0.7	0.7580	0.7611	0.7642	0.7673	0.7704	0.7734	0.7764	0.7794	0.7823	0.7852
0.8	0.7881	0.7910	0.7939	0.7967	0.7995	0.8023	0.8051	0.8078	0.8106	0.8133
0.9	0.8159	0.8186	0.8212	0.8238	0.8264	0.8289	0.8315	0.8340	0.8365	0.8389
1.0	0.8413	0.8438	0.8461	0.8485	0.8508	0.8531	0.8554	0.8577	0.8599	0.8621
1.1	0.8643	0.8665	0.8686	0.8708	0.8729	0.8749	0.8770	0.8790	0.8810	0.8830
1.2	0.8849	0.8869	0.8888	0.8907	0.8925	0.8944	0.8962	0.8980	0.8997	0.9015
1.3	0.9032	0.9049	0.9066	0.9082	0.9099	0.9115	0.9131	0.9147	0.9162	0.9177
1.4	0.9192	0.9207	0.9222	0.9236	0.9251	0.9265	0.9279	0.9292	0.9306	0.9319
1.5	0.9332	0.9345	0.9357	0.9370	0.9382	0.9394	0.9406	0.9418	0.9429	0.9441
1.6	0.9452	0.9463	0.9474	0.9484	0.9495	0.9505	0.9515	0.9525	0.9535	0.9545
1.7	0.9554	0.9564	0.9573	0.9582	0.9591	0.9599	0.9608	0.9616	0.9625	0.9633
1.8	0.9641	0.9649	0.9656	0.9664	0.9671	0.9678	0.9686	0.9693	0.9699	0.9706
1.9	0.9713	0.9719	0.9726	0.9732	0.9738	0.9744	0.9750	0.9756	0.9761	0.9767
2.0	0.9772	0.9778	0.9783	0.9788	0.9793	0.9798	0.9803	0.9808	0.9812	0.9817
2.1	0.9821	0.9826	0.9830	0.9834	0.9838	0.9842	0.9846	0.9850	0.9854	0.9857
2.2	0.9861	0.9864	0.9868	0.9871	0.9875	0.9878	0.9881	0.9884	0.9887	0.9890
2.3	0.9893	0.9896	0.9898	0.9901	0.9904	0.9906	0.9909	0.9911	0.9913	0.9916

Z	0.00	0.01	0.02	0.03	0.04	0.05	0.06	0.07	0.08	0.09
2.4	0.9918	0.9920	0.9922	0.9925	0.9927	0.9929	0.9931	0.9932	0.9934	0.9936
2.5	0.9938	0.9940	0.9941	0.9943	0.9945	0.9946	0.9948	0.9949	0.9951	0.9952
2.6	0.9953	0.9955	0.9956	0.9957	0.9959	0.9960	0.9961	0.9962	0.9963	0.9964
2.7	0.9965	0.9966	0.9967	0.9968	0.9969	0.9970	0.9971	0.9972	0.9973	0.9974
2.8	0.9974	0.9975	0.9976	0.9977	0.9977	0.9978	0.9979	0.9979	0.9980	0.9981
2.9	0.9981	0.9982	0.9982	0.9983	0.9984	0.9984	0.9985	0.9985	0.9986	0.9986
3.0	0.9987	0.9987	0.9987	0.9988	0.9988	0.9989	0.9989	0.9989	0.9990	0.9990

The first column indicates the integer and first decimal of the quantile x for what the corresponding value $N(0.34)$ is to be found. As an example, assuming that the value of $N(0.34)$ is needed, the table must be analyzed as follows

Z	0.00	0.01	0.02	0.03	0.04	0.05	0.06	0.07	0.08	0.09
0.0	0.5000	0.5040	0.5080	0.5120	*0.5160*	0.5199	0.5239	0.5279	0.5319	0.5359
0.1	0.5398	0.5438	0.5478	0.5517	*0.5557*	0.5596	0.5636	0.5675	0.5714	0.5753
0.2	0.5793	0.5832	0.5871	0.5910	*0.5948*	0.5987	0.6026	0.6064	0.6103	0.6141
0.3	*0.6179*	*0.6217*	*0.6255*	*0.6293*	***0.6331***	0.6368	0.6406	0.6443	0.6480	0.6517
0.4	0.6554	0.6591	0.6628	0.6664	0.6700	0.6736	0.6772	0.6808	0.6844	0.6879
0.5	0.6915	0.6950	0.6985	0.7019	0.7054	0.7088	0.7123	0.7157	0.7190	0.7224
...	...	...	...	...	...	...	...	...	...	...

and the corresponding value is

$$N(0.34) = 0.6331$$

If the value of $N(-x) = N(-0.34)$ is to be found, just recall the symmetry property of the normal distribution, such that

$$N(-x) = 1 - N(x)$$
$$N(-0.34) = 1 - N(0.34) = 1 - 0.6331 = 0.3669$$

3 Statistical analysis

Risk management involves knowledge of probability and statistics. Analytical tools are developed to analyse return distributions and time series. Distributions and econometric models are tools for assessing the properties of financial data.

When departing from the assumption of normality, usage of more complicated distributions to fit data becomes crucial. This is especially true for risk, that often concentrates on the tails of the distribution. Extreme events are often the most important.

It is also very important to have knowledge of probabilistic approaches to risk. These are useful when forecasting risk for important projects. When all possible outcomes are taken into account, risk management can identify and prevent risk efficiently.

There are many applications of probability and statistics in financial risk management, from the calculation of mean and variances of returns, to the assessment of project expected outputs. One problem with financial data is to assess the properties of the returns and grasp the properties of future returns. Accuracy in risk measurement goes through the calculations of econometric properties of data.

After studying this chapter you will be able to answer the following questions, among others:

1. What distributions are relevant for risk management analysis?
2. What happens when the assumption of normality of financial returns is relaxed?
3. How are the parameters of Pareto, Bernoulli and Poisson distributions estimated and interpreted?
4. How can probabilistic approaches be used for assessing risk? What are the accuracy and reliability of the approach?
5. What are the main econometric processes for data analysis? What are the features of time series of financial returns?

The first section of the chapter is an introduction to the use of probability and statistics in financial risk management. The second section is about probabilistic approaches, and their use for project planning. The final part is dedicated to time series analysis, econometric models and their estimation.

3.1 Relevant distributions

Learning outcomes

1. Understand the importance of heavy-tailed distributions in finance.
2. Acquire knowledge about risk-related important distributions.
3. Use maximum likelihood for parameter estimation.

3.1.1 Pareto distribution

The probability of a large loss is related to the size of the tail of returns distribution. A heavy tail involves a consistent probability of having a large loss, while a thin tale of the distribution means probability of extreme events is close to zero. Heavy-tailed distributions are better at modelling losses where there's a small but non-zero chance of having a large loss.

Part of good risk management is about analysing data and fitting them into known distributions. The standard distribution of reference, as known, is the normal distribution. However, the assumption of normality fails when dealing with extreme events.

When the point is about catastrophic events and consequences, it is very important to have a realistic description of the tail of the distribution considered. In this case it is worth considering other classes of distributions that fulfil the need of an accurate tail description.

The concept of tail is fundamental in risk management. Compared to other distributions, like the Normal or the Exponential, the Pareto distribution shows a fatter (heavier) tail.

The Pareto distribution is commonly used to model excess of loss in financial distributions, given the good descriptive capabilities of large losses. The survival function of a Pareto variable is

$$\Pr(X > x) = \begin{cases} \left(\dfrac{c}{x}\right)^{\alpha} & \text{if } x \geq c \\ 1 & \text{if } x < c \end{cases}$$

where

c and α are some constants.

The continuous random variable with positive support X is said to have the Pareto distribution if its probability density function is given by

$$f(x) = \frac{\alpha}{c}\left(\frac{c}{x}\right)^{\alpha+1}, \quad x > c$$

The cumulative distribution is

$$F(x) = 1 - \left(\frac{c}{x}\right)^{\alpha}, \quad x \geq c$$

The Pareto distribution has two parameters, c and α. Both parameters can be estimated from the distribution, but usually the parameter c marks a lower bound on the possible values that a Pareto distributed random variable can take on, and in most applications is chosen in advance.

The mean can be computed as:

$$E(x) = \int_c^\infty x \frac{\alpha}{c}\left(\frac{c}{x}\right)^{\alpha+1} dx$$

$$= \frac{c\alpha}{\alpha-1} \int_c^\infty \frac{\alpha-1}{c} dx$$

$$= \frac{c\alpha}{\alpha-1}, \quad \alpha>1$$

It is then possible then to determine the expectation of the square

$$E(x^2) = \int_c^\infty x^2 \frac{\alpha}{c}\left(\frac{c}{x}\right)^{\alpha+1} dx$$

$$= \frac{c^2\alpha}{\alpha-2} \int_c^\infty \frac{\alpha-2}{c}\left(\frac{c}{x}\right)^{\alpha-1} dx$$

$$= \frac{c^2\alpha}{\alpha-2}, \quad \alpha>2$$

and, by the basic property of variance equality (the expectation of the square minus the square of the expectation)

$$Var(x) = E(x^2) - [E(x)]^2$$

$$= \frac{c^2\alpha}{\alpha-2} - \frac{c^2\alpha^2}{(\alpha-1)^2}$$

$$= c^2 \frac{\alpha(\alpha-1)^2 - \alpha^2(\alpha-2)}{\alpha-2(\alpha-1)^2}$$

$$= c^2 \frac{\alpha}{\alpha-2(\alpha-1)^2}, \quad \alpha>2$$

The parameter α can be estimated with maximum likelihood. For this particular distribution the associated log-likelihood function is

$$\mathcal{L}(\alpha) = \ln\left[\prod_{i=1}^n \frac{\alpha}{c}\left(\frac{c}{x_i}\right)^{\alpha+1}\right]$$

$$= n\ln(\alpha) + n\alpha\ln(c) - (\alpha+1)\sum_{i=1}^n \ln(x_i), \quad x \geq c$$

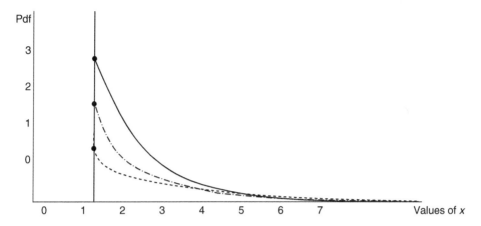

Figure 3.1 Stylized patterns of the Pareto distribution for $c = 1$ and different values of parameter a. Recall that the Pareto is a discrete distribution. A continuous line is adopted here just for guiding the eye of the reader.

It follows that the first order condition on the likelihood is

$$\mathcal{L}'(\alpha) = \frac{n}{\alpha} + n\ln(c) - \sum_{i=1}^{n} \ln(x_i) = 0$$

The solution maximizing the likelihood is

$$\tilde{\alpha} = \frac{n}{\sum_{i=1}^{n} \log\left(\frac{x_i}{c}\right)} \tag{3.1}$$

When a variable X is Pareto distributed, the quantity at denominator $\log\left(\frac{x_i}{c}\right)$ is exponentially distributed. Now recall that the sum of exponential distributions is distributed as Gamma

$$G = \sum_{i=1}^{n} \log\left(\frac{x_i}{c}\right) \sim \text{Gamma}$$

The gamma distribution can be approximated by a two-parameters (β, n) function in the form of

$$f(x) = \frac{\alpha^n}{\Gamma(n)} x^{n-1} e^{-\alpha x}, \quad x > c$$

where

$$\Gamma(n) = (n-1)!$$

is the gamma function.

Given equation (3.1), it follows that

$$E(\hat{\alpha}) = \frac{\alpha n}{n-1} \int_0^\infty \frac{\alpha^{n-1}}{(n-2)!} x^{n-2} e^{-\alpha x} dx$$

$$= \frac{n}{n-1} \alpha$$

and the variance is

$$Var(\hat{\alpha}) = \frac{n^2 \alpha^2}{n-1} \left(\frac{1}{n-2} - \frac{1}{n-1} \right)$$

$$= \frac{n^2}{(n-1)^2 (n-2)} \alpha^2$$

That shows the estimator $\hat{\alpha}$ is biased, as opposed to the alternative estimator

$$\alpha^* = \frac{n-1}{\sum_{i=1}^n \log\left(\frac{x_i}{c}\right)}$$

In particular, the variance

$$Var(\alpha^*) = \frac{1}{(n-2)} \alpha^2$$

is lower than the variance of the biased estimator, confirming α^* is a better estimator than $\hat{\alpha}$.

The two-parameters first type Pareto distribution belongs to the family of Generalized Pareto Distribution (GPD). The generalized distribution has three parameters, and each of them defines a specific feature. The cumulative distribution is

$$F_{(a,\mu,\sigma)}(x) = \begin{cases} 1 - \left(1 - a\frac{x-\mu}{\sigma}\right)^{\frac{1}{a}} & \text{if } a \neq 0 \\ 1 - e^{\left(-\frac{x-\mu}{\sigma}\right)} & \text{if } a = 0 \end{cases}$$

$$x \geq \mu, \quad \mu \leq x \leq \frac{\mu - \sigma}{a}, \quad a > 0$$

where

μ is a location parameter
σ is a scale parameter
a is a shape parameter.

The distribution is obtained for negative values of the shape parameter. For $a > 0$ and $\mu = -\dfrac{\sigma}{a}$ the distribution reduces to the simple Pareto as seen above. Furthermore, it reduces to the uniform distribution for $\mu = 0$ and $a = 1$, and the exponential distribution for $\mu = 0$ and $a = 0$.

The probability density function is given by

$$f_{(a,\mu,\sigma)}(x) = \begin{cases} \dfrac{1}{\sigma}\left(1 - a\dfrac{x-\mu}{\sigma}\right)^{\frac{1}{a}-1} & \text{if } a \neq 0 \\ \dfrac{1}{\sigma}e^{\left(-\frac{x-\mu}{\sigma}\right)} & \text{if } a = 0 \end{cases}$$

The expected value and variance in this case are

$$E(x) = \mu + \frac{\sigma}{a-1}, \quad a > 1$$

$$Var(x) = \frac{\sigma^2}{(a-1)^2(2a-1)}, \quad a > \frac{1}{2}$$

There are many possible applications for the Pareto distribution in Economics, mostly for the analysis of tail (extreme) events.

3.1.2 Binomial distribution

The binomial distribution describes the behaviour of a variable X meeting the following conditions:

- The number of observations n is fixed.
- Observations are independent.
- Observations represent one of two outcomes.
- The probability of first outcome p is the same for each outcome.

These are preconditions to confirm a variable X has a binomial distribution, with two parameters, p and n. The understanding of the binomial distribution and the following arguments require basic knowledge of probability theory.

Define a probability measure $\mathbb{P}$ on a space Ω. Also define an event A occurring with probability $p = \Pr(A)$.

An intermediate step to binomial distribution is to introduce the Bernoulli random variable. A Bernoulli variable X defined on a Ω space takes the values zero or one, according to the realization ω of the event A. In mathematical notation

$$X(\omega) = \begin{cases} 1 & \text{if } \omega \in A \\ 0 & \text{if } \omega \notin A \end{cases}$$

$$X : \Omega \to \{0,1\}, \quad X \sim b(1,p)$$

Given the properties of the Bernoulli distribution, it is possible to define the probability distribution function, as the probability that X equals 1 or 0.

$$\Pr(X = x) = \begin{cases} p & \text{if } x = 1 \\ 1-p & \text{if } x = 0 \\ 0 & \text{otherwise} \end{cases}$$

which can be written as

$$\Pr(X = x) = p^x (1-p)^{1-x}$$

The evaluation of function X over the average value from the occurrences of zeros and ones gives the mean of the distribution as

$$\begin{aligned} \mu_{BER} &= \sum_{x \in \text{Range}(X)} k\mathbb{P}(X = x) \\ &= 0 \times (1-p) + 1 \times p \\ &= p \end{aligned}$$

The variance comes from the basic properties of the moments of the distribution

$$\begin{aligned} \sigma^2_{BER} &= E[X^2] - (E[X])^2 \\ &= \left[0^2 (1-p) + 1^2 p \right] - p^2 \\ &= p - p^2 = p(1-p) \end{aligned}$$

A convenient use of a Bernoulli variable is to write piecewise defined functions that take values $a_1, a_2, ..., a_n$ over different events $A_1, A_2, ..., A_n$.

$$X(\omega) = \begin{cases} a_1 & \text{if } \omega \in A_1 \\ a_2 & \text{if } \omega \in A_2 \\ ... & ... \\ a_n & \text{if } \omega \in A_n \end{cases}$$

The characterization of the binomial distribution is the probability of getting a certain amount of an outcome, over the n independent trials, where each trial has two possible outcomes.

For example, using a binomial distribution, we can determine the probability of getting h heads in n coin tosses. The probability of a head is denoted by p. For n trials you can obtain between 0 and n heads.

The mass function of the binomial distribution is

$$f(x|n, p) = \begin{cases} \binom{n}{x} p^x (1-p)^{n-x} & \text{if } 0 \le y \le n \\ 0 & \text{otherwise} \end{cases}$$

Figure 3.2 The binomial distribution is a discrete distribution in segments.

where

$$\binom{n}{k} = \frac{n!}{k!(n-k)!}$$

The distribution is determined by the quantities n (number of trials) and p (probability of success). The quantity $f(x|n, p)$ represents the probability of exactly x successes out of n trials.

Example 3.1: Consider picking five balls numbered 1 to 5. One person selects blindly at random one ball at a time. Someone else has to identify it. This is done five times, and repeated with other pairs of people. In each trial there is a probability $p = 20\%$ of picking any specific number between 1 and 5. The probability of identifying one card correctly after five attempts is

$$\Pr(X = 1) = \binom{5}{1}(0.2)^1 (0.8)^{5-1} = 5(0.2)(0.8)^4 = 0.4096 \simeq 41\%$$

A binomial distribution gives us the probabilities associated with independent, repeated Bernoulli trials. It is a sum of n independent Bernoulli distributed random variables. It follows from the addition properties for independent random variables, that the mean and variance of a binomial distribution are n times the mean and variance of a Bernoulli distribution.

Therefore the mean of the binomial distribution is

$$\mu_{BIN}(X) = n\mu_{BER}$$
$$= np$$

and the variance is

$$\sigma^2_{BIN}(X) = n\sigma^2_{BER}(X)$$
$$= np(1-p)$$

The maximum likelihood estimator for the binomial distribution is given by

$$L(p|n, p) = \prod_{i=1}^{n}\binom{n}{x_i} p^{x_i}(1-p)^{n-x_i}$$
$$= \left[\prod_{i=1}^{n}\binom{n}{x_i}\right] p^{\sum_i x_i}(1-p)^{n-\sum_i x_i}$$

The log-likelihood is

$$\ln L(p|n, p) = \sum_{i=1}^{n} x_i \ln(p) + \left(n - \sum_{i=1}^{n} x_i\right)\ln(1-p)$$

The first order condition is

$$\frac{d \ln L(p|n, p)}{dp} = \frac{1}{p}\sum_{i=1}^{n} x_i + \frac{1}{1-p}\left(n - \sum_{i=1}^{n} x_i\right) = 0$$

It follows that

$$(1-\hat{p})\sum_{i=1}^{n} x_i + \hat{p}\left(n - \sum_{i=1}^{n} x_i\right) = 0$$
$$\Rightarrow \hat{p} = \frac{\sum_{i=1}^{n} x_i}{n} = \frac{x}{n}$$

For large number of observations and small value of p, calculating the binomial probabilities becomes cumbersome. In this case it is convenient to approximate the binomial probabilities with Poisson probabilities (see below).

3.1.3 Poisson distribution

The Poisson distribution is a discrete probability distribution first derived by the mathematician S.D. Poisson. It gives the probability that a specified number of events will occur in a fixed interval. The events are supposed to occur at some known average rate, and they are independent of the time since the last event occurred.

The Poisson distribution is based on four assumptions.

1.   Event is a countable quantity and occurrences are independent.
2.   The probability of an occurrence is independent from other occurrences.
3.   The average frequency of occurrence in the interval considered is known.
4.   The number of events in an interval is proportional to the size of it.

The Poisson distribution has a single parameter, conventionally indicated with λ. It represents the average number of occurrences in the interval (period) considered. In general if $X \sim Poiss(\lambda)$, the probability mass function is

$$f(x,\lambda) = \Pr(X = x) = \frac{\lambda^x e^{-\lambda}}{x!}, \quad x = 1, 2, \ldots$$

Example 3.2: If the random variable X follows a Poisson distribution with parameter 2.7, the probability that the variable will take a value of 7 is

$$\Pr(X = 7) = \frac{\lambda^x e^{-\lambda}}{x!} = \frac{(2.7)^7 \times e^{-2.7}}{7!} = 0.014$$

In order to derive the mean and variance of the Poisson distribution it is necessary to start from the moment generating function, that is

$$
\begin{aligned}
M_x(t) &= E(e^{tx}) \\
&= \sum_{k=0}^{\infty} e^{tk}\left(\frac{e^{-\lambda}\lambda^k}{k!}\right) \\
&= e^{-\lambda}\sum_{k=0}^{\infty}\frac{(\lambda e^t)^k}{k!} \\
&= e^{-\lambda}e^{\lambda e^t} = e^{\lambda(e^t - 1)}
\end{aligned}
$$

The mean of the distribution can be then derived as

$$
\begin{aligned}
E(x) &= \frac{d}{dt}M_x(t)\Big|_{t=0} \\
&= \frac{d}{dt}e^{\lambda(e^t - 1)}(t)\Big|_{t=0} \\
&= \lambda e^t M_x(t)\Big|_{t=0} \qquad \text{(by chain rule)} \\
&= \lambda e^t e^{\lambda(e^t - 1)}\Big|_{t=0} = \lambda
\end{aligned}
$$

Similarly we can derive the variance through deriving the second moment first

$$
\begin{aligned}
E(x^2) &= \frac{d^2}{dt^2}M_x(t)\Big|_{t=0} = \frac{d}{dt}\left(\frac{d}{dt}M_x(t)\right)\Big|_{t=0} \\
&= \lambda\frac{d}{dt}(e^t M_x(t))\Big|_{t=0} \\
&= \lambda\left(e^t M_x(t) + e^t \frac{d}{dt}M_x(t)\right)\Big|_{t=0} \\
&= \lambda e^t\left(M_x(t) + \lambda e^t M_x(t)\right)\Big|_{t=0} \\
&= \lambda(1 + \lambda)
\end{aligned}
$$

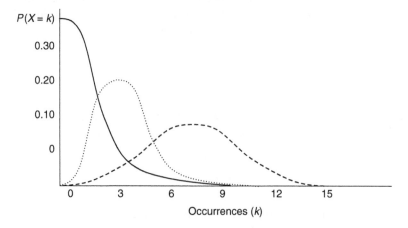

Figure 3.3 The graph shows different shapes for the Poisson distribution for different values of the parameter. The function is only defined at integer values of k therefore the continuous lines do not represent the true distribution and only indicate the path of the dots.

Therefore

$$Var(x) = E(x^2) - \left[E(x)^2 \right]$$
$$= \lambda(1+\lambda) - \lambda^2$$
$$= \lambda$$

There are some empirical ways of checking for a Poisson distribution. A simple method is to see if the variance is roughly equal to the mean for the given data. Poisson data plotted on a histogram show right skewness, and the effect is less pronounced as the mean increases.

Suppose that a series of n random variable $X_1, X_2, ..., X_n$ are independent $Pois(\lambda)$. The maximum likelihood estimator can be derived as follows. The likelihood function is

$$L(\lambda \mid x) = \prod_{i=1}^{n} \frac{\lambda^{x_i} e^{-\lambda}}{x_i!}$$
$$= \frac{\lambda^{\sum_i x_i} e^{-n\lambda}}{\prod_i x_i!}$$

The log-likelihood is

$$\log L(\lambda \mid x) = \sum_{i=1}^{n} x_i \log \lambda - n\lambda - \sum_{i=1}^{n} \log(x_i!)$$

The first order condition is

$$\frac{d \log L(\lambda \mid x)}{d\lambda} = \frac{1}{\lambda} \sum_{i=1}^{n} x_i - n = 0$$

$$\Rightarrow \sum_{i=1}^{n} x_i = n\lambda$$

$$\Rightarrow \hat{\lambda} = \frac{1}{n} \sum_{i=1}^{n} x_i$$

$$= \bar{x}$$

The MLE estimator of the Poisson distribution is the mean of the distribution. Just observe that the same result comes from using the method-of-moments estimation.

If the data are Poisson distributed then they show significant randomness over time, and there should be no evidence of different values of the average occurrence rate over time. Any fluctuations in numbers of accidents are assignable in such cases to random variation.

The Poisson distribution can be seen, under some circumstances, as an approximation of the binomial distribution. When the number of observations is large, the binomial distribution involves complicated calculations. Putting $\lambda = np$, the Poisson terms can, in certain circumstances, be used instead of the binomial terms.

The conditions to approximate the binomial distribution with a Poisson distribution are:

- A large value of n
- A small value of p

The reference values to be considered as large or small are not fixed. The empirical experiments suggest a good interval of values as follows

$$Pois(\lambda = np) \rightarrow B(n, p), \quad \text{for } 0,0008 \le \frac{p}{n} \le 0,0015$$

In order to confirm the strict relationship between the two distributions, it is interesting to observe how the Poisson distribution can be derived as a limiting case of the binomial. The direct way to prove it works is on the mass function of the distribution and a change in variable.

Setting $p = \frac{t}{n}$ the binomial mass function can be written as

$$B\left(n, \frac{t}{n}\right) = \binom{n}{x} \left(\frac{t}{n}\right)^x \left(1 - \frac{t}{n}\right)^{n-x}$$

In order to get the desired result, it is convenient to expand the formula expressing the binomial term

$$B\left(n, \frac{t}{n}\right) = \frac{t^x}{x!} \left(1 - \frac{t}{n}\right)^n \frac{n(n-1)...(n-(x-1))}{n^x} \left(1 - \frac{t}{n}\right)^{-x}$$

As $n \to \infty$ the single terms of the formula converge as follows

$$\lim_{n \to \infty} \left(1-\frac{t}{n}\right)^{-x} = 1$$

$$\lim_{n \to \infty} \frac{n(n-1)...(n-(x-1))}{n^x} = 1$$

$$\lim_{n \to \infty} \left(1-\frac{t}{n}\right)^{n} = e^{-t}$$

Therefore the whole expression convergence is

$$\lim_{n \to \infty} B\left(n,\frac{t}{n}\right) = \frac{t^x}{x!} e^{-t}$$

which is clearly the Poisson distribution.

Another way to approximate the binomial distribution to the Poisson is through the characteristic function.

In statistics, the characteristic function of a random variable X is defined as

$$\varphi_{X,t} = E\left(e^{itX}\right)$$
$$= \int e^{itX} dF(x)$$
$$= \int e^{itX} f(x), \quad t \in \mathbb{R}$$

where

$F(x)$ is the cumulative distribution function of X
$f(x)$ is the probability density function
i is the imaginary unit.

The characteristic function for the binomial $\left(n,\frac{t}{n}\right)$ distribution is

$$C_n(\theta) = \sum_{x=0}^{n} e^{i\theta n} \binom{n}{k}\left(\frac{t}{n}\right)^{x}\left(1-\frac{t}{n}\right)^{n-x}$$
$$= \left(1-\frac{t}{n}+\frac{te^{i\theta}}{n}\right)^{n}$$
$$= \left(1+\frac{t\left(e^{i\theta}-1\right)}{n}\right)^{n}$$

Taking the limit yields:

$$\lim_{n \to \infty} C_n(\theta) = e^{t(e^{i\theta}-1)}$$

which is the characteristic function of the Poisson distribution with mean t.

Snapshot 3.1
Excel statistical functions

The aim of this snapshot is to give a list of the statistical functions embedded into Excel and their outcome. The list includes the major distributions that are dealt with in the book's previous, current and future chapters, and aims at being a guide for the students wanting to apply on Excel the theoretical models presented.

The first table lists the functions to be used for descriptive statistics:

Function	Outcome
AVEDEV	Average of absolute deviations from the mean
AVERAGE	Mean of the distribution
GEOMEAN	Geometric mean
MEDIAN	Median
PERCENTILE	k-th percentile of values in a range
DEVSQ	Sum of squares of deviations from the mean
KURT	Estimator for kurtosis
SKEW	Estimator for skewness
STDEV	Standard deviation
VAR	Estimation for variance
CORREL	Correlation coefficient between two data sets
COVAR	Covariance
FREQUENCY	Frequency distribution as a vertical array

The statistical distributions are defined by the following functions:

Function	Outcome
BINOMDIST	Binomial distribution probability
CRITBINOM	Smallest value for which cum. dist. < criterion
CHIDIST	Chi Square distribution
CHIINV	Inverse of Chi Square distribution
EXPONDIST	Exponential distribution
NORMDIST	Normal cumulative distribution
NORMINV	Inverse of normal cumulative distribution
POISSON	Poisson distribution
TDIST	Student's t distribution

The last table includes the most common linear model and statistical tests:

Function	Outcome
FTEST	Test of equality of the variance of two populations
TTEST	Test of equality of means of two populations
SLOPE	Slope of the linear regression model

3.2 Probabilistic approaches

Learning outcomes

1. Describe the concept of probabilistic approach.
2. Learn how to use scenario analysis and decision trees, for project analysis.
3. Implement simulations in order to analyse potential outcomes.

3.2.1 Scenario analysis

In financial modelling, scenario analysis evaluates the impact of simultaneous changes in a number of sensitive variables. The changes in all involved variables are then applied to evaluate the impact on the investment return.

A first analysis can be done by developing a specific asset in case history should repeat itself. This static technique is called Back Testing and involves the creation of just one scenario of how the situation could evolve.

Scenario analysis goes further and takes into consideration more factors and a deeper view of the historical scenarios to replicate. It takes a more in-depth look at the future, while taking into account historical data and economic knowledge.

General preparation of scenario analysis involves four basic steps:

1. Identify the relevant factors around which to build the scenario.
2. Choose the number of scenarios to be created and analysed for each selected factor.
3. Estimate the outcomes for each possible scenario.
4. Determine the probabilities to assign to each scenario.

Values can be presented as single outcomes for each scenario, or as a weighted average (expected value), assuming probabilities for each scenario can be estimated, in order to weigh the average accordingly.

Each factor gets assigned a value in order to depict a specific scenario. It is common practice for example to simulate a best-case and worst-case scenario in order to bound the range of possible outcomes from some possible investment decision.

Historical data are usually the starting point of the analysis. Past years' returns are taken into account, and constitute the basis for the scenario modelling. In fact, on returns many variables can be calculated as volatility and correlation.

After the scenario is completed and all the above points are fulfilled, the last step is the use of the scenario result to plan strategies.

Example 3.3: Consider the following table summarizing three possible states of the world

Economy	Probability	Stock A return	Stock B return
Boom	20%	15%	10%
Normal	60%	5%	−5%
Recession	20%	−10%	20%

It is possible to calculate expected returns as

$$\mu = \sum_{i=1}^{n} p_i x_i \to \mu_A = 4.0\%, \ \mu_B = 3.0\%$$

and the standard deviations

$$\sigma = \sqrt{E(x^2) - (E(x))^2} \to \sigma_A = 8.0\%, \ \sigma_B = 10.3\%$$

Starting from this first scenario, we can create many others changing values to the probabilities assigned to each state. It is also possible to change the returns assigned to each state. All these changes generate many new scenarios. The ultimate goal is to generate extreme scenarios.

The regulatory framework for scenario analysis is the Basel Accord, stating that financial institutions subject to regulation should use internal and external loss data in order to create scenarios, together with some additional microeconomic factors.

Regulation is very loose about the process of scenario formation given the information used. In the Basel framework the purpose of using the regulated inputs is to calculate regulatory capital.

Results from a scenario analysis can be used internally, as a guide to business planning, or more widely as indicators of market functioning, chasing what might happen to financial market returns, such as bonds, stocks or cash, in each of those economic scenarios. The scenarios may have sub-scenarios, and probabilities may be assigned to each.

3.2.2 Decision trees

Decision trees have many applications. In many fields their use allows for helping with making good choices, especially the ones involving high levels of risk. Using decision trees it is possible to compare different workable choices with a graphic approach.

Compared to other methodologies, decision trees offer some remarkable advantages:

- The approach is graphic, allowing one to visualize at a glance the various alternatives and possible outcomes.
- They allow for a high flexibility, depicting complex alternatives and being easy to modify according to new information. Moreover, there is almost infinite chance to split a tree into sub-trees, allowing for complex analysis.
- They are not in contrast with other forms of decision methods, but arise as a useful complementary tool.

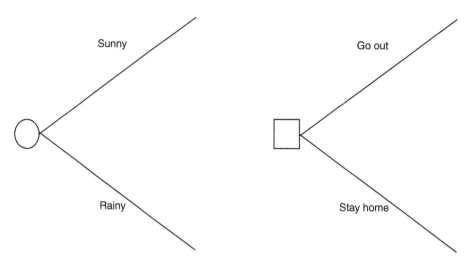

Figure 3.4 Chance nodes (left) are defined as the nodes where some new information is expected afterwards. Decision nodes (right) are the nodes when it is requested to make a decision between the following alternatives.

Trees can be decomposed in pieces in order to focus the analysis on specific actions. However, it is never so good to put too much information on it, in order to preserve the intuition effect.

The construction of a tree starts from the bottom and moves on through ramification. The analysis often involves steps back, in case the further development of the tree discloses the need for changing the information in the previous steps.

The first distinction to make when starting a decision tree is between chance nodes and decision nodes. Chance nodes (commonly indicated by a circle) are the tree nodes followed by an event that is not under control of the agent. Decision nodes (squares) are the nodes followed by some decision.

The purpose of decision tree analysis is to forecast future outcomes, assigning probabilities to possible events. Bayesian probability models help to analyse the problem when the analysis involves complex decisions.

Example 3.4: The expansion of a factory has a cost of €1,500,000. If the management decides to not do anything, and the economy state is good, the expected revenues are €3,000,000. If the economy is bad, revenues will only be €1,000,000. If the expansion is approved, the firm will register revenues of €6,000,000, and €2,000,000 if the economy is bad. Assume there is a 40% probability of a good economy and a 60% chance of a bad economy.

It is possible to represent the problem on a decision tree:
The Net Present values from expansion and no expansion are

$$NPV_{EX} = 0.4 \times 6,000,000 + 0.6 \times 2,000,000 - 1,500,000 = €2,100,000$$

$$NPV_{NE} = 0.4 \times 3,000,000 + 0.6 \times 1,000,000 = €1,800,000$$

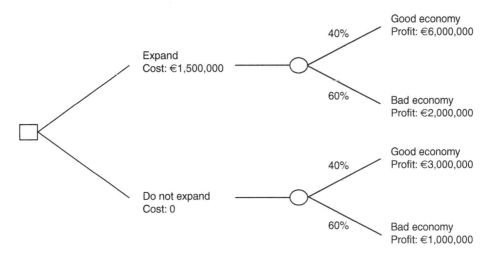

Figure 3.5 An example of a decision tree where decision nodes are alternate with informa-tion nodes, whose output is subject to branching probabilities.

the NPV from expanding is higher therefore the factory should expand.

Given forecasted probabilities for each scenario, given certain economic states, allows determination of the final payoffs. An additional complication that may add up to the model is the degree of dependent uncertainties.

Example 3.5: Now consider an additional alternative to wait and see how the economy goes, bearing the risk that there will not be enough resources available if waiting.

Backward induction on the tree gives a new NPV for the choice of waiting, as

$$NPV_{Wait} = 0.4(0.5 \times 6 + 0.5 \times 1) + 0.6 \times 1 = €2,000,000$$

The new NPV from waiting is higher than not expanding, but anyway lower than in the case of immediate expansion. This is an example of dependent uncertainties, where the dependency is between the uncertainty about the state of the economy and the one about the availability of resources.

3.2.3 Simulations

Simulations involve drawing one outcome from a distribution to generate a set of cash flows and values. Repeating the simulation several times, it is then possible to derive a distribution for the asset value.

The main difference between simulations and other probabilistic approaches, is that the number of variables to be changed and the potential outcomes are not constrained to some limited number.

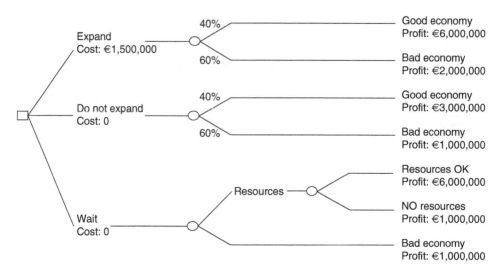

Figure 3.6 An example of a tree where the complication of a resource constraint is introduced. The optimal decision is then subject to the availability of the resources.

When historical data are available for some variables, it is possible to use the data
on differences in a specific variable across existing investments that are similar to the
investment being analysed.

Where historical data do not suffice, it is necessary to pick an appropriate statistical
distribution, capturing the trend of the input variables, and estimate its parameters.
There are simulation packages available in the computer industry, offering a wide range
of possible distributions.

The main issue with simulating variables is that most statistical distributions carry
statistical features that are hardly approximated by real-world variables. In this sense, an
important issue is represented by correlation.

In presence of strong correlation across simulation inputs, a choice must be made
between letting only one input vary, and embedding the correlation algorithm in the
simulation itself, adding more computational burden to the simulation.

The number of simulations required in every case is determined by criteria like the
number of inputs of the simulation, the type of distributions involved and the range of
possible outcomes.

The best possible result of a simulation is not just a single outcome for the expected
value of an asset, but a whole distribution of possible values.

The simulation can be achieved by different means. Monte Carlo is used when limited knowledge of the population is available, and sampling is so complicated that values generation is too cumbersome or expensive.

In the case of an exploratory approach, exogenous variables are changed in order to
generate specific courses of action, defined by models that are usually built from historical data. In some cases, a mixed approach of human decision and artificial intelligence
can lead to interesting results, since it is a real-time type of simulation

Example 3.6: Assume the estimation of some quantity $\theta = E[h(\mathbf{x})]$, where $\mathbf{x} = \{x_1, x_2, ..., x_n\}$ is a random vector in $\mathbb{R}^n$, $h(.)$ is a function from $\mathbb{R}^n$ to $\mathbb{R}$, and $E[|h(\mathbf{x})|] < \infty$ must be carried on.

The following Monte Carlo algorithm can be used

1. for $i = 2$ to n
2. generate $\mathbf{x}_i$
3. set $h_i = h(\mathbf{x}_i)$
4. set $\hat{\theta}_n = \dfrac{h_1 + h_2 + ... + h_n}{n}$

That gives a good estimator for the parameter.

The choice of a good random generator involves a trade-off between speed and reliability. A good uniform number generator has generally overall good performance, in terms of both the criteria mentioned above, being never the top performer over all these criteria.

In choosing an appropriate random number generator one should remember that a faster generator is not necessarily better (while, often, the opposite is true). Moreover, a good equi-distribution is a necessary but not sufficient requirement for a number generator to be good.

Among the various classes of simulation available, in finance the most useful is the explanatory simulation, which does not create a computational burden and is easy to implement. The use of historical data provides realistic modelling of real-world behaviour.

Scenario planning is carried through computer simulation, like for risk-adjusted NPV, which is usually computed from inputs that are not always fixed, even if they are well defined.

The simulation replicates the performance of the project under evaluation, providing a distribution of the NPV over a range of discount rates and other variables.

An example of computational solution of common problems in financial mathematics is the Monte Carlo integration, allowing for the approximation of complicated integrals. Consider the problem of estimating an analytically tricky integral of a function f over some domain D, given by

$$F = \int_D f(\mathbf{x})d\mu(\mathbf{x})$$

where
$\mu(\mathbf{x})$ is the mean of the variable $\mathbf{x}$.

The function f does not need to be one-dimensional. Monte Carlo techniques can be used to solve integrals that cannot be evaluated analytically. Assuming there is a p.d.f. p defined over the same domain, the equation can then be written as

$$F = \int_D \frac{f(\mathbf{x})}{p(\mathbf{x})} p(\mathbf{x})d\mu(\mathbf{x})$$

That is equal to

$$E\left(\frac{f(\mathbf{x})}{p(\mathbf{x})}\right)$$

which is the expected value of $\dfrac{f(\mathbf{x})}{p(\mathbf{x})}$ with respect to a random variable distributed according to $p(\mathbf{x})$. Whenever $f(\mathbf{x}) \neq 0$, this is true for all $p(\mathbf{x}) \neq 0$.

The value of $E\left(\dfrac{f(\mathbf{x})}{p(\mathbf{x})}\right)$ can be also calculated by generating a number of random samples according to p.

Next step is to compute $\dfrac{f}{p}$ for each sample, and calculating the average of these values then.

As the sample size increases, the average converges to the expected value, which is almost surely also the value of the integral. The process of estimating the value of an integral by averaging the value of $\dfrac{f(\mathbf{x})}{p(\mathbf{x})}$ for multiple random samples is called Monte Carlo integration.

3.3 Time series analysis

Learning outcomes

1. Describe and implement standard econometric models
2. Analyse the autocorrelation of financial time series
3. Learn about stylized facts of financial returns

3.3.1 ARCHl-GARCH models

A major concern of financial analysts and economists is the modelling of volatility in asset returns. As a measure of risk volatility is the core of financial analysis and a basis to calculate the premium required by investors.

Modelling and forecasting volatility or, in other words, the covariance structure of asset returns, are very important. Time series analysis is directly connected to the volatility issue. Measuring volatility from past data is the core of econometric models.

The focus of financial time series analysis is the theory and practice of asset valuation over time. It is an empirical discipline with deep roots in statistical inference, making the analysis of financial time series much different from analysis of other types of time series.

The Autoregressive Conditional Heteroscedasticity (ARCH) model is the first model of conditional heteroscedasticity, while GARCH is the generalized version of it. An autoregressive model specifies that the output variable depends linearly on its own previous values.

In order to understand the concept of heteroscedasticity, consider a sequence of random variables $x_0, x_1, ..., x_T$ and a sequence of vectors of random variables $y_0, y_1, ..., y_T$, and the conditional expectations of y_t given the value x_t, in the respective domains.

The sequence $y_0, y_1, ..., y_T$ is said to be heteroscedastic if the variance of y_t conditional on the value x_t, defined as

$$Var(y_i \mid x_i), \quad i \in (1, n)$$

changes with t.

The metrics is also called conditional heteroscedasticity, based on the fact that it is the sequence of conditional variances that changes and not the unconditional variance. Conditional heteroscedasticity in fact can be in some cases observed even when dealing with a sequence of unconditional homoscedastic random variables. The opposite does not hold.

Estimation methods like Ordinary Least Squares (OLS) are based on the assumption of homoscedasticity of variance, therefore returning biased estimates in presence of heteroscedasticity in the series.

Such class of models is useful in case there are reasons to believe the time series will show some characteristic size, or variance. ARCH models describe the current that the variance of the error term is a function to be correlated with the size of previous error terms.

Consider an information set $\mathcal{F}$, generated by a sequence of error terms ε. Then $\mathcal{F}_{t-1}$ is the sigma algebra generated by the term $\varepsilon_{t-i}, i \geq 1$. The ARCH model of ε_t has the following properties.

$$E\left(\varepsilon_t \mid \mathcal{F}_{t-1}\right) = 0$$
$$Var\left(\varepsilon_t \mid \mathcal{F}_{t-1}\right) = \sigma_t^2$$

The error sequence of an econometric model is

$$\varepsilon_t = x_t - \mu_t\left(x_t\right)$$

where

y_t is an observable random variable.

and

$$\mu_t\left(x_t\right) = E\left(\varepsilon_t \mid \mathcal{F}_{t-1}\right)$$

is the conditional mean of y_t given $\mathcal{F}_{t-1}$.

In deriving the ARCH model, the usual assumption is that the $\mu_t\left(y_t\right) = 0$ and the error term ε_t can be decomposed as

$$\varepsilon_t = z_t \sigma_t$$
$$z_t \sim \text{i.i.d.}(0, 1) \tag{3.2}$$

The ARCH model of order q has the form

$$\sigma_t^2 = \omega + \sum_{i=1}^{p} \alpha_i \varepsilon_{t-i}^2, \quad \omega > 0, \ \alpha_i \geq 0$$

The positivity of the conditional variance is guaranteed by the constraints on the model parameters. In case the unconditional variance is not diverging, meaning

$$E\left(\varepsilon_t^2\right) = \sigma_u^2 < \infty$$

the decomposition of the error term in (3.2) shows that the error is the product of a converging standard deviation and an i.i.d. variable, so that ε_t is white noise.

ARCH estimation is usually done using maximum likelihood method. Under the assumption of returns being normally distributed, the density function is

$$f\left(\varepsilon_t | \mathcal{F}_{t-1}\right) = \frac{1}{\sqrt{2\pi}\sigma_t} e^{-\frac{\varepsilon_t^2}{2\sigma_t^2}}$$

The log-likelihood is

$$L(\omega, \alpha) = \sum_{t=1}^{T} \frac{1}{2} \log\left(\sigma_t^2\right) - \frac{1}{2} \log\left(\frac{\sigma_t^2}{\sigma_{u,t}^2}\right)$$

where

$$\sigma_{u,t}^2 = \frac{\omega}{1-\alpha}, \quad \alpha < 1$$

is the unconditional variance.

The Generalized ARCH (GARCH) was introduced by T. Bollerslev in 1986. Compared to ARCH, it adds dependency of the conditional variance on its own lag. The model takes the general form of GARCH(p,q) as

$$\sigma_t^2 = \omega + \sum_{i=1}^{p} \alpha_i \varepsilon_{t-i}^2 + \sum_{j=1}^{q} \beta_j \sigma_{t-j}^2$$

The GARCH(1,1), for $p = q = 1$, is the most widely used in practice, allowing for one lag on both the error term and the variance term. The model is then

$$\sigma_t^2 = \omega + \alpha \varepsilon_{t-1}^2 + \beta \sigma_{t-1}^2$$

Many variations of GARCH formula have been introduced, in order to improve the flexibility of the model. The main issues of the basic GARCH is that it assumes the response to a shock to be independent of the sign of the shock itself, thus ignoring asymmetry.

In order for the GARCH model to work properly, an essential attribute is the stationarity of the time series modelled. Stability is determined by imposing constraints on the parameters estimated with maximum likelihood.

A sufficient condition for the variance of a GARCH(p,q) process to be positive is

$$\omega > 0$$
$$\alpha_i \geq 0, \quad i = 1,...,p$$
$$\beta_j \geq 0, \quad j = 1,...,q$$

which in turn implies

$$\sum_{i=1}^{p} \alpha_i + \sum_{j=1}^{q} \beta_j < 1,.$$

A stationary GARCH can be then simplified by targeting variance, so that the equality

$$\omega = \left(1 - \sum_{i=1}^{p} \alpha_i + \sum_{j=1}^{q} \beta_j\right)\sigma_u^2$$

holds and the estimate of the variance is given by

$$\hat{\sigma}_u^2 = \frac{\sum_{k=1}^{t} \varepsilon_k^2}{t}$$

The conditional variance then converges towards the 'long-run' unconditional variance, and the model contains one parameter fewer than the standard GARCH(p,q) model.

One of the possible methods to estimate a GARCH process is through Maximum Likelihood. In order to estimate the parameters of a GARCH(p,q) model, suppose the noise z_t in the model is standard normal.

It follows that the error term ε_t is Gaussian, with $\varepsilon_t \sim N(0, \sigma_t^2)$, conditional on the history of the process, with past $\varepsilon_k = \varepsilon_{t-1}, \varepsilon_{t-2},....$. A conditioning argument yields the density function $f(x_1, x_2,..., x_t \mid \theta)$ of the distribution with unknown parameters θ, through the conditional Gaussian densities of the error terms, given the realizations $\varepsilon_1 = x_1, \varepsilon_2 = x_2,..., \varepsilon_t = x_t$, in the form

$$f(x_1, x_2,..., x_t \mid \theta) = f(x_t \mid x_{t-1}, x_{t-2},...) \times f(x_{t-1} \mid x_{t-2}, x_{t-3},...) \times ... \times f(x_1)$$

$$= \frac{1}{\sqrt{2\pi\sigma_t^2}} e^{-\frac{(x_t-\mu)^2}{2\sigma_t^2}} \times \frac{1}{\sqrt{2\pi\sigma_{t-1}^2}} e^{-\frac{(x_{t-1}-\mu)^2}{2\sigma_{t-1}^2}} \times ... \times \frac{1}{\sqrt{2\pi\sigma_1^2}} e^{-\frac{(x_1-\mu)^2}{2\sigma_1^2}}$$

where

μ is the mean of the distribution.

It follows that the Gaussian likelihood of $\varepsilon_1,..., \varepsilon_t$, conditioned on parameters θ, is given by

$$L(\theta \mid x_1, x_2,..., x_t) = f(x_1, x_2,..., x_t \mid \theta)$$
$$= f(x_1 \mid \theta) \times f(x_2 \mid \theta) \times ... \times f(x_t \mid \theta)$$
$$= \prod_{k=1}^{t} f(x_k \mid \theta)$$

Table 3.1 Constructing a series of lagged values implies shifting down the observations in order to match the previous time. Then it is possible to get the difference between the old value and the lagged one (first difference).

Time	y_t	y_{t-1}	Δy_t
t	0.5	–	–
$t-1$	0.9	0.5	$(0.9 - 0.5) = 0.4$
$t-2$	-0.1	0.9	$(-0.9 - 0.1) = -1.0$
$t-3$	0.4	-0.1	$(0.4 + 0.1) = 0.5$
⋮	⋮	⋮	⋮

In practice, it is often more convenient to work with the logarithm of the likelihood function, log-likelihood, which is

$$\ln L(\theta \mid x_1, x_2, \dots, x_t) = \sum_{k=1}^{t} \ln \left[\frac{1}{\sqrt{2\pi\sigma_k^2}} e^{-\frac{(x_k - \mu)^2}{2\sigma_k^2}} \right]$$

$$= \dots \tag{3.3}$$

$$= -\frac{t}{2}\ln(2\pi) - \frac{1}{2}\sum_{k=1}^{t}\ln\sigma_k^2 - \frac{1}{2}\sum_{k=1}^{t}\frac{(x_k - \mu)^2}{\sigma_k^2}$$

For a general GARCH(p,q) process it is then possible to substitute

$$\sigma_t^2 = \omega + \alpha\varepsilon_{t-1}^2 + \beta\sigma_{t-1}^2$$

into (3.3), and the likelihood function is maximized as a function of the parameters involved. The resulting value in the parameter space is the Gaussian estimator.

MLE is usually not precise when estimating from small samples, and there are drawbacks like the tendency to be biased even with a small number of failures. Moreover calculating MLE requires substantial computing power and specific statistical packages.

3.3.2 Autocorrelation of financial returns

The value taken by a variable in a precious time point is generally called lagged value. General notational standards indicate as y_{t-1} the one-period lagged value of y_t. The lag can be constructed by shifting all the observation of some variable by one period.

The difference Δy_t between the value of a variable at some point in time t and the value of the same variable at a previous time $t-1$ is called first difference.

$$\Delta y_t = y_t - y_{t-1}$$

In a panel data, once one of the columns is lagged, the first observation is lost. When the lag is higher than one period, it is possible to define a second, third, fourth difference, and so on.

A financial time series is said to show positive autocorrelation if, when the residual at time $t-1$ is on average positive, the residual at time t is likely to be positive as well.

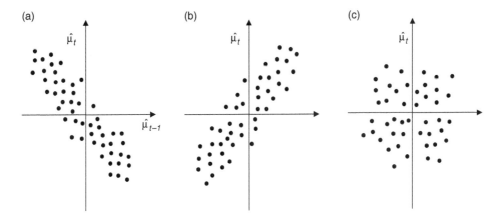

Figure 3.7 In graph a) Most dots lie in the first and third quadrant, showing positive auto-correlation. In graph b) most dots lie in the second and fourth quadrant, showing nega-tive autocorrelation. In graph c) dots are sparse without clear pattern, showing absence of autocorrelation.

Positive autocorrelation indicates that, if the residual at $t-1$ is negative, the residual at t is also likely to be negative.

The opposite holds for negative autocorrelation and in the last case shows no pattern so that autocorrelation is not present, therefore data are randomly distributed.

For a lag h, the autocorrelation coefficient of a time series $x_1, x_2, ..., x_t$ is given by

$$r_h = \frac{c_h}{c_0}$$

where

$$c_h = \frac{1}{t}\sum_{k=1}^{t-h}(x_t - \bar{x})(x_{k+h} - \bar{x})$$

is the autocovariance function and

$$c_0 = \frac{1}{t}\sum_{k=1}^{t}(x_k - \bar{x})^2$$

is the variance function, and $\bar{x}$ is the mean value of the series.

The plotting graph of the autocorrelation against the lags is called a correlogram. It incorporates a lower and upper bound, for an immediate interpretation of the results, and when the value of the autocorrelation is higher (lower) than the upper (lower) bound, then the null hypothesis (absence of autocorrelation) is rejected and there is autocorrelation.

The study of the correlogram is important to understand whether out-of-boundary isolated values really correspond to the presence of autocorrelation. For example a very

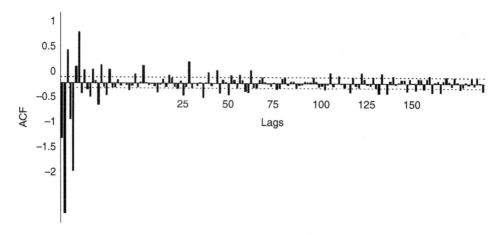

Figure 3.8 Example of correlogram. In this case the values exceed upper and lower boundaries (dotted lines) for many lags. That means there is autocorrelation.

large r_h is less likely to occur by chance than a coefficient barely outside the bands, and a large r_h at a very low lag is more likely to represent persistence than isolated large r_h at higher lags.

There are several statistical tests to detect autocorrelation in financial time series. A famous and widely used one is the Durbin-Watson test.

Developed by J. Durbin and G.S. Watson in two papers (1950, 1951), the test assumes that the error terms ε_t are stationary and normally distributed with mean zero. The test assumes regression errors are autoregressive first-order, so that

$$\varepsilon_t = \rho_\varepsilon \varepsilon_{t-1} + a_t$$

where

ρ_ε is the autocorrelation coefficient

a_t is a $N\left(0,\sigma^2\right)$

If ρ_ε are the error autocorrelations, the null hypothesis is that errors are uncorrelated. This can be written as

$$H_0 : \rho_\varepsilon = 0, \quad \varepsilon > 0$$

against the alternative hypothesis that the errors follow an autoregressive process $AR(1)$.

$$H_1 : \rho_\varepsilon > 0, \quad |\rho_\varepsilon| < 1$$

To test the null hypothesis get the least squares estimates $\hat{\beta}$ and residuals $e_1, ..., e_t$. The statistic is

$$DW = \frac{\sum\limits_{k=2}^{t}\left(e_k - e_{k-1}\right)^2}{\sum\limits_{k=1}^{t} e_k^2}$$

where

e_i is the residual associated with the observation at time i.

As mentioned above, the hypothesis is accepted or rejected according to the value of the statistics compared to the boundary values. In particular

if $DW < d_l$ $\rightarrow$ reject $H_0 : \rho_\varepsilon = 0$
if $DW > d_u$ $\rightarrow$ do not reject H_0
if $d_l < DW < d_u$ $\rightarrow$ not conclusive

where

d_u is the upper bound in the correlogram
d_l is the lower bound.

Given the value r_1 for the sample ACF of the errors at lag 1, it holds that

$$DW = 2\left(1 - r_1\right)$$

Being a correlation, it follows that the DW statistic is bounded between 0 and 4. For heavily positively autocorrelated errors, the statistic is very close to 0. If the errors are white noise, the value of the statistic is 2. Finally, in case of almost perfect negative autocorrelation the statistic is close to 4.

The interpretation of the results depends in which region the statistic falls. In order to correctly interpret the statistic according to its value, when testing for positive auto-correlation for a given confidence level, the following holds:

1. If $DW < d_l$, the error terms are positively autocorrelated.
2. If $DW > d_u$, no evidence that the error terms are positively autocorrelated.
3. If $d_l < DW < d_u$, the test is inconclusive.

When testing for negative autocorrelation for a given confidence level it holds:

1. If $(4 - DW) < d_l$, the error terms are negatively autocorrelated.
2. If $(4 - DW) < d_l$, no evidence that the error terms are negatively autocorrelated.
3. If $d_l < (4 - DW) < d_u$, the test is inconclusive.

Example 3.7: Suppose the DW statistic from a test is 0.86. There are 80 quarterly observations in the multifactor regression. The relevant critical values drawn from the table of DW statistics are $d_U = 1.57$, $d_L = 1.42$, so that $4 - d_U = 2.43$ and $4 - d_L = 2.58$.

The test statistic is clearly lower than the lower critical value, then the null hypothesis of no autocorrelation is rejected for positive correlation.

A drawback of the *DW* test is that the form of the model is assumed to be known, which is very rare in practice. Moreover the test is sometimes inconclusive, so that confirmation of either the null or alternative hypothesis may be complicated.

Also, the failure of the null hypothesis can happen in many ways, other than the $AR(j)$ alternative, with a very low power in detecting the alternatives.

Ignoring autocorrelation (when present) is similar to ignoring heteroscedasticity of data. This makes OLS estimation inefficient (even if still unbiased) although with very large size samples.

3.3.3 *Other stylized facts*

The concept of stylized fact was introduced in 1961 by N. Kaldor, who empirically identified a range of statistical facts related to economic growth, and then developed a theoretical model.

The term then became popular and was adopted to describe, in general, specific regularities of financial time series, that are persistent across different markets, asset types, time scales, etc.

The modern era of financial markets, with the development of electronic trading, has been characterized by the availability of large amounts of data to empirically verify the presence of stylized facts in the time series.

Autocorrelation of returns, described in the previous section, is related to an obvious stylized fact of financial time series, the absence of autocorrelation, which has been empirically observed quite consistently in the last 20 years.

The absence of autocorrelation is an obvious fact to observe, since, if returns were significantly autocorrelated, one could make correct predictions of returns and use them to make profitable investment decisions.

The basic idea about the absence of autocorrelation is that, when this is spotted and exploited, it should disappear quickly, letting the market converge to some equilibrium.

However, a discipline like technical analysis aims at forecasting price trends by studying past price data and finding patterns that can be used as signals to buy or sell.

On the other hand, the autocorrelation for absolute and squared returns has been observed, and it is positive and significant, with slow decay. Moreover, generally the autocorrelation in the absolute returns is much higher than in corresponding squared returns.

Another important stylized fact, which was firstly observed by Kendall (1953), is that distribution of financial returns are non-stationary. Clustered volatility ensures that volatility is not constant over time.

Non-linearity has been tested by several scientists, who investigated daily and weekly changes in major FX rates, indices and commodities, finding evidence of non-linearity in dependence.

More recent studies confirm the significant role played by non-linear serial dependencies, for a very broad range of financial data, even after removing linear serial correlation from the time series.

Scaling laws describe the size of absolute returns as a function of the time interval of measurement. Financial markets actually exhibit scaling laws and a wide range of financial data and time intervals have been empirically tested.

Evidence shows that scaling law is empirically evident in good approximation, giving a direct relation between time interval t and average volatility, when the latter is expressed as a power of the absolute returns observed at those intervals, as outlined by the formula

$$\left[E\left(|r|^{p} \right) \right] = f(p) \Delta t^{d(p)}$$

where

r is the observed return
$f(p)$ and $d(p)$ are deterministic functions of p.

Different choices for p and for the functional forms determine different values for the drift exponent $d(p)$. A typical choice is $p = 1$ which corresponds to absolute returns.

Müller *et al.* (1990) analysed millions of intraday FX prices to observe empirical evidence of scaling in the mean absolute changes of log prices.

Other studies in the second half of the 1990s have interesting findings, such as the tendency of data to retain a unique functional form for a range of time scales. Moreover, Gopikrishnan *et al.* (2000) found the distribution of stock price fluctuations to preserve the same functional form, when considering fluctuations on time scales that differ by three orders of magnitude.

Also volume has been studied by many researchers. Plerou *et al.* (2000) show that trading volumes on common markets exhibit power law decay, long memory and long-range persistence of time correlations.

Calendar effects are another feature of some types of financial data, and refer to cyclical anomalies in returns. The concept resembles intraday effects, weekend effects and the famous January effect, defining a general increase on stock prices registered in the first month of each year.

Another stylized fact concerns the autocorrelation of the squared returns, which is generally positive and higher at higher frequencies, leading to phenomena like volatility clustering and memory effect.

Other facts relate to the moments of the distribution of observed returns. Fat tails are a popular effect observed on several types of assets. Financial returns have been shown to be less concentrated around the mean and more on the tails, compared to the assumption of normality.

Mandelbrot (1963) observed the phenomenon more than 50 years ago, and nowadays, Cont (2001) found the sample kurtosis on the series under consideration to be between 5 and 100, much higher than the kurtosis of the normal distribution, which is equal to 3.

Also skewness has been observed, making the distribution of financial returns asymmetric around the mean, for many observed time series. There is anyway an issue of standard estimators having problems of overestimation.

Summary

The tail of returns distribution defines the probability of a large loss on some investment. Heavy tails involve high probability of a large loss, while thin tails mean that probability of extreme events is close to zero.

When dealing with catastrophic events and their consequences, it is important that description of the distribution's tail is realistic. It is worth considering other classes of distribution, other than the normal distribution.

The concept of tail is crucial for financial risk management and, compared to other distributions, the class of distributions showing a fatter tail than normal or exponential distribution, can capture extreme events in a much better way.

Scenario analysis is a powerful tool to evaluate the impact of simultaneous changes in the set of sensitive variables. The impact on the hypothetical returns is evaluated by applying the variable changes to the general problem of returns estimation.

Decision trees can be applied to many fields, and they offer a good solution to help with choice making, especially if high levels of risk are involved. Decision trees allow comparison of many possible choices in a unique visual approach.

Simulations differ from other probabilistic methods in that a wider number of variables are changed, giving rise to a large range of potential outcomes, not constrained by a limited number, as for other methods.

Time series analysis allows us to model and forecast volatility, as well as determine the covariance structure of asset returns. Econometric models are meant to estimate the volatility from past data.

The main focus of the analysis is the theory and practice of asset valuation in a dynamic framework. As an empirical discipline, it is rooted in statistical inference, and financial returns turn out to be very different from other types of time series.

The development of electronic trading has made large amounts of data available to researchers and analysts, facilitating the identification of stylized facts in the time series, like absence of autocorrelation of returns, volatility clustering, scaling laws and more.

Bibliography

Andersen, T.G., Davis, R.A., Kreiß, J.P. and Mikosch, T.V. (eds). 2009. *Handbook of Financial Time Series*. Springer.

Cont, R. 2001. Empirical Properties of Asset Returns: Stylized Facts and Statistical Issues. *Quantitative Finance*, 1: 223–236.

Durbin, J. and Watson, G.S. 1950. Testing for Serial Correlation in Least Squares Regression, I. *Biometrika*, 37(3–4): 409–428.

Durbin, J. and Watson, G.S. 1951. Testing for Serial Correlation in Least Squares Regression, II. *Biometrika*, 38(1–2): 159–179.

Dutta, K.K. and Babbel, D.F. 2013. Scenario Analysis in the Measurement of Operational Risk Capital: A Change of Measure Approach. *Journal of Risk and Insurance*, 81(2): 303–334.

Forbes, C., Evans, M., Hastings, N. and Peacock, B. 2010. *Statistical Distributions*. Wiley.

Fouque, J.P., Fomby, T.B. and Solna, K. 2008. *Econometrics and Risk Management*. Emerald.

Francq, C. and Zakoian, J.M. 2010. *GARCH Models: Structure, Statistical Inference and Financial Applications*. Wiley.

Gopikrishnan, P., Plerou, V., Liu, Y., Amaral, L. A. N., Gabaix, X. and Stanley, H.E. 2000. Scaling and Correlation in Financial Time Series. *Physica A*, 287(3–4): 362–373.

Gourieroux, C. and Monfort, A. 1995. *Statistic and Econometric Models*. Vol. 2. Cambridge University Press.

Grinblatt, M. and Titman, S. 2002. *Financial Markets & Corporate Strategy*. McGraw-Hill.

Itô, K. 1944. Stochastic Integral. *Proc. Imperial Acad. Tokyo*, 20: 519–524.

Jackel, P. 2002. *Monte Carlo Methods in Finance*. Wiley Finance.

Kaldor, N. 1961. *Capital Accumulation and Economic Growth: The Theory of Capital*. St. Martins Press, 177–222.

Kendall, M. 1953. The Analysis of Economic Time Series. *Journal of the Royal Statistical Society. Series A*. 96: 11–25.

Larsen, R.J. and Marx, M.L. 2006. *An Introduction to Mathematical Statistics and its Applications*. 4th Edition. Pearson.

Lea, R.B. and Cohen, B.H. 2004. *Essentials of Statistics for the Social and Behavioral Sciences*. John Wiley & Sons, Inc.

Mandelbrot, B. 1963. The Variation of Certain Speculative Prices. *Journal of Business*, 36: 392–417.

McLeish, D.L. 2005. *Monte Carlo Simulation and Finance*. Wiley Finance.

McNeil, A.J., Frey, R. and Embrechts, P. 2005. *Quantitative Risk Management Concepts, Techniques and Tools*. Princeton University Press.

Müller, U., Dacorogna, M., Olsen, R., Pictet, O., Schwarz, M. and Morgenegg, C. 1990. Statistical Study of Foreign Exchange Rates, Empirical Evidence of a Price Change Scaling Law, and Intraday Analysis. *Journal of Banking and Finance*, 14: 1189–1208.

Plerou, V., Gopikrishnan, P., Amaral, L. A. N., Gabaix, X. and Stanley, H. E. 2000. Economic Fluctuations and Anomalous Diffusion. *Physical Review E*, 62(3): 3023–3026.

Salvatore, D. and Reagle, D. 2002. *Statistics and Econometrics*. 2nd Edition. McGraw-Hill.

Van der Vaart, A.W. 2004. *Time Series*. Vrije Universiteit Amsterdam.

Von Collani, E. and Dräger, K. 2001. *Binomial Distribution Handbook for Scientists and Engineers*. Birkhäuser.

Werner, R.R. 2010. *Designing Strategy: The Art of Scenario Analysis*. Windjammer Adventure Publishing.

Exercises

Questions

1. Explain the need of non-normal distributional forms in financial risk management, and why normality is not the best choice.
2. Given its features, to what aspects of financial risk management does the Poisson distribution better adapt to?
3. What is the difference between the EWMA (Exponential Weighted Moving Average) model and the GARCH model for volatility estimation?
4. What are the advantages of probabilistic approaches to risk, compared to analytical methods? What about the disadvantages?
5. Describe the steps needed in the implementation of simulations for project and business analysis.
6. Explain how heteroscedasticity impacts on the analysis of conditional variance of financial time series.
7. List and comment the stylized facts of financial time series.

Problems

1. A GARCH(1,1) model has been estimated as

$$h_t = 0.00045 + 0.04r_{t-1}^2 + 0.94h_{t-1}$$

   a.   Calculate the conditional variance at time t if $r_{t-1} = 0.04$ and $h_{t-1} = 0.03$.
   b.   Calculate the unconditional variance of r_t.

2.   Define a stock return Y_t at time and some macroeconomic factor X_t, both at time t. Assume the two variables are related through a GARCH model

$$Y_t = \beta_0 + \beta_1 X_t + \beta_2 X_t^2 + \delta\sigma_t + a_t$$

   where $a_t = \sigma_t \varepsilon_t$, $\sigma_t = \sqrt{1 + 0.3a_{t-1}^2 + 0.2\sigma_{t-1}^2}$
   If the $\varepsilon_t \sim N(0,1)$ random variables, and factor values are $\beta_0 = 0.05$, $\beta_1 = 0.3$, $\beta_2 = 0.1$, $\delta = 0.2$,
   a.   Determine $E\left[Y_t | X_t = 0.1, \ a_{t-1} = -0.6, \ \text{and} \ \sigma_{t-1} = 0.1\right]$?
   b.   Determine $VaR\left(Y_t | X_t = 0.1, \ a_{t-1} = -0.6, \ \text{and} \ \sigma_{t-1} = 0.1\right)$?
3.   Write down the log-likelihood and first order conditions for an AR(1)-ARCH(1) model.
4.   If X is a Gaussian random variable with unknown parameters $\theta_1 = \mu$ and $\theta_2 = \sigma^2$, and given a data vector $\mathbf{x} = (x_1, x_2, ..., x_n)$ derive the maximum likelihood estimators for θ_1 and θ_2.
5.   Define $\mathbf{b} = (b_1, b_2, ..., b_n)$ as a vector of a variable independently distributed as a Bernoulli (p). Derive the maximum likelihood estimator of p.
6.   Show that the third moment for a Pareto distribution of the form $P(x > X) = x^{-2}$ for $x \geq 1$ does not exist.
7.   Assume it has been estimated that 22% of swans in some region in the world are black. By examining 12 swans chosen at random, independently of each other:
   a.   Determine how the number of black swans in a sample of 12 swans is distributed.
   b.   Calculate the mean and standard deviation of the number of black swans in the above sample.
   c.   What is the probability that 7 or more of the 12 swans are black?
8.   Assume a Poisson distribution with mean 0.5 for the profit warnings per month in a specific industry. Find the probability that in a particular month there will be:
   a.   Fewer than two warnings
   b.   More than two warnings
   c.   Fewer than three warnings.
9.   A company has acquired an option to purchase 1,000,000 kg of special material from a foreign government for €5.00 per kg. The company can process the material and would be able to sell for €8.00 per kg after importing it. If a licence is not granted after purchase, the company will have to pay a penalty of €1.00 per kg to cancel the purchase. The company also has the opportunity to wait until the decision on licence is made, before making the purchase, but in this case there is 70% probability that another company will get the deal first. The probability to get the licence or not is equally likely. Construct a decision tree to represent the problem and analyse the NPV of the different alternatives (purchase, do not purchase, wait).
10.   Consider the scenarios defined by the following table for two stocks.

State	Probability	Return A	Return B
Boom	20%	15%	10%
Normal	60%	5%	−5%
Recession	20%	−10%	20%

a. Calculate the expected returns, volatilities and correlations associated with each scenario.

11. Consider the annual returns of stock A and B, as given in the following table.

Year	Stock A	Stock B
1	80.95%	58.26%
2	−47.37%	−33.79%
3	31.00%	29.88%
4	132.44%	30.35%
5	32.02%	2.94%
6	25.37%	−4.29%
7	−28.57%	28.86%
8	0.00%	−6.36%
9	11.67%	48.64%
10	36.19%	23.55%

a. Estimate the average and standard deviation in annual returns in each company.
b. Estimate the covariance and correlation in returns between these companies.

12. Consider the stocks in exercise 11.
a. Calculate the variance of an equally weighted portfolio of the two stocks.
13. Consider the vector of three assets with the following characteristics:

$$\bar{R} = \begin{pmatrix} 0.05 \\ 0.12 \\ 0.14 \end{pmatrix}, \ \sigma = \begin{pmatrix} 0.005 \\ 0.075 \\ 0.092 \end{pmatrix}, \ \Omega = \begin{pmatrix} 1 & -0.17 & 0.25 \\ -0.17 & 1 & 0.45 \\ 0.25 & 0.45 & 1 \end{pmatrix}$$

where r is the vector of expected returns, σ is the vector of standard deviations and ρ is the correlation matrix between the three assets. Your broker offers you two portfolios to choose from: portfolio $\Pi_1 = (0.25, 0.65, 0.10)$ and portfolio $\Pi_2 = (0.35, 0.20, 0.45)$.
a. Calculate the expected return and standard deviation of each portfolio. Which portfolio would you choose?

14. Recalling exercise 13, assume the investor is offered a third portfolio $\Pi_3 = (0.45, 0.00, 0.55)$.
   a.   Calculate the expected return and standard deviation of the portfolio.
   b.   Which portfolio would the investor prefer now?

Appendix: Itô's Lemma

Itô's Lemma is named for its discoverer, the mathematician K. Itô, and plays, in stochastic calculus, the role that is played in ordinary calculus by the fundamental theorem of calculus.

Calculations in financial mathematics, and stochastic calculus in particular, use some form of Itô's Lemma, which is the basis of the whole Itô calculus. It is an analogue for stochastic processes of the ordinary calculus of Leibnitz and Newton.

Changes in a stock price, for example, involve a deterministic component which is a function of time and a stochastic component depending upon a random variable.

When the process followed by a random variable is known, Itô's Lemma gives the stochastic process followed by some function of that variable.

Recalling that the price of a derivative is a function of both price of the underlying and time to expiration, it is then clear how Itô's Lemma plays an important part in the analysis of financial derivatives.

Consider a differential function $f(x,t)$ of a stochastic variable x and time t, driven by the Generalized Wiener process:

$$dx(t) = \mu(x,t)dt + \sigma(x,t)dz$$

which can be discretized as

$$\Delta x = \mu \Delta t + \sigma \varepsilon \sqrt{\Delta t}$$

where μ is the instantaneous expected rate of change in x and σ is its instantaneous standard deviation.

A Taylor's series expansion of $f(x,t)$ gives

$$\Delta f(x,t) = \frac{\partial f}{\partial x}\Delta x + \frac{\partial f}{\partial t}\Delta t + \frac{1}{2}\frac{\partial^2 f}{\partial x^2}\Delta x^2 + \frac{1}{2}\frac{\partial^2 f}{\partial t^2}\Delta t^2 + \frac{\partial^2 f}{\partial x \partial t}\Delta x \Delta t + ...$$

Ignoring terms of order higher than Δt and recalling that $\Delta x \Delta t = 0$ and $\Delta t^2 = 0$ by the properties of Brownian motion, the expansion becomes

$$\Delta f(x,t) = \frac{\partial f}{\partial x}\Delta x + \frac{\partial f}{\partial t}\Delta t + \frac{1}{2}\frac{\partial^2 f}{\partial x^2}\Delta x^2 \qquad (3.4)$$

The next step is to substitute for the process of Δx, which is known, and the process of Δx^2. Recalling again the properties of the Brownian motion, the latter can be derived as

$$\begin{aligned}
\Delta x^2 &= \mu^2 \Delta t^2 + \sigma^2 \Delta z^2 + 2\mu\sigma\Delta t \Delta z \\
&= 0 + \sigma^2 \Delta z^2 + 0 \\
&= \sigma^2 \varepsilon^2 \Delta t, \quad \varepsilon \sim N(0,1)
\end{aligned} \qquad (3.5)$$

The above term contains the stochastic component ε. However, since its variance is 1, the variance of the term $\varepsilon^2 \Delta t$ is very small, and negligible. The value of $\varepsilon^2 \Delta t$ is then equal to its expected value, which is Δt. The process in equation (3.5) becomes then

$$\Delta x^2 = \sigma^2 \varepsilon^2 \Delta t = \sigma^2 \Delta t$$

Substituting Δx^2 and Δx in (3.4) and taking limits, yields

$$
\begin{aligned}
df(x,t) &= \frac{\partial f}{\partial x}(\mu dt + \sigma dz) + \frac{\partial f}{\partial t} dt + \frac{1}{2}\frac{\partial^2 f}{\partial x^2}\sigma^2 dt \\
&= \frac{\partial f}{\partial x}\mu dt + \frac{\partial f}{\partial x}\sigma dz + \frac{\partial f}{\partial t}dt + \frac{1}{2}\frac{\partial^2 f}{\partial x^2}\sigma^2 dt \\
&= \left(\mu\frac{\partial f}{\partial x} + \frac{\partial f}{\partial t} + \frac{1}{2}\sigma^2\frac{\partial^2 f}{\partial x^2}\right)dt + \frac{\partial f}{\partial x}\sigma dz
\end{aligned}
$$

This result is the Itô's Lemma. The expected rate of change in $f(x,t)$ is not simply the sum of its rate of change due to the passage of time, and the expected rate of change in x multiplied by the sensitivity of $f(x,t)$ to x, but it also has a term involving the volatility of x and the second derivative of $f(x,t)$.

As an example of the application of the lemma, consider a bank deposit worth 1 at time zero, earning a continuously compounded interest rate r_f, with a value at time t given by

$$D_t = e^{r_f t}$$

Assume uncertainty in the inflation level, so that the general process for prices π in the economy is

$$d\pi = \mu\pi dt + \sigma\pi dz$$

where

μ is the expected inflation rate
σ is the volatility of prices.

The value in real terms of the deposit is then given by

$$\tilde{D}_t = \frac{e^{r_f t}}{\pi_t}$$

Using Itô's Lemma it is now possible to derive the process for $\tilde{D}_t$ as a function of π_t. The first step is to calculate the derivatives involved, as

$$
\begin{aligned}
\frac{\partial \tilde{D}}{\partial \pi} &= -\frac{D}{\pi^2} = -\frac{\tilde{D}}{\pi} \\
\frac{\partial^2 \tilde{D}}{\partial \pi^2} &= \frac{2D}{\pi^3} = \frac{2\tilde{D}}{\pi^2} \\
\frac{\partial^2 \tilde{D}}{\partial t} &= \frac{rD}{P} = r\tilde{D}
\end{aligned}
$$

It follows that the process for $\tilde{D}$ is

$$d\tilde{D} = \left(\sigma^2 - \mu + r_f\right)\tilde{D}dt + \sigma\tilde{D}dz$$

So that the expected effective real rate of return on the deposit is given by adding to the nominal rate the variance of prices, and subtracting the expected inflation rate.

4 Financial derivatives

Financial derivatives have become important in the last 30 years and are actively traded on exchanges and over-the-counter markets throughout the world. In 2012 the size of the derivatives market has been estimated at almost €1 quadrillion (one thousand trillion, one million million). They are linked to a specific financial instrument or reference, and allow specific financial risks in financial markets to be traded in their own right.

Parties entering positions in financial derivatives are enabled to transfer specific financial risks (interest rate risk, currency risk, equity risk, commodity risk, credit risk, etc.) to counterparties willing, or better suited, to manage these risks.

Derivative securities are increasingly used by many participants in financial markets, including bankers, fund managers, security and currency traders in the world's major markets, but this also increasingly extends to the finance departments of public and private sector organizations.

Common derivative contracts are options, future and forward contracts, interest rate swaps. There are also more complicated derivatives that allow for more exotic payoffs or a complex pricing structure.

There have been many new ideas in risk management and risk measurement. Analysts have also become more aware of the need to analyse what are known as real options.

After studying this chapter you will be able to answer the following questions, among others:

1. What are the types of traders active in financial markets, and what is the purpose of their trading?
2. What are financial derivatives, and how can they be used for speculation and hedging?
3. How can a financial derivative be priced? What models are available?
4. What are the main features of the Black-Scholes-Merton model, and how can it be used to price financial derivatives?
5. What are interest rate derivatives? What are the most common types available?

The first section of the chapter is an introduction to options and futures contracts, their structure and payout diagrams. The second section is about interest rate derivatives, written on interest rates as underlying. The final part deals with the pricing of derivatives, analysing the binomial model in discrete time, and the Black-Scholes-Merton model in continuous time.

4.1 Options and futures

Learning outcomes

1. Describe standard financial derivatives and their payoff structure.
2. Understand the rationale behind the use of financial options, forwards and futures.
3. Learn about types of traders in the market.

4.1.1 Types of traders in the market

There are different types of traders in the market, according to the purpose of their investment decisions. The distinction is particularly meaningful in derivatives markets, since financial derivatives are a powerful tool for both hedging and speculation, given their intrinsic nature, and useful to exploit arbitrage opportunities.

Financial derivatives take their values from the underlying assets they are written on. They help managing financial risks effectively, given the expectations of the investors.

Trading in derivatives is a form of insurance against unexpected price movements, volatility of markets, uncertainty about corporate performance and profits. Derivatives can then serve many purposes and investors in the market are identified according to the purpose by which they choose to trade in derivatives. The main distinction to be made is between hedgers, speculators and arbitrageurs.

All types of traders are very important for the functioning of the market, each one with their specific contribution. Arbitrageurs allow for price discovery, hedgers constitute the economical side of the market, trading for business and economical purposes, and speculators are gamblers, providing liquidity and depth.

Hedgers typically aim at reducing their asset exposure to price variations, taking a position opposite to the one they try to cover. Hedgers primarily look at limiting their exposure risk, by using various tools and limiting losses in case of adverse movements in the underlying asset.

The objective of hedgers is to trade simultaneously on different markets, in order to hedge some risk they are facing due to potential future price changes of some other trades.

Their purpose is not to make a huge profit out of their trades, but to protect existing financial positions. A perfect hedge is rare but investors can reduce their risk which goes against them.

For example, in the producer-consumer space, both hedgers who produce and hedgers who consume have an interest in holding positions in either the underlying commodity, or the derivative written on it.

Recalling basic knowledge about investment strategies, when an investor wants to lock in the price of an asset to purchase in the future, it is opportune to enter a long position in a future. The opposite holds for the case of a future sale (short future).

Since a lower risk translates in a lower expected return, making investing less appealing, the overall purpose of hedging is not to reduce the aggregate risk level, but to cut away the unwanted risks in order to concentrate resources on the wanted ones.

Example 4.1: Airlines companies commonly hedge against increasing oil prices by entering long positions in oil futures contracts on the exchange for the oil required to operate their business activities (short position in the physical market).

There are hedgers who are both producers and consumers of some commodity, like oil refineries, where oil is processed through cracking in order to get all output products, and energy is also consumed in order to feed the process.

A popular method for hedging is through option trading. Hedging strategies in options markets involve holding a position in some underlying stock, while taking the same or opposite position in an option, in order to offset the portfolio gains and losses.

Speculators try to predict future movements in the price of an asset and take positions accordingly, to maximize the profit. Speculators have an extreme appetite for risk and they are in the derivatives markets just to make high profits.

They base their decision on effective forecasts of market trends, and take positions with no guarantee of the investment made. Speculators typically try to forecast market moves by relying on fast moving trends, exposing themselves to huge profits or, equally likely, huge losses. Speculators are typically looking to diversifications of their holdings and aim at maximizing profits in a short period of time.

If a speculator feels the stock price of some entity is expected to fall in a short time, he would typically short sell these shares in a derivative market without actually buying or owning those shares. The opposite holds in case of a bullish forecast, and in case the stock follows the expectation, the speculator can make sizeable profits.

A broad definition of speculation is the temporary take of a position on some assets, not to use or keep it, but for later closing the position out and profit from interim price changes.

A better definition is however needed in order to really distinguish speculators from other types of investors. Generally, traders on the winning side of a bid-ask spread may be referred to as speculators.

From the point of view of the bid-ask spread, it is possible to envision hedgers like the investors willing to close rapidly their planned trades, even standing on the losing side of the spread.

Therefore it could be possible to classify speculation as aiming at realizing high profits by trading with hedgers at a favourable price, gaining on the closing of the position, in the winning side, with their profit being strictly linked to the size of the bid-ask spread.

Beware that such a definition of speculators would also include market makers, which is not the case.

An alternative definition, based on information, was given by Grossman and Stiglitz (1980), who define speculators as traders who incur costs in search of relevant information.

Different speculators gain pieces of information, which altogether contribute to the disclosure of aggregate information on the market. They are then followed by all other types of investors, who spot the opportunities given by that.

In general, it is rather difficult to give an unambiguous definition of speculation. Much easier is to identify properties that characterize every speculator. Tirole (1982) wrote that in a pure speculative market trades should not take place, in that every trader would assume that the other investor wants to trade because he holds better information than him. Therefore trading becomes a zero-sum game.

Financial derivatives are widely used by speculators seeking profits by betting on the future direction of the market. This is why it is possible to consider hedge funds, financial institutions, commodity advisors and operators, and brokers, as speculators.

Speculators can be also differentiated by the time horizons on which they trade, from the market makers, operating at the shortest time horizon, to the investment-type traders, trading at the longest time horizons.

Trading on options is one of the most common and efficient ways to speculate, given the leverage effect. A single claim usually underlines many shares of the underlying assets, so that even a marginal variation in the share price is multiplied many times when you trade in options. This leads to potential big gains or big losses with a single decision.

Expectations on the asset trend determine the type of option and strategy the speculator will choose. A bullish expectation on a stock price leads to a long position in a call price with strike lower than the forecasted price.

In case of a bearish expectation, the natural choice is to go long in put options. In both cases, the profit (if made) will be obviously determined by the absolute value of the differential between the market price of the underlying and the strike price of the option.

The last category of market participants are arbitrageurs, investors making extremely important investment decisions in a very short amount of time. They trade to lock in a riskless profit by simultaneously entering into transactions in two or more markets.

Arbitrageurs exploit market imperfections and inefficiencies to their advantage, given the fact that sometimes assets are overpriced or underpriced compared to a fair theoretical value.

There are many types of arbitrage in the derivatives markets. When the futures price is trading at a premium on the underlying asset, an arbitrageur will take positions in the two assets and money to exploit the opportunity.

Arbitrageurs fulfil the important function of balancing price differences across the markets, especially when price differentials are consistent, continuously tracking prices across the chosen segment.

The arbitrageurs usually have huge capital at their disposal, and take deliveries in one market segment, giving them in another market segment. There is a time gap between giving and taking deliveries, but this should be negligible for the purpose of trade.

On average, arbitrageurs should have no net position open, given the nature of their trading, meaning that for each open position, there is another opposite position in another market.

Arbitrage trading is made of reasonably small returns, with a high frequency of opportunities. Considering that for each transaction there is cost of brokerage, transaction tax, stock exchange charges, making it unviable in many cases.

Moreover the arbitrage opportunity (price differential) stands only for a few minutes or seconds, so that a very fast trading system is needed in order to capture it. If the arbitrageur is unable to close open positions and the market moves against the strategy, a loss will be incurred.

4.1.2 *Option structure and payout*

An option is a financial derivative that gives the right to buy or sell, a reference security (underlying) at a pre-specified price. The two major classes of options are call options and put options.

A call option gives the owner the right to buy a specific asset at a certain price, called *strike*. Settlement happens at a particular maturity date. A put option gives the right to sell a particular asset at a pre-specified price.

Buying an option creates rights but not obligations. The owner of a long position in a call option benefits from the price of the underlying asset being above the strike price of the call at maturity. If the price is below the strike, it is not optimal to exercise the option, and the buyer will let it expire. The payoff from a long position in a call option is

$$c = \max\left(S_T - K, 0\right)$$

where

S_T is the price at maturity T of the underlying
K is the strike price specified in the contract.

A long position is the simplest way to trade a call option. When the outlook on a stock is bullish, the trader can buy call options in order to get the underlying stock for the strike price at maturity, and cash it on the market for a high price.

Investors can also benefit from a short position in call options. When the outlook on the underlying asset is bearish (declining), the seller of the options believes it is possible to benefit from the counterparty not exercising the right attached to the option, and the gain on the option premium cashed at sale.

On the other hand, the buyer of a put option benefits from the price of the underlying being below the strike at maturity. As opposed to a call option, when the price is above the strike, it is not optimal to exercise the option.

The payoff of the long position in the put option is given by

$$p = \max\left(K - S_T, 0\right)$$

A long position in a put option usually has a protective purpose. When the outlook on a stock is bearish, the trader can buy put options to cover a decrease on the underlying price and balance it.

Investors can also benefit from short position in put options. When the outlook on the underlying is bullish, the seller of the options believes it is possible to benefit from the expiring of the option without exercise and the gain on the premium cashed to sell.

Many options are not traded on the regulated exchange. There is also an over-the-counter (OTC) market where financial derivatives are heavily traded. Whereas exchange-traded options are standardized contracts, OTC options are usually tailored to a particular risk.

If an investor has a need to hedge a position in currency or some other underlying asset, for a specific maturity, but the available exchange-traded options cover only part of that, it is then possible to access the OTC market to trade the appropriate instrument.

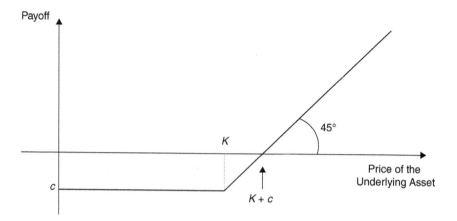

Figure 4.1 The payoff function for a long position in a call is flat, beginning at an underlying asset price of zero and continuing to the strike price, with a loss equal to the call premium (*c*). As the price of the underlying asset rises beyond the strike price, the call comes into the money, and payoff begins to rise with the price of the underlying asset.

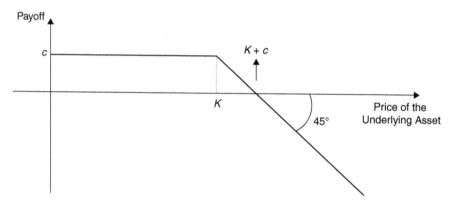

Figure 4.2 The payoff function for a short position in a call is flat, beginning at an underlying asset price of zero and continuing to the strike price, with a profit equal to the call premium. As the price of the underlying asset rises beyond the strike price, the call comes out of the money, and the loss begins to rise one for one with the price of the underlying asset.

4.1.3 Forwards and futures

A forward delivery contract is the most common forward contract. It is negotiated between two parties for the delivery of a commodity at a pre-specified strike, at a certain time in the future.

There is no initial transfer of property on the asset. The agreement is on delivering it at maturity. A forward transaction from the perspective of the buyer establishes a long position in the underlying commodity. For the seller, a forward transaction entails a short position in the underlying commodity.

Main forward markets are the markets of forward on foreign exchange and markets of forward on physical commodities. Forward contracts on both foreign exchange and physical commodities involve physical settlement at maturity.

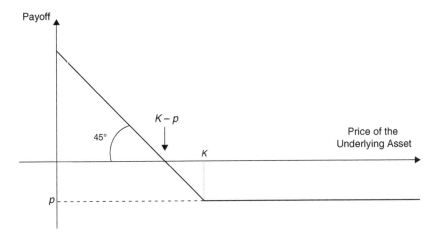

Figure 4.3 The payoff function for a long position in a put option shows the maximum profit at an underlying asset price of zero, which decreases when moving to the strike price. As the price of the underlying asset rises beyond the strike price, the put comes out of the money, and the loss is equal to the premium paid.

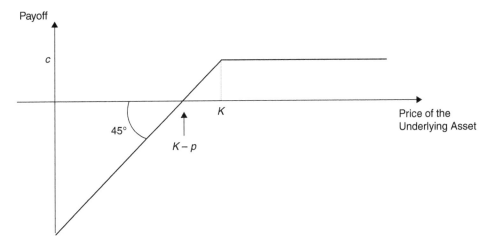

Figure 4.4 The payoff to writing a put option is exactly the opposite of the payoff to buying one. The writer receives the put-option premium so long as the price of the underlying asset remains above the strike price of the put. Once the underlying asset's price falls below the strike price, the payoff to option writer falls one-for-one as the price of the underlying asset falls.

However, a big share of contracts involve cash-settlement instead of physical delivery. At maturity, the short party pays to the long a cash sum if the underlying at maturity is above the contract price. If the spot price on the underlying prevailing at the maturity date of the contract is below the purchase price specified in the contract, then the long makes a cash payment.

The payoff of a forward contract is given by expression

$$F = S_T - K_F$$

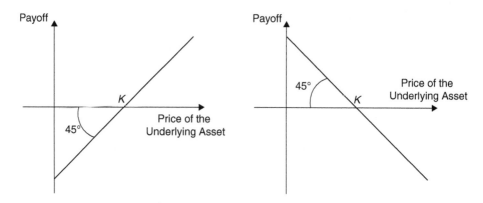

Figure 4.5 The payoff of a forward contract can be positive or negative. The cost of entering a forward contract is zero, so the payoff from the contract represents the investor's total gain or loss from the contract.

where

K_F is the delivery price specified in the forward contract
S_T is the spot price of the underlying at maturity.

From the payoff it is possible to calculate the payout ratio as the ratio of payoff over the spot price

$$R = \frac{(S_T - K_F)}{S_T}$$

The structure of the contract is such that the present value of the payout $(S_T - K_F)$ is zero. It follows that the initial forward price f at the beginning of the contract equals K_F.

The delivery price K_F remains fixed and must be distinguished by the forward price of the contract F that fluctuates over the time horizon, rising and falling with the spot price of the underlying asset.

Example 4.2: Consider a forward contract to exchange 100 kilos of gold in one year at a delivery price of €27/gram. If the spot price of gold rises to €30/gram one year from now, the profit for the purchaser of the contract is

$$\text{Payout} = \left[(30 \times 1,000) - (27 \times 1,000)\right] \times 100 = €300,000$$

Suppose instead that the spot price of gold in a year falls to €25/gram. Then the purchaser of the forward contract has a payoff

$$\text{Payout} = \left[(25 \times 1,000) - (27 \times 1,000)\right] \times 100 = €-200,000$$

If the spot price of gold at maturity is exactly €30,000/kilo, both parties are no better or worse off than if they did not enter the contract.

Table 4.1 Replication of a forward contract by using the underlying asset.

	Cash flows	
Actions	Time t	Time T
A: Buy forward contract	0	$S_T - F$
B: Buy one unit of underlying asset	$-S_t$	S_T
Borrow present value of the forward price	$Fe^{-r\Delta t}$	$-F$
Total	$-S_t + Fe^{-r\Delta t}$	$S_T - F$

Given the spot price S_t of an asset at time t, the forward price of the asset is given by the formula

$$F = S_t e^{r\Delta t}$$

where

r is the continuously compounded risk-free rate of return
$\Delta t = T - t$ is the time interval until maturity.

The result is consistent with no-arbitrage condition on the market, so that it should be the same on normal markets to buy the asset today or hold it and buy the forward contract and take delivery. To account for absence of arbitrage, the cost of both strategies must have the same present value.

To get a proof of the forward-spot price equality, consider a replicating portfolio of the forward contract.

It can be observed that payoffs at maturity are the same for both A and B. In order for the market to be free of arbitrage opportunities the equality of payoffs must hold also at time zero. Therefore

$$-S + Fe^{-r\Delta t} = 0 \implies F = Se^{r\Delta t}$$

When forward contracts have stocks as underlying, there can be the case where the stock pays a dividend. In this case, assuming the underlying asset pays a dividend yield d, the equivalence formula becomes

$$F = Se^{(r-d)\Delta t}$$

When the underlying is a commodity, there are storage costs involved. As for the dividends, these costs can be expressed in terms of a continuous variable s contributing to the discount. As opposed to the dividends, storage costs represent a negative flow, therefore it adds up to the exponent

$$F = Se^{(r+s)\Delta t}$$

For an already existing forward contract, the value today of a long position is given by

$$f = (F - K)e^{-r\Delta t}$$

and, for a short position, by

$$f = (K - F)e^{-r\Delta t}$$

Example 4.3: Assume $K = €270$, $F = €245$, $r = 4\%$, $\Delta t = 1/2$. The value of the forward contract for the buyer is

$$(245 - 270)e^{-0.04 \times \frac{1}{2}} = -€24.50$$

If the forward is to be closed out today, the long party should compensate the short party €24.50.

Given the spot-forward parity it follows, it is possible to express the value of the forward contract for a long and short position, in terms of the spot price, as

$$
\begin{aligned}
f_{Long} &= (F - K)e^{-r\Delta t} \\
&= (S_t e^{r\Delta t} - K)e^{-r\Delta t} \\
&= S_t - Ke^{-r\Delta t} \\
f_{Short} &= Ke^{-r\Delta t} - S_t
\end{aligned}
$$

The same reasoning yields the relationship for dividend-paying stocks

$$
\begin{aligned}
f_{Long} &= (F - K)e^{-r\Delta t} \\
&= (S_t e^{(r-d)\Delta t} - K)e^{-r\Delta t} \\
&= S_t e^{-d\Delta t} - Ke^{-r\Delta t} \\
f_{Short} &= Ke^{-r\Delta t} - S_t e^{-d\Delta t}
\end{aligned}
$$

and for commodities

$$
\begin{aligned}
f_{Long} &= (F - K)e^{-r\Delta t} \\
&= (S_t e^{(r+s)\Delta t} - K)e^{-r\Delta t} \\
&= S_t e^{s\Delta t} - Ke^{-r\Delta t} \\
f_{Short} &= Ke^{-r\Delta t} - S_t e^{s\Delta t}
\end{aligned}
$$

Futures are traded on organized financial markets. They are based on underlying or reference assets. They are regulated and the features are standard in the market, and all specified in the contract.

As opposed to forwards, whose settlement is entirely made at maturity, futures are monitored by the clearing authority of the exchange, so that profits and losses are settled every day. At expiration the only settlement is the change in value from the previous day.

Marking to market is the process of the party who is negative in the value of the contract on some specific day, to cover the negative position by paying a margin to the clearing house.

Besides the different settlement process, a forward contract is equivalent to a futures contract with exactly the same features. In order to prove it consider a simple forward strategy consisting in entering a long position in an amount r^T of contracts, where r is the daily return and T the maturity in days. Payoff at expiry of this strategy is then

$$r^T \left(S_T - F \right)$$

With daily settlement, for the same strategy set in futures, at the end of first day the position is settled for an amount $F_1 - F$, and closed out afterwards. The amount is then invested at a rate r till maturity, yielding an amount defined as

$$r\left(F_1 - F \right) r^{T-1}$$

On the second day, strategy is repeated, and an amount r^2 of futures contracts is bought at a price of F_1. At position closure, $F_2 - F_1$ is received and invested at r^{T-2}, generating an amount

$$r^2 \left(F_2 - F_1 \right) r^{T-2}$$

The process is then repeated every day until maturity generating a total payout equal to

$$r^T \left(F_1 - F \right) + r^T \left(F_2 - F_1 \right) + ... + r^T \left(S_T - F_{T-1} \right) = r^T \left(S_T - F \right)$$

which is exactly the same payoff as the forward.

Snapshot 4.1
Volatility strategy with strangles

It is possible to trade simultaneously on more than one option, in order to generate new strategies and combinations. An example is the strangle, an investment strategy involving the purchase or sale of particular options.

It allows the holder to gain profits based on how much the price of the underlying asset moves, with limited exposure to the direction of price movement. A long position in a strangle is equivalent to buying the involved options, while the sale of the option derivatives is known as a short strangle.

A long strangle is obtained by entering a long position in both a call and a put option, on the same underlying security, with the same time to maturity, but with different strike prices.

The investor in a long strangle makes a profit when the underlying price moves far enough away from the current price, either above or below. This is why the strangle is useful to set a volatility strategy.

So an investor may buy a swap to bet on high volatility of the underlying asset, even not knowing in which direction it is going to move. Such a position has a limited risk, with maximum loss equal to the cost of both options, and unlimited profit potential.

A short strangle position, on the other hand, involves selling both a call and a put option on the same underlying asset. The premium can be chosen by the seller, with the hope that this will cover any potential volatility.

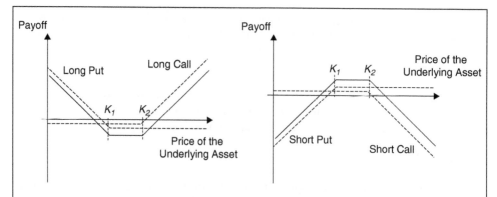

Figure 4.6 The payoff of a long strangle (left) is positive for very low or very high values of the stock price, precisely out of the range bounded by the strike prices. The short strike, conversely, offers limited profit for medium-range prices.

As opposed to the buyer, the seller of the strangle makes a profit if the underlying price stays within the range bounded by the two strike prices of the options. The investor, in this case, wants to take a short strangle position betting on limited volatility of the underlying asset. This position has limited profit and unlimited risk.

4.2 Pricing of derivatives

Learning outcomes

1. Learn how to use binomial trees for option pricing.
2. Understand the rationale behind the Black-Scholes-Merton model for option pricing.
3. Perform pricing of financial options and compute the Greeks.

4.2.1 Binomial trees

The binomial model was suggested by Cox *et al.* in 1979. They assume that stock price movements are composed of a large number of small binomial movements. The binomial model resembles the features of continuous time models for option pricing, in a simplified structure.

Consider a stock with initial price S at time t which has the option of moving up to $S_h = Sh$ according to a multiplying factor $h > 1$ or down to $S_l = Sl$ according to a multiplying factor $l = \dfrac{1}{h} < 1$, at time $T = t + \Delta t$. Let p be the probability of the price rising from S to Sh. The expected price at time $t = 1$ as from the tree is

$$E(S_T) = pSh + (1-p)Sl$$

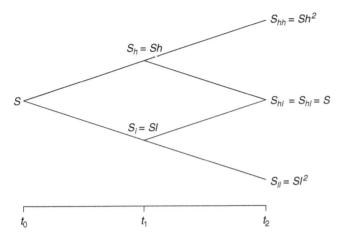

Figure 4.7 An example of a binomial tree for option valuation. At each step, the price of the underlying asset can go up by a factor *h*, or down by a factor *l*.

It is now possible to compare this expectation with the one given by risk-neutral valuation

$$E(S_T) = Se^{r\Delta t}$$

That means that the expected stock price at time $t = 1$ is given by the stock value today compounded at the risk-free rate. Calculating the expected price from the stock at $t = 1$ and making use of risk-neutral valuation,

$$
\begin{aligned}
E(S_T) &= pSh + (1-p)Sl = Se^{r\Delta t} \\
\Rightarrow S_0 &= e^{-r\Delta t} E(S_t) \\
&= e^{-r\Delta t} E(Sh + Sl) \\
&= e^{-r\Delta t} (pSh + (1-p)Sl) \\
\Rightarrow e^{r\Delta t} &= (ph + (1-p)l) \\
&= p(1-l) + l \\
\Rightarrow p &= \frac{e^{r\Delta t} - l}{h - l}
\end{aligned}
$$

This calculated probability is called risk-neutral probability, because it represents the probability of a rise in price of the underlying stock given the assumption of risk neutrality.

Actual probabilities are real-life chances of each event happening. They are also referred to as physical, objective probabilities while risk-neutral probabilities are artificial probabilities that match the observed security prices, given subjective probabilities and risk preferences.

A similar argument gives the formulation of *u* and *d* in terms of the volatility. Consider the variance of the stock price as from the tree, as the difference between the expectation of the square and the square of expected return.

In the case of the binomial tree the return can be expressed as the probability-weighted average of u and d. Therefore the variance has the form

$$ph^2 + (1-p)l^2 - \left[ph + (1-p)l\right]^2 \tag{4.1}$$

It is then possible to equate this variance with its expression $\sigma^2 \Delta t$.

$$\sigma^2 \Delta t = ph^2 + (1-p)l^2 - \left[ph + (1-p)l\right]^2$$
$$= \ldots$$
$$= p(1-p)(h-l)^2$$

Consider the first part of the product

$$p(1-p) = p - p^2$$
$$= \frac{e^{r\Delta t} - l}{h-l} - \frac{e^{2r\Delta t} - 2le^{r\Delta t} + l^2}{(h-l)^2} = \tag{4.2}$$
$$= \ldots$$
$$= \frac{e^{r\Delta t}(h+l) - hl - e^{2r\Delta t}}{(h-l)^2}$$

Substituting (4.2) in (4.1) and recalling that $l = \dfrac{1}{h}$, it follows that

$$h = \frac{\sigma^2 \Delta t + 1 + e^{2r\Delta t}}{e^{r\Delta t}} - \frac{1}{h}$$
$$= \frac{\sigma^2 \Delta t}{e^{r\Delta t}} + \frac{1}{e^{r\Delta t}} + e^{r\Delta t} - \frac{1}{h}$$

The simple condition $e^{r\Delta t} \approx (1 + r\Delta t)$ allows for the following approximations

$$\frac{1}{e^{r\Delta t}} + e^{r\Delta t} \approx 2$$
$$\frac{\sigma^2 \Delta t}{e^{r\Delta t}} \approx \sigma^2 \Delta t$$

Therefore

$$h^2 = (\sigma^2 \Delta t + 2) - 1$$

This is a second order equation with roots

$$h = \frac{\sigma^2 \Delta t + 2 \pm \sqrt{\sigma^4 \Delta t^2 + 4\sigma^2 \Delta t + 4 - 4}}{2}$$

Since both terms $\sigma^4 \Delta t^2$ and $4\sigma^2 \Delta t$ are negligible, what is left is

$$h \approx 1 \pm \sigma\sqrt{\Delta t} \approx e^{\sigma\sqrt{\Delta t}}$$

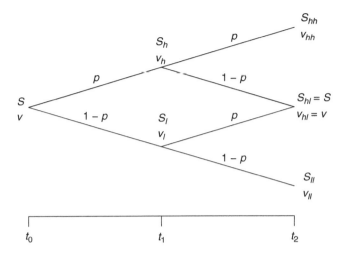

Figure 4.8 The same binomial tree can be used to also show the corresponding values of the option, at each node, given the risk-neutral probability *p* of an upper movement.

Similarly it is possible to derive the relationship for *d* and the result is

$$h \approx e^{\sigma\sqrt{\Delta t}}, \; l \approx e^{-\sigma\sqrt{\Delta t}}$$

This allows us to price an option on the binomial tree knowing only the volatility of the stock, the risk-free rate and the time interval considered.

Once we know the risk-neutral probabilities to assign to up and down movements of the stock, it is possible to price the options on the binomial tree, according to the assumption of risk neutrality.

The pricing on a binomial tree is done moving backward on the tree. Starting from the maturity of the tree, payoffs of the options can be calculated, corresponding to the stock values at each terminal node. After that, the value at each previous node is calculated using the values of following nodes and the risk-neutral probabilities.

Consider a model in one time step, from $t = 0$ to $t = 1$. When the value of the stock goes up to S_h or down to S_l at time $t = 1$, the value of the option associated with those values moves to v_u or v_d respectively. Given the probability of an upper movement, the value of the option at time $t = 0$ is given by

$$v = e^{-r\Delta t} \left[pv_h + (1-p)v_l \right]$$

The model can be then extended for two time steps. In this case each node at time 1 can be seen as the starting node of another one step tree, terminating at time 2. Therefore the pricing of the option at time 1 is

$$v_h = e^{-r\Delta t} \left[pv_{hh} + (1-p)v_{hl} \right] \tag{4.3}$$

And

$$v_l = e^{-r\Delta t} \left[pv_{hl} + (1-p)v_{ll} \right] \tag{4.4}$$

After that, working backward the price of the option at time zero is given again by the general pricing formula. An alternative is to substitute for (4.3) and (4.4) in (4.5) and do some maths to get

$$v = e^{-rT}\left[p^2 v_{hh} + 2p(1-p)v_{hl} + (1-p)^2 v_{ll} \right] \qquad (4.5)$$

The formula gives the value of the option at time zero directly as a function of the expected payoffs at time 2, without going through the intermediate time step.

Recall the payoffs at time 2 for the call and put options at each node are given by

$$c = \max(S_T - K, 0)$$
$$p = \max(K - S_T, 0)$$

Example 4.4: Consider a three-month call option with a strike $K = 21$ on a stock priced €20 today and volatility 19.06%. Assume the current continuously compounded interest rate r (at three-month maturity) is 12%. The high and low factors can be computed as

$$h \approx e^{0.1906\sqrt{0.25}} \approx 1.1, \; l \approx \frac{1}{h} \approx e^{-\sigma\sqrt{\Delta t}} \approx e^{-0.1906\sqrt{0.25}} \approx 0.9$$

It follows that the risk-neutral probabilities are

$$p = \frac{\dfrac{20}{e^{-0.12\times0.25}} - 18}{22 - 18} = 0.65, \; 1 - p = 0.35$$

We can the calculate the value of the call option as

$$c = e^{-0.12\times0.25}(1\times0.65 + 0\times0.35) = 0.63$$

Chapter 11 deals with the hedging techniques that can be implemented with derivatives. What follows is an introduction to hedging positions in financial options, taking some position in the underlying stock.

More specifically, it is possible to hedge a short position $-v$ in an option with δ shares of stock. In order to avoid arbitrage opportunities, the value of the portfolio must be the same in each state. Mathematically we can write this as:

$$\delta S_u - v_u = \delta d S_d - v_d$$
$$\Rightarrow \delta(S_u - S_d) = v_u - v_d$$
$$\Rightarrow \delta = \frac{v_u - v_d}{S_u - S_d}$$

Binomial trees are very useful to value American options, because they can only be valued numerically. The difference when pricing an American option instead of a European option on the tree is not big.

When valuing the payoff at each node at time steps before the last one, a comparison must be made between the European value of the option obtained as $v_u, v_d...$ and the intrinsic value of the option, given by the price of the stock at each node minus the strike.

The higher of the two values must be then taken into account when stepping backward on the tree, to value the option.

4.2.2 Black-Scholes-Merton model

The Black-Scholes-Merton (BSM) model for option pricing is one of the most important concepts in modern financial theory. It was developed by Fischer Black, Myron Scholes and Robert Merton, and it is the most popular options pricing model in the world.

The model is used to the theoretical price of European put and call options, and was originally developed without taking into consideration the effects of dividends paid during the life of the option. The model, once derived, can be adapted to account for the dividends paid on the underlying stock, by determining the ex-dividend date value of the latter.

Stock prices can take any value in the real domain, in a certain time period. Therefore a realistic model of price behaviour is needed to start the analysis. The BSM model applies this concept through extremely complex mathematics, in order to derive pricing formulas for options written on an underlying following a random process.

In order to make the analysis possible, the model is based on several assumptions. However, the assumptions needed to derive the model do not limit the efficiency of the pricing kernel, which can be adapted to frameworks where some of the assumptions are relaxed.

The main assumption of the BSM model are:

1. The stock pays no dividends during the option's life.
2. Options are European style.
3. Markets are efficient, normal and arbitrage-free.
4. There are no commissions or transaction costs.
5. Lending and borrowing happens at the risk-free rate.
6. Prices are lognormal and returns are normally distributed.

The behaviour of underlying asset prices follows a geometric Brownian motion, with a variance rate proportional to the square root of the price. This is stated formally as

$$\frac{dS}{S} = \mu dt + \sigma dW \tag{4.6}$$

where

S_t is the price of the underlying stock
μ is the expected return on S
σ is the standard deviation of the stock returns
W is Wiener process (Brownian motion).

Suppose f is the price of a derivative contingent on S. From Itô's Lemma we get:

$$dv = \left(\frac{\partial v}{\partial S} \mu S + \frac{\partial v}{\partial t} + \frac{1}{2} \frac{\partial^2 v}{\partial S^2} \sigma^2 S^2 \right) dt + \frac{\partial v}{\partial S} \sigma S dW \tag{4.7}$$

Consider forming a portfolio of one share of stock and an amount $\delta = \dfrac{\partial v}{\partial S}$ of the option. The value of such a portfolio is

$$V = S - \frac{v}{\delta}$$

Given this formulation the change in portfolio is given by

$$\Delta V = \Delta S - \frac{\Delta v}{\delta} \tag{4.8}$$

Plugging (4.4) and (4.5) into (4.6), the change in value of the portfolio can be expressed as

$$\Delta V = \mu S \Delta t + \sigma S \Delta W - \left[\left(\frac{\partial v}{\partial S} \mu S + \frac{\partial v}{\partial t} + \frac{1}{2} \frac{\partial^2 v}{\partial S^2} \sigma^2 S^2 \right) \frac{\Delta t}{\delta} + \frac{\partial v}{\partial S} \frac{\sigma}{\delta} S \Delta W \right]$$

$$= \ldots$$

$$= \left(-\frac{\partial v}{\partial t} - \frac{1}{2} \frac{\partial^2 v}{\partial S^2} \sigma^2 S^2 \right) \frac{\Delta t}{\delta}$$

This step shows the rationale of the model intuition. The change in value of the portfolio is no longer dependent on the Brownian motion. The process of the portfolio value has only drift, therefore it is much easier to handle.

In order to avoid arbitrage opportunities the portfolio being riskless must instantaneously earn the risk-free rate r, and the change in portfolio value in the time interval is equivalent to the current value of the portfolio multiplied by the risk-free rate and the time interval itself.

$$\left(-\frac{\partial v}{\partial t} - \frac{1}{2} \frac{\partial^2 v}{\partial S^2} \sigma^2 S^2 \right) \frac{\Delta t}{\delta} = r \left(S - \frac{v}{\delta} \right) \Delta t$$

Multiplying both sides by $\dfrac{\delta}{\Delta t}$, and rearranging terms yields the BSM PDE as

$$\frac{\partial v}{\partial t} + \frac{\partial v}{\partial S} r S + \frac{1}{2} \frac{\partial^2 v}{\partial S^2} \sigma^2 S^2 = rv$$

Solving it, subject to the terminal payoff condition of the derivative it is possible to derive analytical formulas for the call and put option value.

The solution of the BSM PDE is a complicated task. The equation admits analytical solutions, and each solution comes from imposing boundary conditions. The process involves variable transformation, and the heat equation.

What is interesting for our purposes is to analyse the specific solution for the call and put options.

The generic solution for the boundary of an option is

$$c = e^{-r\Delta t} \hat{E}\left[\max(S_T - K, 0)\right]$$

where

$\hat{E}$ denotes expectation under risk-neutral measure
S_T is the price of the stock at maturity of the option T
K is the strike price of the option.

Recall the process for the stock is

$$dS = \mu S dt + \sigma S dz$$

Recall that S is lognormal and

$$\hat{E}(S_T) = S_0 e^{r\Delta t}$$
$$Var(\ln S_T) = \sigma^2 \Delta t$$

Substituting the values for the mean and the variance of the stock gives the specific solution for the call option written on a stock S:

$$
\begin{aligned}
c &= e^{-r\Delta t} \hat{E}\left[\max(S_T - K, 0)\right] \\
&= e^{-r\Delta t}\left[S e^{r\Delta t} N(d_1) - KN(d_2)\right] \\
&= SN(d_1) - Ke^{-r\Delta t} N(d_2)
\end{aligned}
$$

where

$$
\begin{aligned}
d_1 &= \frac{\ln\left[\dfrac{E(S_T)}{K}\right] + \dfrac{\sigma^2 + \Delta t}{2}}{\sigma\sqrt{\Delta t}} \\[2mm]
&= \frac{\ln\left[\dfrac{S}{K}\right] + \left(r + \dfrac{\sigma^2}{2}\right)\Delta t}{\sigma\sqrt{\Delta t}} \\[2mm]
d_2 &= \frac{\ln\left[\dfrac{E(S_T)}{K}\right] - \dfrac{\sigma^2 + \Delta t}{2}}{\sigma\sqrt{\Delta t}} \\[2mm]
&= \frac{\ln\left[\dfrac{S}{K}\right] + \left(r - \dfrac{\sigma^2}{2}\right)\Delta t}{\sigma\sqrt{\Delta t}} = d_1 - \sigma\sqrt{\Delta t}
\end{aligned}
$$

and $N(.)$ is the cumulative standardized normal distribution defined as

$$N(x) = \int \frac{1}{\sqrt{2\pi}} e^{-\frac{x^2}{2}} dx$$

The same reasoning leads to the particular solution for the price of a put option

$$p = Ke^{-r\Delta t} N(-d_2) - SN(-d_1)$$

Example 4.5: Assume valuing a call option on a stock with price €99, strike price €95, time to expiration one year, risk-free rate 5% and volatility 25%. These values make it possible to calculate the BSM theoretical option value, and the first task is to calculate values for d_1 and d_2

$$d_1 = \frac{\ln\left(\frac{99}{95}\right) + \left(0.05 + \frac{0.25^2}{2}\right)1}{0.25\sqrt{1}} = 0.49$$

$$d_2 = 0.49 - 0.25 = 0.24$$

$$N(0.49) = 0.6879, \ N(0.24) = 0.5948$$

It is then possible to calculate the price of the option

$$c = 99(0.6879) - 95e^{-(0.05)(1)}(0.5948) = €14.35$$

The BSM model is based on the assumption that the underlying stock pays no dividend. But once the model is derived, it is possible to use it also to price options written on dividend-paying stocks. Define the continuous dividend rate as q. To obtain the continuous dividend version of the model, we replace S in the regular model with

$$S_q = Se^{(-q\Delta t)}$$

Example 4.6: Recall the previous example and assume the stock pays an annual dividend rate of 1.5%. The adjusted stock price is

$$S_q = 99e^{(-0.015 \times 1)} = 97.53$$

With the new value for the underlying the result of calculation is

$$d_1 = 0.43, \ d_2 = 0.18$$

$$N(0.43) = 0.6665, \ N(0.18) = 0.5715$$

And the resulting call price is €13.36.

It is interesting to investigate how the BSM model relates to the binomial model as seen before. Recall that at any time t the stock price S can move up to S_u with probability p or down to S_d with probability $1-p$. Also recall that risk-neutrality arguments show that

$$
\begin{aligned}
ve^{rdt} &= pv_h + (1-p)v_l \\
&= p(v_h - v_l) + v_l
\end{aligned}
$$

The Taylor series expansions of v_h, v_l and e^{rdt} are

$$
v_h \approx v + \frac{\partial v}{\partial S} dS_h + \frac{1}{2} \frac{\partial^2 v}{\partial S^2} (dS_h)^2 + \frac{\partial v}{\partial S} dt
$$

$$
v_l \approx v + \frac{\partial v}{\partial S} dS_l + \frac{1}{2} \frac{\partial^2 v}{\partial S^2} (dS_l)^2 + \frac{\partial v}{\partial S} dt
$$

$$
e^{rdt} \approx 1 + rdt
$$

Note that $dS_h = dS_l = dS$ by symmetry, and $(dS_h)^2 = (dS_l)^2 = \sigma^2 dt$ so that

$$
v(1+rdt) = p\left(v + \frac{\partial v}{\partial S} dS + \frac{1}{2} \frac{\partial^2 v}{\partial S^2} \sigma^2 dt + \frac{\partial v}{\partial S} dt \right) + (1-p)\left(v + \frac{\partial v}{\partial S} dS + \frac{1}{2} \frac{\partial^2 v}{\partial S^2} \sigma^2 dt + \frac{\partial v}{\partial S} dt \right)
$$

After rearranging terms the result is exactly the BSM PDE:

$$
\frac{\partial v}{\partial t} + \frac{\partial v}{\partial S} rS + \frac{1}{2} \frac{\partial^2 v}{\partial S^2} \sigma^2 S^2 = rv
$$

4.2.3 The Greeks

The BSM PDE is composed of sensitivities of the option price to the various parameters affecting the price. Looking at the PDE it is possible to directly see some of the Greeks, in the form

$$
\frac{\partial v}{\partial t} + \frac{\partial v}{\partial S} rS + \frac{1}{2} \frac{\partial^2 v}{\partial S^2} \sigma^2 S^2 = rv
$$

$$
\rightarrow \Theta + \delta rS + \frac{1}{2} \Gamma \sigma^2 S^2 = rv
$$

The PDE shows then explicitly the sensitivity of the option price to changes in the time to maturity (theta), and in the price of underlying, first (delta) and second (gamma) order.

The other sensitivities not appearing in the PDE are the sensitivity to the change in volatility (vega) and in the level of the interest rate (rho). These are the most important Greeks, but many more can be defined just considering the sensitivity to each parameter at higher orders.

The formula for delta δ of a call option in the BSM framework is

$$
\delta_c = N(d_1) \tag{4.9}
$$

It can be obtained by differentiating the formula for the call price with respect to the price S of the underlying asset. Recall that

$$c = SN(d_1) - Ke^{-r\Delta t}N(d_2) \tag{4.10}$$

where

$$d_1 = \frac{\ln\left[\dfrac{S}{K}\right] + \left(r + \dfrac{\sigma^2}{2}\right)\Delta t}{\sigma\sqrt{\Delta t}}$$
$$d_2 = d_1 - \sigma\sqrt{\Delta t}$$

First of all, the chain rule gives the first order derivatives of d_1 and d_2 with respect to S as

$$\frac{\partial d_1}{\partial S} = \frac{\partial d_2}{\partial S} = \frac{1}{S\sigma\sqrt{\Delta t}}$$

It follows that the derivative of (4.9) with respect to S is

$$\delta_c = \frac{\partial c}{\partial S} = N(d_1) + \frac{1}{S\sigma\sqrt{\Delta t}}\left[SN'(d_1) - e^{-r\Delta t}KN'(d_2)\right]$$

where

$N'(.)$ is the standard normal probability density.

Consider the term in square brackets on the right-hand side. It must be shown to be equal to zero, in order to prove (4.10). Note that

$$e^{-r\Delta t}KN'(d_2) = e^{-r\Delta t}KN'\left(d_1 - \sigma\sqrt{\Delta t}\right)$$
$$= e^{-r\Delta t}K\frac{1}{\sqrt{2\pi}}e^{\frac{-\left(d_1 - \sigma\sqrt{\Delta t}\right)^2}{2}}$$
$$= e^{-r\Delta t}K\frac{1}{\sqrt{2\pi}}e^{\frac{-d_1^2}{2}}e^{\frac{\left(2d_1\sigma\sqrt{\Delta t} - \sigma^2\Delta t\right)}{2}}$$
$$= e^{-r\Delta t}KN'(d_1)e^{\frac{\left\{2\ln\left[\frac{S}{K}\right] + 2r\Delta t + \sigma^2\Delta t - \sigma^2\Delta t\right\}}{2}}$$
$$= e^{-r\Delta t}KN'(d_1)\frac{S}{K}e^{r\Delta t} = SN'(d_1)$$

so that the above statement is true.

The same reasoning leads to the formula for the delta of a put option δ_p, which is defined as

$$\delta_p = -N(-d_1)$$

Again by chain rule, and applying some of the above results, the gamma of a call option can be calculated as

$$\Gamma_c = \frac{\partial \delta_c}{\partial S} = \frac{\partial \delta_c}{\partial d_1}\frac{\partial d_1}{\partial S} = \frac{N'(d_1)}{S\sigma\sqrt{\Delta t}}$$

Some straightforward reasoning and maths show that the gamma of a put option is the same as the gamma of a call option.

Theta is the sensitivity of the option price to the variation of the time to maturity. A similar argument used for the chain rule above shows that

$$\frac{\partial d_1}{\partial t} = \frac{\partial d_2}{\partial t} - \frac{\sigma}{2\sqrt{\Delta t}}$$

The theta of a call option is defined as

$$\Theta_c = \frac{\partial c}{\partial t}$$

$$= e^{-r\Delta t}KN'(d_1)\frac{\partial d_1}{\partial t} - rKe^{-r\Delta t}N(d_2) - e^{-r\Delta t}KN'(d_2)\frac{\partial d_2}{\partial t}$$

$$= e^{-r\Delta t}KN'(d_2)\frac{\partial d_2}{\partial t} - \frac{\sigma e^{-r\Delta t}KN'(d_2)}{2\sqrt{\Delta t}} - rKe^{-r\Delta t}N(d_2) - e^{-r\Delta t}KN'(d_2)\frac{\partial d_2}{\partial t}$$

$$= -Ke^{-r\Delta t}\left[rN(d_2) + \frac{\sigma N'(d_2)}{2\sqrt{\Delta t}}\right]$$

For a put option, theta can be defined as

$$\Theta_p = \frac{\partial p}{\partial t} = Ke^{-r\Delta t}\left[rN(-d_2) - \frac{\sigma N'(d_2)}{2\sqrt{\Delta t}}\right]$$

In order to derive the rho of a call option, note that

$$\frac{\partial d_1}{\partial r} = \frac{\partial d_2}{\partial r} = \frac{\sqrt{\Delta t}}{\sigma}$$

The rho of a call option is defined as

$$Rho_c = \frac{\partial c}{\partial r}$$

$$= SN'(d_1)\frac{\partial d_1}{\partial r} + Ke^{-r\Delta t}N(d_2)\Delta t - e^{-r\Delta t}KN'(d_2)\frac{\partial d_2}{\partial r}$$

$$= Ke^{-r\Delta t}N(d_2)\Delta t + \frac{\partial d_1}{\partial r}\left[SN'(d_1) - e^{-r\Delta t}KN'(d_2)\right]$$

$$= Ke^{-r\Delta t}N(d_2)\Delta t$$

The rho of a put option is

$$Rho_c = -Ke^{-r\Delta t}N(-d_2)\Delta t$$

Finally, to derive the vega of a call option, consider that

$$\frac{\partial d_1}{\partial \sigma} = \frac{\partial d_2}{\partial \sigma} + \sqrt{\Delta t}$$

As a consequence, the vega of a call option is defined as

$$V_c = SN'(-d_1)\sqrt{\Delta t}$$

The proof of the derivation is left as an exercise.
The vega of a put option is

$$V_p = Ke^{-r\Delta t}N'(-d_1)\sqrt{\Delta t}$$

Greeks can be considered the risk sensitivities, risk measures or hedge parameters, and are vital tools in risk management. They allow component risks to be treated in isolation, and rebalance the portfolio accordingly to achieve a desired exposure.

Snapshot 4.2
The BSM pricing formula for dividend-paying stocks

Options are often written on what can be interpreted as an asset that pays a continuous dividend that is proportional to the asset's price. Consider how to value such options for a general case

This case is valid for options on equity indices with a continuous dividend yield q, futures with $q = r$, FX rates with $q = r_f$ (where r_f is the foreign interest rate) and assets without dividends $(q = 0)c_q = e^{-qT}SN(d_1) - e^{-rT}KN(d_2)$ds.
The price of the European call is

$$c_q = e^{-r\Delta t}\left[e^{-q\Delta t}SN(d_1) - e^{-r\Delta t}KN(d_2)\right]$$

with

$$d_1 = \frac{\ln\left(\dfrac{S}{K}\right) + \left(r - q + \dfrac{\sigma^2}{2}\right)\Delta t}{\sigma\sqrt{\Delta t}}$$

$$d_2 = d_1 - \sigma\sqrt{\Delta t}$$

The price of a European put is

$$p_q = e^{-r\Delta t}KN(-d_2) - e^{-q\Delta t}SN(-d_1)$$

If the asset underlying the options pays discrete dividends (known in advance), the process governing the asset price S can be divided in a deterministic part (the present value of all future dividends falling into the lifetime of the option) and a stochastic process followed by S_0 according to

$$S_t = S_0 \left(1-\delta\right)^{n(t)} e^{ut+\sigma W}$$

where $n(t)$ is the number of dividends paid out by time t. The price of a call option on such a stock is

$$c_\delta = e^{-r\Delta t} \left[S_0 \left(1-\delta\right)^{n(t)} e^{rT} N\left(d_1\right) - KN\left(d_2\right) \right]$$

and the price of the put is

$$p_\delta = e^{-r\Delta t} \left[KN\left(-d_2\right) - S_0 \left(1-\delta\right)^{n(t)} e^{rT} N\left(-d_1\right) \right]$$

4.3 Interest rate derivatives

Learning outcomes

1. Define interest rate derivatives and their payoff structures.
2. Acquire knowledge about interest rate swaps.
3. Analyse the structure and payout of interest rate caps, floors and swaptions.

4.3.1 Interest rate swaps

There are five classes of swaps: interest rate swaps, currency swaps, equity swaps, commodity swaps and credit swaps. Plain vanilla interest rate swaps are standardized contracts.

An Interest Rate Swap (IRS) is a contract to exchange payments based on a defined principal amount, for a fixed period of time. The principal amount is not exchanged, only the interest payments are.

There is no generation of new funds from an IRS, but the interest rates get converted on a different rate basis (e.g. from a floating or variable interest rate basis to a fixed interest rate basis, or vice versa).

The payer of a floating rate is by convention defined as the buyer of the swap, making payments that are based on a floating rate of interest, such as the London Inter Bank Offered Rate (LIBOR). The maturity of an interest rate swap is usually between one and fifteen years.

As mentioned above, the notional amount is just a reference and is not exchanged between the counterparties. Therefore it could be an arbitrary number, with no consistency at all during the life of the IRS.

Consider a plain vanilla IRS, with a notional principal L and resembling n interest payments through its maturity date, T. Denote payment dates as $t_i = t_1, t_2, ..., t_n$ and the present value of a future payment (discount factor) made at time t_i as PV_{0,t_i}.

Indicating with r_S the swap (fixed coupon) rate, the present value of the payments, PV_{FD} on the fixed leg, is given by

$$PV_{fix} = L \sum_{i=1}^{n} r_S PV_{0,t_i} \left(\frac{\Delta t}{M} \right)$$

where

L is the notional principal amount.
$\Delta t = t_i - t_{i-1}$ is the number of days between the i-th and the $(i-1)$-th payments.
M is the selected day-count convention (typically 252, 360 or 365 days).

For an existing swap, the value of the floating-leg payments on date t_1 is given by

$$PV_{flt} = L \sum_{i=1}^{n} F_{i-1,i}^{L} PV_{0,t_i} \left(\frac{\Delta t}{M} \right)$$

where

$F_{i-1,i}^{L}$ is the forward rate implied by the relevant curve (typically LIBOR).

The implied forward rate is then given by the discounting equation

$$F_{i-1,i} = \frac{M}{\Delta t} \left(\frac{PV_{0,t_{i-1}}^{L}}{PV_{0,t_i}^{L}} - 1 \right) \tag{4.11}$$

where

PV_{0,t_i}^{L} is the is the discount factor associated with the relevant forward curve.

The present value of the cash flows of the swap is the difference between the values of the two streams of cash flows. Therefore the swap value for the counterparty paying floating and receiving fixed is

$$V_{SW} = PV_{fix} - PV_{flt}$$

while the value for the counterparty paying fixed and receiving floating is

$$\tilde{V}_{SW} = PV_{flt} - PV_{fix}$$

Another valuation methodology is based on basic present value relationships, ignoring principal at maturity, with swap cash flows defined as a combination of a floating rate bond and fixed rate bond.

Similar to valuation of a bond as discounted value of expected future cash flows, the fixed leg of a swap can be valued as the present value of the fixed payments. For a swap lasting for n years this is equal to

$$PV_{fix} = \sum_{i=1}^{mn} \frac{C_S}{m}\left(1+\frac{r}{m}\right)^{-i}$$

where

C_S is the annual swap payment
r is the discount rate
m is the number of payment periods per year.

The floating leg can be seen as a floating rate bond paying no principal, and it is again equal to the present value of its expected cash flows. The value of a floating rate bond with face value B_{mn} is

$$B_{flt} = \sum_{i=1}^{mn} \frac{\tilde{C}_i}{m}\left(1+\frac{r_i}{m}\right)^{-i} + B_{mn}\left(1+\frac{r_{mn}}{m}\right)^{-mn} \tag{4.12}$$

where

$\tilde{C}_i$ is the expected floating coupon at time i
r_i is value of the floating rate at time i
r_{mn} is the value of the floating rate at maturity.

As mentioned above, no actual principal amount is involved in the swap deal, so that only the first term of equation (4.12) represents the value of the floating leg of the swap.
It follows that the equation can be rearranged as

$$B_{flt} - B_{mn}\left(1+\frac{r_{mn}}{m}\right)^{-mn} = \sum_{i=1}^{mn} \frac{\tilde{C}_i}{m}\left(1+\frac{r_i}{m}\right)^{-i}$$

Since at maturity the bond sells at present value, it follows that $B_{flt} = B_{mn}$, so that

$$PV_{flt} = B_{mn} - B_{mn}\left(1+\frac{r_{mn}}{m}\right)^{-mn}$$

Swaps are traded privately in the over-the-counter market, and an important industry has taken place to facilitate swap transactions. Swap dealers are ready to take either side of a transaction (e.g. pay-fixed or receive-fixed) depending on the demand at the time.

4.3.2 Caps and floors

An interest rate cap (IRC) is a financial instrument that limits the highest rate to be paid from a borrower at a floating rate. At interest payment date, if the rate is above the cap level, the IRC pays to the owner the difference between what is owed at the floating rate and what would be owed at the prearranged cap.

An interest rate floor (IRF) is an instrument that puts a lower bound on what is received by lending at a floating rate, by paying the holder the difference between what would be due at the fixed floor rate and what is due at the floating rate.

The OTC market for caps and floors is very liquid, and common policy is to base the floating payment on the LIBOR as of the beginning of each payment period (tenor). A full instrument normally covers many tenors, resulting in portfolios of one period 'caplets' and 'floorlets' with staggered payment dates.

Knowing the value of individual caplets and floorlets with arbitrary fixed rates and expirations covering the whole instrument maturity, the caps and floors themselves can be priced just by adding up the value of the segments.

To price a cap or a floor, it is then necessary to price the single caplets (floorlets) as options. Suppose reset dates of a cap are $t_i = t_1, t_2, ..., t_n$. The caplet can be priced as

$$c_{LET} = L \Delta t \left[\max(0, r_L - r_K) \right] \qquad (4.13)$$

where

L is the notional amount exchanged
r_L is the floating rate between time t_i and t_{i+1}
r_C is the cap rate
$\Delta t = t_{i+1} - t_i$ is the tenor of the caplet.

The floorlet can be priced as

$$f_{LET} = L \Delta t \left[\max(0, r_F - r_L) \right]$$

where

r_F is the floor rate.

Example 4.7: Assume an investor holding a caplet on the six-month LIBOR rate with an expiry of 15 January 2013 struck at 2.7% with a notional of €1,000,000. If the LIBOR rate sets at 3.2% on 15 January, the investor receives

$$1,000,000 \times 0.5 \left[\max(0.032 - 0.027, 0) \right] = €2,500$$

Customarily the payment is made at the end of the rate period, in this case on 1 July 2013.

Interest rate derivatives, like caps and floors, can be valued using the Black model, developed by F. Black in 1976, and also known as the Black-76 model. It represents a modification of the standard BSM model, and allows us to price options on futures contracts as underlying. Therefore, the model is able to price a European option based not on the spot price of the underlying instrument, but on its future price.

Given the relationship between future price F and spot price S, described as

$$F = Se^{r_f T}$$

it follows that, substituting for it in the standard BSM formulas, the Black model formulas for the price of a call and put option in terms of the futures price of the underlying asset take the form

$$c_{76} = e^{-r_f T}\left[FN(d_1) - KN(d_2)\right]$$
$$p_{76} = e^{-r_f T}\left[KN(-d_2) - FN(-d_1)\right]$$

where

$$d_1 = \frac{\ln\left(\frac{F}{K}\right) + \frac{\sigma_F^2 T}{2}}{\sigma_F \sqrt{T}}$$

$$d_2 = \frac{\ln\left(\frac{F}{K}\right) - \frac{\sigma_F^2 T}{2}}{\sigma_F \sqrt{T}} = d_1 - \sigma_F \sqrt{T}$$

and

σ_F is the volatility of future price.

As mentioned above, each single caplet forming a cap can be evaluated using the Black model. Under the assumptions of the model, consider that the underlying rate has a lognormal distribution with volatility σ. Starting from equation (4.13), the present value of a caplet on LIBOR expiring at time t and paying at time T, is given by

$$c_{LET} = L\Delta t P(0, \Delta t)\left[F_L N(d_1) - r_K N(d_2)\right]$$

with

$$d_1 = \frac{\ln\left(\frac{F_L}{r_K}\right) + \frac{\sigma_L^2 \Delta t}{2}}{\sigma_L \sqrt{\Delta t}}$$

$$d_2 = \frac{\ln\left(\frac{F_L}{r_K}\right) - \frac{\sigma_L^2 \Delta t}{2}}{\sigma_L \sqrt{\Delta t}} = d_1 - \sigma_L \sqrt{\Delta t}$$

where

F_L is the forward price of the rate. For LIBOR rates this is given by equation (4.11)
$P(0, \Delta t)$ is the value today of a bond with face value 1, maturing at time T.
σ_L is the volatility of the underlying rate.

Accordingly, the floorlet has a value of

$$f_{LET} = L\Delta t P(0,T)\left[r_K N(-d_2) - F_L N(-d_1)\right]$$

There is a one-to-one relationship between volatility and the present value of the option. Therefore it is possible to quote the price of a caplet by simply quoting its volatility, which is exactly what happens in real markets.

Example 4.8: Consider a €10,000 loan and a contract that caps the interest rate on it at 8% per annum, for three months starting one year from now. The zero-curve is flat at 7% per annum and the volatility for the three-month rate underlying the caplet is 20% per annum. The continuously compounded zero rate for all maturities is 6.9394%. It follows that

$$F_k = 0.07,\ d_k = 0.25,\ L = 10,000,\ R_k = 0.08,$$
$$t_k = 1.0,\ t_{k+1} = 1.25,\ P(0,t_{k+1}) = e^{-0.069394\times1.25},\ \sigma_F = 0.20$$

$$d_1 = \frac{\ln\left(\dfrac{0.07}{0.08}\right) + \dfrac{0.2^2}{2}}{0.2\times1} = -0.57,\quad d_2 = d_1 - 0.2 = -0.77$$

so that the caplet price is

$$c_{LET} = 0.25\times10,000\times0.9169\left[0.07N(-0.57) - 0.08N(-0.77)\right] = €5.2$$

Each caplet must be valued separately, and the cap value is obtained by adding up all the caplets. The same applies to floors and floorlets.

There are two different approaches to the volatility to be input in the Black model. The spot volatility approach consists in using different volatilities for each caplet or floorlet, while the flat volatility approach implies using the same volatility for all caplets, but varying it according to the life of the cap.

4.3.3 Swaptions

A swaption is an option that gives the owner the right to enter into an underlying swap. The buyer of a payer swaption has the right to pay fixed and receive floating on the swap, while the buyer of a receiver swaption has the right to pay floating and receive fixed on the swap.

The right to receive fixed is the same as the right to pay floating, making a swaption analogous to foreign exchange options, where the call option in one currency is the same as the put option in the other currency.

Swaptions are useful to hedge risk on fixed income instruments. In particular they can be used to hedge call or put positions in bond issues, change the tenor of an underlying swap and change the payoff profile of the corporation.

The swaptions market is populated by large institutions, banks and hedge funds. Banks and corporation use swaptions to hedge their core business operations, buying payer swaptions to hedge against rise of interest rates, and receiver swaption to hedge against decreasing rates.

Major banks such as JP Morgan Chase, Bank of America and Citigroup are major market makers in the mostly traded currencies, trading amongst themselves in the swaption interbank market.

Market makers manage big portfolios of swaptions, traded with many counterparties. The exposure resulting from such a structure requires significant investments for monitoring.

Swaptions are traded on the OTC market, as an agreement between two counterparties to exchange the payments. The various counterparties are exposed to each other's failure to make scheduled payments on the underlying swap, but collateral agreements are typically used to mitigate that risk.

Suppose there are n coupon dates for the swap at $t_i = t_1, t_2, ..., t_n$, with equal reset dates on both sides. To derive a pricing formula, consider a swaption with expiration date T, corresponding to the start date of the swap expiring then at date t_n.

The cash flow paid to the buyer of a payer swaption at expiry date of the swaption is defined as

$$\begin{cases} L\sum_{i=1}^{n} e^{-r_f(t_i-T)}(r_s - r_k)(t_i - t_{i-1}) & \text{if } r_s > r_k \\ \\ 0 & \text{otherwise} \end{cases}$$

where

L is the notional principal
r_k is the strike rate
r_s is the market swap rate at time T
r_f is the risk-free rate.

The present value of the above cash flow, when different from zero, is

$$PV_S = e^{-r_f T} L\sum_{i=1}^{n} e^{-r_f(t_i-T)}(r_s - r_k)(t_i - t_{i-1})$$

$$= ...$$

(4.14)

$$= L\sum_{i=1}^{n} e^{-r_f t_i}(r_s - r_k)(t_i - t_{i-1})$$

Taking the i-th term from equation (4.14), this is equal to

$$\max\left[L(r_s - r_k)(t_i - t_{i-1}), 0\right]$$

The equation represents the typical structure of an option payoff. The Black model gives the price for such an option at time zero as

$$Le^{-r_f t_i}(t_i - t_{i-1})\left[r_s N(d_1) - r_k N(d_2)\right]$$

(4.15)

where

$$d_1 = \frac{\ln\left(\frac{r_s}{r_k}\right) + \frac{\sigma_s^2 T}{2}}{\sigma_s \sqrt{T}}$$

$$d_2 = \frac{\ln\left(\frac{r_s}{r_k}\right) - \frac{\sigma_s^2 T}{2}}{\sigma_s \sqrt{T}} = d_1 - \sigma_s \sqrt{T}$$

and

σ_s is the volatility of the swap rate.

An intuitive way to determine r_s for a swap with constant notional principal is through the formula

$$r_s = \frac{1 - e^{-r_f t_n}}{\sum_{k=1}^{n} e^{-r_f t_k}}$$

The price of a payer swaption PS is obtained by summing up all individual options (4.15) over all the tenors involved, so that

$$PS = L \sum_{i=1}^{n} e^{-r_f t_i} \left(t_i - t_{i-1}\right) \left[r_s N\left(d_1\right) - r_k N\left(d_2\right)\right]$$

For the receiver swaption, the same reasoning yields

$$RS = L \sum_{i=1}^{n} e^{-r_f t_i} \left(t_i - t_{i-1}\right) \left[r_k N\left(-d_2\right) - r_s N\left(-d_1\right)\right]$$

As for ordinary equity options, it is possible to express formulas also for the Greeks of swaptions, which turn out to be very similar to the previous ones.

Recall that the delta of an option is the sensitivity of the option to the changes of value of the underlying asset. In the case of a swaption, the underlying is the fixed forward swap rate r_s. Therefore the delta of a payer swaption δ_{PS} takes the form

$$\delta_{PS} = \frac{\partial PS}{\partial r_s}$$

$$= \ldots$$

$$= L \sum_{i=1}^{n} e^{-r_f t_i} \left(t_i - t_{i-1}\right) N\left(d_1\right)$$

The delta for a European receiver swaption is

$$\delta_{PS} = \frac{\partial RS}{\partial r_s}$$

$$= \ldots$$

$$= L \sum_{i=1}^{n} e^{-r_f t_i} \left(t_i - t_{i-1}\right) \left[N\left(d_1\right) - 1\right]$$

The gamma is the second derivative of the price of the option with respect to the underlying, or the first derivative of the delta with respect to the underlying. Therefore the gamma of a swaption is

$$
\begin{aligned}
\Gamma_{PS} &= \Gamma_{RS} \\
&= \frac{\partial^2 PS}{\partial r_s^2} \\
&= \dots \\
&= \frac{L \sum_{i=1}^{n} e^{-r_f t_i} \left(t_i - t_{i-1} \right) N'(d_1)}{\sqrt{T} r_s \sigma_s}
\end{aligned}
$$

Theta is the sensitivity of an option to the time to maturity. For a swaption it takes the form

$$
\begin{aligned}
\Theta_{PS} &= \Theta_{RS} \\
&= \frac{\partial PS}{\partial T} \\
&= \dots \\
&= -r_s PS + \frac{L \sum_{i=1}^{n} e^{-r_f t_i} \left(t_i - t_{i-1} \right) r_s \sigma_s N'(d_1)}{2\sqrt{T}}
\end{aligned}
$$

Finally, vega is the sensitivity of the option price to the volatility parameter. In the case of a payer swaption it is

$$
\begin{aligned}
V_{PS} &= V_{RS} \\
&= \frac{\partial PS}{\partial \sigma_S} \\
&= \dots \\
&= L \sum_{i=1}^{n} e^{-r_f t_i} \left(t_i - t_{i-1} \right) r_s \sqrt{T} N'(d_1)
\end{aligned}
$$

Summary

Several types of traders populate financial markets, classified according to the purpose of their investment strategies. They can be distinguished with respect to the use they make of the money they invest.

Financial derivatives are a powerful tool for both hedging and speculation, being useful also to exploit arbitrage opportunities. Among the types of traders in the market, arbitrageurs enhance the discovery of prices, hedgers trade for business and economical purposes, and speculators are gamblers, providing liquidity and depth to the market.

Financial derivatives are priced in relation to an underlying asset they are written on, and help managing financial risks, given market conditions and expectations of the investors.

An option gives the right to trade on some underlying asset, at maturity of the option, or sometimes before, at some pre-specified conditions. The two major classes of options are call options and put options.

The pricing of derivatives can be done in several ways, one being through binomial trees, which are based on the assumption that stock price movements are made of a large number of small binomial steps.

The Black-Scholes-Merton model for option pricing is a key concept in modern financial theory. The model aims at producing the theoretical price of European put and call options.

Originally developed under strict assumptions, without taking into consideration the dividends paid by the stock, and with other simplifications, the model can be adapted after derivation, to relax many of the original assumptions, and price a wider range of instruments.

Interest rate swaps are meant to exchange payments based on a defined principal amount, for a fixed period of time. There is no actual exchange of the principal amount, but only exchange of interest rate payments.

Swaptions give the owner the right to enter into an underlying swap, at pre-specified conditions. A payer swaption gives the buyer the right to get a fixed payment and receive a floating one, on the swap, and the opposite holds for a receiver swaption.

Bibliography

Avellaneda, M. and Laurence, P. 2000. *Quantitative Modeling of Derivative Securities*. Chapman & Hall/CRC.

Batten, J.A., Fetherston, T.A. and Szilagyi, P.G. 2004. *European Fixed Income Markets: Money, Bond, and Interest Rate Derivatives*. John Wiley & Sons, Inc.

Baxter, M. and Rennie, A. 2006. *Financial Calculus: An Introduction to Derivative Pricing*. Cambridge University Press.

Black, F. 1976. The Pricing of Commodity Contracts. *Journal of Financial Economics*, 3: 167–179.

Black, F. and Scholes, M. 1973. The Pricing of Options and Corporate Liabilities. *Journal of Political Economy*, 81(3): 637–654.

Capinski, M. and Zastawniak, T. 2003. *Mathematics for Finance: An Introduction to Financial Engineering*. Springer Undergraduate Mathematics Series. Springer-Verlag.

Chance, D.M. and Brooks, R. 2008. *An Introduction to Derivatives and Risk Management*. 7th Edition. Thompson South-Western Publishers.

Choudhry, M. 2005. *Fixed-Income Securities and Derivatives Handbook: Analysis and Valuation*. Bloomberg Press.

Cox, J.C., Ross, S.A. and Rubinstein, M. 1979. Option Pricing: A Simplified Approach. *Journal of Financial Economics*, 7(3).

Epps, T.W. 2007. *Pricing Derivative Securities*. 2nd Edition. World Scientific Publishing Co. Pte. Ltd.

Gardner, D.C. (ed.). 1996. *Introduction to Swaps*. London, Pitman Publishing.

Grossman, S.J. and Stiglitz, J. 1980. On the Impossibility of Informationally Efficient Markets. *American Economic Review*, 70 (3): 393–408.

Hull, J.C. 2005. *Options, Futures, and Other Derivative Securities*. 6th Edition. Prentice Hall.

Hull, J.C. and White, A. 1999. *Forward Rate Volatilities, Swap Rate Volatilities, and the Implementation of the Libor Market Model*. Working Paper. University of Toronto.

Hunt, P.J. and Kennedy, J.E. 2000. *Financial Derivatives in Theory and Practice*. John Wiley & Sons, Inc.

Kolb, R.W. and Overdahl, J.A. 2003. *Financial Derivatives*. 3rd Edition. John Wiley & Sons, Inc.

Neftci, S.N. 2000. *An Introduction to the Mathematics of Financial Derivatives*. Academic Press.

Shreve, S.E. 2004. *Stochastic Calculus for Finance I: The Binomial Asset Pricing Model.* Springer Finance.
Shreve, S.E. 2005. *Stochastic Calculus for Finance II: Continuous Time Models.* Springer Finance.
Smith, D. 1991. A Simple Method for Pricing Interest Rate Swaptions. *Financial Analysts Journal,* May–June: 72–76.
Tirole, J. 1982. On the Possibility of Speculation under Rational Expectations. *Econometrica,* 50: 1163–1182.
Williams, D. 1991. *Probability with Martingales.* Cambridge University Press.
Wilmott, P., Howison, S. and Dewynne, J. 1996. *The Mathematics of Financial Derivatives.* Press Syndicate of the University of Cambridge.

Exercises

Questions

1. Carefully explain the difference between selling a call option and buying a put option, in terms of payoff.
2. Why is the expected loss from a default on a swap less than the expected loss from the default on a loan with the same principal?
3. List the main factors that affect stock option prices.
4. Why is the early exercise of an American call option on a non-dividend-paying stock never optimal?
5. What happens to the value of a down-and-out call option when increasing the frequency with which asset price is observed to determine whether the barrier has been crossed? What is the answer to the same question for a down-and-in call?
6. What position is equivalent to a long forward contract to buy an asset at K on a certain date and a put option to sell it for K on that date?
7. What does it mean, in common terminology, that an option is in-the-money, at-the-money or out-of-the-money?
8. In order for a derivatives market to function most efficiently, two types of economic agents, hedgers and speculators, are needed. Explain why.
9. Most futures positions closed out through a reverse trade rather than closed out at delivery. Explain why.

Problems

1. Consider a stock meant to pay a dividend of €0.10 per share in 3 months and 9 months from now. With no other dividend payments within the next 12 months, the interest rate is 5% with continuous compounding.
   a. Calculate the 12-month forward price of the stock if the current market price is €20 per share.
2. Using the data in exercise 1, assume an investor entering a forward contract to buy 100 shares of the stock in one year.
   a. What is the value of the forward contract today?
   b. What is its value in six months, provided the stock is then traded at €18 per share?

3. Assume the current stock price is €27, and a three-month call with a strike price of €28 costs €2.65. You have €6,500 to invest.
    a. Describe two alternative speculation strategies, one in the stock and the other in the option on the stock.
    b. What are the potential gains and losses from each strategy?

4. Prove that the price of a call option satisfies the BSM PDE.

5. Prove that the solutions for the BSM Greeks satisfy the PDE.

6. Companies A and B have been offered the following rates per annum on a five-year loan of €20,000,000:

	Fixed rate	Floating rate
Company A	12.0%	Libor + 0.1%
Company B	13.4%	Libor + 0.6%

Company A requires a floating-rate loan while company B requires a fixed-rate loan.
    a. Design a swap contract netting the 0.1% per annum to the intermediary bank, that will appear equally attractive to both companies.

7. Consider a binomial world in which a stock, over the next year, can go up in value by 20% (by a subjective probability of 55%) or down by 10% (by a subjective probability of 45%). The stock is currently trading at €10. The risk-free return is 5%. Consider a call that expires in one year, with a strike price of €11.
    a. What is the value of the call option?
    b. If the call option was trading for €0.32, can you find an arbitrage opportunity?
    c. If the call option was trading for €0.61, can you find an arbitrage opportunity?

8. Consider a European call option, which is written on a stock whose current value is €8, with the strike price €9 and expiration date in one month. Assume for simplicity that one month later, when the option can be exercised, the stock price can either appreciate to €10 or depreciate to €6. Assume that the risk-free interest rate is zero.
    a. What is the current price of the call option?

9. Suppose that the strike price of an American call option on a non-dividend-paying stock grows at some constant rate g.
    a. Show that if g is less than the risk-free rate, r, it is never optimal to exercise the call early.

10. You would like to speculate on a rise in the price of a certain stock. The current stock price is €29, and a three-month call with a strike price of €30 costs €2.90. You have €5,800 to invest. Identify two alternative investment strategies, one in the stock and the other in an option on the stock. What are the potential gains and losses from each?

11. Consider a binomial world in which a stock, over the next year, can go up in value by 50% (subjective probability of 60%) or down by 33.33% (subjective probability of 40%). The stock is currently trading at €50. The risk-free return is 5%.

a. What is the value of the call option that expires in one year with a strike price of €55?
b. Calculate the expected return from the stock.
c. Is the expected return on the call option higher or lower?

12. For a European put option on a stock with one year to expiry, the stock price is €50, the strike is €50, risk-free interest rate is 4%, dividend is 4% and the price of the option is €6.22. Determine the implied volatility of the stock.

13. Prove that, using this binomial tree, we can find the price of any contingent claim. In other words, any contract paying $h(S_1)$ where h is any function of S_1.

14. Consider options on two different assets (asset 1 and asset 2). Would you prefer to have two different options, one on each asset (with the same strike price K), or would you prefer to own an option on the portfolio of the two assets with a strike of $2K$?

15. Prove that the put-call parity formula for the American options with dividends is:

$$S_0 - D - K \leq C - P \leq S_0 - Ke^{-rT}$$

16. Use the put-call parity relationship to derive, for a non-dividend-paying stock, the relationship between:
a. The delta of a European call and the delta of a European put.
b. The gamma of a European call and the gamma of a European put.
c. The vega of a European call and the vega of a European put.
d. The theta of a European call and the theta of a European put.

Appendix: The market price of risk

The market price of risk is the excess return on the risk-free rate needed to compensate investors bearing risk on the market. In derivatives theory quantities are modelled as stochastic, and randomness leads to risk. The purpose of financial analysis is to determine how much extra return an investor should expect for taking risk.

In the BSM option pricing model the market price of risk is not directly expressed, given that risk in an option position can be hedged away by taking a position on the underlying asset. This is the basis of risk-neutral valuation.

In order to derive the market price of risk it is necessary to consider two different derivatives written on the same underlying variable. Consider the properties of derivatives dependent on the value of a single variable θ, following the stochastic process

$$d\theta = \mu_\theta \theta dt + \sigma_\theta \theta dW$$

where $\mu_\theta m$ and σ_θ are the expected growth rate and volatility of θ respectively. It is assumed that the parameters depend only on the variable itself and the time.

The process of any derivative v_i written on θ, according to Itô's Lemma is

$$dv_i = \left(\frac{\partial v_i}{\partial \theta}\mu_\theta \theta + \frac{\partial v_i}{\partial t} + \frac{1}{2}\frac{\partial^2 v_i}{\partial \theta^2}\sigma_\theta^2 \theta^2\right)dt + \left(\frac{\partial v_i}{\partial \theta}\sigma_\theta \theta\right)dW$$
$$= m_i dt + s_i dW$$

Define the process for $\varsigma_i = \ln v_i$ and apply again Itô's Lemma to get

$$d\varsigma_i = \left(\frac{1}{v_i}m_i - \frac{1}{2v_i^2}s_i^2\right)dt + \left(\frac{1}{v_i}m_i\right)dW$$
$$= \mu_i dt + \sigma_i dW$$

Consider the above process for two derivatives

$$d\varsigma_1 = \mu_1 dt + \sigma_1 dW$$
$$d\varsigma_2 = \mu_2 dt + \sigma_2 dW$$

The next step is to form a portfolio V of relative weights w_1 and w_2 of the two derivatives, with weights summing up to one. Letting Π denote the natural log of the portfolio value, the process followed by $d\Pi$

$$d\Pi = \left(w_1\mu_1 + w_2\mu_2\right)dt + \left(w_1\sigma_1 + w_2\sigma_2\right)dW$$

In order to investigate the risk premium it is crucial to know under what circumstances the above portfolio is riskless. Choosing values

$$w_1 = -\frac{\sigma_2}{\sigma_1 - \sigma_2}$$
$$w_2 = \frac{\sigma_1}{\sigma_1 - \sigma_2}$$

the portfolio process becomes

$$d\Pi = \left(\frac{\sigma_1}{\sigma_1 - \sigma_2}\mu_2 - \frac{\sigma_2}{\sigma_1 - \sigma_2}\mu_1\right)dt + \left(\frac{\sigma_1}{\sigma_1 - \sigma_2}\sigma_2 - \frac{\sigma_2}{\sigma_1 - \sigma_2}\sigma_1\right)dW$$

The term in dW vanishes and the volatility of the process is shown to be zero. The process is then left with just the drift, and in order for the portfolio to be riskless, the drift must be equal to the risk-free rate

$$\frac{\sigma_1}{\sigma_1 - \sigma_2}\mu_2 - \frac{\sigma_2}{\sigma_1 - \sigma_2}\mu_1 = r$$

which implies

$$\frac{\mu_1 - r}{\sigma_1} = \frac{\mu_2 - r}{\sigma_2} = \lambda$$

The parameter λ is the market price of risk of the underlying variable θ. It is independent on the single derivatives and must be the same for all the claims written on the same underlying variable.

It measures the trade-off between risk and return associated with a variable. The excess return can be expressed as the product of the quantity of risk, σ, and its price λ.

It is also called the Sharpe ratio, and is used to assess the level of compensation obtained by the investor for the risk taken.

The Sharpe ratio is useful to compare two assets with different returns and volatility. The asset with the higher ratio gives a higher return in proportion of the risk taken to hold it, therefore representing a better investment opportunity. A good investment strategy is to pick investments with high Sharpe ratios. However, like any mathematical model it relies on the data being correct.

From the risk premium formula derived above, the relation between the risk premium demanded by investors, in terms of excess return, for holding derivative i and the price of risk can be written as

$$\mu_i - r = \lambda \sigma_i$$

Thus, the derivative's risk premium can be interpreted as the market price of risk λ, times the amount of risk derivative i holds, σ_i.

Recall the process followed by any derivative v is

$$dv = \mu v dt + \sigma v dW$$

The assumption in the traditional risk-neutral world is that investors do not demand any compensation for the risk taken, so that the market price of risk is zero. Consequently $\mu = r$, and the process followed by r is

$$dv = rv dt + \sigma v dW$$

It is now possible to describe other words, each one characterized by a specific level of the market price of risk. Generalizing the framework, the growth rate of the process drift can be written as

$$\mu = r + \lambda \sigma$$

so that

$$dv = (r + \lambda \sigma) v dt + \sigma v dW$$

The market price of risk of a variable determines the growth rates of all the securities dependent on that variable.

5 Market risk

Market risk is the risk of losses in a portfolio or trading book, due to changes in the price of the securities included in the portfolio. Reference price may range from equity prices, interest rates, credit spreads, foreign-exchange rates, commodity prices, and other indicators whose values are set in a public market.

Banks have developed various tools to manage market risk. The most popular among them is the Value-at-Risk (VaR) analysis, which has become a well-established standard in the industry over the past 20 years, as a regulatory standard in measuring market risk.

The analysis is also subject to a quantitative analysis based on short-term data. In any case, the main idea behind VaR is that extreme losses are less likely to happen, but are much more dangerous in case of an event occurring.

The adoption of the Basel II Accord starting from 1999 established a worldwide standard for market risk measurement and gave further impetus to the use of VaR as a preferred measure of market risk.

In the last few years, further methods have been developed to overtake the limitations of VaR, giving a new input to the science of financial risk management, and overcoming some weaknesses of traditional measures.

After studying this chapter you will be able to answer the following questions, among others:

1. What is market risk and how can it be measured through quantile metrics?
2. What is the rationale of Value-at-Risk as a quantile metric?
3. How can VaR be calculated? What are the three possible approaches to VaR estimation?
4. How can VaR be decomposed to capture the effects of adding new positions to the target portfolio?
5. What are the analytical approximations of VaR?

The first section of the chapter gives an overview of market risk, with an introduction to the concept of risk metrics and quantile measures. The second section is about the description of linear VaR, and how it can be measured using different methods. The final section deals with advances in VaR analysis, including its main limitations and an introduction to alternative measurement methods.

5.1 Market risk metrics

Learning outcomes

1. Give an overview of market risk.
2. Describe quantile metrics and their application to market risk.
3. Define and comment on the VaR rationale and expectation.

5.1.1 Overview of market risk

Market risk is the risk arising from movements in financial market prices, reflecting the uncertainty as to an asset's price when it is sold. The specificity of market risks depends on what type of asset is under consideration.

The approach to be used in assessing market risk depends on the distributional property of the data, and on the linearity (or non-linearity) of the dependence of portfolio to variations in market prices.

When the assumption of normality is accepted, it is reasonable to assume that market movements follow the normal distribution, and standard statistical tools can be employed. But when positions do not change linearly with changes in market prices it is better to use simulation techniques, compared to analytic approaches.

In case both normality and linearity hold, it is appropriate to use standard risk measures, otherwise it is the case to use scenario analysis combined with simulation techniques.

The introduction of financial derivatives makes most portfolios non-linear, so that a combination of statistical tools and simulation is likely to be the most effective risk measurement approach.

Financial data for market risk measurement come in the form of profit-loss (P&L) data. The P&L of a portfolio can be defined as the excess value generated, over a period t, plus intermediate payments. Therefore it can be expressed as

$$P/L_t = V_t + d_t - V_{t-1} \tag{5.1}$$

where

V_t is the portfolio value at time t
V_{t-1} is the portfolio value at time $t-1$
d_t is the amount of intermediate payments between $t-1$ and t.

Positive values indicate a profit and negative values indicate losses but formula (5.1) does not take into account any time value effect. In order to take time value into consideration, it is more appropriate to define P&L as

$$P/L_t = (V_t + d_t)e^{-r_{\Delta t}\Delta t} - V_{t-1}$$

where

$r_{\Delta t}$ is the appropriate discount rate between $t-1$ and t.
Δt is the time interval between $t-1$ and t.

An alternative formulation takes the value of P&L evaluated at the end of period t.

$$F\left(P/L\right)_t = V_t + d_t - e^{r_d \Delta t} V_{t-1}$$

Differences between the two measures depend on the discount rate and for short periods will be relatively small. In practice, those differences are often ignored, but in theory they can sometimes matter.

When using measures for market risk, like Value-at-Risk, it is usually more convenient to invert the analysis and express the data in terms of losses and profits (L/P), with the simple transformation

$$L/P_t = -\left(P/L_t\right)$$

It is therefore sufficient to change signs, to invert the distribution and assign positive values to losses, and negative values to profits. That kind of transformation allows the implementation of the VaR measure, among others.

Data can also come in the form of arithmetic returns, defined as

$$r_{A,t} = \frac{\left(V_t + D_t - V_{t-1}\right)}{V_{t-1}}$$

which is equivalent to the P&L distribution normalized by the value of the portfolio at time $t-1$.

The arithmetic returns formula implies that the intermediate payment D_t does not earn any further return on its own, so that compounding is not considered. This assumption is valid only on very short terms, since over longer terms the income is usually reinvested, and gains some interest.

In order to account for the compounded return earned on the intermediate payments, returns can be expressed in geometric form as

$$r_{G,t} = \log\left[\frac{\left(V_t + D_t\right)}{V_{t-1}}\right]$$

Considering the return at which the intermediate payments are invested, it is possible to write

$$r_{G,t} = \frac{\left(V_t + D_t\right)}{V_{t-1}} - 1$$

which in turns yield that

$$R_{G,t} = 1 + r_{G,t}$$

so that, for small values, the two returns almost converge. In that case the difference is negligible, especially for a short horizon period.

The advantages of geometric returns over arithmetic returns are that they ensure portfolio value is always non-negative, and bounded. For very low values, arithmetic returns imply negative asset values, which does not make any sense economically.

On the other hand, a very low geometric return implies the asset price to converge to zero, but remaining always positive. Over long time horizons geometric returns allow for taking return compounding into account, therefore yielding more accurate measures.

5.1.2 Quantile metrics and Value-at-Risk

The quantile of a continuous random variable x is a real number such that

$$\Pr(x < x_\alpha) = \alpha$$

Knowing the distribution function $F(x)$ of the random variable, the quantile x_α corresponding to the quantile α can be defined as

$$x_\alpha = F^{-1}(\alpha)$$

Given the α-quantile of the return distribution, the probability of getting a lower return is exactly α.

Example 5.1: Suppose the 5% quantile of a distribution of returns is equal to -0.03. It means that there is a 95% certainty that returns will not be lower than -3%. When α is small, the quantile becomes then a downside risk metric.

When dealing with market risk, the variable X is assumed to be an observation on the P&L distribution, and $\alpha\%$ is assumed to be a small probability so that the α-quantile represents the loss to be not exceeded with $(1-\alpha)\%$ confidence.

The distribution of returns already implies a time frequency, which is the chosen one to measure the market risk. For example, the measurement of returns can be daily, weekly or monthly, according to the purpose of measurement.

Suppose that returns are i.i.d. normally distributed, with mean μ and standard deviation σ. Then, for any $\alpha \in (0,1)$, applying the standard normal transformation gives

$$\Pr(x < x_\alpha) = \Pr\left(\frac{x - \mu}{\sigma} < \frac{x_\alpha - \mu}{\sigma}\right)$$
$$= \Pr\left(z < \frac{x_\alpha - \mu}{\sigma}\right)$$
$$= \alpha$$

where Z is the transformed standardized normal variable.

Example 5.2: Consider a series of returns, normally distributed with mean 8% and standard deviation 20% then the probability of a return being less than 4% is given by

$$\Pr(x < 0.04) = \Pr\left(\frac{x - 0.08}{0.2} < \frac{0.04 - 0.08}{0.2}\right)$$
$$= \Pr(z < -0.2) = 0.42$$

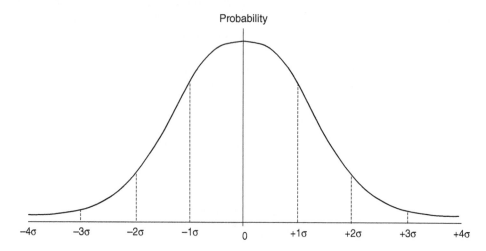

Figure 5.1 The figure shows the corresponding VaR at the 99% level of confidence. In this case, the VaR is determined by the cut-off between the top 99% and bottom 1% of observations, so we are dealing with a 1% tail rather than the earlier 5% tail. In this case, the cut-off point is approximately −2.33, so the VaR is 2.33.

given the fact that −0.2 is the 42% quantile of the standard normal distribution

Example 5.3: Consider a fund with normally distributed future active returns, expected to be 3% in the next year. The standard deviation of the expected active return is assumed to be 5%. The probability of underperforming the benchmark by 2% or more over the next year is given by

$$\Pr(x < -0.02) = \Pr\left(\frac{x - 0.03}{0.05} < \frac{-0.02 - 0.03}{0.05}\right)$$
$$= \Pr(z < -1) = 0.1587$$

There is a 15.87% probability to underperform the benchmark by 2% or more.

The quantile of a distribution is a risk metric that is closely related to VaR. The quantiles are sensitive to changes in the returns that are greater than the target or threshold return, in a symmetric way.

The quantile is affected by positive returns as well as negative returns, which is not necessarily a desirable property for a risk metric, that should focus more on the downside risk.

Anyway, quantiles are mathematically easy to handle and, for every $y = f(x)$, continuous, always non-decreasing function of x, the α-quantile of y is just

$$y_\alpha = f(x_\alpha)$$

where

y_α is the α-quantile of the distribution of y.

There is a bi-univocal relationship between the quantiles of the originary random distribution and the quantiles of the functional distribution associated with it. Assuming that $y = \ln(x)$ and the 1% quantile of x is (for simplicity) equal to 1, then the 1% quantile of the transformed variable y is equal to

$$VaR_y = \ln(VaR_x)$$
$$= \ln(1)$$
$$= 0$$

Downside risk can be measured by the appropriate quantiles of the distributions, defined as values q, limiting an area on their left, representing a given probability p, which is defined as

$$p = \Pr(x \geq q)$$
$$= \int_q^\infty f(x)dx$$
$$= 1 - F(q)$$

Every distribution has specific values for its quantiles, and values are usually summarized in specific tables, like in the case of the normal distribution. Being able to read the table of the normal distribution is a fundamental exercise for any course of studies in finance.

On the other side of the distribution, an important measure, which is complementary to the previous one, is the conditional expected value, defined as

$$E(x \mid x < q) = \frac{\displaystyle\int_{-\infty}^q xf(x)dx}{\displaystyle\int_{-\infty}^q f(x)dx} \qquad (5.2)$$

which gives the additional information on the average size of the loss, when the cut-off quantile is exceeded. This calculation is the basis of the so-called expected shortfall (ES), conditional loss (CL), or expected tail loss (ETL).

The expected shortfall measure is dealt with in Chapter 12, and it is proposed often as an alternative to VaR, showing better properties. ES tells us how much we could lose on average if the measured returns go beyond VaR.

Note that in the case of a standard normal distribution, equation (5.2) takes the form

$$E(x \mid x < -\alpha) = \frac{-N(\alpha)}{F(-\alpha)}$$

Example 5.4: Given the properties of the normal distribution, the conditional expected value below zero is

$$E(x \mid x < -\alpha) = \frac{-\left(\dfrac{1}{\sqrt{2\pi}}e^0\right)}{\dfrac{1}{2}} = -0.8$$

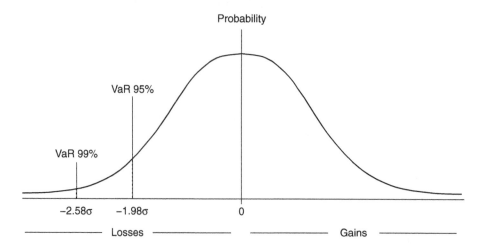

Figure 5.2 Value-at-Risk can be calculated for several confidence intervals.

Value-at-Risk is based on two parameters

- the significance level α (confidence level);
- the time horizon, commonly denoted by *h*, which is the period of time, usually trading days, over which the VaR is measured.

VaR tells what is the maximum expected loss that a firm may suffer over a period of time that has been specified by the user, under normal market conditions and a specified level of confidence.

There are several methodologies to calculate the measure, from historical data, through analytical approach, or by computer simulation.

If the daily VaR with a 99% confidence level for a given position is €1,000,000, it means that during the day there is a 1% probability that the loss in the next day will be higher than €1,000,000.

The measure requires estimation of volatility and correlation between market prices of different positions in a portfolio, and aims at measuring possible losses under normal circumstances.

A common assumption is that financial returns follow a normal distribution, and the measurement is achieved by collecting in a central database all the positions of a firm, and aggregating them into a portfolio.

The significance level to be used is commonly set by regulators. For regulatory purposes this period is at least one year. Hence the data on which VaR estimates are based should capture all relevant daily market moves over the previous year.

Basel II Accord, and Basel III more recently, give freedom to banks that meet certain requirements, to use their own internal model for VaR calculation. In assessing their market risk capital requirement they should measure VaR at the 99% confidence level.

The risk horizon represents the time period over which the exposure to the position holds. Under the Basel banking regulations it is normally ten days.

5.1.3 VaR rationale and definition

Risk managers at a desk level are mostly concerned about liquid market risk, so that they focus on daily risk horizon, while extending it to ten days when an internal VaR model is used to assess risk capital for regulatory purposes. Internal capital allocation requires usually a very long time horizon, of about a year.

As for the time horizon, also the confidence level depends on the application considered. VaR can be used to assess the probability of company insolvency, which depends on its capitalization and risk over a long horizon, of six months to a year.

The confidence level is as well linked on the purpose of the analysis. Market risk is usually measured at a 99% confidence level, but companies aiming at getting a very good rating will then set a higher confidence level so to account for a very low probability of default.

As mentioned above, the Basel Accord allows banks to use an internal VaR model, if they meet some specific requirements. In this case a 99% confidence level must be applied to the VaR model for assessing potential losses over a ten-day (two financial weeks) time horizon. The resulting figure is then multiplied by a factor of approximately $k \approx 3$, to obtain the market risk capital requirement.

The rationale behind the value determined by the regulators is the application of the Chebyshev's inequality to VaR measure, generating an upper bound. The probability for a variable x of falling outside some interval is given by

$$\Pr\left(|x-\mu| > z\sigma\right) \le \frac{1}{z^2}$$

where

μ is the mean of the distribution
σ is the standard deviation of the distribution
z is the standard normal deviate (score).

By symmetry of the normal distribution and assuming the population value of the standard deviation is known, it holds that

$$\Pr\left[(x-\mu) < -z\sigma\right] \le \frac{1}{2z^2} \tag{5.3}$$

which defines the upper boundary for the VaR, defined as

$$VaR_{max} = z\sigma$$

From equation (5.3) the value of a 99% VaR is equal to setting a percentile of 1%, which leads to the calculation as

$$0.01 = \frac{1}{2z^2}$$

and to the solution

$$z(0.99) = 7.07$$

Consider a bank reporting a 99% VaR based on normality assumption. The parametric calculation yields

$$VaR_{99\%} = 2.33\sigma$$

The correction factor can then be calculated by the ratio of the upper bound VaR and the misspecified VaR, so that

$$
\begin{aligned}
k &= \frac{VaR_{max}}{VaR_{99\%}} \\
&= \frac{7.07\sigma}{2.33\sigma} \\
&= 3.03
\end{aligned}
$$

For trading purposes, risk managers work with a much lower confidence level, and a shorter time horizon, because they necessitate, for their activity, a quicker, more frequent (even if less accurate) assessment of risk.

Many institutions work on a second scrutiny basis, setting higher confidence levels for the desks and traders that constantly exceed their VaR limits. A higher confidence level than 95% or a longer risk horizon than one day may give traders too much freedom.

VaR calculation is based on the assumption that the position remains static over time, and risk is assessed at the end of the period. However, positions in a portfolio are continuously adjusted, and the realized P&L accounts for the adjustments in positions and the costs of trades.

In order for the measurement to be accurate, it is therefore essential to express all P&L in terms of present value, discounting all cash flows at the relevant risk-free rate for the period under consideration.

Denote the value of the portfolio at t by V_t and its discounted value after n days as PV_{t+J}. the discounted theoretical P&L over a risk horizon of n trading days is

$$P/L_n = PV_{t+n} - V$$

The future value at time $t+h$ is uncertain, not observable so that the P&L is a random variable. It is then crucial to measure the distribution of that variable, in order to calculate the VaR of the portfolio.

Portfolio P&L is a random variable, so that nothing can be said about it for sure, but a guess can be made, according to some specific confidence level. So a 99% daily VaR is the maximum loss level that we expect to exceed with no more than 1% probability, when holding a portfolio for 24 hours.

Example 5.5: If a VaR measurement is taken, yielding a 5% daily VaR of €1,850,000, there is a 95% probability that the loss on the portfolio will be above the measured VaR, when holding the portfolio for one day.

In distributional terms, a loss is a negative return, and the $\alpha\%$ VaR is the $\alpha\%$ quantile of the discounted P&L distribution (or the $(1-\alpha)\%$ quantile, when looking at the symmetric distribution of L&P).

In terms of frequency the 5% VaR of a weekly discounted P&L distribution is the loss to be incurred and exceeded every 20 days. Assuming the distribution is centred on a zero-excess return, the distribution has zero mean.

The estimation of the n-day VaR at time t is given by the α-quantile, $q_{n,\alpha}$ of the discounted P&L distribution, satisfying the condition

$$\Pr\left(PV_{t+n} - V_t < q_{n,\alpha}\right) = \alpha$$
$$\mathrm{VaR}_{n,\alpha} = -q_{n,\alpha}$$

where

PV_{t+} is the discounted value of the portfolio at time $t+n$.

VaR is expressed in dollar terms, making it a straightforward measure of the potential loss on a portfolio, which is very appealing and easy to understand for top management.

Measuring VaR from P&L distribution is a possible way, but many practitioners prefer to work with returns, because the latter are more of a relative measure, which is independent of the portfolio size at the time of measurement, while P&L is an absolute measure, taken in absolute terms.

The discounted n-day return on a portfolio can be defined as

$$r_{n,t} = \frac{PV_{t+n} - V_t}{V_t}$$

and the α-quantile $x_{n,\alpha}$ of the related distribution satisfies the condition

$$\Pr\left(r_{n,t} < x_{n,\alpha}\right) = \alpha$$
$$\mathrm{VaR}_{n,\alpha} = -x_{n,\alpha}$$

The VaR estimate can be also expressed in value terms by multiplying for the portfolio value, so that

$$VaR_{n,\alpha} = -x_{n,\alpha}V_t$$

Snapshot 5.1
The choice of parameters for VaR

VaR accuracy is based on the right choice of parameters. Recall that a common assumption is that the change in portfolio over time is normally distributed, leading to the formula:

$$VaR = N^{-1}(\alpha)\sigma$$

where
α is the confidence level.

Regardless of the time horizon, in its simplest form the VaR for a particular confidence level is proportional to the volatility.

Banks trading desks usually calculate VaR daily and update portfolios accordingly. Investment funds recalculate their positions monthly, because of the less active trading involved.

For market risks a one-day period is always chosen, scaling then according to

$$VaR_{T-day} = VaR_{1-day}\sqrt{T}$$

Changes in the portfolio from one day to the next are not totally independent. Define ΔP_i as the change in value of a portfolio on day i.

The above formula is only accurate under the assumption of absence of auto-correlation of financial returns on which the volatility is measured.

In case a first order autocorrelation is assumed, the variance of $\Delta P_{i-1} + \Delta P_i$ can be written as

$$\sigma_{\Delta P}^2 = \sigma^2 + \sigma^2 + 2\rho\sigma^2 = 2(1+\rho)\sigma^2$$

where

ρ is the correlation between ΔP_{i-} and ΔP_i.

Generalizing, the correlation between ΔP_{i-j} and ΔP_i is ρ^j, leading to a formula for the variance of the sum of ΔP_i over time $\sum_{j=1}^{T} \Delta P_i$, which is given by

$$\sigma_{\sum \Delta P}^2 = \sigma^2 \left[T + 2(T-1)\rho + 2(T-2)\rho^2 + ... + 2\rho^{T-1} \right]$$

which assumes standard normal distribution of the daily changes in the portfolio of returns.

5.2 VaR calculation methods

Learning outcomes

1. Describe the historical simulation approach to VaR.
2. Describe the parametric approach to VaR.
3. Define Monte Carlo simulation approach to VaR.

5.2.1 Historical simulation approach

There are three main methods for calculating VaR. As with all statistical models, they depend on certain assumptions, the parametric method, historical simulation and Monte Carlo simulation.

The easiest way to estimate VaR is the historical simulation method, relying on the empirical distribution of observed past P&L. After the observations are ordered in magnitude, the distribution is cut at the desired quantile.

In the case of a 95% VaR estimation, with 100 observations available, the confidence level implies a 5% tail. It means that for 100 observations, there are five observations in the tail, and the VaR is then determined as the sixth highest observation.

The relevant quantile is determined by how data are ordered. In case of an L/P distribution, the opposite tail will have to be cut in order to get the VaR measure. More generally, with n observations, and a confidence level of α, the relevant observation is the highest observation defined as

$$VaR_{\alpha,n} = (1-\alpha)n + 1$$

Historical simulation method implicitly assumes that the approach is totally free of any distributional assumption. VaR is determined by the actual price movements, without underlying assumptions of normality driving the conclusion.

Another assumption is that observations in the time series are equally weighted when it comes to measuring the VaR. This can be problematic if there is a trend in the variability making it different over time.

The last important assumption is that the historical simulation approach implicitly relies on history repeating itself, with the observed time period providing a full picture of the risks that the various markets could be exposed to in the future.

On the other hand, most of the assumptions of the approach also constitute its weaknesses. In particular, the strong linkage with the history of data represents a point of vulnerability of the model, especially if one doubts the past could repeat itself.

Another issue is about the equal weighting of the observations, which is controversial because it assumes that the more recent data could play a more important role than the very old ones. If volatility shows an increasing trend, even within the historical time period, the analysis will then understate the Value-at-Risk.

The strict relationship with the past data also implies another bug in the approach, namely the difficulty of adaptation to the new form new risks and assets, for the obvious reason that no historical data are available to compute the Value-at-Risk.

Shortly, the historical simulation approach relieves the scientist from the trouble (and related problems) of making specific distributional assumptions, at the cost of assuming that the distribution of past returns can efficiently represent the expected future returns. In a highly volatile market, characterized by structural shifts occurring at regular intervals, this assumption is difficult to sustain.

In order to overcome some of the above limitations, modifications have been suggested. The most obvious relate to the weighting scheme of the data, following the argument that returns in the recent past can better predict the future, rather than returns from the distant past.

Boudoukh *et al.* present a framework where each return, rather than being weighted equally, is assigned a probability p based on how recent the observation is. For a weighting factor λ, the observations, for the time from t backward, are weighted as

$$t \rightarrow \lambda p$$
$$t-1 \rightarrow \lambda^2 p$$
$$t-2 \rightarrow \lambda^3 p$$
...

approaching zero as time approaches zero (the first observation in the past).

Other methods suggest combining historical simulation with time series models. The idea is to get better estimates of VaR by fitting time series models through the historical data and using the parameters of that model to forecast the VaR.

Empirical works have been done using ARMA (auto regressive moving average) models, fitting the predicted bounds in a better way. Such an improvement is that data fitting makes the VaR more sensitive to changes in the variance of prices (or returns), than with standard historical simulation.

Hull and White (1998) suggest an innovative updating method for historical data. They simply suggest adjusting the historical data to the observed current volatility, when considerably different.

Such an approach involves estimating variance on a day-specific basis over the historical time period. Hull and White use a GARCH model for variance estimation, which allows recent shifts to be captured that are underweighted by the conventional approach.

5.2.2 Parametric method

The parametric approach to VaR is based on assumptions on the distribution of portfolio returns. Moreover it is assumed that the sensitivity of the portfolio price to changes in risk factors is constant, and risk factors are correlated by a constant.

Historical data are needed in order to get the volatility measure for each factor, and after working out the potential effect of each component on the overall portfolio, the overall distribution of the market parameters is constructed from this data.

The risk mapping technique allows us to determine the distribution of profits and loss over m. Normal factors entail a normal distribution for the distribution of portfolio profits and losses.

In order to implement the standard VaR formula the standard volatility must be retrieved and then the appropriate z value multiplied to it. This can be done using historical data, but more commonly using the implied volatility contained in exchange-traded option prices.

Example 5.6: Consider a bond with nominal value €1,000,000, price €100, standard deviation 2.79%. The 95%-VaR critical value is given by

$$x_{VaR} = 1.65 \times 0.0279 = 0.046$$

The portfolio has a market value of €1,000,000 so the VaR of the portfolio is

$$VaR = 1,000,000 \times 0.046 = €46,000$$

the maximum loss the portfolio may sustain over one year for 95% of the time.

When dealing with a portfolio of two assets and their individual VaR, aggregating measure can be done in two ways. The undiversified VaR is the weighted average of the individual standard deviations.

The diversified VaR instead takes into account the correlation between the assets, and the volatility is calculated in the Markowitz framework using the formula that takes into account the covariance among assets.

The volatility for VaR calculation is the square root of the variance of the portfolio. A portfolio exhibiting high volatility will have a high VaR number. An observer may then conclude that the portfolio has a high probability of making losses.

For large portfolios, it is convenient to work with vectors and matrices to express correlations and covariances. This is what the RiskMetrics™ VaR methodology does to obtain the same results.

Once a portfolio starts to contain many assets, the analytical method as described above becomes inappropriate. Matrices allow for calculation of portfolio VaR with many hundreds of assets, which would require assessment of the volatilities and correlations of each couple of assets.

One of the main drawbacks of the normality assumption is that it allows for negative prices. One way to avoid this is to work with geometric returns rather than arithmetic returns

$$u_t = \log\left[\frac{(V_t + d_t)}{V_{t-1}}\right]$$

where

d_t is any intermediate payment made by the portfolio.

Assume that geometric returns are normally distributed with mean μ and standard deviation σ. When d_t is zero or reinvested in the asset, the consequence is that the natural logarithm of V_t is normally distributed, or that V_t itself is lognormally distributed.

Consider the critical value, defined as

$$x_{VaR} = \mu + z\sigma \tag{5.4}$$

The definition of geometric returns can be used to define the critical value V_{VaR} corresponding to a loss equal to the VaR considered

$$x_{VaR} = \log V_{VaR} - \log V_{t-1}$$
$$\Rightarrow \ \log V_{VaR} = x_{VaR} + \log V_{t-1}$$

so that

$$V_{VaR} = e^{(x_{VaR} + \log V_{t-1})}$$
$$= e^{(\mu + z\sigma + \log V_{t-1})}$$

From the critical value, it is then possible to infer VaR

$$VaR = V_{t-1} - V^*$$
$$= V_{t-1} - e^{(\mu + z\sigma + \log V_{t-1})}$$

Lognormal VaR is consistent with the assumption of normally distributed geometric returns. The formula for lognormal VaR is more complex than ordinary VaR, but the lognormal VaR advantage is to exclude the possibility of negative asset (or portfolio) values.

5.2.3 *Monte Carlo simulation*

Similarly to historical simulation, Monte Carlo methodology for VaR calculation is based on the generation of different scenarios that may affect the portfolio value. The difference is that historical simulation scenarios are simulated from historical data, while Monte Carlo involves the simulation of scenarios from a lognormal distribution.

Therefore the Monte Carlo method takes input from both historical simulation and from parametric method in that it uses the same distribution assumption for risk factors.

The method accounts for non-linearity in portfolio positions, to price risk for both linear portfolio and non-linear portfolios. The distribution of profits and losses must not be necessarily symmetric.

Drawbacks of the approach are the fact that, as well as other approaches, Monte Carlo cannot take into account any non-normal distribution, and the simulations are computationally intensive and more time-consuming than either the parametric methodology or historical simulation.

As for the normal linear VaR model, the basic assumption is the multivariate normality of portfolio returns. The covariance matrix is assumed to be positive semi-definite, meaning it captures all the dependencies among risk factors.

Some of the strict assumptions can anyway be relaxed and distributional features can be accommodated, for example using marginal distributions of different types than normal. Distributions of returns other than normal are also possible, for a very high number of simulations.

Monte Carlo simulation is composed of many different steps.

1. Define the time horizon T of the analysis and divide it into n equally spaced intervals of length $\Delta t = \dfrac{T}{n}$. Discretization must ensure Δt is large enough to approximate the continuous pricing observed in the markets.

2. Use a random number generator to simulate the price of the asset at the end of the first time step. Most random number generators follow specific kernels, and either prices or returns can be simulated.

    The model generally used to describe price movements between time i and $i+1$ $(i = 1,2,...,n)$ is the generalized Brownian motion

    $$\Delta S = \left(S_{i+1} - S_i\right) = \mu S_i \Delta t + \sigma S_i \varepsilon \sqrt{\Delta t} \tag{5.5}$$

    So that realized returns are

    $$u_i = \frac{\Delta S}{S_i} = \mu \Delta t + \sigma \varepsilon \sqrt{\Delta t} \tag{5.6}$$

    where
    u_i is the return of the stock on the i-th observation
    S_i is the stock price observed at time i
    S_{i+1} is the stock price observed at time $i+1$
    μ is the sample mean of the stock price
    Δt is the time interval

σ is the sample volatility of the stock price

ε is the random number generated from a normal distribution.

At the end of Step 1 a random number is drawn to determine returns according to (5.6).

3. Repeat Step 2 for all time intervals until T is reached. At each repetition another random number is drawn and (5.5) is applied to retrieve S_{i+2} from S_{i+1}, S_{i+3} from S_{i+2} and so on. The procedure is repeated until determining S_T.

4. Steps 2 and 3 must be iterated a consistent number of times, in order to get different paths for the stock price over the time horizon and take in account a broad universe of possible ways the stock price can take over a period of time.

5. Depending if the measure is taken on prices or realized returns:

   a. Prices: Rank simulated prices from the smallest to the largest and pick the simulated value corresponding to the desired confidence level. Deduce the relevant VaR, which is the difference between S_i and the α-th lowest terminal stock price.

   b. Returns: After calculating realized returns from simulated price, rank them from the lowest to the highest and cut the obtained empirical distribution at the desired confidence level.

The process for the stock price in (5.5) requires us to input the drift and volatility in order for the term ε to be the only random component:

$$\mu = \frac{1}{n\Delta t} \sum_{i=1}^{n} u_i$$

and

$$\sigma = \sqrt{\frac{1}{(n-1)\Delta t} \sum_{i=1}^{n} (u_i - \bar{u})^2}$$

Based on the estimators it is then possible to generate stock prices rearranging the Brownian motion

$$S_{i+1} = S_i \left(1 + \mu\Delta t + \sigma\varepsilon\sqrt{\Delta t}\right)$$

If multiple assets are taken into account, then Monte Carlo begins with the generation of m normal variables with unit variance and correlation matrix. The first step is to apply Cholesky decomposition to the correlation matrix Σ of the factors, yielding a factorization of the kind

$$\Sigma = A^T A$$

The following step is to generate a vector $\mathbf{z}$ of independent univariate standard normal variables. Then build the vector

$$\mathbf{y} = A\mathbf{z}$$

It turns out by construction that the elements of $\mathbf{y}$ have unit variance with the correlation matrix.

Even if time consuming, Monte Carlo simulation has the advantage to be able to model both linear and non-linear instruments, as well as complex derivatives. Extreme events are negligible and the simulation kernel can be chosen to represent any distribution.

The main disadvantage is the computational power required given the exponential rate of increase of complexity. For a portfolio of 100 assets, wanting to run 100 simulations for each asset, the total amount of simulations needed is 10,000. To get accurate results, more simulations are better, therefore working on a large portfolio can be resource- and time-consuming.

Snapshot 5.2
Euler's theorem on homogeneous functions

A risk measure ρ can be defined in terms of the economic capital (EC) required by the portfolio with profit/loss x:

$$EC = \rho(x)$$

is called homogeneous of degree τ if for any $h > 0$ the following equation obtains:

$$\rho(hx) = h^\tau \rho(hx)$$

A function $f : u \subset \mathbb{R}^n \to \mathrm{R}$ is called homogeneous of degree τ if for any $h > 0$ and $u \in U$ with $hu \in U$ the following equation holds

$$f(hu) = h^\tau f(u)$$

Let $u \subset \mathbb{R}$ be an open set and $f : u \subset \mathbb{R}$ be a continuously differentiable function. Then f is homogeneous of degree τ if and only if it satisfies the following equation:

$$\tau f(u) = \sum_{i=1}^{n} \frac{\partial f(u)}{\partial u_i}, \quad u_1, u_2, \ldots, u_n \in u, \quad h > 0$$

It is easy to show that $\dfrac{\partial f(u)}{\partial u_1}$ is homogeneous of degree $\tau - 1$ if f is homogeneous of degree τ. It follows that if f is homogeneous of degree 1 and continuously differentiable for $u = 0$ then f is a linear function (i.e. with constant partial derivatives). Therefore the homogeneous functions relevant for risk management are not differentiable in $u = 0$.

Two functions that are homogeneous of degree 1 are convex

$$f(\eta u + (1-\eta)v) \leq \eta f(u) + (1-\eta) f(v), \quad \eta \in [0,1]$$

If and only if they are sub-additive

$$f(u+v) \leq f(u) + f(v)$$

5.3 Inside VaR

Learning outcomes

1. Explain how VaR can be decomposed to isolate the impact individual positions.
2. Define VaR limitations.
3. List and calculate the analytic approximations to VaR.

5.3.1 Decomposition

The composition of portfolio VaR gives important information about the risk structure of the portfolio. Besides a static measure of risk, what is really important is to know what is the marginal contribution of the individual portfolio components to the diversified portfolio VaR.

On the other hand, it is also important to determine how each individual asset can contribute in proportion to the diversified portfolio VaR, and the incremental effect on VaR of adding a new instrument to the existing portfolio.

Marginal VaR is the partial derivative with respect to the weight of an individual component of portfolio and measures the change in portfolio VaR resulting from adding it. Hence, the marginal return-VaR of component i is given by:

$$\Delta VaR_i = \frac{\partial VaR_p}{\partial w_i}$$

where

w_i is the weight of asset i in the portfolio
VaR_p is the portfolio VaR before adding the new component
V_p is the value of the portfolio before adding the new component.

Recall the formula for the variance of returns in the Markowitz framework. In order to obtain the MVaR measure in terms of portfolio volatility, consider the partial derivative of the variance with regard to the weight of a portfolio of n components.

$$\frac{\partial \sigma_p^2}{\partial w_i} = 2w_i \sigma_p^2 + 2\sum_{j \neq i}^n w_j \sigma_{ij}$$

$$= 2 \, cov\left(r_i, w_i r_i + 2\sum_{j \neq i}^n w_j r_j \right)$$

$$= 2\sigma_{ip}$$

From the properties of derivation recall that

$$\frac{\partial \sigma_p^2}{\partial w_i} = 2\sigma_p \frac{\partial \sigma_p}{\partial w_i}$$

Therefore

$$
2\sigma_{ip} = 2\sigma_p \frac{\partial \sigma_p}{\partial w_i}
$$

$$
\rightarrow \frac{\partial \sigma_p}{\partial w_i} = \frac{\sigma_{ip}}{\sigma_p}
$$

(5.7)

Substitute equation (5.7) into equation (5.4) to obtain

$$
\Delta VaR_i = \frac{\partial z \sigma_p}{\partial w_i}
$$

$$
= z \frac{\partial \sigma_p}{\partial w_i}
$$

$$
= \frac{z \sigma_{ip}}{\sigma_p}
$$

Recall from CAPM that $\beta = \dfrac{\sigma_{ip}}{\sigma_p^2}$ so that the equation of marginal VaR becomes

$$
\Delta VaR_i = \frac{z \sigma_{ip}}{\sigma_p}
$$

$$
= z \beta_i \sigma_p
$$

$$
= \beta_i VaR_p
$$

There is a linear relationship between MVaR and the intrinsic riskiness of the component i. The MVaR is a function of the current VaR of the portfolio, and the beta of the additional component.

Component VaR indicates the change in the measure when deleting a given component of the portfolio. It is defined in terms of marginal VaR and the sum of the component VaR of all portfolio components gives the portfolio VaR.

Total portfolio VaR is the weighted average of the first derivatives of VaR with respect to each component of some amount invested in assets $i = 1, 2, ..., n$, in the portfolio. It will be a linearly homogeneous function of the positions in the instruments. We can apply Euler's Theorem then

$$
VaR_p = \sum_{i=1}^{n} w_i \frac{\partial VaR_p}{\partial w_i}
$$

The formula defining component VaR for asset i is therefore

$$
VaR_{C,i} = w_i \frac{\partial VaR}{\partial w_i}
$$

meaning that

$$
VaR = \sum_{i=1}^{n} VaR_{C,i}
$$

and setting a clear relationship with marginal VaR as

$$VaR_{C,i} = w_i MVaR_i$$

Component VaR can be also expressed as a percentage of total portfolio VaR, showing the actual weight on total VaR of each single component.

$$VaR_{C,\%} = \frac{VaR_C}{VaR_p}$$

As for all weights, the sum of all the single percentage VaR_C is one

$$\sum_{i=1}^{n} \frac{VaR_{C,i}}{VaR_p} = \frac{1}{VaR_p} \sum_{i=1}^{n} VaR_{C,i}$$
$$= 1$$

Incremental VaR is a measure of how VaR changes in the portfolio, due to adding a new asset. Assume the actual portfolio is made of n positions, and consider adding a new position i with weight w_i.

The change in VaR of the portfolio due to the new position can be approximated via first order condition as

$$IVaR_i \approx w_i \left(\frac{\partial VaR_p}{\partial w_i} \bigg|_{w_i \text{ small}} \right)$$

This is the incremental VaR of instrument i. Hence, the VaR of the portfolio after the new position is added can be approximated by

$$VaR_p + IVaR_p$$

Even if they look similar, there is a substantial difference between component VaR, which is an exact measure, and incremental VaR, which is an approximation.

Looking at the incremental VaR one can study the dynamics of the portfolio. For example a highly positive IVaR means that the new position has a significant impact on the overall risk.

A moderately positive IVaR means the contribution to the risk of the overall portfolio is non-zero but not substantial. Negative IVaR means that an added position reduces the overall risk of the portfolio, so that diversification is taking place and the new position has a hedging effect on the original portfolio.

In all cases, the relative size of IVaR rises as the size of new position increases. That happens because the IVaR will increasingly reflect the VaR of the new position rather than the old portfolio.

Being an estimation on the effect of a change in the portfolio composition, incremental VaR can be estimated using a Taylor-series expansion based on marginal VaR. Consider a portfolio p, with a measured VaR level VaR_p.

Assume an additional component i to be added to the portfolio. The hypothetical new portfolio will have a new VaR measure, VaR_{p+i}. At a first approach, the IVaR associated with trade/position i is

$$IVaR_i = VaR_{p+i} - VaR_p$$

The calculation can be time consuming when it involves many new positions to be added. The delVaR approach, as seen before, can be faster and accurate. It is based on a Taylor expansion around VaR_p. The expansion for the value of the augmented portfolio is given by

$$VaR_{p+i} \approx VaR_p + \sum_{i=1}^{n} \Delta w_i \left(\frac{\partial VaR_p}{\partial w_i} \right)$$

and

$$\begin{aligned} IVaR_i &= VaR_{p+i} - VaR_p \\ &\approx \sum_{i=1}^{n} \frac{\partial VaR_p}{\partial w_i} \Delta w_i \end{aligned}$$ (5.8)

It is then possible to rewrite (5.8) in matrix notation

$$IVaR_i \approx \nabla \mathbf{VaR_p} \mathbf{w}_\Delta^{\mathrm{T}}$$

where

$\mathbf{w}_\Delta$ is the vector $(\Delta w_1, \Delta w_2, ..., \Delta w_n)$

It is possible to approximate the IVaR associated with a set of new positions using only the initial estimates of VaR_p and $\nabla \mathbf{VaR_p}$. This approach allows us to estimate and use IVaRs in real time, when assessing investment risks and specifying position limits.

5.3.2 Limitations

Using an axiomatic approach, Artzner *et al.* (1997) have tried to define a satisfactory risk measure, setting out certain attributes that should be a reasonable requirement of any risk measure.

The classical definition of risk measure is such that VaR does not appear to be a risk measure. Consider a set Π of random variables in the real domain. Consider a function $f : \Omega \to \mathbb{R}$ and define the following properties:

Monotonicity: $X \geq 0 \Rightarrow f(X) \leq 0, \ \forall X \in \Omega$
Positive Homogeneity: $X \in \Omega \Rightarrow hX \in \Omega, \ \forall h > 0$
Translation Invariance: $X \in \Omega \Rightarrow f(X+a) = f(X) - a, \ \forall a \in \mathbb{R}$
Sub-Additivity: $f(X+Y) \leq f(X) + f(Y), \ \forall X, Y \in \Omega \mid X + Y \in \Omega.$

A function is said to be a risk measure if it shows all the four properties. VaR is not a risk measure because it is not sub-additive, so that a portfolio made of sub-portfolios risks an amount which is at most the sum of the separate amounts risked by its sub-portfolios.

VaR has become a primary tool for risk management since the introduction of minimum capital requirements. Providing a single measure for all the risk types of a corporation, it is easy to implement and understand.

However, VaR comes with some disadvantages. For example, it cannot distinguish between different liquidities of market positions. The risk measure given by VaR is tailored for short-term and standard market conditions.

Another limit is that VaR is based on precise assumptions about the distribution of portfolio returns, and the cost of an integrated VaR platform for big portfolios can be huge, making it very expensive.

For every type of risk, traditional risk measures can be listed. For example, for a fixed income portfolio, it can be represented by a cash-flow map and quantified on the basis of the sensitivity to movements in a yield curve.

The standard measure of interest rate risk is duration, the average of the present values of all cash flows weighted by the maturities. Yield curve risk is also measured using the present value of a basis point move (PVBP), describing how much the present value of cash flows change for a 1 bp shift in the yield curve.

Traditional equity risk measures are based on the sensitivity of stock prices to risk factors, measured by the beta. The elements contributing to the risk are the variances and covariances of underlying factors, sensitivity of factors and residual risk.

Beta as a measure of risk does not take into account the risk arising from movements in the underlying risk factors and specific risks of a portfolio, in that the only risk that can be eliminated is the diversifiable one.

Sensitivity-based risk measures are anyway limited in that they cannot be compared across different activities to give an overall exposure across all types of securities, so that it is not possible to get an indication of the potential loss, under normal circumstances or extreme events.

VaR is a risk measure that takes into account all sources of risk, and one of its main advantages is that it takes into account the volatilities and correlations of risk factors, so as to give a measure of risk that is comparable across different asset classes.

As a risk measure, VaR has some limitations, the first one being related to volatility, which can be either good or bad. VaR in fact does not take into account volatility direction, therefore failing in capturing the downside effect.

In order to clarify it, consider two portfolios, one showing much of the variation of returns on the up side, the other showing much of the variation on the down side. Under some circumstances the two portfolios could have the same VaR. Volatility itself does not reveal whether returns are concentrated in the positive or negative domain.

Downside risk measures take care of this limit and are based on some benchmark return as a reference for the actual realizations. Markowitz introduced the semi-variance operator in 1959, measuring the variance of lower-than-benchmark returns, which is given by

$$\sigma_{1/2}^2 = E\left\{\left[\min\left(0, r - E(r)\right)\right]^2\right\}$$

where

r is the realized return
$E(r)$ is the expected return.

The approach by Markowitz uses the expected return as the benchmark return, but many other choices are possible. The generalized version of the volatility measure implies the benchmark return can be time-varying or fixed. Dembo and Freeman in 2001 developed the regret operator, which is given by

$$RG = -E\left[\min\left(0, r - r_B\right)\right]$$

where

r_B is the benchmark return.

The straightforward interpretation of the regret operator is to be the cost of insurance against downside risk, because it has the same form as the payoff of a put option with strike price equal to the benchmark return. The measure distinguishes upside risk from downside risk.

The regret operator is a lower order partial moment of order 1, which can be generalized for any order k by the formula

$$RG = -E\left[\min\left(0, r - r_B\right)^k\right]^{\frac{1}{k}}$$

5.3.3 Analytic approximations

A popular approach to VaR is the delta-normal approach, introduced by J.P. Morgan in the RiskMetrics™ suite. It is based on assumption of linearity of change in portfolio value over time, and normality of returns.

The sensitivity of the portfolio to each factor $f_i = (f_1, f_2, ..., f_n)$ can be written as

$$\delta_i = \frac{\partial V}{\partial f_i} f_i$$

Consider a portfolio dependent on n factors, with sensitivities $\delta = (\delta_1, \delta_2, ..., \delta_n)$. The first order Taylor approximation to the portfolio's discounted Profit-Loss is, in vector notation

$$P\&L = \delta^{\mathsf{T}} \mathbf{r}$$

where

δ^{T} is the transpose of the vector of factor sensitivities
$\mathbf{r} = (r_1, r_2, ..., r_n)$ is the vector of factor returns.

Suppose the *m*-day discounted returns on the underlying asset are normally distributed. The approximate distribution of the Δt–day P&L on the portfolio is

$$P\&L_{\Delta t} = N\left(\delta \mu_{\Delta t}, \left(\delta \sigma_{\Delta t}\right)^2\right)$$

where

$\mu_{\Delta t}$ is the mean of the distribution of returns over the time interval Δt

$\sigma_{\Delta t}$ is the standard deviation of the distribution of returns over the time interval Δt.

Option pricing theory is based on the assumption that the expected return on the underlying asset is the risk-free discount rate. To be consistent with this assumption we set $\mu_h = 0$.

$$\Delta V = \sum_{i=1}^{n} \delta_i \Delta S_i$$
$$= \delta_P^T \Delta S$$

where

V is the portfolio price

$\delta_P^T = \left(\delta_{P_1}, \delta_{P_2}, ..., \delta\delta_{P_n} \right)'$ is the vector of net position deltas

$\Delta S = \left(\Delta S_1, ..., \Delta S_n \right)'$ is the vector of changes in the underlying prices.

Equivalently the equation of P&L can be expressed as

$$P/L = \sum_{i=1}^{n} \delta_i^V R_i$$
$$= \delta_V^T r$$

where

$\delta_V = \left(\delta_{V_1}, \delta_{V_2}, ..., \delta_{V_n} \right)$ is the vector of value deltas.

Assuming a multivariate normal distribution for the factor returns

$$VaR_{h,\alpha} \approx N^{-1}(1-\alpha)\sqrt{\delta_V^T \Omega_n \delta_V}$$

where Ω_h is the m-day covariance matrix of the discounted returns on the underlying asset. Non-linearity makes the delta-normal approach not adequate. A better approximation of actual VaR is the delta–gamma approach. For simplicity consider only one risk factor f. Based on the first two terms of the Taylor series expansion, it regards the extra term $(\Delta f)^2$ as another i.i.d. normal variable, which should be treated in the same way as Δf. Changes in portfolio value are then driven by two risk factors, Δf and $(\Delta f)^2$. An example of non-linear product dependent on a factor is a portfolio of options:

$$\Delta V \approx \delta \Delta f + \frac{1}{2}\Gamma(\Delta f)^2$$

The option is then equivalent to a portfolio that is linear in the two risk factors Δf and $(\Delta f)^2$. When estimating VaR, the option is assimilated to a portfolio that is linear in two normal risk factors.

The VaR of the option is therefore equal to z times the portfolio standard deviation, which is given by applying the approximation formula

$$\sigma_p = \sqrt{\delta^2 \sigma^2 + \left(\frac{1}{2}\Gamma\right)^2 \sigma^2}$$

$$= \sqrt{\delta^2 \sigma^2 + \left(\frac{1}{4}\right)\Gamma^2 \sigma^2}$$

Consequently the formula for linear VaR is modified into the corresponding formula for non-linear VaR

$$VaR = z\sigma f \sqrt{\delta^2 + \left(\frac{1}{4}\right)\gamma^2 \sigma^2}$$

Summary

Market risk arises from adverse market price movements, due to the uncertainty about the future. Different securities can give rise to market risk, with specificities linked to the asset class considered.

The distribution of prices and returns plays a crucial role in determining what approach should be used for market risk analysis, including the linearity or non-linearity of the dependence between the portfolio and the market.

The time frequency implied in the distribution of returns determines the horizon of market risk measurement, which can be daily, weekly, monthly and so on, according to the purpose of measurement.

Value at Risk tells what is the maximum expected loss that can be incurred on some specific position, under normal market conditions at a specific level of confidence, over the time period considered.

VaR can be calculated by means of parametric estimation, historical simulation approach or Monte Carlo simulation. The metrics require estimation of volatility and correlation between the market and the various assets in the portfolio.

Risk management at desk level requires quick estimation of risk, and focuses on very short-time horizons. At an internal risk department level, longer-time horizons are usually taken into consideration.

The composition of portfolio VaR for some overall position gives important information about the risk structure of the portfolio, which is important for grasping the marginal contribution of any single asset to the overall risk.

However, VaR has some disadvantages, in that it does not distinguish between different liquidities of market positions, and is tailored mostly for short-term and standard market conditions.

Another limitation is that VaR is based on specific distributional assumptions of portfolio returns, and the cost of an integrated VaR platform for big portfolios can be huge, making it very expensive.

Bibliography

Alexander, C. 2001. *Market Models: A Guide to Financial Data Analysis*. John Wiley & Sons.

Alexander, C. 2008. *Market Risk Analysis: Value-at-Risk Models*. John Wiley & Sons.

Alexander, C. & Leigh, C. 1997. On the Covariance Matrices Used in VaR Models. *Journal of Derivatives*, 4: 50–62.

Artzner, P., Delbaen, F., Eber, J.M. and Heath, D. 1997. Thinking Coherently. *Risk*, 10(11): 68–71.

Basle Committee on Banking Supervision. 1995. *An Internal Model-Based Approach to Market Risk Capital Requirements*.

Beder, T.S. 1995. VAR: Seductive but Dangerous. *Financial Analysts Journal*. September–October.

Berkowitz, J. and O'Brien, J. 2002. How Accurate are Value at Risk Models at Commercial Banks. *Journal of Finance*, 57: 1093–1111.

Berry, R. 2011. *An Overview of Value-at-Risk: Part III – Monte Carlo Simulations VaR*. J.P. Morgan Investment Analytics & Consulting.

Chatfield, C. 2001. *Time Series Forecasting*. Chapman & Hall, 181–214.

Choudhry, M. 2001. *The Bond and Money Markets: Strategy, Trading, Analysis*. Butterworth-Heinemann.

Choudry, M. 2006. *An Introduction to Value-at-Risk*. John Wiley & Sons.

Culp, C.L., Miller, M.H. and Neves, A.M.P. 1998. Value at Risk: Uses and Abuses. *Journal of Applied Corporate Finance*, 10(4): 26–38.

Dembo, R.S. and Freeman, A. 2001. *The Rules of Risk: A Guide for Investors*. Wiley.

Dowd, K. 2002. *Measuring Market Risk*. John Wiley & Sons.

Duffie, D. and Pan, J. 1997. An Overview of Value at Risk. *Journal of Derivatives*, 4: 7–49.

Frye, J. 1997. *Principals of Risk: Finding Value-at-Risk Through Factor-Based Interest Rate Scenarios*. NationsBanc-CRT.

Glasserman, P., Heidelberger, P. and Shahabuddin, P. 2000. Efficient Monte Carlo Methods for Value at Risk. *Working Paper*. Columbia University.

Hallerbach, W.G. 2003. Decomposing Portfolio Value-at-Risk: A General Analysis. *Journal of Risk*, 5(2): 1–18.

Hull, J. and White, A. 1998. Incorporating Volatility Updating into the Historical Simulation Method for Value at Risk. *Journal of Risk*, 1: 5–19.

Irina, N.K. and Svetlozar, T.R. 2000. *Value at Risk: Recent Advances*. Chapman & Hall, 801–858.

Jamshidian, F. and Zhu, Y. 1997. Scenario Simulation: Theory and Methodology. *Finance and Stochastics*, 1: 43–67.

Jorion, P. 2002. How Informative are Value-at-Risk Disclosures?. *The Accounting Review*, 77: 911–932.

Jorion, P. 2006. *Value-at-Risk: The New Benchmark for Managing Financial Risk*. McGraw-Hill.

Markowitz, H. 1959. *Portfolio Selection: Efficient Diversification of Investments*. John Wiley & Sons.

Marshall, C. and Siegel, M. 1997. Value at Risk: Implementing a Risk Measurement Standard. *Journal of Derivatives*, 4(3): 91–111.

Exercises

Questions

1. For what purpose is it advisable to set a long-time horizon for a VaR measure? What about a high confidence level?

2. Assuming normality in the distribution of returns, list the factors that result in a decrease in VaR.
3. List and compare the various approaches to VaR. In particular, what are the benefits associated with each approach?
4. How can marginal VaR for an asset be interpreted?
5. What is the average relationship between component VaR and individual VaR for some specific position?
6. What information is required to calculate VaR through simulation?
7. What are the main drawbacks of Monte Carlo simulation of VaR?
8. Is it possible to convert the daily VaR for some portfolio of derivatives, just by using the standard multiplication by the square root of time?
9. Is the delta-normal approximation of VaR more suitable for a short-time horizon or a long-time horizon? Explain.

Problems

1. Suppose an investment with a 4% chance of a loss of €10,000,000, a 2% chance of a loss of €1,000,000 and a 94% chance of a profit of €1,000,000.
   a. What is the Value at Risk (VaR) for one of the investments with 95% confidence level?
   b. What is the expected shortfall when the confidence level is 95%?
2. From exercise 2, consider adding another portfolio identical to the first one. They are independent of each other.
   a. What is the VaR for a portfolio consisting of the two investments when the confidence level is 95%?
   b. What is the expected shortfall for a portfolio consisting of the two investments when the confidence level is 95%?
3. Consider a return distributed symmetrically with zero mean and $\sigma = 1\%$. Use the Chebyshev's inequality

$$\Pr\left[\left|X - E(X)\right| > x\right] \le \frac{E\left[\left(X - E(X)\right)^2\right]}{x^2}$$

   to show that the 99% VaR of the distribution of returns is lower than 0.1.
4. Consider a portfolio of one share in some stock, with price $S = 100$. Daily returns on the stock are i.i.d. $N(0,0.1)$.
   a. Compute the one-day 99% VaR.
   b. Compute the ten-day 99% VaR.
5. Suppose that the change in the value of a portfolio over a one-day time period is normal with a mean of zero and a standard deviation of €2,000,000.
   a. What is the one-day 97.5% VaR?
   b. What is the five-day 97.5% VaR?
6. Consider the portfolio in exercise 5.
   a. What is the five-day 99% VaR?
   b. How do the answers to the previous points change if there is first-order daily autocorrelation with correlation parameter equal to 0.16?

Appendix: Factor mapping for VaR

The standard framework for VaR estimation implicitly assumes that each position in a portfolio has its unique risk factor, so that a one-to-one relationship holds and every risk factor is projected onto a specific position.

This is not always the case, and sometimes, a number n of positions must be projected onto a number m of risk factors, smaller than n. The process of mapping aims at defining standard building blocks in order to relate positions and risk factors appropriately.

One of the main reasons to do mapping are the reduction of the size of the covariance matrix, given that, for n different positions in a portfolio, the information needed is quite vast and grows geometrically, as n increases.

Another important fact is that the choice of factors that are too correlated to each other, may cause problems in the rank of the covariance matrix. Therefore being able to choose them is an advantage.

Finally, mapping can be useful when data is scarce, so that it is possible to focus the analysis on similar instruments, for which data is sufficient, through risk factors.

Mapping is a process basically divided into three stages:

1. Construct a set of benchmark factors, collecting volatilities and correlations.
2. Derive synthetic replications of the positions held.
3. Calculate VaR using mapped instruments.

The first stage goes through selecting a set of key assets, representative of the positions held in the portfolio. Good proxies of portfolio instruments range from key money market, key equity assets, key currencies, key commodities, and so on.

Another approach involves selecting core risk factors, rather than instruments. Methods like principal component analysis or factor analysis help identify the relevant factors, driving the movements of a group of time series.

Factor analysis commonly shows that few factors are sufficient to explain the movements of a set of instruments. The factors are chosen to be independent from each other, with volatilities being the only non-zero elements in the covariance matrix.

Mapping becomes very specific for different types of position. The crucial point is that the very many types of instruments in the market can be broken down to a definite amount of standard building blocks. The core of mapping is to identify these blocks and the associated risk measure.

The easiest category to analyse in terms of building blocks is the FX positions. When the currencies involved in the positions held are included in the mapping system, volatilities and covariance matrix are immediately available.

Assume the value of the position is constant at V_{FX}, the exchange rate is e, so that the value of the position in domestic currency is eV_{FX}. If the exchange rate is distributed as $N \sim (0, \sigma_e^2)$, the VaR is defined as

$$VaR_{FX} = -\alpha \sigma_e e V_{FX}$$

Another type of standard building block is equity. Consider a portfolio with an equity position of amount V_{EQ}, and missing information about a firm's volatility and correlation data.

It is possible to make an assumption of the equity return R_{EQ} being related to the market return R_M, through a CAPM relationship. Recall that the variance of an asset from CAPM formula is given by

$$\sigma_{EQ}^2 = \beta_{EQ}^2 \sigma_m^2 + \sigma_\varepsilon^2$$

where

β_{EQ}^2 is the beta of the stock
σ_m^2 is the variance of market returns
σ_ε^2 is the variance of the error term.

The assumption of normality with zero mean allows us to express the VaR in the form

$$VaR_{EQ} = -\alpha \sigma_{EQ} V_{EQ}$$
$$= -\alpha \sqrt{\beta_{EQ}^2 \sigma_m^2 + \sigma_\varepsilon^2} V_{EQ}$$

where

V_{EQ} is the value of the stock.

The formula for VaR relies on publicly available data, beside σ_ε^2 which could be available, making things easy, or not directly available. The issue can be handled in several ways.

If the portfolio is well diversified, the idiosyncratic risk goes to zero, so that one can assume σ_ε^2 to be equal to zero. Then VaR becomes

$$VaR_{EQ} \approx -\alpha \sigma_{EQ} \beta_{EQ} \sigma_m V_{EQ}$$

so that the only volatility needed is the market volatility, and the only firm-specific information is the beta.

Finally, it is interesting to analyse the case of the primitive instrument being a zero-coupon bond.

6   Interest rate risk

Interest rate risk is the risk that changes in the level of interest rates may cause the market value of a bond to change. Interest rate risk increases with time. The longer an investor holds a bond, the higher the risk.

Fluctuations in interest rates have an impact on the profitability of any business, making it necessary to manage interest rate risk. For bond investors, rising interest rates mean falling bond prices, while declining interest rates mean rising bond prices. In general, the prices of long-term and low-yield bonds have higher sensitivity to interest rate changes.

Excessive interest rate risk can translate into a significant threat to the earnings and capital base of any financial institution. Changes in interest rates affect earnings by changing the net interest income and the level of interest-sensitive income and expenses.

Shifts in the yield curve have an impact on both short-term and long-term financial positions. Financial derivatives like interest rate swaps, caps and floors, and swaptions, represent a source of interest change, and their value fluctuates with interest rates.

Financial institutions are concerned about the interest rates on assets and liabilities resetting at different times. The assessment of interest rate risk is a very large topic at banks, credit unions, financial companies and among regulators.

After studying this chapter you will be able to answer the following questions, among others:

1. What is the relationship between the price and yield of a bond?
2. What are duration and convexity, and how do they relate to the sensitivity of bond prices to changes in the yield?
3. What are the techniques to achieve immunization of a position on bonds?
4. What are short-rate models of interest rate? How can risk measures in affine models be described?
5. What are the main types of advanced interest rate risk models?

The first part of the chapter is dedicated to an introduction to bond prices and yields, and basic hedging through duration and convexity. The second part is about short-rate models and risk measures in affine models. The final part focuses on more advanced models of interest rate risk, like the LIBOR market model, the M-Absolute and M-Square models.

6.1 The dynamics of interest rates

Learning outcomes

1. Describe the relationship between bond prices and yields.
2. Define fixed income futures and their application to financial risk.
3. Explain how yield shifts impact on portfolio immunization.

6.1.1 Bond prices and yields

Interest on an investment or loan can be calculated in many different ways. The main distinction is between simple and compound interest. The simple interest is paid at the end of every time period, but not reinvested for the following period, so it does not earn extra interest if you leave it in the bank.

$$I_S = L \times r \times \Delta t$$

where

I_S is the amount of simple interest generated by the investment
r is the annual interest rate applied on the nominal amount
L_0 is the nominal amount on which the interest rate is applied.

Compound interest implies that the interest earned on a time period is reinvested in the same account and earns interest in later periods. Define the final value of the investment, called the future value, compounded on t years

$$L_t = L(1+r)^t$$

The formula is valid for annual compounding, meaning that the interest rate is compounded only once every year.

In order to allow for different compounding frequencies, consider an interest rate that is compounded m times per year. In this case the formula is modified as

$$L_t = L\left(1+\frac{r}{m}\right)^{tm}$$

The highest compounding frequency is represented by continuous compounding, which can be approximated by

$$L_{\Delta t} = Le^{r\Delta t}$$

In finance, most of the time it is interesting to look at the present value of an investment knowing the final value and the interest rate applied. Basically the formulas are about inverting the ones for compounding so to get

$$L_t = \frac{L_t}{(1+r)^t}$$

$$L = \frac{L_t}{\left(1+\dfrac{r}{m}\right)^{tm}}$$

$$L = L_t e^{-r\Delta t}$$

Example 6.1: Assume one buys a car borrowing the price. Two equal offers are made to sell identical cars for €29,700. The first seller requires cash on delivery. The second seller provides a zero-interest loan for one year, therefore is the best choice. But if the offer from the first seller goes down to €27,000, in order to make a decision one must be able to determine the present value of each alternative.

At a 10% rate, it is indifferent to buy the car from one seller or the other. Other values of interest rates generate different present values to be compared, therefore changing the optimal choice accordingly.

The concept of effective annual rate is related to the compounding frequencies. Different investments can give different interest based on differently compounded rates. For the same nominal rate r it is possible to calculate the effective rate for all the compounding frequencies m. Table 6.1 summarizes the calculation for the most common frequencies and an example in terms of numbers.

It is clear that a higher compounding frequency generates a higher effective return. This is why usually borrowers prefer to pay interest at low compounding frequency, while the lenders prefer higher compounding frequency.

That is why yield is sometimes referred to as the Internal Rate of Return (IRR) of an investment in bonds for $n = \dfrac{T}{\Delta t}$ periods, where T is the maturity.

The IRR is the interest rate r_y that solves the equation

$$B_0 = \sum_{i=1}^{n} \frac{C_i}{\left(1+r_y\right)^i}$$

where

C_i are the cash flows paid by the bond at each time i
$n = t$ in terms of the notation used so far, in case of annual payments.

The IRR equation can also be expressed in continuous compounding, as

$$B_0 = \sum_{i=1}^{n} C_i e^{-r_y i}$$

In the case of a coupon bond the payments are the coupons and the face value plus the last coupon, at maturity. For a zero-coupon bond, the only payment is the face value at maturity.

Table 6.1 Effective annual rate calculation for different compounding frequencies. The last column shows an example of the calculation applied to a nominal rate of 4%.

Compounding	m	Effective annual rate	r = 4%
Annually	1/1	$r = (1+r/1)^1 - 1$	4.00%
Semi-annually	1/2	$r_S = (1+r/2)^2 - 1$	4.04%
Monthly	1/12	$r_M = (1+r/12)^{12} - 1$	4.06%
Weekly	1/52	$r_W = (1+r/52)^{52} - 1$	4.07%
Daily	1/365	$r_D = (1+r/365)^{365} - 1$	4.08%
Continuous	1/∞	$r_e = e^r - 1$	4.08%

Example 6.2: Consider now two bond yields above (11%) and below (8%) the average return. For a yield of 11% the present value of the bond is (continuous compounding)

$$B_0 = \sum_{i=1}^{7} 8e^{-0.11i} = 83.25$$

Present value of the bond at 8% is

$$B_0 = \sum_{i=1}^{7} 8e^{-0.08i} = 98.31$$

The bond-pricing formula cannot be inverted and solved analytically for r_y. Therefore it must be solved computationally. Another method is to adopt an iterative procedure of trial and error in order to identify the yield that gives the market price.

A guess on the value of r_y is made and put in the formula, to check whether the present value from the calculation matches the actual price of the bond.

There is also an approximation formula that allows for a fair approximation of the yield to maturity of a coupon bond, as a closed form solution. The formula is

$$r_y = \frac{C_i + \dfrac{B_{FV} - B}{t}}{\dfrac{B_{FV} + B}{2}}$$

where

B_{FV} is the face value of the bond at maturity
B is the market price of the bond.

In order to avoid confusion, note that throughout the text, the notation B_{FV} is used as well as B_T, to define the value at maturity (face value) of a bond, which is by convention €100.

Example 6.3: Consider a seven-year bond which pays an 8% coupon rate, face value €100, currently selling at €90. The average return per year is

$$r_y = \frac{8 + \dfrac{100 - 90}{7}}{\dfrac{100 + 90}{2}} = 9.92\%$$

The trial and error approach usually involves bounding the right yield between two extreme values, one higher and the other lower than the actual yield. Define the net present value as the difference between the theoretical price from applying the guessed yield and the market price.

It is possible to get closer to the market price, just changing the guess on the yield appropriately, from a lower rate r_l, yielding a positive NPV_+, and a higher rate r_h, yielding a negative NPV_-. Then the yield to maturity is given by interpolation:

$$r_y = r_l + \frac{NPV_+}{NPV_+ - NPV_-}(r_h - r_l)$$

where

> NPV_+ is the positive net present value, from a low guess on the yield
> NPV_- is the negative net present value, from a high guess on the yield.

Example 6.4: Given the two bonds in Example 6.2, the NPV at 11% is

$$-90 + 83.25 = -6.75$$

NPV at 8% is

$$-90 + 98.31 = 8.31$$

The yield to maturity is then

$$r_y = 0.08 + \left(\frac{8.31}{8.31 - (-6.75)} \right)(0.11 - 0.08) = 9.66\%$$

which is a fair approximation of the initial calculation. Computing the yield numerically gives a value of $r_y = 10.06\%$.

Standard yield to maturity calculations and bond pricing are limited in the sense that they underline the same yield to maturity for all bond payments. If we account for the fact that the payments happen at different points in time, it is natural to assume they should be discounted at different yields.

That means discounting each cash flow by a rate appropriate to its maturity, using a spot rate. The present value of a bond in discrete compounding is given by

$$B_0 = \sum_{i=1}^{n} \frac{C_i}{(1 + r_i)^i}$$

and continuous compounding can be written as

$$B_0 = \sum_{i=1}^{n} C_i e^{-r_i i}$$

where

r_i is the yield to maturity corresponding to time i.

A spot rate for each maturity increases the accuracy of the pricing, and makes assumptions on reinvestment rates unnecessary. The term structure rates incorporates current spot rates, expectations of future spot rates, expected inflation, liquidity and risk premium.

When dealing with pricing over two or more maturities that are shifted from today, it is convenient to work with forward yields. They indicate the expected spot yield at some date in the future and can be derived directly from spot rates.

Define the one-year spot rate r_1 as the rate available now for investing for one year, and the two-year spot rate r_2 as the rate available now for investing for two years. The forward rate between maturity 1 and 2 is the rate implied for investing for a one-year period in one year's time.

This can be generalized to any forward rate between time t_1 and t_2, which can be written as

$$r_{1,2} = \left(\frac{(1+r_2)^{t_2}}{(1+r_1)^{t_1}} \right)^{\frac{1}{t_1-t_2}} - 1$$

where

r_1v is the spot rate at time t_1
r_2v is the spot rate at time t_2

Another important variable of interest is the par yield. It is the theoretical coupon rate r_{FV} that makes the bond calculated price equal to par value. It can be calculated adapting the bond pricing formula as

$$B_T = \sum_{i=1}^{t} \frac{r_P B_T}{(1+r_i)^i} + \frac{r_P B_T + B_T}{(1+r_t)^t}$$

$$= \sum_{i=1}^{t} \frac{C_P}{(1+r_i)^i} + \frac{C_P + B_T}{(1+r_t)^t}$$

where

B_T is the bond face value
r_P is the par yield
C_P is the coupon calculated on the par yield.

Example 6.5: Assume the spot rates in the term structure are:

Year	Spot rate
1	6.00%
2	6.75%
3	7.00%

The par yield on a bond that will be priced at par therefore is:

$$100 = \frac{C_P}{(1.06)} + \frac{C_P}{(1.0675)^2} + \frac{C_P + 100}{(1.07)^3}$$

The solution to the equation is $C_P = 7.21$. Therefore the par yield is $r_p = 7.21\%$.

The par yield curve is used for determining the coupon to set on new bond issues, and for assessing relative value.

For a portfolio of bonds, the aggregate yield is not just the average of the yields of the single bonds. In order to determine the portfolio yield it is necessary to determine the cash flows for the portfolio and then find the interest rate that makes the present value of the cash flows equal to the market value of the portfolio.

6.1.2 Fixed income futures

The no-arbitrage condition for the market equilibrium states that the actual forward price should equate the expected future spot value. In real life, this is generally not true and the condition

$$F = E(S_T)$$

is valid if there is an equilibrium.

This is true because there are two main categories of investors on the market. The hedgers use the market to shift the risk to speculators, who then are demanding a high premium to bear the risk.

The premium exists for

$$F \neq E(S_T)$$

The condition on the market depends on the position chosen by the various types of investors. When the hedgers go short and speculators assume long positions, then the forward price is lower than the expected future spot rate

$$F < E(S_T)$$

When this is the case, speculators expect to have a profit equal to the difference between the two prices

$$E(S_T) - F$$

while hedgers expect a loss of the same amount, that can be seen as the premium paid to the speculators. An inverted argument holds for long hedgers and short speculators.

The above scheme can be replicated at time zero by going long on a futures and lending an amount equal to the present value of the future price at the risk-free rate. The strategy completes by buying the asset for a price F, using the money from the lending at time zero, and selling it for S_T.

The present value of the future price is given by

$$Fe^{-rT}$$

The expected present value on the other position is the present value of the stock price discounted by an appropriate discount rate y, over the time horizon Δt. That is

$$E(S_T)e^{-y\Delta t}$$

The no-arbitrage condition implies the whole strategy to have value zero at maturity, for the equality between forward price and expected spot price. Therefore the same condition implies the whole value to be zero also at time zero. That is

$$
\begin{aligned}
&E(S_T)e^{-y\Delta t} - Fe^{-r\Delta t} = 0 \\
\Rightarrow\ &F = E(S_T)e^{(r-y)\Delta t} \\
\Rightarrow\ &\begin{cases} F < E(S_T) & \text{if } y > r \\ F = E(S_T) & \text{if } y = r \\ F > E(S_T) & \text{if } y < r \end{cases}
\end{aligned}
$$

The condition $F < E(S_T)$ implies $y > r$. The excess of y over r represents the systematic risk associated with the asset.

An important feature of fixed income futures is that, at delivery, the seller has the obligation to deliver and the right to choose which security to deliver.

There are three different types of fixed income future, according to the underlying being an interest rate, a short-term treasury bill or a long-term bond. In order to understand the dynamics of this type of future, what follows is the case of a bond as underlying.

Assume current time is t and an investor who wants to hold one unit of a coupon bond at a future date T. The coupon and price at time t are C and B_t respectively. There are two ways to achieve a long position in the bond at maturity.

a.   Buy a forward contract for delivery of the bond at time T, at a price F_t.
b.   Borrow money to buy the bond.

The following table summarizes the cash flows for both operations:

Strategy	Date	t	T
A	Buy a forward contract on 1 unit of bond	0	F_t
B	Borrow money	B_t	$-B_t[1+r\Delta t]$
	Buy 1 unit of bond	$-B_t$	$C\Delta t$

By summing up all entries in the third column of the table, it is clear that these operations have a null cost at time t. In order to avoid arbitrage opportunities, the strategy must have a null cost at maturity as well.

Therefore, also the entries in the fourth column must equate to zero. That means

$$F_t - B_t\left[1+r\Delta t\right]+C\Delta t = 0$$

It follows that

$$F_t = B_t\left[1+r\Delta t\right]-C\Delta t$$

and, finally

$$F_t = B_t\left[1+r\Delta t - C\Delta t\right]$$

Example 6.6: Consider a forward contract maturing in six months, on a bond with coupon rate 10% and price €115. Risk-free interest rate is 7%. Then the forward price is equal to

$$F_t = 115\left[1+\left(0.07\times\frac{1}{2}\right)-\left(10\times\frac{1}{2}\right)\right]=114.02$$

In fixed income futures the variable of interest is the yield, not the price. The two are correlated but it is more common to settle the contracts based on the basis points, defined as 0.01%.

Shifts in the yield curve generate changes in the settlement of forwards. In general, the owner of a forward contract gains oppositely than what happens for prices. Because you are watching yields rather than price, when you are long you gain when yield falls rather than rises.

Spot rates are such that they cover the interest rate granted over different maturity, from a common starting point (time zero). Using two spot rates $y(0,t_1)$ and $y(0,t_2)$ on different maturities, it is possible to determine the associated forward rate $F(0,t_1,t_2)$, indicating the rate to be applied in between maturities t and T as seen at time 0.

Suppose an investor who wants now to know and guarantee the one-year zero-coupon rate for a €1,000 loan starting in one year. There are two possible strategies to achieve that:

a. Go long in a forward contract with principal €1,000, one-year maturity, written on the one-year zero-coupon rate $y(0,1)$ at a predetermined rate $F(0,1,1)$.
b. Borrow €1,000 to be repaid at the end of year 2, and simultaneously lend the same sum and receive it back at end of year 1.

The cash flows generated by the two alternatives are equivalent. The following table summarizes the case of strategy B:

	Today	In one year	In two years
Borrow	1,000	–	$-1,000\left[1+y(0,2)\right]^2$
Lend	–1,000	$1,000\left[1+y(0,1)\right]$	–
Total	0	$1,000\left[1+y(0,1)\right]$	$-1,000\left[1+y(0,2)\right]^2$

This is equivalent to borrowing $1,000\left[1+y(0,1)\right]$ in one year, repayable in two years as $1,000\left[1+y(0,2)\right]^2$. Again by no-arbitrage argument, the implied rate on the loan is the forward rate $F(0,1,1)$, given as

$$10,000\left[1+y(0,1)\right]\left[1+F(0,1,1)\right]=10,000\left[1+y(0,2)\right]^2$$

or

$$F(0,1,1)=\frac{\left[1+y(0,2)\right]^2}{\left[1+y(0,1)\right]}-1$$

The generalization of the formula is

$$F(0,t_1,t_2)=\left\{\frac{\left[1+y(0,t_1)\right]^{t_2}}{\left[1+y(0,t_1)\right]^{t_1}}\right\}^{\frac{1}{t_2-t_1}}-1$$

which is the formula to extract any forward rate $F(0,t_1,t_2)$ from the spot rates $y(0,t_1)$ and $y(0,t_2)$ covering the time interval of the forward.

As mentioned above, futures contracts move opposite to interest rates. When interest rates fall, a good strategy is to buy futures contracts. When interest rates rise, it is good to sell.

6.1.3 Yield shifts and immunization

When yields change, the yield curve on the graph has a shift. It is possible to distinguish various types of shift, in particular distinguishing between parallel and non-parallel shift.

Parallel shift happens when the yields on all the maturities change in the same direction, all by the same amount, so that the slope of the yield curve does not change.

When the yields for different maturities change differently in amount, the curve has a non-parallel shift. Non-parallel shifts fall into two general categories.

A twist shift happens when the curve has a shift in the slope that makes it flatter or steeper. In case of a flatting twist shift the spread between short- and long-term rates narrows down and the curve becomes flatter.

In a steeping twist shift the spread between short- and long-term rates widens up and the curve becomes steeper.

Butterfly shifts happen when the shift implies a change in the convexity of the curve. In a positive butterfly shift the yield curve becomes less convex. For example, if interest

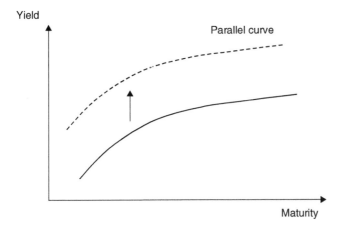

Figure 6.1 A parallel shift in the yield curve involves a full translation of the curve up or down, without changes in the slope or curvature.

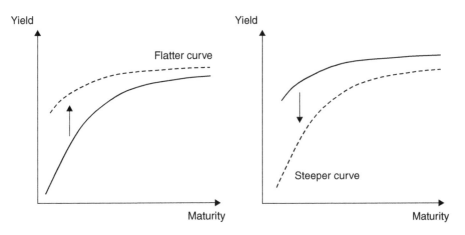

Figure 6.2 Other shifts in the yield curve involve a change in the slope.

rates increase, both short and long maturity yields increase by more than those at inter-mediate maturities.

In a negative butterfly shift the curve convexity increases. When rates increase, inter-mediate term yields increase by more than the long- and short-maturity yields.

A portfolio is said to be immunized when the interest rate changes have no effect on its value. The typical situation is of a corporation having to meet a future fixed obligation. In this case immunization allows the future obligation to be met with a pre-specified amount of available assets.

The strategy consists in holding a portfolio of assets with the same value and modi-fied duration of the liabilities portfolio. In general, when the (modified) duration of both assets and liabilities are the same, as well as the current values, the position is immunized.

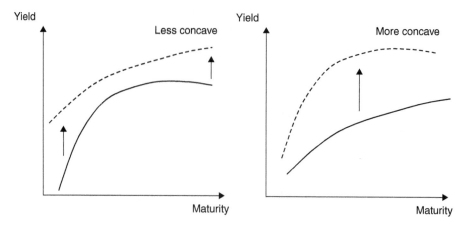

Figure 6.3 A third possible change in the yield curve involves the concavity.

Example 6.7: Consider a liability of €1,000,000 due 10 years from now. In order to immunize it, a portfolio with duration 10 years and future value of €1,000,000 is needed.

Consider a liability to be immunized buying coupon bonds. In case the interest rises during the life of the bond, the position in the bond will guarantee a gain in the reinvestments of the coupon received. But on the other hand, there will be a loss in the resale of the bond at maturity. The opposite will happen if interest rates fall.

When the conditions are satisfied, the losses from compound interest will be balanced by the gains in the resale of the bond, and vice versa.

In order to verify it, consider a liability of amount L_t to be paid at time t. The current reference interest rate is r_y, and the immunization conditions require investment in a coupon bond with specific features.

Assume the bond matures at t as well, so that its face value can be written as

$$B_{FV} = B_t$$

The face value of the bond must be equal to L_t at time t, and this must hold whichever way the interest rate moves. Define

$$B_T = L_t = Le^{r_y t}$$

where

L is the present value of the nominal L.

Consider now the partial derivative of the bond face value with respect to the interest rate r_y

$$\frac{\partial B_{FV}}{\partial r_y} = B_0 t e^{r_y(t-1)} + \frac{\partial B_0}{\partial r_y} e^{r_y t}$$

where

$B_0 = L$ is the present value of the optimal bond future value.

The condition of neutrality of the nominal amount to changes in interest rates, which is basic for defining immunization, can be written as

$$\frac{\partial B_{FV}}{\partial r_y} = 0$$

It follows that

$$\frac{\partial B_{FV}}{B_{FV}\partial r_y}e^{r_y} = \frac{\partial B_{FV}}{\partial r_y} \times \frac{e^{r_y}}{B_{FV}} \tag{6.1}$$

The right-hand side of the above equation is the duration of the nominal amount, meaning that duration is equal to the time length t of the target investment. The solution $\hat{r}_y$ to the above equation is called the critical rate.

In case there is no single bond that can be used for immunization, it is possible to construct a portfolio of bonds. The simplest case is the one with a portfolio of two bonds X and Y with weights w_X and w_Y in the portfolio, respectively.

The right portfolio mix is given as the solution of the system

$$\begin{cases} w_X + w_Y = 1 \\ w_X D_X + w_Y D_Y = D_P \end{cases} \tag{6.2}$$

where

D_X is the duration of bond X
D_Y is the duration of bond Y
D_P is the duration of the portfolio.

Assume the yield curve is flat at some level r_y and any movement preserves the flatness. A flat yield curve means that all the bonds have the same yield to maturity.

A small shift in the yield curve will have the same effect on the current value of the immunizing assets and on the current value of the liabilities, and the former will be enough to meet the target cash flow.

Immunization is not a one-time strategy. The rebalance of the portfolios must be done over time in order to ensure that conditions for immunization are constantly met. As far as time goes, and yields change, the portfolio of assets must be reworked.

Consider an investor whose assets consist of €1,000,000 invested on a 15-year time zero-coupon bond. The investor liabilities are €500,000 invested in a 10-year zero-coupon bond. The duration is

$$D = \frac{1}{B_y}\sum_{t=1}^{T} tC_t e^{-r_y \Delta t}$$

$$= \frac{1}{1,000,000e^{-r_y \Delta t}}\left(15 \times 1,000,000 e^{-r_y \Delta t}\right)$$

$$= 15$$

This proves that the duration of a zero-coupon bond is equal to its maturity. In the same way, the duration of the 10-year bond is calculated to be 10.

When the duration of the assets is higher than the duration of liabilities, the cash inflows from the assets occur at a later time than the outflows on the liabilities side. This makes a rise in interest rates not convenient for the investor.

To see that consider the change in value of the two positions. Through inverting and discretizing formula (6.1), the changes in value are given by

$$
\begin{aligned}
\Delta_{Ass} &= DB_y e^{-r_y} \Delta r_y \\
&= DB_0 \Delta r_y \\
&= 15 \times 1,000,000 \Delta r_y \\
&= €15,000,000 \Delta r_y \\
\Delta_{Lia} &= 10 \times 500,000 \Delta r_y \\
&= €5,000,000 \Delta r_y
\end{aligned}
$$

Therefore a positive change in yield would drive down the assets much more than the liabilities, generating a loss for the investor. In this case immunization involves reworking the portfolios in order to achieve a good hedging on the interest rate. Setting up a system like (6.2) is the right way for it.

It is possible to extend the argument to multiple liabilities. Consider the case of n liabilities. The net present value of the cash flows is

$$
B_0 = \sum_{i=1}^{t} \left(A_i - B_i \right) e^{-yt}
$$

where

A_i is the asset i
B_i is the liability i.

The conditions for immunization require the present value to be zero, and then the usual condition of zero sensitivity to yield changes. Immunization in such a framework can be achieved also by the cash matching technique, so that liabilities can always be immunized with a set of matching zero-coupon bonds.

Another consideration is that duration of course decreases with time, but at a pace which is different from the linear decrease of time to maturity. It is possible in fact to show that the duration of a coupon-bond at maturity is not zero, but positive.

Hedging with duration is meant to offset the price fluctuations of a position in bonds. Usually not all the yields on the market react in the same way to some specific change in the interest rates.

Therefore it is sometimes defined

$$
\beta_y = \frac{\Delta r_{y,B}}{\Delta r_{y,A}}
$$

where

β_y is the so-called yield beta
$\Delta r_{y,B}$ is the change in yield of the liability position
$\Delta r_{y,A}$ is the change in yield of the asset (hedging) position.

The hedge ratio is defined as

$$h = \frac{D_{\$,B}}{D_{\$,A}}\beta_y$$

where

$D_{\$,B}$ is the dollar duration of the liability position
$D_{\$,A}$ is the dollar duration of the hedging position.

The hedging ratio defines the proportion of hedging security with respect to the liabilities, that ensures hedging is accomplished, so that

$$\Delta V_B = h\Delta V_A$$

where

V_B is the value of the liability position
V_A is the value of the asset position.

The whole theory relies on small changes in interest rates. Immunization may not work for the investor against large changes. In practice, this is not usually a problem as the theory is fairly robust. Rebalancing is efficient when interest rates change gradually.

Snapshot 6.1
Compounding frequencies for interest rates

The terminal value of a current amount L, invested for n years, at a rate R per annum, is given by

$$L_n = L(1+R)^n$$

If the interest rate is compounded m times per year, the terminal value of the investment can be written as

$$L_{n,m} = L\left(1+\frac{R_m}{m}\right)^{nm}$$

As the compounding frequency tends to infinity, the computation shifts into continuous compounding, which gives the highest value for the terminal value, and can be written as

$$L_c = Le^{R_c n}$$

The relation between discrete and continuous compounding is given by

$$Le^{R_c n} = L\left(1+\frac{R_m}{m}\right)^{nm}$$

$$\Rightarrow e^{R_c n} = \left(1+\frac{R_m}{m}\right)^{nm}$$

$$\Rightarrow R_m = m\left(e^{\frac{R_c}{m}} -1\right)$$

To show the effect of compounding frequency on an interest rate of 10% per annum, it is possible to apply the above formulas, and the effective rates at different compound frequencies are shown in the table below.

Compounding frequencies	Interest rate
Annual (m=1)	10.0000%
Semi-annual (m=2)	10.2500%
Quarterly (m=4)	10.3813%
Monthly (m=12)	10.4713%
Weekly (m=52)	10.5065%
Daily (m=365)	10.5156%

6.2 Short-rate models

Learning outcomes

1. Describe the term structure of interest rates and the yield curve.
2. Define and comment on single-factor models of the short rate.
3. Define and comment on multi-factor models of the short rate.

6.2.1 The term structure of interest rates

Constant interest rate is a common assumption of most theoretical models in finance. In reality, interest rates vary through time. This occurs primarily because inflation rates are expected to differ through time.

When considering bonds with the same risk, it is possible to compare their yields for different maturities. The relationship between interest rates (yields) and maturities is called term structure of interest rates, and the graph plotting it is called the yield curve.

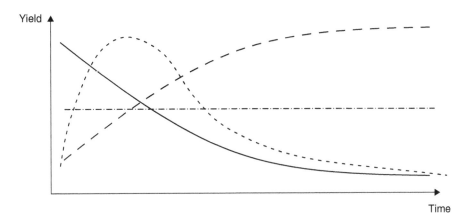

Yield

Time

Figure 6.4 The yield curves, as resulting from most common models of the interest rates, and observed empirically, can take different forms.

Depending on the model for the short rate used the yield curve can take four different shapes. The curve can be upward sloping, downward sloping, flat or humped.
The most common shape is the upward slope, meaning that short-term rates are below long-term rates. This is due to expectations that macroeconomic factors will cause rates in the future to go up.

The rationale behind the upward sloping yield curve is that expectations of higher inflation (with resulting tightening of monetary policy to compensate for it) generate the demand for a higher risk premium due to uncertainty about the future rate of infla-tion. Investors price this risk into the yield curve by demanding higher yields for longer maturities.

If a yield curve is downward sloped, long-run interest rates are below short-term interest rates. This is due to expectations of future economic regression. A flat yield curve indicates expectations on the economy have a negligible effect on the risk pre-mium demand of investors.

A humped curve is due to clustering of demand on intermediate maturities. For example, in recent years investors have demanded high volumes of the 30-year-long bond, whose price has raised to the point that it yields less than the 20-year bond. This has caused the humped curve to be the most common shape in recent years.

In order to have a complete term structure, all maturities must be covered. In prac-tice, in most bond markets, bonds for just a few maturities are issued. Therefore it is necessary to complete the structure by inferring the rates for the other maturities.

A convenient procedure is to use the bootstrapping method. In some markets it is pos-sible to construct some longer-term zero-coupon bonds by forming portfolios of traded coupon bonds. Zero-coupon yields can be derived from the prices of these bonds.

Assume a market with T bonds, one for each available maturity. For simplicity con-sider bonds that make payments at each maturity with identical payment dates. It is then possible to construct zero-coupon bonds for each maturity $1, 2, ... T$.

The next step is to construct discount factors $v_{t+1}, v_{t+2}, ..., v_{t+T}$ for all maturities, defined as the present value of a bond with notional 1, expiring at each maturity involved. From discount factors, yields can be derived to build the curve up to time $t + T$.

Recall the price formula for a coupon-paying bond

$$B = \sum_{i=1}^{T} C_i e^{-y_i t_i} \simeq \sum_{i=1}^{T} \frac{C_i}{\left(1 + y_i\right)^i}$$

where

C_i is the payment made by the bond at time i
y_i is the yield corresponding to maturity i
t_i is the time corresponding to maturity i. For annual compounding $t_i = i$.

Indicating the payment of bond $i = 1,...,T$ at time $t + j$ $(j = 1,...,T)$ with $C_{i,j}$ and the price of bond i with $B_{i,t}$ the discount factors must then satisfy the pricing kernel, as above, given by equations

$$\begin{pmatrix} C_{1,1} & C_{1,2} & \cdots & C_{1,T} \\ C_{2,1} & C_{2,2} & \cdots & C_{2,T} \\ \vdots & \vdots & \ddots & \vdots \\ C_{T,1} & C_{T,2} & \cdots & C_{T,T} \end{pmatrix} \begin{pmatrix} v_{t+1} \\ v_{t+2} \\ \vdots \\ v_{t+T} \end{pmatrix} = \begin{pmatrix} B_{1,t} \\ B_{2,t} \\ \vdots \\ B_{T,t} \end{pmatrix} \tag{6.3}$$

The conditions in the bonds ensure that the payment matrix of this equation system is non-singular so that a unique solution will exist.

Consider now a portfolio of the T bonds, equivalent to a zero-coupon bond paying 1 at $t + j$. Denoting by $\alpha_{i,j}$ the units of bond i needed to replicate the zero-coupon bond maturing at $t + j$, it must hold

$$\begin{pmatrix} C_{1,1} & C_{2,1} & \cdots & \cdots & \cdots & C_{T,1} \\ C_{1,2} & C_{2,2} & \cdots & \cdots & \cdots & C_{T,2} \\ \vdots & \vdots & \ddots & & & \vdots \\ C_{1,j} & C_{2,j} & \cdots & \cdots & \cdots & C_{T,j} \\ \vdots & \vdots & & & \ddots & \vdots \\ C_{1,T} & C_{2,T} & \cdots & \cdots & \cdots & C_{T,T} \end{pmatrix} \begin{pmatrix} \alpha_{1,j} \\ \alpha_{2,j} \\ \vdots \\ \alpha_{j,j} \\ \vdots \\ \alpha_{T,j} \end{pmatrix} = \begin{pmatrix} 0 \\ 0 \\ \vdots \\ 1 \\ \vdots \\ 0 \end{pmatrix} \tag{6.4}$$

Equation (6.4) gives a unique solution associated with the maturity $t + j$. The comparison of (6.3) and (6.4) yields the equality

$$v_{t+j} = \begin{pmatrix} \alpha_{1,j} & \alpha_{2,j} & \cdots & \alpha_{T,j} \end{pmatrix} \begin{pmatrix} B_{1,t} \\ B_{2,t} \\ \vdots \\ B_{T,t} \end{pmatrix} = \sum_{i=1}^{T} \alpha_{i,j} B_{i,t} \tag{6.5}$$

That gives the discount factor corresponding to the j-th entry.

The iteration of the calculation in (6.4) for all $j = 1,...,T$ returns the values for all the zero-coupon bonds. Formula (6.5) can then be applied to get the corresponding discount factors.

Example 6.8: Two bonds are traded on the market. Bond A is a two-year 4% coupon bond; 8% provides payments of €4 in the first year and €104 in second year. Bond B is a one-year zero-coupon bond providing a payment of €104. Assume the price of bond A is €97, while the price of bond B is €90.

$$\begin{pmatrix} 91 \\ 96 \end{pmatrix} = \begin{pmatrix} 5 & 105 \\ 104 & 0 \end{pmatrix} \begin{pmatrix} v_{t+1} \\ v_{t+2} \end{pmatrix}$$

The solution is $v_{t+1} = 0.96$ and $v_{t+2} = 0.91$.

Bootstrapping applies also to non-regular time intervals, as long as the bonds have at most T payments and each bond has no more than one payment day, the technique also applies to the case where the maturities of the T bonds are not all different and regularly increasing as above. If there were more payment dates bonds, the above system of equations would not have a unique solution.

In order to build the term structure from the short rate, consider the price at time t of a zero-coupon bond that pays off 1 at maturity T.

$$P_{t,T} = \hat{E}\left[e^{-\bar{r}\Delta t}\right]$$

where

$\hat{E}$ is the expectation in the risk-neutral world
$P_{t,T}$ is the price at time t of a ZCB paying 1 at maturity T
$\bar{r}$ is the average value of the short rate in the interval $\Delta t = T - t$.

Indicating with $y_{t,T}$ the continuously compounded interest rate at time i for the term $T - t$ we can substitute in place of the average short rate, to get

$$P_{t,T} = \hat{E}\left[e^{-r_{t,T}\Delta t}\right]$$

so that

$$R_{t,T} = \frac{\ln P_{t,T}}{\Delta t}$$
$$= \frac{\hat{E}\left[e^{-\bar{r}\Delta t}\right]}{\Delta t}$$

That enables the term structure of interest rates to be elaborated at any time t directly from the risk-neutral process for the short rate at that time.

6.2.2 Single-factor models

In short-rate models the state variable is the instantaneous forward rate, which is stochastic. Most notable models are Gaussian-based, and incorporate Brownian motion. They are the classical interest rate models.

The stochastic differential equation describing the dynamics of short-rate follows an Itô process

$$dr_t = m_{r,t}dt + s_{r,t}dW_t$$

where

$m_{r,t}$ is a drift parameter dependent on both r_t and t
$s_{r,t}$ is a diffusion parameter dependent on both r_t and t.

Single-factor models have only one driving factor, and take multiple forms, according to what forms of drift and diffusion are chosen. Various choices of the coefficients $m_{r,t}$ and $s_{r,t}$ lead to different dynamics of the instantaneous rate.

The general framework is a stochastic basis (Ω, F, P), (omega space, filtration, probability space). Another condition is that all bond prices are adapted processes, for convention, with $P_{t,T}$ being the price at time t of a bond paying a face value equal to 1 at maturity T, so that $P_{T,T} = 1$.

The market is arbitrage-free, meaning there exists an Equivalent Martingale Measure $\mathbb{Q}$ such that

$$P_{t,T} e^{-\int_0^t r(s)ds}, \quad t \in [0, T]$$

is a $\mathbb{Q}$-martingale, for all $T > 0$, and the denominator is the money market account.

The first category of short-rate models developed are the equilibrium models. They are characterized by constant drift and diffusion parameters, so that the term structure they produce is totally endogenous, without necessity to match the observed structure on the market.

A popular equilibrium model is the Vasicek model (1977). The formulation of the model is

$$dr_t = a(b - r_t)dt + \sigma dW_t$$

The short rate is described by a mean-reverting process, in that the short rate evolves around a fixed constant level b, at a reverting speed a, which is constant as well. All parameters are non-negative constants.

One of the main advantages of the Vasicek model is that it has an explicit expression for the short rate, which is normally distribution. However, given its structure, the model allows for negative rates.

In order to derive the analytical expression of the short rate, it is necessary to introduce the variable change

$$x_t = r_t - b$$

The process in dx_t becomes

$$dx_t = -ax_t dt + \sigma dW_t$$

Consider another change of variable

$$z_t = e^{at} x_t$$

The process becomes

$$\begin{aligned} dz_t &= ae^{at} x_t dt + e^{at} dx_t \\ &= ae^{at} x_t dt + e^{at}(-ax_t dt + \sigma dW_t) \\ &= e^{at} \sigma dW_t \end{aligned}$$

From previous equations

$$z_t = z_0 + \int_0^t e^{as} \sigma dW_s$$

$$\rightarrow e^{at} x_t = e^{a0} x_0 + \int_0^t e^{as} \sigma dW_s$$

$$= x_0 + \int_0^t e^{as} \sigma dW_s$$

so that

$$x_t = e^{-at} \left(x_0 + \int_0^t e^{as} \sigma dW_s \right)$$

Since $x_t = r_t - b$, the short rate can be calculated as

$$r_t - b = e^{at} (r_0 - b) + e^{-at} \sigma \int_0^t e^{as} dW_s$$

$$\rightarrow r_t = e^{at} (r_0 - b) + \sigma \int_0^t e^{-a(t-s)} dW_s + b$$

$$= e^{at} r_0 + b(1 - e^{-at}) + \sigma \int_0^t e^{-a(t-s)} dW_s$$

Generalizing the solution to any time interval $\Delta t = t - s$ gives

$$r_t = e^{a\Delta t} r_s + b(1 - e^{-a\Delta t}) + \sigma \int_s^t e^{-a\Delta t} dW_u$$

Every short rate model carries a specific form for the bond price solution as a function of the short rate. The solution for the price at time t of a bond with face value equal to one, maturing at time T ($\Delta t = T - t$), implied by the Vasicek model is given by the formula

$$P_{t,T} = \Lambda_{t,T} e^{-\Theta_{t,T} r_t}$$

where

$$\Theta_{t,T} = \frac{1 - e^{-a\Delta t}}{a}$$

and

$$\Lambda_{t,T} = e^{\frac{(\Theta_{t,T} - \Delta t)\left(a^2 b - \frac{\sigma^2}{2}\right)}{a^2} - \frac{\sigma^2 \Theta_{t,T}^2}{4a}}$$

The continuously compounded interest rate at time t for a term of $\Delta t = T - t$, can be derived from the bond price using the discount relationship

$$P_{t,T} = e^{-r_{t,T}\Delta t}$$

The point $r_{t,T}$ which determines the term structure in that specific time interval is

$$r_{t,T} = \frac{1}{\Delta t}\ln P_{t,T}$$

As mentioned above, the main drawback of the Vasicek model is the possibility of negative rates. In order to overcome this limitation, Cox, Ingersoll and Ross (CIR) proposed a model incorporating a different form for the diffusion part. The short rate follows the process

$$dr_t = a(b - r_t)dt + \sigma\sqrt{r_t}\,dW_t$$

Multiplying the volatility and Brownian motion by the square root of the rate, the output rates get bounded in the region of the positive numbers. Bond prices in the CIR model have the same general form as in Vasicek's model, but the functions $\Lambda_{t,T}$ and $\Theta_{t,T}$ are given as

$$\Theta_{t,T} = \frac{2(e^{\gamma\Delta t} - 1)}{(\gamma + a)(e^{\gamma\Delta t} - 1) + 2\gamma}$$

and

$$\Lambda_{t,T} = \left[\frac{2\gamma e^{\frac{(\gamma+a)\Delta t}{2}}}{(\gamma + a)(e^{\gamma\Delta t} - 1) + 2\gamma}\right]^{\frac{2ab}{\sigma^2}}$$

where

$$\gamma = \sqrt{a^2 + 2\sigma^2}$$

As in Vasicek, both bond price and continuously compounded interest rate are linearly dependent on r_t. The value of r_t then determines the level of the term structure, but not the shape, which is dependent only on time t.

The main issue with equilibrium models is that the output term structure does not fit the actual structure of interest rates on the market. Parameters can be chosen and calibrated to give the best possible fit, which however always turns out being not perfect.

Investors like to have accurate models for interest rates, given very little movement in interest rates may generate huge movements in the value of associated portfolios.

The problem of fit can be overcome by letting some parameters vary deterministically with time. No-arbitrage models are designed to be exactly consistent with today's term structure of interest rates.

The simplest form of a no-arbitrage model was described by Ho and Lee. They were the first to propose a no-arbitrage model of the term structure, using the current term structure of rates as an input to the model. The process is given by

$$dr_t = \theta_t dt + \sigma dW_t$$

where θ is a non-random function of t and σ is, as usual, a non-negative constant.
    The analytical solution for the rate is

$$r_t = r_s + \sigma(W_t - W_s) + \int_s^t \theta_u ds$$

and the expression for the price of the bond is

$$P_{t,T} = \Lambda_{t,T} e^{-r_t \Delta t}$$

where

$$\ln \Lambda_{t,T} = \ln\left(\frac{P_{0,T}}{P_{0,t}}\right) + \Delta t F_{0,t} - \frac{1}{2}\sigma^2 t \Delta t^2$$

The main drawback of the Ho-Lee model is that it does not incorporate mean reversion of the short rate. This is an empirically verified important feature of interest rates, therefore for a model to be accurate, it must incorporate mean reversion. The solution has been given by the Hull-White model. It is also known as the extended Vasicek model, in that it is basically the no-arbitrage version of it. The process is

$$dr_t = (\theta_t - ar_t) dt + \sigma dW_t$$

In this case, the analytical solution to the model is

$$r_t = e^{-a(t-s)} r_s + \int_s^t e^{-a(t-u)} \theta_u du + \int_s^t e^{-a(t-u)} \sigma dW_u$$

and the price of the bond for the given short rate becomes

$$P_{t,T} = \Lambda_{t,T} e^{-\Theta_{t,T} r_t}$$

where

$$\Theta_{t,T} = \frac{1 - e^{-a\Delta t}}{a}$$

and

$$\ln \Lambda_{t,T} = \ln\left(\frac{P_{0,T}}{P_{0,t}}\right) + \Theta_{t,T}\frac{\partial f_{0,t}}{\partial t} - \frac{1}{4a^3}\sigma^2 \left(e^{-aT} - e^{-at}\right)^2 \left(e^{2at} - 1\right)$$

where $f_{0,t} = -\dfrac{\partial \ln P_{0,t}}{\partial t}$ is the instantaneous forward rate. The drift term has a closed-form solution and the θ_t function for the model can be calculated as

$$\theta_t = \frac{\partial f_{0,t}}{\partial t} + af_{0,t} + \frac{\sigma^2}{2a}\left(1 - e^{-2at}\right)$$

6.2.3 Multi-factor models

One-factor models of short rate describe the yield curve with sufficient accuracy, but given their dimensionality, they only capture parallel shifts in the curve. But in reality, the LIBOR curve is often steepening, so that more complicated models are required.

It is not wise for example to use a single-factor model for pricing fixed income derivatives maturing in a relatively long term. A similar comment applies to a derivative written on an underlying security that does not mature in the near future.

It is often observed that yields at opposite ends of the term structure move in opposite directions. This is a behaviour that single-factor models cannot explain, and more factors are needed for the analysis.

Multi-factor models were introduced primarily to overcome these problems, and their efficiency is given by the fact that they allow for instantaneous correlation between bond returns to be not perfect, leading to higher flexibility of the term structure.

A Gaussian multi-factor model can be specified by setting dependence of the short rate upon a vector of factors $\mathbf{x}$, as given by

$$r_t = \sum_{i=0}^{n} x_{i,t} \tag{6.6}$$

where

$$dx_t = \mathbf{A}\left(b - x_t\right)dt + \Sigma dW_t, \quad x_t, b \in \mathbb{R}^n \tag{6.7}$$

where

$\mathbf{A}$ and Σ are $n \times n$ matrices.

The solution to equation (6.7) is a Gaussian process in the form

$$x_t = e^{-\mathbf{A}t}x_0 + \int_0^t e^{-\mathbf{A}(t-s)}\mu ds + \int_0^t e^{-\mathbf{A}(t-s)}\Sigma dW_s$$

The prices of a ZCB is again defined in affine form, given specific functional forms for the parameters. Gaussian multi-factor models in general are very useful in practice given their tractability and the ability to capture different empirical aspects of the data.

The multi-factor Cox, Ingersoll and Ross (CIR) model is based on independency of the factors $X_{i,t}$, where the short rate satisfies equation (6.6), and the dynamics of each $x_{i,t}$ are derived from the single-factor CIR model, and are given by

$$dx_{i,t} = a_i \left(b_i - X_{i,t} \right) dt + c_i \sqrt{x_{i,t}} \, dW_{i,t}, \quad a_i, b_i, c_i > 0$$

It follows that there exist functional forms $A_{i,t}$ and $B_{i,t}$ such that the expectation of the discounting factor, for each factor x, is given by the affine form as defined by

$$E\left(e^{-\int_t^T X_{i,u} du} \right) = e^{A_{i,\Delta t} + B_{i,\Delta t} X_{i,t}} \tag{6.8}$$

It is then possible to derive the term structure, recalling that the short rate is given by the sum of the single factors, so that

$$E\left(e^{-\int_t^T r_u du} \right) = E\left(e^{-\int_t^T \sum_i X_{i,u} du} \right)$$

$$= \dots$$

$$= \prod_{i=1}^n E\left(e^{-\int_t^T X_{i,u} du} \right)$$

Substituting for equation (6.8) yields the ZCB price as defined by

$$P_{t,T} = \prod_{i=1}^n e^{A_{i,\Delta t} + B_{i,\Delta t} X_{i,t}} = e^{\sum_i e^{A_{i,\Delta t} + B_{i,\Delta t} X_{i,t}}}$$

The two-factor Hull-White model (1994) gives a representation of the instantaneous rate in terms of the current rate r_t and two stochastic variables x_t and y_t, each driving a specific feature in the shape of the yield curve.

The two stochastic variables follow the processes

$$dx_t = -\lambda_1 x_t dt + \sigma_1 dW_1$$
$$dy_t = -\lambda_2 x_t dt + \sigma_2 dW_2$$

where

σ_1 and σ_2 are the instantaneous volatilities.

The Brownian motions are correlated by some typically largely negative coefficient (close to -1), so that parallel moves of the yield curve are inversely correlated with the steepening of the curve.

Short-rate models have many advantages. As an example, they are tractable and suited for Monte Carlo simulation methods. They allow for quick computation of derivatives prices, a very useful feature for risk management, which requires frequent repricing.

They also present some disadvantages, in that they show unrealistic features. The one-factor models imply that movements in the entire term structure can be hedged with only two securities.

Moreover, the correlation of instantaneous returns on ZCBs of different maturities is perfect, which is not realistic as well, but in general can be overcome by using multi-factor models.

Models with two or more factors offer higher flexibility and a better fit to reality. However, when more than three factors are considered, only numerical solutions become feasible.

Other models are more close to reality, like the class of the LIBOR market models, which model directly the observable market quantities, making them straightforward to calibrate.

These models also offer the possibility to easily price interest rate derivatives, just making appropriate distributional assumptions about the evolution of LIBOR rates. In this framework, short-rate models are a useful tool for quality assessment of more sophisticated models.

6.3 IRR management

Learning outcomes

1. List and comment on the sources of interest rate risk.
2. Describe the most common measurement techniques for IRR management.
3. Define duration and convexity hedging.

6.3.1 Sources and identification

Before setting out some principles for interest rate risk management, a brief introduction to the sources and effects of interest rate risk might be helpful. There are several sources of IRR that can be listed.

Repricing risk arises from the differences in the maturity of assets and liabilities of an institution. If a long-term fixed loan is financed through a short-term deposit, there could be a future decrease in value. An increase in the interest rate in fact would result in higher payments to depositors, while the fixed income from the loan would not change.

It is possible to assess repricing risk by comparing the volume of assets and liabilities maturing (repricing) within a given time period. Some banks intentionally take repricing risk in their balance sheet structure, in order to improve earnings.

Given the usual upward shape of the yield curve, it is common for banks to aim at earning positive spreads by setting longer maturities on the assets side, financing them with short-term liabilities. Such a spread is anyway subject to the changes in the interest rates.

When liabilities are short-term oriented, they reprice more frequently, making the bank position liability-sensitive. The earnings of a bank which is liability-sensitive, normally increase when interest rates fall and decrease when they rise. The opposite holds for asset-sensitive positions.

Imbalances in repricing usually do not translate into changes in earnings until some time in the future. Banks can reduce or extend maturities on both sides of the book, according to their risk preferences.

The risk evaluation is, therefore, based not only on near-term imbalances but also long-term ones. Future earnings of a bank get a severe exposure to IRR if the management fails to measure and manage material long-term repricing imbalances.

Another source of risk is the yield curve risk, arising when unpredicted yield curve shifts have a negative effect on the income or underlying value of some bank. When the yield curve steepens, even a position that is hedged against parallel moves of the curve may suffer losses.

Another source of IRR is known as basis risk, and relates to the imperfections in correlated positions. Even if two positions have similar repricing features, and the overall portfolio is hedged, movements of the interest rates may result in unexpected changes in earnings and cash flows.

In general basis risk arises when there is a change in the difference between rates for two different markets or instruments, due to a shift at different times or by different amounts.

For example, two loans of same type, with same maturity repricing at the same frequency, may give rise to basis risk, if they are based on different reference rates. The institution, in fact, is exposed to the risk that the spread between the two reference rates may change unexpectedly.

Since it reflects a differential in interest rates, basis risk has a direct impact in anticipating future cash flows from relevant instruments, affecting in turn the underlying net economic value of the bank.

An interesting aspect of basis risk relates to the relationship between prime rates set by authorities, and the offered rates set by the bank. It is common that when prime rates increase, also deposit demand increases, generating an initial positive imbalance for the bank.

However, after some time, the stabilization of rates may cause the benefit for the bank to be offset by the worsening of the rate spreads in other markets, so that the repricing imbalances turn out to be unfavourable.

In some cases, managers look at this specific type of basis risk as a form of option risk, even if the categorization of the risk is not very important as long as bank management understands the implications for the bank's interest rate risk exposure.

Optionality is a source of IRR that links to option features embedded in fixed income instruments. Various types of bonds and notes embed call or put provisions, loans with the right to prepay balances, deposit instruments giving the right to withdraw funds at any time, without penalties.

The risk arises from the asymmetrical payoff characteristics of such instruments, especially for short position investors, who usually take the risk from the embedded features to be exercised.

Moreover, leverage plays a role in amplifying the risk profiles associated with optionality, given that influence of option positions on the financial condition of the firm can be either positive or negative.

It is now clear that IRR can arise from a variety of sources. Measurement systems vary in order to capture each type of interest rate exposure. The mix of activities in a bank determines what are the most appropriate measurement systems to be used.

The management of the institutions should be able to understand the business and risk profile of the company before making any investigation on the various IRR sources and how they contribute to the overall corporate IRR profile.

6.3.2 *Measurement techniques*

Banks use a variety of methods to measure IRR, with different levels of complexity, depending on the contingent needs. The technique used depends, in part, on whether the institution is focused on earnings or economic value as an indicator of its financial position.

Gap analysis is a method that entails the classification of interest-rate-sensitive assets, liabilities and off-balance-sheet items into time bands. The bands are defined in advance according to the maturity of fixed-rate items, or time to next re-pricing for floating-rate items.

Every single time band is investigated in terms of pertinent assets and liabilities, so as to get a figure of the gap positions. Summing up the gaps for all the sub-periods in a certain period, the cumulative gap for the given period is obtained.

Cumulative positions are then multiplied by the changes in the reference rate, so as to determine the impact of the rate shifts on interest financial flows. It is also possible to use a weighted method to calculate the cumulative gap.

The method assigns a weight to each individual gap, corresponding to the time during which they are exposed to a change in the interest rate. Gap analysis is a popular tool among bank managers, due to its simplicity.

Commercial banks typically show a time mismatch between assets and liabilities, while for other types of banks like building societies, assets and liabilities are tied up mainly in longer time bands with fixed interest rates, with greater time alignment of interest rate-sensitive assets and liabilities.

The method precision depends on the right choice of time band length. Most products are classified from the aspect of their immediate maturity, or re-pricing, but instruments whose forecasted flows are influenced by changes in the market interest rate, are more complicated.

In the latter case, banks should classify individual items into time bands that mostly correspond to reality, also based on previous experience or various simulation methods.

Banks should determine the number of time bands according to the time structure of their balance sheet, so that for longer maturities, a dense structure of bands is chosen, and for shorter maturities, a less dense structure is possible.

There are some downturns in using gap analysis. One of the main weaknesses of the approach is that it does not take into consideration possible changes in the slope of the yield curve.

Gap analysis catches the impact on financial flows in time bands implying the static view that the structure and size of balance sheet items in the bands do not change, as opposed to reality.

Another disadvantage is that in the same time bands, it may happen that assets and liabilities may show different adaptation of the interest rates to a change in the market rates.

As a consequence, a position that looks balanced in a specific time band may entail some IRR that is not perceived by the bank from the point of view of the gap analysis, but may cause an unexpected impact on the interest revenues of the bank.

There are also problems in classifying items with embedded options, or with a non-predefined maturity period. The analysis can be slightly modified in order to adapt to some of the above features, but anyway, the increasing complexity of financial products in the last few years, has made the gap analysis quite useless for most products. Gap analysis nowadays represents an extra instrument for measuring IRR.

Linear descriptions of the bond-yield relationship are imprecise in that they do not consider non-linearities in the relationship between the bond price and the respective yield, so that larger interest changes could lead to substantial mistakes in the calculation.

The simplest attempt to capture convexity effects in the price relationship is given by the Basis Point Value (BPV) method, which helps to calculate a change in the price of the financial instrument if the interest rate changes by one basis point.

The method involves scenario analysis methodology, and consists in calculating the price of some fixed income instrument corresponding to the actual market interest rate, for comparing it with the price on the same instrument calculated for a different interest rate.

The difference between the present values represents a change in the value in the case of interest rate movements and is indicative of the sensitivity of the instrument's price to a change in the interest rate.

Compared to gap analysis, the BPV approach offers a more comprehensive view on the situation of the interest rates on the market. The advantage of BPV is to consider different sensitivities of the instruments, with regard to maturity and coupon.

The approach directly captures the complexity of the relationship between change in interest rates and the corresponding change in the bond prices. The main disadvantage is that it does not account for size effects.

An alternative is offered by simulation methods, which are founded on the evaluation of the potential simulated impacts of interest rates on the simulated price path for assets and liabilities in some portfolios.

Static simulations describe the development of interest rates, while dynamic simulations also add the development of individual balance-sheet and off-balance-sheet items of an institution.

The most frequently used types of simulations are historical simulation, Monte Carlo and the bootstrapping method. Simulations have the advantage of identifying all sources of IRR, and their ability to cover all basic sources depends on the sophistication level.

The growing complexity of financial products available on the market makes simulations very important, enabling the basic shortcomings of gap analysis, linear models and PVBP to be eliminated.

The main disadvantage of the simulation models is the complexity and the high level of computational power required. Generally, the greater the level of sophistication, the greater the difficulty of measuring the interest rate risk.

6.3.3 Duration and convexity hedging

The sensitivity of bond prices to change in yields determines the pattern of cash flows for a bond. The relationship is inverse and non-linear, and in general, the greater the coupon rate, the lower the sensitivity to changing interest rates.

Moreover, the longer the time to maturity, the greater the sensitivity to changing interest rates, and the greater the yield to maturity, the lower the sensitivity to changing interest rates.

The relationship between price and yield for a bond depends on the magnitude of the starting yield and how much it changes. The convexity implies that for smaller changes in the yield, the linear approximation of the change in price is more accurate.

Duration is a measure of the average time length for the bond's cash flows and is used to estimate the sensitivity of the bond price to a change in yield. Mathematically it is expressed as the time-weighted measure of the length of a bond's life.

The higher the duration, the higher the volatility with respect to changes in the yield to maturity. Duration can be measured in some ways for different purposes: Macaulay duration, modified duration and effective duration.

212 *Interest rate risk*

In continuous compounding, the Macaulay duration is defined as

$$D = -\frac{dB_y}{dr_y} \times \frac{e^{r_y}}{B_y}$$

where

r_y is the yield to maturity of the bond
B_y is the price of the bond corresponding to the yield r_y.

It is possible to express the derivative as

$$\frac{dB_y}{dr_y} = -e^{-r_y} \sum_{t=1}^{T} tC_t e^{-r_y \Delta t}$$

where

C_t is the payment made by the bond at time t
Δt is the time interval between payments.

Therefore the formula for duration is

$$D = \frac{1}{B_y} \sum_{t=1}^{T} tC_t e^{-r_y \Delta t}$$

which, in case coupons are paid annually, can be expressed in discrete compounding, as

$$D = \frac{1}{B_y} \sum_{t=1}^{T} \frac{tC_t}{\left(1 + r_y\right)^t}$$

Dollar duration is defined instead as the amount of duration, without price normalization, meaning

$$D_\$ = \sum_{t=1}^{T} tC_t e^{-r_y \Delta t}$$

It is interesting to note that

$$\sum_{t=1}^{T} \frac{C_t e^{-r_y \Delta t}}{B_y} = 1$$

Therefore, the discounted payments divided by the bond price sum up to one, and each of them can be seen as a weight w_t. It follows that

$$D = \sum_{t=1}^{T} tw_t$$

Example 6.9: A five-year bond with face value €100, selling at par, pays a semi-annual coupon rate of 5%. If the yield of the bond is 5% as well, the Macaulay duration of the bond (discrete compounding) is given by

$$D = \frac{1}{100} \times \left(\frac{5}{1.05} + \frac{10}{1.05^2} + \frac{15}{1.05^3} + \frac{20}{1.05^4} + \frac{525}{1.05^5} \right) = 4.55$$

The duration of the bond is 4.55 years.

The duration is a weighted average of the times of payment. Each weight indicates the relative importance of the payments. Larger payments have a higher weight, while smaller payments have a lower weight.

The Macaulay duration tells us what is the percentage change in the bond price given a small percentage change in the yields. It is an elasticity measure.

The modified duration of a bond is defined as

$$MD = -\frac{dB_y}{dr_y} \times \frac{1}{B_y}$$

It can be defined as the negative of the first order derivative of the price, normalized by the bond price. It follows that in terms of cash flows of the bonds modified duration can be expressed as

$$MD = \frac{e^{-r_y}}{B_y} \sum_{t=1}^{T} t C_t e^{-r_y \Delta t}$$

which can be discretized as

$$MD = \frac{D}{\left(1 + r_y\right)}$$

While the Macaulay duration informs on what is the percentage change in the bond price given a small percentage change in the yields, modified duration tells what is the percentage change in prices if the yield changes by any specific amount of percentage points.

Example 6.10: Using the data in example 6.9, the modified duration of the bond is given by

$$MD = \frac{4.55}{1.05} = 4.33$$

The modified duration of the bond is 4.33 years.

Being a first order approximation of the sensitivity of a bond's price to a change in interest rates, duration is more accurate for small changes in yield, and less accurate for large changes in yield.

It is very important to underline that duration and modified duration capture the sensitivity to changes in flat yield curves. When the curve is not flat, or does not shift in parallel, they are not efficient measures.

If there are embedded options in the bond, then effective duration must be used. Macaulay and modified duration are not applicable because the price changes for these securities are not linear in the yield.

$$ED = \frac{B_l - B_h}{2B_y \Delta r_y}$$

where

Δr_y is change in yield
B_h is price of the bond corresponding to the yield going up by Δr_y
B_l is price of the bond corresponding to the yield going down by Δr_y.

By definition, the duration of a zero-coupon bond is equal to its maturity, given the fact that the face value at maturity is the only payment made by the bond. The modified duration instead will be slightly lower than the zero-coupon bond's maturity.

For coupon bonds, instead, the interest shortens the effective maturity of the cash flows and the greater the coupon, the lower the duration, because the bond is repaying back the investment faster than a similar bond with lower coupons. Similarly, the greater the yield to maturity the lower the duration, because the payments are discounted at a high rate, resulting in a lower present value, and the duration.

As a first order approximation, duration is not optimal for large changes in yield. In order to capture the sensitivity of bond prices to larger changes in yield, a second order approximation is needed.

Convexity is a measure of the curvature of the value of a security or portfolio as a function of interest rates. Convexity is related to the second order derivative of the price function. The combined use of convexity and duration can reduce substantially the approximation error in presence of the curvature.

The expression for the second order derivative is

$$\frac{d^2 B_y}{dr_y^2} = \sum_{t=1}^{T} t^2 C_t e^{-r_y \Delta t}$$

Convexity is defined as

$$CV = \frac{d^2 B_y}{dr_y^2} \times \frac{1}{B_y}$$

which can be discretized as

$$CV = \frac{1}{\left(1+r_y\right)^2 B_y} \sum_{t=1}^{T} \frac{t(t+1)C_t}{\left(1+r_y\right)^t}$$

Example 6.11: Using the data in examples 6.9 and 6.10, the convexity of the bond is given by

$$CV = \frac{1}{100 \times (1.05)^2} \times \left(\frac{5 \times 2}{1.05} + \frac{10 \times 3}{1.05^2} + \frac{15 \times 4}{1.05^3} + \frac{20 \times 5}{1.05^4} + \frac{525 \times 6}{1.05^5} \right) = 23.93$$

The convexity of the bond is 23.93.

Following the Taylor series expansion, the change in price sensitivity to the change in yield can then be approximated as

$$\frac{\Delta B_y}{B_y} = -D\Delta r_y + \frac{1}{2}CV\left(\Delta r_y\right)^2$$

As for the duration, an approximation of the convexity is the effective convexity, which can be calculated as

$$ECV = \frac{B_l + B_h - 2B_y}{2B_y\left(\Delta r_y\right)^2}$$

The only approach to IRR that is completely riskless is to construct an asset portfolio with cash flows exactly matching the liability cash flows. This funding method is called dedication. It is an accurate approach but may be infeasible or excessively costly. In some situations, risk managers may want more flexibility.

A more flexible but more risky approach is called matching. The liabilities in a portfolio have a certain market value, that changes as time passes and as interest rates change. Immunization through matching consists in constructing an asset portfolio with the same market value and the same interest rate sensitivity as the liabilities so that the asset value tracks the liability value over time.

The most common form of immunization is achieved through matching the duration and market value of the assets and liabilities, so that the net position is hedged against small parallel shifts in the yield curve.

Summary

There are many ways to calculate the interest on some loans or investments. Simple interest is paid at the end of a time period, while the compound interest earns interest on the interest as well, over periods.

Coupon bonds pay coupons at due dates, and the face value at maturity, while for zero-coupon bonds, the only payment is the face value. Hedgers use the market to shift the risk to speculators, who then are demanding a high premium to bear the risk.

Fixed income futures give the obligation to deliver some specific security, choosing which security to deliver. The underlying can vary among interest rates, short-term bills or long-term bonds.

When the yield curve moves, it is possible to distinguish between parallel and non-parallel shifts, depending on whether the curve just translates on the plane, or gets modified in shape and slope too.

A portfolio of fixed income assets is said to be immunized when the value is not affected by changes in the level of interest rates. The typical situation involves a corporation's future fixed obligation, and immunization allows anticipation of future obligations with a pre-specified amount of available assets.

Short-rate models of interest rates use Brownian motion stochastic processes to describe the movements of the interest rates over time. Commonly known models are Gaussian-based, based on equilibrium or no-arbitrage conditions.

There are many methods that are used by banks and financial institutions to measure interest rate risk. They come with different levels of complexity, depending on whether the focus of the institution is on earnings or economic value.

Duration is the average time length of the cash flows of a bond, and approximates the sensitivity of the bond price to the movements of the yield curve. Modified duration and convexity improve the accuracy of measurement. The mathematical expression of duration, modified duration and convexity involve the time-weighted measure of the length of a bond's life.

Bibliography

Black, F. and Karasinski, P. 1991. Bond and Option Pricing when Short Rates are Lognormal. *Financial Analysts Journal* (July–August): 52–59.

Brigo, D. and Mercurio, F. 2001. *Interest Rate Model: Theory and Practice*. Springer-Verlag.

Cochrane, J.H. and Piazzesi, M. 2005. Bond Risk Premia. *American Economic Review*, 95: 138–160.

Cox, J.C., Ingersoll, J.E. and Ross, S.A. 1979. Duration and the Measurement of Basis Risk. *Journal of Business*, 52: 51–61.

Cox, J.C., Ingersoll, J.E. and Ross, S.A. 1985. A Theory of the Term Structure of Interest Rates. *Econometrica*, 53: 385–407.

Duffee, G. 2002. Term Premia and Interest Rate Forecasts in Affine Models. *Journal of Finance*, 57: 405–443.

Duffie, D. and Singleton, K. 1999. Modelling Term Structures of Defaultable Bonds. *The Review of Financial Studies*, 12: 687–720.

Fabozzi, F.J. (ed.). *The Handbook of Fixed Income Securities*. 6th Edition. McGraw-Hill.

Fama, E.F. 2006. The Behavior of Interest Rates. *Review of Financial Studies*, 19: 359–379.

Filipovic, D. 1999. A Note on the Nelson-Siegel Family. *Mathematical Finance*, 9: 349–359.

Heath, D., Jarrow, R. and Morton, A. 1990. Contingent Claim Valuation with a Random Evolution of Interest Rates. *Review of Future Markets*, 9: 54–82.

Ho, T.S.Y. and Lee, S.B. 1986. Term Structure Movements and Pricing Interest Rate Contingent Claims. *Journal of Finance*, 41.

Hull, J.C. and White, A. 1993. One-Factor Interest-Rate Models and the Valuation of Interest-Rate Derivative Securities. *Journal of Financial and Quantitative Analysis*, 28(2): 235–254.

Hull, J.C. and White, A. 1994. Numerical Procedures for Implementing Term Structure Models II: Two-Factor Models. *Journal of Derivatives*, 2(1): 21–31.

Longstaff, F. 1992. Multiple Equilibria and Term Structure Models. *Journal of Financial Economics*, 32: 333–344.

Merton, R.C. 1974. On the Pricing of Corporate Debt: The Risk Structure of Interest Rates. *Journal of Finance*, 29: 449–470.

Musiela, M. and Rutkowski, M. 1997. Martingale Methods in Financial Modelling. *Applications of Mathematics*, 36. Springer-Verlag.

Vasicek, O.A. 1977. An Equilibrium Characterisation of the Term Structure. *Journal of Financial Economics*, 5: 177–188.

Exercises

Questions

1. Explain what is meant by basis risk when futures contracts are used for hedging.
2. Which bond's price is more affected by a change in interest rates, a short-term bond or a longer-term bond, with all other features fixed? Why?

3. Provide the definitions of a discount bond and a premium bond. Give examples.
4. All else equal, which bond's price is more affected by a change in interest rates, a bond with a large coupon or a small coupon? Why?
5. What is the difference between the forward price and the value of a forward contract?
6. Someone argued that airlines have no point in using oil futures given that the chance of oil price being lower than the futures price in the future is the same as the chance of it being lower. Discuss this.
7. Why is the expected loss from a default on a swap less than the expected loss from the default on a loan with the same principal?
8. A futures price can be assimilated to a stock paying a dividend yield. What is the dividend yield in the futures case?
9. Describe the difference between a swap broker and a swap dealer.
10. If the cost advantage of interest rate swaps would likely be arbitraged away in competitive markets, what other explanations exist to explain the rapid development of the interest rate swap market?

Problems

1. The annual effective yield on a bond is 5%. A three-year bond pays coupons of 8% per year (semi-annual payments). Calculate the duration.
2. Calculate the modified duration and convexity of the bond in exercise 1.
3. Prove that the duration of a portfolio of many assets is the weighted average of all durations of the single assets.
4. Consider the following portfolio:

Bond	Coupon	Maturity	Par value	Price value	YTM
1	7.0	5	10,000,000	9,209,000	9.0%
2	10.5	7	20,000,000	20,000,000	10.5%
3	6.0	3	30,000,000	28,050,000	8.5%

Determine the yield to maturity of the portfolio.
5. Consider the two bonds in the following table:

	Bond A	Bond B
Coupon	8%	9%
Yield to maturity	8%	8%
Maturity	2 years	5 years
Par	€100.00	€100.00
Price	€100.00	€104.055

a. Compute the duration and modified duration for the two bonds.
b. Compute the convexity for the two bonds.

6. Recall the two bonds in exercise 4.
    a. Repeat the calculations of duration, modified duration and convexity, using the shortcut formula, by changing the yields by 0.2%.
    b. Compare the results with those found in exercise 4 and comment.
7. An investor holds 100,000 units of a bond whose features are summarized in the following table. He wishes to be hedged against a rise in interest rates.

Maturity	Coupon rate	Yield	Duration	Price
18 years	9.5%	8%	9.14	€114.181

Characteristics of the hedging instrument, which is here a bond, are as follows:

Maturity	Coupon rate	Yield	Duration	Price
20 years	10%	8%	9.49	€119.792

Coupon frequency and compounding frequency are assumed to be semi-annual. YTM stands for yield to maturity. The YTM curve is flat at an 8% level.
    a. What is the quantity of hedging instrument that the investor has to trade? What type of position should the investor take on the hedging instrument?
    b. Suppose that the YTM curve increases instantaneously by 0.1%. Calculate the corresponding new price for the two bonds.
8. Consider the two bonds in exercise 7.
    a. When the YTM curve increases instantaneously by 0.1%, what happens to the portfolio in terms of profits or losses when the portfolio is not hedged? What if it is hedged?
    b. If the curves shifts by 2% instead, how does the answer to point a. change?
9. A bank is required to pay €1,100 in one year. There are two investment options available with respect to how funds can be invested now in order to provide for the €1,100 payback. The first asset is a non-interest bearing cash fund, in which an amount x will be invested, and the second is a two-year zero-coupon bond earning 10% per year (corresponding to the risk-free rate in the economy), in which an amount y will be invested.
    a. Develop an asset portfolio that minimizes the risk that liability cash flows will exceed asset cash flows.
10. What position is equivalent to a long forward contract to buy an asset at K on a certain date and a put option to sell it for K on that date?
11. How can a forward contract on a stock with a particular delivery price and delivery date be created from options?
12. An insurance company has negotiated a three-year plain vanilla swap, exchanging a fixed payment of 8% for floating LIBOR + 1%. The notional principal is €50,000,000. The LIBOR is expected to be 7%, 9% and 10% at the end of each of the next three years, respectively.
    a. Determine the net dollar amount to be received, or paid, by the insurance company each year.

Appendix: Principal component analysis of the term structure

The Principal Component Analysis (PCA) to the term structure provides an alternative representation of the changes in the term structure (ΔTS), by means of principal components x_i, as defined by

$$\Delta TS = (\Delta x_1, \Delta x_2, ..., \Delta x_n)$$

The method of derivation of coefficients requires knowledge of matrix calculus.

Any realization of principal components implies a corresponding unique change in the key rates. Principal components are linear combinations of changes in the interest rates, given as

$$\Delta x_i = \sum_{i=1}^{n} \eta_{ij} \Delta y_j, \ j = 1, 2, ... n$$

where

η_{ij} are the principal component coefficients
y_j is the yield corresponding to maturity j.

Each component explains the maximum percentage of the total residual variance not explained by previous components. The starting point is the covariance matrix of zero-coupon rates, which is symmetric, with m independent eigenvectors, corresponding to m non-negative eigenvalues. Looking at eigenvalues in order of size, the highest eigenvalue corresponds to a specific eigenvector, whose elements are identified as the coefficients of the first principal component.

The second highest eigenvalue corresponds to another specific eigenvector, whose elements are identified as the coefficients of the second principal component. And so on, for all eigenvalues.

So the variance of each component is given by the size of the corresponding eigenvalue, and the proportion of total variance of the interest changes explained by the i-th principal component is

$$\sigma_{y,i}^2 = \frac{\lambda_i}{\sum_{i=1}^{m} \lambda_i}$$

From condition of independency of eigenvectors, it follows that the matrix of coefficients η_{ij} is orthogonal, so that its inverse corresponds to the transpose. The equation for Δx_i can then be inverted, to get the interest rates, as

$$\Delta y_j = \sum_{i=1}^{n} \eta_{ij} \Delta x_i, \ j = 1, 2, ... n$$

From how the model is built, it is clear that lowest eigenvalues play a very small role in determining the changes in interest rates. Therefore it is possible to reduce the dimensionality of the model to the m highest eigenvalues, as given by

$$\Delta y_j = \sum_{i=1}^{m} \eta_{ij} \Delta x_i + \varepsilon_i$$

where

ε_i is an error term due to the approximation from reduced dimensionality.

Changes in interest rates are then sufficiently well approximated by the first k components and the portfolio sensitivity to these components can be used to define the IRR profile.

The model as shown above implies each principal component to have very different variances, meaning that an even (i.e. unitary) shift in all components would not make them equally likely.

A further step involves giving to each factor a unit variance, so to make changes in each factor comparable. Again from matricial calculus, the unit variance is obtained by multiplying each eigenvector by the square root of the corresponding eigenvalue, so that the model gets the form

$$\Delta y_j = \sum_{i=1}^{m} \left(\eta_{ij} \sqrt{\lambda_i} \right) \frac{\Delta x_i}{\sqrt{\lambda_i}} + \varepsilon_i$$

so that in an equivalent equation, the product of eigenvalue and eigenvector is isolated. The new factor loading in parenthesis measures the impact of one standard deviation move in each principal component.

7 Credit risk

Credit risk is the risk of loss due to a borrower's failure to repay a loan or meet a contractual obligation. Credit risk arises when an obligor is planning to use future cash flows to pay a current debt.

There are many types of counterparties and many different types of obligations, so that credit risk takes many forms. As a general rule, investors are compensated for assuming credit risk by way of interest payments from the obligor.

The credit risk management process involves the identification of potential risks, the measurement of them, and appropriate treatment, through implementation of risk models. Assessment can be analytical and formulaic, or based on qualitative analysis.

Modern credit risk management is recognized by many economic actors, due to recent history of financial failures of banks and other financial institutions. The recent Basel II capital accord articulates new market standards for credit risk management and capital adequacy for banks.

Banks are increasingly facing credit risk in various financial instruments and the settlement of transactions. The ability to discriminate good customers from bad ones is a decisive element to be successful in the credit industry.

After studying this chapter you will be able to answer the following questions, among others:

1. What are the main drivers of credit risk? How can they be combined in order to achieve risk measurement?
2. What are credit ratings, and what is their importance for assessing the riskiness of credit investments?
3. What are structural models of credit risk?
4. What are reduced-form models of credit risk?
5. What are the main models used in the industry for the assessment of credit risk and the elaboration of credit ratings?

The first section of the chapter focuses on the main variables of credit risk, and their analysis. The second section is about structural models of credit risk, based on intrinsic information on the corporation, as implemented by researchers and adopted by the industry. The final part deals with threshold and mixture models, offering a different approach, based on analytical assumptions.

7.1 Basic concepts

Learning outcomes

1. Define default probabilities and their properties.
2. Describe the loss given default and its calculation.
3. Explain how credit ratings impact on credit risk assessment.

7.1.1 Default probabilities

The first step in credit risk modelling is usually the measurement of the probability of default for a corporate exposure over a given investment horizon. Rating agencies publish synthetic measures of creditworthiness, but many investors prefer to apply other methodologies.

The default probabilities determined from historical data are usually different from the probabilities of default implied in bond prices or credit default swaps. These differences are sometimes quite large. Therefore it is important to establish a correct policy for default probability assessment.

The reason for the difference is that asset pricing on financial markets is usually done in a risk-neutral framework. Therefore the implied default probabilities are risk-neutral ones. Historical data, instead, give real-world (physical) probabilities as an output.

As mentioned above, usually default probabilities from bonds are derived in the risk-neutral framework. Consider a treasury (risk-free) bond with maturity T and face value $B_{T,f}$, with a yield r_f, and a similar zero-coupon bond issued by a corporation, with face value $B_{T,c}$ yielding r_c. Define the corresponding prices for the bonds today as $B_{0,f}$ and $B_{0,c}$. The present value of the cost of default is therefore

$$PV_{DF} = B_{0,f} - B_{0,c}$$

Positivity of the cost is guaranteed by the fact that, normally, the risk-free rate is much lower than a corporate yield, so that the discounted risk-free bond price is higher than the one of the corporate bond.

Define the five-year default probability of the corporate bond as p, and assume there is no recovery in case of default. The credit event generates a loss on the face value of the bond. It is then possible to define the expected loss as

$$EL = PV_{DF} = B_{T,c}\,pe^{-r_f T}$$

Therefore

$$p = \frac{PV_{DF}}{B_{T,c}e^{-r_f T}}$$

Example 7.1: Suppose that a five-year zero-coupon Treasury bond with a face value of 100 yields 4% and a similar five-year zero-coupon bond issued by a corporation yields 6.5%.

The corresponding prices are 82.19 for the treasury bond and 72.99 for the corporate bond. The present value of the cost of default is

$$PV_{DEF} = 82.19 - 72.99 = 9.20$$

The risk-neutral probability of default is

$$p = \frac{9.20}{100 \times e^{-0.05 \times 5}} = 0.112 = 11.2\%$$

This is a simplified approach, in that no recovery is considered. Moreover most bonds are not zero-coupon, therefore more complicated calculations are involved.

Duffie and Singleton (1999) derived a relationship between default probabilities and yield of corporate bonds. The basic definition of the spread is

$$s = -\frac{1}{t}\log\left(\frac{B_{0,c}}{B_{0,f}}\right)$$

The present value of the risk-free bond under the risk-neutral measure is given by

$$B_{0,f} = \hat{E}\left(e^{-\int_0^t r_u du}\right)$$

where

$\hat{E}$ denotes the expectation under the risk-neutral measure.

The survival function $F(t)$ is the function defining the probability of the reference to survive until some specified time of default τ, as

$$F(t) = P(\tau > t) = e^{-\int_0^t \lambda_u du}$$

where

λ is the hazard (default-intensity) rate, at some point in time.

The way spread is defined depends crucially on the definition of the recovery rate. Duffie and Singleton assume that a constant proportion R of the bond price at default is recovered. Therefore the price of the bond at time t is

$$B_{0,c} = \hat{E}\left(e^{-\int_0^t r_u + (1-R)\lambda_u du}\right)$$
$$= \hat{E}\left(e^{-\int_0^t r_u du}e^{-(1-R)\int_0^t \lambda_u du}\right)$$

It is easy to recognize the first exponential in parenthesis as the price at time zero of the risk-free bond

$$e^{-\int_0^t r_u + (1-R)\lambda_u du} = B_{0,f}$$

The second exponential can be manipulated as follows

$$e^{-(1-R)\int_0^t \lambda_u du} = \left(e^{-\int_0^t \lambda_u du}\right)^{1-R} = F(t)^{1-R}$$

Therefore the price of the defaultable bond can be expressed as

$$B_{0,c} = B_{0,f} F(t)^{1-R}$$

The solution to the spread becomes

$$
\begin{aligned}
s &= -\frac{1}{t}\log\left(\frac{B_{0,c}}{B_{0,f}}\right) \\
&= -\frac{1}{t}\log\left[\frac{B_{0,f} F(t)^{1-R}}{B_{0,f}}\right] = -\frac{1}{t}\log\left[F(t)^{1-R}\right]
\end{aligned}
$$

From every risky cash flow it is possible to derive the corresponding default probability, as a function of their price and the recovery rate. Suppose that a one-year risky zero-coupon bond trades at B and the risk-free rate is r_f. Market price is given by the multiplicative spread s over the risk-free rate

$$B_{0,c} = B_{T,c} e^{-r_f s}$$

Indicating with π the probability of default of the bond entity, and assuming a zero recovery rate, the bond price is

$$B_{T,c} e^{-r_f s} = e^{-r_f}\left[(1-\pi)\times B_{T,c} + \pi \times 0\right]$$

so that

$$\pi = 1 - e^{-s}$$

Spreads quote in the Credit Default Swap market, and allow for the construction of a credit curve in the same way as interest rate swaps can be used to construct the zero-coupon term structure.

As for swaps, the liquidity in the CDS market covers most maturities, making interpolation necessary only in a few cases. The calculation of the CDS spread is the focus of Section 10.2. This section deals with the use of spread to extract default probabilities.

Example 7.2: Suppose that a one-year risky zero coupon bond trades at 97.53. Assuming the risk-free rate is 4%, the price implies a yield of 6.5%, with a spread of 2.5% over the risk-free rate. This is verified considering that

$$100e^{-0.065} = 97.53$$

If the bond had a recovery value of zero, from pricing the equation we have that

$$e^{-0.04}\left[(1-\pi)\times100+\pi\times0\right]=97.53$$

and

$$\pi = 1-e^{-0.025} = 2.47\%$$

Recovery rates are usually estimated based on experience and historical data. After determining the appropriate level R of the recovery rate the first step is to strip out the effect on the spread.

A standard CDS will pay out the nominal value minus recovery, if the credit event happens, and the market spread s reflects the recovery rate. To compute the spread s_R net of the recovery rate, the following approximation can be used

$$s_R = se^{-R}$$

The default probability can be derived from following the same approach for a zero-coupon bond. The recovery rate is a constant so that there is a direct link between the spread and the default probability:

$$\pi = 1 - \frac{1}{\left(1+\dfrac{s}{1-R}\right)^t}$$

The link established between spreads and default probabilities is as direct as the link in fixed income between interest rates and forward rates.

Example 7.3: Recall Example 7.2. Introducing a recovery rate of 40% for the bond, the probability of default becomes then

$$\pi = 1 - \frac{1}{\left(1+\dfrac{0.025}{0.6}\right)} = 4.00\%$$

7.1.2 Loss given default

Credit exposure defines the amount at risk in the event of default, while the recovery rate is the fraction of loss that can be recovered through bankruptcy proceedings or some other form of settlement.

Exposure-at-default (EaD) is an interesting and difficult parameter to estimate in assessing counterparty credit risk. Banks and other financial institutions are offered many ways to calculate it. The main options offered by regulators include the existing Current Exposure Method (CEM), the Standardized Method (SM) and an Internal Model Method (IMM).

Table 7.1 Credit conversion factors for PFE calculation

Residual maturity	Interest rates	FX gold	Equities	Metals	Other commodities
<1 year	0.0%	1.0%	6.0%	7.0%	10.0%
1–5 years	0.5%	5.0%	8.0%	7.0%	12.0%
>5 years	1.5%	7.5%	10.0%	8.0%	15.0%

The range of models available to calculate EaD includes Value at Risk. The Current Exposure Method relies on the VaR methodology.

The main components involved in the calculation are the current exposure (CE), the current value of the amount at risk, and a potential future exposure (PFE), the maximum amount of exposure expected to occur on a future date with a high degree of statistical confidence. Exposure at default is defined as the sum of them. Therefore

$$E_D = E_C + E_{PF}$$

where

E_D is the amount of exposure at default
E_C is the amount of current exposure
E_{PF} is the amount of potential future exposure.

Sometimes the agreement with a financial counterparty involves some collateral as a guarantee of the operation. In this case the amount of collateral mitigates the amount of EaD, so that

$$E_D = E_C + E_{PF} - C_L$$

The PFE calculation is standardized by applying specific percentages to the notional values in the portfolio at risk. The credit conversion factors (CF) are different for various asset categories and maturities.

Banks that meet specific requirements are allowed to use the Current Exposure Method (CEM). They are allowed to net positions covered by a master agreement, but 40% of the PFE will always remain, even though trades might perfectly offset each other.

These indications translate into the PFE for n positions in a portfolio, with corresponding notional $L_i = L_1, L_2, ..., L_n$ and conversion factors $f_{C,i} = f_{C,1}, f_{C,2}, ..., f_{C,n}$ to be defined as

$$E_{PF} = 0.4 \sum_{i=1}^{n} L_i f_{C,i} + 0.6 N_{GR} \sum_{i=1}^{n} L_i f_{C,i}$$

where N_{GR} is the ratio of current exposure with netting to current exposure without netting.

$$N_{GR} = \frac{\max\left(\sum_{i=1}^{n} V_i, 0\right)}{\sum_{i=1}^{n} \max(V_i, 0)}$$

Example 7.4: Assume the following portfolio of assets

Asset	Notional value
Fixed Income 2 yrs	35,000,000
Fixed Income 10 yrs	−21,000,000
Equities A (2yrs)	13,000,000
Equities B (10 yrs)	25,000,000

The replacement ratio is

$$N_{GR} = \frac{35-21+13+25}{35+13+25} = \frac{52}{73} = 0.71$$

And the PFE is given by:

$$E_{PF} = 0.4\left[(35\times0.005)+(-21\times0.015)+(13\times0.08)+(25\times0.1)\right]+$$
$$+0.6\times0.71\times\left[(35\times0.005)+...+(25\times0.1)\right] = 2.81$$

Loss given default (LGD) is the magnitude of likely loss on the exposure and is expressed as a percentage of the exposure. LGD is specific for any type of transaction because it is influenced by characteristics like the presence of collateral and the degree of subordination.

The Basel Committee has stated rules for the calculation of the loss. The simplest approach is to apply fixed percentages to the EaD in order to get the loss. For example a 50% LGD value applies to unsecured transactions, with a higher LGD (75%) applied to subordinated exposures.

In presence of collateral, the LGD percentage is scaled according to the nature and amount of collateral. When the collateral is real estate, separate rules and calculations apply. All other transactions are viewed as unsecured for this regulatory purpose.

As for other variables, banks meeting some requirements can determine the appropriate loss given default to be applied to each exposure, based on internal analysis to be validated internally.

There are several ways to measure LGD for a portfolio or asset. A simple one is based on market prices of defaultable bonds. Since the future value is known, the comparison of actual price and future value leads to measure of the possible LGD.

The advantage of such an approach is that bond prices are directly observable, and reflect the behaviour of the market. Market transactions are supposed to reflect the investor's expected recovery on discounted principal and missed interest payments, restructuring costs and uncertainty.

The workout methodology is based on observed LGD over the length of a workout, and differs from the market approach in that the timing of cash flows paid by the asset is very important, impacting on the estimates of the actual LGD.

The tricky part is to determine the right discount factors for the various cash flows. The same debt restructuring for example can be more or less risky, according to the output assets. In principle the correct rate would be for an asset of similar risk. The workout LGD on a loan i is defined as

$$L_{GD,i} = 1 - \frac{R_{C,i} - C_{L,i}}{E_{D,i}}$$

where

$R_{C,i}$ is the present value of total cash flows recovered to date on loan i
$C_{L,i}$ is the present value of all costs (direct and indirect) on loan i.

Example 7.5: A bank-only asset is a corporate loan, and the EaD has been calculated as €181,530,000. Assume that after one year, the total amount of cash flows recovered on the loan is €18,000,000. The bank has total costs of €12,000 from the loan, and the risk-free rate is 4%. Ignoring decimals for simplicity it turns out that

$$R_C = 18,000,000e^{-0.04} = €17,294,210$$

The present value of costs is

$$C_L = e^{-0.04}12,000 = 11,529$$

The loss given default is therefore given by

$$L_{GD} = 1 - \frac{17,294,210 - 11,529}{181,530,000} = 1 - 0,095 = 0,905$$

meaning that in case of distress, the loss for the bank on the loan would equate 90.5% of the amount.

In case of recovery, the exposure at recovery (EaR), which is the amount to be recovered in case of distress, reduces the economic loss resulting from a default and the loss becomes

$$L_{GD,i} = 1 - \frac{R_{C,i} - C_{L,i} - R_E}{E_{D,i}}$$

where

R_E is the amount of exposure at recovery.

Example 7.6: Given the data in Example 7.5, assume there is a 40% recovery rate in case of default.

$$R_E = 0.40 \times 172,294,210 = 72,612,000$$

That reduces the loss to

$$L_{GD} = 1 - \frac{17,294,210 - 11,529 + 72,612,000}{181,530,000} = 1 - 0,495 = 0,505$$

Another methodology is the analysis of credit spreads of risky bonds, and to use them to estimate the LGD. This methodology is not widely used, especially in banks. It is used much more on trading floors.

The spread over the risk-free rate reflects the premium required by the investors, including the expectations on loss, the liquidity premia and default probabilities.

7.1.3 Credit ratings

The process for assessing the credit quality of an obligor is called credit analysis. It is a process of both qualitative and quantitative approach to the issue. Procedures like credit scoring mix with human judgement in order to gather a synthetic valuation.

Through the analysis of financial statements and the evaluation of the economic environment, a credit analyst can assess the riskiness involved in entering some obligation. Also the nature of the obligation plays a role, in that for example a senior debt is less risky than a subordinated one.

Based upon the analysis, the credit analysts assign the counterparty a credit rating, which can be used for making credit decisions. The figure of the credit analyst is very important and financial institutions hire their own professional to prepare credit ratings for internal use.

Another side of credit analysis is the world of specialized corporations, called rating agencies, that are in the business of developing credit ratings to be used by investors or third parties. Best known are Standard & Poor's, Moody's and Fitch.

Rating agencies fulfil the role of information intermediary between the bond investors and bond issuers. Their activities are mainly financed by commission fees paid by the banks.

Ratings result from a thorough analysis of public and private information from all relevant sources. Information usually is obtained from public sources. Rated companies also are a source of information through meetings with the senior management. A committee of experts assigns the rating which is communicated to the issuer that asked for it, and ratings are updated on an ongoing basis by the agencies.

Credit ratings are nowadays the main source for assessing the credit quality of an obligor and the riskiness implied by an investment, but their original purpose was to distinguish between investment grade and non-investment-grade debt securities.

Agencies put emphasis not only on the one-time credit analysis and score of an obligor, but even more on the stability of company performance over time. Companies evolve year by year both in business strategies and management structure.

Each rating agency has different standards for indicating the ratings associated with various risk categories. Ratings are in fact commonly indicated by a letter sign, synthetizing the credit information.

Credit ratings are not only issued for private companies. Sovereign credit rating aims at measuring the level of risk when investing in government bonds of a country. While government bills are usually considered risk free, in reality they entail political risk.

Ratings for government bonds are expressed usually in terms of a number (the higher the better) synthetizing various factors like economic performance/projections, structural assessment, debt indicators, access to banks, access to capital markets and other credit ratings.

Analytical and statistical models for credit risk are the focus of the rest of the chapter. It is interesting to mention here one of the most popular and simplest measures for credit rating creation.

Table 7.2 Credit ratings assigned by the major credit agencies

Standard & Poor's	Moody's	Fitch IBCA
AAA	Aaa	AAA
AA+	Aa1	AA+
AA	Aa2	AA
AA−	Aa3	AA−
A+	A1	A+
A	A2	A
A−	A3	A−
BBB+	Baa1	BBB+
BBB	Baa2	BBB
BBB−	Baa3	BBB−
BB+	Ba1	BB+
BB	Ba2	BB
BB−	Ba3	BB−
B+	B1	B+
B	B2	B
B−	B3	B−
CCC+	Caa1	CCC+
CCC	Caa2	CCC
CCC−	Caa3	CCC−
CC	Ca	CC
C	C	C
D		D

Table 7.3 Credit ratings on sovereign countries.
Source: http://www.creditratings101.com/

Rank	Country	Score
1	Norway	93.33
2	Switzerland	90.22
3	Sweden	88.93
4	Denmark	88.80
5	Finland	88.55
6	Luxembourg	88.27
7	Canada	88.26
8	Netherlands	88.20
9	Hong Kong	87.18
10	Australia	86.18

The Altman z-score model makes use of multiple discriminant analysis combining a set of five financial ratios into a unique score. The score uses statistical techniques to make predictions about probability of failure of an obligor, using eight variables from a company's financial statements.

Each of the five financial rations is assigned a specific weighting factor. The financial ratios in the Altman Z-score and their respective weight factors are shown in Table 7.4:

The score is then an indication of the state of the company, according to the following thresholds

$$z > 2.99 \quad \rightarrow \quad \text{Safe zone}$$
$$1.80 < z < 2.99 \quad \rightarrow \quad \text{Grey zone}$$
$$z < 1.80 \quad \rightarrow \quad \text{Distress zone}$$

Table 7.4 Altman's z-score factors and weights

Variable	Definition	Weighting factor
x_1	$\dfrac{\text{Working Capital}}{\text{Total Assets}}$	1.2
x_2	$\dfrac{\text{Retained Earnings}}{\text{Total Assets}}$	1.4
x_3	$\dfrac{\text{EBIT}}{\text{Total Assets}}$	3.3
x_4	$\dfrac{\text{Market Value of Equity}}{\text{Book Value of Total Liabilities}}$	0.6
x_5	$\dfrac{\text{Sales}}{\text{Total Assets}}$	1.0

Example 7.7: Consider the following simplified balance sheet of a company.

Entry	Value
Working capital	35,000,000
Retained earnings	15,000,000
EBIT	20,000,000
Market value of equity	200,000,000
Sales	50,000,000
Tot. assets	190,000,000
Tot. liabil.	50,000,000

The Altman z-score is therefore

$$Z_A = 1.2 \times \frac{35}{190} + 1.4 \times \frac{15}{190} + 3.3 \times \frac{20}{190} + 0.6 \times \frac{200}{50} + 1.0 \times \frac{50}{190} = 3.34$$

The score is good, therefore the company is in a safe zone in terms of credit reliability.

7.2 Structural models

Learning outcomes

1. Describe the KMV-Merton approach to credit risk.
2. Define first passage models.
3. Describe the CreditMetrics™ model.

7.2.1 The KMV-Merton approach

Given the nature of credit risk, one of the main issues is to describe the default processes. The literature has developed two types of model, structural and reduced form models.

Structural models process information on the evolution of corporate structural variables like assets and liabilities, in order to determine the time of default. The approach
allows us to model credit events based directly on economic fundamentals, such as the
capital structure of a company. The driving factors in structural models are the value of
corporate assets and the default threshold.

A popular structural approach is the model developed by R. Merton in 1974. The
model simplifies the company structure; assuming the total value V_t it is composed at
any time t by an amount E_t of equity and an amount of debt represented by a zero-
coupon bond maturing at T, with face value D_T, and value at time t equal to D.

Recall that the equity E of a company can be seen as a European call option on the
total value. This is evident considering that

$$E_T = \max(V_T - D)$$

When the total corporate value is enough to pay back the face value of the debt, the
firm does not default and shareholders receive the amount left after paying debt-holders. When debt is higher than asset value, the firm defaults and bondholders take control of the firm, while shareholders receive nothing.

Assume the firm can only default at time T. The total company value is assumed to
follow a diffusion process given by

$$dV_t = rV_t dt + \sigma_V V_t dW_t$$

where

σ_V is the volatility of company value.

The payoff to bondholders at time T is given by

$$D_T = V_T - E_T$$

It is then possible to apply the BSM pricing formula, in order to price the equity of the
company at time t, using D as the strike price.

$$E_t = e^{-r\Delta t}\left[e^{r\Delta t}V_t N(d_1) - DN(d_2)\right]$$

where

$$d_1 = \frac{\ln\left(\dfrac{e^{r\Delta t}V_t}{D}\right) + \dfrac{1}{2}\sigma_V^2 \Delta t}{\sigma_V \sqrt{\Delta t}}$$
$$d_2 = d_1 - \sigma_V \sqrt{\Delta t}$$

The term $-d_2$ is defined as distance to default (DD), and the probability of default at
time T is given by

$$\pi = \Pr(V_T < D_T) = N(-d_2)$$

The expected loss amount at time T can be defined as

$$L_E = F\left(N\left(-d_2\right) - \frac{e^{r\Delta t}V_t}{D} N\left(-d_2 - \sigma_V \sqrt{\Delta t}\right) \right)$$

The loss given default in this case is:

$$L_{GD} = \frac{e^{r\Delta t}V_t}{D} \frac{N\left(-d_2 - \sigma_V \sqrt{\Delta t}\right)}{N\left(-d_2\right)}$$

The spread can be computed as:

$$s = -\frac{1}{\Delta t} \log\left[N\left(d_2\right) + \frac{e^{r\Delta t}V_t}{D} N\left(-d_1\right) \right]$$

The complication in applying the Merton model is the necessity to estimate the firm's asset value V_t, and volatility σ_V, which are both unobservable. Moreover, the debt structure of the company must be turned into a zero-coupon bond with maturity T and face value D_T.

The maturity of the structured zero-coupon bond can be chosen to match the maturity structure of the debt or simply corresponding to some required time horizon. Merton's model is structured to not allow for a default prior to maturity.

Other models are structured for the time of default to be defined as the first passage time of the value process V to some deterministic or random barrier. In principle, the credit event may occur at any time before the maturity date.

In the reduced form model the time of default is determined by the first jump of an exogenously given jump process. The parameters governing the default hazard rate are inferred from market data.

Those models use the information publicly available on markets, about the debt instruments and CDS, to infer default probabilities and dependencies among counterparties. Of course they lack information about the structure and nature of the company.

The KMV model is based on the Merton structural approach. As for the original work, the model recognizes that neither the underlying value of the firm nor its volatility are directly observable.

Following the model assumptions in the Merton approach, the firm variables can be inferred by the ones observed for the equity, solving a system of simultaneous equations.

From now on, by suppressing the suffix t, for convenience, the value of the equity of the firm can be expressed as

$$E = VN\left(d_1\right) - e^{-r\Delta t}DN\left(d_2\right) \tag{7.1}$$

Using Itô's Lemma it can be shown that the volatility of equity σ_E is given by

$$\sigma_E = \left(\frac{V}{E}\right)\frac{\partial E}{\partial V}\sigma_V$$

In the BSM model it can be also shown that

$$\frac{\partial E}{\partial V} = N(d_1)$$

so that following Merton's model the volatility of equity becomes

$$\sigma_E = \left(\frac{V}{E}\right) N(d_1) \sigma_V \tag{7.2}$$

The first step in the implementation of the KMV-Merton model is to estimate σ_E from either historical stock returns data or from the volatility implied by options written on company equity.

After estimating the equity volatility a forecasting horizon must be chosen as well as a measure of the face value of the firm's debt. Also appropriate values for the firm's equity and the risk-free rate must be chosen.

The final step is to solve the system of equations (7.1) and (7.2) numerically for values of V and σ_V. The distance to default can be then calculated as

$$D_{DF} = \frac{\ln\left(\dfrac{V}{F}\right) + \left(\mu - \dfrac{\sigma_V^2}{2}\right)\Delta t}{\sigma_V \sqrt{\Delta t}}$$

where μ is an estimate of the expected annual return of the firm's assets. The probability of default corresponding to DD is

$$\pi_{KMV} = N(-DD)$$

The market value of the firm's equity, the face value of debt and the volatility of equity are the key inputs to the model. As the market value of equity declines, the probability of default increases.

That defines the main strength and weakness of the model. In fact, the model works properly when the Merton model assumptions are met and markets are efficient and well informed.

Following the same approach, Varicek developed his own model, which treats equity as a perpetual down-and-out option on the underlying of the firm. The model fits with many types of liabilities, including short- and long-term liabilities, convertible bonds, and both common and preferred equity.

The corporate market value and volatility of assets can be derived from the option pricing equations derived in the Vasicek framework. The default point term structure (i.e. the default barrier at different points in time in the future) is determined empirically.

The distance to default (DD) is calculated as the combination of asset value, volatility and the default point term structure, using the standard BSM approach

$$D_{DF} = \frac{\ln\left(\dfrac{V}{D_T}\right) + \left(\mu - \dfrac{\sigma_V^2}{2}\right)\Delta t}{\sigma_V \sqrt{\Delta t}}$$

The formula looks the same as in the KMV-Merton approach, but the main difference is that the value of the firm's debt is time-dependent. Therefore the model estimates a term structure of this default barrier to come up with a DD term structure to be mapped to a default-probability term structure.

The model leads to a term structure of default probabilities named expected default frequency (EDF). From the EDF term structure it is then possible to calculate the related cumulative EDF term structure up to any term T referred to as $CEDF_T$.

That measure is finally converted into a risk-neutral measure through the equation

$$\tilde{\lambda}_{DF,T} = N\left[N^{-1}\left(\lambda_{DF,T} \right) + \lambda\sqrt{\rho_{iM}^2}\,\sqrt{T}\,\right]$$

where

$\tilde{\lambda}_{DF,T}$ is the risk-neutral CEDF
$\lambda_{DF,T}$ is the CEDF
ρ^2 is the square of correlation between the underlying asset returns and the market index returns
λ is the market Sharpe ratio.

Finally, the spread of a zero-coupon bond is obtained as

$$s = \frac{1}{T}\log\left[1 - L_{GD} \times \tilde{\lambda}_{DF,T}\right]$$

which involves a risk-neutral LGD.

The main limitation of the Merton model is that it allows for default only at maturity. Moreover it is not properly correct to assimilate the whole firm to a tradable asset, given that the former does not offer observable parameters for the analysis.

The BSM-like assumption of non-stochastic interest rates sounds totally unrealistic in this framework, and the yield spread curve in calibrated versions of the Merton model typically remains essentially zero for months, in strong contradiction with observations.

7.2.2 First passage models

Several authors have been working on overcoming the main limitation of the Merton model, the limitation of default time to maturity only, proposing structural-type models in which this restrictive and unrealistic feature is relaxed.

First passage models extend the Merton framework by allowing default to happen at intermediate times, even before maturity T. As the name suggests, most of these models define the time of default as the first passage time of the value process V, and outstanding debt with face value D, to a deterministic or random barrier.

Black and Cox (1976) give an extension of the standard framework, taking into account advanced features of debt contracts, as covenants, subordination and restrictions. They state that default occurs when the firm's value falls below some certain time-dependent barrier D_t.

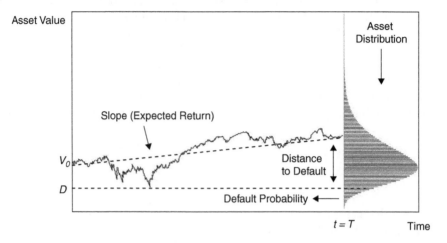

Figure 7.1 The KMV modelling of expected default.

This can be explained by the right of bondholders to exercise a covenant, allowing them to liquidate the firm whenever its value drops below the specified threshold, so that the default time is given by

$$\tau = \inf\left(t > 0 : V_t < D_t\right)$$

A consistent definition of default implies that

$$D_T \leq D$$

Moreover, in order for the time barrier to be meaningful, it must hold that

$$D_t > D$$

Many choices of the time-dependent barrier are possible, but Black and Cox choose the form of an increasing time-dependent barrier, as given by

$$D_t = D_0 e^{kt}$$
$$D_0 \leq De^{-kT}, \quad t \in [0, T)$$

where

k is an arbitrary constant.

When $k = r$, the default barrier is equal to the face value of the debt discounted at the risk-free interest rate.

Recall the Brownian motion process of the firm's value, as in the Merton framework, which stays valid in the framework of the first passage model, given by

$$dV_t = \mu V_t dt + \sigma V_t dW_t, \quad V_0 > 0$$

The first passage time to the threshold can be defined as the first passage time for a Brownian motion, as described by

$$\left(V_t < D_t\right) = \left[W_t + \dfrac{\left(r - \dfrac{\sigma^2}{2} - k\right)t}{\sigma} \le \dfrac{\log\left(\dfrac{D_0}{V_0}\right)}{\sigma}\right]$$

leading to the risk-neutral probability of default, defined as

$$Q\left(0 \le \tau < t\right) = Q\left[\min_{s \le t}\left(\dfrac{V_s}{D_s}\right) \le 1\right]$$

$$= Q\left\{\min_{s \le t}\left[W_t + \dfrac{\left(r - \dfrac{\sigma^2}{2} - k\right)t}{\sigma} \le \dfrac{\log\left(\dfrac{D_0}{V_0}\right)}{\sigma}\right]\right\}$$

After a change of variable, so that

$$A = \dfrac{\left(r - \dfrac{\sigma^2}{2} - k\right)t}{\sigma}$$

$$B = \dfrac{\log\left(\dfrac{D_0}{V_0}\right)}{\sigma}$$

and, from the probabilistic properties of the normal distribution, it follows that

$$Q\left(0 \le \tau < t\right) = 1 - \left\{N\left(\dfrac{A - B}{\sqrt{t}}\right) - e^{2AB}N\left(\dfrac{A + B}{\sqrt{t}}\right)\right\}$$

Other first passage models assume a constant default threshold $D > 0$. Assuming that at time of observation, t, default has not been triggered yet, so that $V_t > D$, the time of default τ is given by

$$\tau = \inf\left(s \ge t : V_s < K\right)$$

Using the reflection principle of Brownian motion yields the default probability between t and T, as

$$\Pr\left(\tau \le T \mid \tau > t\right) = N\left(h_1\right) + e^{\left[2\left(r - \frac{\sigma_V^2}{2}\right)\ln\left(\frac{K}{V_t}\right)\frac{1}{\sigma_V^2}\right]}N\left(h_2\right)$$

where

$$h_1 = \dfrac{\ln\left(\dfrac{D}{e^{r\Delta t}V_t}\right) + \dfrac{1}{2}\sigma_V^2 \Delta t}{\sigma_V \sqrt{\Delta t}}$$

$$h_2 = h_1 - \sigma_V \sqrt{\Delta t}$$

Other forms of the first passage model allow for stochastic interest rates, bankruptcy costs, taxes, debt subordination and more. All the complications increase the degree of accuracy and realism of the models, at the expense of a higher analytical complexity. Bielecki and Rutkowski (2002) provide an extensive review of this class of models.

The default threshold is always positive and can be interpreted as a safety covenant of the corporate debt, allowing bondholders to take control on the firm, acting as a protection mechanism against possible moral hazard of the shareholders and the management.

A direct consequence of introducing stochasticity of interest rates is that a correlation is then assumed between the asset value and the interest rates. This makes the default threshold stochastic, when specified as the discounted value of the face value of the debt.

7.2.3 CreditMetrics™

The CreditMetrics™ model was introduced by J.P. Morgan and Partners in 1997, as a VaR based methodology to value non-traded assets like loans and privately placed bonds.

CreditMetrics™ is built around credit migration, represented by a transition matrix that measures the probability that the credit rating of any given debt security will change over the course of the credit horizon.

Technically, the methodology is made of three main steps:

1. Estimation of the credit exposure amount of each obligor in the portfolio.
2. Calculation of the volatility of portfolio value subject to credit quality changes.
3. Calculation of the correlations among obligors and final risk measure.

In order to estimate the credit quality migrations, it is necessary to use transition matrices containing the migration probabilities. A transition matrix allows mapping the probability of an obligation to downgrade or upgrade in rating over time.

The risk of a position is given by the possibility of the obligor to default, but also to changes in value. Transition matrices give the picture of what are the probabilities associated with entering a default state, or migrating to another credit quality state.

The main statistical assumption is that the credit rating changes for different counterparties are assumed to be dependent. Therefore standard linear correlation fails to capture the dependence among counterparties.

A sophisticated method to model correlation is through copula functions, which are the core topic of Section 12.1. A Gaussian copula model can be used to build up a joint probability distribution of rating changes.

The copula correlation between the rating transitions for two companies is typically equated to the correlation between their equity returns through a factor model, and copula properties of marginal distributions.

Through the CreditMetrics™ approach, credit risk is measured at both volatility and percentile level.

Rating upgrades and downgrades impact on the required credit risk spreads or premiums, therefore affecting the implied market value of the loan. In case a loan is downgraded, the credit spread should rise in order for the discounted loan value to decrease. The reverse is true for a credit rating upgrade.

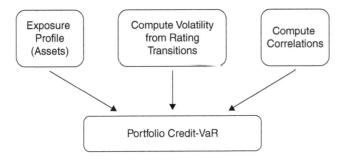

Figure 7.2 Scheme of the procedure for applying the CreditMetrics™ model to a portfolio of assets.

...	...	...	...	...	...	...	...	...
AA	0. 8	90.72	7.42	0.72	0.26	0.08	0.00	0.00
...	...	...	...	...	...	...	...	...
BB	0.01	0.09	0.54	6.62	82.76	7.80	0.63	0.06
...	...	...	...	...	...	...	...	...

$N^{-1}(0.0008) = -3.156$
$N^{-1}(0.0008 + 0.9072) = 1.328$
$N^{-1}(0.0008 + 0.9072 + 0.0742) = 2.101$

$N^{-1}(0.0001) = -3.719$
$N^{-1}(0.0001 + 0.0009) = 3.090$
$N^{-1}(0.0001 + 0.0009 + 0.0054) = 2.489$

Figure 7.3 Rating transition quantiles for the given transition matrix.

In constructing the model representation, consider two companies X and Y, having respectively ratings of AA and BB. Also suppose that the correlation between the equity returns of the two companies has been measured and is equal to some defined value.

Credit ratings between counterparties are assumed to be dependent, and the dependence structure can be measured using a Gaussian copula, so that rating transition thresholds can be set as quantiles of a normal distribution, and the copula correlation, as shown in Figure 7.3, using the data in Table 7.5.

For each rating considered, the transition quantiles can be calculated as the inverse of the normal distribution of probabilities that are obtained by summing up as many of the matrix probabilities in a line, for how many rating steps are considered.

Repeating the calculation so that for any single rating, the thresholds corresponding to all ratings are calculated, it is possible to obtain a map of the thresholds associated with each rating, which are of course normally distributed.

The main point is that, according to what are the estimated rating transitions, the portfolio value must be revalued in order to take this into account. And risk can be measured accordingly. It is useful to see a full example for just one bond.

Transition thresholds are useful in that a further step of the model is the Monte Carlo simulation of the value of the company, and the company is placed into a rating

Table 7.5 A typical example of a credit ratings transition matrix. For each transition from a rating to another, the table shows the corresponding transition probability.

Initial rating	Rating at the end of the year (%)							
	AAA	*AA*	*A*	*BBB*	*BB*	*B*	*CCC*	*Default*
AAA	90.81	8.21	0.74	0.08	0.12	0.03	0.01	0.00
AA	0.80	90.72	7.42	0.72	0.26	0.08	0.00	0.00
A	0.04	2.32	90.84	5.63	0.84	0.24	0.04	0.05
BBB	0.05	0.31	5.78	87.12	5.22	1.21	0.13	0.18
BB	0.02	0.16	0.71	7.52	80.61	8.63	1.12	1.23
B	0.00	0.14	0.26	0.47	6.61	83.52	4.12	4.88
CCC	0.25	0.12	0.21	1.35	2.42	11.12	65.01	19.52

class, according to where the simulated value falls among the ranges bounded by the thresholds.

Once the new simulated rating classes are obtained, another step consists in simulating credit spreads, in order to obtain a new term structure of forward rates, and use them for pricing the bonds.

Finally, a Credit VaR measurement is performed on the revaluated assets, so that a credit-adjusted risk measure is obtained, as a final outcome.

7.3 Reduced-form models

Learning outcomes

1. Describe the Jarrow-Turnbull model of credit risk.
2. Describe the Duffie-Singleton model of credit risk.
3. Define and comment on the CreditRisk+™ model.

7.3.1 The Jarrow-Turnbull model

Reduced-form models are based on exogenous default, risk-neutral measures and the absence of arbitrage. Default is characterized as the first event of a Poisson counting process. Default occurs at some time τ with probability proportional to some time-dependent function, which is given by

$$\Pr(t < \tau < t + dt) = \lambda_t dt \tag{7.3}$$

where

λ_t is the hazard rate.

The hazard rate describes the rate at which default occurs and is given by

$$\lambda_t = \lim_{\Delta t \to 0} \frac{1}{\Delta t} \Pr(D_{t+\Delta t} | S_t) \tag{7.4}$$

where

$D_{t+\Delta t}$ is the event of the company defaulting between t and $t + \Delta t$
S_t is the event of the company surviving at time t.

In terms of logic, it is then possible to define the survivor function $Q_{t+\Delta t}$ of the company, at time $t + \Delta t$, in terms of the events, like

$$Q_{t+\Delta t} = \Pr\left(S_{t+\Delta t} \wedge S_t\right)$$

where

$S_{t+\Delta t} = \bar{D}_{t+\Delta t}$ is the event of the company surviving between t and $t + \Delta t$.

The formula can be expressed in terms of conditional probabilities, as

$$Q_{t+\Delta t} = \Pr\left(S_{t+\Delta t} | S_t\right)\Pr\left(S_t\right)$$

It follows that

$$Q_{t+\Delta t} - Q_t = \Pr\left(S_{t+\Delta t} | S_t\right)\Pr\left(S_t\right) - \Pr\left(S_t\right)$$

Now note that, since $F_t = \Pr\left(S_t\right)$, the formula can be rewritten as

$$Q_{t+\Delta t} - Q_t = Q_t \left[\Pr\left(S_{t+\Delta t} | S_t\right) - 1\right]$$
$$= -Q_t \Pr\left(D_{t+\Delta t} | S_t\right)$$

From (7.3) and (7.4), some mathematics show that

$$\frac{F_{t+\Delta t} - F_t}{F_t} = -\lambda_t$$

Integrating both sides yields the expression

$$\ln\left(Q_t\right) - \ln\left(Q_0\right) = -\int_0^t \lambda_s ds$$

and, from $Q_0 = 1$ (by convention the probability of a company starting the business is equal to one), it follows that

$$Q_t = e^{-\int_0^t \lambda_s ds}$$

which is the expression for the survival probability before time t.

   A popular reduced-form approach for calculating default probability is based on the work by Jarrow and Turnbull (1995). The model assumes that no matter when default occurs, the recovery payment is paid at maturity time T.

The survival probability before time t, when maturity is set at T, is discretized and defined as

$$Q_{t,T} = e^{-\lambda(T-t)}$$

Then the coupon bond value is given by

$$
\begin{aligned}
B_t &= P_{t,T} R \int_t^T -dQ_{t,u} du + \sum_{i=1}^n P_{t,T_i} C_i e^{-\lambda(T_i-t)} \\
&= P_{t,T} R \left[1 - e^{-\lambda(T_i-t)} \right] + \sum_{i=1}^n P_{t,T_i} C_i e^{-\lambda(T_i-t)}
\end{aligned}
\tag{7.5}
$$

where

$P_{t,T}$ is the risk-free discount factor
P_{t,T_i} is the proper discount factor for the i-the coupon
C_i is the i-th coupon
R is the recovery rate.

Conditional default probability disappears in the above formula, so that there is no dependency with the bond price. This holds even for $R = 0$ and the value of λ for a ZCB is also the bond's forward yield spread. This can be seen by showing that

$$D_{t,T} = P_{t,T} e^{-\lambda(T_i-t)}$$

which can be considered a risky discount factor.

A complication of the model that is often used in practice involves letting the intensity parameter to be time-dependent, and allowing for the recovery rate to be paid upon default. Equation (7.5) is then modified as

$$
\begin{aligned}
B_t &= \int_t^T P_{t,u} R_u \left(-dQ_u \right) + \sum_{i=1}^n P_{T,i} C_i Q_{t,T_i} \\
&= \int_t^T P_{t,u} R_u \lambda_u e^{-\int_i^u \lambda_s ds} + \sum_{i=1}^n P_{T,i} C_i e^{-\int_i^{T_i} \lambda_s ds}
\end{aligned}
$$

where

$$Q_{t,T_i} = e^{-\lambda(T-t)}$$

The Jarrow-Turnbull model has the great advantage of calibration, that can be done using a series of risky zero-coupon bonds, in order to get a default probability curve and the corresponding spread curve.

By definition, the difference between two survival probabilities $Q_{0,s}$ and $Q_{0,t}$ at times $s > t$ is the default probability between s and t. Choosing an arbitrary recovery rate, it is possible to retrieve default probabilities from bond prices.

7.3.2 The Duffie-Singleton model

The Jarrow-Turnbull model assumes that recovery payment can only occur at maturity, which is not the general case, and it is far from reality. The two drawbacks are that recovery in reality occurs upon default, and its amount can vary over time.

Duffie and Singleton (1999) developed a reduced-form model that allows the payment of recovery to occur at any time, for an amount proportional to the full value of the bond (fractional recovery), as given by

$$R_t = \delta D_t \tag{7.6}$$

where

δ is a constant recovery factor
D_t is the full (as not defaulted) value of the debt at default time t.

The model implies that as the credit quality of a reference entity default, the price of the corresponding bond decreases, and the corresponding recovery amount is a fraction of that value, instead of being proportional to the final payoff, like in the Jarrow-Turnbull model. In mathematical terms it means there exists some adapted loss process L_t such that

$$L_t = 1 - \delta_t \tag{7.7}$$

which is complementary to the recovery factor.

Debt value at time t is assimilated to a claim, as the expected payoff is weighted by the probabilities of default occurring or not, and it is given by

$$D_t = \left[\frac{p(1 - L_t) E(D_{t+\Delta t}) + (1 - p) E(D_{t+\Delta t})}{1 + r \Delta t} \right] \tag{7.8}$$

where

p is the probability of default
r is the interest rate.

The equation can be solved recursively and gives the value of the debt in case of no default occurring. Considering equations (7.6), (7.7), (7.8), the value of the debt is defined as

$$D_t = \left[\frac{1 - p\Delta t(1 - \delta)}{1 + r \Delta t} \right]^n B_T$$

where

B_T is the value of the debt at maturity as no default occurs
n is the number of periods considered.

By conditioning to $\Delta t = \dfrac{T}{n}$, after some mathematical manipulation, the formula for the debt value simplifies in

$$D_t = e^{-rT - p(1-\delta)T} B_T$$

This formula holds in case all parameters of the exponentials are not time-dependent. In the more general case, assuming time-dependence for the default probability and the interest rate, the Duffie-Singleton model can be written as

$$D_t = E\left(e^{-\int_t^T [r_u + p_u(1-\delta)] du} \right) B_T$$

7.3.3 CreditRisk+ ™

The model CreditRisk+™ was developed by Credit Suisse in 1997. It is the most famous reduced-form model of credit default risk and it is not based on any assumption about the causes of default.

The model assumes default rates to be continuous random variables, incorporating the volatility of default rates to capture the uncertainty in the level of default rates. Macroeconomic factors may cause the incidence of defaults between different obligors to be correlated, even though there is no causal link between them.

Factors are input in the model using default rate volatilities and sector analysis, not modelling default correlations as input into the model. Sectors represent various industrial and geographical categories.

The mathematical approach of CreditRisk+™ is different from the one of structural models, in that it applies techniques widely used in the insurance industry to model the sudden event of an obligor default.

The assumptions underlying the CreditRisk+™ model enable the explicit computation of the distribution of the number of defaults in the portfolio. Each sector is characterized by a specific default rate, driven by a single underlying factor.

The total expected rate of default in a specific sector is modelled as a random variable with specified mean and standard deviation. The volatility reflects how the probabilities of default in the portfolio are distributed around the average levels.

The main reasons are that default correlations between obligors are not stable over time and there is a severe lack of data for empirical analysis. Defaults are in fact rare events, so that it is hard to extract a correlation measure from the data.

It is not possible to forecast the exact time of default of an obligor, nor the exact number of total defaults in a portfolio of many obligors.

In order to understand the mathematics of CreditRisk+™ it is important to derive the basic statistical theory of the process involved in the context of credit default risk. Consider a portfolio consisting of N obligors.

Following the technical document by CreditSuisse (1997), assume each position has a probability p of defaulting over a one-year time horizon. In order to analyse the distribution of losses from an aggregate portfolio, consider the probability generating function

$$F(x) = \sum_{n=0}^{\infty} p_n x^n$$

where

x is an auxiliary variable
p_n is the probability of having n defaults.

In case of a single obligor the formula reduces to

$$F_i(x) = 1 + p_i(x-1)$$

Given independence between events, the generating function of the overall portfolio is the product of the single probability generating functions

$$F(x) = \prod_i \left[1 + p_i(x-1) \right] \tag{7.9}$$

The formula becomes more convenient to work with, when taking the log, and ignoring the higher powers of probabilities, given they are very small. Therefore

$$\log\left[1 + p_i(x-1) \right] \simeq p_i(x-1)$$

Taking logs of equation (7.9) and integrating in the limit, the probability generating function yields

$$\log F(x) \simeq \sum_i p_i(x-1)$$

$$\rightarrow F(x) \simeq e^{\sum_i p_i(x-1)} \simeq e^{\lambda(x-1)}$$

From the probability generating function it is then possible to derive the corresponding form of distribution, by expanding it in a Taylor series

$$e^{\lambda(x-1)} = e^{-\lambda} e^{\lambda x} = \sum_{n=0}^{\infty} \frac{e^{-\lambda} \lambda^n}{n!} x^n$$

from which it is clear that, for small values of individual defaults, the probability of n defaults occurring in the portfolio is given by

$$p_n = \frac{e^{-\lambda} \lambda^n}{n!}$$

The distribution of the number of defaults in the portfolio for a given experiment on a given portfolio of obligors, must be then combined with a distribution of default losses, in order to get the measure of the distribution of default losses.

The distribution of losses is obtained through several steps. First of all it is necessary to group the exposures in the portfolio into tranches. Doing so, the amount of data required for calculation is significantly lower.

Dividing the portfolio into m tranches, the expected loss in terms of probability of default can be expressed, for each tranche, as

$$EL_j = v_j \lambda_j, \ j = 1, 2, ..., m$$

where

v_j is the common exposure for tranche j
λ_j is the expected number of defaults in trance j.

Since λ is the Poisson parameter, the sum of the expected number of default events in each exposure band, it follows that

$$\lambda = \sum_{j=1}^{m} \lambda_j = \sum_{j=1}^{m} \frac{EL_j}{v_j}$$

Define the probability generating function $G(x)$ in terms of multiples of the unit L of exposure:

$$G(x) = \sum_{n=0}^{\infty} p_{nL} x^n$$

where

p_{nL} is the probability of aggregate losses being equal to $n \times L$.

Exposure bands are independent therefore it is possible to write the probability generating function as a product of the single $G_j(x)$.

Treating each exposure band as a portfolio and using the Taylor expansion as for default process

$$G_j(x) = \sum_{n=0}^{\infty} p_n x^{v_j n} = e^{-\lambda_j} e^{\lambda_j x^{v_j n}}$$

it follows that

$$G(x) = e^{-\sum_{j=1}^{m} \lambda_j + \sum_{j=1}^{m} \lambda_j x^{v_j n}}$$

In practice, for the loss severity probability distribution, a lognormal probability distribution is often used. The parameters of this probability distribution are the mean and standard deviation of the logarithm of the loss.

The loss frequency distribution must be combined with the loss severity distribution for each loss type and business line to determine a total loss distribution. Monte Carlo simulation can be used for this purpose. As mentioned earlier, the usual assumption is that loss severity is independent of loss frequency. On each simulation trial, we proceed as follows:

- Sample from the frequency distribution to determine the number n of loss events.
- Sample n times from the loss severity distribution to determine the loss experienced for each loss event.
- Determine the total loss experienced.
- When many simulation trials are used, a total loss distribution is obtained.

Summary

Credit risk modelling involves several steps, including the measurement of the probability for a corporate exposure to default, credit exposure and a given investment horizon.

Credit exposure is the amount at risk in case of default, and the recovery rate represents the fraction of the loss that can be recovered through bankruptcy proceedings or some other form of settlement.

The estimation of the exposure at default is of high relevance in assessing counterparty credit risk. There are many ways that can be used by financial institutions to calculate EAD, also as described in regulatory documents.

The loss given default is the size of the loss which is likely to happen on the exposure, expressed as a percentage of the exposure. It is specific for transaction types, and influenced by elements like the presence of some collateral, and the degree of subordination.

Credit analysis allows us to assess the credit quality of a counterparty, as a process of quantitative and qualitative approach. Credit scoring is a mix of human judgement and quantitative information, merged into a synthetic valuation.

Credit ratings are used to assess credit quality through synthetic indicators, and the riskiness implied by an investment, and are obtained through the implementation of analytical models of credit.

The structural approach processes the available information about the corporate structural assets and liabilities, to determine the default time. It also allows modelling of the credit events on the basis of economic fundamentals.

Reduced-form models are based on exogenous shocks, risk-neutral measures and the absence of arbitrage. Default is characterized as the first event of a Poisson counting process.

Bibliography

Arora, N., Bohn, J.R. and Zhu, F. 2005. *Reduced Form vs. Structural Models of Credit Risk: A Case Study of Three Models.* Moody's KMV Company.

Basle Committee on Banking Supervision. 1999. *Credit Risk Modelling: Current Practices and Applications.*

Berd, A.M., Mashal, R. and Wang, P. 2003. *Estimating Implied Default Probabilities from Credit Bond Prices.* Lehman Brothers.

Bielecki, T.R. and Rutkowski, M. 2000. *Credit Risk: Modeling, Valuation and Hedging.* Springer Finance.

Black, F. and Cox, J. 1976. Valuing Corporate Securities: Some Effects of Bond Indenture Provisions. *Journal of Finance* 31: 351–367.

Brandimarte, P. 2006. *Numerical Methods in Finance and Economics, A MATLAB®-Based Introduction.* 2nd Edition. John Wiley & Sons.

Credit Suisse Financial Products. 1997. *CreditRisk+: A Credit Risk Management Framework.*

Duffie, D. and Singleton, K. 1999. Modeling Term Structures of Defaultable Bonds. *Review of Financial Studies* 12: 678–720.

Duffie, D. and Singleton, K.J. 2003. *Credit Risk: Pricing, Measurement, and Management.* Princeton University Press.

Glants, M. and Mun, J. 2008. *The Banker's Handbook on Credit Risk Implementing Basel II.* Elsevier Academic Press.

Gupton, G.M. and Stein, R.M. 2002. *LossCalc™: Moody's Model for Predicting Loss Given Default (LGD).* Moody's Investor Service, February.

Hamilton, D.T. and Varma, P. 2005. *Default and Recovery Rates of Corporate Bond Issuers.* Moody's Global Credit Research, January.

Jarrow, R.A. and Turnbull, S.M. 1995. Pricing Derivatives on Financial Securities Subject to Credit Risk. *Journal of Finance,* 50: 53–86.

J.P. Morgan. *CreditMetrics Technical Document.* JP Morgan New York.

J.P. Morgan. *Introducing the J.P. Morgan Implied Default Probability Model: A Powerful Tool for Bond Valuation.* J.P. Morgan Securities Inc. Emerging Markets Research.

Kimber, A. 2004. *Credit Risk From Transaction to Portfolio Management.* Elsevier Butterworth-Heinemann.

Mark, R.M. 1999. *Derivative Credit Risk: Further Advances in Measurement and Management.* Risk Books.

Merton, R.C. 1974. On the Pricing of Corporate Debt: The Risk Structure of Interest Rates. *Journal of Finance,* 29: 449–470.

Mun, J. 2010. *Modeling Risk: Applying Monte Carlo Risk Simulation, Strategic Real Options, Stochastic Forecasting, and Portfolio Optimization.* John Wiley & Sons.

Wagner, H.S. 1996. The Pricing of Bonds in Bankruptcy and Financial Restructuring. *Journal of Fixed Income,* (June): 40–47.

Exercises

Questions

1. What are the main factors affecting credit risk, and how do they relate to each other?
2. Describe the Monte Carlo application of CreditRisk+™. How would you sample for default intensity? Why?
3. How would you use a CDS to hedge credit risk on a single zero-coupon defaultable bond? Support your answer with a numerical example.
4. How would you relate the structure and rationale of Collateralized Debt Obligations, and the rising of a financial crisis?
5. How would you apply an interest rate model to credit risk? How would you approach the calculation of default probabilities in that framework?
6. Describe the main features of the Credit Metrics model. What are the main differences with the Credit Risk+™ model?

Problems

1. Consider a bank holding the following portfolio of assets:

Asset	Notional value	Collateral
Fixed Income 2 yrs	32,000,000	7,000,000
Fixed Income 10 yrs	−18,000,000	2,000,000
FX gold 7 yrs	11,000,000	3,000,000
Other Commodities 5 yrs	−13,000,000	4,000,000
Equities A (2yrs)	24,000,000	9,000,000
Equities B (10 yrs)	−5,000,000	1,000,000

Assume the level of current exposure is estimated to be 20% of the net future exposure.

   a. Calculate the exposure at default of the bank.

2. The balance sheet of a company includes the following entries:

Entry	Value
Working capital	45,000,000
Retained earnings	22,000,000
EBIT	18,000,000
Market value of equity	150,000,000
Sales	60,000,000
Tot. assets	210,000,000
Tot. liabil.	90,000,000

Calculate the Altman z-score.

3. Suppose that a ten-year zero-coupon Treasury bond with a face value of 100 yields 4.5% and a similar ten-year zero-coupon bond issued by a corporation yields 6.5%.

   a. Calculate the risk-neutral probability of default.

4. A bank-only asset is a corporate loan, of total €120,000,000. After five years the obligor has made regular monthly payments of €1,000, inclusive of a 50% interest amount. The bank has total costs of €2,000 per year from the loan. Assume a risk-free rate of 5% and a recovery rate of 40%.

   a. Calculate the workout loss given default.

5. A CDS contract offers protection to default of a company, starting on 1 January 2011 and the expiry date is 1 October 2013. The contract rate is 0.50% per annum and the payment dates are 1st April, 1st July, 1st October and 1st January of each year. The contract notional is €7,500,000, and the recovery rate is 40%.

   a. What is the present value of this contract?

6. A loan amount is priced at €104,000,000 at the beginning of the swap period, with a loss of €15,000,000 experienced at the end of the period. Suppose that interest payment plus fees on the loan is 6%.

   a. Calculate the level of the LIBOR corresponding to a total return to the swap buyer of 8%.

7. Suppose that a five-year risky zero-coupon bond trades at €87.33 and the risk-free rate is 4%. Recovery rate is 40%.

   a. Compute the default probability from the multiplicative spread.

8. Given the transition matrix in Table 7.5, retrieve the transition quantiles associated with an A-rated and a B-rated position.
9. An application of CreditMetrics™ analysis produces the following output for a BBB borrower:

Rating	Transition prob.	Value
AAA	0.02%	109.37
AA	0.33%	109.19
A	5.95%	108.66
BBB	86.93%	107.55
BB	5.30	102.22
B	1.17	98.10
CCC	0.12	83.64
Default	0.18	51.13

Calculate the 95% and 99% VaR associated with the portfolio, assuming normality of returns. Repeat the analysis assuming non-normality.

Appendix: The Markov process for transition matrices

A Markov chain is a sequence of variables $X_1, X_2, ..., X_n$ sharing the Markov property, described as

$$\Pr\left(X_{n+1} = x \mid X_1 = x_1, X_2 = x_2, ..., X_n = x_n\right) = \Pr\left(X_{n+1} = x \mid X_n = x_n\right)$$

Assume the variable $x = \left(x_t \mid t = 0,1,2,...\right)$ identifying credit ratings of some exposure, is a Markov chain on the finite state space $S = \left(1, 2, ..., Z, Z+1\right)$, from state 1 being the best credit class, until $Z+1$ designating the default state.

Since it is not possible to move back from default, the $Z+1$ is the absorbing state of the chain, where the state is absorbing if and only if

$$p_{ii} = 1$$
$$p_{ij} = 1, \quad \forall i \neq j$$

where

p_{ij} is the probability to move from state i to state j.
Denote $P(s,t)$ as the $(Z+1) \times (Z+1)$ transition matrix generated by a Markov chain model with transition probability as

$$p_{ij} = P\left(x_t = j \mid x_s = i\right), \quad s < t$$

This is the probability that a borrower rated i at time s migrates to rating j at time t. Let $\bar{P}$ denote transition matrices for the discrete-time estimator.

The first Markov chain model applied to the transition matrix is the discrete-time Markov chain model based on annual migration frequencies. Generally, estimation in a discrete-time Markov chain can be viewed as a multinomial experiment since it is based on the migration away from a given state over a one-year horizon. Let $N_i(t)$ denote the number of firms in state *i* at the beginning of the year and $N_{ij}(t)$ represents the number of firms with rating *i* at date *t* migrated to state *j* at time $t+1$. Thus, the one-year transition probability is estimated as

$$\bar{p}_{ij}(t) = \frac{N_{ij}(t)}{N_i(t)}$$

If the rating process is assumed to be a time-homogeneous Markov chain, i.e. time-independent, then the transitions for different borrowers away from a state can be viewed as independent multinomial experiments. Therefore, the maximum likelihood estimator (MLE) for time independent probability is defined as

$$\bar{p}_{ij} = \frac{\sum\limits_{t=1}^{T} N_{ij}(t)}{\sum\limits_{t=1}^{T} N_i(t)}$$

where *T* is the number of sample years. The estimator of transition probabilities is always modified by the number of firms during the sample years. If $\bar{P}$ denotes the transition matrix for a Markov chain over a year horizon, then the discrete-time transition matrix is as

$$\bar{P} = \begin{bmatrix} \bar{p}_{11} & \bar{p}_{12} & \cdots & \bar{p}_{1C} & \bar{p}_{1,C+1} \\ \bar{p}_{21} & \bar{p}_{22} & \cdots & \bar{p}_{2C} & \bar{p}_{2,C+1} \\ \vdots & \vdots & \ddots & \vdots & \vdots \\ \bar{p}_{C1} & \bar{p}_{C2} & \cdots & \bar{p}_{CC} & \bar{p}_{C,C+1} \\ 0 & 0 & \cdots & 0 & 1 \end{bmatrix}$$

where

$$\bar{p}_{ij} \geq 0, \quad \forall i,j$$

and

$$\sum_{j=1}^{C+1} \bar{p}_{ij} = 1, \quad \forall i$$

8 Liquidity risk

Liquidity risk arises as one of the major types of risk faced by banks and financial institutions. During the recent financial crisis, the role of liquidity risk prominently emerged, as well as the importance of its proper management, as a crucial condition for the viability of banks.

Liquidity risk stems from the difficulty or impossibility to market or close an investment quickly enough to prevent or minimize a loss. It is generally valid that the positions of smaller size are subject to larger liquidity risk.

Liquidity risk management aims at accomplishing two main objectives. On one side, it should assess, in perspective, the funding needed by an institution to meet obligations. On the other side, it must ensure the availability of cash or collateral to fulfil those needs at the appropriate time through coordination of the available funding sources under normal and stressed conditions.

Investors owning long-term assets should take into account the marketability of those assets, in relation to their short-term cash needs. If assets are sold in an illiquid market, in fact, they are difficult to market, therefore carrying a liquidity risk. Liquidity risk may lower the value of certain assets or businesses due to the increased potential of capital loss.

After studying this chapter you will be able to answer the following questions, among others:

1. What is market microstructure and how can the price formation process in the financial markets be defined?
2. What is the difference between funding liquidity and market liquidity?
3. What are the main models for liquidity? How can they be classified?
4. How does regulation deal with liquidity risk and what are the main metrics developed by regulators?
5. What are the main monitoring tools for liquidity risk?

The first section of the chapter gives an introduction to the functioning of financial markets, and price formation, and how liquidity issues can be identified. The second section is about models of liquidity and how liquidity risk can be managed, introducing the most popular models in the field. The final section deals with the regulatory framework, showing how liquidity risk is considered at a supervisory level, and what are the main regulatory provisions.

8.1 Market prices

Learning outcomes

1. Define market microstructure.
2. Describe the price formation process in financial markets.
3. Explain the difference between funding liquidity and market liquidity.

8.1.1 Market microstructure

Market microstructure is a specialized field of finance dealing with the analysis of market kernel and price formation mechanism. The focus is on how the working process of a financial market affects the level of prices. This is done by examining how the market features affect variables like prices and volumes associated with transactions.

When transactions take place on a regulated market, the assets are transferred from one investor to another. This is done at some trading cost, which of course has an impact on the price of that asset. Market microstructure manages to establish a connection between the costs associated with trading, and the bid-ask spread on the market.

Price formation involves a component connected to the structure of the market where the transaction takes place. There are permanent and transitory components in price variations. Permanent components are usually related to the level of information asymmetry on the market, while temporary components are supposed to be related to the past information and therefore quite controversial.

Bid-ask spreads have the power of affecting transactions to some extent. They also affect the statistical properties of the time series because they create spurious volatility in the data, and contribute to explain autocorrelation in returns.

There are several types of market structure, and some markets rely on mixtures of them.

The differences depend on how transactions take place, and the major distinction is between auction and dealer markets.

In a pure auction market investors trade directly with each other without the intervention of dealers. Oppositely, a call auction market takes place at specific times when the security is called for trading. In a call auction market, investors place orders, specifying desired price and quantity of the target security, and trading happens at a specific time following specific rules.

The continuous auction market is characterized by investors trading on orders placed at an earlier time by other investors, while a pure dealer market is made up of major dealers placing bids and offers to be answered by investors.

There are also several types of order that can be input in a market, depending on the mechanism of order satisfaction. A market order is such that the broker trades it immediately at the best price available on the market.

A limit order sets a minimum and maximum price for the trade to take place. A limit order to buy sets a maximum price, above which the investor will not accept to buy. A limit order to sell, on the other hand, sets a minimum price, below which the investor is not willing to sell the security.

In a centralized continuous auction market, the best limit order to buy and the best limit order to sell are the lowest and highest prices in the order book and establish the market level, and the quantities at those prices represent the depth of the market.

Example 8.1: Consider an investor who wants to sell 18,500 shares of stock A at no less than €32.65 per share, but only if the whole quantity can be traded at once, in the current session. Such an investor should then issue an all-or-nothing, day order to sell the shares.

A stop-loss order is placed to buy or sell when the asset reaches a certain price, so to limit the loss of a trader. Setting a stop-loss selling order on a stock, at some percentage less than the price paid to buy it, limits the loss to that percentage.

The advantage of a stop-loss order is that monitoring on the asset price is not needed, once the limit has been set. In case of prolonged absence from the market, it is an efficient tool for trading at the desired price.

The disadvantage is that sometimes the stop-loss price could be activated by a sudden and temporary shock on the asset price, which creates a short-term fluctuation not reflected by the real trend of price.

Example 8.2: Consider an investor who bought a stock for €50. Right after that, the investor could enter a stop-loss order for €45, so that, if the stock falls below that price, the stock is sold at the market price. This limits the loss on the position to

$$50 - 45 = €5$$

with no need of further action after the stop order has been sent.

There is no golden rule on how much below the price at which the asset was bought should an investor set the stop-loss price. Usually it ranges between 5% and 15% of the price of the previous trade.

Once the stop price is reached, the order turns into a market order, so that the effective selling price could be different from the stop price. The difference may be quite considerable in fast-moving markets.

The types of order also set a distinction among investors. Active traders normally issue market orders, given they are keen to trade continuously, while passive traders would normally issue limit orders, to make the best out of limited transactions, therefore earning higher margins from active traders.

Buying on margin involves borrowing funds from a broker to purchase an asset, allowing an investor to leverage a financial position by trading on assets that would not be affordable otherwise.

When a margin account is open, a minimum initial investment is required to the investor, which is the minimum margin. When the account is operational, a certain percentage (initial margin) of the purchase price of a stock can be borrowed.

The loan can amount to some specific fraction of the stock price (usually 50%) and can be kept for as long as the investor wants. The proceeds from selling stocks in a margin account go to the broker up to full payment of the loan.

The marginable securities on the account are collateral of the loan and some interest must be paid to the broker. Interests are accrued on the part of the loan which is not reimbursed, and increase as debt increases.

Example 8.3: Consider an investor depositing €10,000 in a 50% margin account, so that an investment of €20,000 can be afforded. If €5,000 of stocks are bought, €15,000 are left on the margin account. Given that the investor has used only half of the equity in the account, the loan is not active yet, so no interest is due. When securities are bought for more than the equity €10,000, the loan position starts and interests are accrued on it.

Together with the initial margin, the agreement involves also a maintenance margin, which is the amount of equity to be maintained after each trade. If the equity in the margin account falls below the maintenance margin, a margin call is issued, forcing the investor to either liquidate his/her position in the stock or add more cash to the account.

Example 8.4: Recall Example 8.3, and assume the full €20,000 is invested into stocks, so that the whole loan is used. If the market value of the securities goes to €15,000, the value of the equity falls from the original €10,000 to

$$15,000 - 10,000 = €5,000$$

Assuming a maintenance margin is 25%, the amount of required equity to be maintained is given by

$$15,000 \times 0.20 = €3,000$$

Since the equity is higher than this, the situation is fine. If the maintenance margin was 40% instead, the amount of maintained equity would be

$$15,000 \times 0.40 = €6,000$$

which is higher than the €5,000 equity. In this case, a margin call will be issued by the broker and the investor will have to restore an appropriate level of equity.

There are many different players in the markets, from the dominant institutional investors (pension funds, mutual funds, foundations and endowments), to the small individual investors. The structure of markets must accommodate all the different types.

In order to specify in what order transactions are executed, some markets adopt a price criteria, giving priority to orders with the best price and secondary priority to the order posted first at a given price. Some other markets modify secondary priority rules to accommodate large transactions.

Example 8.5: Assume a futures contract is currently selling at bid €123.10 and ask €123.35. Trader A is the bidder with time precedence at that price, and he is defending it. In order to buy at €123.10, a trader B must wait until investor A trades. In order to gain precedence, a trader must improve the bid to €123.15. You then would have price priority over his bid and time precedence over all subsequent bids at €103.15. If A then wants to reclaim his precedence, he would have to bid higher at €123.20. Time precedence encourages traders to jump over each other's prices with improved prices.

The trading process is comprised of four steps. The first step is information, with market giving information of past and current quotes. Second step is order routing, when brokers take orders from investors and forward them to the market.

The third step is the trading process execution, when orders are executed. The last step is clearing, which takes place comparing the transaction orders of buyers and sellers in order to clear them.

The bid-ask spread on the market represents the difference between the asking price and the offer price available to traders. The spread is a reliable measure of the liquidity of a market.

There are several factors that determine the bid-ask spread in a security. First of all, the dealers supplying liquidity to the market and granting continuity in transactions, have order handling costs for which they must be compensated. On the other hand, there are also suppliers of immediacy, who buy at bid and sell at ask price, assuming then huge inventory risk, to be compensated as well.

When dealers place bid or ask prices, they give an option to the market investors to trade at this actual bid and ask, before it changes according to new information hitting the market. Market spread determination incurs in the problem of asynchronous trading. It is implicitly assumed that observations are recorded in equally spaced intervals of 24 hours. That generates biases in the return predictions made by investors.

Example 8.6: Consider an actively traded asset A and a rarely traded asset B. If new information hits the market at closure, the closing price of asset A is more likely to reflect this information than the price of asset B. The returns of asset B will reflect the new information and eventually show autocorrelation. In fact, note that the return of asset B is zero in periods of non-trading, reverting to the cumulative mean return when trading is active. Thus, negative autocorrelation arises due to the mean reversion.

There are several important factors that determine the market microstructure. The concept of liquidity resembles the concept of elasticity, in that a liquid market does not show large changes in price due to shifts in demand. When a market is less liquid instead, the bid-ask spread is much more sensitive to shifts in demand.

Another determining factor is transparency, defined as the amount of information possessed by market participants. Markets that communicate in real time the bids and offers of buyers and sellers, and the prices of executed trades, are considered highly transparent.

There are also econometric issues determining the features of a microstructure. A trading microstructure consists normally of a series of discrete events in continuous time. That defines a point process.

In a perfect market, the price of an asset would be determined at the equilibrium between demand and supply. The reality is not that straightforward because every market has frictions that must be taken into consideration.

As defined by Amihud *et al.* in 2005, the main frictions, ranging from exogenous transaction costs, inventory risk and demand pressure, private information and search friction, are sources of illiquidity that increase trading costs. As a consequence, assets must be valued taking into consideration all the future streams of aggregated trading costs. Brokerage fees, taxes, and other costs, add up to the asset price at each trade, and become a source of illiquidity.

All costs involved in the trading of an asset are reflected in the market price, which carries all the information available until that time. The bid-ask spread reflects all these additions, therefore widening as they increase.

Another source of illiquidity is the absence of natural players on the market, so that investors are obliged to trade with market makers, for immediate transactions. Market makers bear the risk of price fluctuations while holding the asset in inventory, so they must be compensated, widening the bid-ask spread.

Information is the other great determinant for market illiquidity. Usually big players get the best and most complete information about fundamental values on the markets. Since the price in equilibrium reflects all the available information, the asymmetry in information generates a mismatch in the marginal prices for different types of investors, giving rise to disequilibrium.

8.1.2 Price formation

Order driven markets are the focus of recent attention from practitioners. In recent years in fact, most markets in the world have set new rules for handling orders, due to the development of electronic limit order book trading platforms in virtually all of the market centres in the world.

Combining orders on the two sides of the market is not easy. High-valuation investors are willing to buy from the low-valuation shareholders, in order to gain from the price difference. That causes a problem to low-valuation shareholders, since they make no gain from it. The same holds for low-valuation investors trying to buy from low-valuation shareholders.

A popular model of price formation in stocks markets is the Foucault model, which is based on several assumptions. Trading is continuous with a single risky asset in the market, and investors trade one share of it sequentially through market or limit order.

Two groups of investors populate the market, one putting a high value V_h on the asset and the other with a low value $V_l < V_h$. High-value and low-value investors populate the market with proportions h and l respectively.

Investors are risk-neutral and maximized their expected utility. For a buy order processed at price b it is given by

$$E(u) = \eta(V_i - b), \quad i = h, l$$

where

η is the probability of execution of the order.

Similarly, the expected utility from a sell order at a specified price is

$$E(u) = \eta(b - V_i), \quad i = h, l$$

In the absence of a trade, the utility is normalized to zero.

A proportion δ of the investor has access to private information about innovation of asset value, which is worth H_+ or H_- with 50% probability each.

Consider a set of mutual strategies, where each trader has an optimal strategy, given the strategies of the other traders. Each trader must choose a type of order (market vs limit) and (for limit orders) the bid or ask order placement price.

Equilibrium is defined as optimal bid and offer prices b^* and a^*, such that a counterparty in the next period is induced to trade at these prices via a market order.

The expected utility of a limit buy order placed at bid price b can then be rewritten as

$$E(u) = (1-k)\left[(1-p)(V_h - b) - pH\right]$$

where

$p = \dfrac{\delta}{2}$ is the proportion of informed investors weighted by the 50% probability.

A buyer who is uninformed is also indifferent between market order or limit order trading, when the utility from the two different trading methods are the same, as defined by

$$V_h - a_m = (1-k)\left[(1-p)(V_h - b) - pH\right]$$

where

A_m is the market ask price.

It is then possible to express the optimal ask price A^*, that will induce an uninformed coming buyer to trade via a market order, as

$$a^* = V_h - (1-k)\left[(1-p)(V_h - b) - pH\right]$$

On the other hand, the optimal bid price B^* is such that an uninformed coming seller will be induced to trade via market order, and is given by

$$b^* = V_l + k\left[(1-p)(a - V_l) - pH\right]$$

There exist parameter values for V_h, V_l, H, δ, k for which equilibrium bid and ask prices are given by

$$a^* = \lambda V_l + (1-\lambda)(V_h - qH)$$
$$b^* = \mu V_h + (1-\mu)(V_l + qH)$$

where

$$q = \frac{p}{1-p}$$
$$\lambda = \frac{1 - k(1-p)}{1 - k(1-k)(1-p)^2}$$
$$\mu = \frac{1 - (1-k)(1-p)}{1 - k(1-k)(1-p)^2}$$

An interesting example to analyse in order to understand market price formation is the one for commodity futures. In commodity markets, market participants who need a certain commodity at the future time *t*, can buy it in the spot market and store it, or go long in a futures contract to take delivery when the contract expires.

Buying from the spot market implies storage and opportunity costs, given that the commodity has to be stored until time *t*, and the buying funds could be used for alternative investments.

The futures price of the commodity should equate the spot price plus any interest and storage cost, as

$$F = S + I + c_{ST}$$

where

  S is the today spot price of the commodity
  I is the total amount of interest earned from time 0 to t
  c_{ST} is the amount of storage costs from time 0 to t.

The price formation of a commodity future is then linked to financial markets via the interest rate. The demand for storable commodities is satisfied through existing inventories and production.

Therefore the holder of such inventories gets a certain utility from the stock, defined as convenience yield. When inventories are high, the marginal convenience yield is low, and vice versa. Thus the marginal convenience yield is inversely related to inventory levels.

8.1.3 Funding vs market liquidity

Funding liquidity can be defined as the ability to settle obligations with immediacy and a financial institution is said to be liquid when it can face obligations in time. Funding liquidity risk is the possibility that an institution will not be able to meet its obligations over a specific time horizon.

As for credit risk, a distinction must be made between the one particular point in time when the liquidity event may happen, and the risk associated with it, that can take infinitely many values according to the distribution of future outcomes.

For transactions between banks, the central bank plays a pivotal role, in that most economies are centred on the central bank funding provision as the extreme source of liquidity.

Banks can create commercial money, but do not control central bank money. The ability to settle obligations, and hence funding liquidity risk, is determined by the ability to satisfy the demand for central bank money.

A bank is liquid if at each point in time the outflows of central bank money are smaller than the sum of inflows and stock held by the bank.

In order to avoid illiquidity, the conditions to be met are described by the net-liquidity demand (NLD) indicator. It can be calculated as

$$D_{NL} = C_{OUT} - C_{IN} - M$$

where

C_{OUT} is the sum of the outflows at a specified time
C_{IN} is the sum of known inflows
M is the stock of central bank money.

For a bank to be liquid, the demand must be filled, and that happens through interbank market, deposits, sales of assets or central bank funding. That means the following inequality must hold

$$D_{NL} \leq w_D L_D + w_{IB} L_{IB} + w_A A + w_{CB} L_{CB}$$

where

L_D is the amount borrowed from new depositors
w_D is the price of new deposits
L_{IB} is the amount borrowed from interbank market
w_{IB} is the price of interbank market funds
A is the amount of assets sold
w_A is the price of assets sold
L_{CB} is the amount borrowed from the central bank
w_{CB} is the price of central bank funds.

The funding liquidity risk is then driven by two stochastic elements: future developments of NLD and future level of liquidity priced. A negative NLD indicates excess liquidity that can be sold on the market. However, when NLD is positive, and cannot be funded in any way, the bank becomes illiquid.

Market microstructure theory helps to analyse the sources of illiquidity. A way to relate market microstructure with market liquidity is to consider three transactional properties of markets: tightness, depth and resiliency.

Tightness is the cost of closing a position over a short period of time, and it is defined as the difference between the bid and the ask prices. Depth is the volume of trades that it is possible to process without affecting the price of assets. Resiliency is an elasticity measure, defined as the speed at which the price converges to the liquidation value of the underlying commodity.

When a market is liquid, the properties assume specific values. Tightness of a liquid market approaches zero, meaning the bid-ask spread is minimized. The depth of a liquid market is small enough to not affect asset prices, and resiliency is high enough to ensure that prices eventually approach the underlying value, so to avoid arbitrage opportunities.

In a liquid market trading is continuous, bid and ask prices are immediately available to trade even small amounts of securities, and it is possible to trade large amounts at a price that is close to the current market price, for a sufficiently long period of time.

In 1986 Amihud and Mendelson developed a model for the relationship between return and spread. Assume there are m different types of investors, holding assets with different time horizons with different holding periods.

Also assume the market is made of $n+1$ different assets, each carrying a perpetual cash flow d_j and a relative spread s_j reflecting trading costs $(j = 0,1,...,n)$. Given the

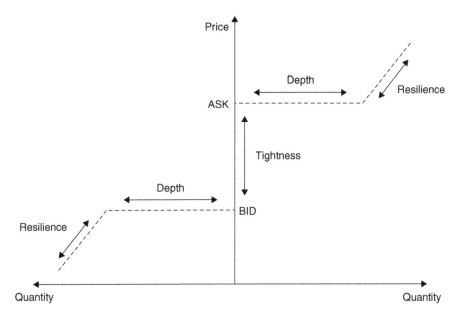

Figure 8.1 The scheme resembles the properties of a market, in terms of liquidity.

relative spread, investors quote an ask price P_j and a bid price $P_j\left(1-s_j\right)$ for every asset. Market makers ensure trading is always possible at those prices.

Given the types of investor and their increasing holding periods, the expected assets holding period for each investor is given by

$$E\left(t_i\right)=\frac{1}{\tau_i}$$

The assets are numbered by increasing relative spreads $\left(s_1 \le s_2 \ldots \le s_n < 1\right)$, and investors are numbered by increasing expected holding periods $\left(\tau_1^{-1} \le \tau_2^{-1} \ldots \le \tau_m^{-1}\right)$. At expiration of the stochastically distributed holding period, the investor sells back to the market makers and quits.

Investor types order is such that investor type $i = 1$ has the shortest holding period, up to investor k having the longest. Investors come in the market at a Poisson rate, with parameter λ_i.

At equilibrium, the number of type i investors active in the market is Poisson with mean

$$m_i = \frac{\lambda_i}{\tau_i}$$

The market makers have an expected zero position since their bid and ask price set equilibrium in demand and supply.

Investors seek to maximize the expected discounted net cash flows, given a set of bid and ask prices. Define $\mathbf{x}_{ij}$ as the vector of quantities j acquired by type i investor. The expected discounted value of portfolio i is the sum of discounted value of inflows over τ_i and the expected discounted liquidation revenue

$$E(V_i) = E\left[\int_0^{\tau_i} e^{-r_f z}\left(\sum_{j=0}^{n} x_{ij} d_j\right) dz\right] + E\left[e^{-r_f \tau_i} \sum_{j=0}^{n} x_{ij} V_j \left(1-s_j\right)\right]$$

which, after some manipulation, yields

$$E(V_i) = \frac{1}{(\tau_i + r_f)} \sum_{j=0}^{n} x_{ij}\left[d_j + \tau_i V_j \left(1-s_j\right)\right]$$

Please note that the risk-free rate r_f enters in the formula as the rate of return on the zero-spread asset.

The utility maximization of investor type i is obtained by solving the optimization problem for maximizing the expected value equation, subject to a wealth constraint and short positions not allowed.

$$\max \sum_{j=0}^{n} x_{ij}\left[d_j + \tau_i V_j \left(1-s_j\right)\right] \tag{8.1}$$

subject to

$$\sum_{j=0}^{n} x_{ij} V_j \leq W_i$$
$$x_{ij} \geq 0 \quad \forall j$$

Market clearing condition is defined as

$$\sum_{i=1}^{k} x_{ij} m_i = 1 \tag{8.2}$$

The solution to the optimization problem (8.1), given the additional constraint in (8.2) is given by a matrix $\underset{k \times (n+1)}{\mathbf{X}^*}$, representing the allocation in equilibrium, and a vector $\mathbf{V}^* = \left(V_0^*, V_1^*, ..., V_n^*\right)$, representing the equilibrium ask prices. The vector of equilibrium bid prices $\mathbf{Z}$ is obtained by the ask vector as $\mathbf{Z}^* = \left(V_0^*, V_1^* \left(1-s_1\right), ..., V_n^* \left(1-s_n\right)\right)$.

Once the equilibrium is derived, the interpretation of results is straightforward. First of all it is now possible to define the spread-adjusted return of asset j and investor i as the gross market return net of liquidation costs, as

$$r_{ij} = \frac{d_j}{V_j} - \tau_i s_j \tag{8.3}$$

The net return is then a non-decreasing function of i, $\forall j$, thus increasing with the holding period. Given the price vector $\mathbf{V}$ an investor of type i wants to form a portfolio that provides the highest return, as

$$r_i^* = \max\left(r_{ij}\right)$$

and the gross return is then given by

$$r_i^G = r_i^* + \tau_i s_j \tag{8.4}$$

The equilibrium gross return is then determined by comparing (8.3) and (8.4), and the optimal solution is the value of asset j corresponding to the minimal required return, as

$$\frac{d_j}{V_j^*} = \min\left(r_i^* + \tau_i s_j\right)$$

so that

$$V_j^* = \max\left[\frac{d_j}{\left(r_i^* + \tau_i s_j\right)}\right]$$

The optimal asset value can be also seen as the difference between the present value of the cash stream d_j net of the present value of expected trading costs associated with the asset.

$$V_j^* = \frac{d_j}{r_i^*} - \frac{\tau_i V_j^* s_j}{r_i^*}$$

The equilibrium implies that investors choose to allocate assets with higher spreads, in portfolios with longer holding periods, and the market gross return is an increasing function of the relative spread.

Snapshot 8.1
Liquidity black holes

A normal market should be in equilibrium and asset prices should not overreact. When prices are low, investors should buy, pushing up the price to some fair level, and vice versa.

Black holes are created when some investors react to a decline in price by selling, instead of buying, and vice versa. There are in fact two types of traders on the financial market.

Negative feedback traders buy when the price is low and sell when the price is high. Positive feedback traders, on the other hand, act in the opposite way. If negative feedback traders dominate, the market is liquid. If positive feedback traders dominate, there are liquidity holes.

Several reasons determine positive feedback trading and black holes in the market. Stop-loss rules, for example, determine traders stop the loss on a position, therefore involving selling assets even when prices are going down.

Another reason for positive feedback trading is dynamic hedging of short positions in options, which involves buying after a price rise and selling after a price decline.

Also the creation of synthetic options entails positive feedback trading, in that a short position in an option is equivalent to creating a long position in the same option synthetically.

It follows that a financial institution can create a long option synthetically by doing the same sort of trading as it would do if it were hedging a short option position.

When trading on margins, sometimes it is not possible for some traders to keep some net worth, so that positions have to be closed out in order to cash out liquidity.

Another phenomenon that generates black holes is leveraging and deleveraging.

When banks are very liquid, they make credit easily available to investors, increasing the demand for assets, whose price therefore rises.

The opposite holds for deleveraging, when banks are less liquid and adopt more restrictive credit policies, so that credit spreads increase, and there is less demand for both non-financial and financial assets, whose prices decrease.

Macroeconomic impacts on the banking activities also play a role, especially in the presence of standardized regulation. In time of crisis banks have to comply with capital requirements.

An increase in volatilities and correlations leads to a proportional increase in market VaR and capital requirements. This fosters banks to reduce their exposures, therefore liquidating assets.

Since banks often have similar positions to each other, they try to do similar trades and that can generate black holes as a consequence.

The same holds for credit risk, because in times of recession, default probabilities increase and capital requirements for loans under Basel II tend to be high. As a consequence banks adopt restrictive lending policies, creating a black hole for small- and medium-size businesses.

8.2 Models of liquidity

Learning outcomes

1. Describe theoretical models of liquidity.
2. Describe traceable models of liquidity.
3. Describe the Diamond-Dybvig model of bank deposits.

8.2.1 Theoretical models

One of the main drawbacks of the VaR approach to risk measurement is that it does not take into consideration the market liquidity impact, with estimates based on mid-prices and it assumes that transactions do not affect market prices.

In order to overcome those limitations, models of liquidity-adjusted VaR (LVaR) have been proposed. Different from the conventional VaR, LVaR takes into account both the size of the initial holding position and the liquidity impact.

Robert Almgren and Neil Chriss (1999 and 2000) developed an optimal trading model in 1999. In the framework of portfolio theory it described how traders can account for both liquidity and transaction costs.

The theory of optimal execution aims at calculating the value of a portfolio under liquidation, supposing that trading happens from the present time to some fixed future time. There are two factors to be considered about the portfolio, the first being the variance-covariance structure of the portfolio. Second, the transaction cost functions of the assets in the portfolio must be known.

Consider a holding period of length T, divided into m intervals of length $\tau = \dfrac{T}{m}$. The trading strategy is defined as the quantity of shares n_j sold in each time interval, where $n_j = n_1, n_2, ..., n_k, ..., n_m$, with n_k being the amount of shares sold in the kth interval.

On the other hand, at time $t_k = k\tau$, the trader plans to hold an amount of shares denoted by h_k.

Suppose the investor holds an initial endowment $L = \sum_{k=1}^{m} n_k$ to be liquidated before time T. The number of units sold between t_{k-1} and t_k is given by

$$n_k = h_{k-1} - h_k, \quad k = 0, 1, ..., m$$

Units sold and held are related by

$$h_k = L - \sum_{j=1}^{k} n_j = \sum_{j=k+1}^{m} n_j$$

A trading strategy can be defined as a rule for determining the amount n_k in terms of the information available at time t_k. The main distinction is between a static strategy (determined in advance of trading) so that the n_k is determined by a rule depending on the available information at time t_0. The dynamic strategy, on the other hand, depends on the information up to time t_k.

The process driving the price dynamics is an arithmetic random walk in the form

$$V_k = V_{k-1} + \sigma \varepsilon_k \sqrt{\tau} - \tau f\left(\frac{n_k}{\tau}\right)$$

where

V_k is the equilibrium price after a sale
V_{k-1} is the equilibrium price before a sale
ε_k is a standard normally distributed random number
$f(.)$ is a permanent impact function.

The term $\dfrac{n_k}{\tau}$ can be referred to as the average rate of trading. Beside the permanent impact, a temporary impact must be also subtracted from the process.

The temporary market impact comes from the fact that the trader who wants to sell a certain number n_k of shares, could do it in small slices, in order to optimize liquidity. When n_k is large the actual price of a transaction may decrease between t_{k-1} and t_k due to the decline of liquidity supply at each following price level. This happens for a very short while and equilibrium is then immediately restored.

The temporary impact affects the actual sale price $\tilde{V}_k$ as

$$\tilde{V}_k = V_{k-1} - g\left(\frac{n_k}{\tau}\right)$$

where

$g(.)$ is a temporary impact function
s is bid-ask constant spread.

The temporary component impacts the actual price per share received, as a function of the previous market price of the previous period, but it does not impact the next market price V_k.

The total proceeds Λ can be calculated by summing the sale values over the entire holding period

$$\Lambda = \sum_{k=1}^{m} n_k \tilde{V}_k$$

$$= LV_0 + \sum_{k=1}^{m}\left[\sigma\varepsilon_k\sqrt{\tau} - \tau f\left(\frac{n_k}{\tau}\right)\right]h_k - \sum_{k=1}^{m} n_k g\left(\frac{n_k}{\tau}\right)$$

The permanent impact defined by the second part of the second term in the formula describes the loss in value due to the price drop subsequent to selling a small portion of the position. On the other hand, the price drop defined by the temporary impact in the last term only involves the units sold in the kth period.

The total cost of trading x_{TC} can be then defined as

$$x_{TC} = LV_0 - \sum_{k=1}^{m} n_k \tilde{V}_k$$

It is an *ex post* measure of cost, and before trading takes place, it is a random variable. Therefore it is possible to calculate its expected value and variance as

$$E(x_{TC}) = \sum_{k=1}^{m} \tau f\left(\frac{n_k}{\tau}\right)h_k + \sum_{k=1}^{m} n_k g\left(\frac{n_k}{\tau}\right)$$

$$V(x_{TC}) = \sigma^2 \sum_{k=1}^{m} \tau h_k^2$$

(8.5)

The model aims at finding trading trajectories x_{TC} such that they solve the minimization problem

$$\min\left[\sum_{k=1}^{m} \tau f\left(\frac{n_k}{\tau}\right)h_k + \sum_{k=1}^{m} n_k g\left(\frac{n_k}{\tau}\right) + \lambda\left(\sigma^2 \sum_{k=1}^{m} \tau h_k^2\right)\right]$$

for various values of λ.

The impact functions can take various forms. The easiest formulations are linear in the rate of trading. The permanent impact takes the form

$$f\left(\frac{n_k}{\tau}\right) = \zeta \frac{n_k}{\tau}$$

where

ζ is the constant permanent impact coefficient.

For the temporary impact, Almgren and Chriss choose a function in the form

$$g\left(\frac{n_k}{\tau}\right) = \theta \operatorname{sgn}(n_k) + \frac{\eta n_k}{\tau}$$

where

θ is the fixed cost of selling, made of half spread plus fees
η is the constant temporary impact coefficient.

The expected value of total cost of trading becomes

$$
\begin{aligned}
E(x_{TC}) &= \zeta \sum_{k=1}^{m} n_k h_k + \sum_{k=1}^{m} n_k \left(\theta \operatorname{sgn}(n_k) + \frac{\eta n_k}{\tau} \right) \\
&= \zeta \sum_{k=1}^{m} h_k (h_k - h_{k-1}) + \theta \sum_{k=1}^{m} |n_k| + \frac{\eta}{\tau} \sum_{k=1}^{m} n_k^2 \\
&= \frac{\zeta}{2} \sum_{k=1}^{m} \left[h_{k-1}^2 - h_k^2 - (h_k - h_{k-1})^2 \right] + \theta \sum_{k=1}^{m} |n_k| + \frac{\eta}{\tau} \sum_{k=1}^{m} n_k^2 \\
&= \frac{\zeta}{2} L^2 - \frac{\zeta}{2} \sum_{k=1}^{m} n_k^2 + \theta \sum_{k=1}^{m} |n_k| + \frac{\eta}{\tau} \sum_{k=1}^{m} n_k^2 \\
&= \frac{\zeta}{2} L^2 + \theta \sum_{k=1}^{m} |n_k| + \frac{\left(\eta - \zeta\tau/2 \right)}{\tau} \sum_{k=1}^{m} n_k^2
\end{aligned}
$$

The search for the right trajectory is crucial in order to minimize the target function, and calculate an explicit formula for the variance as well.

A simple trading strategy is to sell out the endowment at a constant rate, so that the amounts sold and held are the same for every interval as

$$n_k = \frac{L}{m}$$

$$h_k = (m - k)\frac{L}{m}$$

That also means that all signs of transactions are positive (since only sales happen). Therefore

$$\sum_{k=1}^{m} |n_k| = |L|$$
$$= L$$

The impact functions take the form

$$f\left(\frac{n_k}{\tau}\right) = f\left(\frac{L}{\tau m}\right)$$
$$= f\left(\frac{L}{T}\right)$$
$$= \zeta \frac{L}{T}$$

$$g\left(\frac{n_k}{\tau}\right) = g\left(\frac{L}{T}\right)$$
$$= \theta L + \eta \frac{L}{T}$$

Recalling the expressions in (8.5) the formula for $E(x_{TC})$ becomes then

$$E(x_{TC}) = \frac{1}{2} L T f\left(\frac{L}{T}\right)\left(1 - \frac{1}{m}\right) + L g\left(\frac{L}{T}\right)$$
$$= \dots$$
$$= \frac{1}{2} \zeta L^2 + \theta L + \left(\eta - \frac{\zeta \tau}{2}\right)\frac{L^2}{T}$$

Some mathematics shows that the variance is equal to

$$V(x_{TC}) = \frac{1}{3} \sigma^2 L^2 T \left(1 - \frac{1}{m}\right)\left(1 - \frac{1}{2m}\right)$$

The transaction cost function relates the trading rate and the premium or discount on the trade. A quick trade will press the market, so that it will be met at only a premium or discount, on the current market price.

Transaction costs calculations are an important part of microstructure, and become effective only for large numbers of trades, where the prediction errors become small, and well-specified models are useful.

The trade of a large basket of securities involves choosing a trading path, which affects the market according to the rate of trading at each point along the path. Summing up the effects on all points determines the cost of trading, and on top of that, each subsequent point trade will be subject to uncertainty of trading revenue, given market moves.

The trading problem reduces to the choice of the right trading path between trading everything at a glance immediately, to not suffer future market moves, and choosing to trade small quantities over time, to minimize market impact, but being subject to market price moves.

8.2.2 *Traceable models*

Theoretical models generally use optimal trading strategies to minimize the LVaR of a position. The large range of parameters of these models requires empirical estimation techniques, still to be developed.

On the other hand, traceable models have rather obvious empirical specifications, and can be implemented with raw data. The type of data commonly used for model application ranges from daily to intraday data.

As a generic approach, all models presented here are calculated on a standard, daily pace, 99% confidence level. The implementation procedure should always be as straight-forward as possible, given that simplicity is in the DNA of these models.

Define trading fair value as the mid-price $\bar{V}_t$. Liquidity costs L_t for trading a quantity q are assumed to be made of three components

$$L_t = T_c + I_t + D_t$$

where

T_c are direct trading (constant) costs
I_t are impact costs of ordering quantity q at time t
D_t are delay costs.

Traceable models neglect direct and delay costs and focus on the impact costs from trading a specific quantity q at a specific time t.

The first model of the traceable class was developed by Bangia *et al.* (1998). They developed a simple liquidity adjustment of a VaR-measure based on a bid-ask spread.

The measure of liquidity is the bid-ask spread, and risk is determined as the worst achievable transaction price. In order to do so, the worst bid-ask-spread is added to the worst mid-price. The liquidity-adjusted VaR is then defined as

$$LVaR = 1 - e^{z\sigma_{mr}} + z_s \tag{8.6}$$

where

σ_{mr} is the volatility of the mid-price return on the market
z is the percentile of the normal distribution for the given confidence level
μ_s is the mean of the bid-ask spread
σ_s is the volatility of the bid-ask spread
z_s is the percentile spread over the past 20 days, from historical distribution.

In order to improve the accuracy of the measurement, and depart from normality, the percentile z_s must be turned into an empirical percentile $\hat{\alpha}_s$ of the spread distribution in order to account for non-normality in spreads. The relationship is

$$\hat{\alpha}_s = \left(\frac{z_s - \mu_s}{\sigma_s} \right)$$

so that equation (8.6) becomes

$$LVaR = 1 - e^{z\sigma_{mr}} + \mu_s + \hat{\alpha}_s \sigma_s$$

The model acknowledges that spreads are not constant over time. Anyway, the liquidity costs associated with order size beyond the bid-ask spread are neglected, therefore underestimating liquidity risk.

The model relies on the assumption of perfect correlation between asset return and liquidity, which is not realistic. Anyway the model is appealing in that it is simple and easy to implement, also for the large data availability.

Another popular model was developed by Ernst *et al.* (2008). Their model is based on a different way to account for future time variation of prices and spreads.

The Bangia *et al.* model is based on a normality assumption for the distribution of future prices, while taking the historical distribution for future spreads. The Ernst *et al.* model assumes non-normal distributions for both prices and spreads, accounting then for skewness and kurtosis in the distributions involved.

The non-normal distribution percentile is estimated with a Cornish-Fisher approximation, a mathematical expression used to approximate the quantiles of a random variable based only on its first few cumulants.

Starting from the corresponding appropriate percentile z of the normal distribution, the non-normal percentile can be calculated as

$$\hat{\alpha}_r = z + \frac{\gamma(z^2-1)}{6} + \frac{\kappa(z^3-3z)}{24} - \frac{\gamma^2(2z^3-5z)}{36} - \frac{\gamma\kappa(z^4-5z^2+2)}{24}$$

where

γ is the skewness of the distribution
κ is the excess-kurtosis (exceeding the value of 3) of the distribution.

This alternative parametric specification defines relative, liquidity-adjusted total risk as

$$LVaR = 1 - e^{(\mu_{mr}+\hat{\alpha}_r\sigma_{mr})}\left(1 - \frac{\mu_s + \hat{\alpha}_s\sigma_s}{2}\right)$$

where

μ_r is the mean of mid-price return
σ_r is the variance of mid-price return
μ_s is the mean of mid-price spread
σ_s is the variance of mid-price spread.

In his model, Berkowitz (2000) determines liquidity price impact through regressing past trades, and controlling for other risk factors. The future price is driven by risk factor changes and the liquidity impact as

$$\bar{V}_{t+1} - \bar{V}_t = \alpha + \beta n_t + f_{t+1} + \varepsilon_t \tag{8.7}$$

where

β is the regression coefficient
n_t is the number of shares traded
α is a constant

f_{t+1} is the effect of risk factor changes in the mid-price

ε_t is an error term.

Authors do not give details of the form of f_{t+1}, which can therefore be estimated through another regression involving the mid-price. For example, it is possible to introduce a framework where the risk factor is a function of transaction price, as

$$x_{t+1} = f\left(\bar{V}_t\right)$$

Given the estimated value $\hat{\beta}$ of the regression coefficient in (8.7) the continuous liquidity-adjusted net return is

$$r_N = \ln\left[1 + \frac{f\left(\bar{V}_t\right) - \hat{\beta}(n_t + \tilde{n})}{\bar{V}_t}\right]$$

where $\tilde{n} = \dfrac{q}{\bar{V}_t}$ is the price-normalized quantity ordered at time t. The relative liquidity-adjusted total risk can be then defined as

$$LVaR = 1 - e^{\left(\mu_{r_N} + \hat{\alpha}_r \sigma_{r_N}\right)}$$

where $\tilde{n} = \dfrac{q}{\bar{V}_t}$ is the price-normalized quantity ordered at time t.

In 2001 Cosandey proposed a simple framework to estimate price impact from volume data. The total value traded in the market is assumed to be constant and can be split over the number of traded shares n_t.

So, at the time an additional position $\tilde{n} = \dfrac{q}{\bar{V}_t}$ is liquidated, the total value gets split over $n_t + \tilde{n}$ shares, affecting the net return, to be then calculated as

$$\bar{r}_{t+1} = \ln\left(r_{t+1} \frac{n_t}{n_t + \tilde{n}}\right)$$

This model form implies no elasticity of liquidity and no future time-variation of liquidity modelled by $\tilde{n}$.

Similar to Berkowitz, the LVaR is defined as

$$LVaR = 1 - e^{\left(\mu_{r_N} + \hat{\alpha}_r \sigma_{r_N}\right)}$$

Cosandey's model provides an easy implementation and it is based on market volume data only, which is a much easier type of information to access, at transaction, for many assets.

A further step in the analysis is to allow for liquidity cost to increase with order size. There is a family of models that use the liquidity cost measure weighted spread as a measure to calculate liquidity costs compared to fair price when liquidating a position quantity q against the limit order book.

The volume-weighted ask price and bid price of trading v shares is calculated as

$$a_{v,t} = \frac{1}{v}\sum_i a_{i,t} v_{i,t}$$

$$b_{v,t} = \frac{1}{v}\sum_i b_{i,t} v_{i,t}$$

where

$a_{i,t}$ is the ask-price of individual limit order
$b_{i,t}$ is the bid-price of individual limit order
$v_{i,t}$ is the ask-volume of individual limit order.

The model then calculates the weighted spread s_t^w as the price-normalized difference of the bid and ask price, as

$$s_t = \frac{a_{v,t} - b_{v,t}}{V_m}$$

An order of size q is executed against several limit orders until individual limit order sizes add up to q. Note that, given the setting of the model,

$$\frac{q}{V} = v = \sum_i v_i$$

As the bid-ask spread, the weighted spread is the cost of closing a position of size q.

The weighted spread approach has been developed, among others, by Francois-Heude and Van Wynendaele (2001), who propose to calculate relative, liquidity-adjusted total risk as

$$LVaR = 1 - e^{(-z\sigma_{mr})}\left(1 - \frac{\overline{s}_w}{2}\right) + \frac{s_t^w - \overline{s}_w}{2}$$

where

z is the percentile of the normal distribution
σ_{mr} is the standard deviation of the mid-price
$\overline{s}_w$ is the average spread for order quantity q
$s_{w,t}$ is the spread at time t.

The second term on the right-hand side represents the worst mid-price net of the average weighted spread, and the third term is a correction for the difference between the actual spread at time t and the average spread.

8.2.3 The Diamond-Dybvig model

Bank runs happen when depositors feel the possibility of losing their money deposited in the bank, therefore, taking immediate action in order to save their deposits. The run of many depositors will dry the cash of the bank, making it impossible to honour all its obligations, increasing the likelihood of the event that was feared by the depositors.

It is important to prevent bank runs, in that they originate from panic of investors due to subjective considerations, that are not always confirmed by the real state of the world. These runs may have big repercussions on the financial sector as a whole.

In the early 2000s, markets were supposed to be resilient and flexible enough to reduce the resistance to shocks and reduce the probability of liquidity problems threatening individual banks or other market participants.

New financial products, complex derivatives and hedge funds seemed to be important for market stability, by increasing the liquidity on the markets and enhancing the spreading of risk among market participants.

The bad quality of credits given by banks during the pre-crisis years is directly related to the liquidity issues that followed. Comfortable liquidity outlooks in fact gave an incentive to banks to take more credit risks and not screen their borrowers.

In the past decades, literature has tried to explain bank runs to be caused by either depositor panic, or by a downturn in the fundamentals of the economy, and inversion to the bad business cycle.

Diamond and Dybvig (1983) developed a model in an attempt to explain why banks issue more liquid deposits than their assets, and why bank runs happen. Many researchers have used that model to foster the understanding of financial crises.

Banks are assumed to generate liquidity through their offer of highly liquid deposits, compared to the less liquid assets they hold. That gives an incentive to liquidity-loving investors to invest in the bank rather than directly in the assets.

Demand for liquidity comes from the uncertainty about consuming and investing needs of the agents, who then care about the value acquired from liquidating assets on multiple liquidation dates.

The differential in liquidity between deposits and assets is a form of insurance arrangement, in which the depositors cut off some liquidating risk at the price of a loss in returns, compared to investing in the assets.

The Diamond-Dybvig model gives a proper explanation of an important function of the bank, as well as showing that satisfying the high demand of deposits puts the bank at risk of runs, when too many depositors decide to withdraw their funds.

Consider a model is in three periods, *0, 1* and *2*, with an investor endowed of 1 unit of the single, storable good in the economy. The good can be invested at time 0, yielding $R > 1$ at time 2, or the investment can be shut down at time 1, salvaging the initial investment.

Agents are divided into two types, but at time 0 they do not know to which type they belong. They learn it at time 1, and the type is equal to the outcome of a shock θ, which then takes values 1 or 2. Type 1 agents consume at time 1, while type 2 agents consume at time 2. A type 2 agent obtaining goods at time 1 stores them for free until time 2.

Denote by c_T the goods received at time T, so that the consumption of a type-2 agent at time 2 is given by the sum of the good stored at time 1 plus the goods obtained at time 1, which can be written as $c_1 + c_2$. It follows that each agent has a smooth, twice differentiable, utility function, in the form

$$u(c_1, c_2; \theta) = \begin{cases} u(c_1) & \text{if type-1 agent} \\ \rho u(c_1 + c_2) & \text{if type-2 agent} \end{cases}$$
$$1 \geq \rho > R^{-1}$$

where

θ is the state of the world determined by the shock.

The optimal choice of consumption for type-2 agents is given by the maximization of the expected utility.

Now assume that there is a probability λ for the agent to get the liquidity shock $\theta = 1$. Denote as $c_{i,j}$ the consumption at time i of agent type j. If $\theta = 1$, the agent is type 1 and salvages (and consumes) all the unit endowment, so that $c_{1,1} = 1$.

If $\theta = 2$, the agent consumes $c_{1,2}$ at time 1, and $c_{2,2}$ at time 2.

In order to define the optimal deposit contract in the economy, the $c_{i,j}$ can be interpreted as the withdrawal of the agent in period i, for an agent type j which is a consequence of the shock.

The optimal contract offered by banks to the depositors is given by the optimization program given by maximizing the expected utility of a depositor, and can be formulated as

$$\max \lambda u\left(c_{1,1}\right) + \left(1 - \lambda\right)\rho u\left(c_{1,2}, c_{2,2}\right)$$

subject to

$$\left(1 - \lambda\right)c_{2,2} = R\left[1 - \left(\lambda c_{1,1} + \left(1 - \lambda\right)c_{1,2}\right)\right]$$
$$c_{1,1}, c_{1,2}, c_{2,2} \geq 0$$

The choice of a functional form for the utility is needed in order to characterize the optimal deposit contract. Assume therefore a utility in the form

$$u\left(c\right) = \frac{c^{1-RR_x} - 1}{1 - RR_x}$$

where

RR_x is the Arrow-Pratt relative risk aversion coefficient

so that

$$\frac{\left(c_{1,1}\right)^{-RR_x}}{\left(c_{2,2}\right)^{-RR_x}} = \rho R$$

and

$$\left(c_{2,2}\right) = \left(\rho R\right)^{\frac{1}{RR_x}} c_{1,1}$$

The solution to the program leads to the optimal contract being

$$c_{1,1} = \frac{R}{\left(1 - \lambda\right)\left(\rho R\right)^{\frac{1}{RR_x}} + \lambda R}$$

which implies that

$$c_{2,2} = \frac{(\rho R)^{\frac{1}{RR_x}} R}{(1-\lambda)(\rho R)^{\frac{1}{RR_x}} + \lambda R}$$

From the results it can be shown that the boundary condition for the optimal contracts is given by

$$1 < c_{1,1} < c_{2,2} < R$$

which completely characterizes the optimal contract.

It can be noted that the same condition holds for the gross returns on deposits, so that the term structure is upward sloping and the net interest income conditions of the bank are fulfilled, and the condition

$$1 < r_1 < r_2 < R$$

holds, where

r_1 is the gross return on deposits withdrawn at time 1
r_2 is the gross return on deposits withdrawn at time 1.

It is straightforward to conclude that the higher the risk aversion coefficient RR_x, the higher the will of depositors to withdraw funds early, compared to keeping them invested. Therefore, more risk-averse depositors withdraw funds at time 1, while less risk-averse depositors will keep the funds in their deposits until time 2.

8.3 Liquidity risk and regulation

Learning outcomes

1. Describe the regulatory approach to liquidity risk.
2. Define the liquidity coverage ratio and net stable funding ratio.
3. Explain what are the main monitoring tools for liquidity risk.

8.3.1 Liquidity coverage ratio

The Basel Committee has improved the liquidity regulation by developing standards for funding. The liquidity coverage ratio (LCR) aims at promoting short-term resilience of the liquidity risk profile of an institution.

The LCR is composed of high-quality assets (HQA) in stressed conditions and total net cash outflows (NCO) over the next 30 days. It is defined as

$$L_{CR} = \frac{H_{QA}}{N_{CO}}$$

where

L_{CR} is the amount of LCR
H_{QA} is the amount of HQA
N_{CO} is the amount of NCO.

The numerator of the ratio is the stock of HQA, which must be held by the bank for a 30-day period, and be liquid and tradable on the central bank. HQA should include:

- A minimum of 60% 'Level 1' assets, comprising very liquid assets like cash and other sovereign debt qualifying for a 0% risk weight in credit risk calculation. More specifically Level 1 assets include:
  - coins and banknotes
  - central bank reserves
  - claims on sovereigns, central banks, PSEs, traded in large markets and being very liquid by means of historical reputation.
- A maximum of 40% 'Level 2' assets, less liquid than Level 1, with a 20% risk weight in credit risk calculation, including:
  - corporate bonds with rating above AA not issued by a financial institution or any of its affiliated entities
  - marketable securities, with the same features as Level 1 assets, but assigned a 20% risk weight.

In general, HQA are assets that can be converted promptly into cash, without suffering a loss in value. Some assets are such that they are liquid even in time of stress, and generate funds without discounts.

An important feature of HQA is the central bank eligibility in that it adds confidence to the banks that are holding assets that could be used in events of severe stress without damaging the broader financial system, boosting confidence in the safety of the banking system.

The funds involved in HQA should be meant as a source of contingent funds, with no hedging purpose. Net cash outflows are the net differential between outflows and inflows during the stress period. Both inflows and outflows are adjusted according to factors, resulting in a severely stressed scenario.

The value of the ratio should be 100% in a normal financial situation, because the stock of HQA is intended to act as collateral against the potential consequences of a liquidity stress.

The ratio may fall below 100% in times of distress, and banks may use HQA reserves in order to balance the decrease. In this case, the supervising authority should consider the situation and respond accordingly.

The committee uses the term 'unencumbered' to describe the main feature of the assets involved in the stock of HQA. The term describes funds to be absolutely free of any restriction, of any sort, that could limit the ability of the bank to liquidate or transfer the asset.

Also assets that have been deposited with the central bank (or pledged to some other public sector entity) are eligible for HQA, if they have not been used to generate liquidity.

Hedged assets may be included in the stock, provided they comply with the general standards and after taking into account the cash outflow generated by the early liquidation of the hedge.

The asset to the market should be periodically hedged through monetization of the assets, in order to minimize the risk of low liquidity under stressed markets. Ineligible assets should be held for a further 30 days, and asset replacement or stock adjustment should be undertaken.

Banks are expected to face liquidity needs in any currency, being able to turn the assets in the stock into liquidity, in the currency and jurisdiction in which the net cash outflows arise.

Also monitoring of the LCR by currency should be undertaken, as well as supervision of potential currency mismatch. FX liquidity risk should be managed taking into account the fact that currency access and swap rapidly deteriorates in times of financial stress.

It is never possible to anticipate what assets are more likely to remain liquid over time. Therefore it is highly recommended that the stock of HQA should be well diversified within the asset classes themselves.

Net cash outflows are defined as the total expected cash outflows (ECO) minus total expected cash inflows (ECI) in the specified stress scenario for the subsequent 30 calendar days. The outstanding balances of liabilities and commitments are multiplied by the rates of expected depreciation.

Each category of the cash inflows is assigned a specific weight, given the scenario analysed, up to 75% of the total expected cash outflows. Therefore the formula for the net cash outflows takes the form

$$N_{CO} = E_{CO} - \min\left(E_{CI}, \frac{3}{4} E_{CO} \right)$$

where

E_{CO} is the amount of ECO
E_{CI} is the amount of ECI.

Each source of funding is assigned a run-off rate, and calibrated, over the 30 days, according to the stickiness of the system. Unsecured funds from small business customers are assigned particular attention.

The stickiness is defined as the stability of the system, guaranteed by the government and public intervention schemes, length and solidity of the bank-client relationship, purpose of the account.

All these factor contribute in defining stability of funds. In fact, deposits that are not guaranteed by the government, or do not have any public protection scheme, as well as high-profile or quickly withdrawable ones, are considered less stable.

Run-off rates applicable to outflows range from 5% to 100%, depending on the nature of the funding. Highest run-off rates correspond to the funding that is perceived to be less stable. The opposite holds for inflow factors

Double counting of items is not permitted, so that if an asset is included in the HQA stock, its inflows cannot be considered in the ECI calculation. In case of an item to be counted in multiple outflow categories, a bank should take up to the maximum contractual outflow for that product.

Table 8.1 Run-off rates for the major asset categories

Funding categories	Run-off factors
Securities backed by Level 1 assets	0%
Securities backed by Level 2 assets	15%
Secured with central banks, PSEs	25%
All other assets	100%

8.3.2 Net stable funding ratio

LCR takes in account the short-rate funding. In order to promote more medium- and long-term funding of bank activities, the Committee has developed the net stable funding ratio (NSFR) as well.

It also defines a minimum acceptable amount of stable funding, over a one-year horizon, given the institution activity profile. It is supposed to complement the LCR to promote structural changes in the liquidity risk profile of banks and other institutions.

Different categories of liabilities are assigned specific weightings in order to calculate the amount of stable funding available. Both assets and off-balance sheet items are included in the calculation.

The NSFR is designed to make sure that long-term assets are financed with a minimum amount of stable liabilities, to limit over-reliance and incentivize better assessment of liquidity risk across all on- and off-balance sheet items.

The objective of the standard is to ensure stable funding under the specified conditions, in order to accomplish a firm-specific stress scenario, simulating a situation of significant decline in the profitability and solvency of the institution. Moreover also a potential downgrade in the institution's rating and material event putting at risk the creditworthiness of the institution is part of the simulation.

The methodology for NSFR is based on classic definitions like net liquid assets and cash capital, as common among banks, analysts and rating agencies. When computing the right amount of assets that should be backed by stable funding, all assets are included independently of their accountability. Stable funding is also required to cover potential liquidity drains on off-balance sheet commitments.

The formula applied for calculating the ratio involves the available amount of stable funding (ASF) and the required amount of stable funding (RSF), and it is given by

$$R_{NS} = \frac{A_{SF}}{R_{SF}} > 100\%$$

where

A_{SF} is the amount of ASF
R_{SF} is the amount of RSF.

In order for the institution to comply with the standard, the ratio must be greater than 100%. The amount of such funding required of a specific institution is a function of the liquidity characteristics of various types of assets, exposures incurred and activities pursued by the institution.

The available amount of stable funding is defined as equity and liability financing that are reliable to provide funds over the time horizon, even in conditions of distress. There are five categories of stable funding, namely:

1. Tier 1 and Tier 2 capital, net of deduction, long-term equity items and borrowings with maturity higher than one year.
2. Short-term maturity (less than one year) stable deposits and term deposits.
3. Less stable short-term deposits and term deposits.
4. Non-maturing deposits, term deposits with maturity less than one year, provided by any institution.
5. All other liabilities and equity not included in the previous points.

The stability of the funding can be assessed in the same way as for the LCR, and maturities are determined by assuming the earliest possible call for repayment. For option-embedded funding, market repayment standards and reputational factors must also be taken into account.

Borrowings from central bank lending facilities outside regular open market operations, if extended, are not included in the ratio calculation. As a standard, NTFS is supposed in fact to disincentivize banks from relying on central bank funding.

The required amount of stable funding required by supervisors must be measured according to ideal assumptions about the liquidity profile of the assets of the institution involved.

The values of the assets of the institution, included the founded ones, are summed up in order to get an aggregate amount to be multiplied by RSF factors that are different for each asset category. Off-balance sheet activities are multiplied by their specific RSF factor as well.

The RSF factors are such that they amortize the asset amounts, for the portion that could not be monetized on an extended basis, during a liquidity event lasting over the reference period.

The most liquid assets are also the more suited to serve as a source of extended liquidity in case of distress, so that they receive the lowest RSF factors, requiring less stable funding than less liquid (higher RSF) assets.

When the assets are represented by secured funding maturing within one year, the asset to be used at settlement at maturity date is the reference one, and the bank should use the corresponding RSF factor for that asset.

If the assets are not unencumbered, so that some restriction is incumbent, they get a 100% RSF, unless the restriction is going to last less than a year, and the assets are treated as unencumbered. Cash and other perfectly liquid assets get a 0% RSF.

Off-balance sheet liquidity exposures can lead to liquidity drains when the market is under stress. The application of an RSF factor defines the need to set aside stable funding to cover potential drains.

The Basel Committee is yet far from finalizing the treatment of liabilities with maturity less than one year. The Committee supervisors will gather data on an observation period of five years, to end in 2017, to conclude about how to treat these instruments in the NSFR.

Table 8.2 RSF factors for the major category components

RSF category components	RSF factor
- Unencumbered cash	0%
- Unencumbered short-term items, less than one-year maturity left, with no option embedded.	
- Unencumbered items, with maturity longer than one year, guaranteed by central banks, or other institutions.	5%
- Unencumbered corporate bonds, or covered bonds rated AA- or higher, complying with Level 2 assets.	20%
- Unencumbered marketable securities assigned 20% weight in the standardized approach of Basel II.	
- Unencumbered gold	50%
- Unencumbered equity securities	
- Unencumbered corporate and covered bonds eligible for central bank and not issued by financial institution (unless covered).	

8.3.3 Monitoring tools

The European guidance on liquidity risk monitoring is based on the Basel III framework, which implements additional provisions for designing of measures for liquidity adequacy assessment.

The metrics defined by the Committee relate to banks' financial structure, available funding and collateral, and market indicators. Together with the LCR standard, they help supervisors in assessing liquidity risk of an institution.

The metrics should be used by regulators in case potential liquidity difficulties are signalled, due to a downturn in the trend of the metrics, or in case some liquidity position deteriorates.

Liquidity adequacy requirements (LAR) for financial institutions include the set of metrics to be used as monitoring tools.

The first metric defined by the committee is the contractual maturity mismatch, which identifies gaps between inflows and outflows of liquidity at specific time bands. For each time band, maturity gaps indicate how much liquidity could be needed.

In the Basel document it is defined as: 'Contractual cash and security inflows and outflows from all on- and off-balance sheet items, mapped to defined time bands based on their respective maturities'.

Institutions should report the mismatches for relevant time bands, based on residual maturity. It is up to the regulators to define the time bands, and securities with undefined maturity should be reported separately.

All securities flows should be reported, in order to allow for supervisor monitoring of the change in values that generate cash flows, as well as the price movement not resulting in inflows or outflows.

Communication to the supervisor authority is made in terms of raw data, without any comment or elaboration. Data do not reflect any future forecasted flows and contractual maturity mismatch does not capture outflows aimed at protecting the business.

Financial institutions are also asked to perform their own analysis, based on behavioural assumptions of cash flows, under different simulated market conditions.

Authorities should be informed about relevant changes in the business model, providing shocks to projected liquidity mismatch.

Another important metric is the concentration of funding, aiming at identifying funding whose importance is so high that it cannot be reduced without triggering liquidity problems. The metric is defined as:

1. Funding liabilities as a percentage of total liabilities from each significant counterparty, where the definition of significance is given by accounting in aggregate for above 1% of the bank's balance sheet.
2. Funding liabilities as a percentage of total liabilities, from each significant product, where significance refers to the single instrument or product accounting in aggregate amount for more than 1% of the bank's total liabilities.
3. List of assets and liability amounts by significant currency, where a currency is considered to be significant when more than 5% of the bank's liabilities are denominated in that currency.

All metrics should be reported for each of separate three-month span time buckets, from one to twelve months.

The funding counterparty for many types of debt actually cannot be identified, so that the metrics are limited in their use. This must be a clear point for institutions and supervisors.

Available unencumbered assets is a metric aimed at providing information about key features, currency denomination and location of an institution's unencumbered assets, which have a potential to be HQLA as mentioned in previous sections.

The definition of the metrics includes both available unencumbered assets marketable as collateral in secondary markets and those that are eligible for central banks' standing facilities.

The supervising authority should get proper reports on the amount, type and location of the assets subject to be collateral for secure borrowing, or liable to be cut off at reasonable costs.

Also collateral accepted at the central bank, but not used, should be included in the bunch. The collateral can be included in the metrics only when banks have already started the operational procedures required to monetize the collateral.

Items should be categorized by significant currency, and the estimated haircut required for each asset on the market or by the central bank should be reported as well. Also the expected monetized value of the collateral should be reported, in place of the notional amount, and actual location of the assets.

The metrics give a good indication of the bank's potential to generate additional sources of secured funding, defining how quickly LCR can be refilled after a liquidity shock, through markets or the central bank.

Traditional LCR is designed to be met in one single currency. The LCR by significant currency metrics allows for identification of potential currency mismatches by monitoring the LCR in significant currencies.

Again from the Basel Committee definition, the metrics can be defined as

$$L_{SC} = \frac{H_{SC}}{N_{SC}}$$

where

H_{SC} is the stock of HQA in each significant currency

N_{SC} is the total net cash outflows over a 30-day time period, in each significant currency.

There is no minimum globally accepted threshold for the metrics, being a monitoring tool but not a standard. Local supervisors should set minimum monitoring ratios, below which authorities should be alerted.

The point is for the supervisors to evaluate how banks are able to raise funding in foreign currencies, and their ability to transfer funds from one currency to another, when required by liquidity conditions.

Finally, it is possible to identify some market-based monitoring tools, to be used as indicators of potential liquidity difficulties. For example, intraday data may offer as warning indicators of liquidity, in some cases.

Also monitoring of information is an important tool to be used by supervisors. Knowing the direction and level that markets are heading to, as well as market-wide information, is a crucial asset when valuing a funding plan.

Equity and debt market can also be the objective of monitoring, in order to gather financial information about the whole market or subsets of it. Also bank-specific information, regarding equity prices, CDS spreads and other assets, can give an important indication of how the markets perceive the risks in a particular institution.

Summary

Market microstructure is the field of specialization dealing with price formation on financial markets, and internal market functioning, focusing on how the working process of markets impacts on the level of prices.

Investors are defined by the order they place on the market, so that active traders normally issue market orders, while passive traders normally issue limit orders, in order to benefit from different transaction times and resulting prices.

The bid-ask spread identifies the variation of liquidation prices around the mid-market, and it is determined by several factors. The liquidity suppliers guarantee continuity in transactions and have order handling costs for which they must be compensated, and this is reflected in the spread.

Funding liquidity relates to the ability of an institution to settle obligations with immediacy. Funding liquidity risk is the possibility that an institution will fail to meet its obligations over some time horizon.

VaR approach to risk is limited in that it does not take liquidity impact into consideration, basing the estimates on the mid-price and assuming no transaction effects on the prices.

Liquidity adjusted VaR allow the limitations to be overcome by taking into account both the size and liquidity impact of the initial position held by an investor. This is done by using various classes of models.

Theoretical models minimize the Liquidity VaR of a position, through optimal strategies, but empirical estimation techniques for this class of model have not been developed yet.

Traceable models, on the other hand, have clear empirical specifications and raw data can be used for their implementation. The type of data commonly used for model application ranges from daily to intraday data.

Bank runs are a consequence of the panic of depositors, who think they could lose their money, and, therefore, take immediate action in order to save their deposits. When many depositors run to withdraw their funds, the bank's funds dry rapidly.

The Basel Committee has developed several tools for liquidity regulation, developing standards for monitoring the risk. The liquidity coverage ratio (LCR) promotes short-term resilience of the liquidity risk profile of an institution. In order to promote more medium- and long-term funding of bank activities, the Committee has developed the net stable funding ratio (NSFR) as well.

Other monitoring metrics have also been developed, without being set as international standards, but as useful tools for the monitoring of the funding situation of an institution and to detect possible future stress.

Bibliography

Acharya, V.V. and Pedersen, L.H. 2005. Asset Pricing with Liquidity Risk. *Journal of Financial Economics*, 77(2): 375–410.

Almgren, R. and Chriss, N. 1999. Value under Liquidation. *Risk*, December.

Almgren, R. and Chriss, N. 2000. Optimal Execution of Portfolio Transactions. *Journal of Risk*, 3: 5–39.

Amihud, Y. and Mendelson, H. 1986. Asset Pricing and the Bid-Ask Spread. *Journal of Financial Economics*, 17: 223–219.

Amihud, Y., Mendelson, H. and Pedersen, L.H. 2005. Liquidity and Asset Prices. *Foundations and Trends in Finance*, 1: 269–364.

Ball, A., Denbee, E., Manning, M. and Wetherilt, A. 2011. Intraday Liquidity: Risk and Regulation. *Financial Stability Papers*, 11. Bank of England.

Bangia, A., Diebold, F.X., Schuermann, T. and Stroughair, J.D. 1998. Modeling Liquidity Risk, With Implications for Traditional Market Risk Measurement and Management. *Center for Financial Institutions Working Papers*. Wharton School Center for Financial Institutions. University of Pennsylvania.

Basel Committee on Banking Supervision. 2010. *Basel III: International Framework for Liquidity Risk Measurement, Standards and Monitoring*. Bank for International Settlements.

Basel Committee on Banking Supervision. 2013. *Basel III: The Liquidity Coverage Ratio and Liquidity Risk Monitoring Tools*. Bank for International Settlements.

Berkowitz, J. 2000. *Incorporating Liquidity Risk into Value-at-Risk Models*. Graduate School of Management. University of California. Irvine.

Bernardo, A. and Welch, I. 2004. Liquidity and Financial Market Runs. *Quarterly Journal of Economics*, 119(1).

Brunnermeier, M.K. and Motohiro, Y. 2009. A Note on Liquidity Risk Management. *American Economic Review*, 99(2).

Çetin, U., Jarrow, R. and Protter, P. 2004. Liquidity Risk and Arbitrage Pricing Theory. *Finance and Stochastics*, 8: 311–341.

Cosandey, D. 2001. Adjusting Value at Risk for Market Liquidity. *Risk*, 115–118.

Diamond, D.W. and Dybvig, P.H. 1983. Bank Runs, Deposit Insurance, and Liquidity. *Journal of Political Economy*, 91: 401–419.

Drehmann, M. and Nikolaou, K. 2010. Funding Liquidity Risk: Definition and Measurement. *BIS Working Papers*. Bank for International Settlements.

Ernst, C., Stange, S. and Kaserer, C. 2009. Measuring Market Liquidity Risk – Which Model Works Best?. *CEFS Working Paper Series*, 1.

François-Heude, A. and Van Wynendaele, P. 2001. *Integrating Liquidity Risk in a Parametric Intraday VaR Framework*. Working Paper. University of Perpignan.

Handaa, P., Schwartz, R. and Tiwari, A. 2003. Quote Setting and Price Formation in an Order Driven Market. *Journal of Financial Markets*, 6: 461–489.

Jacoby, G., Fowler D.J. and Gottesman, A.A. 2000. The Capital Asset Pricing Model and the Liquidity Effect: A Theoretical Approach. *Journal of Financial Markets*, 3(1): 69–81.

Jarrow, R.A. and Subramanian, A. 2001. The Liquidity Discount. *Mathematical Finance*, 11(4): 447–474.

Keiding, H. 2012. *Economics of Banking*. Preliminary version.

Nikolau, K. 2009. Liquidity (Risk) Concepts Definitions and Interactions. *Working Paper Series*, 1008. European Central Bank.

Stange, S. and Kaserer, C. 2008. The Impact of Order Size on Stock Liquidity: A Representative Study. *CEFS Working Paper Series 2008–09*. Center for Entrepreneurial and Financial Studies (CEFS). Technische Universität München.

Topi, J. 2008. Bank Runs, Liquidity and Credit Risk. *Bank of Finland Research Discussion Papers*, 12.

Exercises

Questions

1. Explain why banks hold more liquid assets than most other businesses.
2. Explain the difference between illiquidity and insolvency. Does the difference matter?
3. Explain why, if the government announces it is abolishing insurance on deposits, a typical bank is likely to face liquidity problems.
4. If yield curves, on average, were flat, what would this say about the liquidity premiums in the term structure?
5. Would you expect the bid-ask spread to be higher on actively or inactively traded stocks?
6. Discuss the moral hazard aspects created by deposit insurance.
7. Describe and compare the different types of trading orders available in the markets.

Problems

1. A bill has a bank discount yield of 6.81% based upon the asked price, and 6.90% based upon the bid price. The maturity of the bill (already accounting for skip-day settlement) is 60 days.
    a. Find the bid and asked prices of the bill.
    b. Calculate the bond equivalent yield of the bill as well as its effective annual yield based upon the asked price. Confirm that these yields exceed the discount yield.
2. Suppose that you sell short 100 shares of IBM, now selling at $70 per share.
    a. What is your maximum possible loss?
    b. What happens to the maximum loss if you simultaneously place a stop-buy order at $78?
3. The table below provides some price information on Marriott:

Bid price	Ask price
37.25	38.13

You have placed a stop-loss order to sell at $38.
    a. By placing this order, what are you in effect asking your broker to do?
    b. Given the market prices, will your order be executed?
4. Consider the following limit order book of a specialist. The last trade in the stock occurred at a price of €45.55.

Limit buy orders		Limit sell orders	
Price	Shares	Price	Shares
35.50	5,000	35.75	1,000
35.25	6,000	35.90	2,000
35.00	8,000	36.00	5,000

    a. If a market buy order for 3,000 shares comes in, at what prices will it be filled?
    b. What will happen if a market order to sell 5,000 shares comes in?

5. Consider the following limit order book of a specialist. The last trade in the stock occurred at a price of €45.55.

Limit buy orders		Limit sell orders	
Price	Shares	Price	Shares
59.75	4,000	55.75	1,000
59.50	5,000	55.80	2,500
59.25	7,000	56.00	4,500

    a. If a market buy order for 1,000 shares comes in, at what prices will it be filled?
    b. At what price would the next market buy order be filled?
    c. You are the specialist: do you wish to increase or decrease your inventory of this stock?

6. You have borrowed $20,000 on margin to buy shares in Disney, which is now selling at $80 per share. Your account starts at the initial margin requirement of 50%. The maintenance margin is 35%. Two days later, the stock price falls to $75 per share.
    a. Will you receive a margin call?
    b. How low can the price of Disney shares fall before you receive a margin call?

Appendix: Liquidity CAPM

Jacoby *et al.* (2000) developed a CAPM-based asset pricing model taking into account liquidity effects. The model is given by

$$E(r_i - c_i) = r_f + \beta_i^* \left[E(r_M - c_M) - r_f \right]$$

where

$$\beta_i^* = \frac{\text{cov}\left(r_i - c_i, r_M - c_M\right)}{\text{var}\left(r_M - c_M\right)}$$

The model is able to capture the impact of liquidity costs on the systematic risk, quantified by the liquidity-adjusted beta β_i^*.

Straight manipulation of the beta equation leads to a decomposition of the covariance term, as given by

$$\begin{aligned}\beta_i^* &= \frac{\text{cov}\left(r_i - c_i, r_M - c_M\right)}{\text{var}\left(r_M - c_M\right)} \\ &= \frac{\text{cov}\left(r_i, r_M\right)}{\text{var}\left(r_M - c_M\right)} + \frac{\text{cov}\left(c_i, c_M\right)}{\text{var}\left(r_M - c_M\right)} - \frac{\text{cov}\left(r_i, c_M\right)}{\text{var}\left(r_M - c_M\right)} - \frac{\text{cov}\left(c_i, r_M\right)}{\text{var}\left(r_M - c_M\right)}\end{aligned}$$

The liquidity-CAPM equation can be then reformulated as

$$E\left(r_i\right) = r_f + E\left(c_i\right) + \left[E\left(r_M - c_M - r_f\right)\left(\beta_i + \beta_i^{L1} - \beta_i^{L2} - \beta_i^{L3}\right)\right]$$

where

$$\beta_i = \frac{\text{cov}\left(r_i, r_M\right)}{\text{var}\left(r_M - c_M\right)}$$

$$\beta_i^{L1} = \frac{\text{cov}\left(c_i, c_M\right)}{\text{var}\left(r_M - c_M\right)}$$

$$\beta_i^{L2} = \frac{\text{cov}\left(r_i, c_M\right)}{\text{var}\left(r_M - c_M\right)}$$

$$\beta_i^{L3} = \frac{\text{cov}\left(c_i, r_M\right)}{\text{var}\left(r_M - c_M\right)}$$

The four beta coefficients resulting from the decomposition can be commented as follows:

- β_i is the classic beta of the CAPM formula, when liquidity issues are not considered.
- β_i^{L1}, or cov(c_i, c_M), represents the *commonality in liquidity*. Expected return increases with the covariance between the asset's illiquidity and the market illiquidity, because investors demand a premium for holding a security that becomes illiquid when their portfolio (market) becomes illiquid.
- β_i^{L2}, or cov(r_i, c_M), measures the sensitivity of asset return to market liquidity. This beta loads *negatively* with expected returns, because investors are willing to give up return on an asset with a high return in times of market illiquidity.

- β_i^{L3}, or cov(c_i, r_M), measures the sensitivity of asset liquidity to market return. This beta also loads *negatively* with expected returns, because investors are willing to give up return on a security that is liquid in a down market. When the market declines, investors are poor and the ability to easily sell becomes valuable.

Acharya and Pedersen (2005) show that, in general, empirically all four betas can help to explain returns in the US equity market.

9 Other risks

Along with the sources of risk examined up until now, there are some others that complete the picture of the financial risk that a company or financial institution may be subject to during its daily activities.

The process of globalization of financial markets, together with deregulation of trades and sophistication in technology, has added complexity to the banking system, changing their risk profiles, with the need to focus on operational risk as a new source of uncertainty.

Financial investors making foreign investments, together with multinational corporates working on import-export, are faced with the global economy. Their activities are therefore subject to an exchange rate risk, with severe financial consequences if not managed appropriately. Exchange rate risk management is an integral part of every firm's decisions about foreign currency exposure.

Volatility risk involves derivatives with embedded options, affecting the underlying asset through a change in the value of the option. Every investment has some level of risk or volatility. This kind of risk can be managed using appropriate financial instruments written on some given financial asset.

After studying this chapter you will be able to answer the following questions, among others:

1. What is operational risk? How can it be treated and what is the regulatory approach?
2. How can currency risk be defined?
3. What are foreign exchange derivatives and how can they be used for FX risk management?
4. What is implied volatility, and how can it be measured?
5. How can variance swaps be used for the management of volatility risk? How do they differ from standard swaps?

The first section of the chapter is dedicated to operational risk, with the description of the methodologies adopted for identification, measurement and management, followed by an introduction to the regulatory environment. The second section is about currency risk, describing the types of currency risks. It also aims to introduce FX derivatives, as well as to show the most common hedging techniques. The final part deals with volatility risk, with the description of the concept of implied volatility, followed by the explanation of the most common volatility-based financial derivatives.

9.1 Operational risk

Learning outcomes

1. Define identification and assessment of operational risk.
2. Explain how operational risk can be treated and controlled.
3. Describe the regulatory approach to operational risk.

9.1.1 Identification and assessment

Traditionally, banks have managed operational risk through internal control mechanisms. Risk management of that type requires specific structures and processes, and inadequate internal controls can lead to significant losses for banks.

The typical weakness historically reported in banks, when managing operational risk, are of many types. For example, for many years the lack of control culture causes managers to give insufficient attention and guidance.

Another type is the wrong assessment of risk related to certain banking activities. New products and services may have a clear impact on the riskiness, as well as changing market conditions.

Finally, control communications failure also represents a major lack in risk management, in that many banks historically failed in creating adequate segregation of control duties, and in fostering communication between different levels and departments.

Identification of operational risk is a major concern for banks and financial institutions. Banks should identify and assess the operational risk inherent in all the activities, processes and systems, and that is especially true for new products and services.

Effective risk identification should be based on both internal and external factors, which can be categorized into different types. For example, people risk is related to the possibility of a bad behaviour from employees. Process risk, on the other hand, is the risk of failures in transactions, control violations and model methodology errors.

Legal risk includes exposure to penalties and damages due to actions of supervisors, or private settlements. Reputational risk is due to losing the esteem and consideration of customers, due to failure in keeping adequate business standards. The summary of external events goes into the event risk category, which resembles the risk deriving from changes in the external environment and macroeconomic variables.

The levels that are subject to operational risk are listed using a three-level procedure. The first level lists the main business groups of the bank, level two lists the sub-departmental teams belonging to each business, while the third level is about the products and services offered by each team.

Risk identification and assessment is a process where several factors including types of customers, activities, products, effectiveness of processes and systems, must be taken into account in order to establish the risk profile of a company and its activities. Moreover, risk tolerance, employee development and the environment surrounding the company play a crucial role.

Self-assessment of risk should build up awareness about operational risk, and serve as a starting point for further risk management processes. They are mostly issued as qualitative tools, in the form of questionnaires and interviews.

Scorecards can be used as evaluation tools, in that they can be easily translated into quantitative parameters, and used to assess both dimensions of operational risk: loss frequency and loss severity. The real meaning of these dimensions will be clear in the following sections.

Risk can be represented as a matrix, in order to get an immediate view on the strengths and weaknesses, and the incumbent threats. Structured questionnaires offer the easiness in recording the answers, very useful in big institutions. Workshops are the right tool to build up awareness across business units.

Corporate culture and management attitude determine the tool to be used. The active involvement of senior managers as well as a participatory culture are factors contributing to the success of a workshop.

After all products are listed in level three, the following step is to record the various risk events associated with them.

Every event is associated with people, process and technology, and can be identified as a historical assessment, for events which occurred in the past. If an entry corresponds to a risk by logic, then it is a judgement assessment.

Intuition assessment relates to the case where the adoption of appropriate measures helped to save the institution from an event, and linked-events recognize the event as resulting from other types of risk.

Historical assessment is based on counting the total number of risk events, the total financial consequences and their impact on the finances of the institution. The exposure at risk due to increase in volumes, and total amount of claims paid out also contribute to the assessment.

Aside self-assessment, loss databases represent another useful tool to assess operational risk management. Collection of loss data within a bank is crucial to analyse the situation and control risk.

Internal databases are usually made of frequent low-impact losses, so to determine a flow of information that is useful to improve the efficiency of the internal processes, rather than help modelling the risk itself.

Major losses occur rarely and carry huge consequences, but they are almost never recorded in internal loss databases. A bank willing to model operational risk must necessarily access external loss databases.

Loss databases take a form which is dependent on the size of the institution. Bigger institutions in general tend to use intranet-based solutions, given they have a complex organization and the flow of loss data must converge in a uniform input.

The key fields in a loss database are date, severity, loss-related compensations, event-type, business line. Secondary entries include the geographical location, relation to other forms of risk, description of causes.

Some losses are not well defined at a specific point in time, but they happen through a life cycle, developing over time. New information changes the loss estimation and it may take a long time before determining the right loss amount.

Unit executives and risk control responsible officers must approve the loss recording, and they receive the reports on the basis of specifically regulated escalation procedures. Also passing of information should be subject to specific rules.

External loss data are collected by consortia and commercial providers, that allow members and customers to exchange loss data in a standard form. The flow of information is anonymous and quality-checked.

The main consortia holding loss databases are the Global Operational Loss Database (GOLD), based in the UK, the Operational Riskdata eXchange (ORX), in Switzerland, and the Database Italiano delle Perdite Operative (DIPO), in Italy.

There is a scaling problem when using external loss data, in that losses that could be easily handled by some banks could be dangerous for others. Therefore scaling is necessary in order to fit each loss data with the structure of the specific bank.

Another tool for risk assessment is business process analysis. Identification of business processes among units is crucial to allocate loss data and determine the risk associated with each process.

In business process analysis, processes are assigned to products, and examined for risk-sensitive items. Loss scenarios can be used to improve the analysis, and documentation of processes helps to improve them and achieve efficiency.

Scenario analyses are mandatory for a bank to gain authorization to run advanced measurement approaches (AMAs). They help to identify impacts that are not historically reported, so to account for extreme cases, emphasizing future aspects, compared to the past.

The objectives of scenario analysis for operational risk are both qualitative and quantitative. On a quantitative basis, scenarios are a basis to run stress tests and complement data used for risk capital computation. Qualitatively, they allow for early detection of risk, help process optimization and weaknesses identification.

In terms of the approach to scenario analysis, the top-down approach involves the identification of potential losses in the range bounded by stress tests. Bottom-up approach, on the other hand, starts with process analysis and assigns frequencies and severity to potential events.

Key risk indicators are a useful tool for assessing potential future losses, in that they make it possible to identify areas at heavy risk. For each indicator, a threshold can be defined.

Commonly used indicators include staff turnover rate, days of sick-leave, information on system failures, frequency of complaints. The problem with the indicators is that they are hardly comparable among units and companies.

Effective monitoring of operational risk is crucial to detect and correct deficiencies, given that proper management of weaknesses reduces the potential frequency and severity of an event.

Early indicators of future losses must be identified in order to anticipate the loss event. Among others, typical potential sources of operational risk are rapid growth, introduction of a new product, system breakdown, employee turnover.

Risk monitoring should be integrated into bank activities, and regular reports should be forwarded to the senior management. Compliance reviews, internal and external auditing, as well as regulator reports should generate those reports.

9.1.2 Treatment and control

As from a paper of the Basel Committee (2001), there are several methods to calculate the regulatory capital. The AMA divides the bank activities into business lines, and defined event types, as specified by the Directive 2006/48/EC of the European Union. An exposure indicator must then be identified for each event type i and business unit j.

The analysis of loss data leads to the calculation of a loss given event and the probability of the event to happen, like in credit risk. The capital requirement is obtained by multiplying all factors as calculated, and a relevant multiplying factor. The formula for capital requirement is then

$$K = \sum_i \sum_j \delta_{i,j} E_{i,j} \pi_{i,j} L_{GE,i,j}$$

where

$\delta_{i,j}$ is the relevant multiplying factor for loss event type i and business line j
$E_{i,j}$ is the exposure indicator for loss event type i and business line j
$\pi_{i,j}$ is the probability of loss event type i and business line j
$L_{GE,i,j}$ is the loss for a given event type i and business line j.

The factors δ_{ij} are determined internally by banks, with the supervision and approval of competent authorities.

Another methodology relies on loss distribution approach, and is based on distributional properties of the loss events. As opposed to AMA, there is no estimation of a relevant factor matrix, but loss distributions are identified on the basis of historical data.

Data sets are used to model loss frequency and severity for each event type and business line, and convoluted then into a cumulative loss distribution using numerical approaches like Monte Carlo. The loss so calculated is the basis for capital calculation.

Finally, scorecards are also used, in the form of interviews, brainstorming, search methods and so on. All the information gathered by using scorecards helps to adjust the risk profile.

There are both qualitative and quantitative criteria involved, and the data obtained are objectified and validated using historical internal and external loss data. Scorecards bring a forward-looking improvement in risk control.

The board of directors and senior management are responsible for establishing and keeping a control culture in the institutions. The integration of operational risk control into other bank activities ensures quick response to changing conditions.

Internal control processes have become more extensive over the years, in order to address all various risks faced by institutions. Appropriate internal control processes are a critical step in banks' profitability at all levels.

Setting up of an internal control system requires setting up a control structure, defined at all business levels. Controls are both physical and documental, and processed through appropriate authorization systems.

Duties are properly spread among employees so as to not generate any conflict of interest and information should be reliable, timely, accessible and provided in a consistent format.

Risk treatment involves four different possible actions to undertake, as mentioned in Chapter 1, which are avoidance, mitigation, transfer and acceptance. The risk matrix obtained by crossing events and business lines helps in choosing the appropriate strategy.

As a general rule, a bank should avoid risk when the expected marginal profit from taking the risk is significantly lower than the cost of taking the risk. Time horizon, expertise and strategic plans guide the choice.

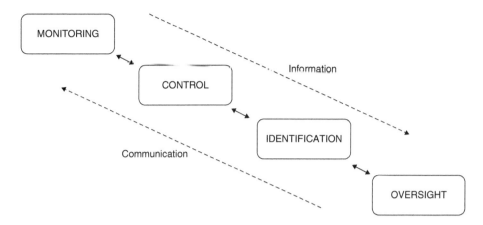

Figure 9.1 The scheme of operational risk process, in an average corporation.

Risk mitigation may go through reduction of either loss frequency or loss severity. The tools for mitigating risk are control measures of such procedures, separation of functions, physical control, coordination checks, disaster recovery.

Report on such controls should be issued in the form of guidelines and instructions to the personnel. Preventive controls are very efficient and also informal control plays a crucial role. Justifications for all decisions made should be traceable.

Risk transfer may happen through either insurance or outsourcing activities. Risk transfer is necessary when internal controls fail in managing the risk, and risk is too high to be accepted.

When taking insurance, cooperation between the risk controlling unit and the unit in charge of buying insurance is crucial. The development of a general insurance framework as a basis to take insurance, and regular coordination with internal risk policies ensure a proper transfer of the risk. Insurance products commonly offered to financial institutions range from the property insurance, business interruption, employment practices, to transport of values.

9.1.3 Basel II approach

According to the Basel Committee on banking supervision, Operational Risk is 'the risk of direct or indirect loss resulting from inadequate or failed internal processes, people and systems or from external events, and includes legal risk'.

The definition does not include reputational and strategic risk, and the main focus is on the causes of operational risk, for better measurement and management of it, even though the corporations seem to be still immature in that respect.

First, distinction must be made between internal and external causes of operational risk. Internal causes include employee behaviour, failures in processes, and the functioning of corporate systems. External causes are all the external events that are not endogenous in the life of the corporation.

Operational risk is characterized by being dependent on all business activities in the firm. It is company specific, meaning that it depends on the company profile and sector. Moreover its handling is influenced by the risk culture of the corporation.

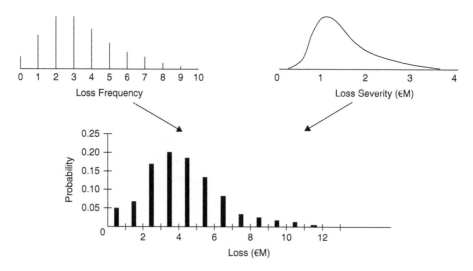

Figure 9.2 The quantification of operational risk management involves merging the loss frequency distribution with the loss severity distribution, in order to get a distribution of losses.

Operational risk is very different from all other forms of risk, in that there is no direct relationship with income, and risk is handled internally with no disclosure of information by the single institution, and a consequent lack of data.

Market and credit risk are better differentiable in the risk factors, due to the general deliberate acceptance of those risks. On the other hand, it is not easy to establish a link between risk factors and severity of losses in operational risk.

The two dimensions characterizing operational risk are loss frequency and loss severity. In order to grasp the difference among the two, consider a car accident and a plane accident. The former is more likely to happen than the latter, but when a plane crashes, consequences will be much more severe than in a car accident.

There is a severity distribution and a frequency distribution, with mean values usually considered for each type. The product of mean values does not necessarily reflect the actual risk accurately, since, as a rule, a higher severity is more than compensated by its related lower probability.

Convolution of information from both distributions is the appropriate methodology to follow in order to assess the risk. Partial information, like frequency of only one means of transport among car and plane, leads to different measures.

A typical convoluted loss distribution shows a level of expected losses (EL) from operational risk events that a credit institution has to expect on average (expected value). It should be absorbed as running costs and managed by internal control measures.

A capital charge for operational risk should cover the unexpected losses due to that specific type of risk. The weak point in the early regulation was that institutions were obliged to book provisions only at time of event.

A basic approach to operational risk is the Basic Indicator Approach (BIA), introduced in Basel II capital adequacy rules. The capital to hold for operational risk is calculated as a fraction of the gross income.

The approach is easy to implement, but only suitable for smaller banks, with a limited range of activities. Counting for the last $i = 1, 2, 3$ years with a positive gross income, the formula for the BIA is

$$A_{BI} = \frac{1}{3} \sum_{i=1}^{3} \alpha I_i$$

where

I_i is the (positive) gross income at time i
α is the fraction of gross income that builds the indicator (typically 15%).

Gross income is defined as net interest income plus net non-interest income. It is intended that this measure should be gross of operating expenses, interest not paid, financial gains or losses, and secondary income sources like insurance.

Further to the BIA approach, the standardized approach is a refinement, differing in that bank activities are divided into a number of standardized business units and business lines.

The standardized approach improves the recognition of different risk profiles across banks, and differentiates appropriately for different lines of business. However, the capital charge is still standardized by regulators.

Every business line has a specific indicator reflecting the size and volume of the bank activities in that specific area. The indicator is a proxy of the amount of operational risk within each of these business lines.

It is possible to summarize the different types of operational risks into seven major categories, as follows.

1. Internal fraud
2. External fraud
3. Employment practices and workplace safety
4. Clients, products and business practices
5. Damage to physical address
6. Business disruption and system failures
7. Execution, delivery and process management

The business activities of a credit institution are divided into eight business lines and assigned a relevant income indicator.

As a consequence, banks must estimate 56 different combinations of business line and risk type. The capital requirement for operational risks corresponds to the sum of capital requirements in the individual business lines.

The indicator for each business line is calculated individually as the average over three years of the sum of net interest income and annual net non-interest income as defined for the BIA.

The last three months of each financial year are considered in order to grasp the value of the indicator. Proxies and estimates can be used in case data are not available for the analysis.

Table 9.1 Operational income factors and indicators for the different business lines in the bank

Business lines	Indicators	Factors α
Corporate Finance	Gross Income	18%
Trading and Sales	Gross Income	18%
Payment and Settlement	Annual Avg. Assets	18%
Commercial Banking	Annual Avg. Assets	15%
Agency Services	Annual Settlement	15%
Retail Brokerage	Gross Income	12%
Retail Banking	Gross Income	12%
Asset Management	Total Funds Managed	12%

Given the corresponding factors for each business line and indicator, the capital requirement for operational risk is calculated using the following formula:

$$A_{ST} = \sum_{i=1}^{8} \alpha_i I_i$$

where

α_i is the factor assigned to business line i.

A variant of the approach is the alternative standardized approach, and it is used by institutions that are authorized by supervisory authority. In fact, banks that want to implement it must fulfil specific conditions.

An alternative approach can be undertaken by banks very active in retail and commercial banking, for at least the 90% of total gross income. Moreover, a consistent part of the assets must carry high probability of default.

Institutions gaining access to alternative standardized approaches are allowed to appropriately modify the indicators for business lines of retail and commercial banking.

Basel II also introduced a more complex way to calculate operational risk, called the advanced measurement approach (AMA). It allows banks to calculate regulatory capital using own internal models.

The approach leads to a significant improvement in risk management processes and mechanisms. Methods like scenario analysis and internal data processing contribute to a better understanding of operational risk, protecting the value of the bank.

There are both quantitative and qualitative criteria to be met by institutions that want to use advanced measurement. Among qualitative criteria, a well-integrated risk management function should be in place, and the institution must have an independent department for operational risk.

Risk exposures and loss events should be carefully reported, and procedures for taking corrective action should be in place. Well-documented risk management and routines to ensure compliance are also prerequisites.

The risk management process should be subject to continuous internal and external reviews, to ensure quality. Authorities should verify the validity of internal validation, and verify transparency of data flows and processes.

Quantitative standards include the ability of the bank to provide measurement methods that are capable of catching tail risk, and capital must be calculated on expected and unexpected losses. The standard must be comparable to a 99.9% confidence level over a one-year period.

The standard must be achieved using internal and external data, scenario analysis and factor analysis. These elements must be merged in order to define a clear strategy for risk measurement.

An important factor affecting aggregate risk is the correlation among individual estimates. Regulation states that institutions can use correlation measurement only if the authorities can verify the validity of the models used to calculate correlation.

The risk measurement system must be internally consistent. In particular it is not allowed to introduce mitigation in the risk measurement, as in other forms of risk, as well as the multiple counting of qualitative assessments.

As mentioned above, the use of AMA is subject to approval by the competent authority. The Basel II document states that banks willing to adopt the standard must submit a series of documents, including a detailed plan, the description of the model to be implemented, and its parameters.

Moreover, an implementation on IT of the model must be submitted along with the responsibilities and reporting agents, a description of the bank's internal risk management process for operational risk, and accurate information about specific training of employees.

9.2 Currency risk

Learning outcomes

1. List and define the various types of currency risk.
2. Describe foreign exchange derivatives and their pricing.
3. Define how FX risk can be hedged.

9.2.1 Types of currency risk

Organizations investing in foreign economies, with a currency other than the domestic one, are exposed to foreign exchange (FX) risk. Corporate treasuries are usually responsible for the handling of currency (or FX) risk. This is a proof of the importance that firms give to risk management issues and techniques.

Madura (1989) gives a common definition of exchange risk as related to the changes in value of a corporation, caused by unexpected currency movements. More specifically, it can be defined as the direct or indirect loss in the financials of the firm, on all the spectrum of the financial statement, causing a loss in the market value of the stock.

Management of currency risk embedded in the daily operation of any multinational corporation requires the accurate determination of the specific type of FX exposure, what hedging strategy is viable and what instruments are available for managing the risk.

Those firms are big players in the currency markets, and they require constant monitoring of the risk involved in foreign currency-denominated operations. Risk can then be measured through the implied VaR from exchange rate moves, provided the type of risk is identified

Following Shapiro (2009) currency risks are commonly classified into three main categories, namely transaction risk, translation risk and economic risk.

Transaction risk involves cash flows, dealing with the effect of exchange rate moves on transactional account exposure. It involves export-related receivables, import-related payables and cashing of dividends.

If the exchange rate changes in the currency of denomination of the contracts involved in the analysis, it will directly impact on the transaction exchange risk affecting the overall firm.

Translation risk relates more to the balance sheet, capturing the changes in valuation of a foreign subsidiary due to exchange rate moves, impacting on the consolidation of the subsidiary to the parent company's balance sheet.

In order to measure translation risk for a foreign subsidiary, the exposure of net assets to potential currency moves must be considered first. Depending on accounting standards, consolidation through translation may be done at the exchange rate as measured at the end of the period, or at the average rate over the whole period.

It turns out that generally, the income statement is translated using the average exchange rate over the period, while consolidation of balance sheet foreign exposure of subsidiaries is done at the exchange rate which is prevailing at the time.

The third type of FX risk is named economic risk, and refers to the risk incumbent on the present value of future operating cash flows, from adverse exchange rate movements.

Such a risk affects both the revenues from domestic sales and exports, and the operating expenses from domestic inputs and imports, and it is applied to the parent company or foreign subsidiary of a company. For good management of currency risk it is essential to identify the various types of currency, and consequently develop efficient strategies.

Transaction exposure differs from operating exposure, in that its size can be easily identifiable, and is confined to a well-defined time interval, making it suitable for hedging with financial instruments.

Example 9.1: Assume an investor puts $25,000 into a European hedge fund. The currency risk is not hedged, and the investor is exposed to changes in the exchange rate between the dollar and the Euro. In the next 12 months the European stock market and the fund itself go up 15% in Euro currency.

If the dollar/Euro exchange is the same after 12 months as when you first made your investment, the investment is now worth

$$25,000 * (1,15) = \$28,750$$

Assume now the dollar appreciated by 27% versus the Euro over 12 months. The value of the investment in dollars is

$$\frac{28,750}{1.27} = \$22,637.8$$

with a loss of $25,000 - 22,637.8 = \$2,362.20$.

Consider now the case of the dollar depreciating by 27% versus the Euro over the 12 months. The holding would now be worth

$$\frac{28,750}{0.73} = \$39,383.56$$

with a gain of $39,383.56 - 25,000 = \$14,383.56$.

Example 9.2: Suppose an American company sells raw materials to a buyer in Germany for €1,000,000. The materials must be delivered 60 days before the payment is made. At the time of agreement the exchange rate is $1.27 per Euro. So the company expects to receive something around $1,270,000. If the American company's cost for producing and delivering the materials is $1,120,000, then the profit expected is $1,270,000 - 1,120,000 = \$150,000$. However if the value of the Euro fell to $1.11, the American company receiving payment would find that it had a $1,110,000 - 1,120,000 = -\$10,000$ loss.

Example 9.3: Suppose the American company required the German company to pay dollars instead of Euro. Then the German company would be bearing the risk. If the exchange rate fell from $1.27 per Euro to $1.11 the amount expected to be paid for buying the €1,000,000 would be given by

$$\frac{1.27}{1.11} \times 1,100,000 = €1,144,144.$$

Transaction risk comes from fluctuations of exchange rates, that may affect business in many ways. A company is exposed to foreign exchange risk also if not involved in foreign business, given that price of international competitors depends on currencies.

Exchange rates fluctuate due to macroeconomic, political, financial factors. From earthquakes to military conflicts and monetary policy interventions, there are several situations that may cause domestic and international currencies to fluctuate.

Companies that do not have any expertise in FX trading usually enter short on currency forwards in order to lock the equivalent amounts they will receive in foreign currency. That allows knowing in advance what profit they are making on a foreign trade.

Some other companies instead decide to speculate on currencies and use the funds to profit on currency speculation. Usually these companies have specialized divisions to handle the currency operations.

Hedging FX risk costs money, and comes at the cost of lower returns. To what extent FX risk is acceptable is controversial. Some investors believe it is possible to ignore it while investing on foreign equity for long periods.

In general, not all investments made out of domestic market expose a company to currency risk. There are many markets whose currencies are linked to another major currency, so that companies trading in the latter can ignore the currency risk.

9.2.2 Foreign exchange derivatives

Foreign exchange (FX) derivatives imply contracts based on which you can purchase or sell currency at a future date. The three major types of foreign exchange derivatives are currency forwards, currency options and currency swaps. If an institution must trade a certain amount of currency in the future, FX forwards allows locking in the value today.

Currency forwards represent the more liquid and used FX derivative products available on the market, trading continuously in the OTC market. The most liquid currencies belong to large European and developed Western countries.

If a company is trading goods or services, from a foreign market, it is at risk of adverse movements of foreign currency. Depending on how the FX rate moves, the transaction value will change, increasing or decreasing the amount of cash flow from the trade.

Example 9.4: Suppose a European company has contracted to buy 100,000 units of raw material from the US in six months, at $5 per unit. At an exchange rate of $1.2/€, that's €416,667. If the exchange rate goes to $1.5/€ the price becomes €333,333.

If the exchange rate goes to $1.5/€, the price is €500,000. The company is exposed to movements in the dollar against the Euro.

An FX forward is an agreement to purchase or sell a set amount of a foreign currency at a specified price for settlement at a predetermined future date, or within a predetermined window of time.

An important distinction is between closed forwards, to be settled on a specified date, and open forwards, setting a window of time during which any portion of the contract can be settled, as long as the entire contract is settled by the end date.

FX forwards can be used to manage currency risk by locking a rate and a date for settlement of some amount of foreign currency. It helps to protect the costs on foreign deals, protect profit margins, anticipate future settlement FX rates by locking them in.

An FX forward with physical settlement is called an outright forward, and has no upfront payment. In case of restrictions to a foreign currency because of limits in non-deliverable forwards provide a way to hedge currencies.

Settlement is made at maturity at a fixed rate, and the amount in the reference currency is paid or received. Given the specific settlement date, FX forward contracts are useful to hedge a single-payment obligation, rather than a stream of cash flows.

Instruments like currency swaps are more suitable to hedge multiple times, but they come at a higher cost than forwards.

Currency forwards are quoted in forward points, which is the basis points amount to add or subtract from the spot rate in order to get the forward rate at a specified time point.

Essentially, FX forwards are interest rate products available wherever there is a market for liquid deposits in the reference currency. The basic idea is to think of a currency like any other commodity, growing at some interest rate.

It is possible then to apply the price relationship between forward price and spot price at time zero as

$$F_0 = S_0 e^{(r_D - r_F)T}$$
(9.1)

where

F_0 is the forward price at time zero
S_0 is the spot price at time zero

r_D is the domestic risk-free rate

r_F is the foreign risk-free rate

T is the maturity date of the forward.

The formula requires the spot rates quoted at the domestic currency, so that

$$S_0 = \frac{S_D}{S_F}$$

where

S_D is the domestic currency

S_F is the foreign currency.

A discrete approximation of formula (9.1) is given by

$$F_0 = S_0 \frac{(1+r_D)}{(1+r_F)}$$

Forward points are given by

$$s_{FW} = F_0 - S_0$$

The principal amount, FX rate, and settlement date are embedded in the contract, and the net settlement is made at maturity in a fully convertible currency. Net settlement is calculated setting the forward exchange rate against the prevailing market 'spot exchange rate' on the fixing date.

Forward points represent the differential between domestic and foreign currency, and can be positive or negative, depending on the ratio between the corresponding interest rates. The currency with the highest rate will get a discount differential.

Example 9.5: A trader has to invest $100,000. Suppose the dollar is trading at $0.79 and the one-year forward is −2 basis points. There are two investment opportunities; one investing in dollars at a rate of 3%, the other buying Euro. Invest them at 2% rate and then short a one-year Euro-for-dollar forward contract. The first strategy yields $103,000 in one year. The second strategy involves buying €79,000, that is worth

$$79,000(1.02) = €80,580$$

in one year, and can be exchanged at

$$\frac{80,580}{0.79 - 0.02} = \$104,649$$

At maturity T, the owner of one FX forward contract for one unit of foreign currency receives an amount equal to the product of the position held (in number of contracts) and the size (the units of foreign currency that can be bought in one contract).

Assuming by simplicity, that one position on one contract is taken, this is equivalent to a position in S_T units of domestic currency.

At the same time, he has to pay an amount equal to the product of position, size and delivery price of one unit of foreign currency, equal to K. It follows that the value of the forward at T is given by

$$F_T = S_T - K$$

Both cash flows must be then discounted to present value, and the difference between the two payments is the value of the FX forward contract, which is given by

$$F = Se^{-r_F T} - Ke^{-r_D T}$$

which can be extended to the general case as described by

$$F = mk\left(Se^{-r_F T} - Ke^{-r_D T}\right)$$

where

m is the number of contracts
k is the size, in units of foreign currency that can be bought with each contract.

Example 9.6: A European company plans to buy equipment from a British manufacturer. The spot quote for the exchange rate is €1.14200/£, the 30-day forward is €1.14511/£, the 60-day forward is €1.14600/£, the 90-day forward is €1.14750/£. Assume the domestic interest rate is 10% and the foreign interest rate is 15%.

The cost of equipment is £1,000,000, with payment due in 30 days, so the company enters a 30-day forward contract to lock the cost of funds at €1,145,110. In order to value the forward contract, the parameters are

$$S = 1.142, \quad K = 1.14511, \quad t = 0, \quad T = 1/12$$
$$m = 1, \quad k = 1,000,000, \quad r_D = 0.10, \quad r_F = 0.15$$

The cost of the forward contract is given by

$$F = (1 \times 1,000,000)(1.14200e^{-0.15 \times 0.08333} - 1.14511e^{-0.10 \times 0.08333}) = -€7,793.22$$

In a non-deliverable forward, the actual funds exchanged on the value date at maturity will depend on the prevailing spot exchange rate. The forward is an asset when the forward rate is higher than the spot rate, and the opposite holds true when spot rates are higher than the original forward rate agreed at inception.

Institutions with significant domestic operations have the advantage to use the domestic currency, and be able to observe deposit flows. Sometimes non-delivery forwards are offered to circumvent these restrictions, because they have cash settlement, and can be hedged using futures or assets.

FX forwards have the advantage to be free of upfront costs and act as a useful tool to fix the exchange rate for a future settlement date. Disadvantages are the counterparty risk embedded into a position in FX forwards and the possible opportunity cost.

The hedging strategy depends on whether the company is receiving or paying the foreign currency in the future. When receiving it, the risk is the devaluation, so that each unit of the currency will be worth less in domestic currency terms.

In this case, the strategy to hedge this risk, is to sell the currency forward and lock in today's rate.

If the company is going to pay the foreign currency in the future, the risk is that the currency will appreciate, because each foreign currency unit will require more dollars to buy. To hedge the risk in this case, the strategy is to buy the currency forward.

Following the BSM approach, Biger and Hull developed a model to price currency options. Based on information about the same parameters as in BSM, the pricing models can derive. The currency option pricing model of Biger and Hull is defined as

$$c_{FX} = e^{-r_F \Delta t} SN(d_1) - e^{-r_D \Delta t} KN(d_2)$$

where

$$d_1 = \frac{\ln\left[\dfrac{S}{K}\right] + \left(r_D - r_F + \dfrac{\sigma^2}{2}\right)\Delta t}{\sigma\sqrt{\Delta t}}$$

$$d_2 = d_1 - \sigma\sqrt{\Delta t}$$

The interest r_F gained on holding a foreign security is equivalent to a continuously paid dividend on a stock share. The key transformation in adapting the BSM model to value currency options is the substitution of exchange rates for stock prices.

As the BSM model, also the Biger and Hull model does not account for early exercise of the option. Currency options in fact are structured like common equity options, with the distinction between European and American options.

Also for currency options, it is possible to derive the put-call parity formula, which is given by

$$p_{FX} = c_{FX} + Ke^{-rT} - Se^{-r^*T}$$

where

> r is the domestic risk-free interest rate
> r^* is the foreign risk-free interest rate
> T is the time to maturity of the option.

Arbitrage possibilities follow the standard conditions of equilibrium, so that if the actual put option premium is different than what is suggested by put-call parity, arbitrage would again be possible. Strategies would then force all prices to converge to equilibrium and arbitrage to disappear.

A currency swap is an agreement to exchange some kind of currency with another one. The swap arises when one party provides a certain principal in one currency to its counterparty in exchange for an equivalent amount of a different currency.

There are three different sets of cash flows involved in a plain vanilla currency swap. At initiation of the swap, there is an actual exchange of cash between the two parties. The currency swap aims in fact at satisfying an actual need for funds denominated in a different currency. This aspect represents the main difference with an interest rate swap, in which both parties deal in the same currency and can pay the net amount.

At a second stage, the parties make periodic interest payments to each other during the life of the swap agreement. Finally, the third step is the termination of the contract, when the parties again exchange the principal.

9.2.3 *Risk hedging in FX markets*

Identification and measurement of FX risk must be followed by a decision on whether to hedge the risk or not. The issue of appropriate hedging strategy is yet to be settled in the literature.

However, in practice, corporate treasurers commonly use various currency risk management strategies. The size of the firm and the prevalence of some type of risk determine the managerial choices.

Regarding transaction risk, the choice is often between a tactical or a strategic approach, to preserve cash flows and earnings. Tactical hedging is mostly used by firms aiming at controlling currency risk on short-term receivable and payable transactions. The strategic approach, on the other hand, is used to hedge longer-period transactions.

Other firms decide to hedge passively, which entails maintaining some hedge structure over regular holding periods, without being concerned about currency expectations, or taking a currency view.

Translation risk involves the balance sheet, and it is usually hedged infrequently, just to avoid major currency impacts on net assets. Long-term foreign exposure, international investments and subsidiaries are involved in the analysis.

Due to its nature, translation risk is not a priority of the management, given that it does not affect the income statement. A common practice is to hedge the net balance sheet exposures (net assets) of the subsidiary under consideration, exposed to the risk.

Economic risk is often considered as a residual risk, due to the difficulty in its quantification, and reflects the potential impact on the present value of future cash flows of exchange rate movements.

Therefore, it may be important to measure how a deviation of the exchange rate from the benchmark rate used for revenue forecasting could impact on the profitability of the company.

The impact on cash flows may be netted out across product lines and markets, and if the exchange rate is connected to the inflation rate differentials between domestic and foreign economy, a subsidiary operating in a high-inflation environment could generate a deterioration in the overall competitiveness of the company.

Kritzman (1993) shows that sophisticated corporate treasuries develop hedging strategies as a more integrated approach to hedge currency risk, compared to buying a plain vanilla hedge to cover certain foreign exchange exposure.

Foreign exchange efficient frontiers measure the efficiency of portfolios in terms of cost of hedging against the degree of risk hedged, so to determine the most efficient strategy at the lowest possible cost.

Optimization approaches can be also used, given some specific currency view of the corporation. Considering both plain vanilla forwards and option strategies, the fully non-hedged position is compared to the fully hedged one, in order to find the optimal strategy.

The optimization approach can be used for all types of currency risk, but an important drawback of the approach is that it relies heavily on the corporate view of the exchange rate (i.e. a possible exchange rate forecast over a specified time period).

The board of a company sets reference exchange rate levels, and the management is required to ensure that the deviation from that budget rate is minimal. This framework determines the frequency and instruments to be used for hedging.

The choice of the benchmark rate is controversial. Some companies use the purchasing power parity rate, especially for hedging short-term positions, while tactical hedging is preferred for longer time horizons.

Other firms prefer to set the budget rate in accordance with their sales calendar and, in turn, with their hedging strategy, so that for the quarterly sales calendar, the next year's quarterly foreign currency cash flows will not deviate more than some percentage.

Another choice of the budget exchange rate could be, as observed by Barton *et al.* (2002), the daily average exchange rate over the previous fiscal year. The firm would then need to use one single hedge over an average-based instrument.

The hedging through average rate is usually implemented on the last day of the previous fiscal year, and also a passive strategy could be implemented, by hedging the average value of an FX currency cash flow over a specified time interval.

Whichever the choice, the budget FX rate used to forecast cash flows must be close to the spot exchange rate, so that possible major changes in the firm's pricing strategy can be avoided.

Common principles for operational framework of best practices may include, as suggested by Jacque (1996), and Allen (2003), the ones listed as

1. Identifying and measuring the types of exchange rate risk the firm is exposed to, specifying what currencies are related to each type of risk.
2. Develop an exchange risk management strategy, specifying currency objectives and whether to perform a partial or full hedge.
3. Create a centralized entity in the treasury department of the company, dealing with practical aspects of FX rate forecasting, risk hedging approach, and more.
4. Develop a set of controls for risk monitoring and appropriate trading management, setting position limits, monitoring through mark-to-market valuation, and establishing of benchmarks for periodic monitoring.
5. Establish a committee for risk oversight, in charge of approving limits on position taking, assess the appropriateness of hedging instruments, and review policies.

As already mentioned in previous sections, the range of hedging instruments for FX risk is wide, including both OTC and exchange-traded products. Among the most common OTC currency hedging instruments are currency forwards and currency options.

It has been shown how to price these types of securities, and it is now possible to show how they can be used for hedging purposes.

9.3 Volatility risk

Learning outcomes

1. Define implied volatility and its measurement.
2. Describe callable bonds and their features.
3. Describe variance swaps as a tool for volatility management.

9.3.1 Implied volatility

The only free parameter in the BSM model is the asset return volatility σ, which is positively related to the value of the option. The price between the option price and the volatility, given all other parameters, is in fact a unique one-to-one mapping.

The specific level of σ, that, input in the BSM model, generates the market observed price, is called implied volatility. It is common practice to quote implied volatilities instead of option prices.

Since an option gives the holder the right but not the obligation to trade on the underlying, volatility movements can only have a positive effect on the option value, that increases for higher volatility values.

Recall that the BSM model implies a constant volatility parameter. Therefore, real market volatility would be constant, if prices behaved like BSM. This is not the case, and in the real world the assumption of constant volatility is consistently violated.

Implied volatilities at different times, for different strikes and times to maturity, are usually different, so that BSM assumptions are violated in reality, and do not represent return volatilities, but still reflect the time value of the option.

A possible interpretation of implied volatility is the market's expectation of future volatility, weighted by the time over the option maturity. The focus is to determine whether there exist natural definitions of expected or average volatility, to be understood as implied volatility.

Empirical studies show consistent statistical properties of implied volatilities across various market indices, looking at various strikes (volatility smile patterns), maturities and time series behaviour.

These properties have been summarized by Cont and Da Fonseca (2002) and can be listed as

1. Implied volatility surfaces have non-flat profile.
2. The shape of the surfaces changes its form over time.
3. There is high positive autocorrelation and mean reversion in implied volatilities.
4. Three principal components (shift in level, opposite movements in put and call, change in surface convexity) are sufficient to explain log-variations in volatility.
5. There is no perfect correlation between implied volatility and underlying asset price.
6. Global shifts in level of implied volatility are negatively correlated with the returns of the underlying asset, while relative movements are lightly correlated instead.

It is common practice on the markets to quote option prices in terms of their BSM implied volatilities. The variation of implied volatility across option strike and maturity can be substantial, drawing the so-called volatility surface.

Differently from option prices, implied volatilities are comparable across different levels of the option parameters, allowing to compare market prices to fair (model) values.

The simplest case to consider is of the volatility to be time-dependent, but not stochastic. In this case the formula for the implied volatility is defined by considering the average variance over the option life, defined as

$$\bar{\sigma}^2 = \frac{1}{T} \int_0^T \sigma_u^2 du$$

Recall the lognormal property of stock prices under the BSM framework, stating that

$$\ln S_T \sim \left[\left(r - \frac{\bar{\sigma}^2}{2}\right)T, \bar{\sigma}^2 T\right]$$

It follows that the price of the call satisfies the BSM formula, for a volatility equal to $\bar{\sigma}$, and the implied volatility σ_{BSM} satisfies

$$\sigma_{BSM} = \bar{\sigma}$$

where

$\bar{\sigma}$ is the quadratic mean volatility from 0 to T.

A common complication of the model is to make the volatility a function of both time and underlying stock, but still deterministic. In this case, the volatility obtained is the local volatility.

The work on local volatilities was pioneered by B. Dupire (1994), who showed that, instead of fixing the strike price and maturity, obtaining a backward PDE for the call price $c_{S,t}$, one can fix the stock price and time of measurement and obtain a forward PDE for $c_{K,T}$.

The dynamics and calculations behind Dupire's model are beyond the scope of this section. In brief, Dupire shows that given some conditions, the above procedure leads to an expression of implied local variance as a function of the option price and the strike price, and the maturity, given by

$$\sigma_{LOC} = \sqrt{\left(\frac{\dfrac{\partial c}{\partial T} + \dfrac{rK \partial c}{\partial K}}{\dfrac{K^2}{2}\dfrac{\partial^2 c}{\partial K^2}}\right)}$$

The shape of volatility surfaces is constrained by no-arbitrage conditions, which are anyway met easily whenever there are no large gradients on the surface.

9.3.2 Callable bonds

A callable bond is a type of bond with an embedded option, that gives the right to repay the face value of the security at a pre-agreed value, before maturity of the security. Some companies issue callable bonds to borrow money.

Embedding a callable feature, bonds are early redeemable, and the issuers usually have to pay the holder the face value of the bonds. In some cases, the issuers will need to pay some premium on top of the face value, as a compensation to lenders.

Given the high degree of optionality left to the borrower by the callable feature, there is usually a call protection period during which the bond cannot be called bad, and a typical bond structure is given by some acronym like 10 NC 5, meaning the bond has maturity of ten years, and it is only callable after the fifth year.

Given the fact that a bond can be called at any time after the protection period, callable bonds do not have a yield to maturity. Other yield measures can be calculated, namely the yield to call, and the yield to worst.

The yield to call is calculated based on the assumption that the bond is redeemable exactly at the end of the protection period, with only this date available. In this case the yield calculation is based on the protection period end time as the new maturity.

Recall that in a standard yield calculation for a bond, the yield to call is obtained by numerically inverting the formula

$$B = \sum_{i=1}^{t_p} \frac{C_i}{\left(1 + r_C\right)^i}$$

or, in continuous compounding

$$B = \sum_{i=1}^{t_p} C_i e^{-r_{Call} i}$$

where

r_C is the yield to call
t_p is the ending time of protection period.

Example 9.7: A two-year callable bond can be only called after one year, at a call price of €100. Current price of the bond is €99, with a face value of €100, and coupons of 8% per annum. If the bond is called, therefore getting a maturity of one year, the resulting payments will be of €4 after six months, and €104 after one year. The yield to call of the bond is therefore

$$99 = \frac{4}{1 + \dfrac{r_{Call}}{2}} + \frac{104}{\left(1 + \dfrac{r_{Call}}{2}\right)^2}$$

Inverting the formula yields a value of

$$r_{Call} = 9.07\%$$

Risk measurement for callable bonds is strictly related to the volatility. Compared to standard bonds, the presence of the option feature makes the risk profile of the bond more complicated.

Duration for a standard bond is a decreasing function of the interest rates, and plotting on a graph the duration against the interest rates, different bonds are represented by different straight lines, where the bonds with longer maturities are represented by higher lines in the plane.

In the case of a callable bond, the maturity is not fixed, and depends on whether the option will be exercised or not. Sticking on the simplest case of a single possible calling date, recalling Example 9.7, the concept can be explained by a graph, like in Figure 9.3.

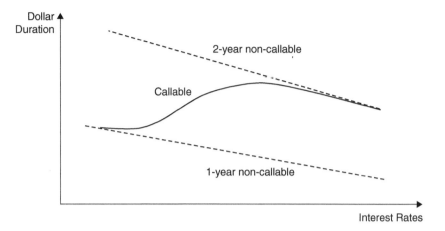

Figure 9.3 The relationship between interest rates and dollar duration for a callable bond is not linear, introducing a degree of complexity for risk calculation.

The duration of the callable bond is comprised between the two straight lines of the bonds representing the shortest and longest possible maturities of the callable bond, and it changes convexity, due to the uncertainty on the effective maturity.

It follows that ordinary formulas for calculating duration cannot be applied to this class of bonds, and an algorithm in several steps must be applied instead. More precisely, in order to calculate the duration of a callable bond, the steps to be followed are given by:

1. Compute the current value of the bond V_0 at the current level of interest rates.
2. Increase the interest rates level by some small amount Δr_y, and calculate the corresponding bond price B_+.
3. Decrease then the interest rates level by the same amount, and calculate the corresponding bond price B_-.
4. The duration of the bond is given by

$$D_{Call} = \frac{B_+ - B_-}{2 B_0 \Delta r_y}$$

Following the same reasoning it is possible to calculate the convexity of a callable bond, which is given by

$$C_{Call} = \frac{B_+ + B_- - 2B_0}{2(\Delta r_y)^2}$$

The intuition behind the convexity formula is the calculation through segments of the distance between the curve representing the yield/price relationship, and the tangent line at the point of initial price and yield, as shown in Figure 9.4.

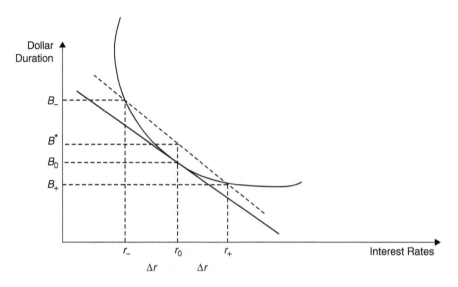

Figure 9.4 Convexity error in the measurement of the change in bond price from the change in the underlying yield.

9.3.3 Variance swaps

A variance swap is a forward contract on annualized variance, the square of the realized volatility. The features of a variance swap include the variance strike, realized variance and the notional, which in the case of the variance swap is expressed in variance units.

The annualized variance is defined as the square root of the sample variance of an n dimensional sample, as

$$\sigma_R^2 = \frac{252}{n-1} \sum_{i=1}^{n} \left[\ln \left(\frac{S_{i+1}}{S_i} \right) \right]^2$$

The payoff at maturity is given by

$$SW_\sigma = L_\sigma \left(\sigma_R^2 - \sigma_K^2 \right)$$

where

L_σ is the variance notional
σ_K^2 is the variance strike.

Since a variance swap is an agreement to exchange

$$\ln \left(\frac{S_2}{S_1} \right)^2 + ... + \ln \left(\frac{S_i}{S_{i-1}} \right)^2 + ... + \ln \left(\frac{S_n}{S_{n-1}} \right)^2 \tag{9.2}$$

a convenient expression for the strike K is such that no money exchange occurs at time zero. Therefore it is

$$K_{SW} = E\left[\ln\left(\frac{S_2}{S_1}\right)^2 + \dots + \ln\left(\frac{S_i}{S_{i-1}}\right)^2 + \dots + \ln\left(\frac{S_n}{S_{n-1}}\right)^2 \right]$$

which can be generalized for any time step $\Delta t \in (0,T)$ as

$$K_{SW} = E\left[\ln\left(\frac{S_{\Delta t}}{S_0}\right)^2 + \ln\left(\frac{S_{2\Delta t}}{S_{\Delta t}}\right)^2 + \dots + \ln\left(\frac{S_T}{S_{T-\Delta t}}\right)^2 \right]$$

In order to determine the right value of K_{SW}, first of all recall that, from the log-properties of the stock price following geometric Brownian motion, it holds that

$$\frac{dS_t}{S_t} - d(\ln S_t) = \frac{\sigma^2}{2} dt$$

Integrating on both sides, the expression for the total variance is obtained as

$$\begin{aligned}\sigma_{TOT}^2 &= \frac{1}{T}\int_0^T \sigma^2 dt \\ &= \frac{2}{T}\left[\int_0^T \frac{dS_t}{S_t} - \ln\left(\frac{S_T}{S_0}\right) \right]\end{aligned}$$

Carr and Madan (1998), as well as Demeterfi *et al.* (1999) show that the fair strike can be calculated using a portfolio of European call and put options with weights inversely proportional to the square of strike.

They argue that in the market defined by a threshold, any twice differentiable payoff function $f(v)$ can be expanded as defined by

$$f(v) = f(k) + f'(k)(v-k) + \int_{-\infty}^{D} f''(k)\max(k-v,0)dk + \int_D^\infty f''(k)\max(v-k,0)dk$$

where

k is some threshold.

They use a replication argument, using a bond, a future and infinitely many options, showing that a short position in the log of a contract replicates a portfolio of positions in futures contract, put and call options.

The replication argument applied to the logarithm of the price ratio, as from the log property of asset prices, can be written as

$$-\ln\left(\frac{S_T}{S_0}\right) = -\frac{S_T - S_Z}{S_Z} + \int_0^{S_Z} \frac{p}{K^2} dK + \int_{S_Z}^\infty \frac{c}{K^2} dK$$

where

S_Z is a threshold value.

A common simplification is to set the cut-off value equal to the current forward price, so that

$$S_Z = F_{0,T} = S_0 e^{rT}$$

The model then simplifies, yielding the formula for the variance swap strike, as

$$K_{SW} = \int_0^{F_{0,T}} \frac{2e^{rT} p}{K^2} dK + \int_{F_{0,T}}^{\infty} \frac{2e^{rT} c}{K^2} dK$$

where

$F_{0,T}$ is the forward price to time T of the option's underlying asset
p is the value at time 0 of the put option with parameters r, K, T, σ, as noted above
c is the value at time 0 of the call option with same parameters as the put.

A convention on the markets for variance and volatility swaps is to impose caps to each payoff, limiting its maximum realization, in order to overtake the impossibility of hedging the contract at times of jumps.

The main problem in defining such a swap is that the payoff equation (9.2) goes to infinite, as $F_{0,t}$ goes to zero. Therefore, a new definition is needed, of a simple variance swap, as an agreement to exchange

$$\left(\frac{S_{\Delta t} - S_0}{F_{0,0}}\right)^2 + \left(\frac{S_{2\Delta t} - S_{\Delta t}}{F_{0,\Delta t}}\right)^2 + \ldots + \left(\frac{S_T - S_{T-\Delta t}}{F_{0,T-\Delta t}}\right)^2 \tag{9.3}$$

so that the denominators in (9.3) are geometrically increasing, for a positive value of the interest rates.

The swap 'strike' is again expressed so that no money is exchanged at time zero. Under all the assumptions mentioned above, the strike is given by

$$k_{SW} = \int_0^{F_{0,T}} \frac{2e^{rT} p}{F_{0,T}^2} dK + \int_{F_{0,T}}^{\infty} \frac{2e^{rT} c}{F_{0,T}^2} dK$$

Traders of variance swaps find them interesting because they allow us to speculate purely on volatility. The same result in fact could be obtained trading in options, but that would require constant delta hedging of the portfolio. The variance swap eliminates the burden of the direction risk of the underlying security.

Moreover, a replicating portfolio of a variance swap requires a whole strip of options, with very high associated costs. Also, one may need to regularly roll the strip of replicating options, to keep it centred around the current price of the underlying security, involving a high degree of complication.

Snapshot 9.1
Gamma swaps

The gamma and vega of a standard variance swap are constant, meaning that the value of the variance swap is not sensitive to changes in F_t.

However, if prices decline, some flexibility to reduce the exposure to volatility is needed, so that a derivative with variance vega and dollar gamma, adjusting with the underlying value, would be beneficial.

Define a gamma (price-weighted variance swap) by the weight $w_t = \dfrac{F_t}{F_0}$. At maturity the buyer receives the realized variance weighted to each t, proportional to the underlying price F_t.

The exposure therefore gains dependence on the path of the variance of F_t. The realized variance paid at expiry of a gamma swap is defined by

$$\sigma_\Gamma = \sqrt{\frac{252}{T} \sum_{t=1}^{T} \frac{F_t}{F_0} \left[\ln\left(\frac{S_t}{S_{t-1}}\right) \right]^2}$$

It can be shown that one can replicate a gamma swap using the following payoff function:

$$f(F_t) = \frac{2}{T}\left(\frac{F_t}{F_0} \log \frac{F_t}{F_0} - \frac{F_t}{F_0} + 1 \right) \tag{9.4}$$

Applying the Carr-Madan argument to payoff (9.4) at time T, the strike of a gamma swap is given by

$$k_{SW} = \frac{2}{TF_0} e^{2rT} \int_0^{F_{0,T}} \frac{p}{K} dK + \frac{2}{TF_0} e^{2rT} \int_{F_{0,T}}^{\infty} \frac{c}{K} dK$$

with first and second order derivative given by

$$f'(F_t) = \frac{2}{TF_0} \log \frac{F_t}{F_0}, \quad f''(F_t) = \frac{2}{TF_0 F_t}, \quad f(F_0) = 0$$

Applying Itô's Lemma to equation (9.4) yields

$$\frac{1}{T}\int_0^T \frac{F_t}{F_0} \sigma_t^2 dt = \frac{2}{T}\left(\frac{F_T}{F_0} \log \frac{F_T}{F_0} - \frac{F_T}{F_0} + 1 \right) - \frac{2}{TF_0} \int_0^T \log \frac{F_T}{F_0} dF_t$$

Summary

Operational risk is 'the risk of direct or indirect loss resulting from inadequate or failed internal processes, people and systems or from external events, and includes legal risk'.

Operational risk management is managed by banks through internal control mechanisms, using specific structure and processes, given that inadequate internal controls can lead to significant losses for banks.

Identification and assessment are the first steps in the management process of operational risk, which includes factors such as types of customers, activities, products, effectiveness of processes and systems, to establish the risk profile of a corporation.

The Basel Committee document on operational risk presents several methods to calculate the regulatory capital, with both qualitative and quantitative criteria involved, estimating the two dimensions of loss frequency and loss severity.

Currency risk is embedded in daily operations of multinational corporations, and requires accurate determination of the exposure, the appropriate type of hedging strategy, and what instruments are available for managing the risk.

Currency risk can be classified into transaction risk, translation risk and economic risk, each with a peculiar role into the overall risk profile of an institution. FX derivatives are based on exchange rate as underlying, and include currency forwards, currency options and currency swaps.

Volatility risk strictly relates to the concept of implied volatility. Real market volatility would be constant, in a world described by the BSM framework, while the real world behaves differently and the assumption of constant volatility is consistently violated.

Bibliography

Allen, S.L. 2003. *Financial Risk Management: A Practitioner's Guide to Managing Market and Credit Risk*. Wiley.

Austrian Financial Market Authority (FMA). 2006. *Guidelines on Operational Risk Management*.

Balland, P. 2002. Deterministic Implied Volatility Models. *Quantitative Finance*, 2: 31–44.

Barton, T.L., Shenkir, W.G. and Walker, P.L. 2002. Making Enterprise Risk Management Pay Off. *Financial Executives Research Foundation*. Prentice Hall, 189.

Basel Committee on Banking Supervision. 2001. *Operational Risk: Supporting Document to the New Basel Capital Accord*. Bank for International Settlements.

Biger, N. and Hull, J. 1983. The Valuation of Currency Options. *Financial Management*, Spring: 24–28.

Carr, P. and Madan, D. 1998. Determining Volatility Surfaces and Option Values From an Implied Volatility Smile. *Quantitative Analysis in Financial Markets*, Vol II. 163–191.

Cont, R. and da Fonseca, J. 2002. Dynamics of Implied Volatility Surfaces. *Quantitative Finance*, 2: 45–60.

Cusatis, P. and Thomas, M. 2005. *Hedging Instruments and Risk Management*. McGraw-Hill.

Cuthbertson, K. and Nitsche, D. 2009. *Financial Engineering, Derivatives and Risk Management*. Wiley.

Da, Z. and Schaumburg, E. 2011. *The Pricing of Volatility Risk Across Asset Classes*. Federal Reserve Bank of New York.

de Fontnouvelle, P., Rosengren, E. and Jordan, J. 2004. *Implications of Alternative Operational Risk Modelling Techniques*. Federal Reserve Bank of Boston.

Demeterfi, K., Derman, E., Kamal, M. and Zou, J. 1999. A Guide to Volatility and Variance Swaps. *Journal of Derivatives*, 6(4): 9–33.

Dupire, B. 1994. Pricing with a Smile. *Risk*, 1: 18–20.

Hakala, J. and Wystup, U. 2002. *Foreign Exchange Risk: Models, Instruments, and Strategies*. Risk Publications.

Jacque, L. 1996. *Management and Control of Foreign Exchange Risk*. Kluwer Academic Publishers.

Johnston, D. 1998. *Callable Securities: An Introduction*. Lehman Brothers. Government Bond Research.

Kelley, M.P. 2001. *Foreign Currency Risk: Minimizing Transaction Exposure*. International Law Section. June/July.

Kritzman, M. 1993. Optimal Currency Hedging Policy with Biased Forward Rates. *Journal of Portfolio Management*, Summer: 94–100.

Labuszewski, J.W. 2010. *Managing Currency Risks with Options*. CME Group.

Lubbe, J. and Snyman, F. 2010. The Advances Measurement Approach for Banks. *The IFC's Contribution to the 57th ISI Session*, 33: 141–149.

Madura, J. 1989. *International Financial Management*. 2nd Edition. West Publishing Company.

Madura, J. 2011. *International Financial Management*. 11th Edition. Cengage Learning.

Marrison, C. 2002. *The Fundamentals of Risk Measurement*. McGraw Hill.

Normand, J. 2003. Currency Risk: Strategy vs. Tactics. *Corporate Finance*, 11(8): 17–20.

Oesterreichische Nationalbank. 2006. *Guidelines on Operational Risk Management*. Austrian Financial Market Authority (FMA).

Shapiro, A.C. 2009. *Multinational Financial Management*. 9th Edition. Wiley.

Smithson, C.W. 1998. *Managing Financial Risk: A Guide to Derivative Products, Financial Engineering and Value Maximization*. 3rd Edition. McGraw-Hill.

Exercises

Questions

1. Suppose a currency increases in volatility. What is likely to happen to its bid-ask spread? Why?
2. How would you define transaction exposure? How is it different from economic exposure?
3. Consider the first part of Example 9.4 in the chapter. Is that a depreciation of the dollar or an appreciation?
4. What risks confront dealers in the foreign exchange market? How can they cope with these risks?
5. Who are the principal users of the forward exchange market? For what reasons?
6. Discuss the basic motivations for a counterparty to enter into a currency swap.
7. In what way can the FX futures market be used for price discovery?
8. Is it true or false that if the foreign exchange market is efficient, a corporation does not need to hedge FX risk at all?
9. Discuss and compare the costs of hedging via the forward contract and the options contract.
10. What is the yield to call and why is it important to a bond investor?
11. If interest rates decline, will the value of a callable bond rise by as much as it would have risen if it was not callable? Explain.

Appendix: Risk-adjusted return on capital

The risk-adjusted return on capital (RAROC) is a risk-adjusted performance measurement tool, which has become important in assessing the profitability of business units.

Generally, risk adjustments compare return with capital employed in a way to incorporate an adjustment for the risk involved in the business, therefore taking into account the fact that the metric is affected by uncertainty. RAROC is the ratio of adjusted income over economic capital

$$RAROC = \frac{R - C - E_L}{E_C}$$

$$= \frac{A_{NI}}{E_C}$$

where

R is the amount of revenues
C is the amount of costs
E_L is the expected loss
E_C is the economic capital
A_{NI} is the adjusted net income.

For a bank issuing a loan, the numerator of RAROC measure for that loan will look like

$$A_{NI} = I - E_L - C_O$$

where

I is the financial income
C_O is the amount of operating costs.

Assuming τ is the corporate tax rate, a step further consists in multiplying the amount obtained by $(1 - \tau)$, in order to get the post-tax RAROC measure.

A further degree of complication can be added by multiplying the economic capital by a compounding factor obtained from the risk-free rate. The amount obtained is added to the numerator of the RAROC equation.

RAROC can be related to CAPM analysis in order to capture the relationship with the hurdle rate. Recall the CAPM equation to be

$$R_i = R_f + \beta_i (R_m - R_f)$$

and

$$\beta_i = \frac{\sigma_{im}}{\sigma_m^2}$$

$$= \frac{\rho_{im} \sigma_i \sigma_m}{\sigma_m^2}$$

$$= \frac{\rho_{im} \sigma_i}{\sigma_m}$$

The CAPM equation becomes

$$R_i = R_f + \frac{\rho_{im}\sigma_i}{\sigma_m}\left(R_m - R_f\right)$$

from which

$$R_i - R_f = \frac{\rho_{im}\sigma_i}{\sigma_m}\left(R_m - R_f\right)$$

and

$$\frac{R_i - R_f}{\rho_{im}\sigma_i} = \frac{R_m - R_f}{\sigma_m}$$

The equation sets an important equivalence for the asset i in the portfolio. The left-hand side is the RAROC of the asset, while the right-hand side is the hurdle rate on the asset. The two are equal.

10 Financial crisis and securitization

The financial crisis that started in 2007 can be considered as the worst event in the last 80 years, hitting the largest financial institutions, causing bailouts of banks by national governments and downturns in stock markets around the world.

In many areas, the housing market also suffered, resulting in evictions, foreclosures and prolonged unemployment.

The crisis originated in the USA, but had immediate worldwide effects, amplified by the economic globalization, leading to growing fears about public debt levels, which contributed to the sovereign debt crises that erupted in Europe.

Securitization got its start in the 1970s, when home mortgages were pooled by US government-backed agencies. A large number of financial institutions still employ securitization to transfer the credit risk of the assets they originate from their balance sheets to those of other investors, such as banks, insurance companies and hedge funds.

Modern securitization took off in the late 1990s and early 2000s, mainly due to the innovative structures implemented across the asset classes, such as Mortgage Master Trusts, insurance-backed transactions, and more uncommon asset classes like the securitization of lottery receivables.

After studying this chapter you will be able to answer the following questions, among others:

1. What have been the main causes and drivers of the most recent global financial crisis? How did the crisis affect Europe?
2. What has been the impact of the global crisis on the financial industry?
3. What are credit derivatives and how can they be classified? How can counterparty risk be incorporated in the analysis?
4. What are the main features of the securitization process?
5. What are collateralized debt obligations? What are the main advantages and disadvantages of using securitized products?

The first section of the chapter is an introduction to the lack in regulation as a main source of instability, that led to the crisis, followed by the description of the impact of the crisis worldwide, especially on the private sector. The second section is about credit derivatives, as a mean for trading and transferring risk among market participants, with pricing insights. The final part deals with securitization, leading to the creation of toxic assets, followed by the analysis of the securitization process, including the advantages and disadvantages of the procedure.

10.1 Crisis and regulation

Learning outcomes

1. Describe the lacks in the regulatory framework that generated the global crisis.
2. Describe how the crisis extended to Europe.
3. Define the impact of the global crisis on the financial industry.

10.1.1 The lacks in the regulatory framework

The term 'credit crunch' identifies the difficulty of obtaining funds on the credit markets, due to the start of the financial crisis. What happened in 2007 was the beginning of the main financial crisis in the history of the world economy. Without any doubt, the driving factor of the crunch was the housing market in the USA.

The initial crisis was the result of two main factors. The low interest rates registered in the years between 2002 and 2005 led to foster and amplify the bad behaviour of some agents, translating into bad mortgage lending practices.

At the beginning of the twenty-first century, the practice of subprime lending to families became quite standard. This type of mortgage is considered much riskier than average.

Given the high risk involved, before the year 2000 subprime mortgages were issued in very few cases. After that, things started changing and lenders started issuing more loans to low-rating counterparties.

Many people who could not normally afford to buy a house had immediate access to mortgages without being fully qualified and creditworthy for it. As a consequence, the demand in real estate rose up, and prices too.

That started a vicious cycle of easy lending and high prices that boosted the practice of subprime lending. Managers were eager to earn commissions on the higher profits, while higher house prices meant that the lending was well covered by the underlying collateral.

On paper, the mortgages were fully covered by the value of the house, thus creating barriers to first comers. Therefore, in order to increase the business volume, lenders had to further relax lending standards, increasing the amount of money lent in percentage of the value of the target house.

On top of that other types of mortgage, with a teasing lower rate for the first amortizing period were issued, in order to make lending more attractive to buyers. Very frequently the information about borrowers was not even properly checked.

The US government policy of home ownership expansion was the main reason why the system could survive without any obstacle from authorities. For decades the US government had had plans to increase home ownership among low-income people.

Even if some single states had a clue as to what was going on, at a federal level there was no interest in regulating the situation. The federal way of dealing with the problem was judicially imposed and the whole machine could keep running at a fast pace.

Some facts and figures give a clear idea of what was going on. The most widely used credit score in the USA was at that time the FICO score, based on different percentages on payment history, credit utilization, length of credit history and more.

According to the *Washington Post*, the median FICO score in 2006 was 723. Many borrowers with a FICO around 450 could obtain mortgages in those years, while 620 was considered the standard threshold for a mortgage to be subprime.

Empirical research has shown the relaxation of lending criteria was quite evident and that many applicants would have been not granted any loan, back in the 1990s. The relaxation took place gradually.

The crisis spread over the world when all the mortgages were packaged into toxic assets and sold to international institutions. Following the failure of Lehman Brothers, all the concerns about the subprime lending developed into banking panic.

Big investors like mutual funds decided to withdraw the money and the central banks had to face a huge loss of private liquidity. At the same time both in the American area and the Euro zone, growth rates started to be largely negative.

The logical consequence of the panic was a cut in the lending from major banks and subsequent lack of liquidity on credit markets. That was due to both banks withholding further credit to borrowers, and corporations demanding fewer funds due to the economic uncertainty and low growth expectations.

Regulation during the crisis lacked efficiency, giving responses that in some way have arguably weakened the foundations of the prior regulatory foundation, and much of the subsequent regulatory agenda has been devoted to cover the weaknesses rather than implementing efficient responses.

The financial community agrees in defining the main factors driving the crisis. First of all the economy showed high leverage, and the consequent high level of prices to make it sustainable.

Governance was not adequate, and the mechanism of internal incentives drove managers to act unethically creating lots of new liquidity, which was primarily invested in countries showing high deficits.

The creation of toxic assets by some financial institutions spread the risk at a global level, creating international interdependencies, that contributed to contagion over continents. Mostly important, the riskiness associated with pooling and creation of the complex assets was not perceived by investors, nor was anything said by banks.

Regulatory failure manifested itself in many ways, through ignorance of risks posed by credit default swaps, low supervision of investment banks, lack of transparency in OTC derivatives markets.

For many years financial deregulation has been sponsored by part of the financial community, as a natural consequence of the free-market rule, which emphasized the efficiency and self-correcting nature of markets.

Regulation seemed to be not necessary and not even able to identify the inefficiencies in the markets, and most people assumed investors to be sufficiently capable and informed to be competent risk managers.

At the beginning of the century, the G20 was established, and took an important role in defining many aspects of the international financial regulation. Meetings, declarations and communications significantly increased in the first decade of the 2000s.

The Financial Stability Board (FSB) was created in 2009, with the responsibility of supervising the work of financial authorities and bodies setting the standards. Moreover the board is supposed to monitor compliance of national rules with the global standards set by FSAP (Financial Stability Assessment Program) of the International Monetary Fund (IMF).

One of the identified bugs in the regulation is procyclicality, meaning that banks are required to increase capital ratios in times of recessions, leading to credit rationing. That generates a path of aggravation of the downturn.

In the last years, investors and regulators have started agreeing that current rules on loss provisioning have a time horizon which is too short. These measures identify risk when it is too late, and foster high risk-taking in time of economic boom.

The Gramm-Leach-Bliley Act in 1999 removed barriers to different financial institutions, allowing each of them to act as any combination of an investment bank, a commercial bank and an insurance company.

Investment banks have an important role in markets, in that they buy and sell financial securities both on behalf of their clients and on their own account. Commercial banks accept insured deposits and make loans to households and businesses.

The new act allowed for merging of the activities thus fostering higher levels of risk taking. In fact the average equity set aside as capital ratio decreased due to the merge, boosting the crisis.

Moreover, since the 1970s regulation fostered the process of going public for investment companies. That allowed firms to raise more equity capital, thus increasing the amount of assets they were allowed to invest in.

Credit rating agencies (CRAs) had a crucial role in the crisis, and are the perfect example of how regulation failed. Their contribution derives from how they handled the securitization process.

As mentioned before, mortgage companies were issuing new loans to unreliable counterparties because they earned fees for each loan and could sell those loans to investment banks and other financial institutions.

On the other hand, investment banks and other financial institutions were keen to take over those mortgages because they earned important fees for packaging the mortgages into toxic assets and could sell them to other financial institutions, including banks, insurance companies and pension funds around the world.

The role of CRAs was crucial in that they certified those assets were safe, thus boosting the demand for them and increasing the attitude of financial institutions to make the poor investments that ultimately toppled the global financial system.

In the 1960s, rating agencies were not important and their role was primarily to give ratings to subscribers asking for them. In 1975 the Nationally Recognized Statistical Rating Organization (NRSRO) certification was issued by the SEC, for the major CRAs.

The new attention of the regulators for ratings and credit risk assessment increased the importance of CRAs and the demand for their services. Many institutions in the whole world started using the NRSRO framework to establish capital adequacy and portfolio guidelines.

Credit ratings became the main tool for prominent regulatory agencies, private investors and mutual funds, which used them for setting guidelines for their investment management policies.

The agencies went from selling ratings to subscribers to issuing them directly to the issuer of the obligations to be rated. As a consequence, every security issuer in the world wanting to have a large market for its securities was forced to buy ratings.

It is easy to get the conflict of interest in the system. Issuers have an interest in paying rating agencies more for higher ratings since those ratings influence the demand for and hence the pricing of securities.

Anyway regulators got convinced that reputational capital would be an incentive to avoid selling better ratings. Agencies claimed that their reputation was based on the sale of objectively appropriate ratings.

Selling favourable ratings for more money would result in a damage of reputation, with consequent long-term profit reduction due to the lack of demand for rating services by new issuers.

But this is not the real story. The structure of the NRSRO rating system was such that demand for new ratings was in practice ensured by the system itself, without a need for reputation.

Regulations made it compulsory-in-practice for new security issues to be certified by the CRAs in the domain of the protocol, and the vast majority of the buyers of securities wanted to use NRSRO ratings in selecting assets.

The growth of complex products at the end of the 1990s intensified the ongoing conflict of interest. Trillions of dollars' worth of assets were packaged, and consequently processed in exchange for a huge amount of fees.

Those fees were cashed by both banks and CRAs, and the latter had no incentive at all in monitoring the issuance and decreasing the rating, in that doing so they would have dramatically decreased their own profits.

This is also proven by the fact that CRAs also started offering consulting services to facilitate the securitization process. Companies had to pay first the agencies for guidance on how to package the toxic assets in order to get a high rating, then pay again for buying the rating itself.

At the beginning of the third millennium it was clear that the securitization development was driving rating agencies to inflate ratings in the name of huge profits. That was also confirmed by the accounting debacle of the early 2000s, when corporations paid accounting firms both to structure and then to audit financial statements.

The warning was clear, also given that the operating margin of CRAs was on average beyond 50% in those years, while the biggest companies in other sectors were averaging between 20% and 36%. Anyway regulatory agencies decided to rely on NRSROs.

It can be said for sure that the global financial crisis had a single cause, but the behaviour of the CRAs is a defining characteristic, and it is difficult to imagine that behaviour without the regulations that created and protected those agencies.

An aspect of deregulation that made it possible to generate the crisis was the possibility above described of merging investment and commercial banking. That increased the leverage of those banks, with the SEC acting as an agreeing spectator.

Many investment banks turned into real holding companies, based in the USA but with branches overseas. European regulators decided to subject those branches to the capital regulations dictated by the Basel Committee on Banking Supervision, through the Basel II agreement.

The SEC then adapted to European laws, showing a trend inversion in the oversight of financial markets. Prior to adoption of the European standard there were no formal regulatory oversights on investment banks' operations, no liquidity or capital requirements.

It is generally agreed that the difficulty in imposing new rules is a clear example of a bad regulatory system. Rating agencies have the potential to be independent and important monitor tools, but in the years of crisis they have failed to do so.

10.1.2 *The crisis in Europe*

The crisis caught the banking system with insufficient capital endowment, so that banks were forced to recapitalize in the middle of the critical years, with objective difficulties in doing so.

The definition of capital itself was not homogeneous among areas in the world. This is a factor that determined the lack of communication and interaction among different banking systems.

In 2010 the Basel Committee set the new definition of quality capital, as a tool for absorbing potential losses and making the institutions stronger. The focus is on common equity as the key component of bank capital.

The Committee adopted a stricter definition of regulatory capital, requiring that deductions be taken from common equity rather than from Tier 1 or Tier 2 capital as was the case in previous regulation.

The new definition of capital was established as a significant improvement in the global capital regime, further enhanced by better risk coverage, the introduction of buffers and higher minimum capital requirements.

During the crisis, many risks were not appropriately covered. For example, some banks had high volumes of complex, illiquid credit products in their books without a sufficient amount of capital to support the risk.

Another issue was the failure in capturing derivative-related exposures, a factor that increased the impact of the crisis. That point was addressed by the Committee in 2009, by strengthening the minimum capital requirements for complex securities.

High risk exposures like CDS, CDO and other securitized products, were given high weights in the calculation of regulatory capital, to better reflect the risk inherent in these products.

In the early 2000s, the start of the Euro currency raised doubts about its stability and duration, given some scepticism on the ability of member countries to stay within the norms under the Growth and Stability Pact.

The financial impact of the introduction of a new currency was rather quick, with the integration of different bond markets into one, and the natural convergence of the government bond yields. The same convergence involved interest rates offered by banks and the short-term domestic rates of the countries in the Euro area.

The spreads on markets across the Euro area narrowed, and the liquidity improved, also thanks to the introduction of the Trans-European Automated Real-time Gross Settlement Express Transfer System (TARGET) system for management enhanced large international payments in the EU.

Interest rates went down converging to the German level (the lowest), and the monetary unification was seen at that time as a sufficient condition for the credibility of the monetary policy on price stability and the accompanying economic growth.

Risk premiums widely narrowed, boosting the growth of credit, and it was much easier for Euro financial institutions to borrow funds easily. The housing sector was the main driver of credit growth, with a parallel growth of the construction industry.

The system started leveraging, and a high level of debt was matched by a boom in house prices, strengthening the effect of debit build-up. The rapid growth distracted the view from the weakness in the fiscal system.

The situation went on until the general worsening of fiscal deficit and public debt in most European countries unveiled it. The rapid growth was in fact accompanied by the rise of imports and consequent account deficit, in the years immediately after.

In most countries the deficit was then financed through debt, and as in many other cases in history, the growth was so consistent, that it was almost impossible to distinguish whether the fundamentals were improving accordingly, or there was an ongoing bubble.

When the growth in the Euro area declined sharply, the financial crisis activated the disclosure of the negatives. The crisis resulted in the annihilation of credit transactions, and interest rates in the EU started diverging, as opposed to what had happened in previous years.

The differential in interest rates, combined with many years of (bad quality) debt accumulation by banks and the large government deficits, resulted in the disruption of the financial system.

In 2008 an extraordinary EU summit in Paris defined joint actions in order to prevent dangerous actions of single countries harming each other. The summit agreed on a rescue plan for banks, and coordination among members, to avoid widespread insolvency and credit shortage.

Unfortunately, the short-term measures adopted by the EU did not achieve any effect, and worsened the fiscal deficit and leverage of the economy. In late 2009 it was unveiled that the fiscal deficit of Greece was about 12.5% of GDP (instead of about 3.5% as communicated before), with a public debt of more than 115% of the GDP.

Other countries like Ireland, Portugal and Spain were also in a bad state, and the yields on some government bonds started widening as well as CDS spreads. By early 2010, a sovereign debt crisis in the Euro zone was clearly there.

As an answer to the situation, in May 2010 the EU and IMF issued a €110 billion bailout package for Greece conditional on implementation of austerity measures. At the same time the 27 member states of the European Union jointly created the European Financial Stability Facility (EFSF).

The facility was structured as an SPV, with the scope of preserving financial stability in Europe, through the provision of financial assistance to troubled Euro-area countries. The EFSF was given the power to sell bonds and lend the proceeds to countries, up to a maximum of €440 billion.

The bonds were backed by the ECB and the IMF, and the facility managed to build up the financial safety to €750 billion. The agreement allowed the ECB to start buying government debt which was expected to reduce bond yields.

Greece was charged to mobilize €60 billion through privatizing public assets and enterprises. At the end of 2010 Ireland was bailed out for the equivalent of €85 billion, and forced to the toughest budget in the country's history. In the meanwhile, markets were struggling to trust Greece, given that serious doubts remained on the ability to service its debt and bond yields started to rise again.

The year 2011 was the year of Portugal, which finally admitted that it was not able to meet its obligations towards international markets, given the very bad state of its own, and asked the EU for help.

The ministers of finance of the Euro area agreed on a €78 billion salvage loan to Portugal, while rating agencies severely lowered the credit rating of Greece bonds to junk status.

In the same year the leaders of European countries started to worry about the possibility of contagion effects, and in a summer summit in Brussels, they decided to issue a further generous bailout to Greece, sponsored by the IMF and private contributions. Again, the EFSF was charged with being the SPV for the disbursement with regular assessment by the Commission in liaison with the ECB and the IMF.

Payment periods were extended and interest rates on the loan were cut. In order to avoid contagion, the EFSF was given preventative powers, with the ability to lend money to the states on the basis of a precautionary program, and issue recapitalization loans to financial institutions. Another innovation was the possibility of intervening on the secondary market to trade in case of a risk for international stability.

The countries correctly applying the relief program got continuous support from the Euro leaders. Portugal and Ireland were granted the same conditions confirmed for Greece, extending the maturity of a minimum of 15 years and reducing the interest rate to 3.5%.

All member states were supposed to strictly adhere to the agreed fiscal targets. In addition to solving their eventual macroeconomic imbalances, member states not involved already in a program were supposed to reduce their deficits below 3% by 2013. The European Investment Bank (EIB) was put in charge of assisting the countries in receiving the funds delivered by the EFSF.

All these measure have not changed the behaviour of investors, since stock markets keep being sceptical about their effectiveness. Besides Greece, all the controversial economies in the Euro area have generated concerns. It is interesting to analyse each country separately

What happened in Ireland was a tout-court nationalization of the banking sector, that drove the country to fiscal distress. The country had been enjoying a period of expansion that started in the late 1990s.

Low corporate taxation boosted investments and with the low level of interest rates, housing credit expanded rapidly in the first years of the 2000s. The downturn of property prices since 2010 put the banks under severe pressure.

In 2009 the crash of property prices, combined with the tightening of credit control, caused the Irish bond yields to increase and the government had to nationalize banks and take over liabilities.

The Irish government supported six major banks in the country with approximately 32% of GDP. Differently from Greece, the problem of Ireland derived mostly from excessive build-up of bank lending rather than public debt, but anyway turning into a fiscal problem and generating a high unemployment rate.

Also Spain came from a good economic period in the early 2000s, with a dynamic economy and significant foreign investment entering the country. The sector driving the boom in Spain was the real estate one, but that changed with the global crisis.

Starting from 2007, house prices fell dramatically, and the end of the real estate boom matched a significant increase in the levels of personal debt. Public finances suffered from a cut in tax revenues and the public deficit increased to over 10% by 2009.

Compared to most countries in Europe, Spain has a relatively low public debt, at about 60% of GDP. The Spanish problem comes from banks being exposed to foreign finances, having relied heavily on wholesale finance from abroad. Moreover, the unemployment rate in Spain (especially among youth) is still one of the highest in the Euro area.

Portugal registered the lowest decline in the GDP growth of the whole Euro zone (about −2.5%), but anyway its fiscal deficit and public debt deteriorated to −10% and 83% in 2009.

Even if both public debt and deficit are lower than Greece, and the economy did not go through the common pattern of boom and bust, as in the other examined countries, Portugal has a large current deficit and high leverage of private sector.

Moreover, it suffers from a low share of population having upper secondary education at least, and a high level of structural unemployment, showing a peculiar problem of low rate of growth.

Being the eighth largest economy in the world, Italy faced a very slow growth of the economy, with an early-2000s GDP growth rate of not more than 1% per annum. The rather low level of fiscal deficit compares to the high level of the public debt.

Besides a large part of debt being held by residents, there is a significant share which is held by foreign investors. With a worrying unemployment rate above 10%, Italy has always been characterized by a north-south divide with the southern parts witnessing chronically high unemployment rates.

Currently, there are important differences among the macroeconomic indicators for the Euro zone economies that are currently in trouble, as well as important structural differences.

Greece had a strong banking system, but the bad situation of the public finances harmed that robustness. In Ireland, on the other hand, the banking system was the weak sector, generating the burden on the fiscal position.

Anyway, regardless of the generating point, the consequences on the whole economy have been the same for all these countries. The markets have been penalizing one economy after another, albeit to different degrees, with a spreading contagion effect.

10.1.3 The impact on the financial industry

When the crisis started hitting on the world financial system, Lehman Brothers (LB) was one of the largest investment banks in the USA, with more than 25,000 employees worldwide, and $639 billion in assets.

LB filed for bankruptcy in September 2008, the largest bankruptcy in history, with an amount of $619 billion in debt. Very few companies invested by the crisis had such a huge amount in assets and debt.

As a consequence, the LB crack was not only the most severe consequence of the financial crisis, but also contributed to the worsening of it, intensifying a process that led to the erosion of almost $10 trillion in market capitalization in just one month (October 2008).

Founded in 1850 by German immigrants, LB grew rapidly into an international powerhouse, surviving all the challenges that the US and world economy had to face in the following decades, until modern times.

After surviving previous crises and economic downturns, LB got hit severely by the American housing collapse, given that the institution had heavily joined the subprime mortgage market.

Everything started in the early 2000s, when LB acquired two subprime lending companies, following the boom of the housing market in the USA. At the beginning, record revenues from Lehman's real estate businesses allowed revenues to grow more than 50% in a couple of years, a faster rate of growth than other businesses in investment banking or asset management.

At the beginning of 2007 LB's stock quotation was above $85, for a corresponding capitalization of almost $60 billion. The housing market started to crack, but LB's management claimed that the risks would have little impact on the firm's earnings. They also claimed that problems in the subprime market would not have impacted on the whole housing market.

At the end of the third quarter in 2007, the situation deteriorated rapidly. LB's stocks fell sharply, and the company had to fire 2,500 mortgage-related people. Offices were closed in some states, but still LB was a big player in the mortgage market.

The fourth quarter was characterized by a general rebound on the markets, with equities going up for a little while. LB did not take the chance to release part of its huge mortgage portfolio.

The leverage of LB was at that point very high, and the progressive deterioration of global market conditions, and immediately after the first bankruptcies of US companies, LB stock lost 48% on concerns it would be the next Wall Street firm to fail.

In April 2008 the company raised $4 billion by issuing preferred stock, gaining back some trust of investors. However, hedge funds start doubting the valuation of the mortgage portfolio and the stock resumed its decline.

In the second half of 2008 the company announced big losses, and a further increase of assets. The management also claimed to have reduced gross assets by $147 billion, reduced its exposure to mortgages and deleveraged consistently.

But it was too late for the situation to revert, and managers unsuccessfully tried to involve new partners. September 2008 was a tough month, and the stock declined more than 75% in value on the market.

At the same time, the spread of CDS on the company's debt peaked by over 65%, and hedge funds started pulling out, with a general cut of credit lines by lenders. Losses became huge and a business restructuring was announced.

Cash drained rapidly and rating agencies announced they would downgrade LB's rating, unless a major stake of the company were sold to external partners. A last unsuccessful takeover trial took place with Barclays PLC and Bank of America.

On 15th September 2008 LB declared bankruptcy, and the stock dropped by 93% in three days. The collapse had a disastrous impact on the whole market, given the size of the company, and its international status. Following the collapse of LB, Bank of America signed an emergency deal to acquire Merrill Lynch, announced on the same day.

Another important crash involved Fannie Mae (FME) and Freddie Mac (FMC), two government-sponsored enterprises (GSE). Their core activity was to buy mortgages from banks, on the secondary market.

After buying the assets, they packaged them into mortgage-backed securities, reselling them on the markets, to investors. The trust behind that sort of trading was put at serious risk by the subprime mortgage crisis.

The two companies were then put into conservatorship by the Federal Housing Finance Agency (FHFA) in September 2008, meaning that the government has had responsibility to manage them since then.

The US Treasury Department bought a huge stake of FMA and FMC preferred equity and securities, in what should have been a temporary intervention. What happened in reality was a lack of improvement in economic conditions, so that it was not possible for the government to sell the shares and let the companies go back to being private.

The congress approved a bailout plan in the second half of 2008, guaranteeing $25 billion liquidity to the companies, that were managing or guaranteeing over $5 trillion of mortgages at that time.

The market started panicking and both FMA and FMC shares lost value considerably, making it impossible for intervention of private investors, to raise additional capital, as was needed to cover the mortgages.

The bailout of the two companies generated side effects that cannot be ignored. First of all, the FHA guaranteed more loans, for a huge amount. Second, tax breaks were approved for homeowners and first buyers.

The FMA and FMC bailout was the greatest in the last 20 years, and was followed by the bailout of the entire banking system, that led to the battle for increasing the limit for the public debt level.

With public debt breaking the ceiling of $10 trillion, there were many concerns about the sustainability of this debt, which keeps downward pressure on the dollar, increasing the price of imports. Such an effect has been limited only because the spread of the crisis over Europe has mitigated the loss in value of the dollar.

10.2 Credit derivatives

Learning outcomes

1. Define asset swaps and their structure.
2. Define credit default swaps and their structure.
3. Describe how counterparty risk can be integrated in CDS valuation.

10.2.1 Asset swaps

Credit derivatives are bilateral financial contracts that isolate specific aspects of credit risk from an underlying instrument and transfer that risk between two parties. Management of credit risk is separated by the ownership of the asset.

Asset swaps are a type of credit derivative combining an interest rate swap with a bond. They can alter the cash flows of the reference bond, and represent a big share of the credit derivatives market, setting the market spreads over the LIBOR rate.

An asset swap transaction involves trading on a bond and then entering an interest rate swap with the same bank that traded the bond. The investor pays a fixed rate, and receives a floating rate, thus transforming the fixed coupon into a floating payment.

Example 10.1: Suppose that a company wants to insure against credit loss from default of the issuer of a bond it is holding. In order to hedge the credit risk of this position the company can enter into an asset swap where the protection seller agrees to pay LIBOR plus or minus a spread in return for the cash flows of the risky bond. In case of default of the reference entity, the protection buyer will continue to receive the LIBOR and a positive or negative spread from the protection seller. In this way the protection buyer has transformed its original risk profile by changing the interest rate and credit risk exposure.

If an investor holds a bond and enters into an asset swap with a bank the value of an asset swap is the spread the bank pays over or under LIBOR. This is based on the value of the coupons of the reference bond compared to the market swap rate, the accrued interest and the premium or discount on value.

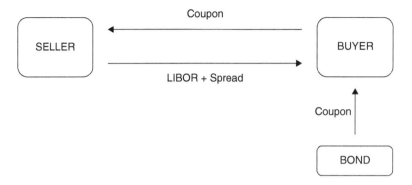

Figure 10.1 The asset swap buyer owns a bond and transfers the coupon to the asset swap seller in exchange for a floating payment of LIBOR rate plus the asset swap spread. In case of default, the buyer loses the coupon and principal redemption on the bond. The swap continues until bond maturity, or can be settled at market value.

It follows that for pricing an asset swap, it is necessary to compare the par value to the underlying bond price, and the spread above or below the LIBOR represents the credit spread between the bond and the swap rate.

Asset swaps can have many different structures. The mostly traded is the par asset swap, which is made by two separate transactions, and involves a long position in a bond from the asset swap seller, at par price, combined with a position into the fixed leg of a swap.

The asset swap buyer gets regular payments of LIBOR plus or minus an agreed spread, in exchange for the fixed payments made on the swap.

The buyer of the asset swap acquires the bond, therefore taking on the credit risk, and in case of default, will lose the coupon payments, but still continue paying on the swap (or close it at market value). The par value of the bond at default is lost, and the asset swap buyer gets only the recovery rate paid. The resulting exposure is both on the swap contract and on the bond redemption (bond price minus recovery).

The purpose of an asset swap is to compensate the buyer for taking these risks. The spread is quoted as a differential on LIBOR, and for highly rated assets and banks then it may be even negative.

The cash flows involved in an asset swap are such that the buyer receives coupons from the bond plus redemption valued off the bond issuer curve, pays coupons on the fixed side of the swap equal to the bond coupons, and receives payments of LIBOR plus spread from the counterparty of the swap.

From the point of view of the asset swap buyer, consider the change in price for a one basis point upward shift in the par curve. The crucial point is that the sensitivity of the bond price to the yield curve shifting parallel, is lower than the sensitivity of the swap to shifts in the LIBOR curve.

This can be true only when the curve of the asset swap issuer is above the LIBOR curve, so that the buyer of the asset swap keeps a residual exposure to interest rate movements.

The market asset swap is structured such that the bond is purchased at the full price, and the notional on the LIBOR floating leg of the swap is scaled accordingly, resulting in a different value of the spread.

As opposed to par asset swap, the bond is not traded at par, but at full market price. When the bond price is above par, the asset swap buyer is exposed to risk, and vice

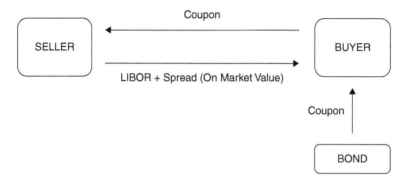

Figure 10.2 In a market asset swap the notional on the floating side is calculated on the market value of the bond, as notional. At maturity the bond market price is exchanged for the face value, 100.

versa when the price is below par. Given this setting, the exposure goes from zero to the maximum at maturity, while the opposite holds for the par asset swap where exposure goes from maximum to zero. At maturity, the par value is exchanged with the original bond value.

Note that the credit exposure of a market asset swap remains the same as a par asset swap.

An asset swap is mainly traded for taking exposure to the credit quality of a bond, without incurring the taxation and accounting burden related to a direct investment. Finally, it allows us to take advantage of mispricing in the floating rate note market.

Beside the classical asset swaps, many different variations exist, to satisfy the various needs of investors wanting to trade risk. The forward asset swap is an agreement today to buy the bond on the forward date at par and then enter into an interest rate swap, whose spread on the floating leg is agreed today.

The asset swap terminates if the bond defaults before the forward date, which is the time for investors to take on the default risk. Given the general upward slope of a credit curve, it is usually cheaper to go long on a forward, than buy the credit today.

Another variation is the cross-currency asset swap, which allows an investor to buy a bond denominated in foreign currency, and contingently enter a swap in the same currency, receiving the floating payments in domestic currency.

The conversion of cash flows is done at a pre-specified exchange rate, and, as opposed to asset swaps, the principal is exchanged at maturity of the swap. The investor can then gain exposure to the credit while reducing their interest rate risk and currency risk.

Callable asset swaps involve callable bonds, so that the buyer of the asset swap needs to be hedged against any loss on the swap, given that they will not be receiving the coupon from the asset.

The asset swap buyer is interested in getting the option to cancel the swap on any of the bond call dates. This can be done by entering a long position in a Bermudan-style receiver swaption.

The asset swap gives a measure of the expected loss on a bond, following default, as a function of the probability of default, market price of the bond and the expected recovery price paid by the issuer following default.

Being dependent on the bond price, the asset swap spread cannot be used to make comparisons across different bonds and different issuers, unless choosing bonds with identical price, which is usually not easy.

O'Kane (2000) shows how to compute the asset swap spread, assuming some structure for the LIBOR course and denoting by $P_{0,t}$ the price today of €1 to be paid at time t.

Assume both swap counterparties are high-rated banks with cash flows priced off the LIBOR curve. For simplicity all payments are annual and made on the same date. Fixed payments are made at dates $i = 1, 2, ..., n$ and floating payments are made at dates $j = 1, 2, ..., m$. When payments are synchronized, then $i = j \ \forall i, \forall j$, but they are not necessarily synchronized.

In order to compute the asset swap spread s_{AS} the present value of all the cash flows is set equal to zero. The seller of the bond gets the par value plus accrued interest, and the net upfront payment is

$$V_{UP} = 100 - B$$

where

   B is the market price of the bond.

The swap payments can be decomposed into the present value of fixed payments

$$PV_{FIX} = C \sum_{i=1}^{n} P_{0,t_i}$$

where

   C is the annual coupon paid by the bond
   P_{0,t_i} is the present value today of a bond that pays €1 at time $t_i = t_1, t_2, ..., t_n$.

and the present value of floating payments

$$PV_{FL} = \sum_{j=1}^{m} a_i \left(r_{L,i} + s_{AS} \right) P_{0,t_i}$$

where

   $r_{L,i}$ is the Libor rate set at time t_i and paid at time t_{i-1}
   a_i is the accrual factor in the corresponding basis
   s_{AS} is the breakeven asset swap spread.

The breakeven asset swap spread s_{AS} is computed by setting the present value of all cash flows equal to zero. From the perspective of the asset swap seller the condition can be written as

$$PV_{AS} = 100 - B + C \sum_{i=1}^{n} P_{0,t_i} - \sum_{j=1}^{m} a_i \left(r_{L,i} + s_{AS} \right) P_{0,t_i} = 0$$

The equation must be solved for the asset swap spread s_{AS}.

In a market asset swap, the notional on the LIBOR side equals the price of the bond, so that the net upfront payment is zero and the notional are exchanged at expiration date. Denoting the market asset spread with s_M, the present value of the floating payments in this case is defined as

$$PV_{FL} = \frac{B}{100} \sum_{j=1}^{m} a_i \left(r_{L,i} + s_M \right) P_{0,t_i}$$

and the final payment is

$$PV_{FP} = \left(100 - B \right) P_{0,t_n}$$

so that the condition on the total present value is

$$PV_M = C \sum_{i=1}^{n} P_{0,t_i} - \frac{B}{100} \sum_{j=1}^{m} a_i \left(r_{L,i} + s_M \right) P_{0,t_i} + \left(100 - B \right) P_{0,t_n} = 0$$

Solving for s_M yields

$$s_M = 100 \frac{s_{AS}}{B}$$

It is also possible to define a zero-volatility spread, which is the continuously compounded constant spread to LIBOR required to recalculate the price of a bond. Denoting the zero-volatility spread by s_{ZV}, it can be defined as

$$P = C \sum_{i=1}^{n} P_{0,t_i} e^{-s_{ZV} t_i} + P_{0,t_n} e^{-s_{ZV} t_{n+m}}$$

The equation can be solved for s_{ZV} using a root-finding algorithm like Newton-Raphson or Brent's method.

10.2.2 Credit default swaps

Credit derivatives markets mostly trade credit default swaps (CDS), a contractual agreement for transferring credit (default) risk from one party to another, given a reference entity.

A CDS provides insurance against the risk of a default by a particular company or obligation. The company is known as the reference entity and a default by the company is known as a credit event.

The buyer of the CDS protection obtains the right to sell a specific bond, the reference obligation. The bond is traded at its par value, which is the notional principal of the swap.

The buyer of a CDS makes periodic payments to the seller, until a credit event occurs or maturity of the contract, and in case of a credit event the swap is settled. Physical settlement requires the swap buyer to deliver the bonds to the seller at the par value.

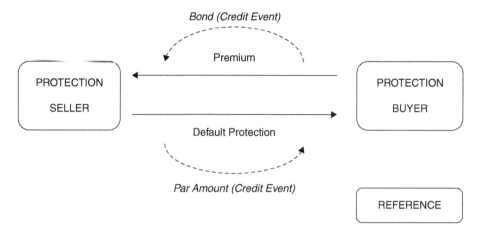

Figure 10.3 The scheme of a CDS, showing the stream of cash flows exchanged between the buyer and the seller of protection. If reference entity defaults, the par amount is exchanged.

In case of cash settlement, some days after the credit event a calculation agent determines the mid-market price of the reference obligation. Denoting this price with V_M the cash settlement is a percentage of the notional principal equal to

$$c_S = \frac{100 - V_M}{100}$$

The amount paid by the buyer of protection, as a percentage of the notional, is the CDS spread, and is often quoted in basis points (100 bp = 1% spread). CDSs are a tool to transfer credit risk, therefore they can be used to hedge a position in a corporate bond.

Example 10.2: Suppose an investor enters a long position in a seven-year corporate bond, with yield 6% and, at the same time, the investor enters a seven-year CDS with a spread of 200 basis points per annum. Such a strategy sorts the effect of converting the corporate bond to a risk-free. In fact, if the reference does not default, the investor earns 6% per year on the face value. If the bond defaults, the investor earns the 6% until default time, receiving then the face value back through the CDS. The money can then be reinvested for the remaining time.

The valuation of a CDS is related to the default probabilities estimation of the reference entity. Given that the existence of a non-negative probability of default is the reason for a corporate (risky) bond to be cheaper than a treasury (risk-free) bond, the difference in value between the two types is the present value of the cost of defaults as

$$PV_{DC} = B_f - B_c$$

where

B_f is the value of the treasury bond
B_c is the value of the corporate bond.

As discussed before in the book, bond prices can then be used to derive default probabilities of a reference entity, given some level of the recovery rate, that can be used to infer the credit spreads.

Hull and White (2000) proposed a model for valuing the spread from CDSs in case of a single reference entity and no counterparty default risk was developed by Hull and White in 2000. Instead of using some hazard rate for the default probability, their model incorporates the unconditional cumulative default probability.

The model starts from considering that the payoff u_{CD} from a CDS is given by

$$u_{CD} = L\left[1 - R\left(1 + a_t\right)\right] \tag{10.1}$$

where

> a_t is the accrued interest on the reference bond at time t, normalized by the face value.

The payoff equation describes the CDS payoff at time of default as the nominal amount minus the amount that is recovered on the entity, including the accrued interest.

The model generates default densities recursively based on assumption of some recovery rate and a set of zero-coupon corporate bond prices combined with a set of zero-coupon treasury bond prices.

The default density term structure is then used to calculate the spread as the premium on the CDS contract. If data on zero-coupon bond prices are missing, they can be bootstrapped from coupon bond prices.

Recall that the probability of default can be defined as a function of the survival probability

$$q_t = 1 - \int_0^T \lambda_t$$

where

> q_t is the risk-neutral probability of no credit event over the life of the CDS contract
> T is the life of the CDS contract
> λ_t is the risk-neutral default probability density at time t.

If a credit event happens before maturity, the present value of CDS payments is given by

$$PV_{CD} = \begin{cases} m\left(k_t + i_t\right) & \text{if credit - event - time} < \text{T} \\ mk_T & \text{otherwise} \end{cases}$$

where

> k_t is the present value of unit payment per year, on payment dates, until t
> k_T is the present value of unit payment per year, on payment dates, until T
> $i_{\Delta t}$ is the present value of accrual payment from previous payment date till t
> m is the total payments per year made by the protection buyer.

The expected value of the payments is then

$$mq_t k_T + m\int_0^T \lambda_t \left(k_t + i_{\Delta t}\right)dt$$

meaning that the expected value in a risk-neutral world is the weighted sum of the possible outcomes (in case of default and in case of no-default before maturity) multiplied by the respective probabilities.

Given equation (10.1), and introducing the risk-neutral framework, the expectation of the payoff for $L = 1$ is

$$u_{CD} = 1 - \hat{R}\left(1 + a_t\right)$$

where

$\hat{R}$ is the risk-neutral expectation of the recovery rate on the reference.

The present value can then be written as

$$PV_{CD} = \int_0^T L\left[1 - \hat{R}\left(1 + a_t\right)\right]\lambda_t v_t dt$$

where

$\hat{R}$ is the risk-neutral expectation of the recovery rate on the reference

v_t is the present value of a unit payment received at time t.

The buyer of the CDS spread has a value V_B given by the difference between the expected payoff made by the position, and the present value of the payments made out to the protection seller.

$$V_{BY} = \int_0^T L\left[1 - \hat{R}\left(1 + a_t\right)\right]\lambda_t v_t dt - mq_t k_T - m\int_0^T \lambda_t \left(k_t + i_{\Delta t}\right)dt$$

It follows that the CDS spread s is the value of m that sets the value to the buyer equal to zero

$$V_{BY} = 0$$

which implies

$$s = \frac{\int_0^T L\left[1 - \hat{R}\left(1 + a_t\right)\right]\lambda_t v_t dt}{q_t k_T + \int_0^T \lambda_t \left(k_t + i_{\Delta t}\right)dt}$$

which is referred to as credit default spread, the total payment per year, as a percentage of the notional principal, paid for a newly issued CDS.

10.2.3 CDS spreads with counterparty credit risk

Again Hull and White (2001) give a description of how to model CDS spreads in the presence of counterparty credit risk, assuming again that default events, risk-free interest rates and recovery rates are independent from each other.

Several cases are possible.

If the reference entity defaults at time t while the counterparty is still alive, the final accrued payment on the CDS implies that the present value of all payments made to date is given by

$$PV_{CC} = m(k_t + i_{\Delta t})$$

In case the counterparty defaults at time t, while the reference does not, the present value of all payments is

$$PV_{CC} = mk_t$$

The same holds if neither the reference, nor the counterparty default before maturity T, so that the expected present value of all payments is

$$E(PV_{CC}) = m\int_0^T [\theta_{\Delta t}k_t + \theta_{\Delta t}a_t + \varphi_t k_t]\,dt + mq_t k_T$$

where, given the notation in the previous section,

$\theta_{\Delta t}$ is the risk-neutral probability that the reference entity defaults between t and $t + \Delta t$, given no default by the counterparty.

$\varphi_{\Delta t}$ is the risk-neutral probability that the counterparty defaults between t and $t + \Delta t$, given no default by the reference entity.

Recall that, in case of a credit event occurring at time t, the expected value of the reference obligation, as a fraction of the face value, is

$$u_{CC} = 1 - \hat{R} - a_t$$

Multiplying the above value by the probability of default of the reference entity, discounting through v_t, and integrating from zero to maturity, yields the present value of the expected payoff,

$$u_{CC} = \int_0^T (1 - R - a_t)v_t \theta_t\,dt$$

so that the value of the CDS to the buyer, represented by the present value of the difference between payoffs and payments made, is

$$V_{CB} = \int_0^T (1 - R - a_t) v_t \theta_{\Delta t} dt - m \int_0^T [\theta_{\Delta t} k_t + \theta_{\Delta t} a_t + \varphi_{\Delta t} k_t] dt + m q_t k_T \qquad (10.2)$$

Recall that the value of the CDS spread is the value of m that makes (10.2) equal to zero, so that, indicating with s_C the spread with counterparty default, it is possible to write

$$V_{CB} = 0$$

which implies a spread

$$s_C = \frac{\int_0^T (1 - R - a_t) v_t \theta_{\Delta t} dt}{\int_0^T [\theta_{\Delta t} k_t + \theta_{\Delta t} a_t + \varphi_{\Delta t} k_t] dt + q_t k_T} \qquad (10.3)$$

In order to solve equation (10.3) it is necessary to assume values for the risk-neutral probabilities of default involved, which is usually done by simulating some credit index process for both the reference entity and the counterparty.

The process, which may take the form of a Brownian motion, is subject to some bottom threshold, so that when the threshold is hit, default occurs. If the reference entity defaults first (credit index for the reference entity falls below the threshold before the process for the counterparty does), payments continue up to default time, and there is a payoff.

If the counterparty defaults first, then payments are made up to default, like before, but there is no final accrual payment, nor payoff.

If neither party defaults during the CDS life, payments continue until maturity, and there is no payoff. If both parties default, by convention a value of 50% is assumed for both $\theta_{\Delta t}$ and $\varphi_{\Delta t}$.

Hull and White (2001) propose an analytic approximation that can be used when default correlation between reference entity and the counterparty is known. Defining with x the percentage reduction in the present value of the expected payoff on the CDS, and with z the percentage reduction on the expected payments, both contingent to default of the counterparty, the equation

$$s = \left(\frac{1 - x}{1 - z}\right) s_C \qquad (10.4)$$

describes the relationship between the spread with and without taking counterparty risk into account.

Assuming π_R and π_C are the default probabilities between 0 and T for the reference entity and the counterparty respectively, and indicating with $\pi_{R,C}$ the joint default probability in the same time interval, and given a 50% probability that the reference entity defaults before the counterparty (and vice versa), the following holds:

$$x = \frac{1}{2} \frac{\pi_{R,C}}{\pi_R} \qquad (10.5)$$

From probability theory, the probability that the counterparty defaults, and the reference entity does not is given by

$$P\left(\text{Def}_C \,|\, \text{No-Def}_R\right) = \pi_C - \pi_{R,C} \tag{10.6}$$

Assume an average 'time distance', when both parties default, between the default of one party and the other is usually a third of the whole timeline. The payments made by the CDS buyer are a third less than if counterparty does not default, leading to

$$z = \frac{\pi_C}{2} - \frac{\pi_{R,C}}{3}$$

Combining (10.4), (10.5) and (10.6), an approximation for the CDS spread is given by

$$\tilde{s} = \frac{1 - \dfrac{1}{2}\dfrac{\pi_{R,C}}{\pi_R}}{1 - \dfrac{\pi_C}{2} + \dfrac{\pi_{R,C}}{3}} s$$

The approximation is based on strict assumptions, and it is heavily simplified, in particular on some basic parameters and excluding discounting for x and z. Anyway it serves for quickly calculating spreads when knowing the default correlation between the two parties has been somehow estimated.

Snapshot 10.2
The Newton-Raphson method

The Newton-Raphson method is an iterative algorithm for root finding, which starts from an initial guessed value, and iterates through consecutive steps in order to find the root.

Each step has a direction, which is determined by both the value and the slope of the target function. Therefore the first derivative of the function $f'(x)$ is involved in the analysis. Recall that the definition of the derivative can be written as

$$f'(x_i) = \frac{\Delta f(x_i)}{\Delta x} = \frac{f(x_i) - 0}{x_i - x_{i+1}}$$

Let x_0 be the guess of root $\tilde{x}$ and let $\lambda = \tilde{x} - x_0$ be the distance between the estimate and the true root. The linear approximation leads to the conclusion that

$$0 = f(\tilde{x}) = f(x_0 + \lambda) \approx f(x_0) + h f'(x_0)$$

So that $\lambda \approx \dfrac{f(x_0)}{f'(x_0)}$

It follows that the real root is approximated by

$$\tilde{x} = x_0 - \frac{f(x_0)}{f'(x_0)}$$

And a new improvement in the x_1 estimate of $\tilde{x}$ is given by

$$x_1 = x_0 - \frac{f(x_0)}{f'(x_0)}$$

The step is repeated many times, so that if x_i is the current estimate, the following estimate is given by

$$x_{i+1} = x_i - \frac{f(x_0)}{f'(x_0)}$$

and the process is iterated until the root is matched.

10.3 Securitization

Learning outcomes

1. Define the securitization structure and participants.
2. Describe collateralized debt obligations.
3. List and comment on the advantages and disadvantages of securitization.

10.3.1 Structure and participants

Securitization is the process of pooling certain types of assets together, and then repacking them into securities earning an interest rate. Both notional principal and interest payments are then transferred to the purchaser of the originated assets.

As a procedure, it rose to prominence in the 1970s, with the US government pooling home mortgages of American home buyers. After that, other types of assets started being securitized, and in a few decades the market grew dramatically.

The following deterioration of the quality of most of those assets, like subprime mortgages, as described in previous sections, undermined investor confidence, and it was perceived that securitization, inadequate valuation methods and insufficient regulatory oversight could severely hurt financial stability.

Securitization is employed by many financial institutions to transfer the credit risk embedded in the assets pooled as underlying. Assets are transferred from the balance sheet of the originators to the ones of other companies.

They process it for various reason, like the cheaper capital that can be raised, and assets being less costly for institutions to hold, compared to the underlying pooled assets, allowing for less strict constraints from the regulators.

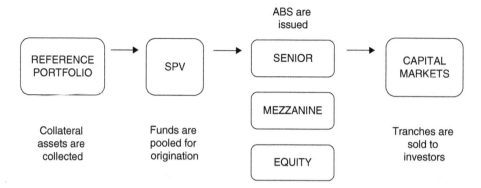

Figure 10.4 The scheme of a securitization process, from asset pooling, to the origination of the securitized assets, and the sale to investors in the market.

The process of origination and consequent distribution initially brought benefits to the participants, by spreading out credit exposures, reducing system vulnerabilities. The impact of securitization before the crisis appeared to be positive.

Advantages and disadvantages of securitization are discussed in the next section, but in general, the main drawback of the whole system was the lack of incentives for originators to ensure minimum standards of prudent lending and risk management.

The securitization process involves two steps. Step one is characterized by a company having a portfolio of loans and other assets generating income. The company, called the originator, identifies which assets are better to remove from the balance sheet.

The assets are then pooled into a reference portfolio, selling the pool to an issuer, which is a Special Purpose Vehicle (SPV), which is an entity appositely set up by some financial institution, with the purpose of purchasing the assets.

In the second step of the procedure, the SPV issues tradable securities to finance the acquisition of the pooled assets. The new securities bear some interest and are sold to the capital markets.

Purchasers of the originated securities receive a fixed payment from a trustee account, which is funded by the cash flows generated by the reference portfolio. The originator usually collects the payments and turns them to the SPV, net of fees for service.

The reference portfolio is divided into tranches, each one with a different level of seniority and risk, offering therefore a different interest to the investor. Both investment return and losses are allocated among the various tranches according to their seniority.

The securitization is usually structured in three tranches, with junior (sometimes called equity) being the bottom one (highest risk, highest return), mezzanine the middle one (middle risk, middle return) and senior the highest one (lowest risk, lowest return).

The least risky tranche (senior) has priority in calling the income generated by the pooled reference portfolio.

The structure concentrates the expected losses of the reference portfolio in the junior tranche, the smallest one, that bears most of the total credit exposure, receiving in exchange a fairly high return.

The mezzanine tranche suffers only when all the junior tranche has been cut off by the losses in the reference portfolios. And the senior tranche is the last one to be hit, therefore being the safest, with little expectation of portfolio losses.

Given the fact that investors often leverage their positions, senior tranches are also the most sensitive to the changes in the sensitivity of underlying asset quality. It is in fact common that, as the junior tranches start suffering losses, the investors on the higher tranches panic, closing out positions and seeking for safer investment opportunities.

After starting with mortgages, securitization soon involved many other types of assets. Basically any asset generating an income is suitable for being securitized. As an example consider corporate and sovereign debt, credit cards, trade receivables.

All these originated instruments, backed by various assets, are usually called asset-backed securities (ABS). Collateralized debt obligations, discussed in the next section, are a special case of ABS.

At the beginning, securitization was started as a vehicle for financial institutions to find new funding. The two options available in this sense are to either move assets off balance sheet, or refinance their origination by borrowing against them.

Example 10.3: Assume a financing company needs to raise cash. Normally, it could take out a loan or sell bonds, or sell the loans directly. But there is no secondary market for individual loans. The solution is then to pool the assets and sell them to an issuer, to turn them into tradable securities.

The flexibility of the securitization process makes it possible to choose the right risk and return combination to match the risk tolerance of target investors, and satisfy the needs of a large share of the market.

This is true also from a dynamic point of view, given that investors can quickly adjust their individual exposure to credit-sensitive assets in response to changes in risk and consumption preferences.

In the last 10 years the role of securitization has changed dramatically, involving many new types of assets, thanks to the improved modelling and risk quantification, encouraging issuers to consider a wider spectrum of assets. Also, it has embraced a larger selection of markets, including emerging economies.

One should consider that when mortgages were securitized, the buyers of the originated assets could get the only important information received loan-to-value ratio (ratio of the loan size to house value) and the borrower's FICO score.

Since these were the only important factors in reselling the mortgage, the lenders considered other information to be irrelevant, even if concerning important aspects of the loan applicant's income, number of years lived at current address, and should not have been ignored.

10.3.2 Collateralized debt obligations

A collateralized debt obligation (CDO) is an asset-backed security (ABS) with an underlying collateral instrument, which is typically a portfolio of bonds or bank loans. CDOs can be classified, according to the debt type, into collateralized loan obligations (CLOs), collateralized bond obligations (CBOs) and collateralized mortgage obligations (CMOs).

A CDO cash flow structure is such that interest income and principal repayments are allocated from a collateral pool of different debt instruments to a collection of CDO securities with different prioritization.

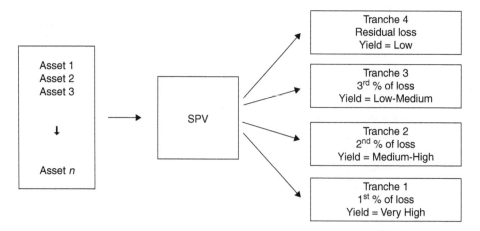

Figure 10.5 The creation of securitized assets involves a special purpose vehicle originating tranches of various riskiness, from the pooling of originating assets.

The bottom tranche, usually known as the equity tranche, covers the first $\alpha\%$ of notional principal, therefore absorbing the first $\alpha\%$ of the losses experienced by the collateral portfolio.

The second tranche, known as the mezzanine, is responsible for the losses above $\alpha\%$, for a level of $\beta\%$ of notional, and absorbs the losses corresponding to the $\beta\%$ (over the equity tranche) experienced by the collateral.

The top tranche, known as the senior, is not touched by losses in the collateral portfolio, until the other tranches have already absorbed the $(\alpha + \beta)\%$ of total losses.

A CDO is backed by portfolios of many types of assets. The most common collaterals are bonds and loans.

In the early 2000s, collateralization was done through firms called Special Purpose Vehicles (SPVs), in charge of purchasing the collateral portfolios and issuing the CDO tranches backed by them.

Being new entities without previous business activities they cannot have any legal liability for events that happened in the past. The bank originator did not transfer any credit risks onto the SPV that were not exposed to bankruptcy risk.

The CDO cannot go into bankruptcy, either voluntarily or through the action of creditors. In fact there is no need for bankruptcy, given that the distribution of the CDO's cash flows is determined in detail at the origination of the CDO.

The bank could earn fees from the SPV, but absolutely not claim the cash flows expected from the assets given to the SPV. The introduction of synthetic securitizations, in the following years, eliminates the need for a special purpose entity.

When the CDO is created with bonds or other fixed income instruments, it is called a cash CDO. Now recall that a long position in a corporate bond has the same credit risk as a short position in a CDS. This leads to an alternative way to create CDOs.

It is then possible to create a CDO forming a portfolio of short positions in a CDS. The credit risks are then passed onto the tranches. This is a synthetic CDO, which is structured so that default losses on the CDS are allocated to tranches whose principal is reduced progressively, as in a cash CDO.

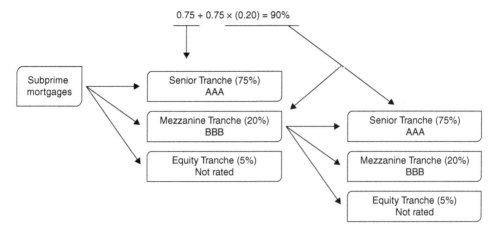

Figure 10.6 The cascade process of securitization implies creating other assets from one of the tranches of a previous securitization. The process involves the recalculation of potential losses.

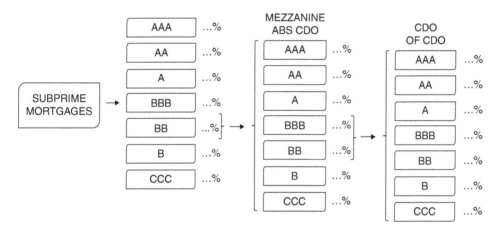

Figure 10.7 The creation of CDOs of CDOs entails processing shares of already processed securities, to generate new assets, with different rating distribution.

On the wave of the success of securitization products, financial engineering developed asset-backed security (ABS) from tranches of already packaged CDOs, named as ABS CDO.

ABS CDOs are structured to split a single tranche of a CDO into three new tranches, thus creating a new scheme. In terms of risks, the consequences are quite severe, in that the process creates also a new senior tranche out of a mezzanine.

The new senior tranche is much more risky than the senior tranche of the previous CDO. The concept is clarified by looking at a numerical example.

The senior tranche accounts for the 75% over equity and mezzanine tranche, meaning that until losses on collateral are lower or equal to 25%, the senior tranche is not touched.

Now consider the scheme of an ABS CDO derived from the mezzanine of the previous scheme. The new structure looks like that in Figure 10.6.

The senior tranche in the ABS CDO now is responsible for the 75% of the CDO mezzanine tranche, meaning that the tranche will be subject to a loss, not after a 25% loss in the collateral portfolio, as before. The mezzanine and equity tranche in the ABS CDO together cover the 25% of the mezzanine they are derived from, which is the $25\% \times 20\% = 5\%$ of the total.

Therefore, the ABS CDO senior tranche is subject to losses after the CDO equity (5%) is lost, and the equity and mezzanine of the ABS CDO (5%) is lost as well. The ABS CDO senior tranche is therefore attacked for a loss of collateral higher than 10%.

Other calculations show that, for example, if losses are 20% on the underlying portfolio, losses on the mezzanine tranche are $15/20 = 75\%$ of the principal. The first 25% is absorbed by the equity and mezzanine tranche of the ABS CDO. The senior tranche of the ABS CDO therefore loses $50/75 = 67\%$ of its value.

The important attributes characterizing a CDO are assets, liabilities, purposes and credit structures. CDOs can be assimilated to a financial company, owning financial assets, such as collateral, and liabilities divided into tranches.

Beyond the seniority and subordination of CDO liabilities, CDOs have additional structural credit protections, and are created to serve the purpose of arbitrage, balance sheet or origination.

An investor with balance sheet purpose aims at reducing the assets in the balance sheet in order to minimize the regulatory and economic capital, or achieve cheaper funding costs. This is an incentive for the investor to sell assets to a CDO.

When the purpose is arbitrage, usually an asset manager wants to improve the fees on assets under management. Assets are then purchased in the marketplace from many different sellers and pooled into a CDO.

Bank origination involves companies willing to increase their equity capital. Sometimes a CDO is created on purpose to absorb liabilities issued by the companies. Usually the operation involves the issuance of unsecured obligations by a bank, to be bought immediately by a CDO.

CDO structures can raise funds at a low cost, leaving the most residual cash flow to the holder of the equity tranche. The debt issued by the CDO is usually floating, but sometimes fixed.

Securitization can be applied to any potential stream of future payments. An important class is consumer receivables, including leases, equity loans, credit card receivables. Student loans are not included.

Mortgage-backed securities represent a huge class in CDOs' origination and they are categorized as residential mortgage loans or commercial mortgage loans. Housing loans by manufacturers are usually categorized separately.

Another class of assets is made of bonds that are backed by television rights, cable subscriptions, and they are also classified as CDOs, even if they best fit into the family of structured finance.

Separate categories incorporate hedge funds of funds, non-performing loans, and investment-grade sovereign bonds. Emerging markets are usually considered as a separate category, and usually have a high yield.

Market value CDOs either pledge assets to a trustee, backing debt at investors' interest, or involve an SPV buying assets and pledging the collateral, to back debt or equity.

This type of CDO absolves obligations on principal and interest by trading assets and gaining interest.

Cash flow CDOs invest in cash assets as collateral, transferring to investors the principal and interest cash flows of the underlying collateral. The cash flow from the collateral pool must meet all deal liabilities from the notes issued by the CDO.

The reference obligations of the CDS backing synthetic CDOs include many types. The so-called managed CDOs have a manager who is active in trading the underlying pool of assets in order to add value. Some managers are more passive, and trade only to avoid losses.

Another class is made of CDOs with the right of substitution, where a bank arranger's structuring group usually handles management activities, allowing them to trade out of deteriorating credit before default and trade into a higher credit quality obligation.

Finally, the category of static pools of CDSs backing a static CDO involves no trading, and there is no planned reinvestment period for the deal. The CDS market allows cash flow maturities to be defined at the deal inception, so that no reinvestments are needed.

10.3.3 Advantages and disadvantages

The securitization of assets offers a wide range of advantages and disadvantages. A general advantage is that economic performance can improve thanks to financial innovation, contributing to the completeness of markets and offering opportunities for risk sharing and risk pooling.

Market completeness is enhanced through the generation of assets that expand the set of risk-return combinations available to investors, lowering transaction costs, increasing liquidity and reducing monitoring and information costs.

Before securitization was introduced in the markets, a long process of disintermediation had taken place. The intermediation role has been then renewed turning from spread banking to conduit banking, originating and servicing loans funded by third parties.

Banks and other financial service institutions are required to maintain certain minimum capital-to-risk-weighted-assets ratios pursuant to the Basle Committee guidelines. In this view, securitization also gives an advantage in terms of capital adequacy, to financial institutions subject to regulation, together with the lack of access to outside capital in the bad modern economic scenario.

Investors got the view of securitized assets as carrying desirable risk properties, and a much higher spread offered compared to most fixed income and equity investments of comparable risk.

Following the wave of globalization and deregulation of financial markets, financial institutions had to face higher competition and new opportunities have risen for financial engineering, to increase lending capacity in absence of other sources of capital.

Moreover, securitization enhances specialization in that loans originated from the process are usually targeted to meet another institution's underwriting standards, while loan servicing may be provided by a third institution.

From the point of view of the financial statement of the company, securitization can offer effects on both the balance sheet and income statement. From the balance sheet point of view there are several advantages.

Capital relief relates to the fact that securitized assets can be taken off the balance sheet of the originator, therefore lowering the amount of regulatory capital required, reducing the total cost of financing by giving capital relief.

More generally, securitization reduces the cost of capital by allowing investors to benefit from access to markets where previously this was not possible, and lowering the required rate of return.

From the point of view of capital planning, securitization is one of the means by which it is possible to increase the capital to total asset ratio. Issuing Tier I or Tier II capital may push prices down, and is subject to constraints. Again, securitization allows us to cut assets off the balance, improving the ratio by cutting the denominator.

By looking at the tables reporting risk weightage for different assets, it is obvious to assume that financial institutions will tend to securitize assets with a high weight, like commercial credit card and auto loans, and invest the funds to generate lower weight assets. Capital relief in turn improves leverage possibilities, with a positive impact on the return of equity (ROE). The higher the leverages, the higher the ROE even with the same ROA.

From the point of view of the income statement, securitization can have many effects. For example, it helps in adjusting the receipt of cash flows as per the needs of the interested party.

Dividing the originated assets into tranches, the redeeming of the principal can be postponed, so that cash flows are effectively directed and controlled for specific purposes. The securitization process helps delivering cash flows at proper times and proper amounts.

Moreover, the procedure improves the credit ratings, easing the fund raising at a cheaper rate. From an income raising point of view, the originator may earn fees for processing loans and also from administration.

Financial ratios are also influenced, and cash generated through securitization has an impact on the balance sheet, that depends on the capital structure budgeting of the corporation.

Also access to the market can be eased through securitization, for example by helping speculative grade institutions to collect funds at an investment-grade rate. Financial institutions in general can benefit from improvement in the rating, and the chance to access new investors.

A very important additional advantage of securitization is the overcoming of market segmentation. Some investors prefer a specific type of asset, with a certain leverage, and choose to invest in it.

The tranches split in securitization allow constraints to be overcome by reallocating risks in a diversified manner. Each tranche collects risks dividing the securities issued into a larger senior class, which is sold at a lower yield than that achievable without segmentation, and allowing borrowers of all sizes to gain access to capital markets.

Since there is no dependence between the originator's rating and the funding through securitization, liquidity is added to the market. Securitization enables originators to increase the rating of debt much higher than that of the issuer, giving access to funding not feasible earlier. Liquidity added to the system can be used as an efficient tool to quickly rework the asset mix in the bank's portfolio.

The nature of the securitization process is to restructure the risk profile of the pooled assets by reallocating risks. Risk gets then reduced and liquidity is higher, so that investors are attracted.

Investors are offered a wide range of possible risk exposures, according to specific rules. The institutions are then able to sell unwanted securities, and buy those ones with better risk profile.

There are also benefits to the originators and the financial system. If transactions are properly structured, originators can relax the focus on capital provision. Funding requires less credit management, allows efficient marketing, reduces costs.

The credit quality is rewarded and cost of credit is reduced, offering an incentive for institutions to improve the process and quality of origination. Originators who ensure better credit quality are rewarded by securitization.

Securitization has also some disadvantages. For example, it is very difficult to synchronize the interest from the backing asset and the interest paid to the purchaser of tranches. There are also complications in some countries regarding the legal aspects of mortgage transfer.

Documentation involved in the process is of a high standard and complexity, to cover every potential risk. It is very time consuming to accomplish all the paperwork and comply with the information duties.

A tricky point is that, once originators no longer hold onto the mortgages, there is no longer responsibility for the stability of the loan. A proof of the argument is the credit crunch that happened in the early 2000s, due to the lowering of credit standards, which allowed the lenders to remove their liability.

Securities purchased by many big investors contained a huge amount of high-risk loans, and when the housing market collapsed, there was a significant decrease in the value of the properties and borrowers started defaulting on their obligations.

Even lenders could verify the downturn of the securitization process, since they ended up abandoning low-risk profile loans, in order to balance out the high-risk loans they pooled in the securitized portfolio.

The cascade process led to the deterioration of credit ratings of the lenders, leaving them with few quality loans left in their portfolio. The fall in ratings hindered them getting new funds, so that they had to stop lending, losing business.

Summary

The first factor that caused the global crisis was the low level of interest rate in the years between 2002 and 2005, leading to the amplification of negative behaviour of some agents, translating into bad mortgage lending practices.

Mortgages were given to households that were not able to afford a home purchase under normal circumstances. These borrowers were unqualified to get the money, and as a consequence, the demand in real estate rose, and prices too.

The packaging of bad mortgages and other assets into toxic securities spread the crisis internationally. The failure of major financial institutions boosted the concerns about the practice of subprime lending and developed into banking panic, with the creation of international interdependencies and the contagion over continents.

The role of the credit rating agencies in the spreading of the crisis was crucial, showing the lack of regulation. Their contribution derives from how they handled the securitization process.

In the early 2000s it was clear that something was wrong and the development of securitization was linked to the tendency of rating agencies to inflate ratings to obtain large profits.

Many risks were not properly spotted or managed during the crisis, and some banks ended up having huge volumes of complex, illiquid credit products on their books without a sufficient amount of capital to support the risk.

Credit derivatives are contracts that transfer credit risk from one party to another, with focus on some specific aspects of the underlying instrument. The management of credit risk is separated by the ownership of the asset.

The mostly traded credit derivatives are credit default swaps, aimed at transferring default risk from one party to another, given a reference entity, in exchange for regular periodic interest payments.

The process of securitization consists in pooling assets together, in order to repack them into new securities, to be issued and sold to investors. Notional principal and interest payments flow to the purchaser of the originated assets.

Securitization can be employed to transfer credit risk embedded in the pooled assets, from one institution to the investors, and cancel them from the balance sheet of the originators, to appear in those of other companies.

A credit default obligation is backed by many types of assets. Bonds and loans are the most widely used collaterals, and the process for the issuance of CDOs is done through firms called Special Purpose Vehicles (SPVs), that purchase the collateral, issuing the CDOs, in tranches.

Bibliography

Anand, M.R., Gupta, G.L. and Dash, R. 2012. The Euro Zone Crisis and its Dimensions and Implications. *eSocialSciences Working Paper Series*. Id:4764.

Andrews, D., Haberlein, H., Olson, K., Moss, J. and Olert, J.S. 2004. *Securitization and Banks: A Reiteration of Fitch's View of Securitization's Effect on Bank Ratings in the New Context of Regulatory Capital and Accounting Reform*. Fitch Ratings Special Report.

Brunnermeier, M.K. 2008. Deciphering the Liquidity and Credit Crunch 2007–2008. *Journal of Economic Perspectives*, 23(1): 77–100.

Cont, R. 2010. Credit Default Swaps and Financial Stability. *Banque de France. Financial Stability Review*, 14. Derivatives. Financial Innovation and Stability.

Davis, K. 2012. Regulatory Reform Post the Global Financial Crisis: An Overview. Report for the Melbourne APEC Finance.

Duffie, D. and Gârleanu, N. 2001. Risk and Valuation of Collateralized Debt Obligations. *Financial Analysts Journal*, 57(1).

Gorton, G.B. and Souleles, N.S. 2005. *Special Purpose Vehicles and Securitization*. FRB Philadelphia Working Paper No. 05–21.

Gorton, G.B. and Souleles, N.S. 2007. *Special Purpose Vehicles and Securitization. The Risks of Financial Institutions*. 549–602.

Hull, J.C. and White, A. 2000. Valuing Credit Default Swaps I: No Counterparty Default Risk. *Journal of Derivatives*, 8(1).

Hull, J.C. and White, A. 2001. Valuing Credit Default Swaps II: Modeling Default Correlations. *Journal of Derivatives*, 8(3).

Jarrow, R.A. and Turnbull, S. 1995. Pricing Derivatives on Financial Securities Subject to Credit Risk. *Journal of Finance*, 50.

Jobst, A. 2008. *What is Securitization?* Finance & Development.

Levine, R. 2011. The Governance of Financial Regulation: Reform Lessons from the Recent Crisis. *International Review of Finance*, 12(1): 39–56.

Lucas, D.J., Goodman, L. and Fabozzi, F.J. 2007. Collateralized Debt Obligations and Credit Risk Transfer. *Yale ICF Working Paper*.

O'Kane, D. 2000. *Introduction to Asset Swaps, Analytical Research Series*. Lehman Brothers International, Fixed Income Research.

O'Kane, D. and Turnbull, S. 2003. *Valuation of Credit Default Swaps, Fixed Income Quantitative Credit Research*. Lehman Brothers.

Tavakoli, J.M. 2003. *Introduction to Collateralized Debt Obligations*. Tavakoli Structured Finance, Inc.

Tuckman, B. 2001. *Fixed Income Securities: Tools for Today's Markets*. 3rd Edition. John Wiley & Sons, Inc.

Exercises

Questions

1. Explain how mortgage-backed securities work.
2. How does risk sharing benefit both financial intermediaries and private investors?
3. Discuss some of the manifestations of the globalization of world capital markets.
4. Why can procyclicality in regulation be considered a factor worsening the crisis?
5. Describe the leveraging process in the early 2000s that characterized the European economy.
6. Describe the heterogeneity registered among European countries who suffered more for the crisis, in terms of the driving factors and peculiar aspects of distress.
7. How is the process of securitization related to the spread of the financial crisis worldwide?
8. Describe the insurance feature of a CDS against credit risk.
9. What are the advantages of a securitization over the issuance of bonds?
10. Is a securitization prevented from achieving a rating which is higher than the rating on the operating company's issued debt? Discuss the point.
11. What are the main balance-sheet effects of the securitization process on the originator?

Appendix: A model of SPVs

Gorton and Souleles (2007) propose a theoretical analysis of SPVs, in the form of a game model of off-balance sheet financing, in order to grasp the source of value in the use of SPVs.

The game involves a financial intermediary (institution) sponsoring the SPV on one side, and a large number of investors on the other side. The intermediary finances a portfolio of two projects, in a one-period setting.

The project quality is determined by the efforts of the institution and determined by the corporate activities. The value of effort, which includes all factors determining the project quality, provides a benchmark for securitization value.

In order to get the value of securitization, the model allows for financing of project through an SPV. Once projects are admitted to investment, the bank chooses an effort level to put on it.

The final step is strategic allocation of the two projects between the balance sheet of the intermediary and the balance sheet of the SPV, after qualities are known, given constraints of various orders (projects cannot be high quality, in order for the model to work).

The institution wants to finance two projects, on a one-period time interval, each one requiring an investment that is set symbolically to €1. The total equity available for the projects is less than €2, therefore funds must be borrowed for an amount equal to

$$D = 2 - E$$

where

E is the amount of available equity $(E < 2)$.

Define as D_T the amount to be repaid at maturity of the debt D. The debt benefits from a tax shield, so that the final net amount to be repaid is

$$\tilde{D}_T = (1 - \tau) D_T$$

where

τ is the corporate tax rate.

The bank puts a high (e_h) or low (e_l) level of effort on the project, with an outcome $(u_l$ or $u_h)$ that is dependent on the level of effort expended. Effort e, which resembles the whole of resources employed for executing the project, has a cost $f(e)$, and projects are independent, so that there are four possible outcome combinations, where either the first or second project has a high outcome, or both have low or high outcomes.

The projects satisfy four basic properties, which can be summarized by the following set of conditions

$$\begin{cases} 2\left[eu_h + (1-e)u_l\right] - f(e) - D > 0, & \text{if } e = e_h \\ 2\left[eu_h + (1-e)u_l\right] - f(e) - D < 0, & \text{if } e = e_l \\ 2u_l - f(e) - D_T < 0, & \text{if } e \in (e_h, e_l) \\ 2u_h - f(e) > u_h + u_l - f(e) > D_T, & \text{if } e \in (e_h, e_l) \end{cases}$$

First of all, for a choice of high level of effort, the net present value of the investment is positive. Second, when a low effort is chosen, the NPV of the project is negative. The third condition is that when both projects have a low return, the default is sure, while in all other states, default does not occur, so that when both projects have a low return, the default is certain, while in all other states, default does not occur.

In the case when securitization is not considered, the institution's problem is to maximize the expected value of the projects, given some choice of effort and debt repayment. That means

$$\max\left(e^2\left[2u_h - f(e) - (1-\tau)D_T\right] + 2e(1-e)\left[u_h - u_l - f(e) - (1-\tau)D_T\right]\right)$$

subject to

$$\left[e^2 + 2e(1-e)\right]D_T + (1-e)^2\left[2u_l(1-c) - f(e)\right] \geq D$$
$$V(e = e_h \mid E(e) = e_h) \geq V(e = e_l \mid E(e) = e_h)$$

where

$E(e)$ is the investors' expectation on the choice of effort of the institution.

The relevant debt level D_T in the formula is the minimum promised amount that a lender would accept, in order to give the funds, namely

$$D_T = \frac{D - \left[1 - E(e)\right]^2 \left\{2u_l\left(1 - c\right) - f\left[E(e)\right]\right\}}{2E(e) - E(e)^2}$$

where

$c \in (0,1)$ is the bankruptcy cost.

The maximization formula is the sum of the aggregate project outcome in both positive cases (the case of both projects having a low outcome is dropped because it generates default, corresponding to an outcome of zero).

The program is subject to both a participation constraint and an incentive constraint. The former, expressed as net cash flow after bankruptcy and effort costs, ensures that the investors populate the market, and join the game with the institution. The latter states that investors have the incentive to choose a high level of effort.

11 Hedging techniques

Several hedging techniques are available to hedge major sources of risk, additionally to the ones already analysed in previous chapters, and beyond the plain duration, linear and normal-assumption-based approaches.

Market risk VaR can be approximated by using sensitivities of asset portfolios to risk factors, based on first and second order derivatives, and accounting for non-linearities in the factor-returns relationship.

Mathematical in-depth analysis allows for defining and pricing of the relevant sensitivities, in order to get the picture of how to hedge risk, and at what cost, in order to resemble the whole BSM framework.

The hedging of credit risk goes through the identification and correct measurement of the exposures involved, together with the estimation of default probabilities associated with each counterparty in the portfolio. The regulatory framework defines standard and advanced methods for risk quantification and capital allocation related to default risk.

Interest rate risk is much more than standard duration and convexity measurement. The calculation of adequate standards for IRR involves using more advanced and complicated models, to overcome limitations of standard methods, including the use of non-linear derivatives.

After studying this chapter you will be able to answer the following questions, among others:

1. What are the main approaches to market risk hedging? How does delta hedging of portfolios work?
2. What are the main steps in credit risk hedging?
3. How does regulation approach the issue of credit risk management?
4. How can the limitations of standard duration and convexity approach be overcome using advanced approaches?
5. How can fixed income derivatives be used for IRR hedging?

The first section of the chapter deals with market risk measurement, delta and gamma hedging and their combination. The second is about credit risk hedging, with an in-depth analysis of exposure measurement techniques and regulatory framework. The focus of the final section is IRR hedging, describing advanced techniques like duration vectors, and the use of fixed income derivatives.

11.1 Market risk hedging

Learning outcomes

1. Describe the delta-hedging approach to market risk.
2. Describe the gamma-vega approach to market risk.
3. Calculate the cost of hedging for single Greeks.

11.1.1 Delta hedging

Recall a Greek of a security is the sensitivity of that security to one of the parameters of the underlying asset. In order to clarify the matter, consider the Greeks for a stock, which is of course dependent only on itself.

The delta of a stock is

$$\delta_S = \frac{\partial S_t}{\partial S_t} = 1$$

This is because, by logic, the value of the stock depends fully on the change of itself.

The delta (hedge ratio) of a derivative f is defined as

$$\delta = \frac{\partial f}{\partial S}$$

so that, for relatively small changes in the stock prices, the change in value of the derivative can be approximated by

$$\Delta f \approx \delta \Delta S$$

A portfolio is hedged, also said to be delta-neutral, when its delta is equal to zero. A trading strategy that dynamically maintains a delta-neutral portfolio is called a delta hedge.

The delta of an option is always comprised, in absolute value, between 0 and 1, and approximates the probability that the option will be in-the-money at expiration. In particular, the delta of a call option is always between 0 and +1, given that its value never moves against the underlying stock.

Example 11.1: An investor holds a portfolio short 2,000 puts, each with $\delta = -0,63$. The portfolio can be hedged by a position in $2,000 \times -0,63 = -1,260$ shares (short position). On the contrary, a long position in put options would be hedged by buying stocks.

The opposite holds for a put option, whose delta is always between -1 and 0. Deep in the money call options have a delta that approaches one, and far out-of-the-money call options have a delta close to zero.

Example 11.2: Consider a hedger who is short 10,000 European calls, on a stock with volatility $\sigma = 30\%$, with $r = 6\%$, $K = 50$, $c = €1.77$. Each option covers 100 shares, so that the total number of shares is $n = 1,000,000$. BSM calculation yields a value for delta equal to

$$\delta_C = N(d_1) = ... = 0.5386$$

so that delta hedging can be reached by buying an amount of shares equal to

$$n_\delta = n\delta_C = 1,000,000 \times 0.5386 = 538,600$$

A position (portfolio) is said to be delta-neutral when it has a zero delta. The delta of a portfolio is the weighted sum of the single deltas of individual assets in it, as described by

$$\delta_\Pi = \sum_{i=1}^{n} w_i \delta_i \tag{11.1}$$

where

  w_i is the weight of the i-th asset in portfolio
  δ_i is the delta of the i-th asset in portfolio.

In order to achieve delta-neutrality, assets with opposite deltas to offset each other must be included in the portfolio, so that the summation in (11.1) is equal to zero.

A delta-neutral position is immunized against any movement of the assets it includes. When delta-neutrality is maintained, adjusting the hedge ratio dynamically, the only factor driving the value arbitrage is the volatility of the underlying.

A negative delta is equivalent to being short in the underlying asset, with a downward price exposure, and the opposite holds for a positive delta, which is exposed to the same directional price risk.

In order to achieve delta-neutrality, it is necessary to trade the right amount of underlying asset when trading on an option. The appropriate number of contracts is determined by the delta or hedge ratio. This is the basis for delta hedging.

Factors driving the option value also affect the delta of a position, thus implying the delta of an option changes as market conditions change. To compensate for these changes, the position on the underlying asset must be adjusted continuously for the portfolio to be kept delta-neutral.

Recall that the delta of a call option in the BSM framework is

$$\delta_c = N(d_1)$$

and the delta of a put option is equal to

$$\delta_p = -N(-d_1)$$
$$= N(d_1) - 1.$$

The delta of a call option on a dividend-paying stock is

$$\delta_{cq} = N(d_1)e^{-q\Delta t}$$

and for a put is

$$\delta_{cq} = \left[N(d_1) - 1 \right] e^{-q\Delta t}$$

Binomial trees can be used to determine the number of stocks and other assets to achieve the hedging of a position in a financial option, by a replication argument. By looking at the bifurcation of the tree, the payoff of a call option in the up and down state can be replicated by a portfolio of stocks and bonds, as from

$$S_h \delta + \left(1 + r_f \right) B = c_h$$
$$S_l \delta + \left(1 + r_f \right) B = c_l$$

where

S_h is the price of the stock on the upper branch
S_l is the price of the stock on the lower branch
c_h is the price of the call option on the upper branch
c_l is the price of the call option on the lower branch.

It follows that the optimal hedging quantity of the bond is given by

$$B = \frac{c_l - S_l \delta}{1 + r_f}$$

while the optimal quantity of underlying stock (delta) is given by

$$\delta = \frac{c_h - c_l}{S_h - S_l}$$

It is possible to extend the analysis to a continuous-time framework, by recalling the BSM framework.

11.1.2 Gamma and vega hedging

Gamma is the rate of change of the portfolio's delta with respect to the price of the underlying asset. When the gamma is small, the delta changes slowly with asset price, so that the portfolio can be rebalanced with a low frequency.

On the other hand, when the gamma is big, then the delta changes quite quickly, meaning a more frequent rebalance is required to keep delta-neutrality of the portfolio.

Gamma measures a derivative's convexity. Its asymptotical properties are

$$\Gamma \to 0 \qquad \text{if } S \to 0$$
$$\Gamma \to 0 \qquad \text{if } S \to \infty$$
$$\Gamma \text{ is high} \quad \text{if } S \approx K$$

When the gamma is high the relation between the derivative and the underlying asset is more convex than linear. The hedging error is therefore more likely to be large in the presence of large moves.

Recall that the change in value of a portfolio can be approximated by a Taylor series expansion, leading to the formula

$$\Delta\Pi = \Theta\Delta t + \delta r S + \frac{1}{2}\Gamma\sigma^2 S^2$$

Making the portfolio delta-neutral implies reducing the change in value of the portfolio to

$$\Delta\Pi = \Theta\Delta t + \frac{1}{2}\Gamma\sigma^2 S^2$$

Gamma involves a second order term of the expansion, thus it is not linear as delta. The gamma of a stock is zero, therefore the underlying asset is not sufficient to hedge against gamma, that requires a position in a derivative that is not linearly dependent on the underlying asset.

Consider a portfolio that is delta-neutral and has a gamma of Γ. A traded option, not written on the same underlying as the portfolio, has a gamma of Γ_H. Adding up an amount of w_H units of the second derivative to the portfolio brings the gamma to

$$\Gamma_P = w_H\Gamma_H + \Gamma$$

In order to neutralize the gamma of the portfolio, the condition to be satisfied is therefore

$$w_H\Gamma_H + \Gamma = 0$$

meaning that

$$w_H = \frac{-\Gamma}{\Gamma_H}$$

After the gamma is hedged, the inclusion of new options in the portfolio will then change the delta, so that the portfolio is no longer delta-neutral. It follows that in order to complete the delta-gamma hedging, a final trade on the underlying asset must be made in order to rebalance the delta.

It follows that simultaneous delta-gamma hedging of a portfolio of option P, requires another (hedging) option H, and the underlying stock S, leading to a system of equations given by

$$\begin{cases} n_S\delta_S + n_P\delta_P + n_H\delta_H = 0 \\ n_S\Gamma_S + n_P\Gamma_P + n_H\Gamma_H = 0 \end{cases}$$

where

n_P is the initial number of options in the initial portfolio
n_S is the solution number of hedging shares of the underlying stock
n_H is the solution number of hedging options
$\delta_S = 1$ is the delta of the underlying stocks

δ_P is the delta of the initial portfolio
δ_H is the delta of the hedging option
Γ_P is the gamma of the initial portfolio
Γ_H is the gamma of hedging option.

That final trade will not affect the gamma again, and the hedging is complete.

Example 11.3: An investor wants to delta-gamma hedge a portfolio with one call option A with $\delta_A = 0.554$ and $\Gamma_A = 0.0361$. Another call option is available on the market with $\delta_B = 0.382$ and $\Gamma_A = 0.0348$.

Finally, it is interesting to learn something about vega hedging. Recall that vega is the sensitivity of the option price to changes in the volatility of the underlying asset. Even if in BSM model, the volatility is assumed to be constant, in practice, volatility changes over time.

As for gamma, vega hedging can be achieved by introducing a traded derivative in the portfolio.

In order to neutralize the vega of the portfolio, the condition to be satisfied is

$$w_H \mathcal{V}_H + \mathcal{V} = 0$$

meaning that

$$w_H = \frac{-\mathcal{V}}{\mathcal{V}_H}$$

A portfolio that is gamma neutral will not in general be vega neutral, and vice versa. In order to achieve both gamma and vega neutrality of a portfolio, at least two different traded options dependent on the underlying asset must be used.

11.1.3 The cost of hedging

It is possible to isolate pure exposure to individual Greeks by hedging all the other risks away. This allows us to price the exposures and figure out how much it costs to get exposed to a given Greek.

Delta is the easiest Greek to price, because the underlying is a pure exposure, having a delta of one. Therefore the cost of a unit exposure in delta is equal to S, and can be formally expressed as

$$P_\delta = S$$

In order to price rho, it is convenient to work with positions on bonds, just recalling that, for a bond

$$\delta_B = \Gamma_B = \mathcal{V}_B = 0$$
$$\Theta_B = rB_{t,T} \qquad (11.2)$$
$$Rho_B = -\Delta t B_{t,T}$$

where

$B_{t,t+\Delta t}$ is the price at time t of a bond maturing at time $t, t + \Delta t$.

Consider a portfolio of a €1 long position in a bond and an opposite €1 short position in a bond. The value of the portfolio is zero, and the overall position is characterized by the Greeks

$$\delta_\Pi = \Gamma_\Pi$$
$$= V_\Pi$$
$$= 0$$
$$\Theta_B = (r \times 1) - (r \times 1)$$
$$= 0$$
$$Rho_B = (-\Delta t_l \times 1) + (\Delta t_s \times 1)$$
$$= T_S - T_L$$
$$\Rightarrow P_\rho = 0$$

where

Δt_l is the time until maturity of the long bond
Δt_s is the time until maturity of the short bond
T_L is the maturity of the long bond
T_S is the maturity of the short bond.

Pricing theta is then straightforward, given that conditions in (11.2) hold. Since it is free to hedge rho, the pure theta exposure is equal to

$$\Theta_B = r B_{t,t+\Delta t}$$

and costs $B_{t,t+\Delta t}$. The theta price for the unit is then given by normalizing the total theta exposure, so that

$$P_\Theta = \frac{B_{t,t+\Delta t}}{r B_{t,t+\Delta t}} = \frac{1}{r}$$

The pricing of gamma and vega is a bit more cumbersome and requires recalling some of the knowledge acquired so far about the BSM framework and the pricing of options.

Knowing the price of each Greek, as derived above, recall the closed formulas for the Greeks of a call option in the BSM framework, given by

$$\delta_c = N(d_1),$$
$$\Gamma_c = \frac{N'(d_1)}{S\sigma\sqrt{\Delta t}}$$
$$\Theta_c = -\frac{N'(d_1)S\sigma}{S\sqrt{\Delta t}} - rKe^{-r\Delta t}N(d_2)$$
$$V_c = \sigma S^2 \Delta t \frac{N'(d_1)}{S\sigma\sqrt{\Delta t}},$$
$$Rho_c = \Delta t K e^{-r\Delta t}N(d_2)$$

where

$N'(.)$ is the p.d.f. of the normal distribution.

The cost of a hedged call option, after cutting away all the Greeks, is given by

$$c_H = c - P_\delta \delta_c + P_\rho \rho_c + P_\Theta \Theta_c$$

$$= SN(d_1) - Ke^{-r\Delta t} N(d_2) - SN(d_1) + \frac{N'(d_1)S\sigma}{2r\sqrt{\Delta t}} + rKe^{-r\Delta t} N(d_2)$$

$$= \frac{N'(d_1)S\sigma}{2r\sqrt{\Delta t}}$$

It is now possible to calculate the sensitivities of this clean price, to all the option parameters, so to obtain new Greeks, which are given by

$$\delta_H = 0, \ \Gamma_H = \frac{N'(d_1)}{S\sigma\sqrt{\Delta t}}$$

$$\Theta_H = 0$$

$$V_H = \sigma S^2 \Delta t \frac{N'(d_1)}{S\sigma\sqrt{\Delta t}}$$

$$Rho_H = 0$$

The price of gamma in this setting is given as usual by the ratio between the call price, and the value of the corresponding Greek. Therefore it is defined as

$$P_\Gamma = \frac{c_H}{\Gamma_H} = \frac{\dfrac{N'(d_1)S\sigma}{2r\sqrt{\Delta t}}}{\dfrac{N'(d_1)}{S\sigma\sqrt{\Delta t}}} = \frac{\sigma^2 S^2}{2r}$$

Now observe that

$$c_H = \frac{\sigma^2 S^2}{2r} \Gamma_H$$

indicating that the price of the clean call option is independent of all contractual parameters. It follows that a unit of cash gives the same amount of gamma, when invested in any call option that is hedged from all other Greeks.

A portfolio of hedged calls is then delta, theta, rho and gamma-neutral, but not necessarily vega-neutral, meaning that vega exposure is free and the price of vega is

$$P_V = 0$$

Finalizing, the value of any claim written on a stock S is given by

$$f = P_\delta \delta + P_\Gamma \Gamma + P_\rho \rho + P_V V + P_\Theta \Theta$$

$$= S\delta + \frac{\sigma^2 S^2}{2r} \Gamma + 0 + 0 + \frac{1}{r}\Theta$$

$$= S\delta + \left(\frac{1}{r}\right)\frac{1}{2}\sigma^2 S^2 + \left(\frac{1}{r}\right)\Theta$$

$$\Rightarrow rf = rS\delta + \frac{1}{2}\sigma^2 S^2 + \Theta$$

which is the BSM PDE, as a function of the option Greeks.

11.2 Credit risk hedging

Learning outcomes

1. Define how to model credit exposure.
2. Describe credit valuation adjustment for credit risk.
3. Explain Monte Carlo methods for credit risk hedging.

11.2.1 Modelling exposure

When a counterparty in a derivative contract defaults, a bank has to close out the position with that specific counterparty. The loss arising from it can be assessed assuming the bank gets a position in an analogue contract with some other counterparty. Upon replacement of the contract, the market position of the bank remains unchanged and the loss can be determined as the cost of replacing the contract at time of default.

If the value of the contract for the bank is negative at time of default, the bank closes out the position paying out the market value of the contract to the counterparty, entering at the same time a new contract, similar to the closed one, with some other counterparty. That allows the bank to receive the market value of the contract and neutralize the net loss.

In case the value of the contract is positive, at closure the bank receives nothing from the defaulting counterparty, and again enters a new similar contract, paying the market value of it, with a net loss equal to the market value of the contract.

Consider an institution holding some position with a counterparty. The value of the portfolio can be defined as

$$V_t = \sum_{i=1}^{n} V_{i,t}$$

where

$V_{i,t}$ is the value of contract i at time t.

It follows by the above definitions that the credit exposure of a bank having a derivative contract signed with some counterparty, is the maximum of the contract's market value (when the value for the bank is positive) and zero (when the value for the bank is negative).

The contract-level exposure for contract i is then given by

$$EX_{i,t} = \max\left(V_{i,t}, 0\right)$$

If the exposure is margined with some collateral H_t, then the exposure is adjusted to be

$$EX_{i,t} = \max\left(V_{i,t} - H, 0\right)$$

The market value of the contract changes randomly over time, so that only the current exposure is known for sure, and the future exposure is stochastic. Moreover, a derivative contract can be both an asset and a liability for the bank, and the risk is bilateral.

When a bank has multiple positions with a defaulted counterparty, with no mitigation of risk whatsoever, its maximum loss is equal to the sum of credit exposure at contract level. The exposure on the counterparty level calculated without netting is

$$EX_t = \sum_{i=1}^{n} \max\left(V_{i,t}, 0\right)$$

The exposure can be reduced through a netting agreement, which is a legal obligation between two counterparties, for aggregating transactions in case of default. Negative-value transactions are used to offset positive-value ones, with credit exposure being represented by the resulting net value.

The total credit exposure calculated out of a netting set is then specified by the maximum between zero and the net portfolio value, as described by

$$EX_t = \max\left(\sum_{i=1}^{n} V_{i,t}, 0\right)$$

At a more general level, some agreements may exclude some of the trades from the netting, and including the others. In this case, the exposure is modelled as a mix of netted and non-netted positions.

Define the k-th netting agreement with a counterparty as NA_k. The resulting exposure is given by the sum of the netted exposure for the k netting-agreed positions, and the exposure of the others

$$EX_t = \sum_{i=1}^{n} \max\left(\sum_{i \in NA_k} V_{i,t}, 0\right) + \sum_{i=1}^{n} \max\left(V_{i,t}, 0\right) \tag{11.3}$$

where the summation in brackets indicates the part covered by only the k-th agreement, which is convoluted in the external summation over i, and the second term is the sum of the exposure for all trades, at contract level, not belonging to any netting agreement.

The three elements for credit exposure calculation are scenario generation, instrument valuation and portfolio aggregation. After simulating different market scenarios, using factor models, an instrument valuation is performed (for each simulation and each trade).

Applying the necessary netting rules, the counterparty-level aggregate exposure is obtained by applying equation (11.3), and the process output is a set of realizations of the exposure, at a counterparty level, at each simulation date.

The calculation is computationally intense, for large portfolios and a high number of simulation dates and market scenarios. The standard in the industry is to use a few thousands of scenarios and various simulation dates.

Scenarios are generated at fixed simulation dates $t_i = t_1, t_2, ..., t_n$, and each scenario realization depends on a set of factors, including interest rates, equity prices, FX prices, affecting the portfolio value.

Path dependent simulation involves the generation of scenarios through time, each simulation describing a path of the factor along a subinterval. Direct-jump simulation instead involves the direct simulation from time zero to the relevant simulation date.

The price of the factor is usually modelled via a stochastic process, which is solvable in closed form. As for many other applications in finance, the typical choice for a price-simulation process is the generalized geometric Brownian motion, in the form

$$dX_t = \mu_t X_t dt + \sigma_t X_t dW_t$$

where both drift and volatility are time-dependent.

The simulation can be run under physical probability, with both drifts and volatilities calibrated to historical prices, or risk-neutral probability, with no-arbitrage calibration of the parameters.

Once simulations are done, future exposure profiles can be obtained by calculation of statistics of the exposure distribution.

For a single transaction, or portfolio of many transactions with the same counter-party, there are two main effects determining the credit exposure over time, going in opposite directions.

Exposure profiles are obtained through calculation of statistics on the exposure distribution, and determine the uncertain future exposure. Profiles obtained from different exposures are usually characterized by different sizes, but similar shapes, and are affected by two main effects in their dynamics.

On one side, greater volatility increases the potential for market prices to move significantly, generating a diffusion effect that increases the exposure. On the other hand, the reduction over time of the remaining cash flows involved in the exposure has an amortization effect, decreasing the exposure over time. So the effects act in opposite directions, the diffusion effect increasing the credit exposure and the amortization effect decreasing it over time.

The exposure profiles also depend on the instruments, and it is different for different types of securities. Moreover, even among the same asset class, different market conditions may lead to different profiles.

Example 11.4: An upward sloping yield curve implies an exposure which is greater for a payer swap than the same receiver swap. Fixed payments in early periods are greater than the floating payments, resulting in positive forward values on the payer swap. The opposite holds for a downward sloping yield curve. In case the curve is humped, the effect is not clear, because the forward value on a payer swap is initially positive and then becomes negative (and vice versa for a receiver swap).

Margin agreements (MA) allow for a further reduction of the counterparty-level exposure, and more and more participants use collateral as a means of credit risk reduction.

An MA entails rules for the correct computation of the collateral amount to be exchanged between parties every trading day, and is a contract that legally binds, requiring one or both of the counterparties to make the relevant payments.

The main features of an MA agreement include:

- A threshold, defined for one or both counterparties, below which no margin is due.
- A grace period, being the number of days from default to the liquidation of the counterparty's position.
- A remargin period, which is the interval in days of monitoring and margin call.
- A minimum transfer amount, the minimum amount for a margin transfer.

Assuming that MAs can be set to cover some netting sets, the collateral held can be written as

$$H_t = \max(V_s - K, 0) \qquad (11.4)$$

where

K is the value of the collateral threshold
s is the remargin date.

In the simple case of daily remargin m, it holds that $m = 1$ and $s = t$. The exposure at default is then defined as

$$E_{X,t} = \max(V_{t+g} - H_t, 0) \qquad (11.5)$$

where

g is the grace period.

Substituting (11.5) into (11.4), and integrating in F (the joint distribution F of V_{t+g} and V_s), gives the expected exposure as

$$E_{E,t} = \int \max\left[V_{t+g} - \max(V_s - K, 0), 0\right] dF$$

Following Gibson (2005), there are four possible combinations of the relevant variables, yielding different values for the exposure. Bounding the integral, for the possible values of the exposure, the expected exposure can be written as

$$E_{E,t} = \int_0^{V_s} V_{t+g} dF + \int_{V_s - D}^{V_s} \left(V_{t+g} - V_s + D\right) dF$$

Gibson assumes a random walk form for V_t, in order to establish the joint distribution F, meaning that

$$V_t = V_0 + \sigma\sqrt{s}X, \quad X \sim N(0,1)$$
$$V_{t+g} = V_0 + \sigma\sqrt{s}X + \sigma\sqrt{t+g-s}Y, \quad Y \sim N(0,1)$$

It is then possible to express the expected exposure in terms of Gaussian increments, in a form given by

$$
E_{E,t} = \int_{-\infty}^{\frac{D-V_0}{\sigma\sqrt{s}}} \left[\left(V_0 + \sigma\sqrt{sx}\right) N\left(\frac{V_0 + \sigma\sqrt{sx}}{\sigma\sqrt{t+g-s}}\right) + \frac{\sigma\sqrt{t+g-s}}{\sqrt{2\pi}} e^{-\frac{1}{2}\left(\frac{V_0+\sigma\sqrt{sx}}{\sigma\sqrt{t+g-s}}\right)^2} \right] N'(x)\,dx
$$
$$
+ N\left(\frac{V_0 - D}{\sigma\sqrt{s}}\right) \left[DN\left(\frac{D}{\sigma\sqrt{t+g-s}}\right) + \frac{\sigma\sqrt{t+g-s}}{\sqrt{2\pi}} e^{-\frac{1}{2}\left(\frac{D}{\sigma\sqrt{t+g-s}}\right)^2} \right]
$$

which is the expected exposure in presence of a collateral, as described above.

11.2.2 Credit valuation adjustment

The derivatives business has been characterized by generally ignoring the counterparty risk involved in the trades, due to the relatively small size of the derivative exposures and the high credit rating of the counterparties which were involved.

But, as the size of the derivative exposure in the portfolio increases, and the credit quality of the counterparties is lower, counterparty credit risk is no longer negligible, and must be appropriately priced and charged for.

Credit valuation adjustment (CVA) is the process of valuation, pricing and hedging of counterparty credit risk. It involves managing counterparty credit risk on both the asset and liability side, and funding risk, analogously to asset-liability management for derivatives.

As a risk assessment methodology, it is very important to enforce the correct incentives for trading and avoid adverse selection. The more risky counterparties, as well as negative funding trade, in fact, tend to migrate to banks without CVA standards.

CVA is the difference between the risk-free value of the portfolio and its true value when accounting for the possibility of default by a counterparty. It therefore resembles the market value of the counterparty risk.

CVA calculation is based on three main parameters

1. Loss given Default (LgD)
2. Expected exposure (EE)
3. Probability of default (PD).

As a general rule, the three parts merge leading to the simplest expression for the CVA, given by

$$
CVA = L_{GD} \times E_E \times P_D
$$

Basel III regulation specifies the features and methodology for CVA calculation. There are two possible methods available to financial institutions adopting the standard:

1. Standardized approach
2. Advanced approach

While the standardized approach is available to all institutions, only banks that comply with the regulatory standards for using the internal model method for counterparty credit risk calculation must use the advanced approach.

CVA is calculated as the difference between the risk-free portfolio and the value resulting from accounting for counterparty default. There are two types of CVA perspectives, unilateral and bilateral.

Denote with $E_{X,t}$ the exposure of the institution towards the counterparty at time t. Assume that in case of default, the institution can recover a fraction R of the exposure.

The risk-neutral discounted expected exposure $E_{E,t}$ (conditional to the counterparty defaulting at time t) is

$$E_{E,t} = \hat{E}\left(D_{0,t}E_{X,t}\right)$$

where

$\hat{E}$ is the risk-neutral expectation

D_t is the discount factor.

The CVA desk of a bank serves the purpose of hedging for possible losses due to counterparty default, or reducing the amount of regulatory capital required. The hedging comes at a cost, quantifiable in the CVA charge.

Assuming independence between exposure and the counterparty's credit quality simplifies the analysis, and the CVA formula becomes

$$CVA = (1-R)\int_0^T E_{E,t}d\pi_{0,t} \tag{11.6}$$

where

T is the longest maturity in the portfolio

$\pi_{0,t}$ is the risk-neutral probability that the counterparty defaults between time 0 and t.

Equation (11.6) requires simulation for the calculation of expected exposure. Discount rates can be simulated using a short-rate model (usually the CIR is appropriate), pricing then the instrument according to the model-specific bond-pricing equation.

The standardized approach for the CVA capital charge as from the Bank for International Settlements (BIS) Document on Credit Risk, is a simplified version of a VaR model capturing the loss on a bank's derivatives position. The model estimates the maximum increase in credit spreads with a 99% confidence level.

Assuming no hedges are used, the standardized method for calculating CVA capital charge K is

$$K = 2.33\sqrt{h}\sqrt{\frac{1}{4}\left(\sum_i w_i E_{D,i}M_i\right)^2 + \frac{3}{4}\sum_i \left(w_i E_{D,i}M_i\right)^2}$$

Table 11.1 Volatility spread approximations

Rating	Spread volatility
AAA	0.7%
AA	0.7%
A	0.8%
BBB	1.0%
BB	2.0%
B	3.0%
CCC	10.0%

Table 11.2 Add-on percentages of the underlying amount for different types of contract

Contract	1 year	1–5 years	>5 years
Fixed income	0.0%	0.5%	1.5%
FX and gold	1.0%	5.0%	7.5%
Other metals	7.0%	7.0%	8.0%
Equities	6.0%	8.0%	10.0%
Commodities	10.0%	12.0%	15.0%

where

K is the one-year risk horizon
w_i is the weight applicable to the counterparty
$E_{D,i}$ is the exposure at default of counterparty i
M_i is the effective maturity of transaction with counterparty i.

A very important element in the CVA standardized approach is the exposure at default (EAD). The regulatory document offers three different approaches to calculate it. The simplest one is the current exposure method (CEM).

The method is based on calculating current exposure from mark to market values, and adding a factor, as a percentage of the notional amount of the contract, to account for the potential future exposure over the remaining life of the contract.

Once the appropriate add-on factor a is selected, the EAD formula is given by

$$E_D = E_C + a$$

where

E_C is the amount of current exposure.

The netting of positions on the CE part can be accomplished from the market values, setting a lower bound of zero.

For the a part a netting factor must be computed, as

$$N_F = \frac{\max\left(\sum_{i=1}^{n} V_i, 0\right)}{\sum_{i=1}^{n} \max\left(V_i, 0\right)}$$

When $N_F = 0$ the whole of positions are netted, and netting is reduced, as it approaches 100% (no netting at all).

$$a = (0.4 + 0.6N_F)\sum_i a_i$$

where

a_i is the adding factor for each counterparty.

When a collateral is put against a netting set, the formula becomes

$$EAD = \max(0, V - C) + a$$

where

C is the collateral amount.

The second approach for EAD calculation is the standardized method which is designed for banks not qualifying for modelling exposure internally. It is therefore calculated in a bit more of a complex way than CEM.

According to the Basel III Document, banks that are IMM-approved must calculate the CVA capital charge by modelling how changes in counterparty's credit spread impact on the adjustments of all derivatives in the portfolio.

The document states that the calculation of CVA capital charge via the advanced method is independent of the accounting method used to determine the CVA, and must be on the formula

$$CVA = L_{GD,M} \sum_{i=1}^{n} \max\left(0, e^{-\frac{t_{i-1}s_{i-1}}{L_{GD,M}}} - e^{-\frac{t_i s_i}{L_{GD,M}}}\right)\left(\frac{E_{E,i-1}P_{i-1} + E_{E,i-1}P_i}{2}\right)$$

where

t_i is the i-th revaluation time (tenor)
s_i is the spread of the counterparty at tenor t_i
$L_{GD,M}$ is the LgD of the counterparty, based on its market instrument or proxy
P_i is the discount factor at time t_i

Now define the value f_t of a derivative, and define a discretized CVA measure, dividing the timeline from 0 to T in n subintervals, corresponding to times $t_i = t_1, t_2, ..., t_n$, so that the equation of CVA can be rewritten as

$$CVA = (1-R)\sum_{i=1}^{n} v_{t_i^*} \pi_i, \quad t_i^* = \frac{1}{2}(t_{i-1} + t_i)$$

where

π_i is the unconditional risk-neutral default probability of default between t_{i-1} and t_i.

Recall that there is a difference between unconditional default probabilities and default probabilities conditional on no earlier default. The former are calculated directly from credit spreads, whose complete term structure is often observable in the market.

The spread and default probability are directly related by the formula for the hazard rate, and the unconditional default probability can be expressed as the probability of defaulting between 0 and t_i, minus the probability of default between and t_{i-1}, as defined by

$$\pi_i = e^{-\frac{t_{i-1}s_{i-1}}{1-R}} - e^{-\frac{t_i s_i}{1-R}}$$

Hull and White (2012) use a delta/gamma approximation; the change in the CVA measure due to a small change in all the credit spreads in the portfolio is given by

$$\Delta CVA = \sum_{i=1}^{n} \max\left(t_i e^{-\frac{t_i s_i}{1-R}} - t_{i-1} e^{-\frac{t_{i-1}s_{i-1}}{1-R}} \right) f_t \Delta s + \frac{1}{2(1-R)} \sum_{i=1}^{n} \max\left(t_i e^{-\frac{t_i s_i}{1-R}} - t_{i-1} e^{-\frac{t_{i-1}s_{i-1}}{1-R}} \right) f_t \left(\Delta s \right)^2$$

which is clearly a form of Taylor series expansion, following the delta-gamma approach. It is based on the first and second order elements of the expansion in order to give an approximation of the real change in the CVA due to its sensitivity to a change in the target variables (credit spreads in this case).

11.2.3 Monte Carlo methods

The key challenge in modelling portfolio credit risk lies in describing the relationship between default events. The main weakness of credit models during the crisis was in fact the failure in modelling the possibility of many simultaneous defaults occurring.

Previous chapters have dealt with a general description of the Monte Carlo methodology applied to finance. Following Brereton *et al.* (2012), it is now possible to adapt the methodology to the various classes of credit risk model.

These classes of models are characterized by a vector of default variables $d_1, d_2, ..., d_n$ and a vector of default probabilities $\pi = (\pi_1, \pi_2, ..., \pi_n)$. The loss L is given by the weighted sum of independent random variables, multiplied by a vector of constants $l_1, l_2, ..., l_n$, and is given by

$$L = d_1 l_1 + d_2 l_2 + ... + d_n l_n$$

Factor models are very important in credit risk modelling. The i-th position in a portfolio defaults when some random variable crosses a preset threshold, where the variables for all positions are dependent on a vector of common factors.

Factors usually are macroeconomic, industry, financial factors, but in general they do not need to have an economic meaning. The most popular models are based on Gaussian distribution.

In a Gaussian factor model the reference random variable X_i is defined as

$$X_i = \alpha_{i1} F_1 + \alpha_{i2} F_2 + ... + \alpha_{im} F_m + \alpha_i \varepsilon_i$$

where

$F_j \sim N(0,1)$ are standard normal distributed factors
$\varepsilon_i \sim N(0,1)$ is a standard normal diversifiable risk.

All factors are chosen such that the marginal distribution of each X_i is $N(0,1)$ as well. The default probability for the *i*-th variable, conditional to

$$F_1 = f_1, F_2 = f_2, ..., F_m = f_m$$

is then given as from normal distribution quantile properties, as

$$\pi_i = N\left[\frac{(\alpha_{i1}f_1 + \alpha_{i2}f_2 + ... + \alpha_{im}f_m) - \theta_i}{\alpha_i}\right]$$

where

θ_i is the threshold for credit event.

A variation on the theme is given by the Student's *t* factor model, which describes the factor polynomial of the reference variable as

$$X_i = \sqrt{\frac{k}{Q_\chi}}\left(\alpha_{i1}F_1 + \alpha_{i2}F_2 + ... + \alpha_{im}F_m + \alpha_i\varepsilon_i\right)$$

where

Q_χ is distributed as a chi-square with *k* degrees of freedom.

In this case, the default probability is defined as

$$\pi_i = N\left[\frac{(\alpha_{i1}f_1 + \alpha_{i2}f_2 + ... + \alpha_{im}f_m) - \sqrt{\frac{v}{r}}\theta_i}{\alpha_i}\right]$$

The loss function is defined as the weighted sum of the constant factors, conditional on each position (defined by the variable X_i) having crossed the threshold. It can then be written as

$$L = l_1 \mathbf{1}_{\{X_1 > \theta_1\}} + l_2 \mathbf{1}_{\{X_2 > \theta_2\}} + ... + l_n \mathbf{1}_{\{X_n > \theta_n\}} \tag{11.7}$$

In order to implement the model into Monte Carlo, the steps required are as follows:

1. Draw the common factors and the idiosyncratic risks.
2. Calculate the values of the random variables, following the above models.
3. Calculate the loss, using formula (11.7).

Another interesting class is represented by intensity models. Define *n* default times $\tau_1, \tau_2, ..., \tau_n$, and assume the portfolio is assessed at time *T*. The Bernoulli default variables are then given by

$$d_1 = \mathbf{1}_{\{\tau_1 > T\}}, d_2 = \mathbf{1}_{\{\tau_2 > T\}}, ..., d_n = \mathbf{1}_{\{\tau_n > T\}}$$

Giesecke (2008) defines a bottom-up approach, where each position in the portfolio is valued separately. Each τ_i is modelled as the arrival time of a point process, with intensity $\lambda_{i,t}$ that represents the rate of arrivals occurring at time t. The default probability of the i-th component is given by

$$P_i = \Pr\left(\tau_i < T\right) = 1 - E\left(e^{-\int_0^T \lambda_{i,s} ds}\right)$$

It is possible to induce the dependency among defaults by characterizing each intensity as a function of a common process Y_t and an individual process $Z_{i,t}$ so that, for example, a convenient form is given by

$$\lambda_{i,t} = Y_t + Z_{i,t}$$

It is very common to model the shared process as a Brownian motion with jumps, in the form

$$dY_t = \mu_{Y_t} dt + \sigma_{Y_t} dW_t + J_t \tag{11.8}$$

where

  μ_{Y_t} and σ_{Y_t} are deterministic functions
  J_t is a jump process.

The jump can be modelled in various forms, but the simplest one is given by

$$J_t = \int_0^t G_t dH_t$$
$$= \sum_{i=1}^{H_t} G_i$$

where

  G_t is an i.i.d. variable.

and

$$H_t = H_0 e^{-\lambda t}$$

is a Poisson decay process starting at H_0 with a probability λdt of a jump occurring between t and $t + dt$, which implies a constant infinitesimal decay and an exponential distribution of the decay process.

Duffie *et al.* (2003) show that under certain assumptions, the default probabilities $\pi_1, \pi_2, ..., \pi_n$ are solutions of a system of differential equations, given by (11.8) and the processes for the idiosyncratic factors, which are modelled similarly.

Through Monte Carlo, it is possible to simulate the process by sampling from an intensity model. The intensity of the point process is given by

$$\lambda_t = \sum_{i=1}^{n} \lambda_{i,t}$$

When the intensity can be bounded between jumps, Ogata (1981) describes a method for simulation. At each process jump, a process λ_t^*, is defined as the upper bound of the process intensity.

A Poisson process with intensity λ_t^* is then simulated, and points are accepted with probability $\dfrac{\lambda_t}{\lambda_t^*}$. The resulting algorithm steps are given by

1. Set $i = 0$ and $\pi_0 = 0$.
2. Find the upper bound of λ_i^*, given the filtration of the process up to $\tau_i \le t \le T$.
3. Simulate arrival times $\tilde{\tau}_1, \tilde{\tau}_2, ..., \tilde{\tau}_n$ for a homogeneous Poisson process with intensity λ^*. Stop after the first accepted arrival time $\tilde{\tau}_i^*$, given that acceptance probability is
    $\dfrac{\lambda_{i,\tau}}{\lambda_i^*}$.
4. Set $\tau_i = \tilde{\tau}_i^* + \tau_{i-1}$.
5. Set $i = i+1$ and repeat steps 2,3,4,5 until $\tau_i > T$.

11.3 Advanced IRR hedging

Learning outcomes

1. Describe the M-Absolute and M-Square models.
2. Define the duration vectors approach to IRR.
3. Explain how IRR can be hedged through fixed income derivatives.

11.3.1 M-Absolute and M-Square models

Both duration and convexity are based on the restrictive assumption of parallel shifts in the term structure of interest rates. There are risk measures that allow interest rate movements to be consistent with empirically realistic shapes of the term structures.

Nawalkha and Chambers (1996, 1997) derived a methodology for improved immunization, the M-Absolute and M-Square models.

The M-Absolute model is straightforward and powerful, including in only one risk measure all the information needed to manage interest rate risk. Moreover, it reduces by more than half the residual interest rate risk not captured by duration.

Recall the standard definition of duration as the weighted average of the maturities of the cash flows of a bond, weighted by the present values of the cash flows, normalized by the bond price

$$D_\$ = \sum_{t=1}^{T} t C_t e^{-r_y \Delta t}$$
$$= \sum_{t=1}^{T} t w_t$$

Recall the standard relationship between instantaneous forward rates and zero-coupon rates as

$$\int_0^t f_s ds = r_{yt} t$$

where

f_t is the instantaneous forward rate at time t.

The zero-coupon rate is an average of the instantaneous forward rate between 0 and t.

If we introduce the term structure of interest rates into the duration formula, it is then possible to express the weights using the forward rates, as

$$w_t = \frac{1}{P} C_t e^{-\int_0^t f_s ds}$$

The equation defines a measure of duration calculated using the entire term structure, instead of just the yield to maturity. It is often referred to as the Fisher and Weil (1971) duration.

Standard duration represents the time horizon τ, at which the future value of a bond is immunized against interest rate movements.

Define the M-Absolute risk measure as the weighted average of the absolute differences between cash flow maturities and the planning horizon. Like in the duration formula, the weights are represented by the present values of the bond cash flows, normalized by the bond price. The formula is then

$$M_{ABS} = \sum_{t=1}^{T} |t - \tau| w_t$$

where

τ is the length of the planning horizon.

The M-Absolute measure is then linked to some specific time horizon. The immunizing model consists in selecting the bond minimizing the quantity M_{ABS}. A straightforward property is that for $\tau = 0$, the measure equates the duration of the bond.

The difference between duration and M-Absolute measure arises from the nature of the stochastic processes assumed for the term structure movements. The performances of the two models compare according to different cases.

If the term structure of instantaneous forward rates has a small parallel shift, the duration model leads to perfect hedging while the M-Absolute model underperforms duration, giving only a limited immunization.

On the other hand, if the term structure shows a general shift in orders higher than first, including slope, curvature and level, the process for risk becomes stochastic and the M-Absolute model outperforms duration.

In general, the duration model completely immunizes against the parallel shifts but cannot target the impact of slope, curvature and other higher order term structure shifts. The M-Absolute model immunizes only partially against the height shifts, but it also reduces the immunization risk caused by the shifts in other parameters.

Numerical solution of the summation over time, for long time periods, can be cumbersome. Therefore a closed form solution has been developed for the M-Absolute measure, as

$$M_{ABS} = \frac{\left(\dfrac{\displaystyle\sum_{t=1}^{T} \left| t - \dfrac{\Delta t_C}{t_C} - \tau \right| C_t e^{-\frac{r_y}{m}\left(t - \frac{\Delta t_C}{t_C} \right)}}{\displaystyle\sum_{t=1}^{T} C_t e^{-\frac{r_y}{m}\left(t - \frac{\Delta t_C}{t_C} \right)}} \right)}{m}$$

where

t_C is the time of the last payment from the bond
Δt_C is the time interval between bond payments
m is the number of payments per year.

The M-Square risk measure is defined as the weighted average of the square of the difference between the cash flow maturities and the planning horizon. As the M-Absolute measure is an alternative to the classic duration, the M-Square stands as an alternative to the convexity measure. Mathematically it is defined as

$$M^2 = \sum_{t=1}^{T} |t - \tau|^2 w_t$$

For the planning horizon tending to zero, the measure converges to the convexity. M-Square and convexity are linked by a linear relationship, which is defined as

$$M^2 = CV - 2D\tau + \tau^2$$

If duration is kept constant, it is clear that M-Square is an increasing function of the convexity.

It is possible to show that the M-Square measure should be minimized in order to achieve better portfolio immunization. On the other hand, it is well known that a higher convexity is beneficial, leading to higher portfolio returns. Given the linear relationship between the two measures, this constitutes a paradox, which is solved by considering that convexity is based on parallel shifts of the term structure, while M-Square resembles a risk measure which fits non-parallel shifts.

11.3.2 Duration vectors

A further improvement in immunization performance, compared to M-Absolute and M-Square methods, is represented by duration vector models (DVMs), described by Nawalkha *et al.* (2005).

The measure immunizes against changes in the shape of the term structure, by using higher order duration. The model therefore captures changes in slope and curvature of the yield curve, providing improved immunization results, based on vector of risk measures $d = (d_1, d_2, ..., d_m)$.

Consider a portfolio of bonds at time 0, paying out C_t at time $t = (1, 2, ..., n)$, and define with y_t the term structure of the instantaneous forward rate. Assume an instantaneous shift in the term structure, from f_t to $f_t' = f_t + \Delta f_t$.

The instantaneous percentage change in value of the portfolio can be defined in terms of a Taylor series expansion, as

$$\frac{\Delta V_0}{V_0} = -d_1 \Delta f_0 - \frac{d_2}{2} \left[\frac{\partial \Delta f_t}{\partial t} - (\Delta f_0)^2 \right] - ... - \frac{d_m}{m!} \left[\frac{\partial^{m-1} \Delta f_t}{\partial t^{m-1}} + ... + (\Delta f_0)^m \right] \tag{11.9}$$

which is the product of the duration vector (dependent on the maturity structure of the portfolio) and a shift vector (dependent on the shifts in the term structure), where

$$d_j = \sum_{t=1}^{n} \left[\frac{C_t e^{-\int_0^t f_s ds}}{V_0} \right] t^j, \quad j = 1, 2, .., m$$

The first duration element in (11.9) is the traditional duration, and the first shift vector element is the change in the level of the forward rate. The second shift vector element, corresponding to the second order element of the Taylor expansion, defines the difference between the change in slope of the forward curve, and the square of the curve shift. And so on along the expansion.

Once the horizon h for immunization is chosen, the implementation of the model requires matching the portfolio duration vector with the duration vector of a hypothetical bond maturing at h.

$$d_1 = \sum_{t=1}^{n} \left[\frac{C_t e^{-\int_0^t f_s ds}}{V_0} \right] t = h$$

$$d_2 = \sum_{t=1}^{n} \left[\frac{C_t e^{-\int_0^t f_s ds}}{V_0} \right] t^2 = h^2$$

...

$$d_m = \sum_{t=1}^{n} \left[\frac{C_t e^{-\int_0^t f_s ds}}{V_0} \right] t^m = h^m$$

As for the standard duration, the duration vector of a portfolio is the weighted average of the duration vectors of the single bonds, and for a portfolio made of q bonds, it is given by

$$d_j = w_1 d_{1,j} + w_2 d_{2,j} + ... + w_q d_{q,j}$$

where

$w_k = w_1, w_2, ..., w_q$ are the weights of each bond in the portfolio.

To immunize the portfolio, funds are invested in a combination of bonds such that the duration vector of the portfolio is equal to a horizon vector, as given by

$$
\begin{aligned}
d_1 &= w_1 d_{1,1} + w_2 d_{2,1} + \ldots + w_q d_{q,1} = h \\
d_2 &= w_1 d_{1,2} + w_2 d_{2,2} + \ldots \mid w_q d_{q,2} - h^2 \\
&\ldots \\
d_m &= w_1 d_{1,m} + w_2 d_{2,m} + \ldots + w_q d_{q,m} = h^m
\end{aligned}
\tag{11.10}
$$

When the number of bonds is equal to the number of constraints, the system allows for a unique solution. No solution exists if the number of assets is lower than the constraints, but the most common case is when the number of assets is higher so that infinite solutions are possible.

In order to identify a unique immunizing solution for the portfolio, a program must be set, with the optimization given by

$$
\min \left(\sum_{k=1}^{q} p_k^2 \right)
$$

subject to (11.10) and

$$
w_1 + w_2 + \ldots + w_q = 1
$$

The minimization function aims at achieving portfolio diversification, reducing diversifiable risk. The solution to the program involves complex matrix calculus that can be performed using specific software.

The model as derived so far is generic, for any form of the term structure shifts. A convenient specification is based upon polynomial functional form for the shifts, which helps to understand how portfolio returns can be decomposed through duration vector modelling.

Following Chambers (1984) it is possible to introduce a polynomial form for the term structure shifts, which implies expressing the Δy as a linear combination. For the zero-coupon yields, the polynomial form is given by

$$
y_t = \alpha_0 + \alpha_1 t + \alpha_2 t^2 + \ldots
\tag{11.11}
$$

where

the αs are the shape parameters of the term structure.

In order to compute the bond prices, the instantaneous forward rates are needed, comparably to the analysis above. Recall that the yield at time t can be written as a function of the instantaneous interest rate, as described by

$$
y_t t = \int_0^s f_s ds
$$

so that the derivative on both sides must be taken in order to solve for f_t. A bit of mathematics shows that, after deriving, and substituting into (11.11), yields

$$f_t = \alpha_0 + 2\alpha_1 t + 3\alpha_2 t^2 + \dots$$

The first three parameters describe the height, slope and curvature, and are essential to correctly capture the term structure, and higher orders can be ignored. Given this setting, the non-parallel shift in the instantaneous forward curve can be rewritten as

$$\Delta y_t = \Delta\alpha_0 + \Delta 2\alpha_1 t + \Delta 3\alpha_2 t^2 + \dots$$

In this case, the percentage change in the value of the portfolio is given by

$$\frac{\Delta V_0}{V_0} = -d_1 \Delta\alpha_0 - d_2 \left[\Delta\alpha_1 - \frac{\left(\Delta\alpha_0\right)^2}{2} \right] - d_3 \left[\Delta\alpha_2 - \Delta\alpha_0 \Delta\alpha_1 + \frac{\left(\Delta\alpha_0\right)^3}{3!} \right] - \dots$$

The shift vector simplifies considerably under the assumption of a polynomial form for the shifts. Note anyway, that the general model is efficient in all other cases, where no specific form for the shifts is specified.

11.3.3 Hedging with fixed income derivatives

Many institutions hedge IRR using financial derivatives. Fixed income derivatives in fact offer a wide range of hedging solutions to the institution, and they come in various shapes and classes.

The simplest way to hedge against some price change, especially for commodities, is to enter a forward contract in order to balance possible future price moves. Sometimes, more than one risk is involved, and a good strategy may involve entering more than one hedging security.

Example 11.5: A European manufacturer uses oil as an input, being subject to oil price risk. In case oil is bought from Saudi Arabia and paid in Saudi Rials, the right strategy is to enter a long position in a forward contract on oil, at a fixed Rial price, and then enter into another forward on the €/Rial exchange rate, in order to lock in the cost in Euro of the oil. In this way, both commodity and currency risk can be hedged simultaneously.

Financial futures and forwards can be used to carry on a micro hedge, when hedging risk on a single specific asset, or macro hedge, when immunizing the overall portfolio of assets.

When a micro hedge is built using a future which has an underlying other than the hedged asset, it is called a cross hedge. When the type of position to take is decided, the amount of hedging instrument to be traded is determined by the hedge ratio.

The ratio tells how many basis points the price of the hedged asset moves, due to a shift of 1 basis point of the hedging instrument. The ratio tells the bank manager the par dollar amount of hedging instrument needed per par dollar of the asset being hedged, and it is calculated as

$$HR = \beta_{AF} \frac{\Delta V_A}{\Delta V_F}$$

where

β_{AF} is the average change in the interest rate of the hedged asset, for a given change in the interest of the hedging contract

ΔV_A is the change in value of the hedged asset

ΔV_F is the change in value of the hedging asset.

The formula is calculated in several steps, the first being the calculation of the ratio between the changes in price. The second step is to calculate the beta term, using statistical analysis of past data.

In case a macro hedge has to be performed on the whole portfolio, or balance sheet of an institution, the amount of hedging instrument to trade is given by

$$V_F = \frac{-D_{GAP} V_A}{D_F}$$

where

D_F is the duration of the underlying bonds in the hedging contract

D_{GAP} is the duration gap of the institution, defined as the difference between the duration of assets and duration of liabilities.

Financial institutions sometimes offer fixed rate commitments, giving customers the option to borrow up to some amount at some specified interest rate. This can be assimilated to a put option sold to the customer.

Selling such an option generates an exposure to risk for the institution, that can be hedged by buying a put option, to offset the virtual put option sold with the commitment.

Given the maturity of the loan committed by the bank, the interest rate on the loan, and the interest rate on the Certificates of Deposit, the number of put options to buy is given through the same analysis as for the futures hedging.

The first step is in fact the calculation of a hedge ratio, using the price of the futures underlying the option. After calculating the hedge ratio, a further step leads to the number of contracts required for the hedge, which is given by

$$p_H = HR \frac{PV_A}{PV_F}$$

where

PV_A is the par value of the asset hedged

PV_F is the par value of the futures contract.

If the interest rate falls, the option is not exercised by the institution, which will not be exposed to additional losses. The advantage of hedging the loan commitment with put options rather than selling future contracts is that in the latter case, there would have been a loss on the futures contract due to a decline in the interest rate.

Interest rate swaps can be used to eliminate interest rate risk for an institution's net worth. The problem is to determine how much notional principal of the swap should be traded in order to fully hedge the interest rate risk on the bank's net worth.

The first step in the process is to calculate the effective duration of the interest rate swap of interest. Recall from basic duration theory that the duration of a swap is given by

$$D_s = D_r - D_p$$

where

D_r is the duration of the payments received
D_p is the duration of the payments made

which is the difference between the duration of the payments received by the institution minus the duration of the payments made.

Exactly as in the case of the macro hedge with futures contracts, the hedge occurs when a rise in interest rates corresponds to a rise of the value of the swap by the same amount, offsetting the decline of the bank's net worth.

This situation is determined by the equality given as

$$D_s L_s = -D_{GAP} V_A \implies L_s = \frac{-D_{GAP} V_A}{D_s}$$

where

D_s is the duration of the swap
L_s is the notional amount of the swap.

The value of the institution is then fully protected against changes in interest rates.

Snapshot 11.1
Convexity adjustment for interest rate derivatives

Interest rate derivatives which are not standard suffer from classic pricing on the relationship between interest rates and bond prices. The standard two-step procedure for valuation can then be modified so that an adjustment is made on the forward value of the variable when calculating payoff.

Consider an interest rate derivative, whose payoff is dependent on a bond yield observed at payoff time. The forward value of a variable S is normally calculated in connection with a forward contract that pays off $(S - K)$ at time T, causing the contract to have zero value for that particular value of K.

The price of a bond at time T, in terms of the yield of the bond, is given by

$$B_T = f(r_{y,T})$$

where
 y_T is the bond yield at time T.
Define the forward bond price at time zero for a contract maturing at time T, as

$$F_0 = f\left(r_{y,0}\right)$$

where
 y_0 is the forward bond yield at time zero.
The price-yield relationship f is not linear. It follows that, when the expected future bond price equals the forward bond price in a world where the bond price maturing at time t is the numeraire, the expected future bond yield does not equal the forward bond yield.
 An approximate expression for the required expected bond yield is

$$E_T\left(r_{y,T}\right) = r_{y,0} - \frac{1}{2} r_{y,0}^2 \sigma_y^2 T \frac{f''\left(r_{y,0}\right)}{f'\left(r_{y,0}\right)}$$

where

 $E_T\left(.\right)$ is the expectation in a world that is forward risk neutral w.r. to $P\left(t,T\right)$.
 σ_y is the forward yield volatility.

Summary

The Greeks represent the sensitivity of a portfolio or security to the change in value of the underlying asset. There is a Greek for each factor having an impact on the price of some dependent security, like a financial derivative.

Delta-neutral immunization against adverse movements of the underlying factors ensures perfect hedging of a linear instrument. The delta hedge can be changed dynamically, so that the only factor driving the value arbitrage is the volatility of the underlying.

A low value of the gamma means delta changes very slowly with the underlying, and the portfolio does not need frequent rebalancing. On the other hand, a high gamma means a very variable delta, and the dynamic hedging must be done more frequently.

In order to isolate the exposure to a Greek, one should be able to hedge all others, allowing to price each exposure and realize how much it costs to get exposed to a given Greek.

In case of default of a counterparty in a portfolio of exposure, the bank must close the position with that specific counterparty. The loss from the default can be assumed to result from taking a position in analog contract with some other counterparty.

Once the position is replaced, the market position of the bank is still unchanged, and the loss is accounted as the replacement cost for the contract at time of default.

Counterparty credit risk can be valuated, priced and hedged through the credit valuation adjustment approach, which involves managing the risk on both the asset and liability side, and funding risk, analogously to asset-liability management for derivatives.

Describing the relationship between multiple default events is crucial to model portfolio credit risk. The main weakness of credit models during the crisis was in fact the failure in modelling the possibility of many simultaneous defaults occurring.

Standard duration and convexity are based on the assumption that shifts of the term structure are parallel, which is limiting and unrealistic. Other risk measures allow interest rates to move consistent with empirically realistic shapes of the term structures.

A powerful approach for non-parallel shifts is the M-Absolute model, which includes in only one risk measure all the information needed to manage interest rate risk, reducing by more than 50% the residual interest rate risk not captured by standard duration.

The M-Square risk measure improves the convexity approach by defining a weighted average of the square of the difference between the cash flow maturities and the planning horizon.

Financial derivatives are used by many institutions to hedge IRR, and fixed income derivatives offer a wide range of hedging solutions to the institution, in various shapes and classes.

Bibliography

Aziz, J. and Charupat, N. 1998. Calculating Credit Exposure and Credit Loss: A Case Study. *Algo Research Quarterly*, 1(1): 31–46.

Bank for International Settlement. 2011. *Basel III: A Global Regulatory Framework for More Resilient Banks and Banking Systems*. Basel Committee on Banking Supervision.

Bank for International Settlement. 2013. *Principles for Effective Risk Data Aggregation and Risk Reporting*. Basel Committee on Banking Supervision.

Brereton, T.J., Kroese, D.P. and Chan, J.C. 2012. Monte Carlo Methods for Portfolio Credit Risk. *ANU Working Papers in Economics and Econometrics*, 579.

Canabarro, E. 2010. *Counterparty Credit Risk*. Risk Books.

Canabarro, E. and Duffie, D. 2003. *Measuring and Marking Counterparty Risk, Asset-Liability Management for Financial Institutions*. Institutional Investor Books.

Chambers, R. 1984. Agricultural and Financial Market Interdependence in the Short Run. *American Journal of Agricultural Economic*, 66: 12–24.

Duffie, D., Filipovic, D. and Schachermayer, W. 2003. Affine Processes and Applications in Finance. *Annals of Applied Probability*, 13: 984–1053.

Fares, Z. and Genest, B. 2013. *CVA Capital Charge Under Basel III Standardized Approach: An Explanation Document, Global Research & Analytics*. Chappuis Halder & Cie.

Fisher, L. and Weil, R. 1971. Coping with the Risk of Interest Rate Fluctuations: Returns to Bondholders from Naive and Optimal Strategies. *The Journal of Business*, 44(4): 408–431.

Fleck, M. and Schmidt, A. 2005. *Analysis of Basel II Treatment of Counterparty Credit Risk, Counterparty Credit Risk Modeling*. Edited by M. Pykhtin. Risk Books.

Gibson, M.S. 2005. Measuring Counterparty Credit Exposure to a Margined Counterparty. November. FEDs Working Paper, 50.

Giesecke, K. 2008. *Portfolio Credit Risk: Top Down vs. Bottom Up Approaches. Frontiers in Quantitative Finance: Credit Risk and Volatility Modeling*. John Wiley & Sons.

Hull, C. and White, A. 2012. CVA and Wrong-Way Risk. *Financial Analysts Journal*, 68(5).

Klacar, D. 2013. Estimating Expected Exposure for the Credit Value Adjustment Risk Measure. Master Thesis. Umea University.

Mishkin, F.S. and Eakins, S.G. 2011. *Financial Markets and Institutions*. 7th Edition. Prentice Hall.

Nawalkha, S.K. and Chambers, D.R. 1996. An Improved Immunization Strategy: M-Absolute. *Financial Analysts Journal*, 52: 69–76.

Nawalkha, S.K. and Chambers, D.R. 1997. The M-Vector Model: Derivation and Testing of Extensions to M-Square. Near Perfect Immunization Against Non Parallel Interest Rate Shifts. *The Journal of Portfolio Management*, 23: 92–97.

Nawalkha, S.K., Soto, G.M. and Zhang, J. 2003. Generalized M-Vector Models for Hedging Interest Rate Risk. *Journal of Banking and Finance*, 27: 1581–1604.

Nawalkha, S.K., Soto, G.M. and Beliaeva, N.A. 2005. *Interest Rate Risk Modeling: The Fixed Income Valuation Course*. Wiley Finance. John Wiley and Sons.

Ogata, Y. 1981. On Lewis' Simulation Method for Point Processes. *IEEE Transactions on Information Theory*, 27: 23–31.

Pykhtin, M. and Zhu, S. 2006. *Measuring Counterparty Credit Risk for Trading Products under Basel II, The Basel Handbook*. 2nd Edition. Risk Books.

Pykhtin, M. and Zhu, S. 2007. A Guide to Modeling Counterparty Credit Risk. *GARP Risk Review*. July/August.

Ziad, F. and Genest, B. 2013. *CVA Capital Charge Under Basel III Standardized Approach: An Explanation Document*. © Global Research & Analytics Dpt. Chappuis Halder & Cie.

Exercises

Questions

1. A company uses delta hedging to hedge a portfolio of long positions in put and call options on a currency. Explain which change gives the most favourable result between a virtually constant spot rate and a wild movement in the spot rate.
2. Explain under what different circumstances are a short hedge and a long hedge appropriate.
3. Does the delta of the option in the binomial tree depend on the risk-neutral probabilities?
4. Bowling Green Savings & Loan uses short-term deposits to fund fixed-rate mortgages. Explain how Bowling Green can use interest rate swaps to hedge its interest rate risk.
5. Chelsea Finance Company receives floating inflow payments from its provision of floating-rate loans. Its outflow payments are fixed because of its recent issuance of long-term bonds. Chelsea is somewhat concerned that interest rates will decline in the future. Yet, it does not want to hedge its interest rate risk, because it believes interest rates may increase. Recommend a solution to Chelsea's dilemma.
6. North Pier Company entered into a two-year swap agreement, which would provide fixed-rate payments for floating-rate payments. Over the next two years, interest rates declined. Based on these conditions, did North Pier Company benefit from the swap?

Problems

1. You are given the following information for two European options:

	50-strike put	55-strike call
Price	0.0230	11.3270
Delta	−0.0072	0.9500
Gamma	0.0040	0.0250

The stock price is 70. Determine the shares of stock and 55-strike calls one must buy or sell to delta-gamma hedge a sale of 100,000 50-strike put.

2. For a one-year European call option on a stock, you are given that the underlying stock's price is 60, the strike price is 65, the continuously compounded risk-free interest rate is 3%. A one-year European put option on the same stock with a strike price of 55, has $\delta = -0.42$ and $\Gamma = 0.04$.
   a. Determine the approximate change in the value of the call if the stock's price decreases to 59 instantaneously.
3. The spot EUR-GBP exchange is €1.18/£, and a one-month put option is written on the EUR with a strike rate of €1.19/£. The volatility of the exchange rate is 12%, the one-month interest rates are 2.2% on the EUR, and 2.4% on the GBP.
   a. Calculate the BSM price of the put option.
   b. What is an appropriate delta-hedge strategy for a long position in the put for an amount of €5,000,000?
4. An investor holds two types of call and two types of put options on a given stock, as in the table:

	Call 1	Call 2	Put 1	Put 2
Delta	0.40	0.55	−0.63	−0.40
Gamma	0.03	0.036	0.028	0.032
Position	1,000 long	500 short	1,000 long	500 short

   a. What is the aggregate portfolio delta?
   b. What is the aggregate portfolio gamma?
   c. If the position is gamma hedged, what is the resulting portfolio delta?
   d. How can the delta-gamma hedging be completed then?
5. A stock currently sells at €100, and in the next period the price will either go up or down by 10%. The risk-free rate is 3%.
   a. Construct a replicating portfolio to value the call, if the strike price is 100.
   b. Calculate the risk-neutral probabilities.
6. Using the information in exercise 6,
   a. Value the call option using the risk-neutral probabilities.
   b. Value a put option written today, with maturity one year, with strike price 100.

12 Beyond normality and correlation

The general assumption of standard models like VaR, is that portfolio returns are normally distributed. Moreover, linear correlation is often assumed to link different assets in a portfolio.

It is possible to relax both normality of returns and linearity of correlation, studying methodologies that allow us to explore new distributional forms, and more complicated correlation types.

Copula functions are an important tool in mathematical finance, in that they allow us to overcome the distributional issues related to the assumption of normality of data, accounting for the convenient modelling of unknown distributions.

Extreme value theory puts the focus of the analysis on the tail of the returns distribution, concentrating on the extreme values and their impact on the riskiness of the portfolio. Extreme events can be modelled using appropriate distributional forms, and convenient risk measures can be obtained.

Backtesting of VaR and the definition of coherent measures is a crucial point in checking for the accuracy of market risk measurement, and to gain coherence in the measurement.

After studying this chapter you will be able to answer the following questions, among others:

1. What are copula functions, and how can they be used to measure correlation between empirical time series? How can they be applied to financial risk management?
2. What are the known measures of dependence among variables?
3. What is extreme value theory and how can it be used for the analysis of the distribution tail? What are the steps for data application?
4. How can the VaR model be verified through backtesting?
5. What is expected shortfall, and how does it overcome the limitations of VaR for market risk measurement? What is conditional VaR?

The first section of the chapter is an introduction to copula functions, with a prime on rank correlation as an alternative to standard linear dependence. The second section is about extreme value theory, GEV distributions and the calculation of tail indices. The final part deals with backtesting of VaR, and the definition of expected shortfall, as a type of coherent risk measure.

12.1 Copula functions

Learning outcomes

1. Define the basic features and properties of copula functions.
2. List and comment on the various measures of dependence among variables.
3. Explain the applications to risk management of copula functions.

12.1.1 Basic properties

There are two main stages in the measurement of portfolio risk: the modelling of the joint movements of risk factors, and the modelling of the impact of changes on each factor, to the portfolio value.

When dealing with a multivariate distribution of the risk factors, it is crucial to know the dependence structure of the risk factor returns. The most common methodologies in portfolio risk measurement use the multivariate Gaussian distribution.

The analytic representation of a multivariate distribution is complex, with cumbersome estimation and use in simulation models. Copula functions offer an efficient approach to analyse and model the correlated default timing of a credit sensitive portfolio.

Copula functions allow us to split the dependence issue into two stages: first of all, the marginal distribution functions are determined, representing the distribution of each factor. Second, the dependence structure of the transformed random variable is determined, given some appropriate copula expression.

Sklar's theorem (1959) states that an n-dimensional copula is a function from the unit n-cube $[0,1]^n$ to the unit interval $[0,1]$, which satisfies specific properties. The first property is

$$C:[0,1]^n \to [0,1]$$

meaning that an n-dimensional copula is a multivariate distribution function C with uniform distributed margins in $[0,1]$. The second property can be expressed as

$$C(1,...,u_k,...,1) = u_k, \quad \forall k \leq n, \quad \forall u_k \in [0,1]$$

so that, knowing the realizations of the first $n-1$ variables have marginal probabilities equal to one, then the joint probability is equal to the n-th marginal probability. The third property is given by

$$C(u_1,...,u_n) = 0, \quad \forall k \leq n, \quad \text{for } u_k = 0$$

meaning that, if the marginal probability of any of the outcomes is zero, the joint probability of all outcomes is zero.

The fourth property says that $C(u)$ is increasing in each component $u_k = (u_1, u_2,...,u_n)$, meaning that the C-volume of any n-dimensional is non-negative.

An n- copula can then be defined as an n-dimensional cumulative distribution function in $[0,1]^n$, with n univariate marginal distributions $U(0,1)$ being uniform in $[0,1]$.

Consider a continuous *n*-variate distribution function $F(x_1, x_2, ..., x_n)$, with univariate marginals given as

$$F_1(x_1), F_2(x_2), ..., F_n(x_n)$$

Now define the inverse functions $F_1^{-1}, F_2^{-1}, ..., F_n^{-1}$, such that

$$x_1 = F_1^{-1}(u_1), x_2 = F_2^{-1}(u_2), ..., x_n = F_n^{-1}(u_n)$$

where

$u_1, u_2, ..., u_n$ are uniformly distributed variates.

Given the conditions above, the function

$$F(x_1, x_2, ..., x_n) = F\left[F_1^{-1}(u_1), F_2^{-1}(u_2), ..., F_n^{-1}(u_n)\right]$$

The simplest copula is the product copula, in the form

$$C(u_1, u_2) = u_1 u_2, \quad u_1, u_2 \in [0,1]$$

The product copula implies that the multivariate distribution is the product of the marginal ones, meaning that it corresponds to independence.

Once the general definition and methodology of copula functions is described, it is convenient to list and comment on the most popular copula functional forms. The most popular copula function is the Gaussian copula, which takes the form

$$C(u_1, u_2; \rho) = \mathcal{N}\left[N^{-1}(u_1), N^{-1}(u_2); \rho\right]$$
$$= \int_{-\infty}^{N^{-1}(u_1)} \int_{-\infty}^{N^{-1}(u_2)} \frac{1}{\sqrt{2\pi(1-\rho^2)}}\left[-\frac{(s^2 - 2\rho st + t^2)}{2(1-\rho^2)}\right] ds\, dt$$

where

$\mathcal{N}[.,.]$ is the bivariate normal distribution, with correlation parameter $-1 < \rho < 1$.

The functional form of the Student's *t* copula is given by

$$C(u_1, u_2; \rho_1, \rho_2) = \int_{-\infty}^{t_{\rho_1}^{-1}(u_1)} \int_{-\infty}^{t_{\rho_2}^{-1}(u_2)} \frac{1}{\sqrt{2\pi(1-\rho_2^2)}}\left[1 + \frac{(s^2 - 2\rho_2 st + t^2)}{2(1-\rho_2^2)}\right]^{-\frac{(\rho_1+2)}{2}} ds\, dt$$

where

$t_{\rho_1}^{-1}(u_1)$ is the inverse of the c.d.f. of the standard univariate *t*-distribution with ρ_1 degrees of freedom.

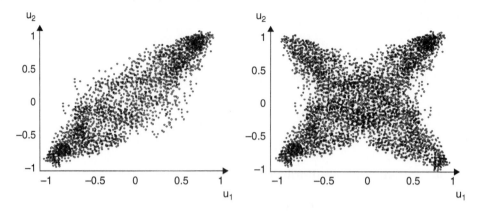

Figure 12.1 A stylized scheme of a Gaussian copula (left) and a Student's *t* copula (right).

The parameter ρ_1 determines the thickness of the tail. The model converges to the Gaussian copula for $\rho_1 \to \infty$.

The Clayton copula was developed in 1978, after original studies from Kimeldorf and Sampson (1975), and it is defined as

$$C\left(u_1, u_2; \rho\right) = \frac{1}{\left(u_1^{-\rho} + u_2^{-\rho} - 1\right)^{\frac{1}{\rho}}}, \quad \rho \in (0, \infty)$$

As ρ approaches zero, the marginals become independent. A limitation of the Clayton model is that it cannot account for negative dependence. It is a type of copula with strong left tail dependence, compared to the right tail, and it is commonly used to study correlated risk.

The Frank copula (1979) is given by

$$C\left(u_1, u_2; \rho\right) = -\frac{1}{\rho} \log\left[1 + \frac{\left(e^{-\rho u_1} - 1\right)\left(e^{-\rho u_2} - 1\right)}{e^{-\rho} - 1}\right], \quad \rho \in (-\infty, \infty)$$

The popularity of the Frank copula is given by the fact that it allows for negative dependence between the marginals, which is not very common among other forms. Moreover it shows symmetric dependence, like the elliptic copulas. Finally, it can model both strong positive and strong negative dependence.

An important drawback is that tail dependence is on average much weaker than the Gaussian copula, with strong dependence concentrated in the centre, making it suitable for data showing weak tail dependence.

The Gumbel copula (1960) is defined as

$$C\left(u_1, u_2; \rho\right) = e^{-\left[\left(-\log u_1\right)^\rho + \left(-\log u_2\right)^\rho\right]^{\frac{1}{\rho}}}$$

Similarly to the Clayton copula, and other forms, the Gumbel copula does not allow for negative dependence. On the other hand, as opposed to the Clayton copula, it exhibits

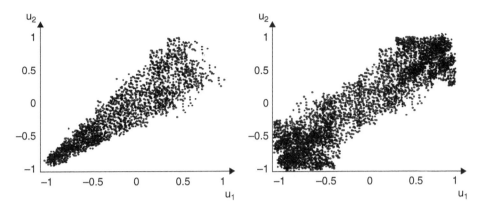

Figure 12.2 A stylized scheme of a Clayton copula (left) and a Frank copula (right).

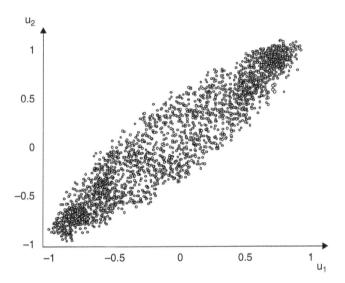

Figure 12.3 A stylized scheme of a Gumbel copula.

strong right tail dependence, while being weak on the left tail, making it a good choice for data that are strongly correlated on high values.

12.1.2 Measures of dependence

Copula functions introduce a new concept of dependence, and new correlation measures. First of all it is useful to recall and summarize the properties of the simple linear correlation, as commonly known.

Linear correlation is a dependence measure whose utility is limited to elliptical distributions, like the Gaussian. In this case, it is a good measure of the dependence among variables, but some properties are violated when other classes of distribution are considered.

For example, in the case of a Student's t distribution, a correlation coefficient of 0 does not necessarily imply independence. Moreover, correlation is invariant under linear transformation, but not for general transformation (i.e. from normal to lognormal).

Another important point is that it is not always possible to generate a joint distribution simply from some marginal distributions and a correlation coefficient.

A common practice to overcome linear correlation is to focus on the ranks of data. As a result, two correlation estimators, Spearman's rho and Kendall's tau have been developed. An interesting feature of them is the invariance with scale, due to ranking of data. Therefore, they are suited to be used with copula functions.

The idea behind Spearman's rho is to take the correlation of the variables resulting from the transformation of applying the empirical c.d.f. to raw data. The correlation of transformed variables is equivalent to the correlation of ranks, and, for a vector of variables, it can be defined as

$$
\rho_S\left(\mathbf{x}\right) = \begin{pmatrix} \rho_{11} & \cdots & \rho_{1j} & \cdots & \rho_{1m} \\ \vdots & \ddots & \vdots & \ddots & \vdots \\ \rho_{i1} & \cdots & \rho_{ij} & \cdots & \rho_{im} \\ \vdots & \ddots & \vdots & \ddots & \vdots \\ \rho_{n1} & \cdots & \rho_{nj} & \cdots & \rho_{nm} \end{pmatrix}
$$

where

$$
\rho_S\left(\mathbf{x}\right)_{ij} = Corr\left[f_i\left(x_i\right), f_j\left(x_j\right) \right]
$$

and

x_i and x_j are random variables with marginals f_i and f_j respectively.

The estimate coefficient of a sample, when sampling observation on two variables x and y is defined as

$$
\hat{\rho}_S = \frac{\sum_{i=1}^{n}\left[r(x_i)-\overline{r}(x)\right]\left[r(y_i)-\overline{r}(y)\right]}{\sqrt{\sum_{i=1}^{n}\left[r(x_i)-\overline{r}(x)\right]^2\left[r(y_i)-\overline{r}(y)\right]^2}}
$$

where

$r(x_i)$ is the rank of observation x_i
$\overline{r}(x)$ is the average rank of variable X
$r(x_i)$ is the rank of observation y_i
$\overline{r}(y)$ is the average rank of variable Y.

Kendall's tau is best described considering two sets of random variables, (x_1, x_2), and (y_1, y_2), the latter being independent of the first set, but with same joint distribution (independent copy). Plotting on a graph the realizations of the two sets (x_1, x_2) and

(y_1, y_2), the line connecting the two points can be either increasing (positive depend-ence) or decreasing (negative dependence).

It is then possible to extend the analysis to multivariate vectors x and y, so that Kendall's tau is then defined as

$$\tau_K(\mathbf{x}) = Cov\left[sgn(\mathbf{x}-\mathbf{y}) \right]$$

where, for each couple of variables x_i and y_i,

$$sgn(x_i - y_i) = \begin{cases} 1 & \text{if } (x_i - y_i) > 0 \\ 0 & \text{if } (x_i - y_i) = 0 \\ -1 & \text{if } (x_i - y_i) < 0 \end{cases}$$

For a bivariate example, with sets of variables (x_1, x_2), and (y_1, y_2) it holds that

$$\tau_K(x_1, x_2) = \Pr\left[(x_1 - y_1)(x_2 - y_2) > 0 \right] - \Pr\left[(x_1 - y_1)(x_2 - y_2) < 0 \right]$$

When the two probabilities are the same, so that upward slopes have same probability of downward slopes, Kendall's tau is equal to zero. A positive value means an upward slope has higher probability, a negative value means that a negative slope is more likely.

Both measures take values in $(-1,1)$ and can be directly derived from the copula C describing the dependence between x_1 and x_2. Spearman's rho can be defined as

$$\rho_S(x_1, x_2) = 12 \int_0^1 \int_0^1 \left[C(u_1, u_2) - u_1 u_2 \right] du_1 du_2$$

and Kendall's tau is given by

$$\tau_K(x_1, x_2) = 4 \int_0^1 \int_0^1 C(u_1, u_2) dC(u_1, u_2) - 1$$

As for Spearman's rho, it is possible to define a sample estimate, as

$$\hat{\tau}_K = \frac{\sum_{i=1}^{n} \sum_{j=1}^{m=n} sgn(x_i - x_j) sgn(y_i - y_j)}{n(n-1)}$$

The concept of tail dependence of copulas includes upper and lower tail dependence. Visually, when plotting the graph of a copula density, the lower left corner corres-ponds to lower tail dependence, and the upper right corner corresponds to upper tail dependence.

Consider a bivariate vector (x_1, x_2) with marginals f_1 and f_2 respectively. The coeffi-cient of upper tail dependence, using standard copula notation, is given by

$$\lambda_U = \lim_{u \to 1} \Pr\left[x_2 > f_2^{-1}(u) \,\middle|\, x_1 > f_1^{-1}(u) \right]$$

If $0 < \lambda_U \leq 1$, the two variables are linked by asymptotical upper tail dependence. If $\lambda_U = 0$, the two variables are upper tail asymptotically independent. The coefficient of lower tail dependence is defined as

$$\lambda_L = \lim_{u \to 1} \Pr\left[x_2 \leq f_2^{-1}(u) \middle| x_1 \leq f_1^{-1}(u) \right]$$

If $0 < \lambda_L \leq 1$, the two variables are linked by asymptotical lower tail dependence. If $\lambda_L = 0$, the two variables are upper tail asymptotically independent.

The bivariate survival function $\tilde{F}_{1,2}$ of a random vector (X_1, X_2) is defined as

$$\tilde{F}_{1,2} = \Pr\left(X_1 > x_1, X_2 > x_2 \right)$$

By working with logic and sets, it is possible to show that the relationship between the survival function and the bivariate distribution of the two variables $F_{1,2}$ is given by

$$\tilde{F}_{1,2} = 1 - f_1 - f_2 + F_{1,2}$$

It is then possible to use this relationship to derive the upper and lower tail dependence coefficients as a function of the copula. Using probability theory and mathematics it is possible in fact to show that

$$\begin{aligned}
\lambda_U &= \lim_{u \to 1} \Pr\left[X_2 > f_2^{-1}(u) \middle| X_1 > f_1^{-1}(u) \right] \\
&= \lim_{u \to 1} \frac{\Pr\left[X_2 > f_2^{-1}(u), X_1 > f_1^{-1}(u) \right]}{\Pr\left[X_1 > f_1^{-1}(u) \right]} \\
&= \lim_{u \to 1} \frac{1 - \Pr\left[X_1 \leq f_1^{-1}(u) \right] - \Pr\left[X_2 \leq f_2^{-1}(u) \right] + \Pr\left[X_1 \leq f_1^{-1}(u), X_2 \leq f_2^{-1}(u) \right]}{1 - \Pr\left[X_1 \leq f_1^{-1}(u) \right]}
\end{aligned}$$

Substituting for the value of the copula function in place of the inverse of marginals, yields

$$\lambda_U = \lim_{u \to 1} \frac{\left[1 - 2u + C(u,u) \right]}{1 - u}$$

Similarly, the lower tail dependence coefficient is given by

$$\lambda_L = \lim_{u \to 1} \frac{C(u,u)}{u}$$

This formulation works well especially with copula functions that have a closed form expression.

12.1.3 *Application to risk management*

Copula functions have many applications in quantitative finance, and in particular for financial risk management purposes. The most interesting frameworks of application are market risk and credit risk.

Market risk application of copula starts from a timeline beginning at any time t (initial time) and a risk measurement on a trading book must be performed through Monte Carlo simulation. The financials are held for a period of length $+-\Delta t$.

Define the random variable $x_{t+\Delta t}$ of portfolio returns and the vector $\mathbf{y}_{t+\Delta t}$ of the underlying risk factors driving the returns. Indicating with f the function of the returns, as a function relating the portfolio returns to the underlying factors, standard notation yields

$$x_{t+\Delta t} = f\left(\mathbf{y}_{t+\Delta t}\right)$$

The estimation of the random variable $x_{t+\Delta t}$ is carried out by analysing the historical time series of the risk factor returns, with m observations back in time, all observed on time steps of Δt. The Monte Carlo kernel simulates n scenarios for the vector of risk factors, assuming a specific analytic form for the multivariate distribution function of $\mathbf{y}_{t+\Delta t}$.

While it is common practice in risk management to assume a multivariate normal distribution, empirical studies prove it to be a wrong choice in that it underestimates the tail heaviness and fails in capturing the dependence structure among risk factors.

Following Romano (2002), an appropriate copula function can be used in place of the assumption of normality, in order to describe the dependence structure among risk factors, while assuming some distributional form for the marginals.

After generating the scenarios and calculating the realizations of $x_{t+\Delta t}$, it is possible to compose the simulated distribution of returns. The estimation of the VaR or any other measure can be done through different methodologies.

It is possible to order the simulated values for positive and negative returns, and cut the simulated distribution at the chosen confidence level, so as to get the value for the chosen risk measure (VaR or ES). Another option is to fit some distribution to simulated data and use it to calculate the desired measure(s). The extreme value theory approach instead entails the estimation of the tail distribution of returns.

Credit risk applications include the Merton latent variable model, to estimate a credit portfolio risk measure over a certain time horizon. Consider a portfolio of n counterparties, and define an indicator variable of the default z_i for each counterparty $i = 1,2,\ldots,n$ such that

$$z_i = \begin{cases} 0 & \text{if no default} \\ 1 & \text{if default} \end{cases}$$

Latent variable models are based on two vectors, to simulate the default or no default state of some counterparty over the specified time horizon. The first (random) vector $\mathbf{x}$ contains the latent variables, the second is the deterministic vector $\mathbf{d}$ of threshold levels.

Each pair of vector elements (x_i, d_i) denotes a latent variable model for the binary random vector $\mathbf{y}$, whose elements are given by

$$y_i = \mathbf{1}_{\{x_i \le d_i\}}$$

In traditional portfolio credit models, such as the KMV model or CreditMetrics™, vector **x** is assumed to be lognormally distributed. This assumption leads to underestimation of probabilities of joint defaults, and can be overcome by assuming any class of univariate distribution for each component of the vector, and a copula function to describe the dependence structure.

Copula functions can be used also to derive conditional default probabilities from CDO contracts. Consider a CDO on n assets, and define as τ_i the default time of the i-th entity.

Define as $Q_{i,t}$ the cumulative probability distribution of company i defaulting at time t. The time to default τ_i is related to some random variable x_i by an equality given as

$$P(x_i < x) = P(\tau_i < t)$$

The default of the n entities in the portfolio can be modelled by a one-factor copula model of correlation to a market factor and individual component, in the form

$$x_i = \alpha_i F_M + \sqrt{1 - \alpha_i^2}\, z_i, \quad -1 \le \alpha_i \le 1 \tag{12.1}$$

where the stochastic elements are all independent from each other, and distributed according to the copula model of choice.

In the case of a Gaussian copula, both z_i and F_M are normally distributed, with correlation between two elements i and j given by $\alpha_i \alpha_j$, due to the common relation to the market.

The one-factor copula model maps the variable x_i to t_i, on a percentile basis, as seen above. Denoting by F the cumulative distribution of x_i and by G the cumulative distribution of Z_i, the realization $x_i = x$ is mapped to $t_i = t$, where

$$x = F^{-1}(Q_{i,t})$$

The one-factor model in (12.1) can be rewritten as

$$Z_i = \frac{x_i - \alpha_i F_M}{\sqrt{1 - \alpha_i^2}}$$

The cumulative distribution G, conditional on the realization of the market variable M is then given by

$$\Pr(z_i < x \mid F_M = f_M) = G\left(\frac{x - \alpha_i f_M}{\sqrt{1 - \alpha_i^2}}\right)$$

which translates into the mapped conditional probability of variable t_i, as

$$\Pr(t_i < t \mid F_M = f_M) = G\left(\frac{F^{-1}(Q_{i,t}) - \alpha_i f_M}{\sqrt{1 - \alpha_i^2}}\right)$$

The variable of interest is not defined directly but mapped through a copula model, so that more handy marginals are considered, and a correlation structure is then defined.

12.2 Extreme value theory

Learning outcomes

1.   Explain what is extreme value theory and what are the related distributions.
2.   Describe the application of EVT to data, in the framework of tail analysis.
3.   Define and comment on the extreme VaR.

Snapshot 12.1
Monte Carlo simulation of copulas

It is possible to implement Monte Carlo simulation of random variables with copula C, simulating a single vector $u = (u_1, u_2, ..., u_n)$, with uniform marginals and the desired copula.

The algorithm proposed here derives the copula from a multivariate distribution, so that simulation is particularly easy.

For a multivariate Gaussian copula the algorithm is as follows:

1.   Generate a covariance matrix of the data, and from it, derive the correlation matrix Ω.
2.   Decompose the correlation matrix through Cholesky, so that $\Omega = \Lambda^T \Lambda$.
3.   Generate a vector $\mathbf{x} = (x_1, x_2, ..., x_n)$ of i.i.d. normal random variables.
4.   Compute the matricial product $\mathbf{y}^T = \Lambda \mathbf{x}$.
5.   Calculate the vector

$$\mathbf{u} = (u_1, u_2, ..., u_n) = \left[N(y_1), N(y_2), ..., N(y_n) \right]$$

For a multivariate t-copula the algorithm becomes:

1.   Generate a covariance matrix of the data, and from it, derive the correlation matrix Ω.
2.   Generate samples x from a multivariate normal distribution, with covariance matrix as in point 1.
3.   Generate independent chi-square terms $\varepsilon \sim \chi_k^2$, with k degrees of freedom.
4.   Calculate the vector

$$\mathbf{u} = (u_1, u_2, ..., u_n) = \left[\frac{t_k x_1}{\sqrt{\varepsilon/k}}, \frac{t_k x_2}{\sqrt{\varepsilon/k}}, ..., \frac{t_k x_n}{\sqrt{\varepsilon/k}} \right]$$

where
t_k is the cumulative distribution function of a univariate t-distribution with k degrees of freedom.

12.2.1 Theoretical background

Extreme value theory (EVT) is the equivalent of the central limit theorem, when dealing with modelling the maxima of a random variable. The main result of EVT relates in fact to the distribution of sample maxima and minima.

Consider a sequence of i.i.d. variables $x_1, x_2, ..., x_n$, distributed according to a smooth function $F(x)$. Denote the sample maximum as

$$M_n = \max(x_1, x_2, ..., x_n)$$

and assume the distribution is subexponential.

In this framework, the tail of the maximum determines the tail of the sum in the limit. The generalized extreme value (GEV) distribution describes the limit distribution of suitably normalized maxima.

Fisher and Tippet (1928) and Gnedenko (1943) described the limit law for the block maxima, given a subsample of size n, starting from a sequence of i.i.d. random variables $\mathbf{x}_n = (x_1, x_2, ..., x_n)$.

Assume a common distribution function, given by

$$F(x) = \Pr(x_i \leq x)$$

For normalizing constants $\delta_n > 0$, $\lambda_n \in \mathbb{R}$, and some non-degenerate distribution function F, the problem is to search for a limit law $G(x)$ such that

$$\frac{M_n - \beta_n}{\delta_n} = F^n(\delta_n x + \lambda_n)$$
$$\rightarrow G(x)$$

Under the specified conditions, it is possible to redefine the normalizing constants so that the distribution function takes one of the three standard extreme value distributions. The first possible form is the Gumbel distribution, which is given by

$$Gumbel(x) = e^{-e^{-x}}, \quad x \in \mathbb{R}$$

The moments of the Gumbel distribution are defined as

$$E(x_G) = \text{Euler's Constant} = 0.5772156649$$
$$Var(x_G) = \frac{\pi^2}{6}$$
$$Mode(x_G) = 0$$

The Frèchet distribution form is given by

$$Frechet(x) = \begin{cases} 0 & \text{if } x \leq 0 \\ e^{-x^{-\alpha}} & \text{if } x > 0 \end{cases}$$

where α is a non-negative constant.

The moments of the Fréchet distribution are given by

$$E(x_F) = \Gamma\left(1 - \frac{1}{\alpha}\right), \quad \alpha > 1$$

$$Var(x_F) = \Gamma\left(1 - \frac{2}{\alpha}\right) - \Gamma^2\left(1 - \frac{1}{\alpha}\right), \quad \alpha > 2$$

$$Mode(x_F) = \left(1 + \frac{1}{\alpha}\right)^{-\frac{1}{\alpha}}$$

where

$\Gamma(.)$ is the gamma function.

The third type is the Weibull distribution, which is given by

$$Weibull(x) = \begin{cases} e^{-(-x)^\alpha} & \text{if } x \leq 0 \\ 0 & \text{if } x > 0 \end{cases}$$

whose moments are given by

$$E(x_W) = -\Gamma\left(1 + \frac{1}{\alpha}\right)$$

$$Var(x_W) = \Gamma\left(1 + \frac{2}{\alpha}\right) - \Gamma^2\left(1 + \frac{1}{\alpha}\right)$$

$$Mode(x_W) = \begin{cases} -\left(1 - \frac{1}{\alpha}\right)^{-\frac{1}{\alpha}} & \text{if } \alpha > 1 \\ 0 & \text{if } 0 < \alpha \leq 1 \end{cases}$$

The three types of distribution can be combined into a generalized extreme value (GEV) distribution, as defined by von Mises (1936), defined as

$$G(x; \mu, \sigma, \xi) = e^{-\left(1 + \xi\frac{x-\mu}{\sigma}\right)_+^{-\frac{1}{\xi}}}$$

where

μ is the location parameter
σ is the scale parameter
ξ is the shape parameter.

The shape parameter determines how the general formula can be reconnected to each of the three distributions described above. In particular, for $\xi > 0$ and $\alpha = \frac{1}{\xi}$, the GEV distribution corresponds to the Frèchet distribution. For $\xi < 0$ and $\alpha = -\frac{1}{\xi}$, it corresponds to the Weibull distribution. For $\xi \to 0$ it corresponds to the Gumbel distribution.

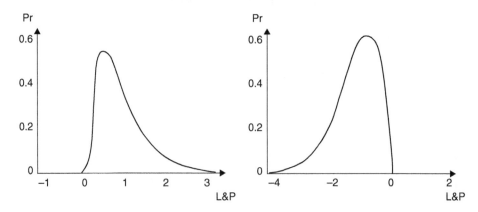

Figure 12.4 The schematic representation of the Frèchet distribution (left) and the Weibull distribution (right).

An alternative representation of the EVT is given by the peak over threshold (POT) method, which takes into account the distribution of the exceedances over some threshold, so that the focus is on estimating the conditional excess distribution of values of x above threshold u, defined as

$$F_u(x-u) = \Pr(x_i - u \le x - u \mid x_i > u)$$
$$= \frac{F(x) - F(u)}{1 - F(u)}$$

where

α_F is the right extreme of F.

There are generally very few observations above the limit threshold, so that F_u may be problematic to estimate. This is a powerful result in terms of conditional excess distribution function.

Picklands (1975) and Balkema and de Haan (1974) showed that a good approximation of the conditional excess distribution function $F_u(x-u)$ for large values of u, and for a large class of distribution functions F, is given by the generalized Pareto distribution (GPD), as given by

$$G(x-u;\sigma,\xi) = \begin{cases} 1 - \left(1 + \dfrac{\xi}{\sigma}\right)^{-\frac{1}{\xi}} & \text{if } \xi \ne 0 \\[2mm] 1 - e^{-\frac{x-u}{\sigma}} & \text{if } \xi = 0 \end{cases}$$

where

$$\xi \ge 0 \Rightarrow y \in \left[0,(\alpha_F - u)\right]$$
$$\xi < 0 \Rightarrow y \in \left[0, -\frac{\sigma}{\xi}\right]$$

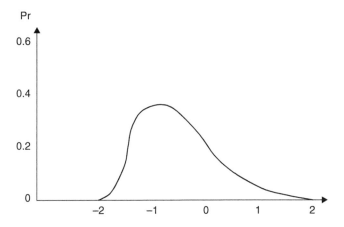

Figure 12.5 The schematic representation of the Gumbel distribution.

12.2.2 Data application

The first thing to do when applying EVT to data is to study the histogram of the data. Recall that most financial series are fat-tailed, so that a graph of the quantiles is the best method to judge the goodness of fit of the series to the model parameters.

Consider a series $x_1, x_2, ..., x_n$ of i.i.d. random variables, and let $x_{n,n}, x_{n-1,n}, ..., x_{1,n}$ be the order statistics. The Q-Q plot graphs the parametric distribution against the variable. Given that the relation

$$F_n(x_k, n) = F^{-1}\left(\frac{n-k+1}{n}\right), \quad k = 1, 2, ..., n$$

where

$F_n(x_k, n)$ is the empirical distribution

$F^{-1}\left(\dfrac{n-k+1}{n}\right)$ is the estimated parametric distribution.

The graph shows a linear form in case the parametric model fits the data. A Q-Q plot therefore gives a good indication of the goodness of fit of the data to a parametric model.

Define the mean-excess function (MEF) of a random variable x, with upper bound x_D, as the mean excess over some threshold h, which can be written as

$$g(x) = E(x - h \mid x > h), \quad 0 \le h \le x_D$$

The form of $g(x)$ depends on the form of the distribution of x. Assuming an exponential form for the variable, the mean-excess function is given by

$$h(x) = \frac{\beta + \xi x}{1 - \xi}, \quad \beta + \xi x > 0$$

Embrechts *et al.* (1997) show that the MEF of a fat-tailed distribution is located between the MEF of an exponential distribution and the MEF of a generalized Pareto distribution.

The choice of the threshold is an important step, and can be done using graphical tools. The Hill graph can be described by considering the ordered statistics $x_1 > x_2 > ... > x_n$ of i.i.d. random variables. The Hill estimator of the tail index ξ using $(k+1)$ ordered statistics is defined by

$$\hat{\xi} = \frac{1}{k}\sum_{i=1}^{k}\ln\left(\frac{H_i}{H_{k+1}}\right)$$

and the Hill graph is constructed by plotting the points in the form

$$\left(k, \hat{\xi}^{-1}\right), \quad 1 \le k \le n-1$$

The threshold u is selected from this graph for the stable areas of the tail index, but the choice is not always clear. The method in fact mostly applies well for a GPD-type distribution.

Several assumptions can be made for the estimation of the parameters of the extreme distribution. It is correct to assume that data are roughly GEV distributed, and parameters and quantiles are estimated for the distribution of excess over a threshold.

The estimation can be done through MLE, observing that there is no closed form solution for the parameters, and numerical methods must be used to get good estimates. The q-quantile can be defined as usual.

12.2.3 Extreme VaR

The estimation of the parameters of the extreme distribution can be done under many assumptions. It can be assumed that extreme values are GEV distributed, following the distribution exactly or roughly.

The assumption that the tail observations follow exactly the GEV distribution allows for MLE to be used for estimation. Numerical methods provide the estimates, given no closed form solution exists.

Define the q-quantile $\hat{x}_q$ of the distribution as the inverse H_q^{-1} of the Hill estimator, so that

$$\ln(q) = \left[-\left(1+\frac{\xi(\hat{x}_q - \hat{\mu})}{\hat{\sigma}}\right)^{-\frac{1}{\xi}}\right]$$

and consequently

$$\hat{x}_q = \hat{\mu} + \frac{\hat{\sigma}}{\xi}\left\{\left[-\ln(q)\right]^{-\xi} - 1\right\}$$

All the three parameters are estimated simultaneously, giving good estimates for time series with positive tail index ξ, which is the case of most financial time series, making MLE a good tool for estimation in the field.

The empirical distribution of extreme observation can be modelled thanks to EVT, and extreme VaR is defined as the q-quantile estimated from the distribution of extreme values.

The underlying assumption is that extreme values follow exactly the GEV distribution, meaning that it can be defined as

$$VaR_E = \hat{\mu} + \frac{\hat{\sigma}}{\xi}\left\{\left[-\ln(q)\right]^{-\xi} - 1\right\}$$

When the assumption is that the extreme values do not follow the GEV distribution not exactly, the VaR can be estimated either in-sample or out-of-sample. The in-sample VaR estimation is given by

$$VaR_{E,in} = \hat{\mu}_n + \frac{\hat{\sigma}_n}{\xi}\left\{\left[n(1-q)\right]^{-\xi} - 1\right\}$$

and the out-of-sample VaR is given by

$$VaR_{E,out} = X_k\left[\frac{n}{k}(1-q)\right]^{-\xi}$$

EVT is adequate for aggregate positions, but is problematic when considering the multivariate case. In a vectorial space with a dimension bigger than one, there is no definition of order, thus extreme observations are hard to identify and define.

As a solution, Longin (1999) proposes to work on the marginal distributions for each asset, solving for as many q-quantiles, for as many assets in the portfolio. Calculating all correlations involved allows us to get a multivariate measure of extreme VaR in the form

$$VaR_E = \sqrt{\sum_{i=1}^{n}\sum_{j=1}^{n}\rho_{ij}w_iw_jVaR_iVaR_j}$$

Beware that the joint distribution of extreme marginal distribution can be different from the whole joint distribution. It is possible that extreme movements in the price change of single assets do not result in extreme movements of the portfolio value.

Recall the POT method for estimation of the conditional excess distribution. The parameter ξ indicates the heaviness of the tail (the larger the parameter, the heavier the tail).

Assuming a GPD distribution for the tail, it is possible to analytically define a VaR and ES measure, as a function of the GPD parameters. First of all, the distribution $F(x)$ can be isolated by writing

$$F(x) = \left[1 - F(u)\right]F_u(x-u) + F(u)$$

It is then possible to substitute for the GPD, and approximating the distribution function of threshold point by

$$F(u) = \frac{n - n_u}{n}$$

where

n_u is the number of observations above u

so that the estimator $\hat{F}(x)$ of $F(x)$ can be written as

$$\hat{F}(x) = 1 - \frac{n_u}{n}\left[1 + \frac{\hat{\xi}}{\hat{\sigma}}(x-u)\right]^{-\frac{1}{\hat{\xi}}}$$

The formula can then be inverted for a given probability p to give

$$VaR_p = u + \frac{\hat{\sigma}}{\hat{\xi}}\left[\left(\frac{n}{n_u}p\right)^{-\hat{\xi}} - 1\right]$$

12.3 Beyond VaR

Learning outcomes

1.   Explain the VaR backtesting procedure.
2.   Describe and comment on the expected shortfall as a coherent measure of risk.
3.   Define conditional VaR and its estimation.

12.3.1 Model backtesting

Backtesting is the statistical comparison of actual gains and losses on a portfolio, to the corresponding VaR estimates. For example, given a 95% confidence interval, it is expected to get one exception every 20 days.

The method consists in checking whether the frequency of exceptions occurring over some time is in line with the VaR confidence interval, in terms of the mere amount of exceptions (unconditional coverage) or considering how they are spread over time also (conditional coverage).

The way exceptions are spread over time is an important indicator, since the clustering of exceptions indicates that the model does not accurately capture the changes in market volatility and correlations.

Assume that on a total amount of n observation, there are m measured exceptions, so that the failure rate is m/n. In case of a confidence interval of 99%, the failure rate should be an unbiased measure of a loss frequency $p = 1\%$.

Each observed return is either an exception or not, so that the sequence of success or failure is binomial distribution. In this specific case, the binomial distribution is given by

$$f(x) = \binom{n}{m}p^m(1-p)^{n-m}$$

As the number of observations increases, the binomial distribution approaches the normal distributions and the number of exceptions is distributed as

$$n \sim N\left(np, (1-p)np\right)$$

As any statistical test with null hypothesis, VaR backtesting is subject to error type 1 (possibility of rejecting a correct model), and type 2 (possibility of not rejecting an incorrect one).

Kupiec in 1995 developed the most popular test of failure rates. Implementing the above discussed approach in a simple way, the test analysed whether the number of exceptions is consistent with the chosen confidence interval.

Also called the proportion of failures (POF) test, it requires as inputs the total number of observations, the number of exceptions and the confidence level. The null hypothesis is

$$H_0 : \hat{p} = \frac{m}{n}$$

The POF is performed as a likelihood-ratio test, which calculates the ratio between the maximum probabilities of an outcome under the two hypotheses. In this case the likelihood ratio L_K is defined as

$$L_P = -2\ln\left[\frac{p^m (1-p)^{n-m}}{\frac{m^m}{n}\left(1-\frac{m}{n}\right)^{n-m}} \right]$$

Under the null hypothesis, the statistic is asymptotically distributed as a chi-square, with one degree of freedom. The null hypothesis is rejected, and the model deemed inaccurate, when the value of L_P exceeds the critical value of the χ^2.

The disadvantages of Kupiec's test are its weakness with one-year sample size (regulatory standard), and, as mentioned above, the fact that it does not consider how exceptions are distributed over time.

In order to overcome the limitations of the POF test, Kupiec, again in 1995, developed the time until first failure (TUFF) test, that measures the time τ until the first exception occurs. In this case the likelihood ratio L_T is given by

$$L_T = -2\ln\left[\frac{p(1-p)^{\tau-1}}{\frac{m}{n}\left(1-\frac{m}{n}\right)^{\tau-1}} \right]$$

The statistic is again distributed as a chi-square with one degree of freedom, with the same acceptance and rejections criteria as the POF test. The main weakness of the TUFF test is the inability to identify bad models.

Both of Kupiec's models fail in detecting the clustering of exceptions, which is an important feature VaR users want to have. Therefore tests of conditional coverage have been developed, to examine not only the frequency of VaR violations, but also the time when they occur.

The most popular conditional coverage model was proposed in 1998 by Christoffersen, as a model based on log-likelihood (as Kupiek's), including separate statistics for the independence of exceptions.

The test is based on an indicator variable, taking a value of one if VaR is exceeded, and a value of zero if there is no violation. Assuming that the indicator in each day is $j \in (0,1)$ conditioned on being $i \in (0,1)$ in the previous day, there are four possible outcomes x_{ij}, for each couple of consecutive days, expressed by

$$x_{00}, \; x_{01}, \; x_{10}, \; x_{11}$$

The probability p_i of observing an exception on some specific day, conditional on state i in the previous day, is given by

$$p_0 = \frac{x_{01}}{x_{00} + x_{01}}$$

$$p_1 = \frac{x_{11}}{x_{10} + x_{11}}$$

so that the unconditional probability is given by

$$p = \frac{x_{01} + x_{11}}{x_{00} + x_{01} + x_{10} + x_{11}}$$

Under the null hypothesis, the exceptions on consecutive days should be independent, so that $p_0 = p_1$. The likelihood ratio for testing independence of exceptions is

$$L_{\perp} = -2 \ln \left[\frac{p^{x_{01}+x_{11}} (1-p)^{x_{00}+x_{10}}}{p_0^{x_{01}} (1-p_0)^{x_{00}} p_1^{x_{11}} (1-p_1)^{x_{10}}} \right]$$

The Christoffersen framework is such that it is possible to obtain an aggregate measure of goodness of fit of VaR model, and the independence of exceptions by just adding $L_{\perp}$ to Kupiec's L_P, so that the conditional coverage is given by

$$L_C = L_{\perp} + L_P$$

Again, the statistics are distributed as a chi-square, but with two degrees of freedom. If the statistics are lower than the critical values, the model is successful and both conditions are fulfilled.

In case the model does not pass the test, it may depend from either failure of VaR model, or clustered exceptions, or both. In order to grasp which effect is determining the failure, the statistics forming L_C can obviously be calculated separately.

12.3.2 *Expected shortfall*

Sub-additivity leads to lower risk for well-diversified portfolios, but VaR shows an opposite behaviour, and diversification leads to an increase of the risk associated with the aggregate portfolio.

Such a property is very important in that it relates to the convexity of the risk surface, therefore playing an important role in portfolio optimization. Convexity of the risk surface ensures the presence of a unique minimum, and no local optimal points.

VaR is criticized for not presenting the whole picture of the risk situation of a portfolio or company. When choosing one measure to describe the risk in a particular situation, the problem with VAR is that, when used in an attempt to limit the risks taken by a trader, it can lead to undesirable results.

Example 12.1: Suppose a bank gives instruction to a trader to keep the one-day 99% VAR below a €10,000,000 threshold. The risk for the bank is that the trader will fulfil the instruction by constructing a portfolio respecting the 99% VaR condition, but at the expense of a 1% chance of a loss of €500,000,000. The trader is satisfying the risk limits imposed by the bank, but is clearly taking unacceptable risks. Most traders would, of course, not behave in this way – but some might.

Recall that, when a risk measure is used for specifying capital requirements, it can be assimilated to the amount of capital required to make a financial position acceptable to regulators.

So it is important to understand how the VaR method can be overtaken and improved in order to give better estimates of the required capital. VaR answers show what is the minimum loss incurred in the α% worst cases, of a portfolio.

Expected shortfall, on the other hand, answers the more elaborated question on what is the expected loss incurred in the α worst cases of the portfolio, describing at full what happens on average when the VaR quantile is exceeded.

If the distribution function of the portfolio is continuous, the answer to this question is given by a tail conditional expectation

$$E_{TC,\alpha}(x) = -E\{x \mid x \le x_\alpha\}$$

where

x_α is the quantile corresponding to α, or $1-\alpha$% VaR.

For generic non-normal distributions the relationship is no longer valid, and another statistic is needed.

Define an order statistics, on an n-tuple of sorted values $(x_1, x_2, ..., x_n)$, given by

$$x_{1,n} \le x_{2,n} ... \le x_{n,n}$$

The number of elements in the sample can be approximated by

$$q = (n\alpha) = \max(m \mid m \le n\alpha),$$

where

$m \in \mathbb{N}$ is an integer
which is the integer part of $n\alpha\%$.

The set of $\alpha\%$ worst cases is then represented by the least q outcomes

$$\left(x_{1,n}, x_{2,n}, \ldots, x_{q,n}\right)$$

A generic natural estimator for the expected loss in the α worst case is given by the expected shortfall, calculated as the average of the last $\alpha\%$ outcomes x_i, with a negative sign, and can be written as

$$ES_{\alpha,n}(x) = -\frac{\sum_{i=1}^{q} x_{i,n}}{q} \tag{12.2}$$

The formula in (12.2) can be expanded using indicator functions in order to get the definition of expected shortfall.

In particular, it is possible to give a simple proof of the sub-additivity of the measure, by considering two variables x and y, with a number of simultaneous realizations

$$\left[\left(x_1, y_1\right), \left(x_2, y_2\right), \ldots, \left(x_n, y_n\right)\right]$$

Consider the risk measure for a portfolio of the two variables, as defined by

$$ES_{\alpha,n}(x+y) = \frac{\sum_{i=1}^{q}(x+y)_{i,n}}{q}$$

The sum of the ordered values picked one by one from each variable, is bigger than the inner sum of the elements x and y in each set of simultaneous realizations, as described above. It follows that

$$\frac{\sum_{i=1}^{q}(x+y)_{i,n}}{q} \leq \frac{\sum_{i=1}^{q}\left(x_{i,n} + y_{i,n}\right)}{q}$$

From the fact that the right-hand side of the inequality is equal to the sum of the expected shortfalls of the two variables, it follows that

$$ES_{\alpha,n}(x+y) \leq ES_{\alpha,n}(x) + ES_{\alpha,n}(x)$$

which proves sub-additivity.

This definition provides a risk measure perfectly satisfying all the axioms of coherency.

Now note that the ordering statistics can be imposed by using indicator functions, so that

$$-\frac{\sum_{i=1}^{w} x_{i,n}}{q} = -\frac{\sum_{i=1}^{w} x_{i,n} 1_{\{i \leq q\}}}{q} \tag{12.3}$$

Let x be the profit/loss of a portfolio on a specified time horizon T and let $\alpha \in (0,1)$ some specified probability level. It can be shown that, after some mathematical passages, this leads to the expanded formulation of equation (12.3) so that the expected shortfall can be written as

$$ES_{\alpha,n}(x+y) = -\frac{1}{\alpha}\left[E\left(x1_{\{x \leq x_\alpha\}}\right) - x_\alpha\left(P(x - x_\alpha) - \alpha\right)\right]$$

The risk measure, formulated in this way, satisfies all the axioms of coherence, as already mentioned.

12.3.3 *Conditional VaR*

Controlling risk over a short time horizon requires conditional VaR estimates, basing the risk measurement for some period $t + \Delta t$, on the information up to time t. It is therefore defined as

$$\Pr\left(R_{t+\Delta t} < -VaR_{t+\Delta t} \mid \mathcal{F}_t\right) = \alpha$$

where

$\Pr\left(R_{t+\Delta t} < -VaR_{t+\Delta t} \mid \mathcal{F}_t\right) = \alpha$ is the portfolio return between t and $t + \Delta t$
$\mathcal{F}_t$ is the filtration up to time t.

There are many methods available for producing robust estimations of conditional VaR (CVaR). RiskMetrics™ produced a model based on a restricted GARCH (1,1) model, with $\alpha + \beta = 1$, modelling the conditional variance as

$$\sigma_{t+\Delta t}^2 = (1 - \lambda) R_t^2 + \lambda \sigma_t^2$$

resulting in an EWMA model. The model has no explicit mean model, and it is therefore applicable to assets whose returns are close to zero. The VaR is given as usual, and can be written as

$$VaR_{t+\Delta t} = -\sigma_{t+\Delta t} N^{-1}(\alpha)$$

The model is attractive in that there are no parameters to estimate, since the correct values of λ to input in the model are directly suggested by RiskMetrics™ based on empirical studies. Moreover, it can be expanded to large portfolios working with matrices and vectors.

The disadvantage of the method is that parameters are not estimated, so that VaR follows a random walk, and the method cannot be adapted to incorporate leverage effect.

Another way to compute CVaR is the fully parametric ARCH method. Assuming a constant mean for the process, the GARCH (1,1) specification of the variance is

$$R_{t+\Delta t} = \mu + \varepsilon_{t+\Delta t}$$

where

$$\sigma^2_{t+\Delta t} = \omega + \beta_1 \varepsilon^2_t + \beta_2 \sigma^2_t, \quad \varepsilon_{t+\Delta t} = \sigma_{t+\Delta t} z_{t+\Delta t}$$

where

$z_{t+\Delta t}$ is an i.i.d. stochastic term, with mean 0 and variance 1.

The parameters of the model are estimated and the conditional VaR at time t is given by

$$VaR_{t+\Delta t} = -\hat{\mu} - \hat{\sigma}_{t+\Delta t} Z_\alpha^{-1}$$

where

Z_α^{-1} is the α-quantile of the distribution of $z_{t+\Delta t}$.

The model provides good flexibility for the modelling of conditional mean and variance, and the specification of the i.i.d. errors. But the density family of the distribution of z must be well specified for the quantile to be right.

Another method of estimation is the Cornish-Fisher approximation, which stands between the parametric and the semi-parametric approach. Compared to the fully parametric ARCH, the conditional variance is expressed by the same formulation.

The only difference is in the distribution of the stochastic term z, which is given by

$$z_{t+\Delta t} \sim g(0,1)$$

where

$g(0,1)$ is an unknown distribution.

Estimation in this case is carried through quasi-maximum likelihood, assuming conditional normality, so that estimated residuals are given by

$$\hat{z}_{t+\Delta t} \sim \frac{\hat{\varepsilon}_{t+\Delta t}}{\hat{\sigma}_{t+\Delta t}}$$

The CVaR is given again by

$$VaR_{t+\Delta t} = -\hat{\mu} - \hat{\sigma}_{t+\Delta t} Z_{CF}^{-1}$$

with the specific innovation of the Z_{CF}^{-1} given by the Cornish-Fisher approximation, which is defined as

$$Z_{CF}^{-1} = N^{-1}(\alpha) + \frac{\gamma}{6}\left\{\left[N^{-1}(\alpha)\right] - 1\right\} + \frac{\kappa-3}{24}\left\{\left[N^{-1}(\alpha)\right]^3 - 3N^{-1}(\alpha)\right\}$$
$$- \frac{\gamma^2}{36}\left\{2\left[N^{-1}(\alpha)\right]^3 - 5N^{-1}(\alpha)\right\}$$

where

γ is the skewness of $\hat{z}_{t+\Delta t}$
κ is the kurtosis of $\hat{z}_{t+\Delta t}$.

The method can be accurate without a parametric assumption, but estimators are not necessarily consistent. Higher moments of standardized residuals may not exist, and anyway, their estimation may be problematic.

The conditional autoregressive VaR was developed in 2004 by Engle and Manganelli, for direct estimation of VaR using quantile regression. The quantile of the return distribution $F_{\alpha,t+\Delta t}^{-1}$ is modelled in the form

$$x_{\alpha,t+\Delta t} = \omega + \beta_1 J_t + \beta_2 x_{\alpha,t}$$

where

$J_{t+\Delta t} = 1_{\{R_{t+\Delta t} < F_{\alpha,t+\Delta t}^{-1}\}}$ is a shock, defined as an exceedance of the previous VaR.

The parameters can be estimated by a minimization algorithm with 'tick' loss target function, as defined by

$$\arg\min \frac{1}{T}\sum_{t=1}^{T} \alpha\left(R_t - x_{\alpha,t}\right)\left(1 - 1_{\{R_t < x_{\alpha,t}\}} x_{\alpha,t}\right) + (1-\alpha)\left(x_{\alpha,t} - R_t\right) 1_{\{R_t < x_{\alpha,t}\}} x_{\alpha,t}$$

This kind of objective function presents many problems when estimating parameters and may result in saddle points and non-differentiability, so that alternative methods of estimation, like genetic algorithms, may have to be implemented.

The VaR is given by

$$VaR_{t+\Delta t} = -x_{\alpha,t+\Delta t} = -F_{\alpha,t+\Delta t}^{-1}$$

It is the method that requires less strong assumptions than any other, and its parametric form provides good convergence to the unknown parameters. The main weakness of the model is the tendency to produce inverted quantiles, so that a 95% VaR may be lower than a 95% VaR.

Summary

The two main steps in measuring portfolio risk are the modelling of joint movements of the risk factors and the modelling of the impact of changes on each factor, to the portfolio value.

Multivariate distribution of risk factors involves describing the dependence structure of the factor returns, and linear correlation is not the best approach to use when dealing with financial data.

Copula functions extend the concept of dependence, and new correlation measures, introducing a new approach. They have many applications in quantitative finance, and in particular for financial risk management purposes.

Copulas find application in market risk and credit risk, where it is common practice, in risk management, to assume a multivariate normal distribution. However, empirical studies prove that normality is the wrong choice, which fails in capturing the dependence structure among risk factors.

Extreme value theory is the modern science of modelling the maxima of a random variable. The main result of EVT relates in fact to the distribution of sample maxima and minima.

The histogram of the data is the first thing to analyse when applying EVT to time series. Most financial time series have been proven to be fat-tailed, so that a graph of the quantiles is the best method to judge the goodness of fit of the series to the model parameters.

The parameters of the extreme distribution can be estimated under several assumptions. It is generally assumed that extreme values follow a precisely defined distribution, the generalized extreme value distribution.

The tail observations can follow the GEV distribution exactly or roughly, depending on the single data set. MLE can be used for estimation, and numerical methods in general provide the estimates, given no closed form solution exists.

The VaR backtesting technique is the statistical comparison of actual gains and losses on a portfolio, to the estimated VaR values. It is crucial to perform backtesting and define coherent measures, when checking for the accuracy of market risk measurement.

Sub-additivity is a key feature in determining the coherence of a risk measure. Due to diversification properties, a sub-additive risk measure allows for reducing risk through combination of several positions.

However, VaR shows an opposite behaviour, and diversification leads to an increase of the risk associated with the aggregate portfolio. VaR is criticized for not presenting the whole picture of the risk situation of a portfolio or company.

Bibliography

Acerbi, C. and Tasche, D. 2002. Expected Shortfall: A Natural Coherent Alternative to Value at Risk. *Economic Notes*, 31(2): 379–388.

Artzner, P., Delbaen, F., Eber, J.M. and Heath, D. 1999. Coherent Measures of Risk. *Mathematical Finance*, 9(3): 203–228.

Balkema, A. and de Haan, L. 1974. Residual Life Time at Great Age. *Annals of Probability*, 2: 792–804.

Basle Committee of Banking Supervision. 1996. Supervisory Framework for the Use of 'Backtesting' in Conjunction with the Internal Models Approach to Market Risk Capital Requirements.

Cherubini, U., Luciano, E. and Vecchiato, W. 2004. *Copula Methods in Finance*. Wiley.

Christoffersen, P. 1998. Evaluating Interval Forecasts. *International Economic Review*, 39: 841–862.

Crouhy, M., Galai, D. and Robert, M. 2000. *Risk Management*. McGraw-Hill Professional.

Damodaran, A. 2007. Strategic Risk Taking: A Framework for Risk Management. Pearson Education.

Embrechts, P., Kluppelberg, C. and Mikosch, T. 1997. *Modelling Extremal Events for Insurance and Finance. Applications of Mathematics*. 2nd Edition. Springer.

Embrechts, P., Lindskog, F. and McNeil, A. 2003. Modelling Dependence with Copulas and Applications to Risk Management. In S. Rachev (Ed.). *Handbook of Heavy Tailed Distributions in Finance*. Elsevier. 331–385.

Fisher, R.A. and Tippett, L.H.C. 1928. Limiting Forms of the Frequency Distribution of the Largest and Smallest Member of a Sample. *Mathematical Proceedings of the Cambridge Philosophical Society*, 24: 180–190.

Frank, M.J. 1979. On the Simultaneous Associativity of $F(x,y)$ and $x + y - F(x,y)$. *Aequationes Mathematicae*, 19: 194–226.

Frey, R. and McNeil, A.J. 2001. *Modelling Dependent Default*. ETH Zurich Preprint.

Frey, R. and McNeil, A.J. 2002. VaR and Expected Shortfall in Portfolios of Dependent Credit Risks: Conceptual and Practical Insights. *Journal of Banking and Finance*, 26: 1317–1344.

Gilli, M. and Kellezi, E. 2006. An Application of Extreme Value Theory for Measuring Financial Risk. *Computational Economics*, 27(2–3): 207–228.

Gnedenko, B.V. 1943. Sur la distribution limite du terme maximum d'une série aléatoire. *Annals of Mathematics*, 44: 423–453.

Gumbel, E.J. 1958. *Statistics of Extremes*. Columbia University Press.

Gumbel, E.J. 1960. Bivariate Exponential Distributions. *Journal of the American Statistical Association*, 55: 698–707.

Jenkinson, A.F. 1955. The Frequency Distribution of the Annual Maximum (Minimum) Values of Meteorological Events. *Quarterly Journal of the Royal Meteorological Society*, 81: 158–172.

Kendall, M.G. 1938. A New Measure of Rank Correlation. *Biometrika*, 30: 81–93.

Kendall, M.G. 1962. *Rank Correlation Methods*. 3rd Edition. Hafner Publishing Company.

Kimeldorf, G. and Sampson, N. 1975. One-Parameter Families of Bivariate Distributions. *Communications in Statistics*, 4: 293–301.

Kole, E., Verbeek, M. and Koedijk, K.C.G. 2007. Selecting Copulas for Risk Management. *Journal of Banking & Finance*, 31(8): 2405–2423.

Kupiec, P. 1995. Techniques for Verifying the Accuracy of Risk Management Models. *Journal of Derivatives*, 3: 73–84.

Longin, M.F. 1999. *From Value at Risk to Stress Testing: The Extreme Value Approach*. Center for Economic Policy Research. Discussion Paper No. 2161.

McNeil, A., Frey, R. and Embrechts, P. 2005. *Quantitative Risk Management: Concepts, Techniques and Tools*. Princeton University Press.

Nelsen, R.B. 1999. An Introduction to Copulas. *Lecture Notes in Statistics*, 139. Springer Verlag.

Pickands, J. 1975. Statistical Inference Using Extreme Order Statistics. *Annals of Statistics*, 3: 119–131.

Romano, C. 2002. *Calibrating and Simulating Copula Functions: An Application to the Italian Stock Market*. CIDEM, working paper.

Sklar, A. 1959. Fonctions de répartition à dimensions et leurs marges. *Publications de l'Institut de Statistique de l'Université de Paris*, 8: 229–231.

Trivedi, P.K. and Zimmer, D.M. 2005. Copula Modeling: An Introduction for Practitioners. *Foundations and Trends in Econometrics*, 1(1): 1–111.
von Mises, R. 1936. La distribution de la plus grande de *n* valeurs. *Selected Papers Volumen II*. American Mathematical Society Providence. R.I. 1954. 271–294.

Exercises

Questions

1. What are the limits of linear correlation, making it necessary to use more sophisticated methods?
2. Define how the ranking of data leads to improvement in correlation measurement.
3. What are the advantages and disadvantages of using a Gumbel copula for modelling dependence?
4. What major types of financial risk benefit more from the application of copula functions?
5. What is the principle behind the use of extreme value theory for data modelling?
6. Explain how backtesting can result in improved performance of VaR modelling.
7. What are the disadvantages of Kupiec's test for VaR accuracy?
8. Explain why expected shortfall is a more accurate risk measure than VaR. What property is the factor in stating so?
9. What are the main changes in VaR estimation, when conditioning to the past information?
10. What are the advantages and disadvantages of applying a Cornish-Fisher approximation method to CVaR estimation?

Appendix: VaR for portfolios of derivatives

When the relationship between factor returns and the change in market value of a portfolio is not linear, the linearity assumption is no longer guaranteed, and the distribution of ΔV will generally be non-normal.

Looking at numerical examples on portfolios containing a non-linear asset, like a financial option, shows that ΔV distribution is far from normality, with high levels of skewness and kurtosis. It follows that standard delta-normal approaches, which are based on linearity, are questionable for portfolios including options.

Recall that the gamma of a portfolio including non-linear products can be defined as

$$\Gamma = \frac{\partial^2 V}{\partial R^2}$$

Such a term is neglected in a linear model for portfolio value. In a portfolio consisting of derivatives on one risk factor, the profit and loss distribution showing a positive gamma tends to be positively skewed and vice versa.

It follows that, for portfolio with positive gamma, linear approximation (and normality assumption) will lead to an overestimate of VaR, and low figures in the case of portfolios with negative gamma.

The quadratic VaR methods are therefore based on a second order Taylor approximation, representing the change in market value of a portfolio, in terms of the underlying factors. For a portfolio made of *n* assets, it is given by equation

$$\Delta V = \delta^{\mathsf{T}} \mathbf{r} + \frac{1}{2} \mathbf{r}^{\mathsf{T}} \Gamma \mathbf{r} \tag{12.4}$$

where

δ is an $n \times 1$ vector of sensitivities to each factor (asset)
$\mathbf{r}$ is an $n \times 1$ vector of factor returns
Γ is the $n \times n$ gamma matrix of adjusted returns.

The VaR quantile, given the non-linearity in (12.4) cannot be calculated in closed form, but the moments of the distribution can be calculated. Given the structure of the portfolio and the normality of factor returns, the expected value of ΔV is given by

$$E(\Delta V) = \frac{1}{2} tr[\Gamma \Sigma] \tag{12.5}$$

where

$tr[.]$ is the trace of a matrix, defined as the sum of the elements on the diagonal
Σ is the $n \times n$ covariance matrix.

The variance is given by

$$Var(\Delta V) = \delta^{\mathsf{T}} \Sigma \delta + \frac{1}{2} tr[\Gamma \Sigma]^2 \tag{12.6}$$

Consider now the standardized variable for ΔV

$$X = \frac{\Delta V - E(\Delta V)}{\sqrt{Var(\Delta V)}}$$

The higher m-th moments of X can be calculated as

$$E(X^m) = \frac{\frac{1}{2} m! \delta^{\mathsf{T}} \Sigma \delta [\Gamma \Sigma]^{m-2} + \frac{1}{2}(m-1)! tr(\Gamma \Sigma)^m}{Var(\Delta V)^{\frac{m}{2}}}$$

In order to calculate the desired quantile, three different approaches are possible. The moment matching approach approximates the distribution of ΔV, by finding a handy distribution, for which quantiles can be easily calculated.

In practical uses, the most common way of applying the method involves the approximation of the distribution of ΔV by a normal distribution with mean and variance given by the equations (12.5) and (12.6).

Another approach involves approximating the target quantile through a Cornish-Fisher expansion. As long as the moments of the distribution are known, the method leads to an analytical approximation of the quantile.

13 Advanced topics

Previous chapters show how standard risk management is built on models like VaR, and the hedging is performed using techniques and instruments, including more or less complex financial derivatives.

The standard time frequency of the measures explored so far ranges from one day to one year, depending on the type of risk to be measured, and the technique or instrument adopted for measurement and hedging.

This chapter aims at moving further in the analysis of financial risk measurement and management, introducing advanced topics, which relax the above assumptions about methodologies, instruments and time frequency.

VaR advances have been developed in order to overcome limitations of standard methodology, regarding the parametric, historical simulation and Monte Carlo simulation approach.

On the instrument side, alternative risk transfer stands as an alternative to standard insurance and reinsurance market. ART methodologies and derivatives provide a different approach to specific types of non-standard risks.

Time series at high frequency behave differently to those at standard frequency. It is therefore important to analyse the behaviour of intraday data, the intraday volatility measurement techniques, and the application to financial risk management of intraday data.

After studying this chapter you will be able to answer the following questions, among others:

1. What are the recent advances in the calculation of VaR, to overcome some of its limitations?
2. What is alternative risk transfer, and how can the ART market be described?
3. How can ART products be used to gain insurance against non-standard types of risk?
4. What is high-frequency finance, and how does statistical analysis change when increasing data frequency?
5. How can heterogeneous volatility be modelled?

The first section of the chapter deals with advances in VaR methods, expressed as modified parametric, historical and simulation approaches. The second section is about the ART market, primary types and products, and insurance derivatives. The final part deals with high-frequency trading, the measurement of intraday volatility and the market risk models for intraday data.

13.1 VaR advances

Learning outcomes

1. Describe modified delta-VaR, and its calculation.
2. List and comment on the steps of the modified historical simulation.
3. Elaborate on how simulations and scenario analysis applied to VaR can be modified.

13.1.1 Modified delta-VaR

Standard VaR methods suffer from implementation risk, which relates to the possibility for the same model to produce different estimates when applied by different users. From the pioneering work of Marshall and Siegel (1997) it can be observed from the VaR results obtained from different risk management system developers, that, when applying different systems, the VaR estimates are different, even if applied to the same portfolio, using the same model.

VaR model sensitivities play a crucial role in the variability of estimates, as well as the portfolio composition. There is a relationship between the type of asset on which risk is measured, and the discrepancies.

Non-linear securities entail higher levels of variability in VaR estimates, compared to linear products, which suggests implementing sensitivity analysis to underlying assumptions, parallel to the VaR computation.

Standard VaR models are meant to fit current information, and observed risks, without being able to capture transition periods, which are often characterized by important structural changes, additional risks, liquidity draining, broken correlations across assets and markets.

Moreover, trading positions are dynamic and change over time, making actual VaR estimates no longer adequate for future developments. There is also a problem of data, which are scarce for some types of assets, while VaR assumes an adequate amount of data is available. This is usually overcome by mapping those assets onto well-known ones, therefore reducing estimation accuracy.

Researchers in the late 1990s started suggesting methodologies to improve VaR, introducing relevant modifications of traditional techniques and new ways of VaR evaluations.

Modern research has developed modifications of traditional ways to measure VaR, as well as new approaches to VaR estimations and interpretations. Standard delta-VaR methods assume normality in the vector $\mathbf{x}_t^\Delta$ of the changes in risk factors, conditional to the filtration till time t, so that

$$\left(\mathbf{x}_{t+1}^\Delta \middle| \mathcal{F}_t\right) \sim N\left(0, \Sigma_t\right)$$

Delta approximation to VaR assumes that changes in portfolio value are a linear combination of the underlying risk factors, so that

$$\Delta V_{t+1} \equiv V_{t+1}\left(\mathbf{x}_{t+1} + \mathbf{x}_{t+1}^\Delta\right) - V_{t+1}\left(\mathbf{x}_{t+1}\right)$$
$$\approx \delta_t^T \alpha_{t+1} \tag{13.1}$$

where

$\mathbf{x}_{t+1}$ is the vector of risk factors at time $t+1$

δ_t is the vector of sensitivities of portfolio price to each factor, so that $\delta_{i,t} = \dfrac{\partial V_t}{\partial \mathbf{x}_t}$

α_{t+1} is the vector of the weighted changes in the factors so that $\alpha_{i,t} = w_i \Delta X_{i,t}$.

The message of equation (13.1) is that the change in value of the portfolio can be expressed as the difference between the value of the portfolio after and before the change in the underlying factor driving it.

The change is then conveniently approximated by the sensitivities of the portfolio value to the various factors, multiplied by the weighted changes in the factors themselves, where each weighted change is given by the product of the weight of the factor in the portfolio, and the change in value of the factor itself.

Recall that a further improvement is to add the second order effect to the approximation in order to get the delta-gamma approach to VaR. The quadratic approximation to the portfolio value changes is given by

$$\Delta V_{t+1} \approx \delta_t^T \alpha_{t+1} + \frac{1}{2} \alpha_{t+1}^T \Gamma_t \alpha_{t+1} \tag{13.2}$$

where

$$\Gamma_t = \frac{\partial^2 (V_t \mid \mathbf{x}_t)}{\partial \mathbf{x}_t \partial \mathbf{x}_t^T}$$

is the gamma matrix of the second order sensitivities at time t.

The main limitation of the delta-gamma approach is that the normal distribution does not approximate the actual distribution of ΔV. Therefore it is no longer possible to use a normal-distribution percentile approach.

It is natural to then move to improvements of the delta-gamma approach. Among others, a popular method is the delta-gamma-Monte Carlo, that approximates the changes in portfolio value following four simple steps.

Summarizing, the algorithm can be described as:

1. Draw random values of $\mathbf{x}_{t+1}^\Delta$ from the relevant distribution.
2. Calculate theoretical values of ΔV at each draw, using delta-gamma approximation.
3. Iteratively repeat steps 1 and 2.
4. Form a distribution of the ΔV values by ordering them.
5. The VaR estimate is the negative of the $(1-\alpha)$-th percentile of the obtained ΔV distribution.

Wilson (1994), Fallon (1996) and Pritsker (1997) developed an optimization approach to VaR. The delta-gamma-minimization method in fact uses a delta-gamma approximation under the assumption of normally distributed changes in risk factors.

The approach uses the formulation as in (13.2), with the weighted factor changes as an input to the program, which is

$$-VaR_t = \min_{Y}\left(\delta_t^T \alpha_{t+1} + \frac{1}{2} \alpha_{t+1}^T \Gamma_t \alpha_{t+1} \right)$$

subject to

$$\alpha_{t+1}^T \Sigma^{-1} \alpha_{t+1} \le \eta_{\chi^2(k)}$$

where

Σ is the covariance matrix of risk factors

$\eta_{\chi^2(k)}$ is the $\eta\%$ critical value of the central chi-squared distribution with k degrees of freedom.

The delta-gamma minimization method offers the advantage of not imposing the assumption of joint normality, also avoiding the computational burden of data generation in Monte Carlo simulation.

Zangari (1996) and Pritsker (1997) developed a method based on delta-gamma approximation, called the delta-gamma-Johnson. The method consists in selecting a distributional form for the model and estimating the parameters, matching moments from first to fourth.

The cumulative density function of the distribution gives the VaR estimate. The strong point of the method is its analytical form. But it uses information up to the fourth moment, which makes it less precise than the Monte Carlo methods.

VaR can also be estimated through a Cornish-Fisher expansion, which approximates through delta-gamma the distribution of ΔV and makes use of the normality assumption for the changes in the risk factors x_t^Δ.

The Cornish-Fisher expansion is used to estimate the $(1-\alpha)$–th percentile of the standardized distribution ΔV_α^{ST}. First of all it is necessary to express the moment generating function of ΔV_α^{ST}, which is defined as

$$M\left(\Delta V_{\alpha,t}^{ST}\right) = E\left(e^{t\Delta V_\alpha^{ST}}\right)$$

The following step is to calculate the cumulants c_i of ΔV_α^{ST}, that can be calculated from the log expansion of $M\left(\Delta V_{\alpha,t}^{ST}\right)$, as given by

$$\ln\left[M\left(\Delta V_{\alpha,t}^{ST}\right)\right] = \sum_{i=1}^{\infty} c_i \frac{t_i}{i!}$$

as given by

$$\Delta V_\alpha^{ST} = N(\alpha) + \frac{1}{6}\left[N(\alpha)^2 - 1\right]c_3 + \frac{1}{24}\left[N(\alpha)^3 - 3N(\alpha)\right]c_4$$
$$- \frac{1}{36}\left[2N(\alpha)^3 - 5N(\alpha)\right]c_3^2$$

Besides the advantage of being an analytical model, the method partially ignores the information, with a lack in accuracy.

13.1.2 *Historical simulation revisited*

The method of bootstrapped historical simulation was suggested by, among others, Duffie and Pan (1997). It generates returns of risk factors via bootstrap from historical observations, drawing data from updated returns.

Starting from the observed returns $r_{i,t}$, at time $t = 1,...T$ on asset $i = 1,...n$, with a covariance matrix Σ, past returns can be updated according to a new estimate of the volatilities, by

$$\tilde{r}_{i,t} = r_{i,t} \frac{\tilde{\sigma}_i}{\sigma_i}$$

where

$\tilde{r}_{i,t}$ is the updated return on asset i at time t
σ_i is the historical standard deviation of asset i
$\tilde{\sigma}_i$ is the new estimate of the standard deviation of asset i.

Another approach updates the past returns using new estimates on both volatilities and correlations. In this case the updated return vector is defined as

$$\tilde{\mathbf{r}}_t = \hat{\Sigma}^{1/2} \Sigma^{-1/2} \mathbf{r}_t$$

where

$\mathbf{r}_t$ is the vector of returns at time t
$\hat{\Sigma}$ is the updated covariance matrix.

An approach that was proposed by Butler and Schachter in 1996 and 1998 combines classical historical simulation with kernel estimation, allowing for improved VaR measurement and construction of confidence intervals.

The first is the approximation of probability density function and cumulative distribution function of the portfolio returns. Standard historical simulation involves piecewise p.d.f. Using kernel estimation, the p.d.f. is defined as

$$\hat{f}_\kappa(x) = \frac{1}{n(0.9\sigma n^{-2})} \sum_{i=1}^{n} \frac{1}{\sqrt{2\pi}} e^{-\frac{1}{2}\left(\frac{x-r_i}{0.9\sigma n^{-2}}\right)} \qquad (13.3)$$

where

n is the sample size
σ is the volatility of ΔV
x is the current point of estimation.

The cumulative distribution function (c.d.f.) is obtained by integrating (13.3) or by the empirical c.d.f.

$$\hat{F}_x(x) = \frac{1}{n}\sum_{i=1}^{n}1_{\{X_i \le x\}}$$

(13.4)

where

$1_{\{\}}$ is the indicator function.

A second step involves the approximation of order statistic corresponding to the chosen confidence level. Denote by k the i-th order statistics, and by $f(k)$ and $F(k)$ the p.d.f. and c.d.f. respectively.

Butler and Schachter estimate both p.d.f. and c.d.f. of the i-th order statistics, employing the above (13.3) and (13.4). The estimate of $f(k)$ is then given by

$$\hat{f}(k) = \frac{n!}{i!(k-i)!}\hat{f}_x(x)\hat{F}_x(x)^{i-1}\left[1-\hat{F}_x(x)\right]^{n-i}$$

and the estimate of is $F(k)$ given by

$$\hat{f}(k) = \sum_{j=i}^{n}\frac{n!}{j!(k-j)!}\hat{F}_x(k)^{j}\left[1-\hat{F}_x(k)\right]^{n-j}$$

The last steps estimate VaR using the first moment (mean) of the returns p.d.f., while the variance reflects the precision of the VaR measure, and leads to the construction of confidence intervals.

The moments of the estimated p.d.f. of order statistics are obtained through a 12-point Gauss-Hermite integration. The mean is then given by

$$\hat{E}(k) = \int_{-\infty}^{\infty}kf(k)dk$$

$$\approx \frac{1}{12}\sum_{j=1}^{12}\omega_j k_j e^{k_j^2}\hat{f}(k_j)$$

The variance is given by

$$\hat{\sigma}^2(k) = \int_{-\infty}^{\infty}k^2 f(k)dk$$

$$\approx \frac{1}{12}\sum_{j=1}^{12}\omega_j k_j^2 e^{k_j^2}\hat{f}(k_j) - \hat{E}(k)^2$$

where

ω_j is the j-th integration weight
k_j is the j-th point of integral approximation.

It follows from the estimation of the variance of the p.d.f., that the estimate of VaR is

$$V\hat{a}R = \frac{1}{12}\sum_{j=1}^{12}\omega_j k_j^2 e^{k_j^2}\,\hat{f}\left(k_j\right)$$

The confidence interval of $V\hat{a}R$ for large samples can be formed using the expression of the standard deviation

$$\hat{\sigma}(k) \approx \sqrt{\frac{1}{12}\sum_{j=1}^{12}\omega_j k_j^2 e^{k_j^2}\,\hat{f}\left(k_j\right) - \hat{E}(k)^2}$$

For large samples, the quantile is normally distributed and the confidence interval can be constructed in the standard form.

13.1.3 *Modified Monte Carlo and scenario analysis*

As explained in Chapter 5, VaR can be estimated, among other methods, through Monte Carlo simulation and scenario analysis. The Monte Carlo method estimates VaR based on simulations of the changes in portfolio value.

The simulation involves the specification of a model for the underlying factors, and the generation of simulated paths for the factors. Prices are simulated in the space of changes in the underlying price differentials, $h_i = h_1, h_2, ..., h_n$, over a time interval $(0, T)$, and are defined as

$$h_{i,t} = x_{i,t} - x_{i,t-1}$$

As an example of that, recall that, when simulating stock prices following a Brownian motion process, which in the discretized form is given by

$$\frac{\Delta S}{S} = \mu dt + \sigma \varepsilon_t \sqrt{\Delta t}$$

the task is to draw the random variable ε_t, of the process, for as many $t = 1, 2, ..., T$ are chosen.

Skipping the standard steps of the classical Monte Carlo simulation method, which should be clear to the student at this stage, it is possible to consider modifications that allow for a more consistent approach to the simulation problem.

Quasi-Monte Carlo methods encompass deterministic schemes with different levels of complexity. MC and QMC methods both approximate an integral over the unit cube. The integral is approximated by

$$\int_{[0,1]^m} f(y)dy \approx \frac{1}{n}\sum_{i=0}^{n-1} f(\mathbf{x}_i)$$

where each of the n vectors $\mathbf{x}_i$ is made of m elements in the hypercube, so that $\mathbf{x}_i = x_{i,1}, x_{i,2}, ..., x_{i,m}$. The approximation discretizes the smooth integral, making it possible to use simulated data to solve the problem.

What differentiates the standard MC from the QMC is that, in the latter, the elements of each vector are chosen to be deterministic, whereas they are selected as random draws from some known distribution, as seen previously.

The basic idea is to use numbers that are deterministic, to be used in place of the usual random numbers, to obtain faster convergence with known error bounds, leading to more efficient numerical procedures and deterministic error bounds.

Scenario analysis for VaR is usually translated into stress testing, that measures the impact of variations in the various financial variables on the value of the portfolio. Other methods have been suggested.

In 1997, Boudoukh *et al.* proposed to apply a measure which is complementary to VaR, the worst-case-scenario (WCS), that evaluates the size of the worst losses, and can be formulated as

$$r_{WS} = \min\left(r_1, r_2, ..., r_i, ..., r_n\right)$$

where

r_i is the *i*-th observed portfolio return.

The WCS measure takes the distribution of losses $F\left(r_{WS}\right)$ during the worst trading interval over a certain time horizon, which can be simulated by random draws from a pre-specified distribution. Boudoukh *et al.* (1997) find evidence of WCS consistently overestimating the losses, compared to VaR.

13.2 Alternative risk transfer

Learning outcomes

1. Describe the ART market and its role in insurance and reinsurance.
2. List and comment on the primary ART contracts and products.
3. Define insurance derivatives and elaborate on their structure.

13.2.1 *The ART market*

Alternative risk transfer (ART) expands the set of possible risks that can be insured. Traditional insurance and reinsurance encounter limits and do not provide coverage for some types of risks.

ART picks up instruments from capital markets, expanding the range of available tools, compared to traditional insurance, providing solutions for problems that are unique, improving the situation of the risk breaker.

Some insurance risks are not related to traditional investment risk, and are not based on any economic factor. An example of this class of risks is the natural catastrophe risk, where the adverse event is represented by a natural element.

The relevant frequency of these types of events should imply a high demand for ART products. Hurricanes, tsunamis and other natural phenomena have the power to cause severe financial strain as well as a number of insurer insolvencies.

The interest in alternative markets is, among other things, a function of the cost of traditional insurance and reinsurance. The market of insurance of property and casualty is characterized by a high cyclicality, meaning that periods of low prices and easy underwriting are followed by periods of rising rates and more restrictive underwriting.

In times of expensive and restrictive insurance, the ART market becomes an attractive source of relatively cheap coverage of risk, and a good substitute for traditional insurance products.

Some sources report that in the early 2000s, at least 50% of the commercial market in the USA has considered migrating to the ART market, with an increasing trend compared to the previous two decades.

Later on, after 2004, the trend has somehow inverted, and the ART market has passed its peak, following a relaxation in the conditions of traditional markets, that reduced the interest in alternative markets.

While it is hard to give a proper definition of ART, it is possible to identify some features that are typical of the wide range of products involved in the process.

Risk can be transferred through alternative carriers (self-insurance, captives, pools), or alternative products (reinsurance, runoff structures, structured finance, new asset solutions).

ART products share features like being customized for client needs, carrying a multi-year coverage (applicable to multiple lines), and having payoffs eventually linkable to multiple factors (events).

The ART application requires interdisciplinary skills, merging insurance and finance knowledge in order to structure complex transactions. Transferring very specific forms of risk, like catastrophe risk, requires professionals from many sectors.

The ART approach to insurance is very peculiar in that it does not rely on traditional sources of capital. Traditional insurance contracts involve the transfer of risk to a single insurance company, while ART transfers the risk to the capital markets.

Multiple solutions are usually combined to create an optimal ART risk management plan. It is possible to divide the analysis into three main categories, namely products, vehicles and solutions.

Products include insurance and reinsurance products, multi-risk products, insurance derivatives and more. Vehicles are channels used to achieve risk coverage, namely captives and risk retention groups, SPV and reinsurers, capital market subsidiaries.

Solutions are represented by combined use of multiple products and vehicles, like enterprise risk management programs.

Companies have traditionally managed risk by transferring it to insurance companies, or by retaining funds internally as a means of self-insurance. Some firms have used a combination of the two.

The demand for insurance in the last year has brought the development of alternatives to commercial insurance. These instruments include:

- Captives are a special type of insurance company set up to insure the risks of its owner (parent companies).
- Risk-retention groups are made up of entities in the same industry sector, that join each other to provide the group members with liability coverage.
- Risk-purchasing groups are made up of entities sharing the same risks, and purchase liability coverage from admitted insurers and other institutions.

The ART market has grown over the last few years, and it is made up of different types of institutions, including reinsurers, corporate end users, brokers and more. Reinsurers provide traditional insurance channels by taking care of the various stages of the process, like underwriting, rate-making, managing risks and investments.

Insurers and reinsurers represent a large share of the ART market, designing products, investing funds of their clients in a range of products, like catastrophe bonds, specifically designed for ART risk management. Moreover, they manage their own risk exposure.

Most insurers in the world are built up as joint stock companies with limited liability, whose equity is made of capitals supplied by the investors themselves. Other big insurers have taken the form of mutual organizations.

Reinsurers, on the other hand, are mostly constituted as joint stock companies, and are based in Bermuda, to benefit from a favourable tax environment, and a less severe regulatory framework.

Both insurers and reinsurers (at least the biggest ones) are expanding their scope developing new products that conglobate insurance and financial elements, to the extent of generating complex products like CDOs, as treated in previous chapters.

13.2.2 *Primary contracts*

Captives were developed in the 1950s, the oldest type of ART vehicle, as a tool to reduce the costs of risk retention and transfer via traditional insurance. In the 1970s they became very popular among the biggest corporations in the world.

A captive is a type of ART, in the form of an insurance or reinsurance company, which is owned by an association of non-insurance firms. The main feature of a captive is that the insured party directly controls the insurer.

After the 1980s, the tax benefit and general convenience of captives were reduced, so that the markets of insurance and reinsurance reverted back to traditional risk transfer and risk financing methods.

At the beginning of the 2000s captives held $130 billion in assets and $25 billion in premiums, and most of them were based in Bermuda, the country with the most friendly legislation, but not the only one so permissive.

In recent years, captives have been subject to a higher level of regulatory oversight, in particular to ensure participants are aware of the risks and to guarantee a minimum level of prudency about liquidity and solvency.

The operational functioning of captives is similar to insurance and reinsurance companies in that they establish reserves for losses and unpaid premiums, set minimum capital aside and apply portfolio diversification.

Captives provide considerable benefits like flexible risk cover, lower cost compared to classic insurance, possible tax advantages, lower earnings volatility and easy access to the reinsurance market.

On the other hand, there are also disadvantages in the use of captives. For example they require an upfront payment of fees, they lead to capital locking (with reduced flexibility). Moreover they require costly reporting and compliance standards.

A pure captive is owned by a single sponsor, writing insurance contracts only for it. Approximately 70% of the world captives at the beginning of the 2000s were pure captives.

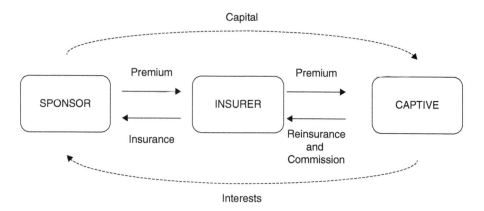

Figure 13.1 The scheme of a captive shows the interconnection between a sponsor company, a hypothetical standard insurer, and the captive, which instead directly gives the insurance required.

The sponsor (writer) has full control over the captive, with direct operational authority in terms of underwriting, investment and premiums. When a loss occurs, the sponsor files a claim to the captive receiving the corresponding refund payment.

Other forms of captive include sister captives, which are owned by a single firm, as the pure captives, but write contracts also for other customers. That increases risk diversification, while still being bounded in a corporate group.

Group captives are insurers owned by a number of companies, writing cover for all of them. Neither ownership nor operations are confined into a single economic area.

A multi-risk product combines various exposures into a single contract, introducing a diversification benefit that reduces the overall cost for aggregate coverage, compared to the sum of the individual parts.

The first class of multi-risk products is the multiple peril products. They are designed to collect all designated exposures into a corporate portfolio, and combine them into a single policy, with a specified premium and a cap. In doing so, it eliminates the individual positions on single perils, aggregating them into a single contract.

A company contracts to have all exposures covered at the same time, therefore no longer worrying about any specific source of risk. The main features of multiple peril contracts include lower transaction costs, eliminating the expenses from contracting each single exposure individually.

Moreover the premium required to the insured part is usually lower, given that risks in the contract are often uncorrelated, and the overall risk exposure is therefore diversified. Another important feature is the lower chance of overinsurance, given that it is very unlikely the firm will have to simultaneously suffer all the losses covered by the contract.

Companies willing to insure multiple perils can use a multi-line policy, containing common conditions and declarations, with the list of specific coverages. The contract may cover properties, business failures, general liability and more.

The commercial general liability policy covers only liability exposure of the client firm, including all ranges of products and damages involved, while the commercial umbrella policy provides protection for very large amounts and a broad range of

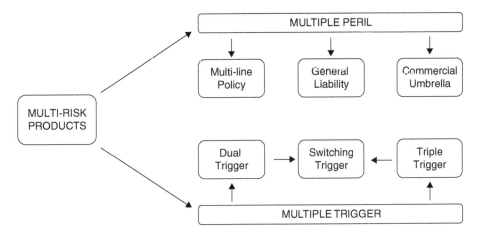

Figure 13.2 Scheme of the structure of a multi-risk ART product.

insurable risks. However, compared to other multi-perils, usually umbrella policies enter in force after a certain amount of losses has already been covered, as an extra coverage on the excess.

The multiple joint coverage can be achieved either through combining several single-line policies, in order to get a master agreement, or using a single text method, where the existing single coverages are rewritten into a new policy, in order to avoid gaps and conflicts that the attachment method may involve.

The second class of multi-risk products includes the multiple trigger contracts. Compared to multiple peril, multiple trigger contracts pay back the insured party only when several events occur at the same time, not just one.

Dual trigger contracts require that two events occur before the payout occurs, while triple triggers require three events to be paid out. These contracts are of course less likely to be liquidated, given the very low combined probability of multiple events occurring.

In general these products are issues on a multi-year basis, with annual trigger resets, coming in different forms. A fixed trigger is a barrier determining whether or not an event occurs, and when a contract will be paid out.

A variable trigger refers to the case when the payout is determined by the level of the trigger itself, which therefore acts as a nominal, not just as a barrier. A switching trigger, finally, varies in relation of the performance of the client's portfolio.

The flexibility of such a scheme makes it possible to create sophisticated structures, permitting resets of the trigger at the time of the event, or aggregation of triggers, to allow multiple event accumulation.

The nature and level of the trigger are normally mutually decided between the parties involved. However, in order to prevent moral hazard, at least one of the triggers is based on external assessment.

In that respect, one should recall that triggers of ART products can be any type of risk, financial or non-financial, threatening the profitability of the client company, so that the range of potential inefficiencies is wide.

The main drawbacks of having multiple triggers is that most contracts involve a high degree of complication, therefore requiring costly efforts to insurers and reinsurers, resulting in higher costs for the clients.

Moreover, they can be considered hybrid products in that they belong to the group of insurance contracts, when hedging non-financial risks, while resulting in being comparable to derivatives when hedging financial risks.

Multi-risk products represent an expanding segment of the ART market, and they are an integral element of the risk management sector worldwide. Even if sometimes they require time and resources, for development, they represent a cheaper alternative to standard insurance and reinsurance methods.

13.2.3 *Insurance derivatives*

As mentioned in previous chapters, financial derivatives can be used to either hedge or speculate, a feature that differentiates them from insurance contracts, which are made exclusively for hedging purposes.

Some insurance derivatives are such that the holder does not have to prove having suffered a loss in order to obtain the benefit from the derivative, so that they are not considered as insurance contracts.

Some features of derivatives contracts make them important instruments in the ART market. These features include a high liquidity, capacity of being cost-effective, flexibility of OTC transactions, no need for the proof of a loss.

Exchange-traded (ET) insurance derivatives have standardized contract terms, generating a mass of liquidity, with lower bid-ask spreads and more effective risk management solutions.

ET catastrophe insurance derivatives are traded on the authorized exchange and can be written on specific indices. They were introduced at the beginning of the 1990s and partially abandoned in the 2000s due to lack of participants.

Temperature derivatives are one of the exceptions to that trend and continue expanding nowadays. They include listed futures and options referencing temperature indices in specific locations.

They were introduced at the end of the 1990s in the Chicago Mercantile Exchange (CME), based on temperatures in ten different cities in the USA. The temperatures involved are taken via official measurement standards, the daily heating degree day (HDD) and cooling degree day (CDD). They are calculated as

$$\text{HDD} = \max\left[0, T_H - \frac{(T_{max} + T_{min})}{2}\right]$$
$$\text{CDD} = \max\left[0, \frac{(T_{max} + T_{min})}{2} - T_H\right]$$

where

T_H is the baseline, a benchmark temperature (typically 18° C)
T_{max} is the maximum daily temperature
T_{min} is the minimum daily temperature.

OTC insurance derivatives are characterized by the high liquidity of the market, and the high customizability of the deals. After both the CBOT contracts and BCOE initiatives have been cut, the OTC market is the only place to deal insurance derivatives nowadays.

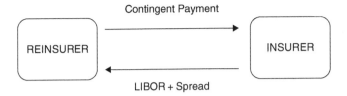

Figure 13.3 The scheme of a catastrophe swap, in terms of the relationship between the insurer and the reinsurer.

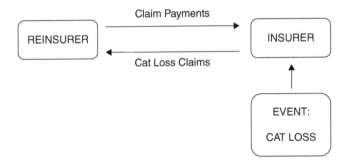

Figure 13.4 A catastrophe swap in case the insured-risk event occurs.

Catastrophe reinsurance swaps are contracts resulting in a synthetic financial transaction, for exchanging a committee fee for a payment based on a catastrophic loss. This allows for getting almost the same protection offered by securitized assets, at a lower cost.

Catastrophe reinsurance swaps are synthetic financial transactions that exchange a commitment fee for a contingent payment based on the onset of a catastrophic loss. the overall strategy gives the same benefits provided by reinsurance or securitization, avoiding the costs and complexity associated with ordinary strategies, or ordinary insurance.

The insurer in a catastrophe swap pays a floating rate (i.e. LIBOR) to a reinsurer, over a period of many years, in exchange for a certain amount of contingent exposure capacity (tied to a defined index, indemnity or parametric event).

If the catastrophe event happens, and a loss is experienced, the reinsurer compensates the counterparty in the swap, and takes over the claim rights through subrogation, otherwise the transaction ends, and the portfolio of the insurer stays unchanged.

Some reinsurers prefer to modify their portfolios through the pure catastrophe swaps, synthetic transactions allowing for an exchange of uncorrelated catastrophe exposure. The actual exposure can be documented through reinsurance agreements, making the deal a swap of reinsurances, rather than a derivative, as commonly defined.

The swap involves risks that are uncorrelated, therefore the insurer involved in the agreement achieves a greater portfolio diversification. For instance, a Japanese reinsurer with an excess of Japanese earthquake risk may swap a portion of its portfolio for other uncorrelated risks, such as North Atlantic hurricane.

Sometimes a swap might involve multiple risks, still uncorrelated. Primary insurance and reinsurance companies in the world, like Swiss Re, Tokyo Marine, and others, have been active in catastrophe swap deals.

Temperature derivatives are customized contracts referencing one or many temperature indices. Starting in the late 1990s, the market for temperature derivatives grew rapidly as more energy companies, then banks and insurers, and then specialized investment funds, began hedging or speculating on US-based temperature indexes.

Also companies from other industries have joined the temperature derivatives market, but corporate by-laws and regulatory restriction often give an incentive to corporations to obtain the temperature cover in the form of standard insurance contracts rather than OTC derivatives.

The main activity on temperature derivatives concentrated on US markets at the beginning, expanding soon to European markets, with trading concentrated on average temperature indices, referencing major European cities.

The market for temperature derivatives in other parts of the world has remained extremely limited, beside major markets like Japan and Australia, due especially to the lack of data.

The industry over the years has developed standardized contracts, setting regular standards like an average tick size, the maximum amount limit, tenor frequencies and reference cities.

Temperature derivatives occur in the form of forwards, swaps, call and put options, as well as combinations like collars (opposite positions on a put and a call with same strike and maturity), straddles (same position on both a call and a put, with same strike and same maturity) and strangles (like a straddle, but with different strikes for the options).

13.3 High-frequency trading

Learning outcomes

1. Describe data filtering procedures for high-frequency data.
2. List and comment on the basic stylized facts of high-frequency time series.
3. Define heterogeneous volatilities and how they can be estimated.

13.3.1 Data filtering

The analysis of high-frequency data has gained relevant importance in recent years, due to traders and investors not being fully satisfied with standard frequency financial market data.

There is a considerable demand for high-quality high-frequency data, at both intra-hour and intra-minute frequency. The analysis of the data allows trading and investment decisions to be made, and sets strategies.

High-frequency data help in understanding the microstructure of the market, to test hypotheses and model development. The improvement of computing power in recent years allows us to collect and store enormous volumes of high-frequency data. Those data have their own characteristics and need corresponding analysing methods.

The main source of high-frequency data are the financial markets, which produce millions of data ticks per day, in term of quotes, prices, volumes, transaction times, and more.

In centralized and regulated markets, like stock exchanges with electronic trading facilities, transaction data are electronically recorded by the exchange and directly provided to interested parties (like NYSE and LIFFE).

High-frequency data sets contain detailed information about transactions and are consistent, while in decentralized OTC markets, data are not recorded by a central institution, and trading goes on for 24 hours per day.

It follows that there is no comprehensive data source, and big data vendors like Reuters and Bloomberg capture the transaction data from the global market, forwarding them to their customers in real time. Data vendors also provide tools to structure customized data sets.

High-frequency data sets are huge by nature, and ticks can reach an amount of 275,000 prices per day for foreign exchange spot rate alone. Such a density of data into a single day represents a source of potential mistakes in the data itself.

As Dacorogna *et al.* underline in their book, the bad ticks must be cleaned, or filtering algorithms have to be implemented, prior to any further analysis. Moreover, given that market transactions take place irregularly, the main feature of high-frequency data is the irregularity in time spacing of the single price.

Inhomogeneous time series introduce specific problems when trying to analyse the data statistically. It might be needed to use interpolation methods to create homogeneous time series for further analysis.

Even if increased computing power has limited the burden of big size of data sets, other features of high-frequency data leave challenges open, in particular about lack of synchrony, bad ticks, time treatment.

Moreover, tick frequencies are different among different securities, and there are intraday seasonal patterns. Yet, perhaps the most difficult aspect of cleaning intraday data is the inability to universally define what is unclean.

Errors can be minimal, like some decimal errors, or significant, like the fractional portion of a number or a trade reported relatively out of sequence. Minimal errors can be easily removed. Treatment of the major errors is more complex, and requires appropriate filtering.

Data filtering involves a trade-off between the purity of the filtered data, and the consistency of the data set properties. In fact, a rough selection would lead to having a useless series, while a finest selection would lead to the change of its statistical properties (overscrubbing).

The marginal scrubbing error is proportional to the tick frequency, but the use of filtering algorithms should be a decision of the single trader, because data processing requires an additional degree of sophistication.

Error definition is unique to the trader and there should be no single correct scrubbed time series applicable to all traders. As research has shown in recent years, the point with high-frequency data is to match real-time data to historical data, rather than obtaining perfect historical data and imperfect real-time data.

Developing a good set of tick filters is equivalent to managing the scrubbing trade-off, so that it can remove spurious data from the series without losing real-time properties of the data.

One of the most common sources of bad data is human error in collecting very high volumes of data, which mostly involve decimal and transposition errors, as well as bad typing of numbers.

Another case relates to bad data from trading processes, when trades are reported out-of-sequence, sold bunched, cancelled, cancelled and replaced, and reported in error, and more.

Data errors may also come from multiple markets trading the same asset simultaneously. In this case there could be mispricing or arbitrage opportunities, generating a differential in price among markets.

In general, the problem at the origin of bad data collection is the asynchronous and voluminous nature of high-frequency financial data. Markets open, generating a high flow of data during the trading hours, to then go off for the closing hours.

Moreover, some types of investors and professionals make trading errors that must be cancelled, replaced or corrected. The human factor is crucial in generating failures, but also technological glitches are sometimes at the basis of data error.

Following Falkenberry (2002), and given all the above aspects, a proper filter should have the following properties:

1. Ability to eliminate outliers from a time series, in terms of a trader's base unit, using techniques and methodologies applicable in real time.
2. Keep the statistical properties of the data set considered, unchanged.
3. Avoid introducing an excessive computational burden, and generating delays due to excessive confirming data points.
4. Show a high degree of flexibility by adapting to securities with different tick frequencies and price levels.

Data filtering can be approached in two different ways. It is possible to search for errors and replace them, through a method that processes the bad ticks in the original time series.

According to the procedure, when a bad price is identified, the choice should be to either cancel it, or substitute the last good value encountered in the series, or replace with some other value not included in the original data set.

Another approach, less realistic and more complicated, involves mapping the basic price activity in a separate synthetic time series, which closely represents the original data. Such a mapping could be done through a moving average of the prices, for example.

High-frequency data have become an unavoidable topic on financial markets theory, given the high potential they offer in helping the understanding of market microstructure.

Moreover, the more technology advances, the easier it is to collect data and process them in order to improve the statistical analysis and the development of intraday risk measurement models.

However, such type of data is difficult to handle, given the spuriousness of large data sets. Moreover, they entail specific statistical issues that cannot be modelled with existing statistical tools.

Research can be heavily influenced by those issues, and the risk is the acceptance of false positive research results, i.e. accepting models based on overscrubbed historical data that fail to recognize the properties of real-time data.

13.3.2 Basic stylized facts

High-frequency data show some behaviours that cannot be observed at lowest frequencies. These facts involve mainly the autocorrelation of return, distributional properties, scaling properties and seasonality, and have been observed on FX markets mostly.

As observed by Goodhart (1989) and Goodhart and Figliuoli (1991), the first order autocorrelation at high frequencies appears to be negative. Very rarely is the phenomenon

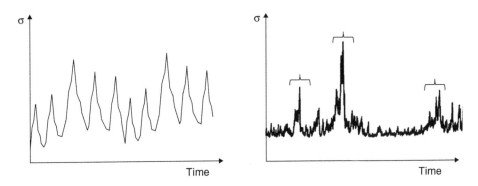

Figure 13.5 Schematic representation of the Seasonality (left) and Volatility Clustering (right) in high frequency financial time series.

observed for lags higher than 5 minutes, down to 1 minute when a uniform tick space is considered.

An explanation of the negative autocorrelation is that traders have heterogeneous beliefs on the effect of information. Moreover, market makers tend to skew the bid-ask spread in the presence of order imbalances.

Price formation in the market also plays a role, due to the existence of discrete transaction prices and the presence of a bid-ask spread. The transaction happens to be closed either close to the bid, or close to the ask price level, so that closing prices bounce between the two boundaries.

High-frequency data are discretely distributed, and show fat tails at various frequencies. This has very important implications in terms of risk management of financial instruments. Discreteness of transaction prices leads to high kurtosis, which increases as frequency increases.

Dacorogna *et al.* analyse the moments of the distributions for major FX rates against USD, and they find that for most of them, both the mean and standard deviation are fairly close to zero.

The absolute values of the third moment (skewness) are generally smaller than one, so that the distribution turns out to be symmetric. The excess kurtosis exceeds zero (the Gaussian value) for almost all time horizons.

While at lower frequencies the assumption of normality is generally acceptable, at the highest frequencies the distribution of financial returns shows fat tails, making extreme events much more plausible than in normally distributed data sets.

A fat-tailed distribution has a higher concentration of values on the tails and extreme values are more frequent than in a normal distribution. The tail index, which is normally infinite for thin-tailed distributions, shows values between 2 and 4 for high-frequency data.

Scaling laws relate to the behaviour of absolute size of returns as a function of the frequency at which they are measured. A wide range of financial data shows scaling laws, which give the relation between time interval and volatility, measured as a power z of the absolute returns.

$$\sqrt[z]{E\left(|r|^z\right)} = f(z)\Delta t^{g(z)} \tag{13.5}$$

where

$f(z)$ and $g(z)$ are deterministic functions of z.

When $z = 1$ the left-hand side of (13.5) indicates the absolute returns. This is a typical choice for implementation of the formula. Taking the logs of the equation, least squares regression gives the estimates for the functions $f(z)$ and $g(z)$. Empirical results indicate a scaling behaviour for hourly to monthly time intervals.

The bid-ask spread bouncing of prices gives a significant contribution to the error of volatility estimation. It is therefore very important to get a precise estimation of volatility, taking into account the bias generated by standard measurement.

The scaling law is applicable for a wide range of time intervals, but it has many limitations when used for long time intervals. Moreover, also the convenience of applying a universal single scaling law is often questioned. Gencay and Selcuk (2006) have found empirical evidence of different scaling behaviour and proposed a multi-scaling approach.

13.3.3 Heterogeneous volatility

Empirical studies show that volatilities measured at different frequencies are not symmetric, given that a rough volatility measure is a better predictor of a finer volatility.

Standard GARCH models are not able to capture the heterogeneity of volatilities at different frequencies, therefore other tools are needed to study volatility at the highest frequencies.

Müller *et al.* introduced the Heterogeneous ARCH (HARCH) process in 1997, with a variance equation that takes into account the returns over intervals of different sizes.

Like any ARCH-based process, the HARCH is based on past square returns, an assumption that works well also for high frequency data, even if they show problems in the convergence of the fourth moment of the distribution.

Following the initial work of Müller *et al.* (1997) and the following tractation by Dacorogna *et al.* (2001), the returns r_t of a HARCH(p) process are defined as

$$r_t = \sigma_t \varepsilon_t$$

where

ε_t is an i.i.d. standard normally distributed random variable.

The term σ_t is the standard deviation, as defined by the HARCH variance equation

$$\sigma_t^2 = \lambda_0 + \sum_{i=1}^{p} \lambda_i \left(\sum_{j=1}^{i} r_{t-i} \right)^2, \quad \lambda_0 > 0, \quad \lambda_n > 0, \quad \lambda_i \geq 0, \quad i = 1,...,p-1 \tag{13.6}$$

Equation (13.6) is a linear combination of the squares of aggregated returns, with a range of extension from the very past up to time $t-1$. The time intervals can take different sizes, forming a heterogeneous set.

HARCH is unique in measuring volatilities of returns over different interval sizes, and can be considered as a special case of the Quadratic ARCH (QARCH), introduced by Sentana in 1991.

Consider that the variance of a HARCH(2) process, defined as

$$\sigma_t^2 = \lambda_0 + \lambda_1 r_{t-1}^2 + \lambda_2 \left(r_{t-1} - r_{t-2} \right)^2$$

can be rewritten as

$$\sigma_t^2 = \left(\lambda_1 + \lambda_2 \right) r_{t-1}^2 + \lambda_2 r_{t-2}^2 + 2\lambda_2 r_{t-1} r_{t-2} \tag{13.7}$$

Equation (13.7) can be identified as an ordinary ARCH(2) process, plus an additional (mixed product) term. The additional term shows how in the HARCH model, the sign of the returns play a role, as opposed to ordinary forms of ARCH.

The mixed product means that two returns with the same sign will contribute to increase the total variance while two returns with opposite signs will offset each other, generating a sort of 'covariance' effect.

It is possible to derive the unconditional variance, in the form of the expectation of squared returns, as

$$E\left(r_t^2 \right) = E\left(\sigma_t^2 \right) = \lambda_0 + \sum_{i=1}^{p} \lambda_i \left[\sum_{j=1}^{i} E\left(r_{t-i}^2 \right) \right]$$

In terms of expectations, there is no cross-product effect, since their expectation is always zero.

Conditions of stationarity impose that

$$E\left(r_t^2 \right) = E\left(r_{t-i}^2 \right)$$

so that, by substituting the above condition in the unconditional variance equation yields

$$E\left(r_t^2 \right) = \frac{\lambda_0}{1 - \sum_{i=1}^{p} i\lambda_i} > 0$$

The finiteness and positivity of the conditional variance is a necessary condition for tractability. It is also a sufficient condition for the stationarity of the process and the existence of the second moment (variance) of the distribution of returns.

While the proof of these conditions is beyond the purpose of the book, an intuitive explanation is to note that the HARCH process is a Markov chain, so that ergodicity and recurrence of Markov chains can be used for proving the stationarity and moment condition.

The computation is particularly cumbersome for the moments above the variance, but as a general result, the expectation for the *m*-th moment is

$$E\left(r_t^m \right) = E\left(\sigma_t^m \right) E\left(\varepsilon_t^m \right)$$

The formula for the expectation of the variance is inserted into the $E(\sigma_t^m) = E(\sigma_t^{2s})$ transforming the power in order to separate the square and multiplying the exponents.

In order to analyse the fourth moment, for example, the value of m is set to 4, therefore $s = 2$.

In the specific case of a HARCH (2) process, a system of size $m \times p = 2 \times 2$ must be solved, where the two equations are the expectation $E(r_t^2 r_{t-1}^2)$ and the fourth moment equation for $E(r_t^4)$.

Recall that the fourth moment for a normal distribution is equal to 3. It follows that, assuming the random variable ε_t has a standard normal distribution, it holds that

$$E(\varepsilon_t^4) = 3$$

and the condition of finiteness of the fourth moment is given by

$$3\left[\lambda_2^2 + (\lambda_1 + \lambda_2)^2\right] + \lambda_2\left[1 + 3(\lambda_1^2 + 6\lambda_1\lambda_2 + 4\lambda_2^2)\right] < 1$$

Dacorogna *et al.* (2001) show that, plotting the second, fourth and sixth moment for a HARCH (2) process, there is a trend of second moments to converge and fourth moments to diverge, for most cases.

Summary

Standard Value-at-Risk methods are subject to implementation risk, implying the possibility that the same model may produce different estimates, when different measurements are performed.

The risk of variability in VaR estimates increases for non-linear securities, compared to linear products, which suggests implementing sensitivity analysis to underlying assumptions, parallel to VaR calculation.

Traditional VaR methodologies have been modified by modern research, and new approaches and interpretations have been introduced.

Alternative risk transfer markets cover risks that are not covered by traditional insurance and reinsurance, overcoming the limits and providing coverage for some types of unusual risks.

Some types of insurance risks are not related to traditional investments, or not even based on standard economic drivers. They therefore require separate treatment and a specific class of assets, for management and hedging.

Insurance derivatives give the holder the chance to hedge against the unusual types of risk, and in some cases, do not have to prove having suffered a loss in order to obtain the benefit from the derivative, so that they are not considered as insurance contracts.

Insurance derivatives contracts show interesting features like the high liquidity, the cost-effectiveness and flexibility of OTC transactions. Moreover, for settlement, no proof of an actual loss is required.

High-frequency data are characterized by specific behaviours that cannot be observed at lower frequencies. Stylized facts observed on intraday data include autocorrelation of absolute returns, scaling properties and seasonality, volatility clustering.

Empirical studies show asymmetry of volatilities measured at different frequencies, and rough volatility measures are better predictors than fine volatility ones. Standard

GARCH models are not adequate to capture the heterogeneity in high frequency volatilities. Therefore other tools are needed to study volatility at the highest frequencies.

Bibliography

Banks, E. 2004. *Alternative Risk Transfer*. John Wiley & Sons, Ltd.

Boudoukh, J., Richardson, M. and Whitelaw, R. 1997. Expect the Worst. VAR: Understanding and Applying Value at Risk. *Risk*, 79–81.

Butler, J.S. and Schachter, B. 1996. *Improving Value-at-Risk Estimates by Combining Kernel Estimation with Historical Simulation*. Office of the Comptroller of the Currency. Economic & Policy Analysis. Working Paper 96–1.

Butler, J.S. and Schachter, B. 1998. Estimating Value at Risk with a Precision Measure by Combining Kernel Estimation with Historical Simulation. *Review of Derivatives Research*, 1: 371–390.

Dacorogna, M., Gencay, R., Müller, U.A., Olsen, R.B. and Pictet, O.V. 2001. *An Introduction to High Frequency Finance*. Academic Press.

Duffie, D. and Pan, J. 1997. An Overview of Value at Risk. *The Journal of Derivatives*, 4: 7–49.

Engle, R.F. and Russell, J.R. 2005. Analysis of High Frequency Finance. *Handbook of Financial Econometrics*. Editors: Y. Ait-Sahalia and L.P. Hansen. Elsevier.

Falkenberry, T.N. 2002. *High Frequency Data Filtering*. White Paper. Tick Data Inc. www.tickdata.com.

Fallon, W. 1996. *Calculating Value at Risk*. Wharton Financial Institutions Center Working Paper Series. Working Paper 96–49.

Fama, E.F. 1963. Mandelbrot and the Stable Paretian Hypothesis. *The Journal of Business*, 36(4): 420–429.

Gabaix, X., Gopikrishnan, P., Plerou, V. and Stanley, H.E. 2006. Institutional Investors and Stock Market Volatility. *Quarterly Journal of Economics*, 121(2): 461–504.

Gencay, R. and Selcuk, F. 2006. Intraday Dynamics of Stock Market Returns and Volatility. *Physica A: Statistical Mechanics and its Applications*, 367(C): 375–387.

Giot, P. 2005. Market Risk Models for Intraday Data. *The European Journal of Finance*, 11(4): 309–324.

Goodhart, C.A.E. 1989. News and the Foreign Exchange Market. *Proceedings of the Manchester Statistical Society*, 1–79.

Goodhart, C.A.E. and Figliuoli, L. 1991. Every Minute Counts in Financial Markets. *Journal of International Money and Finance*, 10: 23–52.

Gopikrishan, P. 1999. Scaling of the Distribution of Fluctuations in Financial Market Indices. *Physica E*, 60: 5305–5310.

Gopikrishnan, P., Plerou, V., Liu, Y., Amaral, L.A.N., Gabaix, X. and Stanley, H.E. 2000. Scaling and Correlation in Financial Time Series. *Physica A: Statistical Mechanics and its Applications*, 287(3–4): 362–373.

Härdle, W., Hautsch, N. and Pigorsch, U. 2008. *Measuring and Modeling Risk Using High-Frequency Trading*. SFB 649 Discussion Paper 045.

Härdle, W., Hautsch, N. and Pigorsch, U. 2008. Measuring and Modeling Risk Using High Frequency Data. *Humboldt Universität zu Berlin, Universität Mannheim*, Discussion Paper, 275–289.

Hartwig, P.R. and Wilkinson, C. 2007. An Overview of the Alternative Risk Transfer Market. *Handbook of International Insurance. Huebner International Series on Risk, Insurance and Economic Security*, 26: 925–952.

International Energy Agency. 2011. The Mechanics of the Derivatives Markets, *Oil Market Report*. April.

Jarrow, R.A. and Turnbull, S. 2000. The Intersection of Market and Credit Risk. *Journal of Banking and Finance*, 24.

434   *Advanced topics*

Jessen, A.H. and Mikosch, T. 2006. Regularly Varying Functions. *Publications de l'Institut Mathmatique. Nouvelle Serie*, 80(94): 171–192.

Khindanova, I.N. and Rachev, S.T. 2000. *Value at Risk*. University of California, Santa Barbara.

Mandelbrot, B. 1963. The Variation of Certain Speculative Prices. *Journal of Business*, 36: 392–417.

Marshall, C. and Siegel, M. 1997. Value at Risk: Implementing a Risk Measurement Standard. *The Journal of Derivatives*, 4(3): 91–111.

Müller, U.A., Dacorogna, M.M., Davé, R.D., Olsen, R.B., Pictet, O.V. and von Weizsäcker, J.E. 1997. Volatilities of Different Time Resolutions: Analyzing the Dynamics of Market Components. *Journal of Empirical Finance*, 4: 213–239.

Pareto, V. 1896. La Courbe de la Repartition de la Richesse. *Réunis et présentés par G. Busino. Euvres completes*. IV. Genève Droz, 1965.

Pritsker, M. 1996. *Evaluating Value at Risk Methodologies: Accuracy Versus Computational Time*. Wharton Financial Institutions Center Working Paper Series. Working Paper 96–48.

Pritsker, M. 1997. Evaluating Value at Risk Methodologies: Accuracy versus Computational Time. *Journal of Financial Services Research*, 12(2/3): 201–242.

Qi, J. 2011. *Risk Measurement and High-Frequency Data: Value-at-Risk and Scaling Law Methods*. Center for Computational Finance and Economic Agents, University of Essex.

Sentana, E. 1991. *Quadratic ARCH Models: A Potential Reinterpretation of ARCH Models*. LSE Financial Markets Group Discussion Paper, 122.

Wilson, T. 1994. Plugging the GAP. *Risk*, 7(10): 74–80.

Zangari, P. 1996. How Accurate is the Delta-Gamma Methodology? *RiskMetrics Monitor*. Third Quarter. 12–29.

Exercises

Questions

1. What aspects of modified delta VaR make it more accurate than standard delta approximation?
2. Discuss the main complications that modified Monte Carlo and scenario analysis introduce, compared to standard simulation methods.
3. List the advantages of ART methods and instruments compared to standard insurance and reinsurance.
4. Which factor among insurance costs and risk aversion plays the major role in choosing ART market for insurance? Explain.
5. Describe the main differences between a catastrophe swap and a standard financial swap.
6. What are the implications of multi-risk products in terms of risk hedging and contract premium, compared to single-peril contracts?
7. Define the main trade-off involved in the filtering of high frequency financial time series.
8. What are the main issues when dealing with high frequency data, in terms of the series roughness? How can the problems be overcome?
9. List and discuss the main stylized facts of high frequency financial time series. How do they differ from stylized facts at lower frequencies?
10. What does heterogeneity in volatility imply for data analysis? How can complications be overcome?

Appendix: Power laws for intraday data

The term power law (PL) identifies the form taken by many regularities in finance. The relation is given by

$$Y = kX^\alpha$$

where

X and Y are the variables of interest
α is the PL exponent
k is a constant.

Pareto (1896) found that the distribution of people with income larger than x shows an upper tail proportional to $\dfrac{1}{x^\zeta}$ for some positive number ζ. A particular case of PL is Zipf's law, which is given by

$$\Pr(X > x) = kx^{-\zeta}$$

corresponding to a density function

$$f(x) = \zeta k x^{-(\zeta+1)}$$

If a variable shows a PL exponent ζ, all moments greater than ζ are infinite, meaning that the law cannot fit properly in bounded systems. The PL distribution of some variable is preserved under addition, multiplication, polynomial transformation, argmin and argmax.

Consider independent random variables $X_1, X_2, ..., X_n$, and some positive constant α. Jessen and Mikosch (2006) perform a survey to show that the following properties for the PL coefficient ζ_{X_i} hold for cumulative and multiplied variables:

$$\zeta_{X_1+X_2+...+X_n} = \min\left(\zeta_{X_1}, \zeta_{X_2}, ..., \zeta_{X_n}\right)$$
$$\zeta_{X_1 \times X_2 \times ... \times X_n} = \min\left(\zeta_{X_1}, \zeta_{X_2}, ..., \zeta_{X_n}\right)$$

Properties hold also for the PL coefficients of minimum and maximum variables in the set, as given by

$$\zeta_{\max(X_1,X_2,...,X_n)} = \min\left(\zeta_{X_1}, \zeta_{X_2}, ..., \zeta_{X_n}\right)$$
$$\zeta_{\min(X_1,X_2,...,X_n)} = \zeta_{X_1} + \zeta_{X_2} + ... + \zeta_{X_n}$$

Finally, the multiplicative and power properties of the PL coefficient can be written as

$$\zeta_{\alpha X} = \zeta_X$$
$$\zeta_{X^\alpha} = \frac{\zeta_X}{\alpha}$$

Applications of PL in finance include intraday stock market activity, where the use of large financial data sets have fostered the understanding of the tail of financial distributions.

Starting from Mandelbrot and Fama, in 1963, to Gopikrishnan in 1999, scientists have analysed hundreds of millions of data points of stock market returns, with frequency from 15 seconds to a few days, identifying an inverse cubic PL of returns, defined as

$$\Pr(|r| > x) \propto \frac{1}{x^{\zeta_r}}, \quad \zeta_r \approx 3 \tag{13.8}$$

The relationship holds for positive and negative returns separately. Plotting the log of x against the log of the cubic PL, the log form of equation (13.8) happens to be defined as

$$\ln\left[\Pr(|r| > x)\right] = -\zeta_r \ln x + \gamma$$

where

γ is a constant.

Empirical studies show that the fit of such a PL is good when the absolute returns are of magnitude between 2 and 80 standard deviations. When the coefficient value is $\zeta = 3$, the variance of the distribution is finite.

Gopikrishnan *et al.* (2000) analysed the trading volumes for the 1,000 largest American stocks, showing they are PL distributed too. Volumes q follow the PL as described by

$$\Pr(q > x) \propto \frac{1}{x^{\zeta_q}}, \quad \zeta_q \approx \frac{3}{2}$$

The origin of the regularities in financial data is not clear, but few models try to predict the tail properties of returns and volumes. Some analysts suggest that fat tails could be a consequence of ARCH effects in the data.

Other explanations (Gabaix *et al.*, 2006) attribute the PLs of trading activity to the strategic trades of very large institutional investors in relatively illiquid markets, creating spikes in returns and volumes, even in an environment of scarce news hitting the markets.

14 The future of financial risk management

The global financial crisis has left many open questions about future developments, and required interventions for settlement. Future financial risk management is therefore an open chapter, still to be written, and full of unknowns.

It is not possible to ignore the role of corporate governance in the crisis, given that managerial behaviour and moral hazard have led to distress in many corporations.

The remuneration system plays a key role in addressing the lack of corporate governance, in that historically, it has been performance-driven, without any link to the market position of the firm and other performance parameters.

The banking sector will play a central role in the overcoming of the crisis, and it is therefore important to analyse the business model, risk management system and areas of potential improvement of banking activities worldwide.

Interbank risk has been identified in the last decades as a major source of the instability of the banking sector, while energy derivatives, on the other side, are supposed to play a central role in future assessment of the industrial sector, given the overall pressure on the worldwide sources of energy.

It is not possible to ignore the effects of sovereign risk dynamics on the stability of the financial sector, given that a large share of financial risk is to be related to the fiscal and economic situation of central governments, in Europe and worldwide.

After studying this chapter you will be able to answer the following questions, among others:

1. What has been the role of corporate governance in the development of the global financial crisis? How do remuneration systems affect governance?
2. How does financial risk relate to the business models in the banking sector?
3. What is interbank risk, and how influential is it in the context of the global crisis?
4. What is the rationale and use of energy derivatives?
5. What is the impact of sovereign risk dynamics on the worldwide contagion due to financial distress?

The first section of the chapter deals with the role of corporate governance in the global crisis, focusing on management failures and the remuneration system. The second section is about the banking sector, its business model and future developments. The final part deals with the future challenges for research, including the analysis of interbank risk, sovereign risk and energy derivatives.

14.1 The role of corporate governance

Learning outcomes

1.   Describe how corporate governance impacted the global financial crisis.
2.   Define the role of the remuneration system on management behaviour.
3.   List and comment on the potential future perspectives of governance.

14.1.1 Management failures

Failures in corporate governance have played a major role in the financial crises, along with other factors. Many institutions that were considered finely structured showed themselves to be weak and tools for corporate governance proved to be ineffective, when pressure started getting very high.

Large industrial corporations as well as big financial institutions suffered from the lack in governance, so that international initiatives, as well as regulatory eyes, started focusing on how to produce an effective response to it.

The international standards for corporate governance are set by the Organisation for Economic Co-operation and Development (OECD). Other institutions, including the BIS and World Bank, rely on the work of the OECD, to set standards.

The OECD, represented by the Corporate Governance Committee (CGC), is responsible for issuing principles that are relevant and field-leading, with a look to the future perspectives.

In the years of the crisis, the committee had the chance to draw conclusions about governance, concluding that the most severe driving factor of governance failure was the wrong implementation of existing standards.

Moreover it was clear from confrontation with other organizations, that the need of new regulation was not so imminent, while focusing more on the application of existing rules appeared to be a more urgent task.

The CGC developed an action plan based on two main pillars. The first pillar includes provisions about specific areas of action, to improve the implementation of the principles. The second pillar focuses on the development of peer review and dialogue, in order to achieve effective monitoring of the situation and promptly identify new problems.

Priority has been given to areas like, among others, governance of remuneration, effective risk-management, board practices, shareholder rights. The main lessons from the crisis have been convoluted into conclusions to be published by the organization.

Remuneration and incentive systems have failed in that they were not based on performance-related criteria. In most cases the link between compensation and performance was weak and difficult to observe. Moreover, compensation schemes were often complicated and obscure.

Remuneration should be determined avoiding conflicts of interests, with the contribution of independent advisors. Shareholders should be involved in the approval of compensation schemes.

The compensation packages should be designed in order to ensure long-term performance, also through postponing parts of remuneration, and adjustments to the related risks.

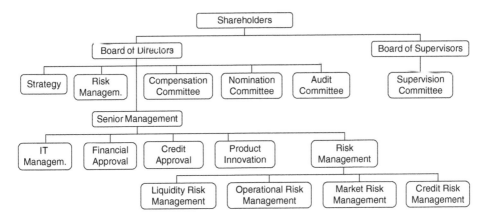

Figure 14.1 An example of a typical board of a medium-big size bank.

Another point is the shift of compensation towards floating components, linked to performance, limiting the fixed part to a minimum. Transparency is a crucial point as well, in that information on remuneration should be available.

The committee also realized that in most cases the boards were not aware of the risks incumbent on the corporation. Risk management was an isolated necessary evil and there was a lack of integration with the general company's strategy.

Profit centres were the core of corporate strategies, and risk management departments were subordinated, so that the disclosure of foreseeable risks was often poor and mechanical.

The main message coming from the committee's analysis is that a major involvement of the board to the establishment of risk management practices is crucial, and risk managers should be independent from profit centres.

Moreover compensation of managers should follow incentive schemes, and be adapted to risk-management aspects, and there should be transparent disclosure of main factors driving the risk perspectives of the corporation, as well as the criteria used for their identification.

In many cases, especially in financial institutions, the board has been found unable to give an objective judgement. The focus has been more on the independence of board members rather than on their competence.

The aspects related to possible conflict of interests have been magnified by the tenure of some board members, and interlocking directorate. Deviations from the optimal board are often not explained.

The OECD principles are widely known as the leading force of corporate governance regulation. Supervisory and regulatory authorities should be properly equipped to face the weaknesses of corporate governance.

The most famous case of bad corporate governance in the last decades is Enron Corp., an American energy, commodities and services company based in Houston, Texas, one of the largest energy companies in the world.

In 2001, the company went through a bankruptcy procedure due to reported institutionalized, systematic and creatively planned accounting fraud, which makes Enron a well-known example of wilful corporate fraud and corruption.

At the end of the 1990s the Enron share price was inflated by the expectations generated by the fake financial figures produced by the management, and by ambitious industrial plans, that seemed to be feasible in light of the financial statements.

The company soon turned from being a utility firm, to being an intermediary clearing house for the market of futures on energy, pretending to be able to price them correctly, due to its combination of an underlying utility business with a market trading overlay.

Enron managers claimed they had invented a new corporate model. The huge revenues registered by the company turned into high compensations for the top managers, high fees paid for consultancy to non-executive board members.

But the rising share price was used to finance off-balance sheet transactions, aimed at inflating further the share price by overestimating the company's earnings. That strategy could not survive the general stock market fall which began in early 2000.

Many other companies tried to follow price-inflating strategies, thus receiving no lesson from the case of Enron. The failure of the big corporation in fact was mostly deemed confined in its effects.

Consequences of the Enron fall on financial markets were huge, and lots of funds which had over-invested in Enron stock suffered significant losses. Big investors with well-diversified portfolios had limited impact, while employees suffered most of the burden, losing their jobs and also their retirement incomes.

Interpreted as an isolated case of fraud and corporate governance failure, the fall of Enron uncovered a scenario of fraud and conflicts of interest which would otherwise have been undiscovered.

But it would be incorrect to think that was all. Enron was operating in the context of the dotcom bubble, with share prices going above sustainable levels in the late 1990s, for a wide range of corporations.

The Sarbanes-Oxley Act (2002) tried to improve the legislation in the USA, based on the convincement that the Enron case was in fact just an example of governance scandal. However, it failed in mitigating the strategy of maximizing share price as a signal of productive activity.

The Sarbanes-Oxley Act made many changes, from increasing the frequency of reporting to widening the range of obligations upon governance. The underlying idea was that the board should be made up of external actors, in order to enforce independence. However, there was no evidence of a link between ineffective monitoring and the lack of independence of directors, either at Enron or elsewhere.

In Europe, in the more recent financial crisis, the main example of corporate governance failure was registered in the UK, with the failure of the British bank and former building society, Northern Rock.

For many years, the regulation of corporate issues in the UK was deferred to British Companies Acts. Since the world global crisis of 1929, the Acts had changed the view on how corporate governance should have been regulated.

Again focusing on interlocking directorates, the Acts have been criticized for not solving the issue of multiple boards of companies of the same group interacting with each other in order to spread the financial matters among different companies. The Acts failed in requiring big groups to publish consolidated balance sheets and income accounts or an interlocking company to publish details of its holdings.

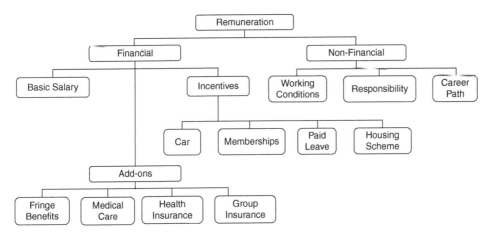

Figure 14.2 An example of a typical remuneration package for top employees and managers.

14.1.2 Remuneration and incentive systems

Even in the years before the crisis fully exploded, the role of executive compensation in driving effectiveness of corporate governance was widely explored. The problem of remuneration was recognized at that time as one of the unsolved problems in the USA.

But the problem has never been confined to American companies, raising concerns also in Europe (Germany and Sweden in particular) and in the rest of the world, including (somehow surprisingly) China.

CEO remuneration had rapidly increased since the early 1990s, in the whole world, standing far above the salaries of average workers. The growth was proportional to the increase in size of the corporations.

The size of the companies is anyway not the only explanation for the compensation rise. Another explanation is that in the early 1990s performance-related pay became more widespread, due to base-salary caps introduced by the legislation.

As mentioned above, the issue of executive compensation had become a major issue not only in the USA, but in many countries in the world, e.g. Australia, Sweden, Germany, Switzerland, the Netherlands and France among others.

In the EU CEO compensation rose by an average 14% per year in the pre-crisis years while other salaries of workers were growing at just about 2%. The gap then grew and the ratio of CEO to average worker pay has thus widened rapidly.

The financial crisis served to make more acute a situation that was already in place in the previous years. It was in fact common for top managers to be rewarded even in case of failure, or to get generous perks such as long-lasting pensions and the continued use of company resources.

The main issue with performance-related compensation was that linkage criteria had been very weak. Compensation of top managers was in fact related to targets having little to do with executive performance such as the level of a company's share price, and not the relative position of the company.

The financial crisis outlined issues, especially in banks, about compensation. Executives had large equity positions in their companies, meaning they shared potential downside risk with shareholders.

This resulted in managers facing high risk, but the very large compensation and bonuses attached to performance seemed to offset the losses on equity holdings, so to remove any incentive for the managers to limit the risk exposure of the corporation.

The result was a risk-taking behaviour of governance that amplified the issues, leading to situations of high risk. In some cases, due to public anger, a number of executives voluntarily renounced their bonuses, in Europe, the USA and in China.

It is rather obvious to consider remuneration and corporate governance an issue related to the very top level of management. However, it was shown that in many companies, the reform of compensation packages should be extended even below.

A number of non-financial companies have faced situations in the past where promotion systems have led to excessive risk taking. Inopportune behaviour included breaches of compliance obligations at all levels with serious consequences for the whole company, and it was evident that strong incentives had to be complemented by adequate risk management systems.

A common issue among firms was the lack of consideration of any risk adjustment in measuring performance for compensation purposes. Being lower level employees not remunerated with stocks, this becomes a major issue.

The lack of risk adjustment leads to a dichotomy of interests between employees and shareholders, and often makes the corporation pay its employees much more than their contribution, in the mid-long term.

The view on the functioning of remuneration systems led the opinions on executive management compensation. One theory states that reaching a decision on remuneration through bargaining necessarily leads to optimality and equilibrium, and therefore the regulators should focus on granting the transparency of the process.

Another theory states that in most cases top managers benefit from asymmetric information and high bargaining power, leading to contracts that are not optimal for the corporation.

Information asymmetry, as well as bargaining power, are important issues, that sum up the lack of guidance in developing trustable performance metrics to build up a wrong remuneration system.

The OECD principles were revised in the years 2003–2004, strengthening them in terms of information disclosure and the consideration of the long-term interest of the corporation in light of business plans.

The principles clearly put the board in charge of developing and disclosed clear remuneration policies covering the board itself and the top management. The long-term relationship between remuneration and interests of the firm should be fully exploited.

The board processes should be adequate to an optimal remuneration policy, also putting non-executive board members in charge of independent judgement about the financial integrity and potential conflicts of interest.

The financial crisis has exposed a lack of appropriate judgement and monitoring of the situation by boards. However, the issue is not necessarily related to the concept of independence.

In many cases the real limit of board actions is the link to their own histories, and to the will of management, so that board members have been shown to be rather more reactive than proactive. Shareholder decisions have often created some turnover, indicating significant path dependency.

Another issue related to the independence of the board is the separation of CEO and board chairman functions. By logic, a good practice should be to separate the functions and disclose information about the current situation.

For companies where the two functions are combined, this should be justified and elaborated to avoid this structure to compromise the effectiveness and independence of the board. The same should hold for the case of a controlling shareholder holding the post of chair, leading to the need to strengthen the legal duties of board members.

14.1.3 Post-crisis perspectives

Future developments of the regulatory framework will have to address corporate governance issues, in order to respond in the near future to developments within financial markets, including share ownership and shifts in investment strategy.

Companies have been threatened by the failure in corporate governance, due to lack of core values such as integrity and trust. Companies would take advantage by the improvement of their reputational value.

Nowadays, ethical behaviour has become a resource, and a company with a reputation for ethical behaviour in today's marketplace engenders both customer and employee loyalty.

Good principles and practices lead to effective corporate governance, combining fairness and honesty in the manner in which companies conduct their affairs. Profits are a legitimate target of the company, to be bounded ethically.

Corporate image and reputation can be built on policies like environmental protection, ethical training. Ethical compliance mechanisms contribute to stability and growth since they instil confidence.

Ethics is going to be an unavoidable element in the process of improved business management. The greed and collusion that drove the system to its lowest point necessitate a total overhaul, in the name of better codes.

The challenge for future corporate governance systems is to manage the trade-off between external regulation and self-regulation, and achieve the right balance. Anglo Saxon countries are a typical example of that dichotomy.

Possible future developments should embrace all aspects of modern corporate governance in the world. It has been observed there should be a new approach in terms of regulatory aspects, self-regulation and the linkage to the market.

Several studies in the late 2000s, from King (2002) to Naidoo (2009) remark how Anglo Saxon countries tend to have well-balanced systems, but are still at risk after the crisis meltdown.

So the choice is between a self-regulation-based system, and a heavily regulated approach, and market based, where the latter could better serve the interests of the shareholders, in the opinion of the aforementioned scientists.

14.2 The banking sector

Learning outcomes

1. Elaborate on the bank risk and business models in the banking sector.
2. Define and comment on the various banking risk management systems.
3. Elaborate on the potential areas of future improvements.

14.2.1 Bank risk and business models

There is a certain amount of literature exploring the relationship between business model characteristics and bank risk, focusing on key factors like capital, operating efficiency, funding sources, and more.

Scientists like Beltratti and Stulz (2012) have focused on the performance factors using stock market information. They observe that banks with more Tier I capital and higher loan-to-asset ratio performed better, in the initial years of the crisis, compared to more shareholder-oriented boards.

The capital structure of banks was characterized by a deregulation period at the beginning of the 2000s, counterbalanced by the provision of a more prominent role in the prudential regulatory process, as from the Basel Accord on capital standards, and subsequent amendments.

The effect of capital requirements on bank risk stays controversial, besides the obvious claim that a higher capital buffer set aside would allow for more control on losses. Moreover, the higher the equity capital, the lower the leverage and, consequently, the risk.

Recent studies from Mehran and Thakor (2011) analyse the possibility that, moral hazard consideration playing a role, there could be an asset-shifting process in favour of riskier assets. The same studies find that higher capital implies a more intensive screening of borrowers, therefore reducing the bank risk associated with bank operations.

The analysis becomes controversial when agency problems between shareholders and managers are taken into account, in that increasing leverage reduces agency conflicts since informed debt-holders intensify the pressure on bank managers to become more efficient (Diamond and Rajan, 2001).

Another situation of positive relationship between capital and risk occurs when regulators force banks more at risk to build equity capital, giving them more risk-absorption capabilities, and therefore enhancing risk-taking behaviour.

Also size can be an important determinant of bank risk, given popular issues like the 'too-big-to-fail' argument, stating that some institutions are so big and interconnected that they cannot be left failing, and governments should support them in times of distress, as underlined by Demirgüç-Kunt and Huizinga (2010) among others.

Securitization is another important factor, allowing banks to off-load parts of their assets from the balance sheet. Right before the crisis there was a rapid growth of off-balance sheet financing by banks, supported by the massive expansion of securitization markets.

Banks' business models had a dramatic change, since the incentive to hedge risk heavily diminished, while the appetite for risk and incentive to take on more rose. The development of securitization allowed banks to turn traditionally illiquid claims into marketable securities.

The sharp reduction in off-balance sheet assets also caused capital requirements to be less restrictive, lowering regulatory pressures, and diversifying their credit portfolios more easily.

Bank funding structure has been heavily influenced by financial innovation developments, leading to an increase in the dependence of the banks on financial markets for their funding, through intense borrowing from wholesale funding, available in the form of mortgage bonds, repo agreements and commercial paper.

An important source of funding is given by retail deposits, having the property of being pretty stable during periods of crisis, therefore allowing banks to have a good prediction of the aggregate level of funding available. Anyway markets stay as a primary source of funding, since banks can borrow at the interbank market a large amount of funding at a relatively low cost.

The crisis has pointed to controversial aspects of wholesale funding, and it has been shown that financiers have lower incentives to monitor the positions. Solvent institutions may be then forced into liquidation due to sudden withdrawals based on negative public signals.

The bank risk is also linked to the income structure. Following the deregulation process in the financial industry, many institutions have gone through geographical expansion, resulting in high rates of credit growth.

The raise in value of the collateral values (due to sharp increases in housing prices), combined with the overall easier access to wholesale funding (due to financial innovation), also enhanced credit growth.

Foos *et al.* (2010) show how loan growth represents an important driver for risk. The global trend towards more diversification in bank income sources and an expansion of non-interest income revenues has provided banks with additional sources of revenue.

Diversification of income sources fosters income stability over time, but no evidence has been shown about the direct impact of non-financial sources of revenues to overall banking risk.

It is a much more volatile type of income than interest-rate-related ones. Therefore, in periods of financial stress there could be a decline in the traditional sources of revenue including fees and brokerage services.

14.2.2 Risk management systems

For quite a long time banks have considered risk management as a tool to control the corporate exposure to the major types of risk, as considered at that time, as credit risk, interest rate risk, foreign exchange risk and liquidity risk.

All the other risks were comprised in the main categories and evaluated using standard procedures, mostly credit procedures. Legal risk is also a concern that has been raised in the last few years, being linked to credit procedures.

Risk management for banks is then focused on the four broad categories, and how they are managed given the constraints posed by each of these risks. Such an analysis must start with a discussion of risk management controls in each area.

The process for credit risk management involves the application of a consistent evaluation and rating scheme to all its investment opportunities. Credit decisions should then be made in a consistent manner and for the resultant aggregate reporting of credit risk exposure should be meaningful.

In order for the process to be smooth, process and documentation must be standardized. Natural consequences of this are the standardized ratings across borrowers and a credit portfolio report on the overall quality of the credit portfolio.

The simplest form of rating involves the association of a single value to each loan, relating to the borrower's underlying credit quality. Some institutions apply a dual system, that rates both the borrower and the lender.

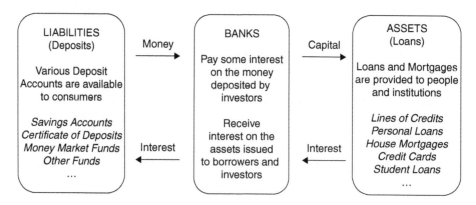

Figure 14.3 A synthetic example of banking activity.

When taking into account both counterparties, the focus of the attention goes to collateral and covenants, while for a single counterparty rating, the general credit-worthiness of the borrower is measured.

Loans are normally rated using a decimal scale, and for each category also a qualitative definition of the borrower is given, with analytical representation of the financials of the borrowing party.

The credit committee achieves good knowledge of the quality of loans and the process in its renovation requires new officers to be introduced to the system, making it easy for the bank to report the quality of its loan portfolio at any time.

All receivables are commonly reported in the same format, and standards are adhered to, so that the senior management gets uniform information unless ratings on loans are changed.

Credit quality reports can change also for other reasons, like the dynamic compliance to the changes of the worthiness of the counterparty overtime. In fact, credit quality reports should signal changes in expected loan losses, if the rating system is meaningful.

The credit quality of assets must be constantly monitored in order to keep the files updated. The standard in the industry of ratings is to review on a quarterly or annual basis to ensure the accuracy of the rating associated with the lending facility.

Internal rating schemes of banks should lead to the same result, by using models that are developing internally. The issue in practical application of this approach is the lack of sufficient industry data to do an appropriate aggregate migration study, so that calculations do not offer the same degree of confidence in their expected loss calculations.

Other reasons for reporting on-the-way changes are the deterioration or improvement of the economic conditions of the borrower, a revaluation of devaluation of the collateral and more. The sum of all the possible changes results in a periodic but timely report card on the quality of the credit portfolio and its change from month to month.

The Financial Accounting Standards Board (FASB) is the authority setting the accounting standards for the monitoring of the value of credit portfolios. Commercial banks are required to have a loan loss reserve account representing the diminution in market value from known or estimated credit losses.

Banks have historically worked on expected loss estimation using a two-step procedure, first involving the estimation of default probabilities, and then moving to the estimate of the loss given default.

The revaluation of the reserve account is done quarterly, and its level reassessed, following the indications about the evidence of loss exposure given by the credit quality report, supported by internal studies.

Many banks started developing concentration reports, not very common before the crisis, in order to indicate the industry composition of the loan portfolio, and Moody's has recently developed a system of 34 industry groups, for classification.

Concentrations by sector are normally compared to benchmarks represented by market indices, so that mutual funds can report their performance in absolute terms and also as a relative position to the market index.

The problem with credit risk is that a loan portfolio does not have a benchmark for comparison, so that specialization by industry sectors of a loan portfolio must be valued by banks according to pros and cons.

The interest rate management procedures are an important area of concern for banks, but historically, the banking sector has dealt with it in a different way, compared to the rest of the financial industry.

Most banks distinguish between trading activity and balance-sheet interest rate exposure, where the former has been commonly assimilated to a form of market risk, while elaborating trading risk management systems to measure and monitor exposure.

Large banks have integrated in their infrastructure the IRR system, but trading risk management systems vary substantially from bank to bank and generally are less real than imagined.

VaR-looking models are implemented in small banks, for IRR measurement, but in most cases they are underdeveloped, and suitable only for banks with very limited trading activity.

Larger banks cannot rely on these types of models, but anyway, in general the banking system has the tendency to aggregate market risk and IRR, implementing VaR as a standard approach.

Daily, weekly or monthly volatilities of the market value of fixed income securities are therefore incorporated into a measure of total portfolio risk analysis, along with market risk for equity, and that of foreign currencies.

Regarding balance sheet interest-rate-sensitive entries, banks generally rely on GAAP standard, avoiding linking their analysis to market values, but mostly looking at cash flows and book values.

The output of the measurement is normally a gap, defined as the asymmetry of the repricing of assets and liabilities, measured in ratio or percentage mismatch terms over a standardized interval such as a 30-day or one-year period.

Moving from cash flows to duration is not so immediate, given the presence of asset categories with no fixed maturity, in the bunch of assets of a bank. The same issue holds on the liabilities side, with retail demand and savings balances.

A large number of banks have tried to move beyond the gap method, which is a static measure of the risk profile of the bank, not fitting well with the dynamics of assets and liabilities value, and spreads fluctuating over time.

The volatility of spreads has been a driver of profitability for banks in the last few years, and currently, many banks are using balance sheet simulation models to investigate the effect of interest rate variation on reported earnings over one- to five-year horizons.

However, simulations are a controversial tool for fixed income analysis, because they require informed repricing schedules, and estimates of cash flows. The analysis requires an explicit response function to the rate movements.

A successfully completed simulation reports the resultant deviations in earnings associated with the relevant scenario for interest rates. The management is responsible for setting limits of acceptance for the simulation outcomes, in terms of deviations from expected income.

Foreign exchange risk management comes with a range of degrees of relevance to banks, depending on how deeply the institution is involved in currency operation and foreign business.

Some banks are only marginally involved into FX operations, so that they take virtually no principal risk, no forward open positions and have no expectations of trading volume.

Also, banks that take part in the FX markets sometimes are just agents for corporate and/or retail clients. Of course the most interesting case is that of institutions that have active trading positions.

Some banks are very active in the area, with large trading accounts and multiple trading locations worldwide. Real-time reporting is ensured by continuous mark to market of positions in spot and forward currencies.

Trading limits are commonly set at desk level and by individual traders, and real-time monitoring is preferred to daily closing in some institutions. Banks with more active trending positions tend to choose real-time monitoring of risk, through VaR systems.

Setting limits is a crucial part of FX risk management, and the derivation of the optimal limits is a controversial task. Some institutions set limits according to subjective variance tolerance, for each currency.

Other institutions derive exposure limits using a method that is analytically similar to the approach used in the area of interest rate risk, combined with stress tests to evaluate the potential loss associated with changes in the exchange rate.

Stress tests are run for both small deviations in the FX rates, and larger changes, mostly to match the highest historical deviations registered in the early past, for major currencies.

Historical data are also used for simulating stress in the variables, by estimating a distribution from which disturbances are drawn. In this case, a one or two standard deviation change in the exchange rate is considered.

These methods are used in most cases to estimate volatility, but not many institutions have been using a covariability approach in setting individual currency limits, or in the aggregating exposure across multiple correlated currencies.

Regarding the incentive systems, there is a widespread conviction that important differences exist between investment banking, where the community trader performance is directly linked to compensation, and other areas of commercial banking.

As already mentioned in Chapter 8, there are several definitions of liquidity risk, the easiest being, in most regards, a notion of liquidity risk as a need for continued funding. This type of liquidity need is forecastable and easily analysed.

Anyway, in the modern capital markets, banks are offered ample resources for growth and recourse to additional liabilities for unexpectedly high asset growth. Analysing liquidity risk as a need for corporate growth, credit lines fulfilment has therefore little relevance to the risk management agenda pursued here.

The liquidity risk type presenting the most relevant challenge is the funding need in time of distress or crisis. Issues become then very different for a financial institution, and standard reports on asset liquidity become very useful in case of continued funding.

What is really required in the analysis of liquidity risk in times of distress is the simulation of worst case scenarios. It is therefore required to simulate bank-specific shocks, in the form of severe losses and systemic crashes.

The purpose of the simulations is to analyse the bank ability to be self-supporting in cases of crisis event, which involves estimating the speed at which the shock would result in a funding crisis.

Response strategies to potential shocks includes adequate balance-sheet shrinkage, with the estimation of the surviving funding to be available in distress time. Results of such simulated crises are usually expressed in days of exposure, or days to funding crisis.

Again, the type of approach is different for different bank sizes, with many banks trying to carefully develop funding plans, and estimate their vulnerability to the crisis with considerable precision.

14.2.3 Areas of future improvements

The level and sensitivity to risk-management-related issues in the banking sector is recently evolving to a higher level of consciousness. Anyway further improvements are possible and necessary.

Common risk management techniques as illustrated by various sections in this book, and reported by regulating authorities, are often the top notch of risk managing, and not the average in the industry.

An important point is that small banks are usually relying on less sophisticated and accurate tools, leaving room for substantial upgrading to reach the level of those reported for top institutions.

A review of possible improvements in the bank industry necessarily comes as an approximate view on a sector that is quite heterogeneous in the size of market participants.

Regarding credit risk management, an important issue is the lack of precision in the credit rating evaluation process. Over time, the approach should in fact be standardized across institutions and across borrowers.

In addition the rating procedures in the banking sector (which is a fundamental part of the capital markets) should be made compatible with rating systems elsewhere in the capital market.

The data issue is important in that credit losses are vaguely related to credit ratings, so that they have to be closely tracked, and demonstrate tightness of credit pricing, credit rating and expected loss. However, as mentioned above, lack of data is an obstacle, given that the industry currently does not have a sufficiently broad database on which to perform the migration analysis that has been studied in the bond market.

Future studies should therefore concentrate on credit portfolio structure and evaluation of gains from diversification, through careful portfolio design. Banks at the moment are not sufficiently managing their credit concentrations by either industrial or geographic areas.

On the interest rate risk side, there have been simulation studies about gap management, accounting measures related to book value, and cash flow losses, being the sectors that create most problem for risk analysis.

Accounting measures based on market figures are the trend that may lead to an improvement of the methodology, especially if related to both assets and liabilities size of the firm book.

Simulations represent a promising tool for interest rate risk measurement and management, and further work must be done in order to incorporate the advances in dynamic hedging that are used in complex fixed income pricing models. Significant improvements should be introduced in making simulations more complex and improve scenario testing.

On the FX risk side, the industry is lacking in the use of ad-hoc approaches, based on VaR for market risk, in setting the trading limits. The use of such tools to a greater degree represents a natural evolution to be explored by banks.

Also models able to capture total risk management have been discussed in the industry and the literature. In particular RAROC and VaR models have been considered, taking into account that the decisions to accept risk and the pricing of the risky position are separated from risk analysis.

The actual situation of the banking system worldwide is of scarce integration of the different parts of the process. In order to be implemented as aggregate measures of risk, both RAROC and VaR assume the time dimension of all risks to be the same.

It follows that a credit risk is similar to a trading risk, creating problems if one considers that market prices are not immediately available for all assets in a bank portfolio, and time dimensions are generally different for different types of risk.

Moreover, such an aggregation process would require deep knowledge of all risks considered, and the methodologies involved. There is no board of directors or example of senior management that can claim such a high level of expertise, making it impossible to ensure the appropriate knowledge required.

The Basel Committee keeps working on initiatives and documents to foster bank resilience, realizing that effective supervision is crucial to ensure stability in the overall banking system.

The financial crisis has uncovered the many lacks in the overall system, and how the existing regulatory capital was not sufficient to ensure proper coverage in times of heavy distress.

This was the main driver of the 2009 enhancements to the regulatory capital framework. At the same time, a review of the trading book framework for financial institutions was deemed as fundamental.

It is controversial whether or not the overall banking activity should be kept separated from the trading book, as it is nowadays. Moreover, definition of trading activities and the way risk in trading books should be linked to regulatory capital, are the focus of the most recent reviews of the Committee.

In a 2010 summit in Toronto, the leaders of the G20 took a position against the role of the external ratings in driving market regulation, and the Committee is working in this direction.

An important aspect of the issue of external ratings has been identified in the review of the various approaches used for calculating regulatory capital for securitizations, in order to disincentivize the reliance on external ratings.

On top of that, the work of the Committee is pointing towards restrictive requirements for the collection of additional information about the exposures and risks underlying a securitization exposure, where failures in doing so would lead to a full deduction from regulatory capital.

Another important point in the work to be done is to ensure appropriate loss absorbing capacity to the systemically important banks, through the indication of a provisional methodology comprising both quantitative and qualitative indicators to assist in assessing the systemic importance of financial institutions at the global level.

Large exposures are a primary concern of regulators for the future of financial stability. The concentration of credit risk has been historically a major source of major failures for financial institutions.

Therefore, it is crucial to set limitations to credit concentration, especially for sensitive banks, given the high contagion impact on the financial system, that may arise from their failure.

A last point of considerable importance for bank regulation is the cross-border bank resolution, based on the Report and Recommendations of the cross-border bank resolution group of 2010.

At both the national and multinational level, efforts have been made to improve the authorities' capability to manage distressed financial institutions and minimize the distress of the overall system.

The principles of the Basel Committee have been used worldwide as a benchmark for assessing the quality of supervisory systems and identifying future work to achieve a baseline level of sound supervisory practices.

Both the IMF and World Bank also base their assessment of banking supervision in different parts of the world, on the principles of the Committee, that has issued a considerable amount of guidance and reporting, especially in response to the financial crisis.

In 2011 a revision of the Core Principles for banking supervision started, to provide a new set of regulatory tools to address topics related to the supervision of systemically important financial institutions.

14.3 Challenges for research

Learning outcomes

1. Describe interbank risk and its role in the global crisis, and after.
2. Define what energy derivatives are, and their use in financial hedging.
3. Explain sovereign risk dynamics in the context of global distress.

14.3.1 Interbank risk

Bank liquidity management heavily relies on the presence of interbank markets in the financial system. With a considerable boom in the last decade, instruments like secured or repo have been a fast-growing segment of money markets.

Repo transactions are backed by a collateral, and they show similarities to the securities used for refinancing operations by central banks, and repo markets are a key part of the transmission of monetary policy.

The interbank market is a reference market for interest rates. For example, the three-month interbank market rate is a benchmark for pricing fixed income securities throughout the economy, with that specific tenor.

The functioning of interbank markets is normally smooth and continuous, with an observed stability of applied rates and consistency across secured and unsecured segments, as well as across different collateral classes.

However, also this sector has been impacted by the financial crisis and since 2007, the functioning of interbank markets faced a worldwide severe impairment.

Until then, the unsecured market and the market secured by government securities were coupled, and interest rate differentials almost nil. But after the crisis hit financial markets, the tensions in interbank markets caused the decoupling.

In the second half of 2007 interest rates started moving in opposite directions, with an increase of unsecured rates and the decreasing of secured rates. They decoupled again in 2009, following the bankruptcy of Lehman Brothers. The decoupling of interest rates was more evident in the USA than in Europe.

Many questions are still open about interbank lending and risk. It is still not clear what are the reasons behind the decoupling of interest rates, and why the effect in the USA was much more severe than in the Euro area.

Moreover, other questions relate to what are the factors underlying the behaviour of interbank markets, and what are the possible policy responses to address the tensions in interbank markets.

So far, some models have been developed that take into account both secured and unsecured interbank lending in the presence of counterparty risk. Credit risk arose as an important framework given its suspected role, together with securitization, in the generation of the financial crisis.

Especially unsecured markets are sensitive to changes in the expectations on the creditworthiness of a counterparty. These considerations are mitigated in the repo market, where a collateral is already in place.

The reaction of most central banks to the tensions in interbank markets, around the world, has led to the introduction of support measures and the support to liquidity of markets in order to avoid insolvency at the institution level.

Heider and Hoerova (2009) examine how the range of collateral accepted by a central bank affects the liquidity conditions of banks and how the lack of high-quality collateral can be faced.

They find evidence of the effectiveness of the above-mentioned measures in terms of tensions reduction in secured markets. However, they are not able to treat the unsecured segment and the associated spill-overs, if those are driven by credit risk concerns.

14.3.2 Energy derivatives

Traditional players in the energy derivatives markets are energy producers, marketers and end-users. In the last few years, a range of new subjects has emerged, namely banks, institutional investors, hedge funds and other investors.

Commodity-linked investments have registered high returns in the last few years, generating an increased interest in the markets. Moreover, they offer a high degree of diversification, being weakly correlated with both equity and fixed income products.

Macroeconomic effects are also related to investing in energy products, like protection against the inflation caused by economic growth, and their correlation with non-financial factors, like the environment.

From the point of view of the product issuers, the attracting feature of energy derivatives is that they can be split into several components, to be used to hedge existing commodity risks, so to overcome market illiquidity.

The most popular energy products available on the market are:

- Energy commodity-linked bonds, issued by Credit Suisse (CH)
- Energy commodity-linked notes, issued by Canadian Imperial Bank (CA)
- Commodity-linked notes, issued by San Paolo IMI (IT)
- Other products involving mostly oil products or natural gas.

Energy prices show a unique behaviour, and their distribution is characterized by some properties. One of them is mean reversion, meaning that the price of the energy commodity is lognormal, like in the BSM framework, with lognormal mean reverting. The process can be written as

$$d \ln S_t = a \left[\theta_t - \ln \left(\frac{S_t}{F_{0,t}} \right) \right] dt + \sigma_t dW_t$$

where

S_t is the spot commodity price at time t
a is a constant non-negative mean-reversion rate
σ_t is the time-dependent local volatility
$F_{0,t}$ is the forward price at time zero for delivery at time t
θ_t is a time-dependent no-arbitrage drift parameter.

The distribution of energy derivatives prices shows fat tails, and returns are leptokurtic and heavily distributed on the tails. Also the seasonality in both prices and volatility are a typical fact of energy derivatives, and in response to cyclical fluctuations in supply and demand, energy prices tend to exhibit strong seasonal patterns in both price and volatility.

Finally, another fact to be considered is the time to maturity effect, meaning that forward/futures prices tend to be less volatile than spot prices.

In the last few years new developments in the energy derivatives market have been registered, and the transactions have considerably increased in volume and complexity. As an example, the issuer of a security guarantees the sum of coupons to be higher than some preset percentage value, where the part not fulfilled at the coupon's payment is settled at maturity.

The new issues have coupons that are linked to the historical path of the underlying commodity, rather than on a specific price observed at coupon payment day. Moreover, they provide the investor with interruption conditions, like a callable feature or a provision that the product expires when the commodity price reaches some specified threshold.

It is also frequent to write contracts on baskets of underlying commodities, mixing energy with other commodities like metals. The development of the Goldman Sachs Commodity Index has made the creation of such baskets much easier in the last few years.

In hybrid products, the final payout of the derivative depends on several factors, which can be market-linked or not. In order to price the instrument, the knowledge of the whole correlation structure of the portfolio is required, in addition to usual volatility measures.

An example of hybrid energy derivatives are the spark spread options, call options written on a basket of correlated commodity products, and having a strike price dependent on the cost of raw materials or emission.

The option is such that the power operator guarantees a constant payments stream, and can use the options to hedge against adverse movements of power prices. Most investors use the spark spread options to replicate the power plant operations through a financial tool. The main challenge in valuing such a contract is the complexity of the correlation structure, given the features of seasonality, and dependence on time to maturity.

Options on basket products are written on portfolios that may include crude oil, equity indices, bonds and more. Rainbow products pay the highest annual return of the basket, Himalayan options pay as the rainbow products, and then the best component is removed from the basket.

The main challenge in this type of derivatives is the difficulty in describing the joint distribution of basket prices, as well as in constructing the overall volatility structure of the basket from the volatility of the single components.

Another important class of energy derivatives includes the commodity-contingent fixed income and equity products. Swaps linked to energy exchange a standard floating rate on LIBOR, with a fixed leg with rate multiplied by the days during which the commodity price stays above a certain threshold.

There are also commodity-contingent swaptions, traded on the markets, and Bermudan-style options, with minimum coupon guaranteed and knock-out features, paying coupons that are dependent on the commodity price at payment time.

The option expires after the total amount of coupons paid out reaches a specified level. Should the level be not reached by all the coupons paid until maturity, the difference is embedded in the last coupon, so that the amount is reached.

Other empirical properties of the energy commodities are the implied volatility increasing with time, and dependent on the strike price. Moreover there are properties of correlation, which depend on the time to maturity, on the time between contracts and also on the strike.

The Heston model (1993) is an example of a stochastic volatility model, aimed at capturing the dependence properties of commodity portfolios. In particular, the volatility process is given by

$$dv_t = a[\theta_t - v_t]dt + \sigma\sqrt{v_t}dW_1$$

where

$$\frac{dV_t}{V_t} = \mu dt + \sqrt{v_t}dW_2$$

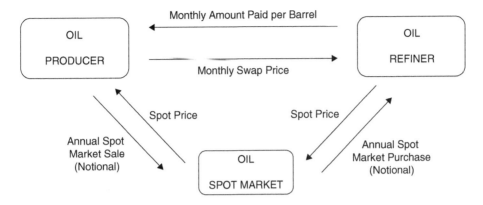

Figure 14.4 Graph of a crude oil swap.

is the price process, and the correlation is given by

$$E(dW_1, dW_2) = \rho dt$$

More complicated models include Levy processes, with jumps, for deterministic and stochastic volatility, and regime-switching models.

Hedging in energy markets is a tricky task, because of mismatches from an ideal world, in which joint distributions, fuel prices and liquidity of hedging instrument would allow for an easy hedge.

In the real world, there is often mismatch between the long maturity of assets and the short maturity of hedges. Moreover the underlying commodity can be both an input or an output of the production process, leading to dirty hedges, where fuel contracts in one location are used to hedge exposure in another place.

There are also liquidity constraints, volume-constrained execution times, wide bid-ask spread and high costs. In practice, only rough and inaccurate hedges are possible, especially when dealing with shorter time horizons.

The short and medium term present problems of stylized facts of the distribution of power prices, as mentioned above. The joint distributions are usually calculated according to a normality assumption, using historical data, which is not realistic.

14.3.3 Sovereign risk dynamics

Before the financial crisis, sovereign credit risk was typically associated with emerging markets. In recent years, also advanced economies have registered credit spreads of a considerable magnitude, and comparable to emerging economies.

Anyway the literature on sovereign risk in advanced economies is still rare and there is room for more research and investigation. Moreover, also the traditional method of investigating sovereign risk through analysis of macroeconomic variables seems to be limited and not exhaustive.

As an example, note that credit spreads rose also in European countries with a very low growth of the public-debt-to-GDP ratio. Furthermore, empirical studies show how, in those countries, sovereign risk is highly correlated to the health of the banking sector.

Sovereign risk has been driven by the fragility of the banking system in that some governments decided to support their banks by injecting capital in the system, because some individual banks are too important and too interconnected to fail.

It is important to understand the nature of sovereign risk, and its importance as a key risk, given the large and rapidly increasing size of the sovereign debt markets. Moreover, sovereign credit risk directly affects the diversification possibilities of financial market participants, for global debt portfolios and may play a central role in determining both the cost and flow of capital across countries.

Global factors play a predominant role in driving sovereign credit spreads, that can be expressed as the sum of a default-related component and an associated risk premium. The Pan and Singleton (2008) framework allows decomposing sovereign CDS credit spreads into components.

The model defines the spread for a *n*-year sovereign CDS contract, as

$$\tilde{s}_t = \frac{2\left(1-\tilde{R}\right)\int_t^{t+n}\tilde{E}\left(\tilde{\lambda}_u e^{-\int_t^u\left(\tilde{\lambda}_s+r_s\right)ds}\right)du}{\sum_{i=1}^{2n}\tilde{E}\left(e^{-\int_t^{t+\frac{i}{2}}\left(\tilde{\lambda}_s+r_s\right)ds}\right)}$$

where

$\tilde{E}$ denotes the risk-neutral expectation
$\tilde{R}$ is the risk-neutral recovery rate on the cheapest to delivery bond, in case of a
 credit event
r_t is the risk-free rate
λ_t is the risk-neutral intensity of a credit event.

The process for $\tilde{\lambda}_t$ is given by

$$d\ln\lambda_t = \tilde{a}\left(\tilde{\theta}-\ln\tilde{\lambda}_t\right)dt+\sigma_\lambda d\tilde{W}_t$$

while the corresponding process for the intensity of a credit event under the objective probability is given by

$$d\ln\lambda_t = a\left(\theta-\ln\lambda_t\right)dt+\sigma_\lambda dW_t$$

The market price of risk is defined as

$$\kappa_t = \alpha+\beta\ln\lambda_t$$

which implies a relationship among the risk-neutral and objective parameters, as given by

$$\tilde{a} = a+\beta\sigma_\lambda$$
$$\tilde{a}\tilde{\theta} = a\theta-\alpha\sigma_\lambda$$

The market price of risk defines the difference between the parameters of the risk-neutral process and those of the objective process, and, therefore, how the probability distributions implied by the risk-neutral and objective processes differ.

The assumption of the model is that λ_t and r_t are independent, so that if no arbitrage condition holds, the market CDS spread is given in the risk-neutral framework, as

$$\tilde{s}_t = \frac{2\left(1-\tilde{R}\right)\int_t^{t+n} B_{t,u} \tilde{E}\left(e^{-\int_t^u \tilde{\lambda}_s ds}\right)du}{\sum_{i=1}^{2n} B_{t,t+\frac{i}{2}} \tilde{E}\left(e^{-\int_t^{t+\frac{i}{2}} \tilde{\lambda}_s ds}\right)}$$

where

$B_{t,u}$ is the price of a risk-free ZCB issued at date t, with maturity u.

It follows that

$$s_t \approx \lambda_t \left(1-\tilde{R}\right)$$

The changes in the spread are approximated by changes in the credit event intensity, and investors demand a risk premium for the risk. The premium is given by the difference between the value of the CDS spread under the risk-neutral process, and the spread under the objective process, where the latter is given by

$$s_t = \frac{2\left(1-\tilde{R}\right)\int_t^{t+n} B_{t,u} E\left(e^{-\int_t^u \tilde{\lambda}_s ds}\right)du}{\sum_{i=1}^{2n} B_{t,t+\frac{i}{2}} E\left(e^{-\int_t^{t+\frac{i}{2}} \tilde{\lambda}_s ds}\right)}$$

where

E denotes the expectation under the objective process.

When $\kappa_t = 0$, the objective process and the risk-neutral process coincide and $\tilde{s}_t = s_t$. The impact of the distress risk premium on the market prices is given by

$$\tilde{s}_t - s_t$$

in absolute terms, or

$$\frac{\tilde{s}_t - s_t}{\tilde{s}_t}$$

in relative terms.

Summary

A big role in the global crisis has been played by failures in corporate governance, when many well-structured institutions had problems and the standard governance tools proved to be ineffective, when put under pressure.

Before the crisis reached its peak, the role of executive compensation as already a major driver in the effectiveness of governance was under investigation. Remuneration policy was considered an unsolved problem for American and worldwide companies.

Management executives resulted in having positions in large stakes of companies' equity, therefore sharing potential downside risk with the other equity holders of the company.

Managers started facing high risks, but they could offset losses on equity positions, through the large bonuses attached to performance levels of the firm, and incentives for managers to reduce the corporate risk exposure were limited.

Deregulation characterized the capital structure of banks at the beginning of the 2000s, which was balanced by strengthening the role of prudential regulation, as from the Basel Accord on capital standards.

Financial innovation and developments influenced the funding structure of banks, leading to increased dependence of the banks on funding coming from financial markets, through wholesale borrowing.

Risk management has been considered by banks, for a long time, as a tool to control corporate exposure to major types of risk. Higher levels of consciousness are emerging in recent years, with a new sensitivity to all related issues.

Interbank markets normally function in a smooth way, with stable applied rates and consistency across secured and unsecured segments, and across different classes of collateral assets.

Both energy producers and consumers are traditional players in the energy derivatives markets, and new agents have started populating the market in the last few years. Moreover, also instruments involved have gone through developments, and the transactions have considerably increased in volume and complexity.

Sovereign credit risk before the crisis was mainly associated with emerging economies, but not considered as an issue for developed areas in the world. The crisis also put advanced economies under pressure, with considerable increase in the credit spreads, comparable in some cases to those of emerging markets.

The main driver of sovereign risk has been the fragility of the banking system, and the decisions made at governmental level on how to intervene to help the situation. Some banks have been saved from bankruptcy simply because they were too big to fail.

Bibliography

Arjoon, S. 2005. Corporate Governance: An Ethical Perspective. *Journal of Business Ethics*, 61(4): 343–352.

Bank for International Settlements. 2011. *The Impact of Sovereign Credit Risk on Bank Funding Conditions*. July. Committee on the Global Financial System.

Beltratti, A. and Stulz, R.M. 2012. The Credit Crisis Around the Globe: Why Did Some Banks Perform Better? *Journal of Financial Economics*, 105(1): 1–17.

Berger, A.N., Imbierowicz, B. and Rauch, C. 2013. *The Roles of Corporate Governance in Bank Failures during the Recent Financial Crisis*. August.

Bollerslev, T. and Domowitz, I. 1993. Trading Patterns and Prices in the Interbank Foreign Exchange Market. *Journal of Finance*, 48(4): 1421–1443.

Christiansen, H. 2009. *Corporate Governance and the Financial Crisis: The Way Ahead.* Corporate Affairs Division. OECD.

Deakin, S. 2010. *Corporate Governance and Financial Crisis in the Long Run.* Centre for Business Research. University of Cambridge. Working Paper No. 417.

Demirgüç-Kunt, A. and Huizinga, H. 2010. Bank Activity and Funding Strategies: The Impact on Risk and Returns. *Journal of Financial Economics*, 98(3): 626–650.

Diamond, D.W. and Raghuram, G.R. 2001. Liquidity Risk, Liquidity Creation and Financial Fragility: A Theory of Banking. *Journal of Political Economy*, 109(2): 287–327.

Filipovic, D. and Trolle, A.B. *The Term Structure of Interbank Risk.* Swiss Finance Institute Research Paper No. 11–34.

Foos, D., Norden, L. and Weber, M. 2010. Loan Growth and Riskiness of Banks. *Journal of Banking and Finance*, 34(12): 2929–2940.

Furash, E. 1994. *Organizing the Risk Management Process in Large Banks.* Risk Management Planning Seminar. Federal Financial Institutions Examination Council.

Heider, F. and Hoerova, M. 2009. Interbank Lending, Credit Risk Premia and Collateral. *International Journal of Central Banking*, 5: 1–39.

Heston, S. 1993. A Closed-form Solution for Options with Stochastic Volatility. *Review of Financial Studies*, 6: 327–343.

Jeanneret, A. 2013. The Dynamics of Sovereign Credit Risk. *Journal of Financial and Quantitative Analysis.* http://papers.ssrn.com/sol3/papers.cfm?abstract_id=1071665.

Kallestrup, R. 2012. *The Dynamics of Bank and Sovereign Credit Risk.* Copenhagen Business School. ISSN 0906-6934.

King Report II. 2002. *King Committee on Corporate Governance.* Institute of Directors Southern Africa.

Longstaff, F.A., Pan, J., Pedersen, L.H. and Singleton, K. 2011. How Sovereign is Sovereign Credit Risk? *American Economic Journal*, 3: 75–103.

McCahery, J.A., Vermeulen, E.P.M. and Hisatake, M. 2013. *The Present and Future of Corporate Governance: Re-Examining the Role of the Board of Directors and Investor Relations in Listed Companies.* European Corporate Governance Institute. Law Working Paper No. 211.

Mehran, H. and Thakor, A.V. 2011. Bank Capital and Value in the Cross-Section. *Review of Financial Studies*, 24(4): 1019–1067.

Mehran, H., Morrison, A.D. and Shapiro, J.D. 2011. *Corporate Governance and Banks: What Have We Learned from the Financial Crisis?* Federal Reserve Bank of New York. Staff Report No. 502.

Mian, A. and Sufi, A. 2009. The Consequences of Mortgage Credit Expansion: Evidence From the US Mortgage Default Crisis. *Quarterly Journal of Economics*, 124: 1449–1496.

Naidoo, R. 2009. *Corporate Governance: An Essential Guide for South African Companies.* Second edition. LexisNexis.

OECD. 2009. *Corporate Governance and the Financial Crisis: Key Findings and Main Messages.*

Pan, J. and Singleton, K.J. 2008. Default and Recovery Implicit in the Term Structure of Sovereign CDS Spreads. *The Journal of Finance*, 63(5): 2345–2384.

Santomero, A.M. 1997. Commercial Bank Risk Management: An Analysis of the Process. *Journal of Financial Services Research*, 12(2–3): 83–115.

Wheelock, D.C. and Wilson, P.W. 2000. Why Do Banks Disappear? The Determinants of US Bank Failures and Acquisitions. *Review of Economics and Statistics*, 82: 127–138.

Exercises

Questions

1. How can the role of corporate governance in the development of the global financial crisis be described?

2. What has been the role of employees and management remuneration in the failure of corporate governance?
3. What are the controversies of wholesale funding for banks, in relation to their business model?
4. Discuss the case of the Enron failure, and explain how it was possible for such a large collapse to build up.
5. Describe the differences in IRR management between banks and the rest of the financial system.
6. What type of interventions at the regulatory level should be made in order to limit contagion in the banking sector, due to bankruptcies?
7. Describe the behaviour of interbank risk at the beginning of the twenty-first century, underlying the difference between the trend pre-crisis and post-crisis.
8. Define and comment on the main steps in the process of FX risk hedging for large banks. How is the issue of setting trading limits handled?
9. Elaborate on Enron's failure and compare it to the major bankruptcies cases that occurred in the financial industry in the first decade of the 2000s.
10. What are the main challenges from a statistical point of view in handling energy derivatives?
11. Explain the differences in how sovereign risk has been considered and handled before and after the financial crisis.

Index

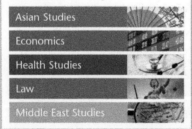